CULTURESCOPE

THE PRINCETON REVIEW

Guide to an Informed Mind

CULTURESCOPE

THE PRINCETON REVIEW

Guide to an Informed Mind

RANDOM HOUSE, INC. NEW YORK 1995

THE STAFF OF THE PRINCETON REVIEW

Culturescope: the Princeton review guide to an informed mind/by the staff of the
princeton review.
College ed./1995 ed., 1st ed.
    p.   cm.
    Includes bibliographical references and index.
    ISBN 0-679-75367-2 $20.00
    1. Handbooks. vade-mecums, etc.   2. United States—Miscellanea.
I. Title
    AG105.M426 1994   031.02–dc20   94-34393 CIP

Manufactured in the United States of America on paper using partially recycled fibers

9 8 7 6 5 4 3 2

First Edition

ACKNOWLEDGMENTS

The Editors of Culturescope would like to thank the following people:

Maria Russo and PJ Waters for lending their lives to the editing, writing, and researching of this behemoth, and for their dogged pursuit of the truth, at any cost.

Kristin Fayne-Mulroy and Bruno Blumenfeld for researching, choosing, and procuring all the groovy photos and artwork.

Meher Khambata, Julian Ham, and Carol Slominski for the rock-solid, market-wise book design.

Kudos must go out to the production team of Adam Hurwitz, John Bergdahl, Glen Pannell, Chris Thomas, Chris Scott, Joe Cavallaro, Lisa Ruyter, Joseph McPartland, Sara Kane, Illeny Maaza, Carol Slominski, Peter Jung, Jessica Brockington, Julian Heath, Russel Murray, Michael Recorvits, Dave Romeo, and Ray Suhler for wrestling the design of this book to the ground and making it scream for mercy. Special thanks to John Bergdahl for his work on the maps and original artwork (like the human "G" nome, our favorite).

Bettmann Archives for their incredible catalog of photographs, without which this book would read a little, well, dry.

Kate Lardner, Eric Banks, Debbie Guest, Louise Weiss, Doug McMullen, and Robert Gooch for fact-checking and proofreading *Culturescope*.

Judy Davis for indexing and cross-referencing the thing in less time than it takes the Editors to smoke a carton of Camels.

Maureen McMahon for her extreme patience, unwavering support, and, most of all, for her deep appreciation of Country Joe and the Fish.

Without these people, culture, as we see it, wouldn't be worth a thin dime.

Chris Kensler and Leland Elliott

Editors

TABLE OF CONTENTS

The word is out—our American educational system is in dire straits. It's hard to turn on a news program or open a paper these days without being hit with doomsday accounts of declining SAT scores, drastic cost-cutting measures at public and private institutions, and the woeful position of educators in our country. It's scary. It's alarming. You may even have heard that Western culture itself is on the wane, possibly as the direct result of Americans' lamentable and overwhelming lack of knowledge about it.

RELAX

It's true that many people, even college-educated, gainfully employed Americans, don't know a lot of basic facts about world culture—the facts that, taken together, make up our collective cultural memory, the knowledge-bank that is at the core of our national psyche. To be culturally literate is to be able to stand comfortably on common ground with the people around you, certainly a goal any individual should work toward and every country should promote. But the notion of a widespread decline in cultural literacy is questionable on several grounds. First of all, we are now more than ever a multicultural society. The "good old days" may have produced higher standardized test scores, but they also had a smaller, more ethnically and economically homogeneous group of Americans taking those standardized tests. Strong, well-funded schools are indispensable and should be more of a national priority, of course, but cultural literacy goes beyond what it's possible to learn in the fixed amount of years we have to get educated. The pool of knowledge required for cultural literacy includes things—like entertainment, sports, architecture, and technology—that may not fit into the already cramped confines of a school day or college semester.

LIFE, IT IS LEARNING

Learning about the complex, ever-changing culture we've inherited should be a lifetime pursuit. And contrary to those "golden age" nostalgists, it's always been difficult to keep straight all there is to know about our culture, no matter what university you've gotten what degree from. Today, with the rise of the global economy and the dawn of the information age, it's more important than ever to have a grasp of the facts of our culture, but those facts seem ever more confusing and overwhelming. And as Americans, we have a special responsibility to understand the many cultures that have coalesced to make our own.

WHERE TO START?

What's the best route to cultural literacy, then? You can always read through the encyclopedia, or you can sit down with one of those sober dictionary-style cultural literacy manuals. This book is something different—a cultural literacy book that's also a good read. Obviously, *Culturescope* does not contain every possible fact there is to know about Western culture. No book could. We've used our considered judgment to decide what's most worth knowing, and we've surveyed college graduates across the country to find out what they do in fact know. We don't make apocalyptic proclamations about the decline of cultural literacy among Americans and its deleterious effect on the unity and purpose of the nation. We just give you lots of interesting, indispensable information that will serve you well in a job interview, a dinner party, when you're reading the newspaper, cruising the Internet, and maybe even when you're sitting in a graduate seminar. We can't guarantee that after you've read this book you'll never confuse Sam Shepard and Tom Stoppard again, but we can say that you'll likely understand many more of the cultural references you hear, and you'll feel confident enough to make some impressive cultural allusions of your own.

THE NUTS AND BOLTS

Culturescope also has some exciting features you won't find anywhere else. With the Culturescope Quiz at the beginning of the book, you'll get a feel not only for what "the experts" think you should know but also for how much other college-educated Americans actually know about each subject. The book's "hypertext" format—all those cross-references you'll see in green—shows you how the facts interrelate, allowing you to jump around and follow those connections as you read. As you delve into the chapters, the question-driven format will help you gauge what you already know about each topic. And, as a final bonus, we give you plenty of recommendations for further explorations—books to read, movies to see, music to hear, and CD-ROMs to experience—so your pursuit of learning doesn't end here.

There are sixteen chapters in *Culturescope*, arranged alphabetically. The chapters cover everything from the arts to history, from science to religion. Some of the chapters you probably saw coming, like Music, while others may be unexpected, like Television and Human Rights. The point is that culture is rich and varied; to be culturally literate, you need to open your mind to the kitsch as well as the canon. You can read the chapters in whatever order you like, and you can follow the trail of whatever interests you most through the green cross-references. Within each chapter, you'll find a discussion that hits the high points of the subject at hand, chronologically whenever possible.

As this book demonstrates, culture is hopelessly interrelated. Many important subjects are covered in more than one chapter of *Culturescope*. In this way, you get a chance to consider a crucial event or historical movement, such as World War I or Romanticism, from a few different angles. No chapter is simply entitled "history," since all of the information in the book collectively makes up what is thought of as history. Within each chapter, we tend to focus on American history, and we try to keep the discussion as up-to-date as possible given the mind-boggling pace of world events these days. You'll also notice that throughout the book important words or phrases and names of key figures are in **boldface**. The *really* significant people get birth and death dates next to their names. These features alert you to the key things you absolutely positively should remember after you read this book and for the rest of your life.

THE HALF-INCH NAILS AND GRAY TAPE

Important stuff is happening in the margins of *Culturescope*. Sidebars and boxes fill you in on cool facts, give you amusing quotations, and provide extra information about what's being discussed in the main text. Plus, look out for these icons:

When we "zoom in" with this symbol, we look closer at a specific aspect of whatever's under discussion. For example, when the Life Sciences chapter talks about the hemispheres of the brain, we "zoom in" to explain left- and right-handedness.

We also "zoom out" to show you the bigger picture surrounding a topic. In the Theater chapter, for instance, next to a discussion of absurdist theatre we "zoom out" to discuss the social factors that influenced the transition from realist to absurdist theatre in the 1950s. Beware—even "zooms" are liable to have cross-references.

With this symbol you'll find further reading on the subject at hand. As you read about boxing in the Recreation chapter, for example, you'll see that we recommend *The Pugilist at Rest*, by Thom Jones, a moving short story collection whose title story is about a retired boxer.

This symbol directs you to good movies that relate to the topic. For instance, as you read about Vincent Van Gogh in the Visual Arts chapter we suggest you check out Robert Altman's film *Vincent and Theo*.

We also turn you on to music that's connected to the events being discussed, such as our recommendation that you listen to "Nutrition" by the Dead Milkmen, which you'll find next to the Life Sciences discussion of nutritional deficiency.

We want you to stay on the cutting edge, and this symbol directs you to CD-ROMs and Internet addresses relating to the subject. For example, when the Geography chapter talks about urban areas we refer you to the CD-ROM *Sim-City*, in which you build your own city.

Go Ahead, Talk To Us

American culture belongs to all of us. But because it is a collective enterprise, culture is always moving, growing and shifting, often in ways that seem chaotic and even anarchic. Culture will never allow itself to be pinned down, even by a book like this. So consider *Culturescope* an exploratory journey into a dynamic field. If you have suggestions for things to include in future editions of this book, write to us at Culturescope, c/o The Princeton Review, 2315 Broadway, New York, New York 10024. You can also e-mail us at books.tpr@review.com.

The Culturescope Quiz

The Culturescope Quiz is a gauge of your cultural literacy and the launching pad for the rest of this book. The questions are in no particular order, and range from obscenely simple to damn hard. Take the test, mark down your answers and then compare them with the answers on pages 25-28. As you check your answers, you will notice that we also refer you to the page or pages of the book where we discuss the topic in question. If you're curious, go right to the page and read on.

So How'm I Doing?

Instructions for scoring the Culturescope Quiz are on page 29. You convert the number of questions that you got right into your personal Culture Quotient. If you're curious to see how college grads from across the country performed on the test, check out the percentages on the answer key. The results are based on a national survey, and you may be quite surprised by what your peers do and don't know. But don't take your score, good or bad, too seriously. The quiz is just for fun.

1. **What is the official game of Canada?**

   (A) Hockey
   (B) Football
   (C) Shinny
   (D) Lacrosse

2. **The term "*film noir*" was coined to describe**

   (A) the black and white photography characteristic of 1920s studio productions
   (B) the French avant-garde movement in cinema
   (C) an American genre of the 1940s and 1950s typically dealing with the underworld
   (D) comedic melodramas of the 1930s

3. **The protest song was a popular kind of what music?**

   (A) Broadway musical show tunes
   (B) Folk music
   (C) Jump band music
   (D) None of the above

4. **One precedent for the American suburb was the design of**

   (A) public parks
   (B) miniature golf courses
   (C) cemeteries
   (D) "Main Street, USA"

5. **What was the name of the plane that dropped the atomic bomb on Hiroshima, Japan in 1945?**

   (A) The Lindy Hop
   (B) The Enola Gay
   (C) The Jefferson Airplane
   (D) The American Spirit

6. **The Aztecs' preferred style for sacrificing humans to the gods was**

   (A) drowning children in sixty-foot-deep wells
   (B) tearing out their hearts with a stone dagger
   (C) boiling them in large vats of oil
   (D) stoning them at frenzied religious festivals

7. **Which of the following statements best describes the aim of cubism?**

   (A) To represent different points of view of a single object
   (B) To represent the geometrical incorporation of several objects into one
   (C) To represent the movement of an object in space
   (D) To represent the movement of an object over time

8. **Who acted as American envoy to France during the Revolution?**

   (A) Thomas Paine
   (B) Benjamin Franklin
   (C) Paul Revere
   (D) John Adams

9. **Which of the following best describes a flying buttress?**

   (A) An interior masonry roof or ceiling constructed on the arch principle
   (B) A new francophile sexual technique
   (C) An exoskeletal system
   (D) A female figure that functions as a supporting column

10. **Who invented baseball?**

    (A) Abner Doubleday
    (B) Alexander Cartwright
    (C) A.G. Spalding
    (D) Cy Young

11. **The French term *"laissez-faire"* most nearly means**

    (A) "the spirit of the times"
    (B) "leave things alone"
    (C) "seize the day"
    (D) "off with their heads"

12. **What British practice contributed to the start of the War of 1812?**

    (A) Four o'clock tea
    (B) Impressment
    (C) Taxation
    (D) Fur trading

13. **Which state was the first to secede from the Union?**

    (A) South Carolina
    (B) Virginia
    (C) Georgia
    (D) Maryland

14. **Which romantic poet was also an important artist?**

    (A) Eugène Delacroix
    (B) Joseph Turner
    (C) John Constable
    (D) William Blake

15. **Cast-iron architecture was a significant technological advance because for the first time a designer could do what?**

    (A) Select building parts from a catalog
    (B) Avoid working with the notoriously corrupt Woodworkers Union
    (C) Open a chic gallery without much capital
    (D) Construct a building more than five stories high

16. **Which Soviet leader paved the way to the fall of the Berlin Wall and the Iron Curtain?**

    (A) Krushchev
    (B) Gorbechev
    (C) Stalin
    (D) Yeltsin

17. **Who invented detective fiction?**

    (A) Edgar Allan Poe
    (B) Raymond Chandler
    (C) Mickey Spillane
    (D) Sir Arthur Conan Doyle

18. **The medieval versions of labor unions were called**

    (A) barterdoms
    (B) abbeys
    (C) guilds
    (D) tribunals

19. **Who is considered the father of the modern Olympics?**

    (A) Woodrow Wilson
    (B) Otto von Bismarch
    (C) Baron Pierre de Coubertin
    (D) Jean-Jacques Rousseau

20. Which of the following countries currently employs a communist economic system?

    I. Cuba
    II. Poland
    III. Thailand

    (A) I only
    (B) III only
    (C) I and II only
    (D) I and III only

21. Which of the following correctly identifies the five members of the League of the Iroquois?
    (A) Shoshone, Pomo, Shawnee, Miwok, and Paiute
    (B) Mohawks, Oneidas, Onodagas, Cayugas, and Senecas
    (C) Calusa, Seminole, Utina, Yamasee, and Biloxi
    (D) Crow, Arapaho, Cheyenne, Pawnee, and Omaha

22. Which of these stars popularized professional football in the 1920s?
    (A) Y.A. Tittle
    (B) Frank Gifford
    (C) Vince Lombardi
    (D) Red Grange

23. By the end of his career, Leonardo da Vinci saw painting as
    (A) a poor method of conveying his ideas about the world
    (B) the truest revelation of God's will
    (C) a lucrative profession
    (D) a good road to scientific discovery

24. Which general was in charge of U.S. military operations in Korea?
    (A) Dwight D. Eisenhower
    (B) Sun Myung Moon
    (C) Douglas MacArthur
    (D) Robert McNamara

25. The urban plan of Washington, D.C. was developed according to a European philosophy that made possible
    (A) free speech for all citizens
    (B) the abolition of slavery
    (C) the virtues of democracy to thrive
    (D) the suppression of protest against the state

26. Adam Smith conceived which of the following metaphors to explain how markets coordinate the economy?
    - (A) The venerable spirit
    - (B) The invisible hand
    - (C) The stealthy tongue
    - (D) The omniscient eye

27. A founder of the school of abstract expressionism is
    - (A) Jasper Johns
    - (B) Jackson Pollock
    - (C) Louise Nevelson
    - (D) Frank Stella

28. The acronym NAFTA stands for
    - (A) Native American Fair Treaty Alliance
    - (B) North American Free Trade Agreement
    - (C) Nations Against Foreign Tariff Associations
    - (D) Nations Against Free Trade Altogether

29. Dante is considered a major literary figure of which of the following periods?
    - (A) Medieval
    - (B) Renaissance
    - (C) Gothic
    - (D) Enlightenment

30. ABC was once part of which network?
    - (A) Fox
    - (B) NBC
    - (C) DuMont
    - (D) CBS

31. In early America, the popular genre of the captivity narrative consisted of
    - (A) accounts of possession by the devil or witches
    - (B) accounts of the experiences of Africans brought to the New World as slaves
    - (C) accounts of the experiences of whites held as war hostages by Indians
    - (D) accounts of forbidden romance among the Puritans

32. What was a major cause of the spread of the Protestant Reformation?
    - (A) An overabundance of living saints
    - (B) A revival of paganism
    - (C) The printing press
    - (D) A conflict regarding celibacy

33. Which of the following statements best captures the aesthetic philosophy of modernism?
    (A) It celebrates the integrity of the individual consciousness.
    (B) It is indebted to classical ideas of proportion and beauty.
    (C) It favors open-endedness, fragmentation, and multiple perspective.
    (D) It finds beauty in the small, homely details of everyday life.

34. Which one of these TV attachments was introduced in 1975?
    (A) Atari game system
    (B) Sony Betamax
    (C) VHS recorder
    (D) Pong

35. Which of the following countries does NOT contain any tropical rainforests?
    (A) Angola
    (B) Zaire
    (C) Brazil
    (D) Indonesia

36. The Beat Generation writers were influenced by
    (A) drugs, Buddhism, and jazz
    (B) technology and science fiction
    (C) natural healing, vegetarianism, and mysticism
    (D) dadaism and surrealism

37. Which sitcom inspired the "The Flintstones," "The Jetsons," and "The Simpsons"?
    (A) "All in the Family"
    (B) "Happy Days"
    (C) "The Honeymooners"
    (D) "Father Knows Best"

38. What primarily caused the demise of feudalism?
    (A) Continental drift
    (B) The dramatic growth of the Christian church
    (C) Attacks by nomadic warriors
    (D) The advent of private property

39. Which of the following countries' topography is over 95 percent desert?
    (A) Saudi Arabia
    (B) Morocco
    (C) Israel
    (D) Sudan

40. Early in his career, Matisse was associated with the style of painting called
    (A) fauvism
    (B) realism
    (C) cubism
    (D) colorism

41. Match the Greek to his play:
    (A) Aeschylus   __ Frogs
    (B) Euripides   __ Antigone
    (C) Sophocles   __ Medea
    (D) Aristophanes   __ Oresteia

42. How did French philosopher Jean-Jacques Rousseau characterize life in the state of nature?
    (A) As more favorable than life under the social contract
    (B) As not much different than it is now
    (C) As like a box of chocolates
    (D) As very complex

43. The early Renaissance painter known for breakthroughs in three-dimensional realism is
    (A) Botticcelli
    (B) Giotto
    (C) Titian
    (D) Tintoretto

44. The primitive kinship between an individual or group and an animal, plant, or natural object is known as
    (A) animism
    (B) fetishism
    (C) shamanism
    (D) totemism

45. Many of the British Invasion bands drew on what kind American music
    (A) Swing music
    (B) Country music
    (C) Chicago and Delta blues
    (D) Zydeco music

46. The prominent nineteenth-century American movement in landscape painting was called
    (A) The Mississippi school
    (B) The Frontier school
    (C) The Hudson River school
    (D) The New England school

47. Which of the following religions does not demand a belief in God?
    (A) Buddhism
    (B) Roman Catholicism
    (C) Islam
    (D) Judaism

48. Who wrote *The Birthday Party*?
    (A) Tom Stoppard
    (B) Edward Albee
    (C) Arthur Miller
    (D) Harold Pinter

49. The world's longest river is the
    (A) Amazon
    (B) Mississippi
    (C) Nile
    (D) Volga

50. Televangelist Jim Bakker was incarcerated for which of the following crimes?
    (A) Indecent exposure
    (B) Grand larceny
    (C) Fraud and conspiracy
    (D) All of the above

51. British economist John Maynard Keynes espoused which of the following methods of bringing nations out of the Great Depression?

    (A) Increased government spending combined with programs designed to stimulate demand and consumption
    (B) Decreased government spending combined with programs designed to stimulate supply and production
    (C) Strict barriers on foreign competition in domestic commodities markets
    (D) A government spending freeze combined with programs designed to halt production

52. How many continents were there on Earth when the first dinosaurs roamed?

    (A) Nine
    (B) Seven
    (C) Two
    (D) One

53. What is the historical significance of the Monroe Doctrine?

    (A) It established the first serious foreign policy of the United States.
    (B) It created peace treaties with several Native American tribes west of the Mississippi.
    (C) It recognized Mexico and Canada as sovereign nations.
    (D) It prohibited interstate trade.

54. Which of the following countries is NOT one of the "Four Dragons" of the Pacific Rim?

    (A) South Korea
    (B) Taiwan
    (C) Thailand
    (D) China

55. Humanism is based on

    (A) a rejection of the material world
    (B) an embrace of family and communal values
    (C) an emphasis on imagination over reason
    (D) a combination of Christianity and classical learning

56. Which is not considered a synoptic gospel?

    (A) Mark
    (B) John
    (C) Luke
    (D) Matthew

57. In 1994 what was the most watched show in the world?

(A) "The Simpsons"
(B) "Beverly Hills 90210"
(C) "Baywatch"
(D) "Murder She Wrote"

58. Which is the most linguistically diverse country?

(A) Papua New Guinea
(B) China
(C) United States
(D) Brazil

59. In what year was the Nineteenth Amendment to the Constitution, granting women the right to vote, passed?

(A) 1890
(B) 1899
(C) 1909
(D) 1919

60. What famous TV show did NOT get its start on radio?

(A) "Amos 'n' Andy"
(B) "Howdy Doody"
(C) "Marx Brothers"
(D) "The Perry Como Show"

61. Which of the following has the lowest latitude?

(A) Brownsville, Texas
(B) San Diego, California
(C) Key West, Florida
(D) New Orleans, Louisiana

62. Which was the first company to establish the concept of radio advertising?

(A) Coca Cola
(B) AT&T
(C) Ford Motor Co.
(D) McDonald's

63.   Match the Shakespearean quotation with the character who said it:

(A)   "Brevity is the soul of wit"   __ Polonius
(B)   "I have come to bury Caesar, not to praise him"   __ Mark Anthony
(C)   "Hath not a Jew eyes?"   __ Shylock
(D)   "Now is the winter of our discontent made   __ Richard III
        glorious summer by this sun of York"

64.   What was rated the most severely polluted and polluting city in the world in 1994?

(A)   Mexico City
(B)   Bangkok
(C)   Detroit
(D)   Moscow

65.   Assume that you are the architect placed in charge of building the Great Pyramid of Giza. The Pythagorean theorem would be most useful in calculating

(A)   the amount of materials that will be needed to complete the job
(B)   the complete ridiculousness of such a monumental undertaking
(C)   the slope of the sides of the pyramid
(D)   the number of hours of slave labor that will be required

66.   The two main characters in *Waiting for Godot* are

(A)   Rosencrantz and Guildenstern
(B)   Vladimir and Estragon
(C)   Gilbert and Sullivan
(D)   Porgy and Bess

67.   Who was the host of "Your Show Of Shows"?

(A)   Ed Sullivan
(B)   Milton Berle
(C)   Groucho Marx
(D)   Sid Caesar

68.   Which of the following is true about a near-sighted person?

(A)   She will have a positive power prescription with concave lenses in her glasses.
(B)   She will have a negative power prescription with concave lenses in her glasses.
(C)   She will have a positive power prescription with convex lenses in her glasses.
(D)   She will have a negative power prescription with convex lenses in her glasses.

69. Which play did Sam Shepherd NOT write?

    (A) *Curse of the Starving Class*
    (B) *Burn This*
    (C) *Tooth of Crime*
    (D) *Fool For Love*

70. After 400 years of European infiltration of North America, the Native American population is what percentage of its original size?

    (A) 2 percent
    (B) 25 percent
    (C) 40 percent
    (D) 60 percent

71. What was the first music video ever played on MTV?

    (A) "Video Killed The Radio Star" (The Buggles)
    (B) "Paradise By The Dashboard Lights" (Meatloaf)
    (C) "Candy O'" (The Cars)
    (D) "Rebel, Rebel" (David Bowie)

72. Which of the following accurately describes the difference between identical and fraternal twins?

    (A) Identical twins—one egg and one sperm; fraternal twins—one egg and two sperms
    (B) Identical twins—one egg and one sperm; fraternal twins—two eggs and two sperms
    (C) Identical twins—two eggs and one sperm; fraternal twins—two eggs and two sperms
    (D) Identical twins—one egg and two sperms; fraternal twins—two eggs and two sperms

73. Who is considered "the father of American football"?

    (A) Walter Camp
    (B) Clark Shaughnessy
    (C) Knute Rockne
    (D) Jim Thorpe

74. The city in which Rosa Parks refused to give up her bus seat to a white man, setting in motion the civil rights movement, was

    (A) Selma, Georgia
    (B) Charleston, South Carolina
    (C) Oxford, Mississippi
    (D) Montgomery, Alabama

75. In which country did chess originate?

(A) England
(B) France
(C) India
(D) Syria

76. Which planet has (i) the longest year, (ii) the longest day?

(A) (i) Mercury, (ii) Pluto
(B) (i) Pluto, (ii) Mercury
(C) (i) Neptune, (ii) Venus
(D) (i) Earth, (ii) Mars

77. Jerome Kern and Oscar Hammerstein's _____ was an early example of the transition from the revues of Ziegfeld to musical theatre based on narrative.

(A) *Oklahoma!*
(B) *Showboat*
(C) *Anything Goes*
(D) *Carousel*

78. What happened at the Stonewall Inn in New York City's Greenwich Village on June 27, 1969?

(A) A riot to protest arrests of gay bar patrons
(B) A riot to protest arrests of straight bar patrons
(C) A riot to protest arrests of black bar patrons
(D) A riot to protest arrests of white bar patrons

79. Which has the lowest probability of occurring?

(A) Being struck by lightning
(B) Being struck by lightning twice
(C) Winning a multi-state lottery
(D) Being born

80. Salsa, which according to George Castanaza on "Seinfeld" is now the second most popular condiment in the United States,

(A) causes heartburn because it is acidic
(B) causes heartburn because it is basic
(C) acts as an excellent cleanser of pennies
(D) Both A and C

81. When was Gregorain Chant developed?

    (A) The seventh century
    (B) The ninth century
    (C) The eleventh century
    (D) The thirteenth century

82. The influence of the French new wave movement was most evident in which of the following late 1960s American films?

    (A) *Barbarella*
    (B) *The Graduate*
    (C) *2001: A Space Odyssey*
    (D) *Faster Pussycat! Kill! Kill!*

83. Which of the following is an example of a fungus?

    (A) Baker's yeast
    (B) Truffles
    (C) The cause of athlete's foot
    (D) All of the above

84. Which of these four elements is the best conductor of electricity?

    (A) Aluminum
    (B) Silver
    (C) Gold
    (D) Copper

85. Who was Nat Bacon?

    (A) A wealthy farmer from Virginia
    (B) A freed slave who returned to Africa
    (C) A rebellious merchant in Boston
    (D) A radical student at Harvard

86. The left hemisphere of the brain controls all of the following abilities EXCEPT

    (A) speaking
    (B) spatial construction
    (C) reading and writing
    (D) calculating and analytical thinking

87. **Which of the following studios did Charlie Chaplin help found?**

    (A) Paramount
    (B) 20th Century-Fox
    (C) Warner Brothers
    (D) United Artists

88. **Group psychology differs from individual psychology in that**

    (A) people may behave differently in groups than as individuals
    (B) counseling takes place in groups instead of individually
    (C) theories are developed by groups instead of individuals
    (D) in a group psychology, individual viewpoints are not considered

89. **In which city did bossa nova originate**

    (A) Santiago
    (B) Caracas
    (C) Rio de Janeiro
    (D) Buenos Aires

90. **The term "nickelodeon" refers to**

    (A) the first device invented for viewing motion pictures
    (B) Edison's first film projector
    (C) the first permanent movie theaters
    (D) vaudeville theaters which featured live acts accompanied by films

91. **Who wrote the quintet known as *The Trout*?**

    (A) Gustav Mahler
    (B) Ludwig van Beethoven
    (C) Robert Schumann
    (D) Franz Schubert

92. **Which of the following describes the principles of behaviorism, or learning theory?**

    (A) Monkey see, monkey do.
    (B) If the carrot doesn't work, use the stick.
    (C) The squeaky wheel gets the grease.
    (D) All of the above

93. **Which of these jazz musicians did NOT directly contribute to the creation of the bebop style?**

    (A) "Dizzy" Gillespie
    (B) "Yardbird" Parker
    (C) "Bud" Powell
    (D) "Satchmo" Armstrong

94. The first permanent movie theater in the U.S. was established in
    (A) 1896
    (B) 1902
    (C) 1906
    (D) 1910

95. The term "hogan" means
    (A) "home place"
    (B) "hero"
    (C) "hollow"
    (D) "holy earth"

96. Who was the first African American to win an Academy Award?
    (A) James Earl Jones
    (B) Oscar Micheaux
    (C) Hattie McDaniel
    (D) Sidney Poitier

97. All of the following may be caused by nutritional deficiency EXCEPT
    (A) anemia (low red blood cell count)
    (B) a malformed skeleton and stunted growth
    (C) disturbances in vision and brain functioning
    (D) cancer

98. Who is credited with the invention of the "narrative" film?
    (A) Edwin S. Porter
    (B) Georges Méliès
    (C) Jean-Luc Goddard
    (D) Sergei Eisenstein

99. The Law of Demand states that
    (A) the quantity demanded increases when price increases, other things constant
    (B) the quantity demanded decreases when price increases, other things constant
    (C) the quantity demanded does not change when price increases, other things constant
    (D) the quantity demanded increases when price increases, no matter what

100. Which of the following studios has never been found in violation of federal anti-trust laws?

(A) Paramount
(B) Universal
(C) 20th Century-Fox
(D) SONY Pictures

Answers to the Culturescope Quiz

Question Number	Correct Answer	% of Survey Respondents Answering Correctly	Explanation on Page
1.	D	21	Answer is explained on page 432
2.	C	51	Answer is explained on page 113
3.	B	71	Answer is explained on page 326
4.	C	43	Answer is explained on page 53
5.	B	99	Answer is explained on page 654
6.	B	72	Answer is explained on page 471
7.	A	67	Answer is explained on page 604
8.	B	81	Answer is explained on page 627
9.	C	57	Answer is explained on page 39
10.	B	19	Answer is explained on page 442
11.	B	92	Answer is explained on page 81
12.	B	47	Answer is explained on page 629
13.	A	59	Answer is explained on page 632
14.	D	52	Answer is explained on page 594
15.	A	15	Answer is explained on page 47
16.	B	90	Answer is explained on page 665
17.	A	23	Answer is explained on page 277
18.	C	93	Answer is explained on page 75
19.	C	17	Answer is explained on page 437
20.	A	74	Answer is explained on page 85
21.	B	63	Answer is explained on page 619
22.	D	58	Answer is explained on page 447
23.	D	27	Answer is explained on pages 584
24.	C	74	Answer is explained on pages 656

Question Number	Correct Answer	% of Survey Respondents Answering Correctly	Explanation on Page
25.	D	21	Answer is explained on page 46
26.	B	77	Answer is explained on page 80
27.	B	73	Answer is explained on page 613
28.	B	98	Answer is explained on page 95
29.	A	21	Answer is explained on page 249
30.	B	41	Answer is explained on page 518
31.	C	47	Answer is explained on page 255
32.	C	50	Answer is explained on page 494
33.	C	49	Answer is explained on page 271
34.	B	96	Answer is explained on page 535
35.	A	60	Answer is explained on page 146
36.	A	62	Answer is explained on page 280
37.	C	57	Answer is explained on page 533
38.	D	34	Answer is explained on page 74
39.	A	60	Answer is explained on page 142
40.	A	61	Answer is explained on page 603
41.	D,C,B,A	22	Answer is explained on page 542
42.	A	62	Answer is explained on page 395
43.	B	23	Answer is explained on page 579
44.	A	41	Answer is explained on page 470
45.	C	62	Answer is explained on page 326
46.	C	47	Answer is explained on page 599
47.	A	67	Answer is explained on page 479
48.	D	23	Answer is explained on page 573
49.	C	50	Answer is explained on page 142

Question Number	Correct Answer	% of Survey Respondents Answering Correctly	Explanation on Page
50.	A	46	Answer is explained on page 509
51.	A	29	Answer is explained on page 89
52.	D	59	Answer is explained on page 135
53.	A	87	Answer is explained on page 411
54.	C	46	Answer is explained on page 148
55.	D	27	Answer is explained on page 250
56.	B	39	Answer is explained on page 489
57.	C	65	Answer is explained on page 538
58.	A	21	Answer is explained on page 153
59.	D	68	Answer is explained on page 189
60.	D	29	Answer is explained on page 517
61.	C	63	Answer is explained on page 151
62.	B	5	Answer is explained on page 516
63.	A,B,C,D	40	Answer is explained on page 547
64.	B	11	Answer is explained on page 148
65.	A	1	Answer is explained on page 340
66.	B	62	Answer is explained on page 569
67.	D	41	Answer is explained on page 522
68.	B	28	Answer is explained on page 360
69.	B	34	Answer is explained on page 573
70.	A	75	Answer is explained on page 174
71.	A	51	Answer is explained on page 536
72.	B	63	Answer is explained on page 222
73.	A	31	Answer is explained on page 446
74.	D	78	Answer is explained on page 197

Question Number	Correct Answer	% of Survey Respondents Answering Correctly	Explanation on Page
75.	C	41	Answer is explained on page 463
76.	B	75	Answer is explained on page 335
77.	B	25	Answer is explained on page 564
78.	A	76	Answer is explained on page 203
79.	B	36	Answer is explained on page 343
80.	D	58	Answer is explained on page 369
81.	B	27	Answer is explained on page 294
82.	B	14	Answer is explained on page 117
83.	D	78	Answer is explained on page 214
84.	B	45	Answer is explained on page 352
85.	A	17	Answer is explained on page 622
86.	B	34	Answer is explained on page 229
87.	D	49	Answer is explained on page 105
88.	A	62	Answer is explained on page 244
89.	C	24	Answer is explained on page 331
90.	C	16	Answer is explained on page 101
91.	C	52	Answer is explained on page 300
92.	D	51	Answer is explained on page 237
93.	D	32	Answer is explained on page 311
94.	B	26	Answer is explained on page 99
95.	A	24	Answer is explained on page 42
96.	C	30	Answer is explained on page 103
97.	D	89	Answer is explained on page 227
98.	B	24	Answer is explained on page 100
99.	B	82	Answer is explained on page 66
100.	D	61	Answer is explained on page 108

DETERMINING YOUR SCORE

STEP 1 Using the answers on the preceding pages, determine how many questions you got right.

STEP 2 List the number of correct answers here. This is your raw score.

STEP 3 To determine your real score, take the number from Step 1 above and look it up in the left column of the Score Conversion Table on page 25; the corresponding score on the right is your score on the exam.

THE PRINCETON REVIEW CULTURE QUOTIENT CONVERSION TABLE

Raw Score	Scaled Score	Raw Score	Scaled Score	Raw Score	Scaled Score	Raw Score	Scaled Score
80-100	800	59	640	38	470	17	290
79	790	58	630	37	460	16	290
78	780	57	620	36	450	15	280
77	780	56	620	35	440	14	270
76	770	55	610	34	430	13	260
75	760	54	600	33	420	12	250
74	760	53	590	32	420	11	240
73	750	52	580	31	410	10	240
72	740	51	570	30	400	9	230
71	730	50	570	29	390	8	220
70	730	49	560	28	380	7	210
69	720	48	550	27	370	6	200
68	710	47	540	26	370	5	200
67	700	46	530	25	360	4	200
66	700	45	520	24	350	3	200
65	690	44	510	23	340	2	200
64	680	43	510	22	330	1	200
63	670	42	500	21	320	0	200
62	660	41	490	20	320		
61	650	40	480	19	310		
60	650	39	470	18	300		

WHAT YOUR SCORE MEANS

We have given the Culturescope Quiz to college grads across the country and scored their tests to give you an SAT-like scale for your cultural literacy. Just like the SAT, your converted score is a number between 200 and 800. The average student gets a 500.

IF YOU SCORE BETWEEN 710 AND 800

You have a profound knowledge of culture. You can carry on a conversation with anyone. Your parents, college professors, and perfect strangers are impressed with you. Still, there are things in this book that you will not know and find interesting. Pay special attention to the sidebars and boxes in order to glean movie and book suggestions as well as *fascinating* trivia.

IF YOU SCORE BETWEEN 610 AND 700

You have a great understanding of American culture. Read the sections where you have the most to learn and heed the movie and book suggestions. You don't have very far to go, so working with *Culturescope* should produce immediate results.

IF YOU SCORE BETWEEN 510 AND 600

There are a few holes in your cultural education—but not to worry! We wrote this book with you in mind. Make *Culturescope* your personal Bible. Read it in the car, in the can, on the train, at the beach—you get the idea.

IF YOU SCORE BETWEEN 410 AND 500

There are some serious deficiencies in your cultural knowledge, and you will need too spend some time with this book. But don't worry, you're really going to get your money's worth. Keep *Culturescope* available, and open it up whenever you can. It won't be long before you're dropping obscure quotes at dinner parties.

IF YOU SCORE BETWEEN 200 AND 410

Party's over. You've had your fun; now let's get down to business.

Architecture contains a huge amount of information about the culture that creates it—about its religion, its technologies, its family relations, its political systems. Architecture is often a forum for the highest achievements of a society. But architecture is hardly a continuum of discrete styles created by infallible masters—it's a continuing aesthetic debate that takes place all around you.

1. What is a ziggurat thought to have been?

(A) A cave painting
(B) A stairway to heaven
(C) An early architectural tool
(D) A god of shelter

The roots of Western architecture are found in Mesopotamia (p. 154), where monuments were built strictly in the service of religion. The most

CULTURESCOPE

Blade Runner (1982), directed by Ridley Scott. Check out the ziggurat associated with twenty-first century corporate power.

The pyramid at Saqqara

Imhotep, architect of Zoser's pyramid, was a man of many talents. Besides his busy architectural practice, he achieved renown for his wisdom as a priest, astronomer, magician, and healer. After his death he was mythologized as a healing deity. It's been downhill for the profession ever since—nowadays, architects are happy to get a project built and to publish the occasional article.

Napoleon's scholars calculated that the blocks in the three pyramids at Giza were enough to build a 1' x 10' wall around France.

Aztec (1980), by Gary Jennings. This soapy adventure yarn is set in Tenochtitlan before the coming of Cortez, and it vividly depicts Aztec society and architecture.

distinctive structure of a Mesopotamian colony was the **ziggurat**. A ziggurat is a rectangle measuring a little more than 200 by 150 feet, with an original height of about seventy feet. It is built on three successive levels with ramplike stairs leading to a shrine on the top. Although its exact derivation and use are not entirely known, this enormous, multi-tiered, mud brick structure was thought to have functioned as the stairway by which the gods of the country mounted to heaven every night. The ziggurat at **Ur** (c. 2100 B.C.) still remains from the New-Sumerian period.

South of Mesopotamia, ancient Egyptians felt that a house was only a temporary lodging; it was the tomb that was the permanent abode. Thus, while Egyptian houses were built of baked brick and papyrus stalks, the **pyramids** and their associated temples were constructed of durable stone and on the largest scale possible. Early Egyptian pyramids had stepped sides like the Mesopotamian ziggurats; the tomb of King Zoser at Saqqara, attributed to history's first known architect, **Imhotep**, is one example. Later pyramids evolved into the pure geometric forms we know so well, epitomized by Cheops' Pyramid, the oldest and largest of the **Great Pyramids of Giza**.

Mayan pyramid

The pyramid-temple ziggurat form has a long and rich history in the Americas that rivals the better-known architectural forms of Sumeria and Egypt. The religious complexes at Tiotihuacan (Toltec, c. 100 A.D.), Tikal (Maya, c. 700 A.D.), Cuzco (Inca, c. 1500), and Tenochtitlan (Aztec, c. 1500) were the equals in grandeur and sophistication of any in the Old World. As a symbol of pre-Columbian culture, the ziggurat form still evokes powerful associations in modern Latin American architecture.

2. **What are the three classical orders of ancient Greek architecture?**
   - (A) Periclean, Peloponnesian, and Aeolian
   - (B) Athenian, Spartan, and Cretan
   - (C) Platonic, Aristotelian, and Socratic
   - (D) Doric, Ionic, and Corinthian

Ancient Greek architecture is divided into the three classical **orders**, each of which combines a different type of **column** and **entablature**, the horizontal part that rests on the column. Each column, in turn, is made up of a **base**, **shaft**, and **capital**, the wide stone placed on the very top of the column below the entablature. The order of a monument determines its entire style. What's amazing is that each order dictated a precise, even rigid style, and no one knows why or how the particulars arose.

The **Doric** order, which originated around the fifth century B.C., was the simplest and most austere. It lacked a base and had a plain, unembellished capital. The **Parthenon**, a temple dedicated to the goddess Athena, for whom Athens was named, is the perfect example of Doric architecture. The temple, located in the **Acropolis** (Greek for "high city"), the sacred citadel on a hill above Athens, brought graceful, balanced proportions to the Doric scheme. The **Ionic** order developed soon after the Doric and was first found in Asia minor. Recognizable by its scrolled (or **"volute"**) capital,

The Classical Orders

Doric   Ionic   Corinthian

Key:
A. Entablature   F. Capital
B. Column   G. Shaft
C. Cornice   H. Base
D. Frieze   I. Plinth
E. Architrave

the Ionic column was slightly more elaborate than the Doric. The fanciest of the three Greek orders was the **Corinthian**, which is really just a variation of the Ionic. With its capital shaped like an upside-down bell and lushly carved with leaves, the Corinthian order developed in the late fifth century B.C. A fourth order,

The Acropolis: on top of the world

called **Tuscan**, is thought to have originated with the Etruscans (p. 387), the civilization that preceded Rome on the Italian peninsula, but no examples of it survive.

3. **What is the "agora"?**
   (A) A material for expensive sweaters
   (B) A political and social gathering place
   (C) An inspiration for cruciform church design
   (D) A desire to isolate the boudoir in residential architecture

The core element of the classical town plan in ancient Greece was known as the **agora**. This center of civic and commercial life originated as an open space centrally located within the town. The multipurpose space functioned as a marketplace and a location for political assembly, ceremonies, and spectacles. The agora evolved from an irregularly shaped space loosely surrounded by buildings into a more formal arrangement surrounded by civic buildings and temples. As a center for commercial and social exchange, the agora is a precursor of the later Italian **piazza**. A good example of a typical agora can be seen in the city of Cyrene, a colony established by the Greeks in 630 B.C. A magnet for many artists, writers, and philosophers, Cyrene was known as one of the great cultural centers of Greek civilization. During Roman rule, the city buildings and spaces, including the agora, were kept intact, but adapted for other uses.

Hippodamos of Miletus (500-440 B.C.), a political theorist credited with being the first **urban planner**, is associated with the rebuilding of the Greek city of Miletus around 479 B.C., after the city was sacked by the Persians. Archeologists have discovered that Miletus was laid out according to a rigid **grid system**, also called a **gridiron**, directly over the natural topography of a peninsula surrounded by two harbors.

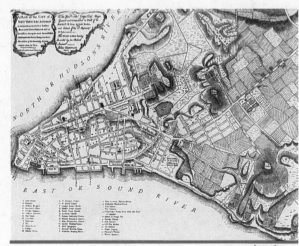

Pre-grid Manhattan

ARCHITERMS

Arcade: *a series of arches supported by piers or columns.*
Colonnade: *a series or row of columns, usually spanned by lintels.*
Stoa: *in ancient Greek architecture, an open building whose roof is supported by a row of columns parallel to the back wall.*

Two distinct grids of regularized building blocks were organized around a seemingly random zone of public buildings. Where the grids merged became the agora. The grid ends at the city limits, where a fortification wall surrounds the city on its land side. The use of the **fortification wall** as a barrier *and* a city planning element is characteristic of many Greek cities, and was developed through the Renaissance. Although the city took many decades to evolve fully, the preimposed gridiron plan laid an organized framework for future growth. The gridiron represented an attempt to impose order and simplify the problems of land use and ownership, and in some form or another the grid sytem can be found in most American cities today. In Manhattan, for example, the idea of 155 streets running east-west and twelve avenues running north-south was introduced in 1811. The pre-grid southern tip of Manhattan grew in a more loosely organized, organic fashion, a direct result of the carving up of the land for farming.

4. **The term "superimposed orders" refers to**

   (A) orders of architecture placed one above the other in an arcaded or colonnaded building

   (B) orders of architecture placed one next to the other in an arcaded or colonnaded building

   (C) orders of architecture that have been stripped of all ornamentation

   (D) None of the above

The **superimposition of orders** is the term for a style in which all three classical orders are placed one on top of the other, usually in this sequence: Doric columns on the ground level, Ionic columns on the second level, and Corinthian columns above that. Superimposed orders first occurred in Greek **stoas,** or walled **porticoes** (roofed porches), but Roman and Renaissance builders also stacked orders. The **Colosseum** in Rome, built 75-80 A.D. as a stadium to hold gladiatorial games (p. 433), used the superimposition of orders to adorn each structural **bay,** or compartment, separately, maintaining the integrity of the structure at each level. The basic bay unit of the Colosseum was made up of brick arches supporting a **barrel vault,** a deep, rounded arched structure forming a ceiling or roof. The massive ground floor base was adorned with Doric columns, the "heaviest" of the three orders. The middle tier was made up of the slightly more elaborate Ionic columns,

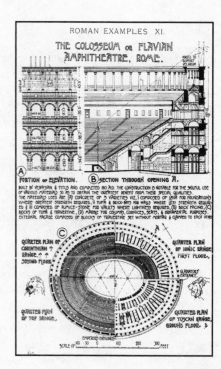

while the "light" top layer features the decorative, relatively delicate-looking Corinthian columns.

Another of the great masterpieces of Roman architecture was the **Pantheon**, the Roman version of a temple to the gods. The awesome interior space of this round, domed building is made even more dramatic by an **oculus** (or "eye," a round opening) that punctures the dome, allowing a stream of light to illuminate the interior and giving it a cave-like effect. Roman architects also designed many **basilicas**, long buildings that filled several civic functions, serving primarily as a dignified setting for judicial business. The plan of the basilica, a long central hall (called the **nave**) flanked by columns, usually with an aisle on each side, was adapted by early Christians for their churches and later became the standard design for Christian churches throughout Europe.

Marcus Vitruvius Pollio (flourished 46-30 B.C.) was a Roman architect during the reign of the Emperor Augustus, to whom he dedicated his ten-book treatise *De Architectura*, the only surviving Roman architectural text. Dealing with all aspects of town planning, building materials, construction, public health, astrology, and mechanics of war, the book demonstrates the central position architecture held in the culture. Vitruvius also includes a lengthy discussion of the Doric, Ionic, Corinthian, and Tuscan orders, with frequent references to the Greeks, making clear that the Romans were aware of the Greeks' significant architectural contributions. But while Roman architecture built on Greek foundations, unlike in other areas, such as sculpture (p. 578), the Romans actually superseded the achievements of the Greeks and developed their own distinctive style. The Romans introduced bricks and concrete, and it was they who invented the vault, the arch, and the dome. The arch and vault were used not only in public buildings like the Colosseum but also for construction projects such as sewers, bridges, and **aqueducts**, many of which are still—amazingly—around today, testaments to the genius of Roman engineering as well as to the value the society placed on order and permanence.

CONCRETE FACTS

Concrete, mortar mixed with small stones, is often thought of as a modern building material. In fact, the first widespread use of concrete was in ancient Rome, and its use was characteristic of much of Roman architecture. Combined with the vault and the arch, it allowed Roman architects great plasticity of form and enabled them to enclose large spaces without interior supports. The celebrated Roman aqueducts are made of brick and concrete, and the masterful Pantheon is topped with a concrete dome. After the fall of the Roman Empire, the use of concrete disappeared and was not revived until the 1700s. Experiments with steel reinforcement in the late 1800s solidified (heh heh) concrete's role as a strong and versatile building material.

ARCHITERMS

Caryatid: *a carved female figure that functions as a supporting column.*

5. **Which of the following best describes a flying buttress?**

   (A) An interior masonry roof or ceiling constructed on the arch principle
   (B) A new francophile sexual technique
   (C) An exoskeletal system
   (D) A female figure that functions as a supporting column

The architecture of ancient Rome experienced a revival in Western Europe from the eighth to the twelfth centuries, known as the period of **Romanesque** architecture. With a burgeoning religious enthusiasm marked by such events as the Crusades (p. 490), Romanesque architecture sprang up all over feudal Europe, marking pilgrimage routes and monasteries. Although Romanesque religious architecture incorporated local idioms as well as Roman influences, it was typified by interiors that were simply organized and enclosed by massive walls with round arches. Some of the finest examples of the style are in Burgundy, in the Cluny monastery. The Atun Cathedral there prefigures the next style in cathedral building, **Gothic architecture,** in its use of the **pointed arch** and **buttresses**.

The Gothic style was originally named by Italian Renaissance artists, who hated it so much that they attributed it to the barbaric **Goths** who sacked Rome. The elements most identified with Gothic architecture, such as the pointed arch and the rib vault, all had their antecedents in Romanesque architecture. The first completely Gothic building was the abbey church of St. Denis outside of Paris.

Between 1194 and 1220 a new cathedral was built for the city of Chartres, France. Generally considered the first building of the High Gothic period, the **Chartres Cathedral** is also the first building designed fully with the **flying buttress** structural system characteristic of High Gothic architecture. With Chartres, the massive, heavy proportioning of the Romanesque period evolved into the elegant and organic proportioning of the Gothic. This new gracefulness was largely due to skeletal structural innovations such as the flying buttress, an external inclined piece carried on an arch or series of arches and a solid masonry structure to which it gives lateral thrust. Its main purpose was to strengthen the nave walls, allowing for a higher, more dramatic vertical dimension. Similar methods had been used in the architecture of Romanesque

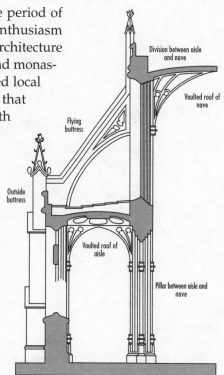

Labels: Division between aisle and nave; Vaulted roof of nave; Flying buttress; Outside buttress; Vaulted roof of aisle; Pillar between aisle and nave

Flying buttress system for a Gothic cathedral

Cathedrals often took more than 100 years to construct, with the position of master builder passed down from father to son to grandson to great-grandson. The penalty for a structural failure, or collapse, was often immediate execution.

cathedrals, but in those cases the buttresses were completely concealed under roofing. The buttress permitted the construction of a skeletal structural system that was self-supporting and thus eliminated the need for solid, heavy walls. It also allowed for larger windows, which let more light into the space.

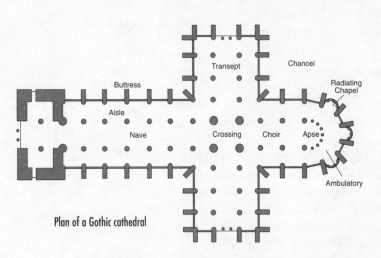

Plan of a Gothic cathedral

Renaissance critics looked down on Gothic architecture for not conforming to the standards of Greek and Roman architecture. Later, **Rationalists**, led by the theorist Viollét-le-Duc, looked back to the Gothic tradition and praised the proportioning and structural integrity of an architecture that was not inspired by the classical tradition. Gothic tradition ultimately became a precursor to the architecture of twentieth-century skyscrapers.

6. Who was the first architect of the Renaissance?

(A) Antonio Averlino Filarete
(B) Anna Maria Alberghetti
(C) Filippo Brunelleschi
(D) Leone Battista Alberti

ARCHITERMS

Lintel: *a beam of any material used to span an opening.*
Pediment: *the feature over a door or window. Its sides can be straight or curved.*

The Renaissance (p. 579) marked the emergence of the architect as we know her today: no longer a craftsperson, but a skilled artist who sees buildings as an expression of some profound aesthetic truth. Architects in fifteenth-century Italy tried to rediscover the essence of ancient Roman architecture by studying the monuments of the past and the treatise of Vitruvius, and to elucidate its mathematical virtues by the study of arithmetic, geometry, music and anatomy. **Filippo Brunelleschi** (1377-1446) formulated the laws of linear perspective, and his Ospedale degli Innocenti (Foundling Hospital) and dome of Florence Cathedral are considered to be the first architectural works of the Renaissance. Michelangelo (p. 585), who occasionally knocked off a piece of sculpture or a fresco, was also one of the great architects of the time. Though most of his projects remained unfinished in his lifetime, his **Biblioteca Laurenziana** (Laurentian Library) is considered one of the masterpieces of Florence. **Leon Batista Alberti** (1404-1472), architect and theorist, continues to influence architecture through his treatise, *On the Art of Building in Ten Books* (1452), which crystallized Renaissance ideals of proportion, the orders, and town planning.

Architecture and books have had a long history together, dating back more than 2000 years. The most comprehensive architectural library in the world is The Avery Library of Columbia University in New York City. It contains over 500,000 volumes on architecture, including original editions of Alberti's and Palladio's treatises.

7. **Which of the following design strategies was characteristic of a sixteenth-century city concerned with military defense?**
   - (A) A perimeter wall
   - (B) A radial scheme of streets
   - (C) A central square or piazza
   - (D) All of the above

With the advent of artillery warfare, a major concern of the ruling class of any town was protection against invasion. Provisions were made in the overall layout of a city to make it as difficult as possible to attack. First laid out in 1593 and completed in 1623, the city of Palmanova, Italy represented the state of the art in urban defense planning. The exterior rim was a nine-sided polygon with a bastion at each point. This was enclosed by a nine-point star wall. The in-between space was used for ceremonial military parades and barracks. A series of radial streets ran from the perimeter wall and converged inward toward the central hexagon-shaped piazza. The piazza could be protected by sealing off the radial streets that intersected it. The civil residential areas were located off of the radiating streets, and gates were placed where the streets intersected the interior perimeter wall. Additional perimeter walls were built in the late 1600s and the early 1800s.

Very few of these ideally fortified cities were actually built. There were several drawbacks, including the fact that it was prohibitively expensive to build an **earthwork**, an embankment made of earth, to form the vast perimeter walls. The isolation between the city and countryside inherent to the plan, fostered by the physical and psychological barrier presented by the wall, also hindered commercial and agricultural growth. However, many features of the city fortress were adapted and modified to serve the needs of other cities. In Karlsruhe, Germany, an old hunting lodge was replaced by a palace that became the point of convergence of thirty-two radiating roads. The roads were not bounded by a wall, however; they ran out toward the forest. In other cities, like Berlin, gridded extensions were grafted onto the original medieval walled city.

AND THE WALLS CAME TUMBLING DOWN

The fortified hill towns of the Kingdom of Naples withstood a seven-year assault by Charles VIII of France due to the height of the walls. But when a technological advance in the design of bullets allowed them to be aimed slightly higher, the town fell to the enemy in eight hours, its walls rendered useless.

Today, the notion of a fortified city can be seen in the "gated communities" of American suburbs. They come complete with security walls, their own police forces, and maintenance fees.

8. The term "hogan" means

(A) "home place"
(B) "hero"
(C) "hollow"
(D) "holy earth"

A Montana tribe and their teepee

Native American architecture before the arrival of Columbus (p. 174) was incredibly rich and varied, and its forms are deeply imbedded in the American psyche. Indeed, with its profound sense of place and the use of appropriate materials and integration of form and meaning, Native American architecture continues to inform and inspire modern architecture. The **teepee**, the **igloo**, and the **pueblo** all resonate with associations of beauty, spirituality, and an ecological harmony that modern architecture envies, and yet these are just a few examples of the diverse forms of Native American building traditions. The more than three hundred nations who lived in North America built their homes and villages according to principles shaped by inherited traditional forms and handed down from generation to generation. These traditions were their blueprints and their building codes.

In the Northeast, a land thick with pine and hardwood forests, the basic building system consisted of bark sheets or woven reed mats lashed to a structural frame of saplings. Along the St. Lawrence River to the shores of Lake Ontario, the Iroquois and Huron built communal **longhouses**, often 100 feet or more in length, covered in sheets of elm

A pueblo in Taos, New Mexico

bark. Single families occupied sleeping compartments along each side of a central aisle, and the entire arrangement was symbolic of the tribes' social solidarity. So strong was this symbol of the longhouse as a unifying force that the five tribes of the Iroquois Confederacy (p. 620) called themselves the "people of the longhouse," and they spoke metaphorically of their domain as a giant longhouse.

Like the civilizations of Central and South America, the people of the Southeast built shaped earth mounds to entomb the bodies of dignitaries and support temples on their flattened summits. The layout of the mounds often defined open-air plazas and fields for athletic events. The central pyramid at **Cahokia**, near present day St. Louis, was the largest structure north of Mexico.

The tribes of the Northwest built plank houses along the Pacific Coast, using massive logs for their post and beam frames, and split cedar and redwood planks for the walls and roofs. The houses, like those of other Native American cultural groups, were not just dwellings but manifestations of mythology and complex social organization. Painted and carved with stylized and symbolic decoration, the plank houses and their associated **"totem poles"** displayed the ancestry, status, prestige, and wealth of the individuals within.

The tribes of the Southwest built a variety of structures adapted to their hot, dry climate. The Navajo called the six-sided log dwellings **hogans**, meaning "home place." The roof was built of stacked pinion logs and covered with earth. Hogan doorways always faced east, and, as with the other examples we have mentioned, the entire process of planning and building the structure was of great symbolic meaning and import.

A Navajo hogan

9. **What is the architectural significance of the Parson Capen House in Topsfield, Massachusetts?**

(A) It is the only house of seventeenth-century New England that can be dated precisely.
(B) It was the first American house to be built out of brick.
(C) It was the first house to install central air conditioning.
(D) One of the Salem Witches resided there until her death in 1644.

Built in 1683 (the date of the house raising, June 8, 1683, carved on the chimney, is the only evidence we have of the precise date of a seventeenth-century New England structure), the **Parson Capen House** in Topsfield, Massachusetts, offers a good example of the way in which the architectural style of the late medieval period in England was adapted by the Puritans (p. 500) in New England. The house was built according to the traditional British **timber construction**, consisting of a heavy oak frame positioned in place with **mortise and tenon joints**. Vertical studs and horizontal joists support the walls and floors, respectively, inside the tremendous frame. The roof is steeply **gabled** (forming a vertical triangle) and the exterior is sided with simple clapboard. The house looks

Parson Capen House: nothing fancy

Mortise and tenon joint

unadorned, with decoration only in two places. Through this simple design and the choice of austere building materials, Reverend Capen managed to express Puritan ideals in the architecture of a dwelling.

The basic elements of this New England house became the foundation upon which Puritan villages, towns, cities, and the dwellings within them were built. The location of Parson Capen's house in the center of the village **common,** or **green,** represents the focal role of the minister in the Puritan community. The New World village green was a direct descendant of the Greek and Roman agora and the Italian piazza. The simple Parson Capen House presents a striking contrast to neoclassicism, the next architectural movement that made its way across the Atlantic Ocean.

10. To which of the following architectural movements would a pattern book be most applicable?

(A) Romanesque
(B) Neoclassicism
(C) American Colonialism
(D) High Victorian Gothic

The term *charrette* is used by architects to express a period of continuous work that spans several days without sleep as part of the creative process. The term is derived from the French word for "small cart," one of which would circulate throughout the studios of *L'École des Beaux-Arts* in the morning to collect the students' assignments—hence they were working until the arrival of the *charrette*.

L'École des Beaux-Arts, founded in the late eighteenth century in France, was the first architecture school in the world. The theoretical approach of the school reflected the ideals of the Enlightenment (p. 396): the goal was to discover a complete, rational system of order that expressed humanity's place in the universe. Under the influence of the *École*, for the first time in history an architectural movement, **neoclassicism**, became a universal standard followed by all architects rather than a regional movement by country. Neoclassical buildings in France, England, and the U.S., among other places, followed principles of geometry and symmetry rooted in the Roman architecture of classical antiquity. The **Prix de Rome** was the coveted and well-respected award for the winner of the annual architectural competition sponsored by the school. Students were praised for their ability to reinterpret—essentially regurgitate—the principles of classical antiquity based on a strict code of forms and techniques.

The church of Ste-Geneviève, also known as the **Pantheon**, Paris, begun in 1755, was designed by Jacques Germain Soufflot and is considered the epitome of French neoclassicism of the Enlightenment era (in addition to being a feat of engineering) with its Greek cross plan, temple porticoed front, and hemispherical dome. The structural flying buttresses are hidden.

Paris's Pantheon

11. Which American patriot designed the University of Virginia?

(A) Ethan Allen
(B) George Washington
(C) Thomas Paine
(D) Thomas Jefferson

Across the Atlantic, architects such as Thomas Jefferson (p. 405) in Virginia and Alexander Parris in Boston adapted neoclassicism to the American environment. Jefferson's home at Monticello is considered a masterpiece that tailors neoclassical principles to Jefferson's individual vision. Another example of early American neoclassicism is Parris's Quincy Market in Boston. **Charles Follen McKim** (1847-1909), a student at *L'École des Beaux-Arts* from 1867-1870, designed Low Library, Columbia University, a classical masterpiece, with his firm, **McKim, Mead, and White**, designers of many prominent neoclassical buildings. The **Greek Revival** period immediately followed the neoclassical period in America. Greek Revival buildings adhere much more strictly to the proportions and character of the Greek orders and the Greek ornamental system. Many courthouses and post offices around the U.S. were designed in the Greek Revival style, including the U.S. Supreme Court building.

Recognizing the importance of cultural liberty to political independence, Jefferson pegged architecture as the perfect discipline through which the democratic ideals of a new nation could be reflected. The first American architect to discard British architecture as the sole model, he was especially drawn to the classical elements of Renaissance architecture, in particular the classical principles of proportion and ornamentation embraced by the sixteenth-century Italian architect **Andrea Palladio** (1508-1580). Jefferson's plan for the University of Virginia, built 1817-1826, came from his revolutionary view of education and the new American university. All matters of academia and discipline, including chosen courses of study, were done under a democratic system that brought together administrators, faculty, and students. To Jefferson, the previous architectural models of the American campus and English quadrangle did not fit this new type of educational institution. Jefferson's UVA **Rotunda**, the central building that is the point from which the rest

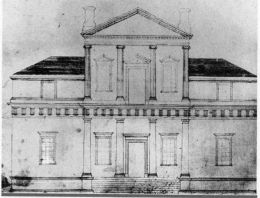

Jefferson's orginal design for Monticello

Even though they are the smallest and least comfortable rooms on the campus, it is considered a great honor to live in the original student housing designed by Jefferson at the University of Virginia.

Thomas Jefferson's Monticello was built and rebuilt over a period of more than twenty years, and Jefferson's daughter accused him of loving to tear down walls even more than build them up. The house was completely redesigned at least twice, reflecting Jefferson's evolving tastes and restless mind. There is evidence to suggest that Jefferson himself never considered the house complete; he referred to it as his continuing "architectural essay" in brick and wood.

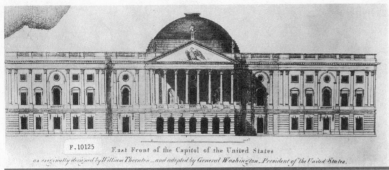

Design for the Capitol of the U.S.: neoclassicism on the Hill

of the campus radiates, was a clear descendant of Palladio's **Villa Rotunda** in Vincenza, Italy, which in turn had the Pantheon as its precedent. The strength of both structures lies in their monumental simplicity and great scale. Both are domed round buildings fronted with rectangular porticoes (Villa Rotunda actually has four identical ones). The domes are uninterrupted by vertical supports.

12. **The urban plan of Washington, D.C. was developed according to a European philosophy that made possible**

   (A) free speech for all citizens
   (B) the abolition of slavery
   (C) the virtues of democracy to thrive
   (D) the suppression of protest against the state

Pierre Charles L'Enfant (1754-1825), a French Engineer, was appointed in 1791 to devise a layout for the new capital city of **Washington, D.C.** The District of Columbia was the first city to be laid out on paper before actually being built. The scheme was based on three main components: straight and diagonal streets (the **trivium**); a meeting or divergence of three radial streets; and urban monuments and markers. In L'Enfant's plan for D.C., major avenues radiated from two focal points, the Capitol Building and the White House.

L'enfant terrible

L'Enfant superimposed a rigid right-angle grid onto the system of interlocking avenues and parks. This urban model, designed to quash the threat of civil disobedience and make any protest easy to suppress, is a clear example of how city planning can be used as a tool by the state. The nooks and crannies and crooked streets of the old medieval city were seen as potentially subversive of the idea of a central ruling power. In contrast,

The first fully mechanized American factory was built in 1814 in Waltham, Massachusetts, and was followed in 1823 by the first American factory town, named **Lowell**, after its founder, **Francis Lowell**. Lowell was designed to take advantage of the most readily available cheap labor: unmarried farm girls from surrounding areas. The "factory girls" lived under strict supervision, with rules designed to ensure morality, and gained international renown for their intellectual pursuits, including a literary magazine called *The Lowell Offering*.

the broad straight street was developed to promote public order and to connect any two points directly, facilitating transportation and communication.

In France in the period during and after the **French Revolution** in 1789, riots and skirmishes flourished in the medieval streets of Paris. Feeling threatened, **Napoleon III** (1808-1873) called in **Baron**

Georges-Eugène Haussman (1809-1891) to devise an urban-planning solution to the unrest. His plan, carried out between 1853 and 1870, was not unlike the plan for D.C. and tremendously altered the face of Paris. Tangled webs of medieval streets were essentially bulldozed to make way for broad boulevards that cut through neighborhoods with little regard for history or the people then living there. Haussman wrote of the **Boulevard de Sebastopol**: "It meant the disemboweling of the old Paris, the quarter of uprising and barricades, by a wide central street piercing through and through this almost impossible maze, and provided with communicating side streets."

13. **Cast-iron architecture was a significant technological advance because for the first time a designer could do what?**
    - (A) Select building parts from a catalogue
    - (B) Avoid working with the notoriously corrupt Woodworkers' union
    - (C) Open a chic gallery without much capital
    - (D) Construct a building more than five stories high

The Industrial Revolution brought advancements in the development of ferrous metals in the following order: **cast iron**, **wrought iron**, and **steel.** Presaging the mail-order frenzy of our own time, iron was developed to a point where it could be prefabricated to predetermined specifications and sold through mail order to the construction industry. Although cast iron was used in bridges, it was far from the ideal bridge-

 One of the bridges most symbolic of the Industrial Revolution is aptly named **The Iron Bridge**, over the Severn River at Coalbrookdale, England, 1779 by **Abraham Darby** (1750-1791). The cast iron was five times stronger than wood and, therefore, required one-fifth the amount of material to carry the same load.

Killer Bridge!

building material. Its heavy, brittle nature works well when used in **compression** (squishing together), but not so well when used in **tension** (pulling apart). **Thomas Telford** (1757-1834), the founder of the world's first engineering society, looked upon the "visual lightness" and strength of the cast-iron bridges as opening up a whole new world that eventually became known as **structural art**: the synthesis of aesthetics and engineering. The visually stunning **Brooklyn Bridge**, designed by **John Roebling** (1806-1869), who died just before work on the bridge commenced, was built by his son and daughter-in-law, Washington and Emily. The Brooklyn Bridge is one of the premiere examples of a **suspension bridge**. By putting all of its forces in tension through the use of steel cables, the suspension bridge was able to span distances previously unheard of.

👁 *Straight Out of Brooklyn* (1991), directed by Matty Rich. Seventeen-year-old Rich's rough-edged debut offers a cinematic illustration of how the Brooklyn Bridge functions simultaneously as a physical passage and a conceptual barrier.

These engineering advances and new building materials and techniques also contributed to the architecture of buildings. Joseph Paxton's groundbreaking **Crystal Palace**, which looked like a giant greenhouse (Paxton in fact originally built greenhouses for a living), was built in London in 1850-1851 for the first great International Exposition. Constructed almost entirely of glass and iron, the building was made possible by the prefabrication and standardization of its structural members. Equally as important, Paxton's design combined elegance and engineering so beautifully that there could be no debate as to whether ironwork was compatible with architecture.

14. **What was Louis H. Sullivan's most significant contribution to American architecture?**

   (A) The development of corporate architecture
   (B) Innovations in reinforced concrete
   (C) The invention of the blueprint machine
   (D) His design for the Ideal City

In the late nineteenth century, the economy of Chicago was booming, with industry and technology leading the way. The earliest roots of what is known as the **"new architecture"** took place in the relatively young Midwest (p. 154), far from the conservatism of what was happening in the more established Northeast (p. 154). But it was Philadelphia architect **Frank Furness** (1839-1912) who led the way with his ornamental motifs inspired by the organic forms of animals and plants. In Chicago, **Henry Hobson Richardson** (1836-1886) sought to convey a feeling of massiveness reminiscent of the Romanesque in his buildings. The **Marshall Field Wholesale Warehouse**, a solid, dignified-looking building constructed almost exclusively of natural material, reflected the new importance of commercial buildings in the Midwest. The exterior walls were of heavy uncut blocks of rock-faced red Missouri granite, with a series of arcades that brings to mind Roman aqueducts. This exterior was completely self-supporting. A skeletal interior structure, made of steel, held up the building's seven floors. Richardson is also well known for his **Trinity Church**, the historic focal point of **Copley Square** in Boston, which recalls without simply mimicking Romanesque architecture.

Richardson's work was an inspiration to **Louis H. Sullivan** (1856-1924), who has been called "the father of American architecture." Sullivan developed the architecture of corporate office buildings, which he designed with his partner, **Dankmar Adler** (1844-1900), at their firm in Chicago. Influenced by the ornamentation of Frank Furness, Sullivan ran in the same circles as Furness and William Le Baron Jenney, who was later known as the pioneer of steel frame construction. Adler and Sullivan practiced at a time of abundant opportunities in the building trades. The booming Chicago economy and the need to rebuild much of the city after the Great Fire of 1871 gave Sullivan the chance to master advanced methods of construction, including the fireproofing of steel frames by encasing them in masonry (cast iron buildings had failed in the fire). Developments in steel construction allowed vertical rather than horizontal construction of buildings, introducing multi-story rentable space. Designed by Sullivan between 1899 and 1904, the **Carson, Pirie, Scott Building** in Chicago is an example

> " *Form ever follows function.*
>
> ——Louis Henry Sullivan "

Chicago's State Street features the vertical building types developed by Sullivan.

ON THE UP-AND-UP

*It wasn't until **Elisha Otis** (1811-1861) got inside an elevator equipped with one of his new safety locks and purposely cut the cable to demonstrate its effectiveness that passenger elevators became widely used. With the advent of the electric elevator in 1889, also popularized by Otis, buildings of more than four or five stories became feasible. The earliest passenger elevator was invented about 250 B.C. by the Greek scientist and mathematician Archimedes, but these primitive elevators were limited in the amount of weight they could lift, and the height they could reach. These elevators were not for the faint of heart: there was nothing to stop an elevator from crashing down when the ropes broke, as they often did.*

PRAIRIE HOME JOURNAL

Plans and elevations of Frank Lloyd Wright's Prairie-Style homes were published in the magazine Ladies' Home Journal *in the early 1900s and were available for purchase.*

of the unification of exterior and interior via the skeletal frame. The minimal amount of structural steel allows for large windows. The original swirled motifs on the bottom two floors attest to Sullivan's fascination with organic ornamentation; he believed that "nature manifests herself in art through structure and ornamentation." In **The Guaranty Building**, Buffalo, NY, 1894, the form of the building begins to express the function. The arrangement of the ornamentation on the attic facade has been described as swirling in such a way as to metaphorically reflect the mechanical system inside.

15. **Name the American architect who made the following statement:**
    "**The prairie has a beauty of its own and we should recognize and accentuate this natural beauty, its quiet level. Hence . . . sheltering overhangs, low terraces and out reaching walls, sequestering private gardens.**"

    (A) Louis Sullivan
    (B) Henry Hobson Richardson
    (C) Eileen Gray
    (D) Frank Lloyd Wright

The early-twentieth-century American Midwest was the birthplace of **Frank Lloyd Wright's** (1867-1959) revolutionary **Prairie-Style** architecture. With its horizontal format inspired by the prairies of the Midwest, the Prairie Style transformed the notion of the dwelling into an expression of the earth. Wright, known as the first truly modern architect, was Sullivan's student. In his Prairie-Style homes, Wright tossed out practically all of the then-familiar domestic architectural vocabulary. He rejected the common gabled and **gambrel** (with two joined slopes, the top one less steep) roofs in favor of low-lying **hipped** (sloped but almost flat) roofs, and got rid of shingles, double-hung windows, and the compartmentalized floor plan typical of the nineteenth century. The W.W. Willits House in Highland Park, Illinois, built in 1902, was an early synthesis of Wright's principles. The house is of wood-stud construction, but covered with stucco. A very low-hipped roof covers a cruciform plan. The interior space seems to flow around an inner "core" of a vertically rising hearth, a plan taken directly from Wright's studies of Japanese domestic architecture, which features a ceremonial core for contemplation (p. 482).

The culmination of Wright's experimentation is the **Robie House**, Chicago, Illinois, 1908, the most perfect example of the organic architectural principles of the Prairie School. The Robie House broke almost completely

FALLING WATER, RISING MILDEW

Kenneth Frampton, an authority on modern architectural history and theory, raves about Falling Water: "Falling Water defies photographic record. Its fusion with the landscape is total . . . its interior evokes the atmosphere of a furnished cave rather than that of a house in the traditional sense. That the rough stone walls and flagged floors intend some primitive homage to the site is borne out by the living room stairs which, descending through the floor to the waterfall below, have no function other than to bring man into more intimate communion with the surface of the stream." As beautiful as it was to look at, Falling Water apparently wasn't as nice to live in: Edgar Kaufman Sr., the original owner of the house, called it "Rising Mildew."

Frankly revolutionary: the Robie House

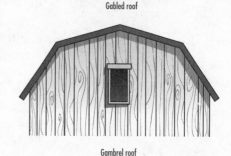

Gabled roof

Gambrel roof

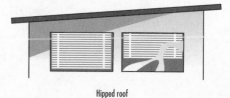

Hipped roof

Types of roofs

with previous architectural understandings of what made a home. In 1936, with new advances in concrete, Wright was freed from the previous constraints of technology as well, and built his **Falling Water** at Bear Run, Pennsylvania, a complete synthesis of architecture with the landscape. The reinforced concrete structure is **cantilevered** (extended out beyond the length of the support) from a huge rock dramatically poised over a waterfall and landscape of trees. The Prairie school movement was only the beginning of Frank Lloyd Wright's profound influence on modern architecture; Wright also made his mark on the architecture of the suburb and the corporate office.

16. **Which of the following architectural movements was based on a passionate criticism of capitalist society in the name of a return to medieval guilds?**

    (A) The Deutsche Werkbund
    (B) Art nouveau
    (C) Neoplasticism
    (D) Arts and Crafts

> **"**
>
> *A real building is one on which the eye can light and stay lit.*
>
> ——*EZRA POUND*
>
> **"**

In 1853, John Ruskin (1819-1900) (p. 260) devoted an entire chapter of *The Stones of Venice* to a discussion of **craftsman art**. Railing against the industrial division of labor (p. 80) and the degradation of the operative into a machine, Ruskin longed for the "ethical cohesion of the preindustrial community" and believed it could be achieved by a return to medieval craftsman guilds. The **arts and crafts** movement, sparked by Ruskin and British designer and architect William Morris (p. 595), sought to carry these ideas out in the fine arts and architecture, among other professions or "crafts." The movement extolled careful craftsmanship in all arts, stressing the moral as well as the aesthetic value of honest individual craft.

These principles were tested in the design and construction of Red House, built in 1859 in Kent, England, by **Philip Webb** (1831-1915). Webb's project used local building materials, carefully integrated forms, and demonstrated his respect for fine craftsmanship. An overhanging slate roof, wrought iron gutter brackets and heavy rough-cast walls punctured by small windows were all recognizable as characteristics of an arts and crafts home. This design approach soon became all-inclusive, with furniture and wallpaper designed along with the house itself. In the early 1900s, Charles Rennie Mackintosh took this philosophy to the extreme with his design for every last detail of the Glasgow School of Art.

The architects associated with the late-nineteenth- early-twentieth-century art nouveau were hailed as modern, although they were the last group to be associated with the Arts and Crafts movement in Britain. Like the Arts and Crafts movement,

HOUSING THE URBAN POOR

Tenements came to American cities in the mid-nineteenth century. "Tenements" at first referred simply to subletting or subdividing a large property into smaller ones. With the exponential growth of the urban poor due to immigration and industrialization, the word began to refer to densely inhabited apartment buildings. Often four or more extended families shared a small floor, with a common sink in the hallway and privies in the basement. Windows were sparse, and ventilation was poor. By the beginning of the twentieth century, after the squalor and degradation of tenement life was revealed to the middle class by photographers such as Jacob Riis, legislation was passed that made these conditions illegal.

art nouveau architects attempted to resist what they perceived as the dehumanizing aspects of technology. Art nouveau designs drew inspiration from natural forms. **Victor Horta** (1861-1947), for example, experimented with the structural and decorative aspects of metal in the stair hall of the Hôtel Tassel, in Brussels. At the base of the stair a freestanding iron column "grows" upward, like a vine reaching up toward the curved iron beam above. Through his innovative designs, the Catalan **Antonio Gaudi** (1852-1926) also conveyed a deep respect for nature and declared an independence from traditional materials and methods of construction. Sectional drawings of his Sagrada Familia Church, Barcelona, completed in 1909, are hauntingly reminiscent of Gothic cathedrals of the twelfth century, yet the look is strikingly modern. Gaudi's famous **Casa Milá** looks like a sandcastle, with its deliberate hodgepodge of plastic lines and forms.

17. **One precedent for the American suburb was the design of**
    (A) public parks
    (B) miniature golf courses
    (C) cemeteries
    (D) "Main Street, USA"

Nature goes formal in Central Park

Poltergeist (1982), directed by Joe Dante. Suburbs and cemetery clash in epic struggle over land rights.

The Waterworks (1994), by E.L. Doctorow. This is a vision of the urban conditions in New York at the time of the construction of Central Park.

Père Lachaise is the Paris cemetery where Jim Morrison is buried. If you wander through the thousands of monuments, you may notice that cryptic directions are carved on many surfaces directing the visitor to the final resting place of the lead singer of the Doors.

The exponential growth of urban populations of the cities of North America and Europe as a result of industrialization caused conditions of intense overcrowding and squalor within cities. Older urban districts, due to their location near centers of production, transformed into slums, while the upper middle class developed greens and squares to improve their residential neighborhoods. The **English Park movement** attempted to mimic the look of an aristocratic country estate in the city. The movement promoted an image of the picturesque, derived from the landscape painting tradition (p. 584), which featured neoclassical structures placed in an irregular landscape, even if that irregularity had to be completely manmade. In a period when the public park had not yet been invented, cemeteries often doubled as retreats from dense urban life, since they had to be close to the urban center. The Parisian cemetery **Père Lachaise**, built on a former landscaped estate close to the expanding city limits, served as an ideal burial ground *cum* recreation center. The living could get their exercise strolling about the grounds, intellectual stimulation from the sights of the funerary monuments, and pay a visit to the remains of great-aunt Bertha to boot.

While the rigid grid system was being used in cities to maximize economic gain and promote political order, the irregularity of the picturesque began to appear in public parks as a new method of "civilizing" the urban masses. **Frederick Law Olmstead** (1822-1903) and **Calvert Vaux's** (1824-1903) Central Park in New York City borrowed the picturesque landscape design technique from England. Olmstead's slightly contradictory goal was "to intefere as little as possible, [but on the other hand,] to increase and develop landscape effects." The park is a series of picturesque landscapes developed by manipulating the pre-existing natural features "saved" by its designers, while architectural features, or **follies**, were placed into the landscape like the funerary monuments of a cemetery.

As the nineteenth century ended, two uniquely American forms of urban development emerged—the **"highrise downtown"** and **"suburban sprawl."** The invention of the passenger elevator and the structural steel frame led to the advent of the **skyscraper**, dramatically changing downtown areas. At the same time the development of the electric tram and commuter railway allowed the middle class to move away from the production core of the city to the less crowded suburbs. The suburbanization of America really hit its stride after World War II, with the development of the **Levittowns**. Builder William Levitt brought mass production techniques to home building and spurred a nationwide increase in home ownership by the middle class. The government helped out by offering extremely lenient credit terms to buyers, including no down payment, so that buying a home actually became cheaper than renting. The first Levittown was created on Long Island, New York, under a government contract to build houses for returning war veterans. Seventeen thousand, four hundred and fifty homes went up from 1947 to 1951. Constructed of all prefabricated components, Levitt's houses were simply designed in a uniform style that employed inexpensive materials, giving rise to the later charge that the unimaginative design of the homes and the monotonous look of the hundreds of identical houses created a suburban culture of boredom, conformity, and escapism.

 Edward Scissorhands (1990), directed by Tim Burton. The film verges on bland infantilism, but you should see it for its ominous Day-Glo suburban-Gothic set.

18. **What was the Bauhaus?**

(A) A natatorium
(B) An animal shelter
(C) A manifesto
(D) A school

In the early part of the twentieth century, various groups tried to reconcile the growing schism between art and industry. In 1909, the Italian Futurists (p. 606), led by Filippo Marinetti, made an iconoclastic attack upon bourgeois culture, and especially high culture in the arts, claiming that modern technology should serve as the new model of beauty. In Germany, in contrast, the **Deutsche Werkbund** was formed by industrialists and craftsmen who understood that art, industry, and design could work together to mass-produce quality goods for wealthy foreign markets. Embracing no particular

 Japanese traditional wood architecture is probably the most sophisticated in the world, with intricate hand-crafted mortise and tenon joints that eliminate the need for nails. Even more important than the artistry of Japanese woodworking to the modernists was the spatial organization of traditional Japanese interiors—rooms could be reduced or enlarged by sliding screens. This open plan was a central tenet of modernism, and it established a link between Japan and the Western architectural avant-garde that continues to this day.

The other Ludwig—Mies van der Rohe

In the 1990s, graphic design suddenly found a rekindled interest in neo-plastic design. Many advertisements, in print and on television, use a de Stijl compositional sensibility. ESPN Sportcenter's logos and score update graphics are noticeable examples.

Bauhaus 1979-1983 (1985), by Bauhaus. This posthumously released double album of all their best tracks reveals Bauhaus, a gloomy post-punk band (p. mus), in all their glory. Critics call their music Goth-rock because of its dark, sensual, death-obsessed sound (more akin to Gothic fiction [p. 257] than architecture). Who knows why they named their band after a German architectural school with a clean, airy, abstract aesthetic? Probably just liked the sound of it. (If you like Bauhaus, also try Love and Rockets, one of several Bauhaus spinoff bands.)

aesthetic, the Werkbund searched for a new common language in which quantity and quality were not mutually exclusive. The architect **Pieter Behrens** (1868-1940) was named chief of design for the AEG, the German Electric Company, and began to design industrial objects, posters, and factories for the industrial giant. Behrens' studio achieved an extraodinary synthesis between production, design, the factory, and the city. Three of Behrens' young apprentices, **Ludwig Mies van der Rohe** (1886-1969), **Le Corbusier** (1887-1966), and **Walter Gropius** (1883-1969), went on to become great masters of twentieth-century architecture.

The **Bauhaus** school, organized in 1919 in Weimar, Germany under the direction of Walter Gropius, was dedicated to exploring the connections between artists and craftsmen and producing high-quality objects. The cross-disciplinary studios in wood, glass, textiles, metal, and color had a devoted faculty that included the artists Paul Klee (p. 608) and Wassily Kandinsky (p. 607) as well as the architects Mies van der Rohe and Adolf Meyer. At about the same time, the **De Stijl** movement in Holland promoted similar goals. De Stijl architects and designers called for a new balance between the "individual" and the "universal," or a liberation from tradition and the forces of individualism. Their aesthetic combined abstract concepts developed by the mathematician M.H. Schoenmakers and images of the early work of Frank Lloyd Wright. Wright's Prairie-Style, horizontal plane constructions, along with the painter Mondrian's sense of unequivalent proportion and exclusive use of the primary colors, yellow, blue, and red, inspired the designer/architect **Gerrit Rietveld's** (1888-1964) 1924 de Stijl masterpiece **The Schroder House** in Utrecht.

19. Le Corbusier's book *Towards a New Architecture* was significant because

(A) it summarized the new spirit in architecture and became the guidebook for modernists
(B) it ridiculed the engineer as a servant to technology
(C) it permanently connected the fine arts to architecture
(D) it inspired the design of the mobile home

Credited with bringing architecture into the modern era, the French architect Le Corbusier captured the spirit of **modernism** in his *Towards a New Architecture*. Le Corbusier (his real name was Charles Éduard Jenneret—Le Corbusier means "the crow") sought to integrate the engineer's functional rationalism with allegorical, sculptural beauty. He expressed this new spirit in small residential projects such as the Villa Savoye of 1929, in large projects such as Chandigarh, and in urban plans such as the Ville Radieuse of 1935. Here, Le Corbusier introduced the "skyscrapers in the park" plan of the modern city. The principles included incredible density in a park setting, separate layers of cars and pedestrians, and broad terraces for the inhabitants of a leisure society to stroll around. In the period between the World Wars, modernism gained favor among architects, governments, and clients, thanks to its combination of rigorous theoretical origins and economic viability.

In 1932, **Philip Johnson** (1906-) and **Henry-Russell Hitchcock** (1903-) published *The International Style*, a catalogue from the Museum of Modern Art's exhibition of the same name. Johnson and Hitchcock coined the phrase "International Style" to market **European modernism** to the American public. In general, International Style designs were characterized by asymmetrical compositions, cubic geometry created by a metal framework, horizontal bands of windows and an absence of ornamentation. Typically, they favored white finishes and an open floorplan, where the weight of the building was carried on thin steel columns, allowing interior wall partitions to be placed freely about the floor without concern for load bearing. The weight of the building is carried by thin steel columns rather than thick stone or brick walls, opening the interior "space" to the exterior "skin" with floor-to-ceiling bands of windows.

> "
>
> *The physician can bury his mistakes, but the architect can only advise his clients to plant vines.*
>
> ——FRANK LLOYD WRIGHT
>
> "

FUTURE SHOCK

Brasilia, the Brazilian capital, was the modernists' opportunity to realize their dream city. With its principle buildings designed in 1956 by Oscar Niemayer (1907-), who worked with Le Corbusier, Brasilia is the realization of the Corbusian ideal of the mechanized, formally unified motor city created by the single architect. Whether or not it is as successful in reality as in theory depends on whom you talk to: architects and design enthusiasts rave about the bold gestures of the Presidential Palace and the Palace of Three Powers; urban planners and theorists like Bruno Zevi decry modernism as sterile and oppressive in its regimented layout and sculptural sensibility.

Le Corbusier's ideas were later misinterpreted by American architects in the housing projects that sprung up under the Great Society (p. 425). These high-rise projects (with notoriously unreliable elevators) became barracks for the urban poor. Some sociologists posit that the isolation and anonymity fostered by these uniform, high-density buildings invites both malaise and crime.

20. **Why would architects call a building brutalist?**
    (A) It has ruthlessly colliding, rough concrete components.
    (B) It forces smaller buildings to be demolished for its construction.
    (C) Its appearance causes people to fight over its appropriateness.
    (D) It emanates a scent of cheap cologne.

The Chrysler Building: the hood ornament as skyscraper

The tremendous task of rebuilding Europe after World War II was undertaken by huge government-sponsored projects that necessited austerity and a strict functionalism. **Brutalism,** a term first used in England, describes the buildings designed by Le Corbusier and his followers after the war, in which exposed rough concrete and large-scale components violently clash in previously unheard-of proportions. With its look of resurrected decay, brutalist architecture seems like the appropriate outgrowth of a war-torn civilization. Le Corbusier's *Unité d'Habitation*, Marseilles, France, 1947, is a good example of the style. The plan united over 300 housing units with interior "streets," a rooftop running track and a children's pool, all cast out of rough-hewn, textured concrete. James Stirling's Engineering Building at Leicester University, England, 1959, incorporated the inherent contradictions of brutalism: labs form a horizontal industrial-looking block, while classrooms and offices are in a glass-skinned free-standing tower.

21. **What is the tallest building in the world?**
    (A) The Chrysler Building, New York City
    (B) The Empire State Building, New York City
    (C) The Sears Tower, Chicago, Illinois
    (D) The World Trade Center, New York City

In 1929-1932 **George Howe** (1886-1955) and **William Lescaze** (1896-1964) designed the Philadelphia Savings and Fund Society building, the first American skyscraper to make the transition from the ideals of the *Beaux-Arts* to the functional clarity of European modernism. Its design

The Seagram's Building: The birth of the Glass Box (that must have hurt).

King Kong (1933), starring Fay Wray. Big stars, big ape, big building.

owes much to the philosophy of the school of **Russian Constructivism**, which used the forms and details of industrial production. Another American skyscraper used a different approach toward modernism by nodding to the myth of industrial luxury that took shape during the 1920s, which included the streamlining of the locomotive, passenger ship, and automobile. William Van Alen's **Chrysler Building** of 1928-1930, detailed with enormous hubcaps and hood ornaments, was influenced by the sleek **art deco** style. The Chrysler building was the world's tallest building until the **Empire State Building** was completed one year later.

Skyscraper design in the United States was unparalleled after World War II, fully embodying the International Style of the 1930s and its successor, the **Glass Box** aesthetic of the 1950s. The most "radical" of these designs are the **Lever House** building of 1952 by Skidmore, Owens, and Merrill and, in 1958, Mies van der Rohe's thirty-nine story **Seagram's Building**, both in New York City. Although both are based on theories developed by the European avant-garde of the 1920s, they set a new standard by which all skyscraper design is still judged. The Seagram's Building, set back ninety feet from its allowable building line on Park Avenue, is the ultimate symbol of corporate America's power and prestige. Its bronze and brown glass facade is a perfect balance of steel and glass, rising with dignity over its solid granite plaza. Thousands of subsequent glass box buildings have been built all over the world since then, including the **Sears Tower**, the tallest building on earth, but few match the combination of proportion, grace, and restraint of the Seagram's Building.

Technological advances in the field of lightweight, long-span structures beginning in the late nineteenth century revived interest in the architectural possibilities of

The Sears Tower: is bigger better?

DOME SWEET DOME

The eccentric genius R. Buckminster Fuller (1895-1983) was interested in the idea of lightweight structures that would be quick to assemble and inexpensive to build. In 1927, he created his first Dymaxion House (he created the word to signify both "dynamism" and "maximum"), an aluminum hexagon suspended from a central mast, which he described as a synthesis of the American skyscraper and the oriental pagoda. It looked something like a flying saucer, and despite its low cost, the idea never really took off. In 1933, he patented the Dymaxion Car, and he went on to patent the Dymaxion Bathroom, Dymaxion Catamaran, Dymaxion Maps . . . you get the idea. Real success, and enshrinement as a pop icon, came with Fuller's Geodesic Dome in 1959, in which maximum space was enclosed with a minimum of materials. Because of the ease with which they could be built, and their groovy shape, domes became a staple of World's Fair stadiums everywhere.

the **tent** form. The German architect **Frei Otto** (1925-) and British engineer Ted Happold collaborated on developing and constructing economical long-span tented structures, most notably the German Pavilion built for the Montreal Exposition of 1967 and the stadium roof for the 1972 Munich Olympics (p. 438). The Carrier Dome, Syracuse, NY, designed in the late 1980s, is a sports stadium with an inflatable teflon (p. 369) roof, commonly referred to as a tension or "tent" structure. The product of many years of evolution in fabric and the technology of long-span structures, the Carrier Dome design enables fabric in the form of teflon panels to be inflated, deflated, and retracted, while spanning vast amounts of space. Further technological advances produced lightweight, Teflon-coated polyester fabrics which, ounce for ounce, are actually stronger than steel in tension. Fabric tensile structures are currently being used with tremendous success in major projects such as Denver International Airport and the Pier 6 Pavilion in Baltimore, Maryland.

22. **What does deconstructivist architecture aim to do?**
    (A) Employ architects to tear down buildings in novel ways
    (B) Disorient the viewer
    (C) Create moveable buildings
    (D) Inspire serenity in the viewer through precise proportions and details

The fall of the Berlin Wall has been a bonanza for architects who have had the opportunity to visit many of the landmarks of modern architecture that had been hidden behind the iron curtain for more than a generation.

If the guiding philosophy of modernism and the International Style could be summed up as "less is more," then postmodernism's retort, in the words of Robert Venturi, was "less is bore." Venturi's books, *Complexity and Contradiction in Architecture* (1966) and *Learning from Las Vegas* (1972), articulated the desire to ditch the sterility of modernism and make a virtue of decoration. Postmodernist architecture, like Michael Graves's Portland Building in Portland, Oregon, embodies

Venturi's notion of the "decorated shed"—a willfully eclectic, graphic, and witty facade attached to a generic modern interior. A different approach was taken with the Centre Pompidou in Paris, designed in 1977 by Richard Rogers and Renzo Piano, which aimed to use technology to create a space that is completely transformable—there are no fixed walls inside but rather partitions that can be rearranged for any number of purposes. The structure's outside, meanwhile, seems like it has been turned inside-out, giving it a high-tech look that reveals the building's inner mechanics. Yet it's also playful: in a touch reminiscent of postmodern movements in the visual arts, such as pop art (p. 615), different areas of the building are painted in bright, funky colors according to their functions.

The postmodern movement called **deconstructivism**, like its literary counterpart deconstruction (p. 279), can be characterized by a focus on exposing internal structure and an aversion to the idea of unity and definitive answers. The goal is to reveal how buildings have traditionally been put together, then to recombine elements in order to put buildings together in new ways. Deconstructivist architects often start with a basic form, such as a rectangle or a trapezoid, and distort it by cutting or overlapping the pure geometry. The idea is to disorient the viewer and force her to question her preconceptions about both form and function. Critics smirk that this is simplistic, merely a material representation of an abstract idea. Fans of Bernard Tschumi's Parc de la Villette in Paris, Zaha Hadid's The Peak in Hong Kong or Rem Koolhaas' Netherlands Dance Theatre in the Hague argue that these projects are technologically and intellectually sophisticated buildings that reflect the angst, alienation, and ambiguity of meaning in modern society. Wow!

As the rise of deconstructivism suggests, in recent years there has been an unprecedented exchange of ideas between architecture and other disciplines such as the arts, philosophy, politics, finance, science, and literary criticism. Architects have realized architecture can rarely be separated from the ideological context in which it is produced. The postmodernist philosophy of **Michel Foucault** (1926-1984), for example, explores the ways in which power is instilled in the state and expressed through more concrete structures, including architecture. All of this cross-pollination of ideas has lead to an increased emphasis on writing and criticism for the development of new architectural ideas. In fact, strange as it may seem, many of the more recent significant events in architecture are not even buildings at all.

From Bauhaus to Our House (1981), by Tom Wolfe. Having trouble buying all of this modern theory? So does Tom, and he's funny, too.

Lawnmower Man (1992), starring Pierce Brosnan. If you can bear the corny plot, this movie gives you an inkling of what it's like to move within virtual reality.

23. Are there architects in cyberspace?

(A) Yes
(B) No
(C) Yes and no
(D) What's cyberspace?

Technology allows you to virtually explore an Egyptian temple.

Like just about everything else in modern life, architecture has been profoundly affected by the computer age. Of course, as a tool, the computer has a tremendous number of applications in the practice of architecture. The speed and accuracy with which engineering, design, and drafting calculations can be performed using **CAD** (computer aided design) software is revolutionizing the representation and construction of architectural projects. Another growing use is the incorporation of computers to monitor and adjust a building's energy, security and structural systems for maximum efficiency—so-called **"smart buildings."** But the computer is much more than a speedy and sophisticated tool. The real potential of computers within architecture is conceptual: they challenge the way architects have traditionally conceived of space. Many cultural theorists, architects among them, believe that the computer, and its network of connections called **cyberspace**, have created a whole new way to think about, and design for, "reality." Real-time graphics and 3-D display systems can allow architects to create virtual buildings and cities that people will inhabit as fully as they do their built environment.

There are also more tangible and immediate repercussions of the information age for architecture. One byproduct of computer networks is the fading importance of the office building, a showpiece of architectural and economic power since the industrial revolution. Much of modern work takes place in a "space" of informational flows rather than the physical space of, say, Toledo or Seattle, and the architectural monuments of the future will have to successfully reflect this. Time will tell if

BUILD ON THE NET

Get on the Internet if you want to keep in touch with architecture as it moves into the twenty-first century. Some suggestions:

Help design Oceania, a new country for the new millennium at http://oceania.org

Participate in public policy debate with the Carter Institute:

http://www.emory.edu/CARTER_CENTER/homepage.htm

Explore Amsterdam from the comfort of your workstation in the Digital City at http://www.dds.nl/]

some of the varied attempts to rethink the workspace now under way, like Steven Holl's minimalist composition for D.E. Shaw & Co.'s Global Securities or Gaetano Pesce's exuberant space for Chiat/Day Advertising, which includes both real and virtual meeting rooms, will provide new answers to the oldest question in architecture: "How will I inhabit my world?"

Answers

1. B	2. D	3. B	4. A	5. C	6. C	7. D	8. A	9. A	10. B
11. D	12. D	13. A	14. A	15. D	16. D	17. C	18. D	19. A	20. A
21. C	22. B	23. A							

Economics

Every large society in history has maintained a functioning economic system or perished. Many thousands of people usually compose a society, and the resources and raw materials for production are limited. Hence, those brave souls who would wrangle with the what, the how, and the who of economic systems are faced with a massive coordination problem. What should a society produce? Well, bread would be good, but how much? And who will make it? How about semi-automatic weapons? Grateful Dead (p. 327) bootlegs? Once these production decisions are settled, someone has to determine the best production methods. Finally, of course, someone has to decide who ends up with all the goodies. Economics is the science that tackles these questions.

MICRO VS. MACRO

Economics is divided into two principal disciplines. **Microeconomics** *is the study of how individual members of society are affected by economic forces; it proceeds from the parts to the whole.* **Macroeconomics** *proceeds from the whole to the parts; it emphasizes the relationship among unemployment levels, overall rates of economic growth, and other aggregate factors.*

1. **What is the function of prices in an economic system?**
   (A) To combat inflation
   (B) To make trade more efficient
   (C) To encourage competition
   (D) To allocate scarce resources

Her muted colors will match any livingroom suite.

Underlying all economic dilemmas is the fundamental problem of **scarcity**. At any given point in time, the amount of corn, the number of diamonds, and the number of Holy Grails in the world cannot possibly satisfy the virtually limitless whims, desires, wants, and needs of each individual member of each society. **Prices** exist to allocate these scarce resources. Essentially, prices function as a relative standard of worth in an economic system; they provide coordination between the desires and the available resources of a society.

A price, then, is a reflection of **value**. Rare and highly prized goods command higher prices than do ordinary ones because rare and highly prized goods are more valuable to members of society. The one and only Mona Lisa (p. 585), for instance, would fetch a very high price (if it were for sale) because millions of people would like to hang it in their living rooms. The price of other goods, like gravel, is lower because gravel can be more easily obtained and few people feel strongly about its use. Economists have conceptualized the relationship between the availability of goods and society's desire to have them in the model of **supply and demand**.

2. **The Law of Demand states that**
   (A) the quantity demanded increases when price increases, other things constant
   (B) the quantity demanded decreases when price increases, other things constant
   (C) the quantity demanded does not change when price increases, other things constant
   (D) the quantity demanded increases when price increases, no matter what

A ROSE BY ANY OTHER NAME

Instead of just saying other things constant, *many economists and intellectual types use the term* ceteris paribus. *This fancy phrase sounds more dignified because it's in Latin, but it means the same thing.*

The **Law of Demand** states that the quantity demanded decreases when price increases, other things constant. Consumers will want to buy more of a product the lower its price, assuming all other variables remain unchanged. As might be expected, the **Law of Supply** states that producers will want to sell less of a product the lower its price, other things constant.

In the perfectly competitive markets of economic theory, individuals cannot establish how much a good costs. Instead, the interaction of many buyers and sellers continuously pushes prices toward equilibrium, that magical price at which demanders can consume all they want and suppliers can sell all they want. Of course, equilibriums are perpetually fluctuating because individual consumers and producers shuffle among many markets, and because the tastes and preferences of consumers are constantly changing. The imperfect and complicated markets of economic reality never reach an equilibrium.

In a standard supply-and-demand diagram, price is measured on the vertical axis and the available number of units of a product is measured on the horizontal axis. Since sellers will respond to higher prices by increasing production—thus increasing quantity supplied—the **supply curve** slopes upward. Conversely, the **demand curve** slopes downward because consumers respond to lower prices by making more purchases.

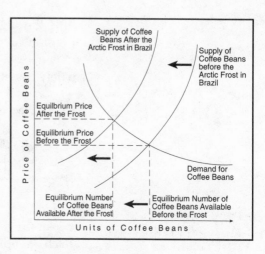

3. **Which of the following factors is NOT a shift factor of supply and demand?**

   (A) Price
   (B) Tastes
   (C) The weather
   (D) Technological advance

Thank God for Juan Valdez.

A **shift factor** is any factor—except price—that affects how much of a good consumers will demand or how much firms will supply. Some of these many determinants of supply and demand include income, taste, technological advance, the weather, and the price of everything else. While a change in price causes movement along supply-and-demand curves, a shift factor causes the entire curve to move.

If, for example, an arctic frost devastates coffee crops in Brazil, farmers could harvest fewer total coffee beans.

Even political causes can be shift factors of supply and demand. For example, wearing a fur coat just isn't the fashion statement it used to be. However, dead critters have not become harder to procure lately, nor have higher production costs caused the demise of the fur industry. Instead, animal rights activists have convinced many potential buyers that there are more humane ways to keep warm. This change in consumer preferences has caused a decrease in the overall demand for furs.

Thus, the aggregate coffee supply available to the market would decrease. In graphical terms, such a chain of events would cause the supply curve for coffee to shift inward (to the left). In reality, bad weather in Brazil ultimately translates into a more expensive cup of joe.

4. **What is opportunity cost?**
   (A) All the benefits forgone by choosing a certain activity
   (B) All the costs of a good paid by society as a whole
   (C) The retail price of a good plus sales tax
   (D) The cost per unit of manufacturing a good

Opportunity cost manifests itself in real life every time individuals and societies make a decision. Ordering Peking duck at your favorite Chinese restaurant, for example, means forgoing Moo Shu pork (or any other delectable treat on the menu). Financing an undergraduate education might mean forgoing delectable treats altogether for years.

Life is full of tough choices. Do you pay out the nose for health insurance or do you play the odds and hope you don't go under a bus? Do you watch old episodes of "Mary Tyler Moore" (p. 519) on television or do you finally start that term paper on the human condition? Do you have your cake or do you eat it? Whenever you choose a course of action, you must effectively *not* choose all other courses of action. Thus, choosing a certain activity necessarily means forgoing all the potential benefits that could be derived from other courses of action. In a stroke of politically correct (p. 429) genius, economists have coined the term **opportunity cost** to describe these sad facts of life.

Using the concept of opportunity cost, individuals and societies can obtain an accurate measure of the **real cost** of a particular good. For an individual consumer, the real cost of a $16 compact disc is about fifty postage stamps. The real cost to society of building more prisons could be a decrease in agricultural subsidies, a slew of ballistic missiles, or a national health care plan.

5. **Approximately when did agriculture first appear among primitive human societies?**
   (A) 40,000-25,000 B.C.
   (B) 10,000-5,000 B.C.
   (C) 5,000-1,000 B.C.
   (D) 1,000 B.C.-100 A.D.

For thousands of years prior to 10,000 B.C. (give or take a millennium), the human species roamed the earth in small nomadic tribes on a constant quest for sustainable food sources. The male members of these **hunter-gatherer** societies mostly hunted and gathered while female members mainly cared for children and maintained the settlement site.

The economic system of a prehistoric society was pretty simple: food was the primary supply concern and there was always a demand for it.

Over the next 5,000 years or so, as the last remnants of the most recent Ice Age (p. 139) disappeared, all of these primitive clans either invented agriculture independently or borrowed the concept from neighboring peoples. Since men spent much of their time hunting, the first farming methods were probably developed by women. Over several generations, as all people recognized that farming was the best thing to come along since opposable thumbs, primitive tribes expanded and refined agriculture, and the first industry in human history was born.

The advent of agriculture and the eventual domestication of herd animals generated dramatic changes in every aspect of human life. Staying in one place necessitated the first permanent dwellings. Formal governing bodies developed within tribes in response to the need for greater social organization. Food surpluses led to accumulations of wealth and provided tribe members with more opportunities for relaxation and reflection. All this extra free time produced aggregate increases in rates of technological advancement, overall standards of living, and, of course, population. Moreover, since farming required more complicated divisions of labor, agriculture also created the first genuine **class** distinctions.

The hunters' gathering

NOTABLE MOMENTS IN ECONOMICS

6700 B.C.	Coins first used (Iran)
3600 B.C.	First known system of taxation
2100 B.C.	First known welfare system (Egypt)
2000 B.C.	Coins in broad use
2000 B.C.-500 A.D.	Trade flourishes
100 B.C.	First corporation (Rome)
105 A.D.	Paper invented in China
301 A.D.	Emperor Diocletian enacts the first wage and price controls
700-1400	Feudalism prevails throughout Europe and Asia
1275	First tariffs instituted in England
1400-1800	Feudalism replaced by private property and mercantilism
1600-1800	Economic activity controlled largely by governments
1700-1800	Development and widespread use of paper money
1750-1900	Industrial Revolution and the age of unfettered capitalism
1776	Publication of Wealth of Nations by Adam Smith
1860-1960	Social security and unemployment insurance developed in Germany
1867	Publication of Das Kapital by Karl Marx
1917	Communists win control of Russia
1932-1970	Integration of socialist institutions into capitalist economic systems
1988-present	Trend toward capitalism dominates most economic systems

By about 5,000 B.C., nearly all primitive tribes had permanently adopted an agrarian lifestyle. Fertile land had become a legitimate commodity and, not surprisingly, societies competed for its use. With diplomacy not yet a viable option, societies sometimes waged the competition for land on the battlefield. In addition to gaining obvious territorial benefits, the society on the winning end of a war could exploit the conquered people themselves. However, constantly sending potential laborers into combat proved too costly for all but the most savage peoples. Thus, most societies found some mutual advantage in exchanging surplus commodities peacefully.

6. Where were the first known civilizations on earth located?
    (A) North America and China
    (B) Central Africa and Madagascar
    (C) Mesopotamia and Egypt
    (D) The Indus Valley and Northern Europe

Despite all the achievements and improvements it generated, the development of civilization definitely had a downside. Technological advancements created new and exciting ways to die. As farming and trading became a way of life, diseases (p. 212) spread rampantly in the concentrated populations. In exchange for the security and convenience produced by food surpluses, each individual member of society lost an immeasurable degree of freedom. Civilization also introduced oppression, slavery, and large-scale warfare to the world.

The first civilizations originated in the richly fertile river valleys of Mesopotamia and Egypt between 4,000 and 3,000 B.C. Mesopotamian civilization developed in the land between the Tigris and Euphrates; Egyptian civilization emerged along the Nile (p. 142). As these civilizations grew, and as others arose in China, North America, the Greek mainland, and the Indus Valley (p. 154), **trade** between and within societies flourished.

Societies used the additional wealth gained through trade to construct large **cities** and to support the growth of more centralized governments. As trade between formerly disconnected societies increased, the interchange of new technology and diverse ideas further facilitated the spread of civilization. People with goods to exchange flocked to the cities, and the growth of commerce also gave rise to a new profession—traders or **merchants**. With all the riches they were able to accumulate, merchants quickly became a politically powerful class in all societies.

7. Money functions primarily as
    (A) the standard by which banks measure their assets
    (B) a medium of exchange
    (C) the root of all evil
    (D) a measurement of economic stability

By definition, **money** is generalized purchasing power; it can be freely substituted for virtually all commodities produced in a society. A unit of money is unique because, although the amount of stuff it can buy may fluctuate, each unit will always be worth exactly what every other unit is worth in the marketplace. As a consumer, you can exchange money for anything you want because sellers know they can exchange it for anything they want. Thus, money is primarily valuable as a common medium of exchange; it is the **currency** through which buyers and sellers exchange the value of different commodities.

Before the development of money, traders could only exchange their goods for other goods. This **barter system** proved extremely inefficient and, by 2000 B.C., most trading involved some form of money. Traders first used objects with intrinsic value for money. Examples of ancient currencies include salt, which can be used to preserve food or to improve its taste, and gold coins, which can be converted into jewelry. These days, most countries use printed paper notes and cheap metal coins as money. Ultimately, such currency derives its value from government **fiat**; it is valuable because the government issuing it says so. Paper money maintains its relative value as long as a national government remains strong enough to back up its currency, and as long as the citizens retain faith in that government.

8. What caused the ultimate demise of the first civilizations in Europe and Asia?

   (A) Rampant plagues
   (B) A rash of natural disasters
   (C) Attacks by nomadic warriors
   (D) A massive decrease in birth rates

Beginning around 1700 B.C., nomadic tribes began sweeping through Europe and Asia, overrunning the economically thriving (but politically weak) civilizations in Egypt, Mesopotamia, China, and the Indus Valley that stood in their way. Shortly after these attacks, another wave of nomads defeated the original conquerors. By 1,100 B.C., all of Western civilization had been basically destroyed. As a result, trade among societies virtually ceased, and societies once again organized themselves into small farming communities.

From the ashes of destruction arose several new civilizations. Small kingdoms, like the Hebrew state of Israel (p. 487) and the Assyrian empire, gradually evolved into new civilizations. Most of these societies,

THAT'LL BE TWO PACKS, PLUS TAX

Much like the ancient merchants who settled on intrinsically valuable objects as a common medium of exchange, the inmates of maximum security prisons have devised a currency system based on an object of inherent value: the cigarette. In the economic confines of penitentiaries, prisoners are willing to trade virtually all goods and services for cigarettes with the knowledge that they can convert cigarettes into other goods and services.

Although the tribes that conquered the earliest civilizations were certainly ruthless, their leaders were probably not especially more ruthless than the leaders they displaced. Furthermore, these tribes didn't just come sweeping through the fertile valleys of civilization for the sport of it; they were probably migrating in response to famines and generally poor living conditions in the places from which they came.

however, are mere footnotes in the history of economic systems. Real economic action did not occur again until about 800 B.C., when the civilizations of the Greek city-states, Rome, and, to a lesser extent, Persia and India began gaining prominence.

Because of their unique geographic situation on the Mediterranean Sea, Greek and Roman cities provided hubs of commerce for all of Western civilization. For roughly 1,200 years, the exchange of goods and ideas flowed freely from the east and the west through the Greek and Roman cities on the Mediterranean. Societies were once again able to share and trade their resources, their products, and their cultures. As a result, technological innovation and increases in aggregate wealth flourished throughout Europe and Asia.

Eventually, European and Asian civilizations came under the military influence of four great empires: the Roman Empire, the Persian empire, the **Gupta** Dynasty (India), and the **Han** Dynasty (China). During the height of this second wave of Western civilization, these empires were able to preserve the relative peace and harmony necessary for successful trade. The central organization of these empires also made possible the building and maintenance of aqueducts, irrigation systems, and an extensive system of roads that connected the ancient cities.

THE NUMBERS GAME

The relative peace maintained by the Gupta Dynasty allowed art, literature, and commerce to extend throughout much of eastern Asia. Chess (p. 463) was also invented during the Gupta reign. The most significant achievement developed in India during this time, however, was the Hindu-Arabic number system. This system, which contained the digits 1 through 9 and zero (the most special digit of all) made mathematics infinitely less cumbersome. Over many centuries, all other peoples gradually adopted the Hindu-Arabic system, thus making possible countless technological and scientific innovations.

9. What caused the ultimate demise of the second wave of European and Asian civilizations?

    (A) Rampant plagues
    (B) A rash of natural disasters
    (C) Attacks by nomadic warriors
    (D) A massive decrease in birth rates

The decline of the four great empires of Rome, Persia, India, and China in the third through fifth centuries A.D. involved absolutely no irony whatsoever; history merely repeated itself. The **Huns**, a fairly mysterious but definitely fierce group of nomads from Mongolia, overran the Han Dynasty in China and the Gupta Dynasty in India. Like the Roman

Empire, which was conquered by a multitude of **Germanic tribes**, the Han and Gupta Dynasties had grown despotic and stagnant, and their extended empires had been weakened by internal strife and massive administration problems. The Persian Empire, although it was eventually able to repel all attacks from nomadic tribes, was extensively weakened by warfare. Without other empires to trade with, its thriving economic system slowly crumbled into chaos.

Over the next 500 years, political and economic chaos ravaged the civilized world. Plagues and nomadic plunderings caused the formerly immense cities to degenerate into sparsely populated ruins. Waves of invaders—the **Vikings** for instance—were constantly attacking someplace from somewhere with some success, and competing warlords continually fought over the lands previously claimed by dissolved empires. Eventually, as the strongest warlords began establishing tiny protectorates, a new political and economic system called feudalism (p. 389) emerged in Europe and much of Asia.

Corporate takeover—Viking style

10. Members of the lowest social class in feudal society were called

    (A) vassals
    (B) fiefs
    (C) lords
    (D) serfs

After reaching maturity as an economic system around 800 A.D., feudalism dominated most of Western civilization until the middle of the fifteenth century. Members of feudal societies lived on small, walled **estates**. In exchange for political protection, all individuals within the walls of each estate swore their enduring allegiance to their **lord**, or political leader. The lord employed **vassals** to serve in the army, to oversee the basic economic and political functions of the estate, and to settle legal disputes. In exchange for these services, the lord granted his vassals a **fief**—a small plot of land for agricultural production. In exchange for the fief, the vassals gave the lord a percentage of everything produced on their land. **Serfs**—the great majority of society who did not directly serve the lord of the estate—were employed by vassals and, eventually, as feudal estates expanded, by the vassals of vassals. Most serfs were farmers who lived and died on the plot of land where they happened to be born. For over 700 years, this unsophisticated pyramid scheme provided enough stuff for enough of the population.

Serf's up!

The economic and political structures inherent to feudalism allowed for very little social mobility. With the exception of war, **tradition** was the exclusive social mechanism of feudal society: tradition required the descendants of lords and vassals to become lords and vassals, and the children of serfs to become serfs. As a result of their fortuitous social positions, lords and vassals had a strong economic incentive to perpetuate this hierarchical state of affairs. Needless to say, serfs did not. Over several generations, thousands of serfs migrated to what remained of the decayed, bygone cities. In the absence of lords and vassals bent on enforcing the traditional social structure, many of these serfs were able to trade their way to great fortunes.

11. **What primarily caused the demise of feudalism?**

    (A) Continental drift
    (B) The dramatic growth of the Christian church
    (C) Attacks by nomadic warriors
    (D) The advent of private property

By the end of the fifteenth century, vibrant cities were again flourishing as the centers of civilization. The material wealth of the newest merchant class began to dwarf the fortunes of many feudal nobles. These former serfs had not only accumulated extensive amounts of money—which had reared its head again after largely disappearing for centuries—but all manner of neat stuff as well. The lords and the vassals wanted some neat stuff, too. Alas, the landed nobility had very few goods worth trading and virtually no money; all they really had was the sacred dirt on which their walled feudal estates stood. Eventually, some perceptive vassal probably divined the idea of exchanging a small portion of land for enough money to buy an Oriental rug or, perhaps, some nice pottery. Once the ball got rolling, the exchange of property quickly became all the rage in Europe and, to some degree, Asia, thus undermining feudalism at its very base.

12. **The medieval versions of labor unions were called**

    (A) barterdoms
    (B) abbeys
    (C) guilds
    (D) tribunals

As the merchant class grew in power and prestige, they began organizing themselves and throwing their new economic weight around in the political arena; they used their wealth to fund the armies of their favorite feudal lords. With the financial resources to raise bigger, better armies, these feudal lords were able to expand their territories into powerful nation-states. In exchange for underwriting military campaigns, the merchants expected the feudal lords to safeguard their business interests.

The invigoration of cities also created a flood of new economic activities. City dwellers in similar occupations organized themselves into **guilds**, which were the medieval version of modern labor unions. These guilds helped finance the leaders of nation-states (p. 392) (who had taken to calling themselves **kings**) in the hope that the kings would protect their interests, too.

A medieval guild of stone masons evolved into an eighteenth-century secret society.

13. **Feudalism evolved into which of the following economic systems?**

    (A) Mercantilism
    (B) Colonialism
    (C) Socialism
    (D) Monasticism

Since the kings and queens of nation-states relied upon the merchants and guilds to fill up their coffers with cash and commodities, they were obliged to grant these groups the protection they desired. Thus, feudalism evolved into **mercantilism**—an economic system in which the state uses its political power to determine who has the right to undertake various economic activities. Under mercantilism, governments used raw force to legitimize and encourage the growth of a multitude of new commercial pursuits. However, because the state had to quash certain industries in order to protect the ones that had bought its favor, the state also limited much economic activity.

14. **Which of the following was a by-product of mercantilism?**

   (A) Atheism
   (B) Imperialism
   (C) Consumerism
   (D) Externalism

POLITICAL ACTION COMMITTEES

Money can still legally purchase political influence. By contributing to the campaign funds of individuals running for elected office, modern businesses and corporations buy the favor of politicians in much the same way that merchants gained political influence under mercantilism.

Despite all the economic injustices inherent to mercantilism, the period in which it flourished (approximately 1400 to 1700) was marked by an overall improvement in the quality of life for nearly all of Europe and Asia. The Renaissance (p. 579) raised art and culture to a new level, and new economic and political freedoms allowed members of society to question previously immutable religious dogmas. Thus, scientific knowledge and technological advancement increased at a feverish rate. Merchants were able to produce more commodities than ever before. All the excess wealth created by increases in trade and production made European nations restless. As a result, monarchs and merchants worked together to find new societies to trade with and, unfortunately, in most cases, plunder.

European explorers and the settlers that followed them across the Atlantic between about 1500 and 1700 were not the kindest of people. Upon discovering that the Native American societies were no match for their military

The buck stops here.

technology, the explorers and settlers quickly lost interest in peaceful trade. Instead, the Europeans just took as many valuable commodities as they could get their hands on for themselves and for the nations they represented. With the discovery of the Americas, the age of Western **imperialism** had begun. Existing societies in any place stumbled upon by Western civilization could expect to be ruthlessly conquered at best. At worst, members of these societies were sold into slavery or just killed off by the more "civilized" Europeans.

> ## THE FINANCING OF COLUMBUS
>
> *The thriving trading companies of the mercantile era were always looking for new trade routes through which they could increase their business. When, for example, **Christopher Columbus** came up with the nutty idea that he could reach Asia faster and more efficiently by sailing west, he appealed to Queen Isabella and King Ferdinand of Spain for financial support. The monarchs, in pecuniary cahoots with the trading company, commissioned the voyage. With three fully outfitted ships, a tactful letter of goodwill, and an Arabic interpreter in tow, Columbus embarked on his westward voyage.*

15. **Which of the following nations was NOT a major force in colonial America by 1700?**
    (A) Portugal
    (B) Spain
    (C) England
    (D) France

England, France, and Spain had gained almost exclusive control over South America and the eastern region of North America by 1700. In exchange for military protection, colonial settlers from these countries sent raw materials and paid various taxes to the governments back home. This situation of taxation without representation was not well received by the settlers and soon the colonies were demanding independence. The British colonists in North America were particularly angered by their political and economic conditions; in 1776, they became the first of many colonial societies to declare and subsequently gain independent nation status.

16. British historian Thomas Carlyle called economics

(A) the naked science
(B) the dismal science
(C) the science of the gods
(D) the science of plenty

By the early 1800s, economics had come into its own as a distinct social science and already **Thomas Malthus** (1766-1834) and other prominent economists of the time were predicting that the sky would surely fall. Commenting on these gloomy forecasts, **Thomas Carlyle** (1795-1881) dubbed economics **the dismal science**.

Malthus contended that a society's prospects for the future are necessarily dim because populations tend to grow exponentially (at an increasing rate) while society can only produce food arithmetically (at a constant rate). As more and more people must depend on a static food supply, at least some part of the population will ultimately starve to death.

ECONOMIC BASES OF THE AMERICAN REVOLUTION

The American colonists, like all other colonists, paid taxes to a European government (in their case, the British) in exchange for military protection; that was part of the deal. Thus, whether or not the Americans actually had anything to bitch about—much less revolt over—remains an interesting question. Whatever the case, American colonists became more and more incensed as the British monarchy imposed several increased or additional taxes through the 1760s and 1770s.

Embodied in this prediction is **the law of diminishing marginal productivity**. As additional variable inputs (people) are added to an existing fixed input (the earth), total output will eventually begin to decrease.

To understand this concept, suppose you are the lone fry cook at a popular diner. No matter how fast you flip burgers, you cannot possibly keep up with the flood of orders. Seeing your plight and possessed with the compassion only she could have, your boss hires two new workers. With the extra help, burger production doubles. Delighted with this success, your boss continues to hire labor until wall-to-wall fry cooks fill the kitchen. Alas, since no one can move, burger production dwindles to virtually nothing. Likewise, on this little greasy spoon we call earth, potentially productive members of society will only take up precious, limited space if the population increases beyond a certain level.

An Essay on the Principle of Population (1798), by Thomas Malthus. In a fit of merriment over the immense technological innovation spawned by the Industrial Revolution, Malthus later eliminated his gloomier predictions of the future from *An Essay on Population*. However, this book still remains a classic justification for population control, if you're into that sort of thing.

Put your money where your Malthus.

17. **Which was the first struggle in recorded history between capitalists and socialists?**

    (A) The Peloponnesian War, which pitted militant Sparta against enlightened Athens
    (B) The fist fight that broke out between two angry Yippies and an unlucky stockbroker at the 1968 Democratic Convention
    (C) The fallout among Catholics, Lutherans, and Calvinists after the conclusion of the Council of Trent in 1563
    (D) None of the above

While there are as many economic theories as there are economists, most theories of the last 300 years have been variations on two major themes: **socialism** and **capitalism**. Both systems are richly layered with subdivisions and conflicts. Students of socialism and capitalism do not merely disagree with each other—they disagree among themselves. **Anarchists**, for example, have taken capitalism to its most radical extreme. **Communism** is socialism on speed.

Long before economists gave them names, variants of socialism and capitalism waxed, waned, and overlapped throughout human history. Initially gaining mainstream respectability in Plato's *Republic* (p. 385), socialism has existed since the advent of government itself. Feudalism and, to a lesser degree, mercantilism are manifestations of socialism. Capitalism, which requires a lack of government control to flourish, is even older. Thousands of years and political upheavals after these systems first tussled for power, a good argument could be made that neither system can function in the complete absence of the other, on the premise that elements of each can be found in nearly every successful civilization. For instance, even the most burgeoning capitalist nations maintain an army to protect the state.

> "
>
> *In capitalism, man exploits man; in socialism, it's the other way around.*
>
> —— ABBA LERNER
>
> "

18. **Capitalism makes which of the following assumptions?**

    (A) Individuals cannot know what is good for them.
    (B) Conflict between the lower classes and the wealthier members of a society is inevitable.
    (C) Private ownership of property is inherently wrong.
    (D) Individuals will consistently act in a rational manner.

CULTURESCOPE

Atlas Shrugged (1957), by Ayn Rand. Rand's novel defends capitalism as the only morally justifiable economic system.

Basically, anything that goes into the production of goods is called a factor of production. These are traditionally classified into three broad categories: land, labor, and capital. Land represents the location and the inputs of production. Labor is the human effort responsible for changing the inputs into something consumable. Capital is the machinery used in production.

All over the world, individual **consumers** buy all kinds of different stuff. In classical Anglo-American economic theory, consumers are perfectly rational beings acting exclusively in their own perfectly rational interests. **Firms**, the makers and providers of stuff, act in their own perfectly rational interests, too. Based on this logic, if your firm can increase its profits by laying off 2,000 workers, there's really no reason not to do so. And so it goes in capitalist economies.

Capitalism is an economic system based primarily on the private ownership of property and the **factors of production**. **Profit** is gained through the investment of capital and the employment of **labor** (except, of course, in the case of laborers, for whom the only sources of income are **wages**). Self-interest is its basic unit of progress; **free enterprise** is its guiding principle; and the functions of the capitalist state are minimal. In capitalist societies, individuals are free to choose their own courses of action; each individual then reaps the rewards or suffers the consequences of those actions.

19. **Adam Smith conceived which of the following metaphors to explain how markets coordinate the economy?**

    (A) The venerable spirit
    (B) The invisible hand
    (C) The stealthy tongue
    (D) The omniscient eye

Despite the fact that he died over 200 years ago, **Adam Smith** (1723-1790) remains to this day the quintessential poster boy for capitalism. Smith argued that markets could get along just fine or, more likely, even better, without incessant hampering by the state. In the absence of government intervention, an **invisible hand** would guide the production of commodities toward the general good. Smith believed that suppliers, left to their own devices, have no choice but to produce the goods consumers want at an affordable price.

If a particular good—say, egg noodles—is in short supply, its market price will necessarily be high relative to the prices of other goods. In response to a high price, entrepreneurial firms will enter the egg noodle market with the belief that they can gain profits. As these firms enter into the market, though, the increase in the aggregate availability of egg noodles will ultimately cause prices to decrease. Eventually, there will be a glut of egg noodles on the market, and some firms will fold.

Adam Smith lays his visible hand on *The Wealth of Nations*.

As egg noodles become more and more difficult to obtain on the consumer market, the market price will increase. Ultimately, the cycle endlessly repeats itself naturally and beautifully, and nobody gets hurt (unless you count the employees of egg noodle factories who will unavoidably be laid off from time to time).

20. **The French term *"laissez-faire"* most nearly means**
    (A) "the spirit of the times"
    (B) "leave things alone"
    (C) "seize the day"
    (D) "off with their heads"

The most recent heyday of capitalism in Europe and the United States climaxed shortly after the turn of the century. For the previous 150 years, Western governments had largely left economic systems alone; they had taken a *laissez-faire* approach to the economic events that shaped their nations. The rapid change and innovation of the **Industrial Revolution** brought about immense economic and social restructuring during this era and, according to some, provided the foundation for the indecent wages, squalid living conditions, and general exploitation of the period.

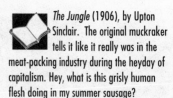

The Jungle (1906), by Upton Sinclair. The original muckraker tells it like it really was in the meat-packing industry during the heyday of capitalism. Hey, what is this grisly human flesh doing in my summer sausage?

21. **Which of the following countries is currently moving toward a capitalist economic system?**
    I. France
    II. Romania
    III. Japan

    (A) I only
    (B) III only
    (C) I and II only
    (D) I and III only

The United States is the current hotbed of non-interventionist capitalism, espousing it in theory and occasionally really practicing it. Other capitalist nations, like Germany, have more centralized economies designed by a consortium of business people, labor representatives, and bureaucrats. Still others, like France and Romania, are currently experiencing transitions from socialism to free-market economic systems.

Germinal (1885), by Emile Zola. This is a realistic account of life in a nineteenth-century French coal mining town.

22. Which of the following nations has a neomercantilist economic system?

(A) Sweden
(B) Canada
(C) Iraq
(D) Japan

After its crippling defeat in World War II (p. 650), **Japan** quickly began to rebuild itself. The Japanese government worked closely with industries to finance a fledgling economy that, within the span of three decades, developed into an economic superpower. Under the influence of the **Ministry of International Trade and Industry (MITI)**, Japanese firms are encouraged to cooperate in competition against the firms of the world. In many cases, MITI does not allow firms that produce goods similar to the ones produced by Japanese firms into the Japanese market. MITI also influences the production decisions of Japanese firms and controls the number of firms in each industry. Although the Japanese economic system is very capitalistic in nature, it is more aptly called **neomercantilist** because the Japanese government wields so much economic influence.

Neomercantilists off to a power lunch

In light of Japan's immense success, many U.S. economists have argued that the United States would do well to adopt a similar system. The United States, after all, has a larger pool of labor and immeasurably more natural resources. If Japan can be successful with a small population on a tiny island, the U.S. can be a lot more successful with millions more people on the better part of a continent. Critics of this reasoning point to the fact that hard work, wise investment, and a commitment to excellence lacking in the United States have propelled Japan to economic superiority. Without constant government interference, they say, the economic growth in Japan over the last fifty years would have been even more profound.

23. **Which is NOT a characteristic associated with socialism?**

    (A) A society without class divisions
    (B) Limited government
    (C) Guaranteed employment
    (D) Collectivized ownership of industry

While capitalism is technically not a political ideology, it produces distinct and formative political effects in profit-driven societies. **Socialism**, by way of contrast, is both a political ideology and an economic system advocating collective or centralized ownership of property and the means of production. Industries are not motivated by profit. Instead, cooperation and social service are emphasized over competition and self-interest. In an ideal socialist society, class differences do not exist.

Great thinkers of all eras have envisioned societies in which every member would work for the good of all members. Earlier socialists, like Sir Thomas More (p. 250), were usually **utopians** who stressed cooperation in combination with a theological ideology. Since the nineteenth century, socialism has taken two divergent paths: revolutionary socialism led to communism, while evolutionary socialism best manifested itself in the social democracies of Europe.

The political and economic roots of modern socialism can be traced to the **French Revolution**, a turbulent struggle that began around 1789 and culminated twenty-six years later with Napoleon's ignominious defeat at Waterloo. Over the next century, workers seeing little gain from their labor rebelled with varying degrees of success against wealthy industrialists and the **landed gentry** left over from feudal times. Full-fledged socialism, though, did not really find its way out of the ivory towers and idealistic closets until 1917, when the **Marxist Bolshevik party** successfully seized power in Russia.

Tired of paying his workers indecent wages to toil in squalid conditions, nineteenth-century British utopian and industrialist **Robert Owen** (1771-1858) decided to create a better life for the employees of his cotton mill. He moved his factory to a better location and provided universal education, improved housing, and low-cost goods and services for his workers and their families. Based on the success of this community, Owen moved to the United States in 1825 and established a more radical collective—which he christened "New Harmony"—in Indiana. Internal strife turned the project into a disaster for everyone involved and, by 1828, Owen was bankrupt and his voluntary experiment in socialist utopia had completely collapsed.

"Gilligan's Island." Seven castaways collectively share limited resources on an uncharted tropical island. From an economic perspective, it's a case study of a successful socialist economic system.

ECONOMIC BASES OF THE FRENCH REVOLUTION

Suppose you live in a powerful nation that has managed to rack up a huge national debt over the last 100 years through wasteful spending and the financing of military campaigns and revolutions all over the earth. What if the politicians, land owners, and clergy who got your country into this mess were exempt from paying the taxes that supported these imperialistic activities? Middle-class French lawyers and merchants were very upset when this situation occurred in their country. When middle-class leaders tried to form their own legislative body to combat the arrogance and excesses of the aristocracy, the aristocrats became outraged. The resulting class warfare, combined with peasant rioting fueled by coincidental food shortages, sparked a long and politically complicated revolution in France that drastically altered the course of European history.

24. Karl Marx argued that

(A) capitalism would inevitably be replaced by socialist economic systems

(B) the technological achievements brought on by the Industrial Revolution were mostly beneficial to the lower classes of society

(C) free markets should be allowed to operate without interference from governments

(D) rampant inflation would cause Western societies to revert to feudalism

During **Karl Marx's** (1818-1883) life, capitalism reigned supreme in the industrialized nations of Europe. Marx predicted that these capitalist systems would inevitably be abolished by the **proletariat**— the **serfs** of the nineteenth century—who were getting mercilessly ripped off by wealthy industrialists. Just to make sure, though, he and **Friedrich Engels** (1820-1895) spent the better part of their lives encouraging the lower classes to overthrow their leaders.

Marx believed that human history was composed of a series of class struggles. When a social system declined, it was initially replaced by a completely different system. Eventually, this new system would itself be replaced by a more perfect synthesis which utilized the best components of the two previous ones. The progression of history prior to 1800 shows that Marx may indeed have been onto something. Because mercantilism was replaced by industrial capitalism, Marx expected the synthesis of these systems—which he called **communism**—to occur. Under communism, governments would control industries for the betterment and enrichment of every member of society.

Karl Marx: a Kapital fellow.

25. Which of the following countries currently employs a communist economic system?

    I. Cuba
    II. Poland
    III. Thailand

    (A) I only
    (B) III only
    (C) I and II only
    (D) I and III only

Keeping up with the political and economic fortunes of socialism and communism has become an increasingly difficult task these days. Communists have maintained control over most of mainland China since winning a long civil war in 1949. North Korea is a communist country; South Korea is not. Vietnam is a socialist country. Russia isn't quite sure what it is any more. In many social democracies, socialists have been voted in and out of power since the end of World War II in 1945. In England, the **Labor party** represents mainstream British socialism. The **Social Democratic party** is the leading socialist party in Germany.

In the U.S., long before baseball seasons ended in salary cap disputes, before the **United Auto Workers** could collectively bring General Motors to its knees, even before **Jimmy Hoffa** (1913-1975) discovered the adhesive power of cement, socialist leaders were organizing labor strikes to force higher wages and improve the working conditions of the American proletariat. If only briefly, North American socialism blossomed into a significant political force during the early twentieth century, as class antagonisms were perpetuated by resentment against the grossly unequal distribution of national wealth. Under Eugene V. Debs (p. 191), the Social Democratic Party attracted notable figures like **Helen Keller** (1880-1968), and managed to garner over one million votes in the presidential election of 1920. However, people in smoke-filled rooms and high places detested the socialist platform of shared wealth and power. In 1919, helped by a patriotic zeal brought on by World War I and an anti-communist fervor provoked by the Russian revolution, **Attorney General A. Mitchell Palmer** launched a "Red Scare" of McCarthyesque

Reds (1981), starring Warren Beatty, Diane Keaton, and Jack Nicholson. This movie portrays the Russian Revolution through the eyes of Western intellectuals.

> From each according to his ability, to each according to his need.
>
> ——*Karl Marx*

Hoover puts the finishing touches on his blacklist.

proportions. Palmer appointed J. Edgar Hoover (p. 198) to head the General Intelligence Division, a new agency created to weed out socialists, communists, and other "undesirable" elements. Under Hoover, mass arrests and deportations of labor leaders and alleged communist sympathizers drove the socialist movement underground, where it has largely remained to this day.

26. Cuba's economy has deteriorated for which of the following reasons?

(A) Decades of popular uprisings have caused political turmoil.

(B) Cuba has been losing ground in its perpetual conflict with neighboring Jamaica.

(C) Former Communist-bloc nations are no longer able or willing to trade with Cuba.

(D) Recent droughts have wiped out precious tobacco crops.

Since 1959, when he led a popular overthrow of the previously pro-American regime, **Fidel Castro** (1926-) has been the hippest despot in the whole hemisphere. Because Castro is an unabashed communist, and because Cuba is geographically situated only ninety miles off the coast of Florida, he has also been an unremovable thorn in the side of American foreign policy. With financial assistance from the Soviet Union and all of Eastern Europe as guaranteed trade partners, Cuba was relatively prosperous throughout the 1960s and 1970s. When the aid dried

Dictatorship is such a drag.

Batting Against Castro (1993), by Jim Shepard, published in *The Paris Review* (issue #127). Two American baseball players experience revolution-bound Cuba and get to bat against you-know-who.

up and the conclusion of the Cold War ended Cuba's unique trading status, Castro could no longer mitigate the fact that Cuba is simply not blessed with enough land, labor, or capital to support itself. By all accounts, present-day Cuba is in desperate economic straits. Without enough fuel to run the industries or enough food to feed the people, Castro's days seem numbered. Although predicting the demise of

Cuba has become something of a sport in the last decade, Castro is not to be underestimated.

27. **In what year did the "Great Crash" of the American stock market occur?**
    (A) 1919
    (B) 1927
    (C) 1929
    (D) 1930

The 1920s, sometimes called "the Jazz Age," was an exciting time to be alive in the U.S. World War I (p. 643), "the war to end all wars" according to Woodrow Wilson, was over. The Industrial Revolution had brought about fantastic technological advances and a new confidence in the human spirit. Drinking was illegal, but drunken partying continued (at least among privileged city-dwellers). **Rugged individualism** and **flappers** were all the rage, as the national economy chugged along. With a little luck and some perseverance, any American could put a chicken in the pot and a car in the garage without the help of the government or anybody else. At least that was the official line from **Herbert Hoover** (1874-1964) in his successful campaign for the presidency in 1928. Indeed, before the **Great Depression**, capitalist economists had convinced many world leaders that markets could run themselves, using competition as the sole stabilizing force.

The Great Gatsby (1925), by F. Scott Fitzgerald. Read it again, for the first time.

Unfortunately, sustained economic growth couldn't last forever. In the fall of 1929, a trickling of European investors began to withdraw from American markets, causing stock prices to tumble a bit. American brokers, seeing stock prices fall, began demanding that investors pay the balance on stocks purchased with borrowed money. These investors had no choice but to convert their assets into cash to pay back the loans. Thus began a vicious cycle: stock prices continued to fall as more and more investors frantically searched for somebody to buy their stocks. On October 24, 1929, **Black Tuesday**, thousands of investors who

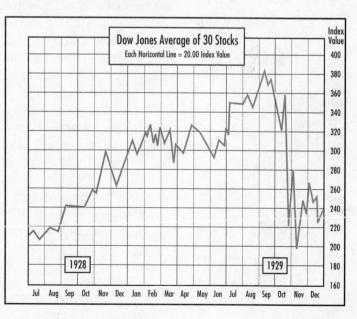

Dow Jones Average of 30 Stocks
Each Horizontal Line = 20.00 Index Value

had waited patiently for an opportunity to sell their stocks got their chance. In about the time it takes you to say "vastly inflated and over-priced stocks," thirty billion dollars and the whole ball of wax had vanished into thin air. Investors who had nursed small fortunes into huge ones watched the onslaught of selling cause their paper wealth to shrink to virtually nothing.

In retrospect, a market crash of serious magnitude was inevitable. By 1929, too many people had speculated in basically worthless and unregulated stocks for entirely too long. Banks, held to virtually no scrutiny, lent money to anyone with a pulse. American businesses of all sizes produced more goods than the markets could bear. These factors and many, many others contributed to the creation of an economic depression.

28. **At the height of the Great Depression, what was the unemployment rate in the U.S.?**
    (A) 10 percent
    (B) 25 percent
    (C) 33 percent
    (D) 50 percent

The Grapes of Wrath (1939), by John Steinbeck. The Joad family struggles to survive the Great Depression.

The business of America is business.

——CALVIN COOLIDGE

The **Great Depression** had severe effects both at home and abroad. In the U.S., thousands of banks closed. Without lending institutions to provide necessary capital, many more thousands of businesses and factories closed their doors. These bank, business, and factory failures ultimately caused the loss of millions of jobs: sixteen million of them, to be exact. In 1933, the unemployment rate in the United States was at a whopping 25 percent, or one in every four potential workers.

In Germany, where the national economy had yet to recover from World War I, the wholesale effects of war reparations and global tumult led to the ascent of the **National Socialists**, whose attempt to mitigate the social and economic needs of a desperate people had disastrous results. The National Socialists—**Nazis** for short—decided that ridiculous increases in military spending and an attempt to rule the world were the best ways to create prosperity. The leaders of Japan had the same idea. The formula worked for both countries, but the military build-up eventually culminated in World War II.

29. British economist John Maynard Keynes espoused which of the following methods of bringing nations out of the Great Depression?

(A) Increased government spending combined with programs designed to stimulate demand and consumption

(B) Decreased government spending combined with programs designed to stimulate supply and production

(C) Stricter barriers on foreign competition in domestic commodities markets

(D) A government spending freeze combined with programs designed to halt production

John Maynard Keynes (1883-1946) maintained that an economy in recession or depression could be cajoled toward economic growth by increases in government spending. Keynes argued that government intervention could bring the market into an equilibrium, albeit an artificial one. Basically, Keynesian theory maintains that people will buy things if they have money, so a very good way to encourage people to buy things is to give money to them. Demand creates its own supply. Keynesian theory heavily influenced American economic policies during the 1930s.

In response to the Great Depression, the Roosevelt administration dramatically expanded the scope of the federal government through a series of programs designed to increase employment and lower commodity prices, known collectively as the **New Deal**. Some of these programs, like the **Works Progress Administration** (**WPA**) which appropriated millions of dollars for the construction of hospitals, roads, and government buildings, effectively stimulated the economy. Others, like the **National Industrial Recovery Act**—a failed attempt to stimulate industrial production—didn't pan out so well. The New Deal was by no means an instant and unblemished success, although something was better than nothing for the millions of Americans the Depression had cast into poverty. Complete economic recovery was not fully achieved until 1941, when the United States officially entered a brand-new world war.

The General Theory of Employment, Interest, and Money (1936), by John Maynard Keynes. In this book, Keynes outlines the model that still serves as the foundation of all modern macroeconomic analysis.

Welcome to "Masterpiece Theater." I'm your host, Maynard.

Keynes also provided the foundation for the post-World War II economic policies of most of the free world. With the help of federal aid and government programs, the United States was able to ease millions of newly unemployed G.I.s into the work force. Critics of Keynes and his disciples charge that instead of bringing the market into equilibrium, constant stop-gap government expenditures have created a perpetual disequilibrium and a mountain of debt. Furthermore, Keynesian economics, which has been nothing short of brilliant in stabilizing employment levels, has never quite been able to solve the problem of constantly rising prices.

30. **Which of the following is a cause of inflation?**
    (A) An increase in consumer purchasing power
    (B) A decrease in government spending
    (C) An increase in the costs of production
    (D) A decrease in the gross national product

CRASH, BANG, BOOM

Stock market crashes wreak havoc on entire societies. As stocks decrease in value, the capital available to the firms that issued the stocks shrinks. Firms cannot borrow money from banks and lending institutions because, with their investments shot, the banks don't have any money to lend. Ultimately, many firms (and many banks) go out of business, causing higher and higher unemployment, as both demand and supply dwindle in the marketplace.

Basically, **inflation** is the official word for constantly rising prices. Prices rise when any of the factors of production become more expensive to obtain, or when there is too much money floating around in the economy (on the simple premise that when more of something exists, all of it is worth less). Suppose you want to bake a cake. If a drought wipes out much of the world's sugar cane crop, the sugar supply will decrease while demand remains unchanged. The resulting increase in the price of sugar will increase your **costs of production**. To earn a profit selling your cake, you would have to charge a higher price than last year. Increasing the

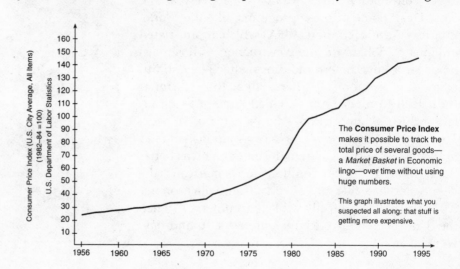

The **Consumer Price Index** makes it possible to track the total price of several goods— a *Market Basket* in Economic lingo—over time without using huge numbers.

This graph illustrates what you suspected all along: that stuff is getting more expensive.

salary of your trusty baking assistant or remodeling your kitchen would raise production costs, too.

Government spending, however, is usually the primary cause of inflation. Not surprisingly, when the government spends money, it buys things. All this spending stimulates aggregate market demand. Firms respond to increased demand by making more stuff. Since firms must hire more labor if they want to increase production, the national employment level increases. Wages increase as firms offer additional cash as an incentive to lure the most productive workers available. That extra money has to come from somewhere, though. To remain profitable, firms must raise the cost of their products in order to offset the cost of higher wages, which in turn diminishes the actual value of the higher wages.

 More than anything else, Americans caught in the middle of the Great Depression needed jobs so they could buy things and get the economy going again. So the Roosevelt administration put them to work. The *Tennessee Valley Authority* undertook massive projects that required massive amounts of labor. The WPA hired citizens to plant trees and construct government buildings. In fact, if you live in the Midwest, it's a good bet that your post office was built by temporary government employees during the Great Depression.

31. When economists, reporters, and budget wonks speak of "pork" they are usually talking about

(A) the festive all-you-can-eat sausage bars found at many restaurants in the Washington, D.C. area
(B) the aggregate dollar amount spent each year in the United States on consumable goods
(C) strict laws that regulate the quality of American livestock
(D) money appropriated by Congress for publicly financed projects in specified locations

Taxes are a government's primary source of **revenues**, and U.S. lawmakers have devised none too few of them. Once collected, tax revenue is appropriated to various agencies and all manner of federal, state, and local programs. In addition to weighty responsibilities like maintaining a national defense, members of Congress must provide for the people who gave them a job. They've got to bring home funding for improving schools and filling potholes to satisfy those ever-fickle voters. The federal money earmarked for a certain use in a certain state or district is colloquially called **pork**. But tax revenues only go so far. Over fifty years of pet programs and a single decade (the eighties) of massive **deficit spending** have come at a price: a debt that puts the entire net worth of other nations to shame.

The government takes in a certain amount of money each year, which it then spends on various goods and services. When the government spends more money than it has, the difference is called the **budget deficit**. To cover the deficit, the government borrows money from banks, money that must eventually be repaid with interest. The total of all outstanding loans and interest deficit is called the **budget debt**. The finances of the United States government are surrounded by a certain mystique, but the national budget is just a complicated version of your checkbook. Of course, the legislators who spend your tax dollars would prefer you didn't know this, as it makes them look like idiots.

THE AMERICAN BUDGET: AN ANALOGY

Sally is an investment banker who enjoys building roads in her backyard and adding to her already formidable collection of heavy artillery. She also has an extended family of geriatrics and unemployed cousins to support. Each month, she earns $10,000 and spends $12,000. Thus Sally has a monthly budget deficit of $2000. She must obtain loans to cover this outstanding amount. At the end of one year, Sally will have accumulated a budget debt of $24,000, plus the accrued interest on her loans. If the interest rate continues to hover around 8 percent, Sally will owe a bunch of money before long. Refer to the events leading up to the French Revolution to see what may soon become of Sally.

---

32. **In what year was the U.S. Constitution amended to include a national income tax?**
    - (A) 1899
    - (B) 1902
    - (C) 1911
    - (D) 1913

For fifty-odd years after the end of the Civil War (p. 633), the United States government tried to institute a federal income tax. The idea was largely detested among the electorate, though, and that pesky **Constitution** kept getting in the way of a permanent income tax structure. Finally, thanks in part to the social reform movement that swept the nation around the turn of the century, the Constitution was amended in 1913 to include an income tax.

Obviously, the advocates of a national income tax wanted to increase federal revenue, but, more importantly, they hoped to create some measure of economic equality between the wealthiest members of society and the increasingly disenfranchised poor.

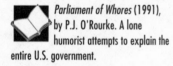
Parliament of Whores (1991), by P.J. O'Rourke. A lone humorist attempts to explain the entire U.S. government.

33. What kind of income tax structure does the federal
government currently utilize?

(A) Proportional
(B) Regressive
(C) Progressive
(D) Dismissive

Ever since the income tax was originally instituted, politicans
have been searching for the appropriate rates of taxation. They can't
be zero, because then government revenues would be zero. They
can't be 100 percent, because then nobody would work voluntarily
and, thus, revenues would be zero. It has to be somewhere in
between. The current federal tax structure is progressive in nature:
the more you make, the higher percentage you pay in taxes.

In 1980, a Democratic Congress and a Republican president
voted to reduce all but the lowest tax rates. The idea was simple:
lowering tax rates would cause individual citizens to work more.
Since people who work more make more money, more tax revenues
would ultimately be collected. This **supply-side** notion did increase
federal revenues slightly. However, across-the-board increases in
government spending—especially of the military variety—effectively negated the increase in revenues and quickly pushed the
national debt to new heights.

34. Which of the following is a benefit of a national trade
deficit?

(A) Foreign wealth flows into the United States.
(B) Dollars flow out of the economy.
(C) A larger selection of quality goods is available.
(D) Allowing foreigners to sell their wares in domestic
markets gives military leaders access to new
technology.

A **trade deficit** occurs when a nation consumes more imported goods
than the nation's firms sell in other countries. The United States, for
instance, has a foreign trade deficit because the millions of foreign products purchased annually by American consumers are worth more than all
the American goods purchased in other nations combined. On the one
hand, this situation is bad because precious U.S. dollars flow out of the
country every time an American consumer buys a foreign product. On the
other hand, foreign competition in the domestic market affords American

> 66
>
> *Do you think you could
> find me a one-armed
> economist?*
>
> ——*Harry S Truman*
>
> 99

The combustible Pinto was just one of the cars that caused the U.S. to lose its dominance in the auto industry.

consumers significantly more quality alternatives. Any time the level of competition in a market increases, all firms producing similar commodities must deliver the best possible product in the most efficient manner and at the lowest possible price if they hope to survive. The automobile market provides an excellent example. Over the last fifteen years, lean and mean foreign competition forced corpulent domestic auto makers to produce better, more affordable cars.

35. **What is a tariff?**

   (A) A universal currency
   (B) A provision designed to foster free trade
   (C) A limit placed on the quantity of imported goods
   (D) A tax on an imported good

In order to encourage domestic consumers to purchase domestically produced commodities, governments tax imported goods as they enter the country. These taxes on international trade are called **tariffs**. Tariffs effectively raise the retail prices of foreign goods and services relative to domestic ones and all nations utilize them to some extent.

Quotas, which limit the number of imports allowed into a country, are another popular type of trade restriction. Both tariffs and quotas create higher prices for consumers. However, unlike a tariff, which is a straightforward tax, a quota on a particular good gums up the economic works by keeping quantity supplied lower than quantity demanded. Because foreign producers cannot export beyond a certain quantity—their quota—domestic producers of a product can keep its prices artificially high by producing some quantity below the level of market demand.

36. **What was the name of the 1930 U.S. tariff that sparked an international trade war?**

   (A) The Harvey-Diebold Tariff
   (B) The Hawley-Smoot Tariff
   (C) The Harley-Davidson Tariff
   (D) The Haskell-Cleaver Tariff

Slapping or raising a tariff on manufacturers in a particular nation virtually guarantees retribution. Nations that aren't careful can find themselves embroiled in a trade war very quickly. In a futile attempt to protect American interests and rein in the unemployment effects of the Great Depression, Congress passed **The Hawley-Smoot Tariff** in 1930. Instead of achieving its goal, it caused other nations to respond with their own tariffs. International trade shriveled, unemployment worsened, and many manufacturers were forced out of business. Between the foreign tariffs abroad and the unemployment at home, those firms that remained had trouble selling their products to anyone.

Following World War II, the leaders of many nations, hoping to avoid a debacle similar to the one caused by the Hawley-Smoot Tariff, met to formulate the **General Agreement on Tariffs and Trade** (GATT). Due to regularly convened GATT conferences ever since, peacetime trade barriers have been reduced and the general use of trade restrictions has been curtailed by all nations.

37. The acronym NAFTA stands for
   (A) Native American Fair Treaty Alliance
   (B) North American Free Trade Agreement
   (C) Nations Against Foreign Tariff Associations
   (D) Nations Against Free Trade Altogether

In 1957, several western European nations formed an economic confederation called the **European Economic Community**. Since then, they have shortened the name to the **European Union,** but their ultimate goal of maintaining a free trade zone has remained unchanged. In response to the European Union, the United States, Canada, and Mexico have recently entered into their own free trade pact, the **North American Free Trade Agreement (NAFTA).** The agreement, which will be phased in over the next fourteen years, allows firms from all three nations to establish production facilities in the other two, provided that the firms adhere to the environmental and labor regulations of the nation where the goods are produced. Firms can then sell their commodities in all three nations without being subjected to trade restrictions.

There's free trade and then there's NAFTA free trade. In response to political pressure from special interest groups, the authors of NAFTA have provided for many, many exceptions. Among them are maritime services, telecommunications, and aviation transportation.

Proponents of NAFTA envision immense growth in all sectors of the North American economy. Free trade, they say, will create more jobs. Furthermore, NAFTA will foster competition and increase aggregate supply, thus driving down aggregate prices. Detractors don't buy it. They say smart firms will set up shop in Mexico, where labor is cheap and

As President Clinton signs NAFTA into law, Gerald Ford and Al Gore hold invisible balls of energy that only they can see.

environmental regulation is somewhere between lame and nonexistent. According to their scenario, big business operators will flood the market with low-priced goods. In the end, smaller firms will be forced to fold. Though critics and proponents agree that employment in Mexico will increase, critics contend that millions of Americans will lose their factory jobs.

Whether or not NAFTA will succeed or fail depends largely on the political and economic fortunes of Mexico. If the Mexican people and their government can tame their economy, which has quivered into and out of **third world** status for decades, NAFTA will pave the way for Mexico to become a serious player in the economic world. If the current economic chaos in Mexico persists, no firms will build factories there nor will Mexican consumers be able to afford imported commodities.

ANSWERS

1. D	2. B	3. A	4. A	5. B	6. C	7. B	8. C	9. C
10. D	11. D	12. C	13. A	14. B	15. A	16. B	17. D	18. D
19. B	20. B	21. C	22. D	23. B	24. A	25. A	26. C	27. C
28. B	29. A	30. C	31. D	32. D	33. C	34. C	35. D	36. B
37. B								

A product of technology made possible by the second Industrial Revolution, film is inextricably tied to the modern era. As the rare art form that does not predate the U.S., movies have grown up along with American culture. Today, the U.S. has the largest film industry in the world, one that exports a steady flow of American culture to any country with a theater. As an art form, as entertainment, and as a visual and aural phenomenon, film has both reflected and influenced American culture on a spectacular scale.

1. **Who invented the first motion picture camera?**

   (A) Thomas Edison
   (B) W.K.L. Dickson
   (C) Étienne-Jules Marey
   (D) The Lumière brothers

CULTURESCOPE

TECHNOLOGY TIME LINE

1837	Telegraph
1876	Telephone
1878	Phonograph
1880	Roll Film
1888	Kodak Camera
1889	Motion Picture Film
1891-1893	Edison's Motion Picture Camera
1895	Marconi's Wireless
1895-96	Motion Picture Projector

The projection device invented by the Lumière brothers was a streamlined version of the kinetograph that weighed about ten times less than Edison's machine, making it more portable and creative. It was dubbed the Cinématographe, a term that still defines the art of motion picture photography: cinematography.

The kinetoscope: the extent of Edison's vision

Photography, motion pictures, and even sound recordings were merely some of the cultural transitions that became part and parcel of the aftermath of the Industrial Revolution. At the turn into the twentieth century, mass production and mass persuasion were becoming the norm. For the first time, there was a profitable consumer market for mass-produced goods such as clothes, furniture, food, as well as for motion pictures and other amusements.

In 1889, **Thomas Edison** (1847-1931) acquired some of George Eastman's strip film and wanted to develop the idea further. Edison commissioned a laboratory assistant named **W.K.L. Dickson** to create a motion picture camera. The first attempts at this were made on photographic cylinders in a process similar to recording sounds on phonographic cylinders, and proved to be less than successful. Dickson ultimately accomplished the deed with the invention of the **kinetograph** (although Edison would take credit for the invention himself), the first motion picture camera.

Cinema did not begin as a mass experience. The first mini-movies were shown on a **kinetoscope**, an apparatus designed by Thomas Edison to show a fifty-foot filmstrip in an endless loop. Kinetoscope parlors, containing a number of machines where a single strip could be viewed for about five cents, caught on across the country as the nineteenth century came to a close.

Edison was resistant to developing projection technology—he was already making a handy profit selling kinetoscopes to exhibitors at $1,000 a pop. He figured that if projectors caught on, then exhibitors would only have to purchase a single machine. An avaricious Edison lost out to the even greedier exhibitors and the technical expertise demonstrated by the Europeans. About a year after the

FRED OTT'S SNEEZE

In the Edison laboratory in West Orange, NJ, the first cinematic record created in America was the undoubtedly poignant Fred Ott's Sneeze. *True to its title, the film simply depicted laboratory mechanic Fred Ott sneezing.*

first kinetoscope parlor opened, **projection devices** perfected by Frenchmen Louis and Auguste Lumière, as well as Edison's under-appreciated assistant Dickson, went on the market. Projection film was an immediate sensation. When the Lumières first showed their film *L'arrivé d'un Train en Gare* (*Arrival of a Train at a Station*) audiences are said to have run from their seats in fear of the oncoming train.

2. The first permanent movie theater in the U.S. was established in

(A) 1896
(B) 1902
(C) 1906
(D) 1910

A new era of mass-consumed entertainment began with the advent of projection. For the first time in history, people were being amused en masse without live performers. Edison possessed a facility for tapping into popular American trends and obsessions. At the end of the nineteenth century, the "Wild West" was in vogue, and Edison shot a scene called *Cripple Creek Barroom* (watch for the sensational sequel—*A Lynching at Cripple Creek!*). The **screen western** was born. Movies were not only exciting—they were easy and inexpensive to reproduce. While exhibitors still tended to package these projected films or "attractions" in tandem with music, lectures, or live variety acts, they could simply reap the benefits of the product

Spaghetti western icon Clint Eastwood

CULTURESCOPE

without any responsibility for creativity. Movie theaters had been around in Europe since 1896, but it was not until 1902 with the opening of the **Electric Theater** in Los Angeles (of course) that the first permanent movie theaters appeared in the U.S.

3. Who is credited with the invention of the "narrative" film?
   (A) Edwin S. Porter
   (B) Georges Méliès
   (C) Jean-Luc Godard
   (D) Sergei Eisenstein

Even though the "movies" had been around since the 1890s, the cinematic "language" that we take for granted today, such as the use of editing to juxtapose shots and increase the storytelling power of the images, developed a decade later. In 1902, Frenchman **Georges Méliès** (1861-1938) made history with *A Trip to the Moon*, the first narrative film. The film is also considered the first "effects" film because Méliès employed double exposures, animation combined with live-action footage, and trick editing to create a reality separate from the "actual" reality recorded on celluloid. The result was a spectacle the likes of which no one had ever before experienced, paving the way for filmmakers to exploit the new medium to its fullest extent. Until *A Trip to the Moon*, films had essentially been documentaries, simply recording everyday actions in the motion-picture format, uninterested in how that reality could be edited to create an entirely separate story. In 1902 and 1903, **Edwin S. Porter's** (1869-1941) films *Life of an American Fireman* and *The Great Train Robbery* made history as the first American narrative films. *The Great Train Robbery* recreated the infamous heist that Butch Cassidy and the Wild Bunch had perpetrated just a few years previously.

Of course, these films, like all films until 1929, were silent and therefore had conventions and narrative devices that were much different than sound films. Since you are not able to hear the dialogue the characters on

KING KONG

The powerful illusions that can be created by the film medium were realized with a vengeance in RKO Studios' 1933 classic King Kong. *The towering ape who terrorized New York and 5'3" actress Fay Wray was in reality only 18" tall.*

screen are relating to each other, story lines remained relatively simple and actions had to speak much louder than words. In fact, you might consider some of the acting in silent films to be exaggerated or even hammy, but remember these actors had to convey a wide range of emotions without the benefit of their voices or musical soundtracks to underscore the mood (imagine watching *Jaws* without the shark's theme—it would be pretty ludicrous). All crucial plot developments were literally posted on screen in a dialogue box just to insure that audiences didn't get confused. Of course, this interupted the flow of the film and was kept to a minimum. Characters were introduced via dialogue boxes, as were locations and complicated situations. Dialogue was kept to the bare minimum and whenever silent films projected dialogue on the screen it was usually to tell a joke or to reinforce the dramatic position of the actors on screen. While the silent era might seem limiting, it actually forced filmmakers like Charlie Chaplin, Buster Keaton, D.W. Griffith, and Sergei Eisenstein to be extraordinarily creative storytellers, expanding and inventing the visual "language" of film. When "talking pictures" became a reality, many of the biggest stars of the silent era were unable to make the transition because their diction or their accents and sometimes their voices were found to be unacceptable by audiences and studios alike.

4. The term "nickelodeon" refers to

   (A) the first device invented for viewing motion pictures
   (B) Edison's first film projector
   (C) the first permanent movie theaters
   (D) vaudeville theaters that featured live acts accompanied by films

In 1905, **Harry Davis** held a grand premiere (prefiguring many to come) at his new theater in Pittsburgh, PA, the **Nickelodeon**. The introduction of the nickelodeon, as all early movie theaters came to be called, made motion pictures a collective experience. Before 1906, when movies were packaged with other amusements, the price was in reach only of the middle class, who had some disposable income. This precluded most working-class viewers from frequenting theaters, as they had decidedly less spare change and restricted leisure time. At the initial cost of a nickel and with a much shorter time frame than previous film-oriented amusements, nickelodeons were a great draw for the working class. The popularity of narrative films such as *The Great Train Robbery* and *A Trip to the Moon* created a boom in the motion-picture market. By 1910, twenty-six million Americans from various backgrounds were attending over ten thousands nickelodeons per week. Suddenly, Americans were sharing a collective cultural experience. While never truly classless, the movies began a tradition that continues to simulate the American ideal: a universal community of middle-class consumers.

The cathedral of the motion picture was the **movie palace**, which came into being in the second decade of the twentieth century. Vast, lavishly decorated, and heavily adorned with gilt, the movie palaces of the early twentieth century boasted organs, orchestras, uniformed ushers, and even choruses. Movie viewing once again became a multi-media experience. Elaborate floor shows were often thematically linked to the feature presentation. Movies were becoming respectable. More complex narratives allowed the form to compete with other middlebrow diversions such as theater and concerts. The increased luxury of the experience made it a viable middle-class entertainment, filled with luxury and elegance, unlike the honky-tonk storefronts of the nickelodeons. Among the first movie palaces were New York's Regent (1913), Los Angeles' Million Dollar Theater (1917), and Chicago's Central Park (1917).

African Americans had their own movie theaters under the Jim Crow laws of the post-Civil War South. Movie theaters had separate, and not always equal, facilities for blacks. Balconies were generally relegated to the "minority trade."

5. Who made *Birth of a Nation*?

(A) Samuel Goldwyn
(B) D.W. Griffith
(C) Erich von Stroheim
(D) Buster Keaton

Birth of a Nation: D. W. Griffith's controversial epic

In 1915, **D.W. Griffith's** (1875-1948) *Birth of a Nation* opened with the highest ticket price of the day—a whopping two dollars. Audiences were astounded by its well-developed narrative and seamless editing. It was also three hours long (a total of twelve reels and 1,375 separate shots), providing competition for multi-reel films emerging from Europe (which were generally composed of 100 separate shots). *Birth of a Nation* is a milestone in the development of modern cinema. Griffith continued where Mèlies had left off, developing through his experiments with editing the fundamental narrative structure of the cinema as we know it.

Originally titled *The Klansman* but renamed for its premiere in New York, *Birth of a Nation* depicts the Reconstruction era (p. 183). A fictionalized account of conflict between the North and South, it focuses on a feud between an abolitionist and a former slave owner. The film's plot includes a melodramatic family saga and a glorified account of the genesis of the Ku Klux Klan. Modern-day audiences have been shocked by the blatant racism threaded throughout the film. Griffith's masterpiece provides invaluable insights into American cultural history and the social attitudes of the era in which it was made. It really must be seen to be believed.

6. **Who was the first African American to win an Academy Award?**
   - (A) James Earl Jones
   - (B) Oscar Micheaux
   - (C) Hattie McDaniel
   - (D) Sidney Poitier

Even though the industry was already dominated by white males, in the early years of filmmaking an all-but-forgotten pioneer set up his own studio, known as the **Film Corporation**, on West 125th Street in Harlem. He was **Oscar Micheaux** (1884-1951) and he is regarded as the first black film maker. Micheaux produced and directed his own films, which dealt with "Negro" life in America. These films were not widely distributed—the bias against blacks in all aspects of the film world was plain to see in the way African Americans were portrayed in films like *Birth of a Nation*. It was not until 1939, when **Hattie McDaniel** won the **Academy Award** for Best Supporting Actress (and even then for playing a slave turned servant) in *Gone With the Wind* that Hollywood acknowledged African Americans' contributions to film.

7. **Who developed the dialectical theory of *montage*?**
   - (A) Jean Renoir
   - (B) D.W. Griffith
   - (C) Sergei Eisenstein
   - (D) Erich von Stroheim

Griffith's pioneering work in narrative structure was surpassed only by his Soviet contemporary, **Sergei Eisenstein** (1898-1948). Eisenstein developed the theory of *montage* (taken from the French verb *monter*, "to

REELSPEAK

ADR: Automatic Dialogue Replacement—*dialogue recorded in a studio after the fact. Sometimes the sound was bad on a set or location, and sometimes the talent hit the margaritas a little too hard the night before. Also used for dubbing dialogue in a film in another language.*

MUSIC AND METAPHOR

Alexander Nevsky (1938) is considered by many to be Eisenstein's masterpiece. It is a sweeping historical drama depicting the Russian army's successful fight against invading German forces, the Teutonic Knights, in the thirteenth century. Eisenstein's film goes far beyond historical epic. Alexander Nevsky was politically important because its patriotic subject matter was again topical with the Nazis posing an undeniable threat to Russia even through the tenuous Nazi-Soviet Non-Agression Pact of 1939. It was also Eisenstein's first sound film and he used it as an opportunity to realize his theories of contrapuntal sound, a theory in which Eisenstein envisioned using the sound medium not to recreate a sense of reality but to enhance emotional response by having the sound-track alternately compliment and conflict with the visual rhythms of the film. The task was incredibly ambitious and with the help of a magnificent score by Sergei Prokofiev, Eisenstein created one of the greatest achievements in film history. The German knights are always presented in rigid geometric formations while the Russian army is disorganized but energetic, and Prokofiev's score works as Eisenstein envisioned it, as another metaphorical device.

assemble"), an approach to **film editing** (the cutting together of different shots) entirely different from Griffith's straightforward dramatic use of the process. Where Griffith was representational, Eisenstein saw the opportunity for metaphor. The technique of montage is a type of editing that aims for expressive or symbolic effects, as opposed to a reality-based or representational

"I am Sergei Eisenstein: Super Genius."

technique, which links together images in order to simulate a realistic flow of events. The images in montage don't necessarily follow a logical order or have an empirical structure; instead, they are assembled in a manner that enhances the emotional and symbolic impact of a narrative. Simply put, where Griffith was an essayist in film, Eisenstein was a poet.

Eisenstein completed only seven films in his twenty-three-year career, but his films, in addition to his theoretical essays, have had greater influence on modern cinema than did any other body of work. Eisenstein's strides in cinematic innovation were not matched until the French **new wave** movement nearly thirty years later. Eisenstein's *Battleship Potemkin* (1925), one of the most influential films ever made, is considered to be the definitive example of film structure. The film commemorates the 1905 revolution against tsarism, specifically the mutiny aboard the tsarist battleship Potemkin and the bloodbath that followed. The most famous sequence from the film, and one of the most highly regarded sequences in film history, is the **"Odessa steps"** sequence, filmed at the port of Odessa where the massacre occurred. The influence of *Battleship Potemkin* and Eisenstein's narrative techniques can be seen even today, not only in film but in the editing used in music videos (p. 536). One direct homage to Eisenstein's "Odessa steps" sequence was in Brian De Palma's *The Untouchables* (1987).

8. Which of the following studios did Charlie Chaplin help found?

(A) Paramount
(B) 20th Century-Fox
(C) Warner Brothers
(D) United Artists

The **studio system**, which served to stabilize production, originated in the second decade of the century. The first studios were based in New York City and the industry flourished there, allowing for more than a dozen studios to come and go during the decade. Initially, the industry was regulated by Thomas Edison's Motion Picture Patents Company (MPPC). Developed by a group of individuals interested in breaking Edison's grip on the industry, the studio system capitalized on the content of movies and the personalities of the stars who appeared in them. Many producers moved to a suburb of Los Angeles to distance themselves from the shady tactics of the MPPC. Undoubtedly they counted on their proximity to the Mexican border to protect them from injunction should the need to flee arise. However, Edison's MPPC was a dying animal, and with the introduction of sound, Edison could no longer compete with what was going to become one of the most powerful corporate entities in America: the movie studio.

As is usually the case within the film industry, artistic growth took a

THE SCREWBALL COMEDY

The screwball genre is defined by quick, wisecracking dialogue, furious pacing, and burlesque and slapstick elements derived from the silent cinema. A classic example of screwball comedy is Howard Hawks's Bringing Up Baby *(1938). Filmmaking brothers Joel and Ethan Coen gave the screwball comedy a modern nod with their 1994 film* The Hudsucker Proxy.

MAJOR PLAYERS IN THE STUDIO SYSTEM

The Actors	The Actresses	The Directors
Cary Grant	Marlene Dietrich	John Ford
Gary Cooper	Greta Garbo	Howard Hawks
Humphrey Bogart	Lauren Bacall	Alfred Hitchcock
Jimmy Stewart	Katharine Hepburn	George Cukor
	Grace Kelly	William Wyler
		Frank Capra

Cary Grant

Greta Garbo

HOLLYWOOD IN NEW YORK

Although everyone associates Hollywood with the movie industry, the capital of American filmmaking from the 1890s through World War I was the Big Apple. Edison's Motion Picture Patents Company housed its studios in West Orange, NJ and East 21st Street in Manhattan. In addition, D.W. Griffith, Adolph Zukor, Vitagraph, Biograph, Universal, Goldwyn, Metro, Fox, and Paramount (then Paramount-Artcraft) all operated studios in New York and Fort Lee, NJ. The subsequent move to California was inspired less by sunny weather than the urge to come out from under Edison's monopolistic hold on the industry through his MPPC.

backseat to the bottom line—money. The development of the studio system brought the industrial nature of movie-making to a head. In order to ensure a consistent product for the consumer and profits for the producers, the studios were developed to provide a system of brand names—either through the star system of bankable personalities, the cult of the director, or the concept of the recognizable genre. Stars signed on to large

STUDIO SYSTEM CASUALTY

Charlie Chaplin and Buster Keaton were two of the most powerful men in the industry in the 1920s, producing some of the best, most innovative, and largest-grossing films of the day. Keaton is held by many to have been Chaplin's superior, but the introduction of the studio system halted his artistic growth, as he was forced to take on roles that essentially destroyed his career.

contracts and directors were given less control over their pictures. This forced artists like **Charlie Chaplin** (1889-1977), who helped establish **United Artists**, to form their own studios. While the studio system did not completely curtail creativity and artistry onscreen, it resulted in the kind of "cookie-cutter" formula fare that the major studios are still churning out today.

The **star system** had its crude beginnings in 1910, when Biograph studios actively promoted **Florence Lawrence** as the Biograph Girl. This paved the way for other companies to market their films based on the actors in them. A new industry arose around these "stars." As well, fan clubs and fan magazines provided plenty of free publicity, as did the regular press, which fed their readerships' yen for glamour. Meanwhile, the mass audience was on its way out—viewership began to fragment into a demographic audience composed of different age, gender, and interest groups—and the studio

Buster Keaton with bevy

system was the perfect engine to exploit these new markets.

The stability the studios insured, their monopolistic natures, and the introduction of sound spurred an unprecedented rise in film production throughout the thirties. With sound, **musicals** became viable screen projects for the first time, and a new genre was born. The studios each claimed its particular talents in the field. Warner Brothers and Samuel Goldwyn banked on Busby Berkeley, while RKO pictures made a mint on the dancing duo of **Fred Astaire and Ginger Rogers**. Meanwhile, **Walt Disney** was producing the Silly Symphony series of cartoons, which paved the way for **animated musicals**, today among the highest grossing films ever made (Disney's 1994 film *The Lion King* made over 700 million dollars in less than a year).

Other genres proliferated as well. The **gangster film** made stars of **Edward G. Robinson** (1893-1973) and **James Cagney** (1899-1986) with films like *The Public Enemy* (1931). The gangster genre came out of America's obsession with figures like Al Capone and the genre was marked with the uncompromising formula of the rise to power of the corrupt central character and his inevitable demise and the heartbreak it would cause those who once loved him. Plenty of seediness, violence, and moralizing—the bad guys always finished last. Studios were anxious to secure multi-picture deals with the likes of the **Marx Brothers**, **W.C. Fields**, and **Mae West**, pioneers of **comedy**, then and today the most bankable of all film investments. The "screwball" comedy enjoyed success throughout the thirties and made directors like **Preston Sturges** and **Howard Hawks** assets to studios as well. The **horror film** also became a recognizable genre with the advent of sound. The classics *Dracula* (1931), *Frankenstein* (1931), and *The Mummy* (1932) all met with huge success, paving the way for the unforgettable experience of *King Kong* in 1933, a film that would itself create another genre, the **monster film**, whose legacy includes *Godzilla* (1956) and films like *Alien* (1979). The horror film genre differs from the monster film genre in that a horror film doesn't necessarily have to include inhuman beasts and has its principle interests in the pyschological horror of its subject matter (Hitchcock's *Psycho* for example) in which humankind explore the dark recesses of their own capacity for evil. The monster film genre interests itself with alien beings or toxic mutations anywhere from the size of a rodent to the size of a building who usually enjoy dining on human flesh and have no interest in finding their own humanity but are definitely interested in killing all of the characters in the story or destroying a large metropolitan area. Both genres share the same ending though: the good guys win, either by coming to grips with their own fears or dropping a nuclear bomb on the beastie.

The unprecedented avalanche of film production (7,500 feature films between 1930 and 1945) also required unprecedented capital, and Wall Street was more than happy to accommodate. The film industry was one of the safest industries to invest in during the Depression. Studios were run by businessmen, and the role of the **producer**, who coordinates all the people involved in a film from writers to technical help, originated under the studio system. Hollywood became a very efficient production line. In the absence of the MPPC, the studios controlled almost every aspect of the moviegoer's experience. In addition, studios had their own production facilities, distribution channels, and exhibition outlets. All of the eight studios were under the control of the Morgan and Rockefeller groups, and the corporate .giants Morgan and Rockefeller owned between them all of the major patents that made sound pictures a reality. In short, Hollywood was a monster that no one could stop—until the government took an interest in the studios' business practices and the **Catholic Legion of Decency** came down on the moral content of their product.

STUDIO SYSTEM FAMILY TREE

1912-1928	1994
The Majors:	**The Majors:**
Paramount	20th Century-Fox
Loews/Metro-Goldwyn-Mayer	Sony Pictures
	Disney
Fox/20th Century-Fox	Paramount
Warner Bros.	**The Minors:**
The Minors:	Miramax
Universal	New Line
Columbia	Tribeca Productions
United Artists	

9. Which of the following studios has never been found in violation of federal anti-trust laws?

   (A) Paramount
   (B) Universal
   (C) 20th Century-Fox
   (D) SONY Pictures

Of course, all of this incestuousness (or cooperation, depending on how you look at it) made everyone tons of money. But the U.S. has always been leery of this mode of operation. The **Paramount Case**, begun in 1938 and concluded in 1948, was part of a movement by the government to uncover hidden corporate trusts after World War II. The five major studios were determined to be in violation of federal anti-trust laws and the three minor studios were found guilty of conspiring with the majors to retain their monopolies. The studios were forced to divest themselves of their exhibition operations, a process that wasn't fully completed until the

1960s, but nonetheless marked the end of the studio system and the "Golden Age" of Hollywood. And as the studio system broke apart, so too did the star system.

10. **The guidelines instituted by the Hays Office resulted in**
    (A) more efficient and economical film productions
    (B) the creation of unions within the studio system
    (C) censorship of films released in America
    (D) federal regulation of studio distribution practices

The Jazz Age (p. 307) of 1920s America created a "new morality" in which the public was more accepting of social "deviance" than it had ever been. In much the same way major-league baseball whitewashed a national bribery scandal and a "fixed" World Series (p. 446) by appointing a conservative federal judge to oversee its operations, Hollywood was given the **Production Code** by the **Hays Office**, officially known as the Motion Picture Producers and Distributors of America. Headed by Will H. Hays, this body regulated the moral content of films. In the late 1920s, a list of "don'ts" was supplied to the production community by a Jesuit priest, Father Daniel Lord, and a prominent Catholic businessman, Martin Quigley. The Depression was having no effect upon the antics of Hollywood personalities, and the scandals were flying. Too much money and too much "fun" ruined the career of many a star and was beginning

PARTY LIKE A MOVIE STAR

Fatty Arbuckle, the silent-screen comedian and rubenesque favorite of kids of all ages, had a peculiar idea of a fun time. In September of 1921, Arbuckle was charged with the rape and murder of starlet Virginia Rappe. Indicted for manslaughter, Arbuckle was never convicted due to lack of evidence, but it is alleged that he sodomized Rappe with a champagne bottle, then crushed her beneath his 270-pound frame. Needless to say, Arbuckle never worked in pictures again and paved the way for the moral overhaul of Hollywood.

EARLY VERSION OF THE PRODUCTION CODE (1927)

"Resolved, that those things which are included in the following list shall not appear in pictures produced by the Association, irrespective of the manner in which they are treated":

1. *profanity*
2. *nudity or the suggestion thereof*
3. *illegal drug traffic*
4. *any inference of sexual perversion (read: homosexuality)*
5. *white slavery*
6. *miscegenation*
7. *sex hygiene and venereal disease*
8. *scenes of actual child birth—in fact or in silhouette*
9. *children's sex organs*
10. *ridicule of the clergy nation, race, or creed*
11. *willful offense to any nation, race or creed*

to tarnish Hollywood's image. The idea was to provide for "self-censorship" to avoid the threat of government or church-sanctioned censorship, but the Church was behind the sanctions nonetheless. By 1934, the Catholic Legion of Decency had instructed all Catholics to shun any film it did not recommend. Threatened by the potential loss of many viewers, the studios weighed art and the bottom line; the Production Code Administration was born the same year. The studios agreed not to distribute any film that had not received the Hays Office's seal of approval.

11. **Filmmaker Leni Riefenstahl produced her most innovative work under the leadership of**

(A) Sergei Eisenstein
(B) Georg Wilhelm Pabst
(C) Adolf Hitler
(D) Werner Herzog

FRITZ LANG

Before the Nazi party ruled Germany, Fritz Lang was one of the most important filmmakers during the Weimar Period (1919-29). Lang's Metropolis *(1926) is one of the most famous of all silent films. It depicted a nightmarish totalitarian society in which humanity was a slave to its own productivity. Despite the fact that Lang was condemning the very machinization of humanity that Hitler hailed,* Metropolis *was purported to be Hitler's favorite film. With his classic* M *(1930), Lang cemented his reputation as a filmmaker, and in 1933 Josef Goebbels offered Lang the leadership of the German film industry. Half-Jewish and a liberal, Lang fled to Hollywood. He enjoyed success in Hollywood through the 1950s, directing such films as* Ministry of Fear *(1944) and* The Big Heat *(1953).*

The potential influence of the film medium on mass morality seemed like a small threat in America, but in the 1930s the German cinema was being overrun by the Nazi party, who used it for their own "moral" agenda. The Nazis approached film as a propaganda tool, essentially crushing any "deviant" artistic endeavors. The Nazi propaganda film was a powerful weapon. Hitler commissioned "educational" films that depicted the German Jews as the equivalent of rats. The films contained exaggerated, stereotypical views of Jews and even used special effects to show metamorphoses of Jews into rodents spreading disease. However, two truly remarkable films did come out of Nazi Germany, both made by German actress and filmmaker **Leni Riefenstahl** (1902-). The majority of Riefenstahl's collaborators had been deported to prison camps or exiled, but Hitler was impressed by her talent and in 1934 commissioned her to film the largest Nazi rally in history in Nuremberg. The film that resulted was *Triumph of the Will* (1935).

Leni Riefenstahl, directing, not saluting.

At once a frightening, fascinating, and unflinching look at the fanaticism of the Nazi party, it is the definitive propaganda film (although Reifenstahl denies ever having been a Nazi herself) and an impressive work despite its subject matter. *Triumph of the Will* was banned in the United States, Britain, and Canada because of its mesmerizing imagery. The U.S. released its share of propaganda war films and documentaries as well (the most famous of which is **Frank Capra's** *March of Time* series of faux newsreels), but none of them had the power or impact of Riefenstahl's work.

Hitler was so impressed by Reifenstahl's film that he again commissioned her in 1936 to document the Berlin Olympics (p. 437), an event Hitler was determined to use to prove the superiority of the Aryan race. Essentially unable to turn down Hitler's request, Reifenstahl managed to let her artistic aspirations come through despite Hitler's whims. The film, *Olympia*, remains one of the greatest documentaries ever made, climbing above its unfortunate supremacist subtext to stand as a testament to athletic achievement. Riefenstahl introduced innovative filming techniques in **slow-motion photography** and the use of **telephoto lenses** (a lense that enables the camera to zoom in closely on action that it is actually quite far away from, opening up a wide and variable spatial range for the camera to capture) that immediately inspired other filmmakers. The director refused Hitler's request to change the sequence in the film that captures Jesse Owens (p. 441) winning the gold medal, which led to the charged moment, also intact in the film, where Hitler leans over in front of his countrymen and adorns Owens with not just one, but four, gold medals.

Ironically, these two impressive documentaries of Nazism are the biggest, most expensive productions ever by a woman director. And to this day, no woman has won the Academy Award for Best Director.

12. **Who was the youngest nominee for Best Director in the history of the Academy Awards?**
    (A) John Singleton
    (B) Orson Welles
    (C) Quentin Tarantino
    (D) Charlie Chaplin

While France was occupied by the Nazis and the whole of Europe was embroiled in World War II, **Orson Welles** (1915-1985) came to Hollywood, and at twenty-six, directed, wrote, produced, and starred in *Citizen Kane* (1941). *Citizen Kane* was a failure with audiences when it premiered, and even some critics were less than favorable toward it, but today it is

Before directing the legendary Citizen Kane, Orson Welles was infamous for a broadcast on his radio series Mercury Theater of the Air which he based on the H.G. Wells story War of the Worlds (1898). The faux documentary/news broadcast told of an alien invasion overrunning the earth and caused a real nationwide panic among its listeners. The 1984 film The Adventures of Buckaroo Banzai Across the 8th Dimension pays homage to Welles's radio broadcast and his influence.

REELSPEAK

DA: Director's Assistant—*to be distinguished from the AD. The director may have one or more personal assistants whose functions range from the fetching of Snapple to the outlining and storyboarding of every shot as well as propping the director up as she attempts to convey said information to the AD.*

regarded as one of the best films ever made. It is a masterpiece of cinematic innovation and storytelling, well ahead of its time in employing several film techniques: deep-focus photography, extended tracking shots, backlighting effects, the use of matte photography and miniatures, and camera acrobatics that had never been seen before in the cinema. In order to accomplish all of this, Welles and his cinematographer invented lighting elements and camera lenses during production, experimenting until they achieved what they were after. The deep focus lens was literally invented on the set of *Citizen Kane* and it allowed the camera to achieve a focus impossible for the human eye; Welles used this device to great effect. Shooting on large sets, Welles used the lens to keep the entire shot in focus, so that the foreground of the scene was equally as sharp as the background, creating the opportunity for cinematic detail that had never

Orson in 1941: weary, brilliant, and relatively thin.

existed before. Backlighting effectively silhouetted all of the action on screen and created sharp contrast, black and white compositions and ghostly images, not exactly the typical Hollywood aesthetic. Welles used matte photography, the process of optically printing different shot elements (such as a shot of a man and a separate shot of a lunar background) into one composition (the man is now on the moon) to achieve shots that couldn't have been done conventionally, at least not without great expense. While tracking shots were nothing new, (literally affixing the camera to a track or dolly so that it could be moved smoothly through a series of rooms or angles), Welles used them in coordination with camera and optical effects to create a seamless, impossible reality. *Citizen Kane* is full of marvelous examples of the culmination of all these techniques in which live action would be combined, or matted, with a shot of a miniature or a photo-realistic painting, in order to create on screen something which never actually existed. In other words, it is the landmark film that all others have followed in the search to create a wholly believable, hyper-realistic screen universe.

13. The term *"film noir"* was coined to describe

(A) the black and white photography characteristic of 1920s studio productions

(B) the French avant-garde movement in cinema

(C) an American genre of the 1940s and 1950s typically dealing with the underworld

(D) comedic melodramas of the 1930s

Despite the collapse of the studio system, America was still the reigning influence on world cinema throughout the 40s and early 50s. One genre of film that developed in America after World War II was the *film noir* genre. This term was coined by French critics (it means "black film") and *cinéphiles* (film lovers) who perceived a new and unapologetic cynicism in American crime films and melodramas in the post-war period. This new toughness was seen as a reaction to the demoralizing horrors of war and the hypocrisies of post-war American society. What made these films a breed apart from others in the crime or melodrama genres was the absence of pity or love for their characters. There were no truly innocent or sympathetic heroes in *film noir*. In fact, *film noir* stories were populated with anti-heroes: ruthlessly scheming, murderous *femme fatales*; burnt-out, morally ambiguous, paranoid private detectives; con men completely lacking humanity; and madmen, miscreants, and degenerates of all types. The classics of the *film noir* genre remain Billy Wilder's *Double Indemnity* (1944), John Huston's *The Maltese Falcon* (1941), and Orson Welles's grim masterpiece *Touch of Evil* (1958).

Much of the subject matter for *film noir* came from the popular literature of the 1930s and 1940s, especially the hard-boiled detective novels of Raymond Chandler and Dashiell Hammett (p. 278). The underbelly of American culture was being exposed to film in a highly stylized, unforgiving manner. Just as *noir* literature became increasingly brutal in the 1950s under such authors as Jim Thompson, so did film. Many of these films had problems getting around the production code—*Double Indemnity* came close to being banned by the Hays Office. The *noir* genre also handed down an indictment of American society unprecedented in film, offering social commentary that would not again be so scathing until the 1960s.

LET'S STAY HOME AND WATCH TV

In 1946, nearly two-thirds of the entire population of America went to the movies. But by 1949, the challenger had arrived—there were one million privately owned television sets. By 1959, there would be fifty million television sets. In the 1960s however, with the combined influence of foreign cinema, the French new wave, and the collapse of the Production Code, Hollywood would get a much-needed injection of creativity that would eclipse even the convenience of television.

It's a noir thing.

14. **The Hollywood Ten refers to**
    (A) the major studios at the end of 1947
    (B) the biggest box-office successes of all time
    (C) the filmmakers who refused to testify to the House Committee on Un-American Activities
    (D) the highest paid actors in the business

The Cold War took its toll on Hollywood. In September of 1947, the House Committee on Un-American Activities (p. 656) began summoning witnesses from the Hollywood community who would prove their patriotism by exposing leftists and communist sympathizers in the film community. Among the producers, executives, and actors to testify against their peers was one B-list actor named Ronald Reagan (p. 427). The **"blacklist"** era began. Anyone in the film business who was found to be a "Red" was ruined, his career effectively over. Charlie Chaplin put himself into exile in England as a result of the accusations against him. In October of 1947 ten filmmakers who had been subpoenaed to testify in court refused to do so. They were found in contempt of Congress and served jail time. McCarthyism, more than anything ever had, stifled creativity in Hollywood for nearly a decade and ruptured the film community that was still accustomed to the cozy days of the studio system.

Ironically, while the rest of the country was under Senator Joseph McCarthy's form of political censorship and Hollywood itself was still reeling from the practice of blacklisting, filmmakers began pushing the envelope of acceptable subject matter (although these films seem tame by today's standards). Daring films such as *The Man With the Golden Arm* (1956), starring Frank Sinatra (of all people) as a heroin addict, did not receive the Production Code's approval, and Elia Kazan's *Baby Doll* (1956), concerning a child bride, became the first film to be condemned by the Legion of Decency. But the two films were financial successes, and this time it was the Legion of Decency that fell victim to Hollywood's bottom line.

The studio system collapsed in the 1950s, and with it went the

COMMIES FROM OUTER SPACE

While McCarthyism was ripping its way through Hollywood, the science fiction genre was mirroring the prevalent American fear of communism with such films as The Day the Earth Stood Still *(1951),* Invaders From Mars *(1953), and* Invasion of the Body Snatchers *(1956). In* The Day the Earth Stood Still, *although the alien is benevolent, he is viewed as a threatening, unseen force. The citizens of Washington, D.C., become so fearful that he wants to take over the United States that they effectively use witch-hunt tactics to track him down and destroy him. The latter two films, like so many films of the 1950s, use the premise that aliens are coming down to take over mankind through brainwashing or, in the case of* Body Snatchers, *completely replacing the original person with a servile proletarian worker. Yikes!*

effectiveness of the Production Code. Foreign and independent feature films did not need to have approval for studio release, since theaters were now independently owned and could run films other than the ones cranked out by the studios. As a result, the code became totally ineffectual and was abandoned in the 1960s. Hollywood was given the freedom to explore sexuality overtly on screen for the first time in twenty years, and other social taboos such as drugs, alcoholism, and race relations were also now available to be explored in the American cinema. This new-found freedom of expression was heavily influenced by the films of foreign countries, which had freely explored a much broader subject matter.

15. The term *mise-en-scène* refers to

   (A) the process of film editing
   (B) the composition and elements of a shot
   (C) the number of shots called for in a script
   (D) processed matte shots

In the 1950s, directors began to put new importance on *mise-en-scène*, ("placing-in-the-scene"), the elements within a frame of film, from the blocking of the actors within the shot, to the set decoration, to the placement and movement of the camera. The theory behind the new interest in *mise-en-scène* held that the creation of mood and emotional response should have less to do with editing than with the depth, composition and length of the shots in the film. The "long take," a shot held for longer than usual without cutting, was favored. While its supporters and theorists were initially French, Welles's *Citizen Kane* was an early example of a film dependent on *mise-en-scène* for its emotional effect. Hitchcock's *Rope* (1948) was another early American experiment with the long take and *mise-en-scène*, the entire film being shot in ten-minute-long takes.

16. The *auteur* theory of filmmaking was a term
    coined by

   (A) François Truffaut
   (B) Andrew Sarris
   (C) Pauline Kael
   (D) André Bazin

The **French new wave** was the most influential cinematic movement since Eisenstein rewrote the cinematic language. One of the tenets of the new wave was the *auteur* theory, a phrase coined by American film critic

REELSPEAK

DP: Director of Photography— *the head of the camera department. He is responsible for the lighting and camera movement, which are both essential in determining the look and feel of the film. The DP is usually both an experienced gaffer (p. 119) and camera operator, but often will neither gaff nor operate. Instead he'll call for "Just one more light! Just one!" at inopportune moments.*

WHO ARE YOU CALLING AN *AUTEUR*?

Many of the French critics who developed the mise-en-scène and auteur theories—François Truffaut, Jean-Luc Godard, and Eric Rohmer—went on to become new wave auteurs themselves. Yet it is interesting to see who they considered to be auteurs. Among those they lauded were Orson Welles, Alfred Hitchcock, Howard Hawks, Fritz Lang, John Ford, Jerry Lewis, and Roger Corman. Some of the choices make absolute sense; Welles and Hitchcock, aside from being thoroughly recognizable directors stylistically, are among the greatest masters of mise-en-scène in film history. However, Jerry Lewis's cinematic accomplishments never came close to those of Buster Keaton and Charlie Chaplin. And Roger Corman, however endearing and intrepid a director he was, had made films such as Swamp Women *(1955) and* Teenage Caveman *(1958) before producing a decade's-worth of low-budget horror films in the 60s. Admittedly, these films are fun to catch on "Mystery Science Theater 3000" (Comedy Central)."*

Francois Truffaut and an actor are crestfallen when they both show up wearing the same coat.

Andrew Sarris (1928-). Sarris based his theory on a theoretical essay by **François Truffaut** (1932-1984), who would go on to become one of the definitive directors of the French new wave movement. The basis of the *auteur* theory is that the director is the commanding force behind a film, and the medium is used to express the personal artistic goals of the director. The best films are therefore ones in which the director, or author (*auteur*), clearly leaves his imprint as an artist. The *auteur* theory favored directors whose films were clearly the result of one artistic vision. By personalizing film to such a degree, the directors of the French new wave allowed themselves an artistic freedom of expression and style that created diverse work. Arguably, not all directors considered *auteurs* are great directors. Ed Wood (*Glenn or Glenda, Plan 9 From Outer Space*) is best known as the worst director of all time, but his films are all so distinct, and his oddball vision so recognizable, that he could be considered an *auteur*. The theory of the director as author has been challenged by many and accepted by few. Cinéphile and film critic Pauline Kael wrote an essay called "Circles and Squares" (1963), refuting Sarris's theory so harshly that the two never reconciled their differences, personally or professionally.

17. All the following were directors "discovered" by the cinematic new wave movement EXCEPT

   (A) Jean Jacques Beineix
   (B) François Truffaut
   (C) Jean-Luc Godard
   (D) Eric Rohmer

Directors François Truffaut, **Jean-Luc Godard** (1930-), and **Eric Rohmer** (1920-) were all products of the new wave movement. While the theories that came about during the new wave were met with much criticism, these critics-turned-directors were able to defend their cinematic ideas by actually applying them to the films they made. Truffaut's *Les quatres cents coups*, or *The 400 Blows* (1959), put the new wave on the international map and garnered the accolades of critics and audiences, winning Truffaut the award for Best Director at the prestigious **Cannes Film Festival** in 1959. Jean-Luc Godard's *Breathless* (1959), written by Truffaut, is just as famous. Films of the new wave were necessarily made on shoestring budgets (they were not produced with large studio backing) and this necessary frugality added to the new wave's anti-establishment aesthetic.

Breathless contains all the elements of the new wave, both technically and aesthetically, such as the use of the shaky **hand-held camera**, the use of **location settings** as opposed to the mock reality of a set, the use of natural lighting, improvisations of both dialogue and plot by the actors and director, and direct sound recording as opposed to **voice-overs** and artificial ambient sound. The definitive mark of the new wave film was its aggressive use of editing and the introduction of the **"jump cut."** The jump cut was used to eliminate spatial and temporal continuity from the viewing experience. In contrast to the traditional method of using "establishing shots" to ease the transition from one scene to the next, jump shots called attention to the power of the director over the film's reality. The new wave filmmakers did not want to be slaves to the "invisible" editing techniques that had become the norm since the days of Griffith, nor did they want to rely on montage to create metaphorical cinematic language. They were out to confuse, challenge, and beguile their audience with a new cinematic syntax.

18. The influence of the French new wave movement was most evident in which of the following late 1960s American films?

(A) *Barbarella*
(B) *The Graduate*
(C) *2001: A Space Odyssey*
(D) *Faster Pussycat! Kill! Kill!*

THE NEOREALISTS (1940-1951)

During World War II the Italian cinema reacted to Fascism in the form of the cinematic movement called **neorealism**. *Abandoning the dependence on plot-driven stories and professional actors, neorealists encouraged improvisation and experimentation, creating their own sociopolitical cinematic form. Other notable filmmakers who came out of the neorealist movement in Italian cinema were Roberto Rossellini and those he inspired, such as Federico Fellini and Michelangelo Antonioni. The neorealists' influence on the French new wave and the move away from "traditional" narrative film structures is undeniable. And if you've ever seen Fellini's* Satyricon *(1970) or Antonioni's* Zabriskie Point *(1970), you know just exactly how far away from the norm their films can be.*

CULTURESCOPE

While it was by no means a new wave film, Mike Nichols's *The Graduate* (1967) was one of the first mainstream American films to use new wave techniques such as the jump cut and the jittery hand-held camera. *The Graduate* earned Nichols an Oscar for Best Director and popularized elements of new wave filmmaking. *2001: A Space Odyssey* (1968) is more avant-garde than anything, although director Stanley Kubrick is undoubtedly considered an *auteur*. *Faster Pussycat! Kill! Kill!* is a silly Russ Meyer film, but if having a signature style in which all of your films concern well-endowed, dominatrix-like women qualify you as an auteur, then Meyer is definitely an *auteur*. *Barbarella* (1968), although directed by new wave pioneer Roger Vadim, is an extremely silly American-Italian-French production from which the 1980s glamour band Duran Duran took their name and features Jane Fonda doing things that Ted Turner would never approve of. The conventions that the new wave movement introduced have become part of the cinematic lexicon and are now even commonly employed in television commercials and programs such as "NYPD Blue" and nearly any video on MTV. Next time you see a commercial where the camera has an annoying tendency to move around and do anything but focus on its subject, you can blame the new wave.

Dustin Hoffman contemplates a formal invitation in *The Graduate*.

19. Who is known as the father of the nonfiction film, i.e., the documentary?

   (A) Victor Flemming
   (B) Dziga Vertov
   (C) David Maysles
   (D) Robert Flaherty

20. The term *cinéma verité* originally referred to

   (A) new wave cinema
   (B) avant-garde cinema
   (C) documentary cinema
   (D) the neorealist cinema

An under-appreciated form, the documentary goes back to the beginnings of motion picture film. However, it was not until the early 1920s that it came into its own. **Dziga Vertov** (1896-1954), who came to be known as the father of the documentary film, and his disciples published a series of essays denouncing narrative cinema and calling for a new cinema dominated by "camera-recorded documentary material."

Originally an editor of **newsreels** for the Moscow Cinema Committee, Vertov released a series of documentaries entitled *kino-pravda* (literally, "film truth"). Vertov's documentaries, while full of complex images and illusions, use these elements not to convey a sense of convincing reality, but to call attention to the process of filmmaking itself. They thus deconstruct (p. 229) the process of cinematic illusion and expose the "reality" of how subjects are documented by the camera. He also used many experimental camera techniques, including trick photography, multiple exposures, animation, and microphotography. Vertov's innovations also touched the creative hearts of the new wave directors—Jean-Luc Godard named his production company after him. Though he himself has been largely forgotten, Vertov has been influential across the decades, even extending to 1990s documentary-style television shows such as "Cops" and "Rescue 911." We're sure he would be proud.

The term *cinéma verité* was coined by documentary filmmaker **Jean Rouch** to describe the **documentary film** as the

REELSPEAK

Gaffer: *the technical lighting expert on set. The DP tells her what it should look like, the gaffer makes it happen, and makes sure that there will be enough light to get an exposure.*

DOGS

The cinéma verité *techniques that so inspired the new wave filmmakers have become the common lexicon of film language. Quentin Tarantino used the verité style with brutal success in his 1992 film* Reservoir Dogs. *Taking the form even one step higher was the 1992 Belgian faux-documentary production* Man Bites Dog, *which spoofs cinema verité by having the film crew follow a serial killer around in his day-to-day life, documenting all of his crimes and vicious slayings. At one point the sound cuts out because the soundman in the film crew has been accidentally murdered during a gun fight. Rather than stop filming, they get another soundman.*

"cinema of the truth." Rouch saw documentary film-making as a sort of guerrilla cinema in which the camera is not simply observing a situation, but is actually an active participant in the action it's recording. The advent of the new wave saw the term *cinéma verité* applied to narrative films as well because so many of the new wave techniques (such as hand-held cameras, unmixed sound, and natural light) originated in documentary films.

21. **Box office receipts were at their lowest in the year**
    (A) 1934
    (B) 1942
    (C) 1956
    (D) 1962

Godard (center) directing *Contempt*, just one of the foreign films that challenged Hollywood in the 1960s.

The availability of foreign films to the American market hurt the Hollywood machine in the mid-1960s. A new generation was going to movies—one that had grown up with television and was visually sophisticated. Hollywood was stuck in its formula rut, churning out films that differed little from its earlier offerings, and could not compete with the easy entertainment of television and with the far more ambitious and creative foreign cinema. The average production cost to studios in the mid-1960s was three million dollars a picture and audience attendance was at an all-time low by 1962. The social and political tumult of the 1960s caught up with Hollywood in the last part of the decade, and American directors challenged the conservative Hollywood aesthetic in both subject matter and technique. The new wave and America's more liberal social climate influenced American directors such as **Sam Peckinpah** (*The Wild Bunch* [1969], *Straw Dogs* [1971]), **Arthur Penn** (*Bonnie and Clyde* [1967],

Alice's Restaurant [1969]), and **Robert Altman** (*M*A*S*H* [1970], *McCabe and Mrs. Miller* [1971]). Audiences welcomed the resurgence of exciting filmmaking in Hollywood, essentially saving the industry from folding in on itself.

Hollywood also recognized the financial wisdom of using younger, less experienced directors to entice audiences back to theaters. Novice directors worked for lower salaries and delivered what the public was hungry for—a new product. The most famous film to come out of this new order was *Easy Rider* (1969), directed by a thirty-two-year-old Dennis Hopper. The ad copy for the film read that it was the story of two young men who go out "in search of America, but they can't find it anywhere." *Easy Rider* is famous for many reasons, not the least of which is **Jack Nicholson's** (1937-) endearing appearance in the film, but it's most renowned for capturing the attitude of youth in 1969. Produced for $375,000, Hopper's movie had the unglossed, guerrilla feel of the new wave films, and dealt unabashedly with the hot topics of sex, drugs, and prejudice. It returned $50,000,000 to its producers, who sang peace and love all the way to the bank. Hollywood was convinced that the youth market was ready for more. Independent producers like Roger Corman were given the chance to invest meager budgets in non-studio productions to foster new talent. Among Corman's discoveries are Francis Ford Coppola, George Lucas, Joe Dante, and Jonathan Demme.

22. The first X-rated film to win an Academy Award was
    (A) *The Devil in Miss Jones*
    (B) *Midnight Cowboy*
    (C) *Deep Throat*
    (D) *A Clockwork Orange*

Hollywood unbuttoned its top button, but all was not fair game, even in the absence of the Production Code. In 1968, the **Classification and Ratings Administration** was created by the **Motion Picture Association of America (MPAA)** and an association of theater owners. The ratings system that emerged was yet another self-censorship measure to prevent increased government involvement in the industry. Films were given ratings, from "G" (General Audience) to "X" (no one under eighteen admitted) based on whether they included nudity, sex, violence, strong language, or "adult situations." The very next year John Schlesinger's *Midnight Cowboy* (1969) received an "X" rating, usually reserved for pornography, essentially crippling it at the box office despite its critical

REALSPEAK

Gofer: *the guy who "goes for" stuff, like the aforementioned Snapple, when the DA is too busy.*

REELSPEAK

Best Boy: *first electrician and major assistant to the gaffer. These are the people who provide electricity at three A.M. from a streetlight after the generator has gone down, or wire an entire swamp for electricity without killing one alligator or featured player. The name is a major holdover from the bad old days of film when most of the women on set were called script girls.*

acclaim. *Midnight Cowboy* went on to win three Academy Awards for Best Screenplay, Best Picture, and Best Director. This oversight was not corrected by the MPAA until 1990, when the "NC-17 rating" was created for films that deal with very risqué subject matter but are clearly not pornographic. The rating system still has its problems, but it's better than the censorship that came before. When you're watching a film made between 1927 and 1969, remember that so many of them were neutered by the censors. People were just as perverse and depraved then as they are now.

23. **All of the following films are examples of the blacksploitation genre EXCEPT**
    (A) *Shaft*
    (B) *Blacula*
    (C) *Black Sunday*
    (D) *Cleopatra Jones*

Sometimes referred to as the decade of decadence, the American cinema of the 1970s saw some of the greatest, most popular, and most lucrative American films ever produced, among them Coppola's *The Godfather* films (1972 and 1974), Lucas's *American Graffiti* (1973) and *Star Wars* (1977), Altman's *Nashville* (1975), Spielberg's *Jaws* (1975), and Woody Allen's *Annie Hall* (1977) and *Manhattan* (1979). It also saw budgets for single films skyrocket up to twenty million dollars. Many films of the 1970s reflected the cynical outlook of the post-Vietnam War American public: Alan J. Pakula's *All the President's Men* (1976) and Michael Cimino's *The Deer Hunter* (1978) are prime examples. Subcultures also began to come into the spotlight in films like *Taxi Zum Klo* (a very graphic account of New York's gay community), John Badham's *Saturday Night Fever* (1977), and **Martin Scorsese's** *Taxi Driver* (1976), among others.

Most iconoclastic among these subculture films was the genre particular to the 1970s, the **blacksploitation** film. Films such as *Shaft* (1971) and its sequels, *Blacula* (1972), *Coffy* (1973), and *Cleopatra Jones* (1973) appealed not only to the black audience, but to any moviegoer who enjoyed grandiose and over-the-top style bordering on kitsch. Immensely popular, especially in large cities, these relatively cheap pro-

THE FORMULA FOR A FORMULA PICTURE

Murder Mystery → *ends with: she did it!*

Action/Adventure → *ends with: I made it!*

Horror → *ends with: we killed it! (until the sequel)*

Love → *ends with: wedding bells (or the modern equivalent)*

ductions were usually marked by lots of violence and sex. But for a refreshing change it was the white characters who were made out to be inept and stupid. The blacksploitation genre eventually paved the way for a new generation of black filmmakers like Spike Lee, John Singleton, the Hudlin Brothers, and Carl Franklin to break through the picket fence of Hollywood.

The creative momentum of Hollywood in the late 1960s and 1970s was slowed in the 1980s as bigger and bigger, and less and less artistically ambitious, productions became the norm. Each successive year saw a new film earn the dubious title of "the most expensive film ever made," a trend that unfortunately continues to this day. The "me decade" can also be said to be the **action film** decade for Hollywood. Mirroring the social mores of the decade—the fitness craze, the obsessions with appearance and possession and status (read: yuppies), and the look-out-for-number-one attitude—the action film became Hollywood's number-one ticket in the 1980s. The artistic and intellectual side of filmmaking (except for the efforts of stunt coordinators, editors, and effects houses such as ILM) got the short end of the stick. It seemed once again that Hollywood had found its formula.

Of course, all of these big productions meant big money for movie stars, who are now arguably the most powerful people in Hollywood—quite a change from the old days of the studio system when the movie producer was the overlord of the lot. What is the second most powerful group, then? If you guessed the stars' agents, you are correct, and the monster that is **Michael Ovitz's CAA** (Creative Artists Agency) is testimony to that fact. Then come the producers and, in some cases, the directors. It still won't help anybody to sleep with the screenwriter.

24. **What country's film industry produces the most films per annum?**
    (A) The United States'
    (B) Japan's
    (C) India's
    (D) China's

Today, **India** cranks out more films each year than the United States, and the cinema of **Hong Kong** is closing in on Hollywood's financial monopoly of the world market. Hong Kong produces films that regularly gross nine-digit returns, thanks to directors and stars like Chow Yun-

---

BREAKING THE BANK

George Lucas, with his Star Wars *trilogy and Steven Spielberg, with films such as* Close Encounters of the Third Kind *(1977) and* E.T. *(1982) proved that a film costing upwards of $30 million could be a sound investment. A lot of producers, directors, and stars took this to heart with disastrous results. Bruce Willis spearheaded one of Hollywood's biggest bombs,* Hudson Hawk *(reportedly $50 million). Producer Mario Kassar of Carolco has put his studio close to bankruptcy on a few occasions, spending close to $100 million for films like* Total Recall *(1990) and* Terminator 2 *(1991). Both of these films were directed by James Cameron and starred Arnold Schwarzenegger, the pair who, with 1994's* True Lies, *broke the record for the most expensive film ever made ($100 million). Elizabeth Taylor is associated with the biggest bomb Hollywood ever produced,* Cleopatra, *which cost $10 million when it was made in 1963.*

Fat, Jackie Chan, and John Woo (the latter two having already crossed over into the American market with Hollywood-backed productions). The SONY corporation's large investment in Hollywood itself in the form of SONY Pictures Studio is making money for foreign investors and conglomerates, not only the American film machine. Hollywood remains, though, at the top of the industry's heap with the largest production companies, the biggest and most advanced **effects houses** in the industry, the most recognizable and bankable collection of movie stars in the world, and our nation's own relatively high standard of living providing steady audiences. People can still afford to go to the movies. The industry has become more competitive as smaller, independent studios release highly successful films. For example, Miramax studios, unknown ten years ago, has released several highly successful films, including *My Left Foot* (1989), *Cinema Paradiso* (1989), *The Crying Game* (1992), and *Pulp Fiction* (1994). The recent growth of many independent studios also allows talent that might otherwise have been missed by the majors to get their shot at the big time. Directors such as Julie Dash, Nick Gomez, and Quentin Tarantino have all started with low-budget independent features. But have no fear, the Hollywood machine still loves formula and films like *Lethal Weapon* (1987) and *Die Hard* (1988) are probably here to stay.

FORTY AMERICAN FILMS YOU SHOULD SEE

All That Jazz (1979), directed by Bob Fosse. *All That Jazz* is an autobiographical account of talented director and choreographer Bob Fosse's life. The film recounts his achievements in film and stage, his penchant for womanizing, and his troubles with alcohol. Fosse lets the film slip surreally between drama and musical as he presents a less-than-flattering look at himself. The upbeat and erotic dance numbers counterbalance the brutal honesty of Fosse's examination of his own life. The mixture works to create a vivid, if bleak, motion picture and a notable artistic statement. *All That Jazz* proved that Bob Fosse still had the chops that made him great in his earlier films *Cabaret* and *Lenny*.

Apocalypse Now (1979), directed by Francis Ford Coppola. Orson Welles once tried to adapt Joseph Conrad's *Heart of Darkness* but abandoned the project. Coppola took up Conrad's story about the darkness of humanity and set it rather ingeniously against the backdrop of the Vietnam War. Some thought this was pretentious and overambitious, and others thought it brilliant, but in any case this is an intensely original and challenging film. Kurtz is played somewhat lethargically by Marlon

Brando, but Martin Sheen is excellent in the role of Marlowe. Coppola spins a rich metaphorical web that has a synergistic effect. While not all of the parts seem to work toward a coherent whole, at the conclusion they somehow add up to even more. You might also want to see the documentary on the making of the film, *Hearts of Darkness: A Filmmaker's Apocalypse* (1991), which is in some ways even darker than the movie.

Badlands (1973), directed by Terrence Malick. Malick took a stylistic cue from Arthur Penn and Sam Peckinpah with *Badlands*. Inspired by the Starkweather-Fugate murder spree of the 1950s, the film is presented as a road movie—one of Hollywood's more low-brow genres. However, Malick uses the road motif to turn expectations upside-down and accentuate the dark subtexts of his story, setting the tale of young love, frustration, and murder against some of America's most beautifully desolate landscapes. A rewarding film experience once you accustom yourself to its unusual and ambitious narrative logic.

The Big Sleep (1946), directed by Howard Hawks. Adapted from the Raymond Chandler (p. 278) novel by three writers, including William Faulkner (p. 272), *The Big Sleep* stars Humphrey Bogart as detective Philip Marlowe and Lauren Bacall as the moll. Not all the ends are tied together in this mystery thriller, but Hawks's direction is so tight, the dialogue so evocative, and the performances so commanding that you don't really complain if one or two larcenous acts remain unaccounted for. This movie is Hollywood entertainment at the top of its form, with no superfluous elements—something they seem to have forgotten how to do.

Blue Velvet (1986), directed by David Lynch. Eight years after making the experimental and avant-garde *Eraserhead* (1978) which both repelled and mesmerized audiences with its Kafka-esque style, Lynch went on to make a truly American classic in *Blue Velvet*. A dark comedy that exposes America's obsession with repressing violence and sex and features some of the oddest Americana ever put on screen, Lynch's film takes us into the American heart by way of the gutter—you can see Lynch as a kid adding scatological touches to Norman Rockwell prints. The film is full of details that one viewing can't even hope to catch. An original, daring, and very funny film, although not for all tastes.

Bonnie and Clyde (1967), directed by Arthur Penn. Based on the true story of Bonnie Parker and Clyde Barrow (played in the film by Faye Dunaway and Warren Beatty), Arthur Penn's film was initially panned by critics and its violence shocked many others, but it was the most popular film of 1967 and ended up receiving ten Academy Award nominations. *Bonnie and Clyde* is now hailed as an American classic that played a significant role in changing American cinema.

Cabaret (1972), directed by Bob Fosse. Set in pre-World War II Berlin, *Cabaret* is the melding of the Broadway musical of the same name, Christopher Isherwood's book *Goodbye to Berlin*, and the John van Druten play *I Am a Camera*. The film is a great example of dramatic counterpoint, contrasting flamboyant musical numbers and an exotic romance against the onslaught of Nazi occupation and a world headed into holocaust. Director Bob Fosse brought all of the elements together beautifully, and the film was rewarded with eight Academy Awards including Best Actress (for Liza Minelli), Best Supporting Actor (for Joel Grey, who reprised the role on Broadway in 1993), Best Score Adaptation, Best Cinematography, and one for Fosse as director.

Casablanca

Casablanca (1942), directed by Michael Curtiz. What can you say about this film that hasn't already been said in a thousand books, documentaries, commercials, and rip-offs? *Casablanca* is the definitive Hollywood film. The cast is a Who's Who of Hollywood stars, and rarely does dialogue get any better. Unlike most of the films made in Hollywood in the 1940s, *Casablanca* transcends the era in which it was made and has become one of the most enduring stories in movie history. If, for some strange reason, you haven't seen this film, see it now or you will regret it, maybe not today, maybe not tomorrow, but someday and for the rest of your life.

Chinatown (1974), directed by Roman Polanski. Polanski's modern *film noir* gives us Jack Nicholson as a Raymond Chandler/Dashiell Hammett-type private eye in 1930s Los Angeles. The dialogue is a stand-out in this film—the screenplay deservedly won an Oscar. A movie made in the classic Hollywood mold, *Chinatown* takes an old formula and gives it a modern spin.

Citizen Kane (1941), directed by Orson Welles. Even before the term *"auteur"* had entered the film world's lexicon, Orson Welles undoubtedly was one. With *Citizen Kane*, Welles rewrote the book on filmmaking, breaking away from the conventions of Hollywood to create a work unlike anything that preceded it. Welles created an original and powerful narrative structure to tell the story of Charles Foster Kane, a fictional man who bears an uncanny resemblance to real-life publishing magnate William Randolph Hearst. Welles's innovations and distinctive directorial style were not met with adulation when the film was first released (although his screenplay did win an Oscar), but today *Kane* remains the film all others are compared to.

City Lights (1931), directed by Charlie Chaplin. A common choice of critics as Chaplin's best film, this bittersweet comedy features his indomitable character, **The Little Tramp**. As always, the Tramp is played by Chaplin, but the character explores a new emotional range in *City Lights*. The story illustrates the difficulties of surviving against great odds during hard times, much as *Modern Times* does five years later, but the emphasis in *City Lights* is on feelings. Studios were nervous about the film because at the time they were releasing sugary, escapist fair for depression-riddled Americans, and although Chaplin described the film as "a comedy romance in pantomime," his sociopolitical criticisms still came through loud and clear. The romance of the film still managed to bring in the audiences, regardless of the characters' grim circumstances, and secured the film's status as a classic.

Close Encounters of the Third Kind (1977), directed by Steven Spielberg. Arguably Spielberg's best film, this was the second-most-popular film in 1977, after *Star Wars*. The film manages to capture a sense of wonder hidden in the threat people feel when confronted with something they don't understand. Speilberg uses the film's myriad special effects to convey these mixed emotions with great success. A magical film that, unfortunately and inexplicably, is no longer available in its original version, which was better than the version Spielberg recut and called the Special Edition.

Dr. Strangelove (1964), directed by Stanley Kubrick. This classic dark comedy about the nuclear age and the cold war features Peter Sellers in a triple role. The film is still topical today, and its examination of the ridiculousness of warfare has rarely been equaled.

Easy Rider (1969), directed by Dennis Hopper. The film that defines the mood of America in the late 1960s. The story of two free-livin' dope dealers who like nothing more than to ride their choppers across the country, *Easy Rider* is less a cinematic achievement than a social study. The film nonetheless acknowledges the avant-garde new wave movements of the 1960s in the way it was directed and edited by Hopper. Absolutely of its time, but it's still a kick to see Peter Fonda and Dennis Hopper cruise their bikes along the highway with Jack Nicholson in tow.

From Here to Eternity (1953), directed by Fred Zinnemann. Although the film's source material (James Jones's novel of the same name) was considerably watered down for Hollywood, *From Here to Eternity* was still risqué enough to raise a few eyebrows when it was released. While the much-touted love seen between Burt Lancaster and Deborah Kerr is tame by today's standards, the film nonetheless has an openness unusual for a 1950s Hollywood production. The tale of Army life in Hawaii just prior to the bombing of Pearl Harbor (p. 650) won eight Academy Awards, including Best Picture, Best Director, Best Screenplay, Best Cinematography, and both Best Supporting Actor awards (for Donna Reed—yes, Donna Reed—and Frank Sinatra).

Gates of Heaven (1978), directed by Errol Morris. Documentary filmmaker Errol Morris enjoyed commercial success when *The Thin Blue Line* was released in 1988, but before he brought popularity to documentary film he made the hilarious *Gates of Heaven*. *Gates* is concerned with the strange culture of people in Southern California who insist on burying their pets in a cemetery, and with the people who run the pet cemetery to cater to their needs. The film manages never to be flippant or condescending to its subjects—they basically speak for themselves. Morris aims not only to observe eccentric behavior but also to create an allegory on the bastardization of American values and the absurd priorities of an increasingly commercialized society. Great food for thought and very entertaining, the film is about as far removed from Stephen King as it could be.

The General (1927), directed by Buster Keaton. Chaplin's cinematic equal, the great filmmaker of the silent era Buster Keaton created a masterpiece with *The General*. The film tells the story of a heroic Confederate soldier trying desperately to foil the Union army's attempt to bring military supplies into Confederate territory. Unlike Chaplin, Keaton was not trying to make a political statement with his story. As a filmmaker, Keaton was much more concerned with the use of the camera and its unique narrative potential than Chaplin was. Exciting, full of action, and beautifully shot, *The General* was quite a technical achievement when it was released. Bear in mind that Keaton performed all of his own stunts (a situation that would cause studios today to collapse and die from unheard-of insurance rates) and watching his reckless physical courage alone is a wonderment.

The Godfather (1972), directed by Francis Ford Coppola. Coppola took what was essentially good pulp fiction and lifted it beyond its own boundaries. Coppola co-wrote the screenplay to *The Godfather* with Mario Puzo (author of the novel), assembled an exceptional ensemble cast, and added excellent art direction, cinematography, and music to create the modern-day equivalent of *Gone With The Wind*. *The Godfather* has all the spectacle and drama of an opera, and with an equivalent running time of nearly three hours. The film won Oscars for Best Picture, Best Actor (for Marlon Brando, who declined the award because of his disgust with the portrayal of Native Americans by Hollywood), and Best Screenplay. *The Godfather II*, released two years later, is as good as the original and became the only sequel in history to win the Academy Award for Best Picture.

Gone With the Wind

Gone With the Wind (1939), directed by Victor Fleming. The granddaddy of the Hollywood epic, this is the model Hollywood film. It swept the Oscars and is still one of the most popular movies of all time. If you haven't seen it, you're missing references to it in today's films, in books, even on *The Simpsons*. It's long, but it's gorgeous, and the performances are movie stars at their best.

Lenny (1974), directed by Bob Fosse. This bio-pic of 1950s comedian Lenny Bruce and his wife, brilliantly portrayed by Dustin Hoffman and Valerie Perrine, is backed by exceptional direction by Fosse. At once a moving look at a troubled artist and an examination of the time in which Bruce's brand of raw, scathing humor got him arrested, *Lenny* has a gritty, stark look well-suited to its subject.

The Manchurian Candidate (1962), directed by John Frankenheimer. A fine political thriller examining the effects of war and McCarthyism, topics that only a few years before couldn't have been addressed in a Hollywood production. Frank Sinatra is well-cast against his type.

The cast of *M*A*S*H*

M*A*S*H (1970), directed by Robert Altman. Released at the height of the war in Vietnam, *M*A*S*H* was a big theatrical and critical success. It boasts a great cast and gave director Robert Altman a chance to do one of the things he does best: black comedy. The film took audiences and Hollywood by surprise with its mixture of sophomoric high jinks, political commentary, and insouciant satire of the Korean War. The television show it inspired is a much-watered-down version of the film.

Midnight Cowboy (1969), directed by John Schlesinger. Crippled at the box office by a misguided "X" rating, *Midnight Cowboy* remains one of the best American films ever made. Adapted from James Leo Herlihy's potent novel, the film depicts male prostitution (the sexually discomfitting context the reason for its rating), but it is essentially a dramatic, squalid "buddy" movie. Voigt plays a hayseed from the Midwest who, setting off for the Big Apple to make his fortune as a "stud," encounters a homeless man named Ratzo Rizzo (Dustin Hoffman) who becomes his only friend. The subject matter is serious and the depiction of low-life New York is jarring, offering sharp insights into what the American dream had become at the end of the decade of peace and love.

Modern Times (1936), directed by Charlie Chaplin. Although he made this movie a decade after synchronized sound had been introduced to motion pictures, director Charlie Chaplin felt the discipline of silent cinema best fit his tale of the struggle to survive in an ever-more-industrialized age. Chaplin's decision resulted in a powerful and comical satire that enjoyed unexpected commercial success. The clarity and sharpness of Chaplin's satire (and his obvious political stance) made Chaplin some enemies in the U.S. and caused the film to be banned in Germany and Italy. At once a metaphor of Chaplin's own career and record of the dehumanizing effects of the machine age, *Modern Times* remains a dark comment on the marriage between technology and the corporate power structure. The film has inspired many later filmmakers, including Jacques Tati, whose *Mon Oncle* pays homage to Chaplin's themes and directorial style.

Even the 1987 film *Robocop* contains an homage to the Chaplin classic.

Notorious (1946), directed by Alfred Hitchcock. Following his visual collaboration with Salvador Dali (p. 610) on *Spellbound*, Hitchcock made his most romantic film to date with *Notorious*. A tale of spies, hidden identity, and double-cross set in post-World War II South America, *Notorious* puts a love story at the center of a nest of vipers. Hitchcock takes the tension inherent in the story's situation and manages to manipulate it to a fever pitch without even having the characters raise their voices. The movie is a great example of Hitchcock's talent, and has the added attraction of Cary Grant, Ingrid Bergman, and Claude Rains.

One Flew Over the Cuckoo's Nest (1975), directed by Milos Forman. Ken Kesey reportedly has refused to see the film adaptation of his novel, and that's a shame. Together with Kubrick's *A Clockwork Orange* (1971) and Mike Nichols's *Catch-22* (1970), this is one of the best film adaptations of a book ever made.

On the Waterfront (1954), directed by Elia Kazan. Articles by journalist Malcolm Johnson inspired novelist Budd Schulberg to write this story of two brothers whose lives are affected by the corruption of harbor unions in New York City in the early 50s. Elia Kazan created a small masterpiece out of this simple tale, thanks not only to his unwavering and focused direction but also to just about everyone else involved in the production. *On the Waterfront* won eight Academy Awards, for Kazan, Marlon Brando, and itself, as well as Best Supporting Actress for Eva Marie Saint, and Best Story, Screenplay, Cinematography, Editing, and Art Direction.

Paths of Glory (1957), directed by Stanley Kubrick. Before teaming again on *Spartacus*, Kirk Douglas starred in Stanley Kubrick's adaption of Humphrey Cobb's factual novel based on events within the French army during World War I. *Paths of Glory* is one of the best anti-war films ever made and it works on many levels: as a courtroom drama, psychological drama, and black comedy. The film tells the tale of a general who is so angry with his troops for retreating from a massacre that his first wish is to have them all shot for disobeying the order to continue the attack. The fact that the enemy is never even revealed to the viewer makes Kubrick's study on the absurdity of war even more biting. The film never loses sight of what it wants to achieve, all the way down to the memorable final scene.

Psycho (1960), directed by Alfred Hitchcock. Hitchcock's notorious introduction of the knife-wielding psychotic to the silver screen unintentionally doomed audiences to countless imitations and a legacy of slasher films. *Psycho* is a canny mix of an intense Oedipal disorder, sexual repression, built-up tension, beautifully calculated shocks, and good old

American depravity. While *Psycho* is not even Hitchcock's best film, it illustrates his mastery of film technique, narrative structure, and a control over the suspense-thriller genre that no film-maker has yet to equal.

Raging Bull (1980), directed by Martin Scorsese. This is one of the best American films ever made, on all levels. Based on the memoirs of boxer Jake LaMotta (who acted as creative consultant on the film), *Raging Bull* is an unflinching look at a man at war with himself and everyone else. One of the most emotional, brutal films you'll ever experience, it won the Academy Award for Best Picture, but director Scorsese was overlooked—first-time director and Hollywood favorite Robert Redford won for *Ordinary People*.

Rocky (1976), directed by John G. Avildsen. This is the first and the best. Old story, old formula, well done, the film won Oscars for Best Picture and Best Director. A perfect example of Hollywood film-making and a simple, uncomplicated good time.

Safety Last (1923), directed by Fred Newmeyer and Fred Taylor. This famous silent comedy starring Harold Lloyd features a standard bumpkin-comes-to-the-big-city-to-make-it-big-plot, but the humor, both subtle and slapstick, makes it an extremely enjoyable ride. Lloyd succeeds in making his character separate from those of his two contemporaries, Keaton and Chaplin, even though he borrows much from both of their styles. Good direction also makes the gags work perfectly: Lloyd's famous stunt sequence involving scaling a building is both very nerve-wracking and funny.

The Searchers (1956), directed by John Ford. Western genre *auteur* John Ford filmed this adaptation of Alan Lemay's novel about a man's search for his kidnapped niece across the wild west. Cowboy archetype John Wayne stars along with Natalie Wood, and if you can make it past the requisite slaughtering of Native Americans you will be rewarded with a surprisingly insightful and emotional film. One of Ford's many triumphs on his familiar territory.

Straw Dogs (1971), directed by Sam Peckinpah. Flawlessly directed by Peckinpah, *Straw Dogs* stars Dustin Hoffman as a pacifist wrestling with his ideas of right and wrong. Extremely controversial when it was

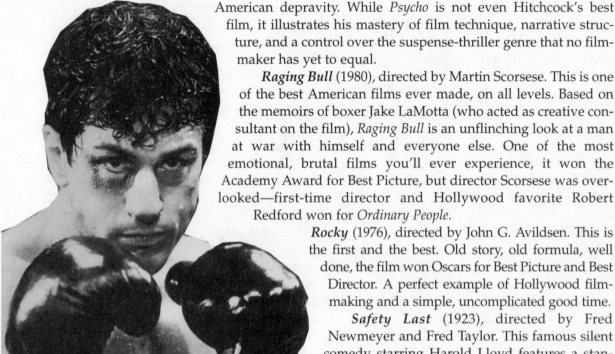

Raging Bull

released, the film is extremely violent. The movie's violence raises important issues for which it offers no simple answers. You be the judge.

Sunset Boulevard (1950), directed by Billy Wilder. Prolific and skilled director Billy Wilder and an excellent cast (including revered silent-era director Erich von Stroheim) created one of the classic black comedies of American cinema. Biting, involving, and funny, the script won an Oscar. Recently adapted for Broadway, the movie has been immortalized for introducing aging star Norma Desmond.

Taxi Driver (1976), directed by Martin Scorsese. Scorsese's second film was controversial for its violence and its subject matter, but it is a riveting study of a skewed personality amidst the chaos of New York. This unforgettable film has a performance by a twelve-year-old Jodie Foster that nearly eclipses De Niro's portrayal of the title character, Travis Bickle. The screenplay was penned by Paul Schrader.

Touch of Evil (1958), directed by Orson Welles. The famous long-take opening shot of this film starts the viewer on a journey through another Welles stylistic masterpiece—a great example of *film noir*. The story takes place in a seedy Mexican border town full of murder, drugs, and kidnapping. A corrupt cop (played so convincingly by Welles that you can almost smell him) makes sure things stay well mixed. To let on any more would ruin the experience. This is a dark, unforgettable film full of stunning photography.

2001: A Space Odyssey (1968), directed by Stanley Kubrick. The film that blew audiences away in 1968 is still an incredibly cerebral experience, but if you're watching it at home, beware: so much of its majesty is lost on a small screen that it doesn't seem nearly as impressive. Kubrick spent two-and-a-half-years and ten-and-a-half million dollars bringing this science-fiction epic to the screen. As with most science fiction, the futuristic

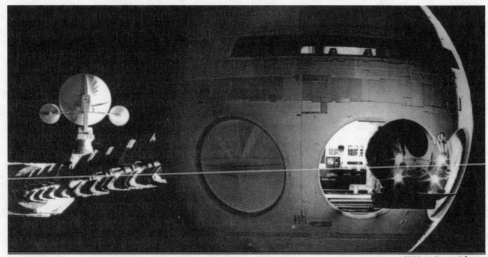

2001: A Space Odyssey

premise is a jumping-off point for social commentary. Kubrick expands on the idea of man's relationship to technology explored in his previous *Dr. Strangelove* (1964). Audiences were riveted not only by the innovative effects but by the timely theme: the relationship between nuclear technology and humankind, which had become an everyday worry.

The Wild Bunch (1969), directed Sam Peckinpah. Peckinpah, along with Arthur Penn, revolutionized the use of violence in American films, and *The Wild Bunch* is a glorious example of Peckinpah's almost balletic treatment of bloody carnage. The story concerns a band of outlaws (William Holden, Ernest Borgnine, and Warren Oates among them) who find the country growing too old for their wild-west lifestyles. But the law still wants to catch up with them. True to form, Peckinpah opens this film with the type of massacre-style shoot-out that usually concludes most Westerns. A classic of the American cinema, it ranks with *Straw Dogs* (1971) as one of Peckinpah's best films.

The Wizard of Oz (1939), directed by Victor Fleming. A twist on Lewis Carroll's *Through the Looking Glass*, *The Wizard of Oz* is Hollywood's best fairy-tale adventure, complete with catchy Oscar winning songs, childhood innocence, mythical creatures, triumph over evil, and oblique references to drugs. *Oz* is gleefully silly, and its production design and art direction anticipate the pop art movement (p. 615). The film is an American classic and a perfect example of a Hollywood crowd-pleaser, but Dorothy's wonderland over the rainbow is not all smiles and flowers, which makes the film enjoyable even to the cynics in the crowd.

ANSWERS

1. B	2. B	3. B	4. C	5. B	6. C	7. C	8. D	9. D	10. C
11. C	12. B	13. C	14. C	15. A	16. B	17. A	18. B	19. B	20. C
21. D	22. B	23. C	24. C						

Geography

Hold on! Don't turn the page because you think a chapter on geography is going to ask you the capital of North Dakota. Geography is an all-encompassing discipline that takes an interest in the world and all that's in it, with a *spatial* perspective (hence all the maps). Geography—*geo*, earth + *graphein*, to write—deals with physical stuff—the origins of oceans, the retreats of great glaciers, the distribution of rain forests, volcanoes, and such, as well as the cultural side of human life on earth, from population growth to the demographics of disease. So whether you're an armchair traveler or a veteran of wanderlust, leave the passport at home and take a trip around the world.

1. How many continents were there on earth when the first dinosaurs roamed?

    (A) Nine
    (B) Seven
    (C) Two
    (D) One

200 million years ago

135 million years ago

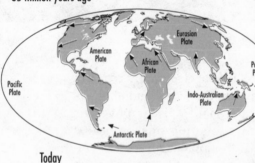

65 million years ago

Today

Continental Drift

Pangaea may be no more, but continental drift continues right under our noses. In Eastern Africa today, tensional forces between Earth's crustal plates seem to be pulling eastern Africa eastward, just as Arabia once pulled apart to create the Red Sea. If the pressure keeps pulling the land for a few more million years, Ethiopia and much of the eastern continent will pull apart, volcanos and other disturbances will reign, and the Red Sea will become ocean.

More than 200 million years ago, the continents as we know them were probably all connected as one large landmass which scientists call Pangaea—*pan* = all, *gea* = earth. Africa formed the core of this supercontinent, which consisted of two major parts, **Laurasia** in the north and **Gondwana** in the south. Over the millenia, the continents slowly moved away from Pangaea through the process of **continental drift**, creating the continents and oceans as we know them today.

The theory of continental drift was effectively defended in **Alfred Wegener's** (1880-1930) book *The Origins of Continents and Oceans* (1915). Using scientific disciplines ranging from geophysics to paleontology, he conceived of an original, single continent—Pangaea—which over geologic time has split into the continents today. Conclusive pieces of evidence were the similarity in rocks and fossils between continents now separated by oceans and the discovery of tropical plant and animal fossils in present-day arctic latitudes.

Scientists believe that the **Dwyka Ice Age** occured just before the break-up of Pangaea, creating the Gondwana part of the supercontinent. All the landmasses of Gondwana were affected by the ice sheets of Dwyka. Today, Eurasia and North America are remnants of Laurasia, while South America, India, Australia, Antarctica, and Africa form the main fragments of Gondwana. Africa's unique position at the heart of what was once Pangea gives it distinct geographical features, such as few deep bays along its coastline (making shipping ports in short supply), the absence of mountain belts like the Andes or the Alps, few extensive coastal plains, deep interior basins, an unusual course of rivers that seem to correspond to interior basins rather than present-day coastlines, dramatic coastline cliffs (in the south), and the rift that separated the **Arabian Peninsula** from Africa and opened up the **Red Sea**.

"Ain't No Mountain High Enough," by Diana Ross. " . . . ain't no valley low enough, ain't no ocean wide enough . . . to keep me from you."

2. **When Earth's crustal plates collide and spread, the result is**
   - (A) earthquakes
   - (B) volcanoes
   - (C) mountains
   - (D) All of the above

Earthquakes, volcanic activity, and mountain ranges mark the pathway of earth's crustal collisions. From the **Himalayas** and the **Andes** to **Mount Vesuvius** and the abysses of **Ethiopia**, the world owes much of its diverse landscapes to the endless movement of the earth's crust. Though the hypothesis of continental drift and crustal crashing was proposed just after the turn of the twentieth century, it was the new sonar equiment of the 1960s which revealed that oceanic ridges were not just underwater versions of mountain ranges, but rather a pipeline for hot, liquid lava that made the ocean floor continually move and spread and reconfigure itself, moving the earth's crust and continents along with it. The crust is fragmented into large plates, on top of which sit the continents we know today. There are seven large plates and numerous smaller ones around the globe, all constantly in motion.

The Earth's crust is thinner than the shell of an egg relative to the planet's diameter. The crust varies in thickness, ranging from about five to fifty miles deep.

Plates spread, collide, and overlap, moving both vertically and horizontally to create a range of dramatic results. A **subduction zone** is a tectonically active region where a plate is consumed by sliding into the earth along the abutting plate. The world we know today is full of crash sites and overlaps between crustal plates. When the Indian-Australian plate collided with the Eurasian landmass, the Himalayas were formed at the zone of contact. Similarly, the collision zone between the plates in the northern and western **Pacific Ocean** created island arcs and archipelagoes such as the **Aleutians** and **Japan**, and in part created the active earthquake and volcano zone along the rim of the Pacific Ocean. The explosive results of crustal plate movement have radically modified our natural environment and changed the course of human history.

About 3,500 years ago, the Greek island of Thera was the Hong Kong of the eastern Mediterranean, an economically powerful outpost of the dominant Minoan civilization. One volcano changed all that. When the volcano Santorini blew up, it decimated Thera, and left a couple of inches of ash on neighboring Crete (also Minoan-dominated), which ruined crops and poisoned the soil. The disaster gave rival culture Mycenae the upper hand, and regional power soon shifted to them. Not only did Santorini's eruption change that course of history, but it may also account for the Bible's famous "parting of the seas" by Moses (p. 486), which actually may have been seismic sea waves resulting from the Santorini eruption.

Where in the World Is Carmen Sandiego? and Where in the USA Is Carmen Sandiego? These crime stopping chases around the globe/USA respectively are lessons in geography for any age.

3. **Where is the San Andreas fault?**

(A) Mexico
(B) Peru
(C) California
(D) Brazil

The **San Andreas fault** marks the boundary between the Pacific and North American crustal plates that are sliding past each other in opposite directions. This **strike-slip fault** runs from the Pacific Ocean north of **San Francisco** down to the Gulf of California, separating Mexico's **Baja California** from the Mexican mainland. Baja California and southern California, including the city of **Los Angeles**, are sliding north/northwest at an unusually high speed, estimated to average more than three inches a year.

Most faults are merely fractures in the crust within one of the Earth's major plates, but the San Andreas fault is a unique point of horizontal contact between plates. It has resulted in a series of intense earthquakes in recent years, several in the Los Angeles area. Since 1987, more than ten major earthquakes have rocked the Los Angeles basin. Experts agree that more are on the way. The state is no stranger to earthquake damage: the San Francisco earthquake of 1906 triggered fires that destroyed the city. Between earthquakes and mudslides and miscellaneous social mayhem, it's no wonder that many Californians have flocked to other states.

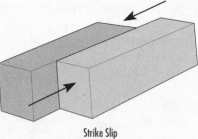

Strike Slip

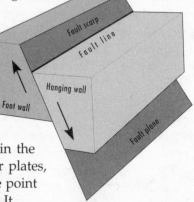

Features of a Fault

THE RICHTER SCALE

We always hear how earthquakes measure on the Richter scale, but what does it really mean? The scale measures the intensity of the waves of energy that radiate from the epicenter of the earthquake. Each whole number on the scale signifies a ten-fold increase in magnitude. On a scale of zero to nine, an earthquake measuring four on the Richter scale makes windows rattle; measuring six means poorly constructed buildings get destroyed; measuring seven makes steel bend and causes widespread damage; measuring eight results in near total destruction.

4. **During the Ice Age, the Bering Strait linked what are today**

   (A) Woody Allen and Mia Farrow
   (B) Italy and Africa
   (C) Alaska and Russia
   (D) Africa and Russia

Although scientists are unsure how the first humans came to **North America**, the most likely theory is that they came about 20- to 30,000 years ago by traversing the **Bering Strait**, a fifty-five mile watery gap connecting the Pacific and Arctic oceans, between today's **Russian Federation** and **Alaska**. No, these hominids didn't paddle prototypes of kayaks or swim the breast stroke of their lives—they were living in the midst of the **Wisconsin Ice Age**, during which there seems to have been a kind of corridor of ice that connected the continents, allowing adventuresome *Homo*

ERA	M.Y.A.	PERIOD	THE GEOLOGIC TIME SCALE	AGE OF
CENOZOIC	3	QUATERNARY	• Glaciers overspread large areas in several stages	Humanity
	6		• Cascades and Sierra Nevada formed	
	25	TERTIARY	• Large deposition of sediments on costal plain of Gulf of Mexico and Atlantic Ocean; also in Pacific coastal areas	Mammals
	40			
	60			
			• Rocky Mountains formed	
MESOZOIC	65	CRETACEOUS	• Mountain-building movements and great granitic intrusions in Sierra Nevada region	
	130	JURASSIC		Reptiles
	190	TRIASSIC	• Appalachian Mountains formed	
	220			
			• Coal-bearing layers deposited	
PALEOZOIC	270	PERMIAN		
	310	PENNSYLVANIAN	• Much crustal activity and granitic intrusion in New England	Reptiles
	350	MISSISSIPPIAN		
	400	DEVONIAN	• Much deposition of marine sediments; crustal folding in eastern and western North America	Amphibians
		SILURIAN		
	440	ORDOVICIAN		
	500	CAMBRIAN	• Great sequences of deposition and crustal deformation; not well-known	Fishes Marine invertebrates
	625	PRECAMBRIAN		

What kind of Neanderthal would trek across the frozen tundra to search for greener pastures? Cultural innovation often occurs under stress: as populations grew, early humans faced increasing competition for hunting/gathering terrain. Our ancestors who crossed the Bering Strait may simply have been acting human in adapting to changing circumstances.

After the Ice Age: The Return of Life to Glaciated North America (1991), by E.C. Pielou and *Patterns in Prehistory: Humankind's First Three Million Years* (1990), by R.J. Wenke. These are two great books about mankind's ancient history.

sapiens to make a mad dash on foot to new frontiers. Many scientists also believe that a Bering land bridge connected Asia to the glacial North America, and that the bridge probably opened and closed with fluctuations in climate until its permanent opening around 8,000 B.C. This would account for the southward migration of the Bering Strait travelers to **Mesoamerica**, where civilization is believed to have been successfully living and farming by 7000 B.C., and eventually to the rest of today's United States.

5. **Glaciers**

   (A) move through plastic deformation
   (B) sometimes leave scour lines called striations
   (C) can be found on the equator
   (D) All of the above

Antarctia

The Antarctic ice sheet covers an area of about five million square miles, equivalent to the size of Canada plus the contiguous United States, or nearly 10 percent of the land area of the entire earth. During the **Pleistocene epoch**, glaciers covered three times that much. That's one big ice cube. In profile, it creates a giant dome shape so tall that Antarctica has the highest average elevation of all the earth's continents. Buried underneath this mass of ice are entire landscapes, including a plateau as large as Australia and a mountain range comparable to the Andes in South America. At the center of the glacial sheet, just east of the South Pole, the ice is over 13,000 feet thick.

In the Northern Hemisphere, the Greenland glacier is about one-eighth the size of Antarctica, much smaller than it was a few million years ago. The ice sheets of Antartica and Greenland are the remains of **continental** glaciers. The next classification, **piedmont**, refers to the union of numerous mountain glaciers in a major range (for example, the Andes). Finally, alpine glaciers dot the landscape in all latitudes, even on the equator (Mt. Kenya).

Glaciers move by plastic deformation. Once they reach a critical mass (starting at twenty meters thick) the ice on the bottom melts and squishes out the bottom. As it scours a mountain valley, carving a typical "U"-shaped terrain, a glacier may leave characteristic marks such as striations—lines cut in bedrock—and glacial polish.

 About 85 percent of all the fresh water on Earth is presently locked up in Antarctic ice. The weight of the ice is so great that the continent has sunk thousands of feet into the ocean over the years.

6. **Why did Christopher Columbus land on North America by accident instead of at his original destination, the East Indies?**

(A) Wind storms
(B) Inaccurate compass
(C) Badly drawn map
(D) Wrong calculation of earth's dimensions

Christopher Columbus (p. 174) landed in North America instead of the East Indies because his voyage was based on the *Guide to Geography* by Roman geographer Ptolemy (p. 336), who wrongly estimated the Earth to be a third smaller than it is. Ptolemy's miscalculation made his determinations of **latitude** and **longitude** way off, causing Columbus to miscalcuate the placement of continents on his transatlantic voyage.

Why did Columbus rely on some guy's calculations from thirteen centuries earlier? Because the influence of the **Roman Empire** was so paramount in Europe that challenging Roman beliefs was, if no longer personally risky (as in feeding Christians to the lions), still unlikely. Ptolemy's miscalculation is an example of Romans being better imitators than originators, because about four centuries earlier, Greek scientist **Eratosthenes** (276-194 B.C.), a follower of Aristotle (p. 386), remarkably estimated the Earth's circumference at 26,700 miles—it's actually 24,900—without a calculator, in an era when distance was measured by how long it took to get somewhere. Maybe he had a fast camel?

 At the time, Eratosthenes's work calculating the Earth's circumference was an innovative stance, as not everyone believed the Earth was a sphere. Eratosthenes, a Renaissance man centuries before the Renaissance (p. 579), is also credited with coining the term "geography."

7. The world's longest river is the

(A) Amazon
(B) Mississippi
(C) Nile
(D) Volga

1993 brought the most devastating flood in U.S. history, the Great Midwest Flood, caused by a slew of unrelenting rainstorms and unusual weather systems. The flood took fifty lives, left nearly 70,000 people homeless, and caused an estimated $20 billion in damages. It lasted eighty days. Of the region's 1600 levees (riverside embankments built to prevent flooding), nearly 1100 broke or overflowed. On August 1, the Mississippi River at Saint Louis, MO crested at nearly fifty feet.

Flowing for 4,160 miles through three nations, the **Nile** is the world's longest river. It features a notoriously fertile **delta**, which normally occurs when fast-moving rivers or streams run into slower-moving water in bays, oceans, and lakes. Silt and sand accumulate at the intersection to create a delta. Land, too, is sometimes built up around rivers from the sediment dragged along and dumped off by the waters. When this sediment is rich in minerals, it may create a welcome riverside valley ripe for farming. Fertile sediment has settled generously along the Nile Valley and Delta for thousands of years, creating opportunities for our prehistoric ancestors along its route. The Nile has carried on alongside waves of human empires: Egyptian, Assyrian, Persian, Roman. Today, the Nile traverses the modern nations **Egypt**, **Sudan**, and **Uganda**. And the fertility of the Nile Valley and Delta endures, testified by the presence today of about sixty million residents, many of them farmers cultivating the rich riverine soil just like the old days.

"Old Man River" (1936), sung by Paul Robeson in the movie version of *Showboat* (p. 565). "I'm tired of livin' and scared of dyin', but old man River he just keeps on rollin' along."

8. Which of the following countries' topography is over 95 percent desert?

(A) Saudi Arabia
(B) Morocco
(C) Israel
(D) Sudan

LET IT RAIN

The rainiest spot on Earth is in the middle of Hawaii's island, Kaui, at Mount Wai'ale'ale. It receives an average of 440.22 inches a year.

Covering an area as large as Western Europe, the Kingdom of Saudi Arabia is one big desert. The most arid part of the country is called The Empty Quarter. The country's only reliable rainfall is in the southern province. Fortunately for the royal family, the country also houses the word's biggest oil and gas reserves. If you visit, don't try to sneak any souvenir oil—stealing is still punished by amputation under the nation's strict Islamic laws (p. 495)

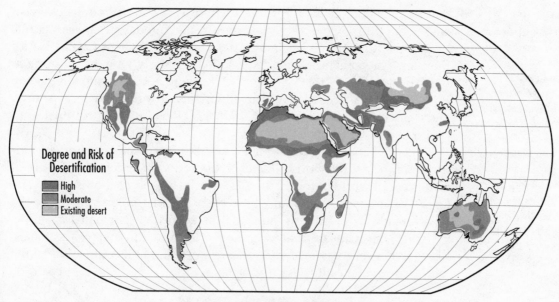

Desertification risk

The country is part of a global phenomenon of **desertification**, the spread of desertlike landscape into arid and semi-arid environments. This is caused by a combination of climatic changes and human activity, such as overgrazing by livestock and **deforestation**. A full one-third of the world's land area is subject to the threat of soil erosion and desertification. While desert spread is occurring in Asia, Latin America, and even the Southwestern U.S., Africa faces the most severe threat of soil erosion. In **Ethiopia**, for example, drought and famine have been rampant, and also exacerbated by civil war. The best recourse against desert spread is tree-planting programs and better land management.

9. **Which of the following does not have natural coal resources in its soil?**

   (A) China
   (B) Japan
   (C) United States
   (D) Russian Federation

Those Americans who may fret over the seeming economic upperhand held by Japan should get a grip on the basics: our societies run on energy, not Walkmans. In fact, Japan has such limited domestic resources

Nonfuel mineral resources, including metals and minerals, are also essential resources that can be processed into steel, aluminum, glass, and other products. Almost all of these are contained in the earth's crust. South Africa is one nation notoriously rich in gold and other natural resources, yet the overwhelming majority of its citizens—black South Africans—still live without electricity. Which just goes to show that it's not what you've got, but how you use it. At least **Nelson Mandela's** at the helm to steer the nation on a more humane course.

that its enormous economy would die if it were cut off from its overseas energy suppliers. Coal, a crucial energy source today, was used as fuel during the Roman Empire and perhaps earlier in ancient China. But for thousands of years human societies relied primarily on wood burning as their fuel-of-choice for heating and cooking. By the late eighteenth century, coal was recognized as an abundant and valuable energy source, and it essentially fueled the entire Industrial Revolution of the nineteenth century.

Today, China, the United States, and the Russian Federation, including **Ukraine**, are the world's largest coal producers, accounting for about 60 percent of world output. (China is also the biggest coal consumer.) The largest exporter is **Australia**, whose best customer is Japan. Despite the widespread use of oil, gas, and nuclear energy, coal remains an indispensable energy resource around the world. And although coal is a nonrenewable resource, world supplies are so great that it could still fuel the world for several centuries.

10. **What country has the world's largest known oil and gas reserves?**

   (A) Saudi Arabia
   (B) Russia
   (C) Iraq
   (D) Iran

Natural gas, often found near oil reserves, is a highly efficient, versatile fuel that has a less detrimental impact on the environment. The U.S. consumes more natural gas than any other single country in the world—more than half of American homes are heated by it.

Saudi Arabia may be mostly desert, but it also contains the world's largest oil and gas reserves and is among the top ten traders of all the world's major industrialized nations. When the United States charged into Iraq for Operation Desert Storm (p. 664), it was trying to protect its interests in oil-rich **Kuwait** and Saudi Arabia. Kuwait was actually the world's first oil-rich state, yet it is the Russian Federation which, in its former life as the U.S.S.R., was the world's largest producer of oil and natural gas. The Russian Federation is also believed to house the most extensive reserves of oil and gas, much still unexplored, as well as abundant caches of diamonds, gold, coal, nickel, timber and other resources. Regional disputes over resources within the former Soviet Union persist, as in the Siberian region of **Krasnoyarsk Krai**, which contains the majority of Siberian oil and struggles with Moscow for greater control over the wealth it produces.

Crude oil (in its refined form, **petroleum**) became a major energy resource in the mid-nineteenth century, when the first wells were drilled in Pennsylvania. Today the U.S. is the world's third biggest producer of oil and natural gas, with large reserves in Texas and Alaska. The U.S. is also a top consumer, and its dependence on foreign oil spawned not just the Gulf War but also the big **OPEC** crisis of the 1970s, where Mideast nations cranked up the prices, Americans freaked out about the cost of gas, and the U.S. government issued an embargo.

11. **Which is the biggest national park in the continental U.S.?**
   (A) Everglades
   (B) Yellowstone
   (C) Grand Canyon
   (D) Boundary Waters

Crossing state lines of Idaho, Montana, and Wyoming, **Yellowstone National Park** is the United States' oldest park, officially created by President Ulysses S. Grant (p. 635) in 1872. Covering almost 3,500 square miles, it is larger than Delaware and Rhode Island combined. Yellowstone has the world's greatest cluster of hot-water geysers and hot pools, starring world-famous geyser **Old Faithful**. What makes Old Faithful blast a hundred or more feet of hot steam nearly every hour of the day? Geysers are pressure cookers of water held by underground volcanic soil that shoots out boiling water and steam at intervals. Old Faithful erupts on average every sixty-five minutes, up to 170 feet, while Yellowstone's Grand Geyser explodes irregularly in rocket-like jets up to 200 feet high.

 Besides Yellowstone, the only other main geyser regions of the world are in new Zealand and Iceland. The only other natural geysers in the U.S. are in Beowawe and Steamboat, Nevada.

Yellowstone is also famous for its abundant wildlife, its **Lake Yellowstone** (at 7,733 feet, one of the largest high-altitude lakes in the world), and hundreds of miles of fishable streams. The park is one of over 350 parks throughout the United States run by the **National Park Service**. Along with the **Grand Canyon**, which has a seven-year waiting list for raft rides, Yellowstone is still an all-time favorite, and the only one that features the world's largest log hotel, the **Old Faithful Inn**.

The Grand Canyon

PC USA (Bröderbund), a computerized atlas of the U.S., and *Travel Planner* (Expert), covering the continental U.S., Alaska, Canada, and Mexico. These programs let you experience the sights and sounds of a cross-country voyage without leaving your living room.

GET OFF YOUR DUFF

To experience the great outdoors, write the National Parks Service at:

The Department of the Interior

National Park Service

Office of Public Inquiries

P. O. Box 37127

Room 1013

Washington, D. C. 20013-7127

E-mail: http://www.nps.gov

There are National Parks in the U.S. just itching to provide you with the rudiments of comfort and tons of slightly trampled nature. 268.6 million people visited National Park areas in 1994 (equal to the population of the U.S.). The most frequently visited park is the Great Smoky Mountain Park in Tennessee and North Carolina. The largest park is Wrangell-St. Elias in Alaska at 13.2 million acres.

12. **Which of the following countries does NOT contain any tropical rainforests?**

(A) Angola

(B) Zaire

(C) Brazil

(D) Indonesia

Tropical rainforest is one of the major plant/animal zones of the globe—the techno term is **biome**—a major division of the earth's surface generally corresponding to a particular climate. Deserts, forests, and savannas are other examples of biomes. Tropical rainforests are also extremely complex **ecosystems**—communities of organisms linked by exchanges of energy in the environment. Tropical rainforests, which extend across Asia, Latin America, Africa, Hawaii, and Puerto Rico, house a greater diversity of both animal and plant species than all the other world biomes combined. Costa Rica, for example, is about half the size of South Carolina but contains as many bird species as all of North America and more species of insects. One cluster of rainforest in **Kalimantan** (formerly Borneo) contains as many species of trees as exist in North America. And the forests yield abundance of chemical products used for medicinal purposes—half of all modern drugs come from tropical forests. Tropical rainforests also play a major role in maintaining the oxygen and carbon balance of the earth, hence the Amazon forest's pet name, "lungs of the world."

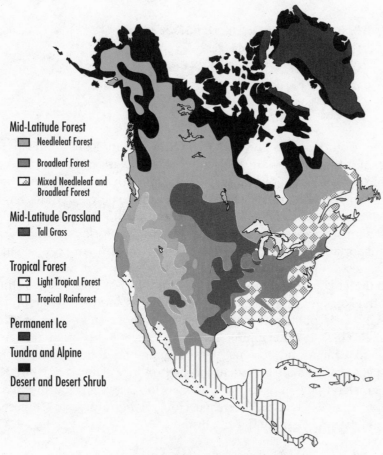

Mid-Latitude Forest
　▩ Needleleaf Forest
　▩ Broadleaf Forest
　▩ Mixed Needleleaf and
　　 Broadleaf Forest

Mid-Latitude Grassland
　▩ Tall Grass

Tropical Forest
　▩ Light Tropical Forest
　▦ Tropical Rainforest

Permanent Ice
　▬

Tundra and Alpine
　▬

Desert and Desert Shrub
　▬

The natural vegetation of North and Central America

Forests have been chopped down for centuries, of course, first for use as fuel for domestic and industrial use, then for houses, boats, charcoal, paper, and so on. Spain's vast plateau once was covered with forests which disappeared during Spain's colonial expansion (p. 77). When Spain colonized Mexico, massive forests there also fell to the ax. Today, two-thirds of Hawaii's, nearly half of Asia's, seventy percent of Central America's and about forty percent of South America's rainforests are gone. The United Nations estimates that at the current rates of logging, Nigeria and other West African nations will be similarly depleted. Deforestation by fire adds significantly to the depletion of the ozone, to global warming (p. 377), and to soil erosion.

13. Which of the following countries is NOT one of the "Four Dragons" of the Pacific Rim?
    (A) South Korea
    (B) Taiwan
    (C) Thailand
    (D) China

WHEN IS A RIVER NARROWER THAN IDEOLOGY?

During the *Korean War (p. 656)* the politically free state of Thailand and the communist-controlled *Laos* were separated by one kilometer of the Mekong River.

The "Four Dragons" of the **Pacific Rim**—South Korea, Taiwan, Hong Kong, and Singapore—are high-growth exporters in the current global economy. Thanks to low labor costs, stable governments, and foreign investment, growth in the Pacific Rim over the last three decades has been at least double that of the U.S. or Western Europe. **South Korea** is the world's most successful shipbuilder, and has a notoriously efficient public transportation system. Los Angeles-based Korean-Americans make up the greatest proportion of visitors to South Korea. Separated from North Korea under U.S. auspices after World War II (p. 82), South Korea still suspects the North of militaristic intentions. The island of **Taiwan**, off mainland China, is politically divided between those successors of **Chiang Kai-shek** (1887-1975) claiming **Taipei** as the capital of both Taiwan and mainland China, and the mainland Beijing-based powerbase insisting China is a unified state that includes the province of Taiwan. **Hong Kong**, another island off China, is one of the world's leading trade and financial centers. All eyes are on 1997, when Hong Kong returns to Chinese rule after ninety-nine years under the British.

14. What was rated the most severely polluted and polluting city in the world in 1994?
    (A) Mexico City
    (B) Bangkok
    (C) Detroit
    (D) Moscow

Traffic congestion in **Bangkok** is so bad that it's a serious hindrance to the country's economic activity. (Thailand is the chief world exporter of rice and rubber, and has big business in tourism—resorts, golf, and sex.) Scientists say that breathing the air in Bangkok is comparable to smoking three packs of cigarettes a day. Cities all along the Pacific Rim, from **Shanghai** to **Beijing**, lie perpetually engulfed in a haze of pollution. Makes Los Angeles look like a country field.

Around the globe, urban areas actually generate their own climate, through emission of smoke, gases, heat, and dust into the atmosphere.

Denver's brown cloud hovers due to temperature inversion.

YOU THINK L.A.'S BAD?

Donora, Pennsylvania is a valley town polluted by numerous factories and industrial plants. An unusual temperature fluctuation in October of 1948 interrrupted the valley's natural ventilation system, trapping almost unbreathable amounts of sulpher dioxide and other pollutants in the air. Half of the town's population became ill, and twenty people died.

Some European cities lose up to one-half of their incoming sun rays due to the smog domes overhead. With so many dust particles in the air around which water droplets can form, cities experience from 60 to 70 percent more foggy days than the countryside, where the grass is still greener and the air more breathable.

15. Who made the Galapagos islands famous?

   (A) Margaret Mead
   (B) Charles Darwin
   (C) Gilligan
   (D) Paul Bowles

The **Galapagos** islands are part of the **Republic of Ecuador**, whose capital city **Quito** was once the capital of the Inca Empire. Charles Darwin made these equatorial islands famous from his visit in 1835. The unusual animal and plant life of the islands contributed to the formation of Darwin's ideas on natural selection. The **archipelago**, named after the old Spanish word for giant land tortoise, is now the only spot on Earth where the tortoises are not extinct. They are believed to have the longest life span

ADAPTIVE RADIATION

This occurs when a biome is thoroughly isolated, as in the case of the Galapagos islands. When a single species faces intense competition for limited resources, the species will often fragment its population. After a period of isolation, a variety of new species evolves, each species filling a separate niche. An example can be found on the Galapagos islands—the thirteen species of finches that evolved from a common ancestor.

of any creature on the planet. The Galapagos also features the highest percentage of indigenous forms of animals— all the reptiles and most of the bird species are native to the Galapagos alone. The islands are also unusual in that species of Antarctic origin, such as penguins and fur seals, live alongside tropical animals.

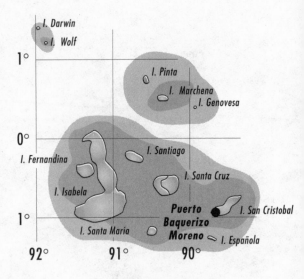

Galapagos Islands

Ecuador deemed the Galapagos island part wildlife sanctuary in 1935, and access to the islands is restricted to 40,000 visitors a year. Despite these conservation efforts, the growth of tourism, both legal and illegal, in the Galapagos islands has upset the delicate ecosystem to the point that the land iguana has become sterile. The local Charles Darwin biological station and other conservationists work to protect the indigenous flora and fauna.

16. **Which Caribbean island has the largest landmass?**

(A) Jamaica
(B) Guadeloupe
(C) Cuba
(D) Haiti

Fuel shortages caused by international economic sanctions make transportation in Cuba unique. Cuban residents rely heavily on black bicycles to get around, imported by the thousands from China. Decades-old Chevrolets and Oldsmobiles also lend a quirky charm to traveling in Havana, and keep inventive automobile spare-parts shops in business.

Originally inhabited by the Arawak people, Cuba was claimed by Columbus (p. 174) for Spain in 1492. The development of the sugar industry, using imported slave labor from Jamaica and elsewhere made Cuba the world's third largest producer of sugar by 1860. Today sugar is the country's major export. Cuba is the only communist state in the Caribbean, led by cigar-chomping **Fidel Castro**, leader since 1959. The United States views the nation as less of a threat than in 1962's Cuban missile crisis (p. 658), when Cuba accepted Soviet nuclear missiles on the island aimed at American cities and nearly triggered war between the superpowers. Still, the U.S. continues to impose economic sanctions on Cuba. Since the collapse of the Eastern European communist bloc, Cuba's traditional trading partner, living standards in the country have fallen.

Iran and the Russian Federation are now major trading partners and two of Cuba's few supporters worldwide.

17. **Which of the following has the lowest latitude?**

    (A) Brownsville, Texas
    (B) San Diego, California
    (C) Key West, Florida
    (D) New Orleans, Louisiana

Blackbeard in sunny Florida

Lying 755 miles further south than Los Angeles and a mere 50 miles from Cuba, **Key West** is on the island of Key West in the Florida Keys. The island, only one and a half miles long and four miles wide, was claimed by **Spain** in 1513 and dubbed Cayo Hueso—**"Bone Key"**—after bones left by local Indian tribes who, either for religious reasons or because of the hard limestone ground, did not bury their dead. During the late eighteenth century, Key West became home to rich shipping merchants, as well as legendary pirates **Blackbeard** and **Captain Kidd** who took advantage of the cargo-rich boats.

Key West became wealthy from salt and cigar industries, and although it was officially declared a port of entry to the U.S. and protected by the Navy in the 1820s, the seas were not made safe from pirates for another decade. Frequented by **President Truman** for regular vacations starting at the end of the 1940s, Key West was once the workplace of Tennessee Williams (p. 570) and Ernest Hemingway (p. 286), who shared his home with dozens of felines.

To Have and Have Not (1937), by Ernest Hemingway. Sometimes called Hemingway's worst novel, it's still Hemingway, and it's set in the Keys. Also check out the movie of the same name starring Humphrey Bogart.

The Florida Keys are home to America's largest living coral reef, a 128-mile stretch. Corals have been around for about 200 million years. Individual corals can have a life span of centuries, but grow only two inches or less a year. Coral reefs cannot survive exposure to water under 68 degrees F, and are usually within 22 degrees north or south of the equator. The slightest human touch on a coral reef can introduce harmful bacteria that will eventually destroy thousands-year-old growth.

18. **Which European country is the source of most of the continent's rivers?**

    (A) Austria
    (B) France
    (C) Germany
    (D) Switzerland

Switzerland lies at the center of Western Europe geographically, and is sometimes called Europe's water tower because from it stem the **Po**, the **Rhine**, the **Rhône**, and the **Inn-Danube** rivers. These connect Switzerland to Germany, France, Italy, and Austria. Though it is the source of crucial waterways to other countries and a major freight transit route for Europe, Switzerland has stayed politically neutral through every major European

 Switzerland is an environmentally conscientious country with government conviction behind it. In 1994, a government referendum voted to ban all commercial truck traffic from the Swiss Alps by the year 2004.

Modern Europe

conflict since 1815, and currently wrangles with its role vis-à-vis the European political and economic community. **Geneva** has retained its position as a center for international organizations such as the United Nations and Red Cross, and has been host to the **Camp David** accords, nuclear reduction treaties, diplomatic attempts at resolving the conflict in former Yugoslavia and more. What about the secret Swiss bank account? It's safe, don't worry. Banking secrecy laws attract foreign capital—almost half the world's investment capital placed outside the investor's own country is in Switzerland. Switzerland is the world's wealthiest country— per capita income is over $33,000. In the United States, it's $22,475.

Interactive Encyclopedia (Compton), *Encarta* (Microsoft), and *Multimedia Encyclopedia* (Grolier's). For general geographical reference, take a trip through these sources.

19. **Which is the most linguistically diverse country?**

   (A) Papua New Guinea
   (B) China
   (C) United States
   (D) Brazil

Go figure—this small nation that occupies a few little islands and only half of a big one is the most linguistically diverse country in the world. Though Papua New Guinea's official languages are pidgin English and Motu, it also harbors over 750 local language groups. In 1975 Papua New Guinea proclaimed independence from its southern neighbor Australia, which had taken over from the British, who had taken over from the people who'd lived there for centuries (the Germans annexed the western half of the island). Among the native ethnic groups, the main distinction is between lowlanders, who have frequent contacts with the outside world, and the notoriously isolated, but increasingly threatened, highlanders. Traditional ethnic tensions are rampant among the highlanders, with family group vendettas that rival *The Godfather* (p. 129).

Sweden, Portugal, Egypt, and Japan are among the minority of countries that are monolingual, but most places are multilingual. Switzerland features German, Italian, French, and Romansh; India speaks about fifteen major languages, most of them Indo-European. China contains the the most concentrated population on Earth

GULLAH SPOKEN HERE

"He en gut no morratater fer mak no pie wid." Say what? That's Gullah for "He has no more sweet potatos for making pie." Gullah is spoken right here in the U.S. on the coastal mainland of South Carolina and Georgia and the adjacent Sea Islands. It's an innovative blend of English and traditional African languages such as Fanti, Yoruba, and Bambara, developed by the ancestors of former African slaves in that region. Today there are about a quarter-million Gullahs keeping the language alive.

Growing Up In New Guinea (1930), by Margaret Mead. This is the anthropologist's seminal work on adolescence and sex in New Guinea.

speaking one language, Chinese. Some consider so-called dialects of Chinese such as **Mandarin** and **Cantonese** to be distinct languages since they are mutually unintelligible when spoken, like the difference between Indo-European languages Spanish and Italian, for example, though they share the same written characters.

20. **Which is the most heavily populated region of the United States?**

(A) Northeast

(B) Midwest

(C) South

(D) West

In the 1940s the South was like another country, with an agricultural economy based on cheap labor and little industrial activity, scarred and fissured by Jim Crow (p. 185) laws on racial segregation. World War II jolted industry development along the Gulf Coast, the cotton harvest became mechanized, and the U.S. federal goverment intervened to end legally sanctioned racial discrimination.

The U.S. Bureau of the Census divides the United States into four regions: the **Northeast** (including New York, Pennsylvania, New Jersey, and the New England states); the **Midwest** (from Ohio west to the Dakotas, Nebraska, and Kansas); the **South** (from Maryland and Delaware to Texas, including West Virginia and Kentucky); and the **West** (from the mountain states to California, and including Hawaii and Alaska). Over the last three decades, the Midwest and Northeast have lost residents to the South and West. Perceived economic opportunities in these regions play a part in the regional migration, along with the fact that the majority of immigrants from outside the U.S. arrive on western and southern shores, or cross southern land borders. In the decade from 1980 to 1990, eight states gained enough population to attain increased representation in Congress: California, Florida, Texas, Washington, Arizona, Georgia, North Carolina, and Virginia.

21. **The cultural landscape of a place includes**

(A) buildings

(B) agricultural centers

(C) distinguishing noises and odors

(D) All of the above

The cultural landscape of any place can never be respresented on a map, as it includes not just the spatial organization of a place but also its visual appearance, its noises, odors, rhythm of life, and all other human-generated effects. In the history of humanity there have been a handful of distinctive **cultural hearths**, cradles of culture groups whose systems of livelihood and lifestyle created distinctive cultural landscapes that spread beyond their boundaries. The major culture hearths of the world emerged as early as 5500 years ago, in Egypt, Mesopotamia, the Indus Valley of the

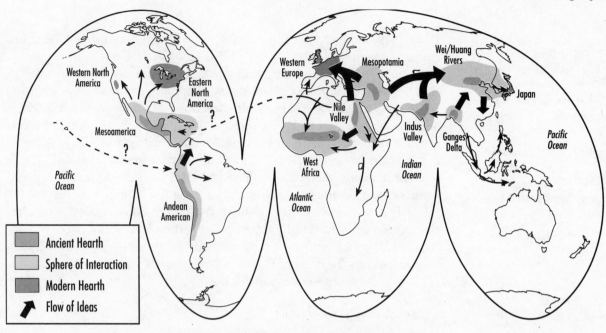

Culture hearths and early diffusion routes

Indian subcontinent, northern China, Southeastern Asia, various locations in Africa, the Americas, and elsewhere. All these hearth areas produced what we call civilization: writing (or other form of record keeping), metallurgy, long-distance trade connections, astronomy, mathematics, social stratification and labor specialization, formalized government, and a structured urban society.

 The elaborate aesthetic impact of Hindu temples and shrines, the pervasiveness of holy animals, and the traditional garb of followers still dominate the landscape of India and parts of Pakistan.

22. **The legend of El Dorado comes from**

    (A) South America
    (B) Central America
    (C) East Africa
    (D) American Southwest

El Dorado is a legendary country in South America, supposedly over-flowing in gold and precious stones, sought by sixteenth-century Spanish explorers. The myth apparently stems from the ruler of an indigenous group near Santa Fe de Bogotá, in present-day Colombia, who was annointed yearly with gold dust. From this minor incident arose the legend of "the gilded one," *el dorado*, which inspired much of the sixteenth-century exploration of South America. It's not the only incident of lands being reached in the pursuit of mythical locales. Medieval European legends spoke of islands located beyond the setting sun that

El Dorado (1967), starring John Wayne (Ed Asner's in it too—yes, Lou Grant goes West). An aging gunfighter helps a buddy in a range war.

Twenty Thousand Leagues under the Sea (1869-1870), by Jules Verne. Submarine explorers discover the remains of drowned Atlantis.

Portuguese explorers were searching for when they ran into America as much as two decades before Columbus set sail.

One of the most famous mythical locales is **Atlantis**, the lost continent that has tantalized philosophers, poets, historians, explorers, and scientists for more than 2,000 years. **Plato** described Atlantis in writings from around 355 B.C. that picked up on the dialogues of his much earlier work, *Republic* (p. 385). In these later dialogues, Plato makes reference to Atlantis, citing extensive architectural, engineering, and ceremonial detail. Plato's student **Aristotle** claimed that Plato had fabricated the Atlantis story and contrived the continent's catastrophic demise (by earthquake and floods), while Plato's followers insisted he was reconstructing history passed on through oral history via Egyptian priests. The controversy over whether Atlantis was fact or fiction continued for centuries—some said Minoan civilization was the basis of Plato's Atlantis, others said it predated Mayan culture. The mystery remains to this day.

23. **The Kurdish nation is in**

   (A) Turkey
   (B) Iran
   (C) Both A and B
   (D) Neither A nor B

While a **state** is an independent political unit occupying a defined, permanently populated territory, a **nation** is a group of people with a common culture occupying a particular territory. **Nation-states** are states whose territorial extent coincides with the occupation of a distinct population. The **Kurds** are an example of a stateless nation—they number some twenty million people divided among six states and dominant in none of them. Kurd populations thrive in Turkey, Iran, and Iraq, with smaller communities in Syria and Armenia. Many Kurds would love to see an independent Kurdistan come into statehood, but this is yet a distant dream. Kurds are not the only stateless nation in the world today: **Palestinians** wrestle for sovereignty in the Middle East, **Basques** do the same in France and Spain, and **Cree Indians** live mainly in the Canadian Prairie Provinces.

QUAGMIRELAND

The recent peace talks between Northern Ireland and Great Britain herald change in this century's political makeup of Ireland. Although Ireland proclaimed independence from the British in 1921 after the three-year Anglo-Irish war, Northern Ireland chose to stay with the Crown (the United Kingdom). Since then, the pro-independence Irish Republican Army of Northern Ireland has waged battle that has included violent methods, against British rule, which is still marked by the pervasive presence of the British military in Northern Ireland. The conflict has caused several thousand civilian casualties over the years.

24. The territory of the Russian Federation covers about how many square miles?

(A) 1 million
(B) 3 million
(C) 6 million
(D) 13 million

Russia, almost twice as big as the United States, covers six million square miles and is the largest country in the world. It's bound by the Arctic and Pacific oceans on its northern and eastern coasts, and has land boundaries with thirteen countries. With the formal breakup of the former Soviet Union, Russia became an independent sovereign state struggling to contain ethnic tensions within its boundaries (as in the 1995 violent suppression of Chechnya in the southwest of the nation by Russian military.) There are fifty-seven nationalities with their own territories within the Russian federation, and ninety-five nationalities without a territory.

With most Russians grossly disappointed in the post-communist leadership which has hardly improved standards of living, the demise of the system that once kept prices of bread and other staples at a few cents year after year has hit the elderly and other vulnerable groups very hard. At the same time, privatization of former state-held industries and new capitalist opportunities have helped create a growing middle class. Russia has vast natural resources, from oil to gold, but many of these caches are located in national territories struggling against Russia for greater autonomy and control over their own terrain.

The Russia House (1990), starring Michele Pfieffer and Sean Connery. A Soviet woman dupes a British publisher into espionage.

Dr. Strangelove, or: How I Learned to Stop Worrying and Love the Bomb (1964), directed by Stanley Kubrick. Peter Sellers stars as the U.S. president (and two other characters) in this brilliant, dark comedy.

25. Appalachia is

(A) an educational district
(B) an economic region
(C) a state
(D) a beer

Appalachia is a loose reference to the part of the eastern United States associated with the Appalachian mountain range. Geologically speaking, Appalachia is a landmass that formed the Appalachian mountains more than 200 million years ago. During the 1950s, the economic stagnation and decline of Appalachia made it dramatically poor, underdeveloped, and uneducated. In the 1950s, employment levels in the coal mining industry of the Appalachian area (still the largest known source of coal in the world) dropped 60 percent (in contrast to a national rate of 1 percent), and farm jobs declined 52 percent (national decline was 35 percent). In the

Deliverance (1972), starring Jon Voight and Burt Reynolds. Four Atlanta businessmen meet some unfriendly natives in an unforgettable canoe trip.

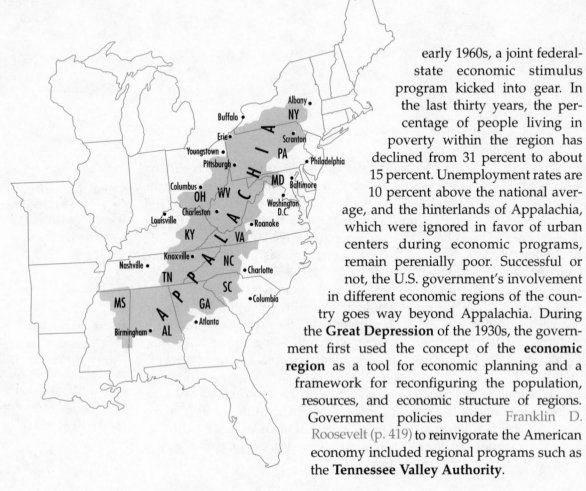

early 1960s, a joint federal-state economic stimulus program kicked into gear. In the last thirty years, the percentage of people living in poverty within the region has declined from 31 percent to about 15 percent. Unemployment rates are 10 percent above the national average, and the hinterlands of Appalachia, which were ignored in favor of urban centers during economic programs, remain perenially poor. Successful or not, the U.S. government's involvement in different economic regions of the country goes way beyond Appalachia. During the **Great Depression** of the 1930s, the government first used the concept of the **economic region** as a tool for economic planning and a framework for reconfiguring the population, resources, and economic structure of regions. Government policies under Franklin D. Roosevelt (p. 419) to reinvigorate the American economy included regional programs such as the **Tennessee Valley Authority**.

26. **Which of the following countries colonized Africa?**

   (A) France
   (B) Portugal
   (C) Germany
   (D) All of the above

The roster doesn't stop there—the three above along with Great Britain, Belgium, Italy, and the Netherlands took a grab at the great continent over the course of four centuries. Colonial empires are nothing new in human history. These European nations were able to march in uninvited by local powers and claim their colonial empires because they were economically strong. In turn, the colonial acquisitions enabled the small European countries to become imperial powers, controlling human numbers far in excess of their domestic populations. The same can be said of Japan in its territorial expansion to French Indochina, its invasion of China, the U. S. occupation of Puerto Rico in 1898, and multitudinous acts of famous empires of yesteryear—the Persian Empire, starring **Alexander the Great**, several hundred years B.C., and so on. On the other hand, strong economies alone do not make powerful nations or empires. China, the third largest economy behind the U.S. and Japan in the early 1990s, is so overpopulated that its chances of per capita economic growth are pathetic with over 1.2 billion people (and sixteen million more every year) grabbing at the national pie.

The Last Emperor (1987), directed by Bernardo Bertolucci. Inspired by the true story of Pu Yi, the last emperor of China, who grew up in the hidden Forbidden City until he was kicked out by communist revolutionaries and forced to fend in the unforbidden world.

27. Why do human populations migrate to other countries?

(A) Perceived economic opportunity
(B) To preserve culture
(C) To get the hell out of Dodge
(D) Any of the above

People leave their homes for faraway lands for any number of the reasons above, as well as to escape local armed conflict, as in the 1980s Afghanistan/Soviet conflict during which millions left their homes. Environmental reasons like the late-nineteenth-century Irish potato famine that induced mass migration to North America; modern information flow, including news of job opportunities (Turks heard about Germany's need for labor via modern communications technologies); political circumstances (in 1972, Uganda's Idi Amin expelled 50,000 Asians from his country); to preserve their culture (Jews who could finally leave the culturally oppressive Soviet Union); and "The Grass is Always Greener" syndrome: all lead to mass migrations.

One of the worst refugee crises in modern history occured in Rwanda, an East African country the size of Maryland where ethnic conflict between the historically powerful Tutsi minority and the numerically dominant Hutu had been going on long before Rwanda and neighbor Burundi's independence from European colonialism. By the last week of July, 1994, an estimated 5.5 million out of 8.3 million Rwandans were either dead, dying, or dislocated, the rest left with decimated land and abandoned farms.

28. Refugees differ from voluntary migrants in that

(A) they get first option for labor opportunities
(B) they have more fun moving
(C) they move with only the personal property they can carry
(D) they are mentally incapacitated

Millions of the world's migrants are **refugees** driven from their homes in desperation, in search of relief from terror or disaster at home.

CULTURESCOPE

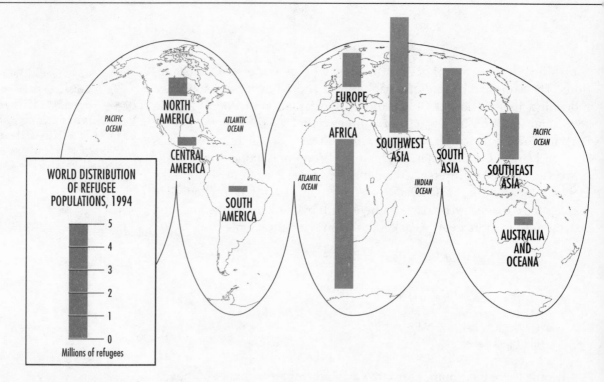

WORLD DISTRIBUTION OF REFUGEE POPULATIONS, 1994

5
4
3
2
1
0

Millions of refugees

If the world as-is just doesn't satisfy, try spawning your own society with MicroProse's *Sid Meier's Civilization* (mixed with historical fact, you build a world empire) and MicroProse's *Sid Meier's Colonization* (you create a new nation).

Some of the world's most massive waves of migration have not been voluntary but forced. Witness the Atlantic slave trade, in which as many as 30 million Africans were forcibly taken from their homes, ripped apart from families, and sent into slavery in the Americas. Though nothing in human history compares to this slave trade, other forced migrations in recent history are notable: tens of thousands of convicts were shipped from Britain to Australia during the late eighteenth century; millions of non-ethnic Russians were ruthlessly moved to the remote regions of the Soviet Union during Joseph Stalin's reign of terror.

Refugees don't necessarily know where they're going when they leave home, and are not often welcomed or easily integrated into the countries they enter. Recent history teems with massive refugee problems: more than a million people escaped from Liberia when it was mired in civil war in 1990; fighting in Afghanistan in the 1980s drove millions to Pakistan and Iran; residents of former Yugoslavia streamed wherever they could from their war-torn country; and millions of Ethiopians fled into Sudan as civil war created impossible living conditions.

Not all refugees' efforts at escape succeed, as evidenced by events in the U.S. in the early 1990s. Haitians who tried to escape political oppression and economic hardship were detained in U.S. military bases and forced to return to their country. The United Nations High Commission for Refugees estimates that there were more than twenty million world refugees in 1994, and geographers estimate as many as thirty million additional intranational refugees—those dislocated within the boundaries of their own country.

29. **Gerrymandering means**

   (A) tilling the soil
   (B) manipulating political district boundaries
   (C) putting people named Gerry into jail
   (D) opening avenues of mass transit in cities

There are more than 85,000 local governmental entities in the United States, of which half are municipalities, townships, and counties. The remainder are school districts, sanitary districts, water-control districts, airport authorities, and other single-purpose divisions. Boundary lines among these multifarious districts change with time in response to shifts in population. When there is a certain number of seats for representatives in an elected legislature such as Congress, there must be a fixed number of electoral districts from which those representatives are elected. Since the congressional seats are based on state population totals, each state must draw its own map of districts, which should, theoretically, allow minorities an opportunity to elect their own representatives. In reality, though, if a state is 80 percent white, 10 percent African American, and 10 percent Asian and Hispanic, an electoral districting map may likely end up with white majorities in all districts and no minority representation.

Strange-shaped districts configured to attain certain political ends are old news in American politics. In 1812, Governor Elbridge Gerry of Massachusetts signed into law a district designed to favor his Republican party. Ever since, the term "gerrymandering" has been used to indicate redistricting for distinct political goals and advantage.

"One Nation Under a Groove" (1978), by the Funkadelics. Petty squabblers over political districts should remember this national credo: "One nation under a groove, gettin' down just for the funk of it . . . ."

30. **"Land of the South Slavs" refers to**

   (A) Bulgaria
   (B) Yugoslavia
   (C) Transylvania
   (D) Lithuania

Long-dormant centrifugal forces shattered Yugoslavia in a violent, tragic, heavily documented civil war. Yugoslavia was a country thrown together on maps without consideration after World War I, a land of seven major and seventeen smaller ethnic and cultural groups. The north was Roman Catholic (p. 491), where Slovenes and Croats were dominant, the south was Serbian Orthodox, and several million Moslems (p. 495) lived in Christian enclaves throughout. Local animosities between these various groups are longstanding and pre-date the recent conflict. In World War II, Nazi-supporting Croats fought against anti-Hitler Serbs; Muslims fought non-Muslims

Two-thirds of the population of Serbia and Montenegro (former Yugoslavia) are currently living below subsistence level, many suffering from malnutrition. Elderly pensioners are especially poor—in 1993, monthly pensions were worth under two dollars, and pensioners in Belgrade were reported to be committing suicide at a rate of four a week.

after the collapse of East bloc communism. Out of the recent collapse of the former Yugoslavia have come the new states of Slovenia, Croatia, Bosnia, Serbia-Montenegro, and Macedonia. The scourge of the recent conflict in former Yugoslavia resulted in the flight of the middle class: an estimated 100,000 professionals left Serbia during the fighting. The absence of this skilled and educated tier of society may hinder economic recovery when when international sanctions are finally lifted.

31. **Which is Canada's largest province?**

(A) Ontario
(B) Alberta
(C) Quebec
(D) British Columbia

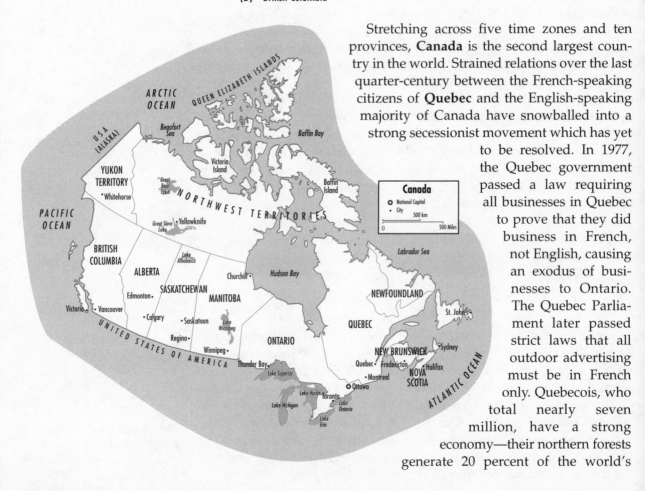

Stretching across five time zones and ten provinces, **Canada** is the second largest country in the world. Strained relations over the last quarter-century between the French-speaking citizens of **Quebec** and the English-speaking majority of Canada have snowballed into a strong secessionist movement which has yet to be resolved. In 1977, the Quebec government passed a law requiring all businesses in Quebec to prove that they did business in French, not English, causing an exodus of businesses to Ontario. The Quebec Parliament later passed strict laws that all outdoor advertising must be in French only. Quebecois, who total nearly seven million, have a strong economy—their northern forests generate 20 percent of the world's pulp and paper, and Quebec is the world's fourth largest hydro-power producer. Still, secession would be costly, especially in jobs, since it would have to embrace free trade to survive. It's presently very protectionist.

32. **Industrial centers are characterized by**
     (A) natural resources
     (B) good transportation
     (C) cheap labor
     (D) All of the above

Industrial centers, as opposed to agricultural centers, are areas where manufacturing and service industries thrive, such as in Japan, the United States, Europe, Russia, and the Pacific Rim. Industrialization was not born of the Industrial Revolution (p. 81) of the nineteenth century. India's textile industry was so successful that British textile makers rioted in 1721, demanding legislative protection against the Indian competition that was overwhelming local British markets. China also possessed a substantial industrial base long before the modern Industrial Revolution.

The first steps in the Industrial Revolution were the invention of the steam-powered weaving loom and the use of coal, instead of charcoal from dwindling wood supplies, to use as fuel for power looms, ships (the first steam-powered vessel crossed the Atlantic in 1819), and locomotives (the first railroad in England was opened in 1825). The Industrial Revolution spread quickly around the world. Some industrial regions emerged because of the combination of their local raw materials, others were based around large urban centers where there were more transportation facilities and plenty of cheap labor, such as the twelve-hour shifts for working children in Britain 200 years ago.

33. **The rate of illiteracy among adults in India today is around**
     (A) 10 percent
     (B) 25 percent
     (C) 50 percent
     (D) 75 percent

Although **India** has one of the world's highest rates of college science graduates and has produced much extraordinary talent, the rate of illiteracy is 48 percent. The figures reflect the fact that nearly one-third of India's population, mostly in rural areas, lives below the poverty line.

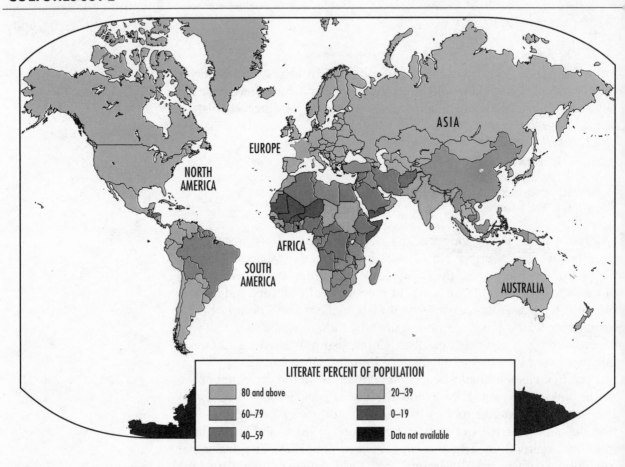

LITERATE PERCENT OF POPULATION

80 and above	20–39
60–79	0–19
40–59	Data not available

The rate of adult illiteracy in the United States is around 9 percent. It is 0 percent in Denmark, 80 percent in Eritrea, 60 percent in Yemen, 66 percent in Cambodia, 43 percent in Nicaragua (but decreasing since the Sandinistas created a literacy crusade during the last decade to educate the masses).

Urban poverty is rampant, too—over 100,000 people live in the streets in **Bombay** alone, and over 20 percent of **West Bengal** live in appalling slum conditions. (That's where **Mother Theresa** runs her mission.) Bombay, the country's commercial capital with a reputation for making people rich, juxtaposes "Bollywood," India's movie industry center and their version of Hollywood (including the glamorous Malabar Hills neighborhood) against a 2.8 mile sprawl of sewerless shanty-towns in central Bombay, said to be the world's biggest slum.

34. **What country raises the most hogs?**

(A) India
(B) Brazil
(C) United States
(D) China

China has the honor of growing the greatest number of **hogs** in the world, followed by the former USSR and the United States. **Cattle** are most prevalent in India (where they mean it when they say "holy cow"—the mostly-Hindu nation won't allow cattle to be killed), Brazil, the former USSR, the United States, and China. **Sheep** mostly speckle the countrysides of the former USSR, Australia, China, New Zealand, Turkey, India, the United Kingdom, and others.

The deliberate cultivation of plants and the herding of livestock started over 12,000 years ago, probably first in parts of China, Southeast Asia, and the Middle East, followed by Mesoamerica, West Africa, the Mediterranean, and beyond. The domestication of animals made certain regions associated with particular animals, as with agricultural crops. Chickens and pigs dominate Southeast Asia, cattle South Asia, camels Southwest Asia, llamas, alpacas, and turkeys the Americas, and yaks inner Asia. Communities that successfully combined the cultivation of plants with the domestication of animals succeeded most in human evolution, as they had more food options.

35. **The level of manufacturing in North America in the last thirty years has**

    (A) increased
    (B) stayed the same
    (C) decreased
    (D) disappeared

Manufacturing employment has fallen dramatically in recent U.S. history, a far cry from the post-World War II economy (p. 82) built on low-skilled, high-waged employment. The main concentration of the North American manufacturing belt is the northeastern United States and adjacent areas of southeastern Canada. Though it covers less than 5 percent of the land area of the continent, the manufacturing belt contains the majority of urban population, the densest and best-developed transportation network, and most of the continent's heavy industry.

Anglo-American manufacturing started in New England in the early nineteenth century. Water-powered textile mills, iron plants, and other small-scale industries that developed there afforded the new United States a great measure of freedom from total dependence on Europe, especially England. The heart of the manufacturing belt was Appalachia (p. 157), in the valleys of the **Ohio River** and its tributaries, and along the shores of the **Great Lakes**. After the 1850s, railroads provided the link between the agricultural and industrial regions of the country.

Transport Tycoon (Microprose). Develop a transportation empire, moving either passengers, mail, or goods.

36. France is famous for its skill in producing

(A) aviators
(B) wine
(C) perfume
(D) All of the above

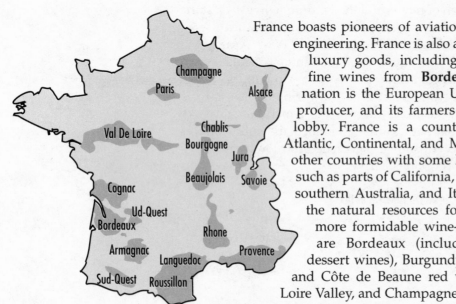

France boasts pioneers of aviation and is today a leader in engineering. France is also a world leader in producing luxury goods, including cosmetics, perfumes, and fine wines from **Bordeaux** to **Champagne**. The nation is the European Union's largest agricultural producer, and its farmers form a powerful political lobby. France is a country with three climates—Atlantic, Continental, and Mediterranean. Along with other countries with some Mediterranean agriculture, such as parts of California, central Chile, South Africa, southern Australia, and Italy, France has developed the natural resources for good wine. Among the more formidable wine-making regions of France are Bordeaux (including delicious Sauternes dessert wines), Burgundy (featuring Côte de Nuits and Côte de Beaune red wines), Rhône, Beaujolais, Loire Valley, and Champagne (for the genuine bubbly).

37. African American population is highest in

(A) Texas
(B) Missouri
(C) North Carolina
(D) Tennessee

There is a widespread population of African Americans throughout the rural South, and **Missouri** is the home of more African Americans than any other state. One of the two biggest human population migrations within the borders of the United States was the northward move of African Americans from the rural South to the urban North. The other big migration was the gold rush out West. The northward stream was small until the years after World War I, when growing northern industries began to recruit African American workers from the South, and African Americans responded to the new opportunities by moving from the South by the hundeds of thousands. At the turn of the century, only 10 percent of the African American population lived outside of the South—by 1990 about 50 percent did. Today, about 80 percent of African Americans living in rural areas remain in the South. And although the urban North still hosts the greatest concentration of African Americans in the U.S., there has been a recent trend of urbanized northerners returning to the urban South for perceived economic and personal opportunities.

38. **Which government has instituted population control policies in the last fifty years?**

   (A) India
   (B) China
   (C) former Soviet Union
   (D) All of the above

In the 1970s China, a draconian population control policy was implemented by the government of China that allowed each couple a limit of one child. Because boys remained the more desired sex, female **infanticide** became a pervasive consequence of the official policy. Though population control policies have weakened in recent years, one still finds billboards in Chinese cities encouraging one-child families. Certain Indian states have enforced population control through male sterilization, and the former Soviet Union promoted pro-growth programs that encouraged increased population growth.

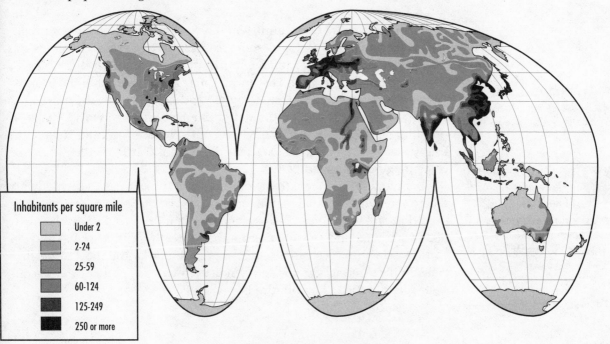

Inhabitants per square mile

Under 2
2-24
25-59
60-124
125-249
250 or more

World population density

The six billionth inhabitant of this planet will be born in late 1997 or early 1998. The world's population at the start of this century was about one-fourth as large, just over one and a half billion. The world population growth exploded in the 1960s and 1970s, and continues to thwart people's economic betterment, stress local environments, cause malnutrition, exhaust soils, damage water supplies, and cause the starvation of thousands every year. These casualites are not from overpopulation alone—in fact, these problems often come down to who holds resources and how they are distributed.

MEGAMANIA

The major focus of North American population is in the urban complex along the eastern seaboard from Boston to Washington, which includes New York, Philadelphia, and Baltimore. This urban mass is called Megalopolis by urban geographers, who predict that it's just a matter of time before the whole area becomes one MEGAcity.

39. **How many Republic of Singapore citizens live in an urban setting?**
    (A) 25 percent
    (B) 50 percent
    (C) 75 percent
    (D) 100 percent

Singapore is the only country in the world that is 100 percent urban. This island state, linked to the southernmost tip of the **Malay peninsula**, was largely uninhabited from the fourteenth to the eighteenth century. In the early 1800s, the **British East India Company** honed in on the islands' strategic position on key trade routes, and established Singapore as a trading settlement. Singapore today promotes itself as a world leader in providing the perfect urban environment. There is no litter, thanks to heavy fines, and you'd better leave the Bazooka at home, Joe, because chewing gum is banned by law.

Bangkok is another extreme of urbanism. It's an overly crowded city, where a network of canals serves as streets, such that boats provide transportation on the water, stores open onto it, laundries do their washing in it, and garbage and sewage are dumped directly in it. Mexico City, the world's second-largest urban area, was once one of the most appealing cities in the Americas but is today noisy, crowded, polluted, traffic-congested, and encircled by hundreds of slums.

SIM CITY/ SIM CITY 2000 (Maxis). Can't find the perfect city on earth? Design your own.

AIDS (acquired immune deficiency syndrome) has infected millions of people worldwide and continues to escalate as a deadly killer without a cure or an accurate understanding of its cause. AIDS is now the leading killer of Americans ages 25-44.

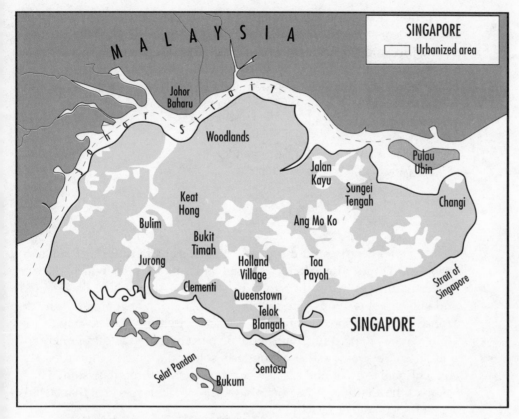

40. Compared to thirty years ago, today's global infection rate of malaria is

(A) much higher
(B) much lower
(C) about the same
(D) a little lower

The infectious disease of **malaria**, transmitted by mosquito, has killed or incapacitated countless millions of people, a huge proportion of them children, and continues to ravage human populations today. Malaria has so afflicted whole populations that towns and regions have been abandoned. Historically, the abandonment of well-developed irrigation systems and apparently fertile lands may have been due to the advance of malaria rather than climatic changes often ascribed to these population shifts.

The Seventh Seal (1957), directed by Ingmar Bergman. This is a thoughful, dark tale of a theater troupe traversing bubonic plague-struck Europe in the Middle Ages.

The Slow Plague: A Geography of the AIDS Pandemic (1993), by Peter R. Gould.

Yellow fever, also transmitted by mosquito, is now confined to tropical and near-tropical areas, but once wreaked havoc far beyond these boundaries and has been one of the great killers of world population. The United States, Europe, and Middle and South America were struck hard by devastating yellow fever epidemics and outbreaks. The last major outbreak in the U.S. was in 1905, and struck southern cities such as **New Orleans** especially hard.

41. **Which country generates nuclear electricity?**

   (A) Japan
   (B) United States
   (C) Spain
   (D) All of the above

We've all heard about those little mishaps at **Chernobyl**, Ukraine, in 1986 and **Three-Mile Island**, Pennsylvania, in 1979, in which nuclear power plants emitted radioactive fuels into the atmosphere that injured and killed people, crops, and livestock. Considering the dangers, why do France and Belgium still get half their electricity from nuclear power, the United States 20 percent, Spain about 35 percent and so on? Proponents of nuclear energy point to it as a long-term solution to energy shortages. The conventional form of nuclear power production is through fission, which involves the splitting of an atom of uranium that releases heat that creates steam to generate electricity.

The Russian navy dumped more than 17,000 contaminated nuclear containers and the old nuclear reactor off the icebreaker ship *Lenin* into the Barents Sea in northern Russia.

Unfortunately, safety problems inherent in conventional nuclear fission plants have not been resolved, and nuclear utilities in the United States alone report several thousand "mishaps" a year. On top of which, **radioactive wastes** are deadly contaminants that have caused and could create more disastrous ecological and human consequences, despite the most valiant efforts to bury the barrels deep in the

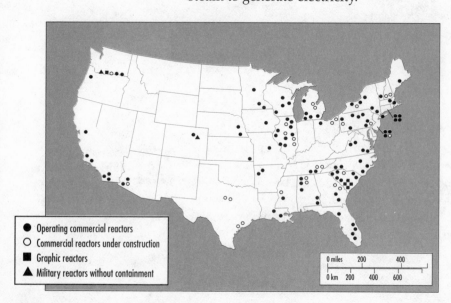

● Operating commercial reactors
○ Commercial reactors under construction
■ Graphic reactors
▲ Military reactors without containment

0 miles   200   400
0 km   200   400   600

ocean or ground. For years, nuclear fusion (p. 381), the merging of two radioactive atoms, has been espoused as the answer to all our energy troubles, since fusion creates many times more energy without the side effect of radioactive waste. Too bad scientists haven't figured out how to convert the method to commercial use. Some nations, including Denmark, Greece, and Australia, have committed to a nuclear-free lifestyle and have no nuclear power plants, and others, like Sweden, are phasing their plants out. To date, the United States produces the largest amount of nuclear power of any individual country.

42. **In the next fifty years Americans will eat**
    (A) more dairy
    (B) fewer grains
    (C) more Pop Tarts
    (D) less meat

Though some of us may be contributing to answer C, the fact is that we'll all be eating less meat, less dairy, and more grains and beans in the next few decades, and not because McDonalds and Burger King are bombing each others' outlets. Energy shortages, exhausted land, scarce water, and a doubling in the population are the catalysts of change here. American agriculture depends heavily on oil—about 140 gallons for every acre of corn—and domestic oil wells will be exhausted in the next twenty years. Importing foreign oil will raise the cost of food at home, on top of which water for irrigation will be less available and more costly, millions of acres of farmland will be lost to urbanization and soil erosion.

Because meat and dairy products are the most expensive and wasteful to produce, they'll become less common in the average American diet over the next several decades. It takes as much as 12,000 pounds of grain to feed a cow until it weighs 1,000 pounds. Slaughtered and eaten by humans, that cow may yield barely 100 pounds. Had the humans eaten the 12,000 pounds of grain directly, they would have gained the 1,000 pounds themselves. Seems like a lot of waste for a slab of steak, no matter how sizzling.

 The U.S. produces close to half of the world's supply of corn. The U.S. is also the leading exporter of both corn and wheat and is second to Thailand as an exporter of rice.

 Soylent Green (1973), starring Charlton Heston and Edward G. Robinson. New York City, in the year 2022, an overcrowded hellhole with dire shortages of food and water and a wicked government secret.

ANSWERS

1. D	2. D	3. C	4. C	5. D	6. D	7. C	8. A	9. B	10. A
11. B	12. A	13. C	14. B	15. B	16. C	17. C	18. D	19. A	20. C
21. D	22. A	23. C	24. C	25. B	26. D	27. D	28. C	29. B	30. B
31. C	32. D	33. C	34. D	35. C	36. D	37. B	38. D	39. D	40. C
41. D	42. D								

Human Rights

The term "human rights" refers to the civil and political rights of the individual in relation to the state. Human rights are at issue everywhere, including the United States. In America, this relationship has been most troubled for members of groups not part of the nation's original power structure: Native Americans, African Americans, women, poor or land-less white men, immigrants. Indeed, the story of human rights in America is the story of power—who has had it, and how others have tried to get their share of it. These struggles—for power, for equality, for representation—have enriched the nation as a whole, making the United States a place where the idea of human rights is central to our national identity.

1. What did Christopher Columbus ask of the Arawak Indians of the Bahama Islands upon landing in the New World?

   (A) Directions to India
   (B) Help to repair the Santa Maria
   (C) Pottery
   (D) Gold

1492 (1992), directed by Ridley Scott; and *Christopher Columbus—the Discoverer* (1992), directed by John Glen. Whatever you do, avoid these two movies. One of them has the fine actor Gerard Depardieu and the other doesn't. It doesn't matter. They're both terrible.

Leif Erickson was the first European to reach America. Most likely the ancestors of the Native Americans on the continent when Columbus and Erickson showed up arrived via the Northwest Passage.

When **Christopher Columbus** (1451-1506), aboard the *Santa Maria,* reached the shores of the Bahama Islands, he immediately began devising strategies to recoup the money that had been advanced him to finance his voyage to find India and to prove the world was round. Unbeknownst to Columbus, a continent or two lay in his path and his mileage calculations were off by about a third. Nevertheless, upon meeting the Arawak Indians, Columbus was overjoyed by these people who brought food, water, and gifts to him and his crew. He wrote in his captain's log that they "would make fine servants . . . with fifty men we could subjugate them all and make them do whatever we want." Columbus did manage to subjugate the Arawaks, and, spying the gold ornaments dangling from their ears, demanded they take him to the source of their gold.

From the Bahamas he sailed to Cuba (p. 150), then to Hispaniola, now the island of Haiti and the Dominican Republic. He found gold in the rivers and a local Indian gave him a gold mask. He wrote back to the court of Madrid that he'd hit Asia and had more gold and spices than he knew what to do with—a fiction designed to extract more money from Spain. Furthermore, he added, just in case the gold and spices run out, you can always use these Indians. They make great slaves. On the home front they bought Columbus's story completely, and he later returned with seventeen ships for two purposes: gold and slaves. Columbus raided one Caribbean island after another, taking hundreds of slaves. On the island of Cicao off Haiti the Spaniards instructed the Indians to show up with gold and they'd get copper coins to hang around their necks. If an Indian was found without a coin, his hand was chopped off.

2. After 400 years of European infiltration of North America, the Native American population was what percentage of its original size?
   (A) 2 percent
   (B) 25 percent
   (C) 40 percent
   (D) 60 percent

No one can be sure exactly how many Native Americans were living on the North American continent when Columbus arrived, but estimates are generally in the range of 9.8 to 12 million. By the year 1890—after the broken treaties, after the raids, after the expansions, after dime novels that glorified the slaughter of the "Red Man," and after the infamous words

"The only good Indian is a dead Indian" (actually, "The only good Indians I ever saw were dead") were spoken by Philip Henry Sheridan—there were only 250,000 Indians left on the continent, or about 2 percent of the original population.

Columbus and the Spanish and Portuguese colonizers who followed him had found a niche in what is now Central and South America, where they sought riches and plentiful, concentrated populations to enslave. In North America, meanwhile, Europeans lusted mainly for land, which they steadily acquired from the native populations through war, outright occupation, and purchase. The relationship of people to the land is perhaps the largest and most ominous cultural difference between Europeans and Native Americans, and misunderstandings abounded from the start. Private property, the idea that an individual or group can "own" land, is a European concept foreign to Native American tribal culture. As they signed over their ancestral territories to whites, Indians often thought they were agreeing merely to share the land use for hunting, fishing, and gathering food.

Throughout most of the eighteenth century, as coastal tribes were mostly overwhelmed by the English, interior tribes were able to hold their own, in part by playing English and French forces off each other as they battled for empire. Once French imperialism in North America petered out, the Revolution came, and most tribes sided with the English. The establishment of a unified power on much of the continent was bad news for Indians, especially since the new United States treated Indians who had supported England as conquered enemies. After the Revolution, U.S. policy began moving toward the duplicity that marked American nineteenth-century dealings with Native Americans: recognizing Indians' right

Lonesome Dove (1985) and *Anything for Billy* (1989), by Larry McMurtry. Both these books deal with the mythologized West, but *Anything for Billy* shows how different from reality the glorified stories that made it back East really were.

Makah tribe relocation

> **"**
> *Sell our country! Why not sell the air, the clouds, and the great sea?*
>
> —— THE SHAWNEE CHIEF TECUMSEH
> **"**

MANIFEST PROFIT

Westward expansion as practiced by Andrew Jackson was not just inspired by wanderlust or an abstraction like "manifest destiny." After he killed a slew of Indians, he made a financial killing by selling the land from which he had just "removed" them.

Discovery Channel's television series, "How the West Was Lost" (1995). This series explores Manifest Destiny from the Native American perspective.

Unforgiven (1992), directed by and starring Clint Eastwood. Gunfighters were real people with real feelings. They simply plunked their moral misgivings into a whisky bottle. This is an unblinking look at the Wild West.

to exist as sovereign nations, but at the same time buying and stealing as much land from them as possible.

Andrew Jackson (p. 630), the U.S. President from 1829-1837, spearheaded a plan given the horrifyingly practical name **"Indian removal."** Several defeated tribes were sent westward to the so-called "Indian Territory," which later became Oklahoma. Whites pushed across the Mississippi River Valley and into Texas and the Southwest, erecting forts, building roads, and doing battle with Indian nations in their way. Treaties were signed and promptly disregarded. Disease, malnutrition, and alcoholism also took their toll on embattled native peoples. The phrase to which most Westward Expansionists clung was **"Manifest Destiny,"** taken from an 1845 magazine article that declared it was "our manifest destiny to overspread the continent allotted by Providence for the free development of our yearly multiplying millions."

3. **Which Indian nation brought a lawsuit against the state of Georgia in 1831?**

    (A)   The Choctaw
    (B)   The Cherokee
    (C)   The Mohegan
    (D)   The Seminole

One infamous episode in the chronicle of Indian removal occurred in 1831, when the **Cherokee Nation** brought suit against the state of Georgia. The Cherokee had existed peaceably on their native lands within Georgia, farming and ranching and developing a sophisticated governmental system that included a constitution similar to that of the U.S. When Georgia declared all Cherokee laws void, the tribe turned to the U.S. Supreme Court. The case was dismissed, and **Chief Justice John Marshall's** decision coined the phrase held over Indians' heads from then on: Indian tribes were **"domestic dependent nations"** unable to turn to the U.S. courts to redress grievances. In another case a year later, Marshall defied President Jackson and held that Georgia's laws were not enforceable within Indian territory either, establishing the doctrine that the U.S. government alone would deal with Native American affairs. Georgia ignored the decision and proceeded to send all Cherokees on forced marches to the Indian Territory. This arduous and often fatal migration, called the **Trail of Tears,** came to symbolize white injustice toward Indians. By 1889, a land rush into the Indian Territory made the Indians' situation even more precarious, as did the spread of the railroad and the demise of the buffalo elsewhere. These legal, social, and technological forces, perhaps even more than the military might the U.S. brought to bear, left Native American populations in the twentieth century greatly reduced—but by no means had Native Americans disappeared, as popular mythology would have it. The nostalgic idea that the continent had seen *The Last of the Mohicans*, as the novel by James Fenimore Cooper (p. 258) described, was a convenient fiction that diverted attention from the problems faced by living Indians. The Battle of Wounded Knee (p. 641)—actually a massacre of the Sioux by the U.S. Army—marked the end of Indian armed resistance to U.S. forces and was a symbolic turning point in a centuries-long struggle.

Scene from the massacre at Wounded Knee

The publication in 1881 of **Helen Hunt Jackson's** *A Century of Dishonor*, which surveyed the federal government's history of unjust dealings with Indians, inspired a turn in U.S. policy that many Indians consider a grave mistake. The **Dawes Severalty Act** of 1887, intended to help Indians assimilate into white society, converted all tribal lands to a system of individual ownership rather than the common ownership central to Indian societies. Indians were given American citizenship and received uniform individual land grants of 160 acres per family head, 80 for single adults. The government sold off "extra" land—in total about 60 million acres—to white settlers. Supporters of the Dawes Act saw it as promoting a more "American," and less "nomadic" life. In reality, the legislation severely undermined tribal life while

Trail of Tears

ZITKALA-SA

*Native American activist Gertrude Bonnin, or **Zitkala-Sa** (1876-1938), a Yankton Sioux who founded the first twentieth-century pan-Indian movement, defied government efforts to assimilate Native Americans. Using the media and lobbying before Congress to argue for the preservation of Native American culture on reservations, she stressed the importance of tribal identities, and explored Indian history and identity in two collections of stories, Old Indian Legends (1902) and American Indian Stories (1921).*

Bury My Heart at Wounded Knee (1970), by Dee Brown. This is a heartbreaking and innovative account of the history of the American West as seen from a Native American perspective.

doing nothing to foster integration into white society. It wasn't until 1934 that the worst aspects of the Dawes Act were mitigated with the passage of the **Indian Reorganization Act**, which acknowledged the importance of Native American cultural institutions such as common ownership and allowed some "surplus" lands to be reinstated as tribal holdings.

4. In America in the seventeenth century, which of the following groups was the largest?

   (A) Black slaves
   (B) White indentured servants
   (C) Free-born blacks
   (D) Native American slaves

Slavery in the New World was the answer to a chronic labor shortage when white settlers wanted to exploit the commercial possibilities of large-scale agriculture, primarily tobacco and rice. In the seventeenth century, British and German **indentured servants** greatly outnumbered African slaves. Indentured servants were people (usually young unmarried men) who, unable to afford the passage across the Atlantic, signed a contract or "indenture" promising a fixed number of years of service to their master in exchange for passage and maintenance during their service. Indentured servants had some legal rights, including the right to bring suit, own property, and get protection from the courts against

A diagram of the deplorable conditions to which kidnapped Africans were submitted on European slave ships

abusive masters—none of which were given to slaves. Like slaves, however, indentured servants could not marry without their masters' permission, had little control over the conditions of their labor, and could be sold without their consent. By the beginning of the nineteenth century, indentured servitude had almost completely disappeared, replaced by the more profitable system of slavery.

While it's true that slavery had existed since ancient times, and was even in practice among the rival tribes of Africa, the Atlantic slave trade eclipsed all other historical institutions of slavery in several ways, including its huge volume, its exclusively racial nature, and the immense distance those kidnapped as slaves were transported. White slave traders employed African middlemen, who knew the terrain, to do the initial dirty work of rounding up prospective slaves. Then came the long, brutal trip across the Atlantic, called the **Middle Passage**, so unbearable it drove scores of kidnapped Africans to suicide. Shackled in unsanitary conditions in the bowels of ships, the prisoners suffered horribly, and many died en route. More than half of all those brought to the present U.S. arrived between 1760 and 1808, when the Atlantic trade was abolished (though an illegal trade was maintained until the Civil War). But by 1808 the slave trade was no longer necessary anyway—slavery had become a self-sustaining system, with the slave population tripling between 1808 and the Civil War.

Slavery in the Southern U.S. had many different faces. The **"peculiar institution,"** as it was known, differed in cities and rural areas, and ranged from large plantations to small households

DIVIDE AND CONQUER DEPARTMENT, PART I

Some historians argue that black slaves and white Irish workers were segregated for fear the two groups would realize their common lot. Slaveowners further devised an ingenious method of limiting the possibilities of slave rebellion with underclass whites as abettors: they employed poor whites as overseers, who functioned as buffers and repositories for black anger toward white oppression.

THAT TROUBLESOME CLAUSE

The basic premises of the American nation are stated eloquently in the Declaration of Independence: "We hold these truths to be self-evident, that all men are created equal, that they are endowed by their creator with certain unalienable rights, that among these are life, liberty, and the pursuit of happiness." The government was instituted "to secure these rights"; the power of the government "derives . . . from the consent of the governed." Yet it's important to remember that the document's purpose was above all pragmatic—to demonstrate to the nations of the world that King George III had been an unjust ruler, and that the colonies were justified in seeking to cut loose from England. In this light, it's easier to understand the decision of Jefferson, who was himself a slaveholder, to include a clause that stated that the king had "waged a cruel war against human nature" by carrying off "a distant people" into "slavery in another hemisphere." It's also easy to see how Southern delegates convinced him to remove the clause, arguing that slavery was not in conflict with the rights to "life, liberty, and the pursuit of happiness." At the same time, women, Native Americans, and white men who were not landowners were not intended to share in the power invested in the "people" of the new democracy. Yet despite its dubious status as a beacon of equality, the Declaration of Independence has proven to be a remarkably flexible document. The very groups that were excluded from the nation's original vision have held up Jefferson's words over the centuries as the lofty goal the nation has never quite achieved.

> **"**
>
> *That execrable sum of all villanies, commonly called the slave trade.*
>
> ——JOHN WESLEY
>
> **"**

with only a servant or two. Slaves made up about a third of the population in the South, and most lived on small farms, in close proximity to their masters. This was in contrast to slaves in Caribbean countries, who formed over 90 percent of the population and rarely saw their masters. Southerners prided themselves on their close relations to their "people," claiming that they cared for them when they were sick and treated them like family. No doubt close and complex ties did develop between blacks and whites in the antebellum South. But an unstable atmosphere of enforced dependency and mutual suspicion prevailed, kept in place by whippings, the systematic sexual abuse of slave women by white men, degrading and arbitrary regulations, the breaking up of families through sales to different owners, and the denial of all legal rights to slaves.

5. Under the Missouri Compromise, Missouri was admitted as a slave state and which other state was admitted as a free state?

    (A) Maine
    (B) Rhode Island
    (C) Ohio
    (D) Nebraska

The **Missouri Compromise** of 1820 aimed to quell animosities caused by Missouri's request to be admitted to the union as a slave state, which would have tipped the balance in Congress to twelve slave states and eleven free states. Southerners held that a new state was free to choose its own status; Northerners argued that Congress could prohibit slavery in a newly admitted state. The compromise bill admitted Missouri as a slave state and Maine (then part of Massachusetts) as a free state, and established the latitude 36/30 as the line north of which slavery was illegal.

The **Dred Scott case** of 1857 declared the Missouri Compromise invalid. In this complicated, controversial case, Scott, a slave in Missouri, was left to a relative of his owner who lived in Illinois, and sued for his freedom, claiming Missouri citizenship. In the appeal to the Supreme Court, Northern justices argued that Scott should be freed under the Missouri Compromise because he had traveled north of 36/30. The notorious ruling that came from the pen of Chief Justice Roger B. Taney nullified the Missouri Compromise, and held that blacks—even free blacks—could not be citizens and that slaves could not become free by traveling north of 36/30.

Dred Scott

The Compromise of 1850 allowed Congress to put off for several years the increasingly divisive issue of slavery in the new territories. California was admitted as a free state, while Utah and New Mexico were created as territories with the question of slavery to be put to a popular vote, and the slave trade was ended in Washington, D.C. The most infamous aspect of the compromise was the **Fugitive Slave Law.** This law established federal commissioners who had authority to enlist all citizens in the cause of catching runaway slaves under penalty of fine, imprisonment, or both. Runaway slaves who were caught in the North were denied trial, and could be hauled back to the South on the basis of a supposed owner's affidavit. The commissioners were to receive ten dollars for returning an accused fugitive to slavery—but only five if they freed him. Many long-free Northern blacks were torn from their families and sent into slavery, and a sinister slave-catching trade burgeoned. Northern states responded to the measure by passing personal freedom laws of their own, but the Supreme Court ruled that states' laws

Slaves preparing cotton for the gin

could not contradict a federal law. **Abolitionists** and others opposed to slavery were galvanized, including Harriet Beecher Stowe (p. 265), who wrote *Uncle Tom's Cabin* in the wake of the outcry aroused by the law.

The abolitionist movement had begun during the 1830s, its crusaders spurred by the Second Great Awakening of the previous decade. Early abolitionists considered slavery a subversion of God's will. As the nation marched toward war, the abolitionists kept attention focused on the moral degradation they claimed the Southern states were bringing down on the entire country. **William Lloyd Garrison** (1805-1879), a devout Baptist (p. 503),

FREEDOM TRAIN

*Most slaves who escaped their masters did so on their own, and probably in a spontaneous, rather than planned, fashion. The legendary underground railroad, though, did play a small but significant role in providing safe passage to the North for escaped slaves. Most of the "conductors" who led fugitives from one safe house to the next were northern free blacks. The most famous of these was an escaped Maryland slave named **Harriet Tubman** (1821-1913). She made nineteen forays back to the South during the 1850s, rescuing about three hundred people. Later, Tubman collaborated with militant abolitionist John Brown (but was not present for his raid on Harpers Ferry) and was a scout and spy for the Union during the Civil War.*

began publishing his anti-slavery newspaper *Liberator* in 1831 and founded the **American Anti-Slavery Society** two years later. Along with his partner, lawyer and orator **Wendell Phillips** (1811-1884), Garrison tirelessly attacked the institution of slavery and the lack of zeal among most of abolitionism's supporters. The movement was often divided over how much women should participate, and white abolitionists were notoriously condescending to their black comrades. In 1865, after the passage of the Thirteenth Amendment, Garrison declared abolitionism's goals met and proposed that the American Anti-Slavery Society be disbanded. Some abolitionists, including Phillips, were horrified, contending that the Society's work would not be done until all black Americans were granted equal rights. Phillips became the Society's president and kept it active until the adoption of the Fifteenth Amendment.

6. **Which of the following insurrections against slavery was led by a white man?**

   (A) John Brown's
   (B) Nat Turner's
   (C) Frederick Douglass's
   (D) Denmark Vesey's

While Southern propagandists tried to assuage abolitionists' moral outrage by maintaining that slaves were happy—"Just listen to them sing. Is that the voice of an unhappy soul?"—there were many slave rebellions prior to the Civil War. One historian has counted over two hundred plots, conspiracies, and insurrections led by slaves. A constant source of inspiration and enticement was the slave revolt of 1790s, led by **Toussaint l'Ouverture**, which overthrew French rule in Saint Domingue and established the nation of Haiti. **Gabriel's Rebellion**, which took place in 1800 in Richmond, Virginia, was led by Gabriel Prosser, a blacksmith, and his brother Martin, a slave preacher. Invoking the Declaration of Independence and the Biblical story of the Israelites' flight from bondage in Egypt, Gabriel orchestrated a plan for slaves from all surrounding plantations to march on Richmond, killing all whites except Quakers, Methodists, and the French. The rebellion fell through when a storm washed out the roads to the city on the chosen night. Another plot, led by Denmark Vesey, was exposed in 1822 in Charleston, South Carolina, and the organizers were executed. **Nat Turner**, a Virginia slave who was a visionary preacher, organized the most famous slave revolt in U.S. history in 1831. Turner and a group of slaves went from house to house killing all the whites they found, fifty-five in total: thirteen men, eighteen women, and twenty-four children. By the end of the twelve-hour spree sixty slaves had joined Turner. Turner escaped but was later captured and hanged, and fear and paranoia spread through white Virginia, leading to strict laws regulating blacks' freedom of movement, as well as one stating that a white must be present at all religious services led by black preachers.

The Confessions of Nat Turner (1967), by William Styron. Styron offers a strange and captivating fictional version of Nat Turner's story.

John Brown (1800-1859), a white abolitionist raised in Ohio, represented the extreme version of abolitionism that held that violent overthrow was the only way to end slavery. Along with twenty-one followers, Brown set out to establish a site in northern Virginia as a haven for escaped slaves and a base for future military actions. From a rented farm in **Harpers Ferry**, Brown collected weapons and in 1859 his "army" occupied the federal arsenal there. Brown's force was quickly subdued by troops under the command of Col. Robert E. Lee (p. 632).

A scowling John Brown

Depicting himself as a selfless martyr for moral and religious principles, the wounded Brown became a cause celebre when he defended himself from a stretcher on the courtroom floor. He was found guilty of treason and executed. Brown's raid on Harpers Ferry contributed to the growing suspicion and fear between North and South that eventually led to the Civil War.

7. **How many blacks won Senate seats during the 1869 elections?**
    (A) Zero
    (B) Two
    (C) Eight
    (D) Twenty

Reconstruction, the period immediately following the Civil War when the nation debated what would become of the defeated, post-slavery South, is a fascinating chapter in U.S. history, and its failure perhaps influences decisions a century later. At first, **President Andrew Johnson** designed a plan that pretty much left former Confederates and plantation owners alone and gave blacks no political power at all. Southern whites rushed to institute **Black Codes** designed to re-establish the general economic and social system of slavery: blacks were required to sign yearly labor contracts, unemployed blacks would be declared vagrants and hired out to white landowners, and black children were to be sent out on forced "apprenticeships" to white employers. Many freed slaves refused to sign the labor contracts, waiting for the the government to give them the **forty acres and a mule** they thought were coming to all former slaves. This promise never materialized, and instead the system of **sharecropping** developed. Sharecroppers were able to work their own plots but had to divide the crops with the landowners at the end of each year. In some areas of the South, however, the destruction of machinery and irrigation systems wrought by the war prevented white planters from getting back on their feet right away, and blacks often ended up acquiring small pieces of land to farm on their own. But economic developments (such as factories) that might have attracted black laborers were stymied by the planters, who were busy consolidating their position as the owning class of the South, even though they were themselves increasingly dependent on Northern financiers and industrialists.

Congress and the controlling Republican party soon put an end to Johnson's vision of reconfigured slavery in 1867, when they endorsed black (male) suffrage and set out to remake Southern state governments. In the most southern of Southern states, Mississippi, two black people, **Hiram Revels** and **Blanche Bruce**, gained election to the U. S. Senate in 1869; sixteen blacks in all served in Congress during the Reconstruction, and hundreds more served in state legislatures and local offices from sheriff to dogcatcher. Meanwhile, Northern carpetbaggers, so named for their suitcases hastily made of carpet, tramped across the financial welcome mats placed at the South's doorstep by Congress. Once entrenched, the carpetbaggers abused their staying privileges. Graft and scandal became rampant in the reconstructed South, and it comes as no surprise that most whites blamed blacks in the legislature for this development.

All of these factors led to the rise of the **Ku Klux Klan**. Members of the former ruling class, humiliated by the sight of those they had once owned enjoying public spaces, political clout, and relative prosperity, plotted to regain what had been theirs. Now, however, the former Southern elite had to hide their faces in white sheets for fear of the law sweeping down from the North. The Klan's terror campaigns, featuring beatings and lynchings (the infamous burning crosses were a later development), were aimed initially at Republican leaders as well as at blacks

Spike Lee (p. 123), the noted African American movie maker, named his film company after a promise—"40 Acres and a Mule."

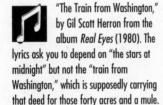

"The Train from Washington," by Gil Scott Herron from the album *Real Eyes* (1980). The lyrics ask you to depend on "the stars at midnight" but not the "train from Washington," which is supposedly carrying that deed for those forty acres and a mule.

who asserted their rights. Despite legal and military victories over the Klan, the force behind Reconstruction began to fade by the 1870s as Republican power declined and Southern states effectively ignored the Fourteenth and Fifteenth Amendments by once more denying blacks the right to vote.

8. **Plessy v. Ferguson allowed what type of institution to segregate blacks into "separate but equal" facilities?**

(A) Railroads
(B) Public schools
(C) State legislatures
(D) Lavatories

In 1896, the Supreme Court handed down a decision cementing the **"Jim Crow"** laws that meant legal oppression of African Americans in the South (and the North) for another seventy years. Ruling in *Plessy v. Ferguson*, a Louisiana case, the Court decreed that railroads could legally separate whites and blacks if the races received equal quarters. Thus the illogical doctrine of **"separate but equal"** was born. Only one voice on the court dissented: **John Marshall Harlan** (1833-1911), a former Kentucky slave owner. He argued that the Thirteenth Amendment banned slavery and applied to individual slave owners; ergo, the Fourteenth Amendment should also apply to the individual. Further, he wrote, discrimination was a badge of slavery and fell under the rubric of the Thirteenth Amendment. But mostly his argument began and ended with the phrase, "Our Constitution is color blind . . . ." The rest of the Court and the country remained deaf to his logic and the era of **segregation** began.

THE SCOTTSBORO BOYS

On March 23, 1931, nine black boys and young men ranging in age from twelve to twenty-one were taken from a freight train in Alabama and charged with the gang rape of two white women who had been riding in the same boxcar. While the evidence against the defendants was flimsy, it took only two weeks for an all-white jury to convict them. All but the youngest were sentenced to the electric chair. The communist-backed International Labor Defense (ILD) took up the case, appealing to the Alabama Supreme Court, which upheld the convictions. But the ILD was organizing protests across the country and public sympathy had begun to turn in favor of the "Scottsboro Boys." The United States Supreme Court heard the case and, in 1935, reversed the convictions on the grounds that the defendants had been denied due process by the all-white jury. Five of the men were retried and convicted again in 1937. The last of them was not paroled until 1950.

Despite a hostile and unpredictable political climate, blacks made social, economic, and educational gains at a brisk pace. Under Reconstruction, the

Freedmen's Bureau had established some four thousand new schools in the South, which educated a quarter of a million former slaves and their children, and the important black colleges and universities, like Spelman, Morehouse, and Howard, were also founded. Blacks left white churches in growing numbers, establishing their own sects as well as many interconnected fraternal, benevolent, and mutual aid organizations. By the beginning of the twentieth century, African Americans could be divided into two schools of thought, represented by **Booker T. Washington** (1856-1915) and **W. E. B. Du Bois** (1868-1963). Washington, an educator and founder of the Tuskegee Institute, a school devoted to the "industrial and moral education of blacks," held that blacks should be conciliatory towards whites, accept segregation, and focus on their own economic and educational progress before they sought political and social equality. Du Bois, a historian, sociologist, and writer (most notably of *The Souls of Black Folk* [1903], a hauntingly beautiful collection of essays tied together with the lyrics and bars of old "Negro spirituals"), also called on African Americans to reach their fullest potential.

Booker T. Washington

But Du Bois rejected Washington's accomodationism, arguing instead for the necessity of protest and agitation if blacks were to win basic human and civil rights in a hostile environment. The dispute between Washington and Du Bois, which culminated in a famous debate over "industrial" versus "classical" education for blacks, gradually tilted toward Du Bois's side. In 1909, the **National Association for the Advancement of Colored People (NAACP)** was founded to fight segregation and continuing legal injustices against blacks.

W.E.B. Du Bois

9. Which woman of the American Revolutionary era asked her husband to "remember the ladies" in drawing up the Constitution?
   (A) Martha Washington
   (B) Dolly Madison
   (C) Emma Willard
   (D) Abigail Adams

It's often forgotten that, until the middle of the nineteenth century, married women in America had no legal status. Once a woman married, she could no longer buy, sell, or own property; everything she owned became the property of her husband. Having no legal status, married women could not sue or be sued, enter into contracts, or be paid their own wages. In the rare case of divorce, the father was automatically granted custody of children—they were his property, too. **Abigail Adams** (1744-1818) was no doubt referring to these unjust laws when she wrote a letter to her husband, **John Adams** (1735-1826), asking him to "remember the ladies" in the blueprint of the new nation: "I desire you would remember the ladies, and be more generous and favorable to them than your ancestors. Do not put such unlimited power into the hands of the husbands. Remember all men would be tyrants . . . " He did not comply, and it wasn't until 1895, with the final passage of a series of **Married Women's Property Acts** that married women obtained legal standing in the U.S.

In the early decades of the nineteenth century, education became the central issue for those concerned with fostering independence and equality for women. "Female Academies" were founded by educators such as Emma Willard, and (affluent white) girls had access to formal education for the first time. Women also banded together to form moral reform societies dedicated to ending male "licentiousness and seduction," and the **temperance movement**, determined to end the wife and child abuse and delinquency they blamed on a culture of heavy drinkers, was adopted as a political cause by many women. Women also played a big role in the abolitionist movement, which introduced women such as the **Grimké** sisters, **Sarah** (1792-1873) and **Angelina** (1805-1879) to politics. The sisters tried to draw other Southern white women to the anti-slavery cause. Attacked in the press for daring to speak in public—an unheard-of transgression for women—they nonetheless embarked on a lecture tour in 1837-1838, and Angelina became the first American woman to address a legislative body when she testified before the Massachusetts legislature.

The mind has no sex but what habit and education give it.

——FRANCES WRIGHT

The term "feminism" did not come into use until around 1910.

The first women's rights convention, organized by **Lucretia Mott** (1793-1880) and **Elizabeth Cady Stanton** (1815-1902), was held in **Seneca Falls**, New York, in 1848. The convention drew about three hundred women and men and produced the **"Declaration of Sentiments."** Modeled on the Declaration of Independence, the document called for equal rights for married women, equal access for women to education and employment, and equal roles for women in politics and religion.

By the end of the nineteenth century, the question of **suffrage**, the right to vote, had become the focus of the women's rights movement. Led by Stanton and **Susan B. Anthony** (1820-1906), membership in the **National Woman Suffrage Association (NWSA)** was divided on whether to enlist men in the cause and whether to support black suffrage. The **women's club movement** grew as well during this time, as women, denied access to official channels of power, sought alternative forums to discuss political and cultural issues. The **settlement movement,** led by women such as Jane Addams and Lillian Wald, provided a training ground for many turn-of-the-century middle-class women who sought involvement and power in the world beyond the domestic sphere. The movement attempted to help immigrant slum-dwellers through establishing "settlement houses"

Women lawyers in a suffrage parade

staffed by educated white middle-class workers, allowing women to become involved in public policy even though they had no legal and political clout.

10. In what year was the Nineteenth Amendment to the
    Constitution, granting women the right to vote,
    passed?
    (A) 1890
    (B) 1899
    (C) 1909
    (D) 1919

When the Nineteenth Amendment, granting women the right to vote, was finally passed in 1919, the women's movement came to a crossroads. The focus on suffrage rather than a broader agenda of women's rights had obscured growing conflicts within the movement. Disputes centered on the difficult question of whether women should be treated as equal to men or as different from men and therefore deserving of special treatment. Fearful that "equal rights" would mean losing special laws protecting female workers and mothers, many women opposed the idea of an Equal Rights Amendment to the Constitution, first proposed in 1923. Women who made strides in politics during the 1930s, such as Frances Perkins, Labor Secretary for President Franklin Delano Roosevelt (p. 419), often came out of settlement and reform movements rather than women's groups such as the National Woman's party and the League of Women Voters, which lost influence and focus in the succeeding decades.

The **birth control movement**, turned into a crusade by **Margaret Sanger** (1883-1966), gained momentum only in the second decade of the twentieth century. A nurse and mother of three, Sanger became convinced after working with the poor on the Lower East Side of Manhattan that the right to control their sexual and reproductive lives was central to women's freedom and well-being. Contraception was a charged issue in the turn-of-the-century U.S.; it was illegal not only to practice contraception but to disseminate information about it. This prohibition was linked not only to the nation's puritanical streak, but to racist fears of white Protestant **"race suicide"** in the face of massive immigration and high African American birth rates. By 1916, birth-control clinics were beginning to open in every major city, in defiance of the law, and in 1921 the Birth Control Conference organized by Sanger resulted in the American Birth Control League, which became **Planned Parenthood** in 1942. Contraception was legalized by many states only as late as the 1960s, and some feminists feel its legalization reflects something of a compromise, as birth control has come to be seen as a medical issue, rather than a woman's right, and access to most contraceptive methods requires the permission of a doctor.

TAKE TWO ASPIRIN AND CALL ME MA'AM

Women's entry into the professions was a hot issue at the turn of the century, with many arguing that women just couldn't hack the pressure and intellectual rigor of professional work. Male-dominated professions like medicine welcomed women only slowly and reluctantly. The first women doctors, including Elizabeth Blackwell (1821-1910) and Mary Jacobi (1842-1906), found themselves mistrusted by patients and ignored by colleagues.

11. The first nationwide strike in the U.S. occurred in

(A) 1801
(B) 1862
(C) 1877
(D) 1898

The **labor movement** in the U.S. began in the nineteenth century with the development of **trade unions**, uniting skilled craftsmen in a single city. In 1852, the National Typographical Union, the first national organization that brought together local unions of the same trade, was formed. Early trade unions used **strikes** and **boycotts** to wrest better conditions and a fairer share of the profits from owners, while a broader **labor reform** movement aimed more generally to protect the rights of the working class. The **Knights of Labor**, begun in 1869 as a secret society of Philadelphia tailors, went on to organize workers from various industries across the country and fought for reforms such as the eight-hour day, the abolition of child labor, equal pay for equal work, and a graduated income tax. The **American Federation of Labor**, cofounded by **Samuel Gompers** (1850-1924), a Jewish immigrant from London, rose to become the nation's most powerful labor union (though it represented only the most privileged of workers) in the twentieth century, especially after it consolidated with the **Congress of Industrial Organizations** (CIO) in 1955.

Militia hold striking millworkers at bay in Massachussetts.

American strikes have tended to be longer and more violent than their European counterparts. Known as "the year of violence," 1877 saw the first nationwide strike in the U.S. and set a bloody precedent. A flagman at a railroad station in Pittsburgh refused to perform a task he deemed too dangerous, and the rest of his crew backed him, as did the other workers on the tracks. The strikers multiplied, and freight trains came to a halt. The Trainsman's Union, although not responsible for the action, endorsed it. Railroad officials called in the National Guardsmen from Philadelphia, assuming that the Pittsburgh militia would not shoot at their fellow city dwellers. When the Philadelphia troops confronted the crowd, the crowd replied with rocks, which guards answered with gunfire. Within a short time, twenty-four were dead and nineteen buildings lay in ashes. What happened in Pittsburgh reverberated throughout the nation. In total, in 1877, 100,000 workers went on strike, a thousand saw the inside of a jail cell, a hundred died, and over half of the nation's rails went cold from lack of use. The **Pullman strike** of 1894 established the hard-line position the U.S. government and business interests would take toward labor. **George Pullman**, the inventor of the railroad sleeping car, fired a full one-third of his workers, ordering a 30 percent cut in wages for the remainder, while refusing to cut prices for food or housing in the company village he had built to house employees. The American Railway Union president, the tireless and articulate labor spokesman **Eugene v. Debs** (1855-1926), ordered a strike. Replacement workers were hired. Federal troops ordered by **President Grover Cleveland**, who sided with Pullman, broke the strike, and Debs was sentenced to six months in jail for contempt of court. Debs came out of the experience in great demand as a speaker, and convinced that trade unions could not ultimately challenge the power of owners under the capitalist economic system. Debs embraced socialism and ran for President five times as the Socialist party candidate.

12. **For what wage did women at the Triangle Shirtwaist Company work in 1911?**
    (A) Three cents per hour
    (B) Seventy-three cents per hour
    (C) One dollar per hour
    (D) Three dollars per hour

The fire at the **Triangle Shirtwaist Factory** in 1911 resulted in the deaths of 146 women workers who had labored for three cents an hour in terrible conditions. When flames broke out, the women were trapped in

DIVIDE AND CONQUER DEPARTMENT, PART II

*While **Samuel Gompers** (1850-1924) and the other leaders of American Federation of Labor paid lip service to the brotherhood of all workers, they were sensitive to the fears and bigotry of their constituents. Blacks, eastern European immigrants, and women were generally excluded from most unions. In 1902, blacks made up only about 3 percent of the total AFL membership, most of them consigned to segregated locals. As W. E. B. Du Bois observed, "The net result of all this has been to convince the American Negro that his greatest enemy is not the employer who robs him, but his fellow white workingman."*

Norma Rae (1979), directed by Martin Ritt. Sally Field gives an Oscar-winning performance as a southern textile worker who takes up the union cause.

the building because management had blocked off all exits and fire escapes to prevent workers from taking breaks. The tragedy profoundly affected women's trade unionism and brought to light the issue of job safety. The factory owners were indicted but acquitted by a jury, intensifying public outcry against abuses by factory owners.

The national trade union movement had virtually excluded women, who were shut out of the highly skilled jobs that were embraced by organizations such as the AFL. The fledgling **International Ladies Garment Workers Union** was spurred by the Triangle Shirtwaist fire to increase efforts to improve conditions in the hot, dirty, noisy **sweatshops** where most women worked ten- and twelve-hour days, six days a week, for wages far below those of their male counterparts. In women, most of whom aspired to leave industrial work upon marriage (although that was more fantasy than reality, especially for immigrant women), owners had a docile and malleable workforce. By the 1920s, women workers turned to protective legislation rather than unions to better their lives. Laws were passed in most states establishing minimal standards for working conditions, minimum wages, and shortened hours for women; but there was a cost in women's freedom and mobility. Since these laws aimed to protect women for their "real" job of motherhood, there were also restrictions on what jobs women could do, and on hours—even unmarried women could not work the night shift.

Mother's Love

Radical labor leader **Mary Harris Jones** (1830-1930), known as "Mother Jones," organized coal miners in Pennsylvania beginning in the 1890s and later made a name for herself as a colorful figure who fought tirelessly and ingeniously for oppressed workers. Mother Jones had an acerbic wit and flair for public relations. One protest she organized had miners' wives banging on tin pans late at night to block strikebreakers coming in for the morning shift; another was a week-long march of child laborers to the New York home of President Theodore Roosevelt. Yet for all her radical politics, Mother Jones was anti-woman's suffrage and felt women's most important work was in the home. Today, there's an exuberantly muckraking, leftist magazine called Mother Jones.

Under the New Deal (p. 419), labor's power was solidified by a series of measures such as the **National Labor Relations Act,** which established workers' right to **collective bargaining.** By the end of World War II, over 12 million American workers belonged to unions and collective bargaining was par for the course in industry. Yet the labor movement's impact has steadily declined in the second half of this century. From the 1950s to the end of the 1980s, the percentage of American workers who were unionized fell by half, to 17 percent, and problems of corruption as well as a changing economy continue to diminish unions' power to fight for the rights of wage-earners.

13. The Haymarket affair of 1886 revealed Americans' fears of

(A) immigrants
(B) anarchists
(C) socialists
(D) All of the above

The **Haymarket affair** began with a workers' rally organized by a small anarchist group to protest the killing of a striking worker by police a few days earlier. The police arrived and demanded that the crowd of about three hundred disperse. Suddenly a bomb exploded near the policemen. Seven policemen were killed in the blast, and four protesters died as police shot wildly into the crowd. Across the nation, paranoia spread against all immigrants, anarchists, and socialists. Hundreds of socialists and anarchists were rounded up in Chicago, and eight anarchists, seven of whom were German by birth, were charged with conspiracy in the case, though none was actually charged with throwing the bomb. The trial against the eight was evidently biased, and seven were sentenced to death. Four were hanged, one committed suicide in jail, two had their terms commuted to life sentences, and one got fifteen years in prison. The case became a benchmark in a growing nativistic movement against immigrants and radicals.

DIVIDE AND CONQUER DEPARTMENT, PART III

"This government is menaced by a great danger. . . . That danger lies in the votes possessed by males in the slums and the ignorant foreign vote. . . . There is but one way to avert this danger—cut off the vote of the slums and give it to women . . . ."

——*Carrie Chapman Catt*

The explosive Haymarket affair

CULTURESCOPE

WASH THOSE GENES

The pseudo-science of Eugenics, originated in the late nineteenth-century, came increasingly into play in the twentieth. Eugenics is the study of ways in which the mental and physical qualities of a population can be manipulated through selective breeding. While they were made most notorious by the Nazis, eugenic measures have been proposed and adopted throughout this century in the U.S., often in the service of racist ideologies. Eugenic ideas also have been aimed at the mentally and physically handicapped.

Sacco and Vanzetti handcuffed on their way to court

The **Sacco and Vanzetti** case in the 1920s also became a benchmark of American anti-immigrant and anti-radical sentiment. In this case, too, the state-sponsored execution of apparently innocent immigrants with vaguely anarchist ties exposed many fault lines in American society. In 1920, two Italian immigrants, **Nicola Sacco**, a shoemaker, and **Bartolomeo Vanzetti,** a fish merchant, were arrested by the Brockton, Massachusetts, police and charged with murder in connection with the holdup of a shoe factory two weeks earlier. The government tried and convicted them on evidence that under scrutiny seems flimsy at best. In 1927, after seven years of appeals and against a background of protests and marches that attracted some of the nation's best-known celebrities, the pair died by the electric chair. The case reflected the beginning of the **Red Scare** that brought anti-communism (p. 422) from a right-wing movement into the mainstream of American life in the 1940s and 1950s, where it became a catchall home for anti-labor and anti-immigrant ideologies as well.

14. The first legislation to ban immigration to the U.S. by a particular national group was aimed against
    (A) Chinese immigrants
    (B) Irish immigrants
    (C) Italians immigrants
    (D) Russians immigrants

Although a nation of immigrants, the U.S. has always had an ambivalent attitude toward immigration. Beginning with the **Know-Nothing party** in the 1850s, which aimed to exclude immigrants and Catholics from political life, the nineteenth century saw the rise of nativism in all quarters. The labor unrest of the second half of the century was consistently tied to

The first television show to center on an Asian American character did not appear until 1994 with the sitcom *All-American Girl,* starring comedian Margaret Cho.

"foreign" ideas brought by immigrants. The first law restricting immigration was the **Chinese Exclusion Act**, which banned immigration from China for ten years starting in 1882, and was made permanent in 1902. Japanese were excluded as well starting in 1907. Concerns for white "racial purity" became tied up in the hysteria over the **"Yellow Peril"** presented by Asian immigration. And while Chinese made up only .002 percent of the population, declining wages and economic stagnation was blamed on Chinese workers, especially in the West. Chinese remained barred from U.S. citizenship until 1943.

LEADING SOURCES OF IMMIGRANTS TO THE U.S.

1820-1975		1976-1986	
Country	*Number*	*Country*	*Number*
1. Germany	6.9 million	1. Mexico	720,000
2. Italy	5.2 million	2. Vietnam	425,000
3. Ireland	4.7 million	3. Philippines	379,000
4. Austria-Hungary	4.3 million	4. Korea	363,000
5. Canada	4.0 million	5. China-Taiwan	331,000
6. USSR-Russia	3.3 million	6. Cuba	258,000
7. England	3.1 million	7. Dom. Republic	211,000
8. Mexico	1.9 million	8. Jamaica	200,00
9. West Indies	1.4 million	9. United Kingdom	150,000
10. Sweden	1.2 million	10. Canada	129,000

One of the more disturbing episodes in American mistreatment of immigrants and their descendants occurred during World War II, when the U.S. seized the property of people of Japanese descent in California and throughout the West and herded them into **"internment camps."** Ostensibly, the government feared that those of Japanese descent would aid the enemy, but the racial animosity was clear—German Americans and Italian Americans were not so treated.

The **Johnson-Reed Act** of 1924 established annual immigration quotas favoring northern Europeans over those from southern and eastern parts of the continent and the rest of the world, and this remained the precedent until the **Immigration Act** of 1965 abolished national quotas and instead allowed entry to 170,000 people from the Eastern Hemisphere and 120,000 from the

The U.S. Army supervises the evacuation of Japanese Americans during World War II.

BLOOD SEGREGATION

During World War II, the Red Cross instituted a "segregated" blood donor program—white donors' blood would only go to white patients, and vice versa. Ironically, the blood bank system was developed by a black physician, Charles Drew (1904-1950). He was fired when he protested "blood segregation."

Western, with the exception of family members of immigrants already here. What Congress did not anticipate, however, was that Asians and Latin Americans, not Europeans (who were enjoying economic improvement), would make up the vast majority of newcomers. The racism lurking not far behind the issue of immigration has continued to manifest itself periodically in the public response to this new face of immigration. The **Immigration Reform Act** of 1986 sought to stem a perceived tide of **illegal immigrants**, especially from Mexico, by imposing penalties on employers who hire illegal aliens—a practice winked at for decades in states near the U.S.-Mexico border. Recent legislation in California has continued this trend, with ballot initiatives passed by popular vote intended to drive away nonlegal residents by means such as denying them emergency medical care and schooling.

15. Who was the attorney who argued successfully before the Supreme Court in *Brown v. Board of Education of Topeka, Kansas?*

   (A) Earl Warren
   (B) Thurgood Marshall
   (C) Orval Faubus
   (D) Clarence Darrow

Desegregating the U.S. in the twentieth century was a slow and arduous process, and education has been the standard-bearer of these efforts. In a seminal court decision that was the legal forerunner of the Civil Rights Movement of the 1960s, **Thurgood Marshall** (1908-1993), who later became the first black Supreme Court Justice, successfully argued the 1954 case *Brown v. the Board of Education, Topeka, Kansas.* Marshall convinced the Supreme Court that the standard of "separate but equal" established in *Plessy v. Ferguson* was self-contradictory. To be separate, argued Marshall, was by definition to be unequal. The *Brown* decision, written by **Chief Justice Earl Warren** (1891-1974), affected public schools across the country, not only in places where there was

The nine African American students being escorted by troops into Little Rock Central High School

actual legal segregation but also where de facto segregation was the norm. The courts ruled that school boundaries must be readjusted to insure a racially mixed student population. Marshall argued that while Jackie Robinson (p. 442) had garnered positive attention as he integrated baseball via the "slow trickle" method, the more successful approach belonged to the armed services, which had simply declared integration the rule with no room for public debate. Yet the courts chose the "baseball" method of integration as the model for the public school system, a process that ended up being slow and painful.

Orval E. Faubus (1910-1994), then governor of Arkansas, refused to comply with a federal court order to allow black children into **Little Rock Central High School**, and ordered the National Guard to prevent nine African American children from entering the doors of the then all-white school. The bizarre scenes that followed—the vigil-like steadfastness of white adults who made sure the black children stayed outside the school doors, the few roughneck white students who shouted racial slurs out the windows, the coven of reporters on guard every morning, the rantings of Faubus himself—turned the Little Rock Crisis into the first mega-television event. Eventually **President Dwight Eisenhower** (1890-1969) got General Maxwell Taylor to send a thousand riot-trained soldiers to Little Rock. The crisis ended immediately, but the wounds continued to fester for decades.

The path to the desegregation of America has had to cover psychological as well as legal ground, and the integration of baseball (p. 442) was a huge but hard-fought victory that paved the way for the twentieth-century Civil Rights Movement. General manager Branch Rickey of the Brooklyn Dodgers selected Jackie Robinson to break the "color barrier" in professional baseball in 1946 after hearing reports that Robinson was tough and backed down from no one. In the segregated army, for example, Robinson had regularly faced racist white military policemen and officers, and stood up for himself with dignity when a white officer attempted to have him court-martialed.

"Fables of Faubus" from *Mingus Ah Um*. This satiric piece by jazzman Charles Mingus (p. 313) was inspired by Faubus.

16. **The city in which Rosa Parks refused to give up her bus seat to a white man, setting in motion the civil rights movement, was**

    (A) Selma, Georgia
    (B) Charleston, South Carolina
    (C) Oxford, Mississippi
    (D) Montgomery, Alabama

When **Rosa Parks** (1913-), riding home from work on a public bus in Montgomery, Alabama, in 1955, refused to give up her seat to a white man at the bus driver's demand, the post-*Brown* phase of the civil rights movement was born. The driver had Parks arrested, and in protest African Americans boycotted all city buses for more than a year. **Dr. Martin Luther King, Jr.** (1929-1968), then a twenty-seven-year-old minister from Atlanta, emerged as a leader of the boycott movement. Influenced by the nonviolent methods preached by Mahatma Gandhi (p. 476) as well as the philosophy of Henry David Thoreau (p. 264), King

REFRIED WALLACE

Governor George Wallace (1919-) of Alabama also attempted to fight integration, promising his supporters "Segregation now! Segregation tomorrow! Segregation forever!" Wallace ran for president twice. In his last attempt, he was shot and paralyzed. Amazingly, in 1980, he won back the govenorship of Alabama. His campaign slogan—"The Candidate for Racial Harmony." The reborn Wallace made more political appointments of blacks than any governor in Alabama history.

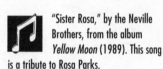 "Sister Rosa," by the Neville Brothers, from the album *Yellow Moon* (1989). This song is a tribute to Rosa Parks.

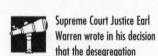 Supreme Court Justice Earl Warren wrote in his decision that the desegregation process should be performed across the land "with all due speed." Twenty years after the decision, various parts of the South still had not complied with the order and remained "lily white."

Dr. Martin Luther King starts the last leg of the Selma-to-Montgomery civil rights march.

helped organize peaceful direct-action tactics, such as **sit-ins** at "whites only" lunch counters across the South. As the movement gained momentum, the **Southern Christian Leadership Conference**, headed by King, organized **Freedom Rides** (the illegal interstate transporting of whites and blacks in the same buses), voter registration, and protest marches in various cities. King met with violence, abuse, and jailings from whites and local southern governments, as well as harassment from the paranoid **J. Edgar Hoover** (1895-1972) of the Federal Bureau of Investigation, who considered Dr. King a rabble-rouser and communist sympathizer. With the help of able lieutenants like Ralph Abernathy, Stanley Levinson, Stokely Carmichael, and Maya Angelou, to name just a few, the movement forged on. A symbolic high point was reached in 1963 with the March on Washington, at which King delivered his inspiring **"I Have a Dream"** speech to 200,000 people.

In the White House, President John F. Kennedy (p. 423) and his younger brother, Attorney General **Robert Kennedy** (1925-1968), at first offered King only lukewarm encouragement, but soon pushed for passage of a new **Civil Rights Act**. After President Kennedy's assassination, former Vice President and newly sworn-in President **Lyndon B. Johnson** (1908-1973) pleaded with Congress to honor Kennedy by passing the

Civil Rights Act of 1964, which outlawed segregation in public facilities and racial discrimination in employment and education. Congress passed the bill, and Johnson launched his **Great Society** program, which he said would "rest on abundance and liberty for all. It demands an end to poverty and racial injustice, to which we are totally committed in our time." Victories in the cause of desegregation were joined by gains in voting rights, culminating in the **Voting Rights Act of 1965**, which increased the number of southern blacks eligible to vote.

17. **In which of these cities were there significant riots following the assassination of Dr. King?**

    (A) Washington, D.C.
    (B) Newark, New Jersey
    (C) Oakland, California
    (D) All of the above

Frustrated by the slow pace of civil rights gains in the face of the poverty and injustice that were still the daily reality for millions of African Americans, many blacks in the 1960s were attracted to a new militancy

MARCUS GARVEY

*A forerunner of black nationalist leaders of the 1960s was **Marcus Garvey** (1887-1940), who brought an urban style to his calls for black economic independence and aimed to link American blacks to Africans with projects such as the Black Star Line, an international shipping company that lasted from 1919 to 1922.*

Smoke billows from L. A. on day four of the six-day Watts riot.

advocated by organizations such as the **Black Panthers**, led by **Huey Newton** (1942-1989). Proponents of **black nationalism** advocated not only economic and psychological self-sufficiency for African Americans but also radical measures that alienated most whites, such as paramilitary training for all black youths. The extreme teachings of Elijah Muhammad, leader of the Lost-Found Nation of Islam, (also known as the Black Muslims), attracted **Malcolm X** while he served time in jail after a youth of petty crime. Converting to Islam (p. 495) and changing his last name from Little to X to symbolize the African identity stolen by slavery, Malcolm became an uncompromising voice against racism and for the empowerment of blacks. After a pilgrimage to Mecca, Malcolm rejected Muhammad's thesis that whites were "devils," and returned to the U.S. to preach a conciliatory message of racial harmony, but was assassinated by wary Black Muslims in 1965. The year 1968 saw two more assassinations that revealed the still-explosive nature of race relations. While running for the presidency, Robert Kennedy, who had become an eloquent and outspoken voice for racial minorities and the powerless in general, was killed by Sirhan Sirhan. Dr. Martin Luther King, Jr. suffered a similar fate at the hands of James Earl Ray. Grief-stricken and enraged, blacks took to the streets in Watts, Washington, D.C., Harlem, Oakland, Atlanta, Newark, and Detroit.

The big picture of the modern civil rights movement reveals a revolution still in many ways unrealized, particularly in terms of economic equality for blacks, but the gains of the 1950s and 1960s nonetheless permanently altered American society. State-sponsored segregation and overt discrimination were ended, anti-black violence declined, and African Americans entered the political life of the nation, winning public office in many communities in which they had once been unable to vote.

Mississippi Burning (1988), starring Gene Hackman and Willem Dafoe. This film about the investigation into the disappearance of three Civil Rights workers in 1964 Mississippi ignores the prominent roles of blacks in the investigation, but it's still a moving account.

Do the Right Thing (1989), directed by Spike Lee. A tour-de-force film that uses the often-conflicting proclamations of Martin Luther King, Jr., and Malcolm X to explore the tensions that exist in a contemporary black urban neighborhood.

18. Who was the author of *The Feminine Mystique*?

(A) Betty Friedan
(B) Kate Millett
(C) Gloria Steinem
(D) Simone de Beauvoir

With the publication of **Betty Friedan's** bestselling *The Feminine Mystique* in 1963, the feminist movement entered a new phase. Friedan's exploration of "the problem that has no name"—the boredom, anger, and frustration of educated middle-class women doomed to lives of domestic drudgery while their husbands and brothers participated in the life of the world at large—came at just the moment women were beginning to question the role they had been assigned in post-World War II American society. Women began to enter the workforce in growing numbers, and to challenge the ideology that held that their "natural" place was at home. Inspired by the Civil Rights Movement, women began to organize. In 1966, the **National Organization for Women (NOW)** was born, determined to fight the widespread discrimination against women in the workplace, the legal system, and the family. NOW took up anew the cause of the Equal Rights Amendment, which remained a divisive issue until its failure in 1982. On the intellectual front, women such as Kate Millett, author of *Sexual Politics*, sought to build on the work of pioneering French feminist **Simone de Beauvoir** (1908-1985), who had exposed the ways in which social systems such as marriage and the nuclear family were arranged to keep power in the hands of men.

One of the biggest victories of the women's rights movement was the case of *Roe v. Wade* in 1973, which established the right to abortion in the stage of pregnancy before a fetus could survive outside the womb. Despite abortion being legal, the issue has continued to prove an incendiary one, as **pro-choice** advocates seek to protect women's right to legal abortion against the efforts of **right-to-life** advocates, who have increasingly turned to violence as their legislative efforts to establish the rights of fetuses have failed.

Isaac Asimov and Betty Friedan partying at Lincoln Center in New York

Still at issue, and varying by state, are laws placing restrictions on abortions, such as efforts to block government funding for abortions.

Efforts to change the way the law deals with victims of rape and domestic violence have also been successful for feminists. Most states no longer require corroborating eyewitness testimony or proof of resistance to convict a rapist, and evidence about a rape victim's sexual past is now excluded. Women

DE BEAUVOIR AND THE EXISTENTIALISTS

*Simone de Beauvoir had a long relationship with the French existentialist philosopher **Jean-Paul Sartre** (1905-1980), author of the novel* Nausea *(1937) and the treatise* Being and Nothingness *(1943). Sartre held that people's awareness of their own freedom results in an intolerable anxiety from which they try to flee. He and other existentialists such as **Albert Camus** (1913-1960), author of the novels* The Outsider *(1942) and* The Plague *(1947), appear in thinly disguised form in de Beauvoir's novel* The Mandarins *(1954).*

have made gains in almost all the traditionally male professions, such as law, medicine, and business, though studies still show the existence of a

The National Organization for Women demand "equity for women—now."

glass ceiling that reserves upper-level positions for white men.

Yet the contemporary feminist movement has been troubled as well as strengthened by its roots among educated, white, middle-class women. Few African American women were involved in the early feminist movement, though more have become involved recently, fostering a long-overdue spirit of debate and diversity. The tendency of white feminists to see all women as in the same boat has angered many minority and less-privileged women. As one black participant at a women's conference said in the 1970s, "My problem is not that I want to get out of the kitchen. I want to get out of *your* kitchen." Another problem of the movement has been its failure to attract the younger generation, who can now take many of the gains their mothers fought for for granted, and are often put off by what they see as strident rhetoric out of touch with a changing social reality. The issues confronting feminists now reach deep into the economic and social systems of the nation, such as the availability of affordable day care for working mothers, who now make up the majority of American mothers.

19. What happened at the Stonewall Inn in New York City's Greenwich Village on June 27, 1969?

(A) A riot to protest arrests of gay bar patrons
(B) A riot to protest arrests of straight bar patrons
(C) A riot to protest arrests of black bar patrons
(D) A riot to protest arrests of white bar patrons

The **gay rights movement** was also born in the 1960s, when patrons at the **Stonewall Inn** in Greenwich Village fought back for the first time against the frequent and degrading police raids on gay bars. Police had routinely arrested people in gay bars for decades—in the 1950s, arrests of gays in Washington, D.C., averaged one thousand per year. The Stonewall incident was followed by three nights of rioting, and almost overnight a massive movement was born, as homosexuals increasingly "came out of the closet" and publicly took on gay identities. By 1973 there were some eight hundred gay organizations throughout the nation, and by 1990 there were several thousand. These groups fought successfully for legal changes that affected the lives of lesbians and gay men. Half the states decriminalized homosexual behavior, and in 1974 the American Psychiatric Association took homosexuality off its list of mental illnesses. The Civil Service Commission eliminated a long-standing order barring homosexuals from most federal jobs. Some religious denominations, such as Unitarians and Reform Judaism (p. 488) welcomed gay ministers and rabbis.

In the 1980s, the AIDS epidemic (p. 213), tragic as it was for the hard-hit gay community, provided a further spur to organizational and political efforts by gays. The **Gay Men's Health Crisis** and the more militant **ACT-UP** were formed, making political involvement an established part of gay life. Recent issues such as gays in the military and ordinances barring equal rights laws for gays have had mixed results, but have shown the savvy and determination of gay organizers to fight for their rights in a still-resistant society.

And the Band Played On (1987), by Randy Shilts. The first years of the AIDS epidemic are recounted in this nonfiction account, later made into a celebrated HBO movie.

Angels In America (1992), by Tony Kushner. This celebrated play was written in two parts that ran simultaneously on Broadway. Part One takes one of the most anti-everything characters in American history, Roy Cohn, a wildly influential attorney who got his start as a henchman for Joe McCarthy (p. 422), and exposes him as a closeted homosexual dying of AIDS.

Gay Rights march in Albany, NY on March 14, 1971

20. What is affirmative action?

(A) The systematic elimination of all white men from positions of power

(B) The use of self-esteem-enhancing techniques to boost achievement by minorities and women

(C) The use of racial, ethnic, or sex preferences in areas such as employment and education

(D) No gender, racial, or ethnic preferences in areas such as employment and education

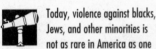 Today, violence against blacks, Jews, and other minorities is not as rare in America as one would like to think. The White Supremacist, Skinhead, and American Nazi movements of the Pacific Northwest attract much publicity and many members.

Education, always at the center of human rights issues in the U.S., has been the battleground for the latest episode. With unprecedented legal victories won by minority groups in the last few decades, attention has shifted to a much more nebulous question: Who decides how to tell the story of America? The movement for **multiculturalism** has worked for more inclusive school curriculums that represent the stories and cultures of all the people of the world, not just the privileged few who have wielded the most power. Opponents argue that multiculturalism is shorthand for a decline in educational standards, and that it's more important for American children to learn about their own culture than any other. The debate has proved to be as productive as it is divisive, as all sides have acknowledged that the U.S. is an increasingly ethnically, racially, and religiously diverse nation.

To be sure, political debates about the meaning of human rights in America are by no means dead. **Affirmative Action**, the program designed to redress past discrimination by reserving places in educational and governmental institutions for minority group members and women, has been attacked both from the left and the right as unfair and damaging to the self-esteem of minorities and women. Native Americans, who recently made big economic gains, especially in the area of gambling casinos on reservations, are still fighting in court for such issues as the return of their ancestral remains from museums like the Smithsonian. Mothers denied custody of children simply because they, like fathers, work outside the home are challenging court decisions. From the Rodney King incident to the O.J. Simpson trial, America continues to be riveted by the ongoing (and perhaps impossible) fight to forge a system where everyone is treated equally.

ANSWERS

1. D	2. A	3. B	4. B	5. A	6. A	7. B	8. A	9. D	10. D
11. C	12. A	13. D	14. A	15. B	16. D	17. D	18. A	19. A	20. C

Life Sciences

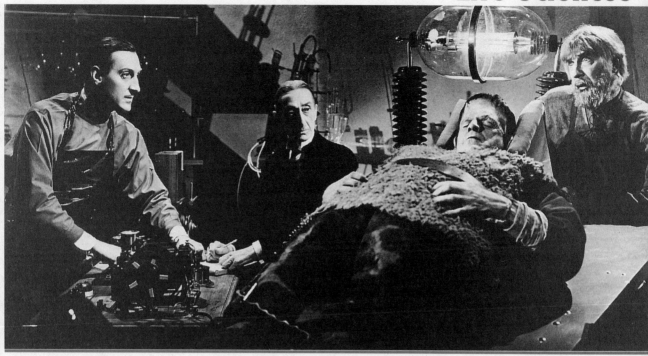

Humans have always wondered about the force that animates them. The life sciences study the bewildering variety of organisms that populate our planet, and in the process, how species have adapted and changed over time. We also turn our gaze inward, toward ourselves. Psychology, anthropology, linguistics, and sociology are sometimes disparagingly called the soft sciences, because they overlap a scientific outlook (hypothesis, experimentation, generalization) with a philosphical one (interpretation). Yet, it can never be possible to be completely objective about our own existence. The human body, a subject of the discipline of biology, is a world unto itself, with territories we have just begun to explore.

1. Which of the following statements is true?
   (A) Man was partially responsible for the extinction of dinosaurs.
   (B) Dinosaurs were predators of early humans.
   (C) Dinosaurs were extinct over fifty million years before humans appeared on the scene.
   (D) Humans and dinosaurs existed at the same time, but lived in different areas of the Earth.

 Astronomers now believe that a meteorite approximately the size of Manhattan (six miles in diameter) slammed into the earth sixty-five million years ago, leading to the extinction of the dinosaurs and all other species that weighed over fifty pounds. It is currently believed that the meteorite made impact at a site near Mérida, Mexico (Yucatan Peninsula) and that the resultant 150-mile-diameter crater is buried under more than a half mile of sediment.

Much (if not all) of our information about the period before written recordkeeping existed, which geologists call **prehistory,** comes from the **geological record**. If you dig out your entire backyard to a depth of one hundred feet, you will be able to tell what was going on sometime in the distant past. Exactly how long ago you are looking at cannot be determined unless you know the particulars of your site (sedimentation rates, erosion rates, history of massive construction projects, etc.), and/or have access to an equal radiocarbon dating service.

To get the whole picture, you would probably need to consult your neighborhood geologist or archaeologist. She would tell you that any two things you've happened to find on the same level of dirt at your site must have been **contemporaneous** (around at the same time). Archaeologists and geologists use the age of different soil levels, in conjunction with the fossils and artifacts they find there, to determine things like how long ago dinosaurs walked the Earth and when the various ice ages occurred. These levels are divided into four major **geologic intervals**—the **Precambrian, Paleozoic, Mesozoic,** and **Cenozoic**. We are currently in the Cenozoic interval, which started approximately sixty-five million years ago. The geologic intervals are further divided into **periods.**

Dinosaurs roamed the earth during the Jurassic and Cretaeceous periods of the Mesozoic interval, between sixty-five and 190 million years ago. Most experts now theorize that dinosaurs became extinct after a large meteor struck the earth. Approximately fifty million years after this event, some arboreal monkeys evolved out of their tails into opposable thumbs, and decided to try walking upright (some are still trying).

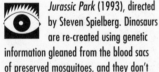 *Jurassic Park* (1993), directed by Steven Spielberg. Dinosaurs are re-created using genetic information gleaned from the blood sacs of preserved mosquitoes, and they don't seem too happy about it.

2. Fossils give all of the following types of information EXCEPT
   (A) clues to the ultimate origin of life on earth
   (B) structures of early bacteria and algae
   (C) the eating habits of dinosaurs
   (D) evidence for the theory of evolution

The term fossil (p. 136) once referred to any curious object dug from the ground. Now, the term refers only to preserved remnants of organisms from the geologic past. For aficionados of **paleontology** (the study of fossils) a handy rule of thumb is, "If the remains stink, it's a zoological sample. If not, lemme see it." Fossils are of differing types. Remains of relatively recent animals may be close to their original form. Bones, teeth, and shells are common; far less common are entire animals, such as the frozen mammoth remains from the arctic tundra of Alaska.

Over time, organic remains are likely to be modified by either **petrification** or **carbonization.** Petrification is a process whereby the original substance, such as a bone, is literally turned to stone, either by replacement or by augmentation. Carbonization works particularly well for preserving leaves or delicate animals. In this process, the organism becomes encased in sediment. Eventually, the increasing pressure caused by the thickening sedimentation pushes out the liquid and gaseous components of the specimen, leaving behind a thin carbon film. Another method by which delicate specimens are preserved is in **amber.**

The fossil record contains evidence of bacteria that are over three billion years old, and shows that algae probably evolved from bacteria about two billion years ago. The shapes of fossilized dinosaur teeth and the presence or absence of associated bones can tell us whether they were herbivores or carnivores. However, fossils do not reveal how life originated on Earth. Scientists hypothesize that the earliest oceans contained a **primordial soup** of chemicals including methane and ammonia. Solar radiation or lightning strikes could have initiated the formation of more complex organic chemicals, then molecular aggregates, and finally living cells.

"Fossil fuels" are composed of the remains of ancient plants and animals. Oil and gas are derived from organisms such as phytoplankton. Coal comes from 250-million-year-old plants and trees, which turn first into peat, then coal.

Wonderful Life: The Burgess Shale and the Nature of History (1989), by Stephen J. Gould. This is a fascinating account of the weird fossilized remains found in an area of the Canadian Rockies.

A common fossil

3. **Who were the Neanderthals?**

(A) Primitive people with no evidence of tool use or culture
(B) Ape-like creatures; not a progenitor of modern man
(C) Contemporaries of Cro-Magnon man
(D) The earliest known specimens of *Homo sapiens*

PILTDOWN MAN

One of the most successful scientific hoaxes of all time was based on faked human remains. In 1911 and 1912, Charles Dawson claimed to have found fossils of "Piltdown man." The remains combined a modern human skull with the jaw of an orangutan. The bones had been filed down and chemically treated to simulate the wear and tear of extreme age. The hoax was not fully discredited until 1953.

Iceman (1984), starring Timothy Hutton. A 40,000-year-old Neanderthal is thawed from a glacier and finds himself in the modern world.

PICTURE YOURSELF ON A BOAT ON A RIVER

Lucy is named after the Beatles' (p. 325) song "Lucy in the Sky with Diamonds," which was playing on the radio as she was discovered.

Our ancestors began to resemble humans more than apes at the moment when they became **bipeds:** that is, when they started to walk on only two feet. Some posit that an erect posture allowed **hominids** to see farther in the grassy savannas in which they lived and thus to spot potential prey or predators. However, baboons also live in savannas, and while they are capable of standing erect, they don't do so at all times. Others correlate bipedalism to the freeing of the hands for carrying food or weapons. In any case, it is clear from the fossil record that several other changes occurred as a result of bipedalism, including an increase in brain capacity. The first bipedal hominids were of the genus *Australopithecus* and lived between three and four million years ago. The fossil called "Lucy" is perhaps the most famous australopithecine, and perhaps the last common ancestor of modern humans and the now extinct *Australopithecus* line.

Fossils definitely belonging to the *Homo* line date back at least 1.5 million years, as we know from **Louis Leakey's** finds of *Homo habilis* at Olduvai Gorge. The Olduvai Gorge site also sheds light on the vastness of culture that had been developed by the early hominids—tool use, gender roles, and shared food. Next came *Homo erectus* (Java man), who cooked with fire and quite possibly practiced cannibalism. *Homo erectus* evolved into *Homo sapiens:* first the **Neanderthal** *Homo sapiens*, then modern humans (*Homo sapiens sapiens*). Neanderthals owe much of their reputations to cartoon imagery, but they have been misrepresented! A Neanderthal could probably walk unnoticed in a cross section of today's world population. Neanderthals made stone flaked tools, built houses, and believed in an afterlife. They buried the dead with food, tools, and

The work of a prehistoric Renoir found in southern France

perhaps flowers. There is evidence of a family structure, since Neanderthals have been found interred in groups containing a male adult, female adult, and children.

The hominids known as **Cro-Magnons** may be the earliest known *Homo sapiens*. Cro-Magnons lived contemporaneously with Neanderthals, and there is little doubt that it was Cro-Magnons who evolved into modern humans. Neanderthals' place in the lineage is still debated. Some believe that Neanderthals evolved into Cro-Magnons, while others believe that Neanderthals were the big losers in a race war with Cro-Magnon.

The Clan of the Cave Bear (1981), by Jean M. Auel. This is romance and adventure, prehistoric style.

4. **Which of the following is unique to humans?**
    (A) Communication
    (B) Symbolic communication
    (C) Spoken symbolic communication
    (D) An opposable thumb

Birds do it, bees do it . . . communicate, that is. In fact, many animal species have been observed to communicate, using sound, smell, or body movements to get across specific messages across like "Good eats over here" or "Get the hell away from me!" **Language** takes communication one step further: it relies on a system of shared **symbols** that stand for **concepts**. For the most part, these symbols are arbitrary—that is, they have no intrinsic relation to the concept they represent. Language was once thought to be the differentiator of man from the rest of the animal kingdom, but when chimpanzees and apes successfully learned sign language, our claim to uniqueness had to be restricted to spoken language.

Human languages have three components: a system of symbols (sounds or hand signs), a vocabulary, and a system of grammar. These vary a great deal. The Kung bushmen of the Kalahari Desert use clicking noises as part of their symbol system; the vocabulary of the Alaskan Eskimo contains over a hundred words for snow; and the Germans prefer to end their sentences with a verb. Moreover, even within a language, people use different dialects and levels of formality, depending on their context. Do you speak the same way when hanging out with your friends as you do in a job interview? Another feature of language is that it is constantly changing, adding new words and dropping or changing the meaning of obsolete ones.

Like other languages, Japanese has imported many words from foreign sources. However, Japanese is unique in that all foreign words are written in its own special alphabet, so that it is possible to tell at a glance which are which.

IF I COULD TALK TO THE ANIMALS

Koko, a California resident who happens to be a gorilla, has been communicating with trainers in American Sign Language for over twenty years. She uses it to express emotions, make up names for new objects, and even lie. She appears to understand human speech and is learning to read. Kanzi, a chimpanzee, has gone one better by learning to "type" on a special keyboard which produces an electronic voice.

5. The division of humanity into races

(A) is based on genetic differences between groups
(B) distinguishes closely related species
(C) is a convenient but increasingly arbitrary designation
(D) is a universally agreed-upon method of classification

Startide Rising (1983), by David Brin Brin. This book envisages a future in which chimpanzees and dolphins have been genetically engineered for greater intelligence and the ability to communicate in spoken form.

HEAD BUMPS

Just as pseudoscientists argue that skin color, an external characteristic, can reveal information about intelligence or other personality traits, the now-discredited theory of **phrenology** *suggested that the size of, and bumps on, a person's skull revealed the functions of the brain and the nature of a person's character.*

Zebrahead (1992), directed by Anthony Drazan. *Zebrahead* offers a look at race in today's United States.

The Evolution of Racism: Human Differences and the Use and Abuse of Science (1994), by Pat Shipman. Racism did not "officially" exist until science created it. This book examines the misuse of science in the name of racial superiority.

Yay! I'm an American! Which way to The Gap?

Race is increasingly a cultural concept, not a scientific one. Long ago, when humans lived in geographically isolated populations with little or no intermarriage between groups, it might have made sense to distinguish "races" based on observable physical differences—skin color, the shapes of eyes or noses, and so on. However, today members of what is called a "race" may have greater genetic differences with each other than with someone of a different race. Moreover, there are no genetic traits that serve to classify people into culturally recognized racial categories (White, Black, Asian, Native American). The ever-growing population of "interracial" people further highlights the arbitrary classification system: in America, children with an African American parent are usually treated as Black, while children with an Asian parent may be seen as White. Other societies differ in their definition of racial boundaries. For example, Mulatto is a racial classification used in Brazil to identify people of mixed ancestry. Note that Mulatto is a socially recognized category that is viewed as a distinct group—not just a descriptive label.

If race is a nonscientific classification, it follows that any attempt to correlate biological race to factors such as intelligence, health, athletic ability, or artistic ability are also unscientific.

6. Approximately how many cells are contained in the human body?

(A) One
(B) One million
(C) Several billion
(D) Several trillion

The **cell** is the unit of life. It occurs in many specialized forms, from single-celled bacteria to hard-walled plant cells to the cells of the human body. However, these all have in common an enclosing **cell membrane**, an interior fluid called **cytoplasm**, and some genetic information which may or may not be contained in a central nucleus. At any given time, there are several trillion cells in the body.

Human life begins as a single cell—the product of an ovum and a sperm. This cell divides itself into more cells by the process of **mitosis**. A developing human is termed a **zygote** until the single cell has divided into up to 128 new cells. By definition, any single cell from a zygote can develop into a complete new organism. The actual number of cells that a human zygote can possess is not known, because ethical reasons have prevented experimentation on how many cell divisions are permissible. After a certain point, the zygote becomes a **morula**. Individual cells from a morula are too specialized to produce an entire organism. From the morula stage, the developing human becomes a blastula and a gastrula.

At the stage of the gastrula, the cells differentiate into the **germ layers**. Once a cell has been "assigned" to one of the three germ layers, its final destination has finally begun to be determined (e.g., pancreas, muscle, bone). As development proceeds, the cell's fate is further determined as its neighbors push against one another and exert "peer pressure." Hey, we're all pancreas cells, why don't you become a pancreas cell too? No one really understands this process of **determination**—i.e., how and when a cell becomes a pancreas cell, rather than just a human cell.

The observation of cells was facilitated by the development of the microscope by Anton van Leeuwenhoek. Using his new toy, van Leeuwenhoek confirmed the discovery of sperm in 1677 (and shocked his peers, who wanted to know where he got it from). He correctly concluded that sperm were a source of reproduction, not a disease as had been earlier thought.

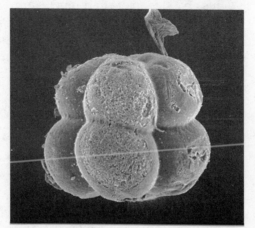

Dividing cell

Who Goes There? (1938), by John W. Campbell, Jr. A superbly written, still terrifying story of cell-mimicking aliens, Antarctic wilderness, and psychological drama. It was the basis for both movies titled *The Thing* (1951 and 1982).

7. Bacteria

    (A)   are germs that always cause disease
    (B)   are used in the manufacture of vinegar, cheese, linen,
           and even some antibiotics
    (C)   are small living creatures made up of only a few cells
    (D)   cannot exist without oxygen

PASS THE SLUDGE, PLEASE

Bacteria are not picky about what they eat. Several kinds of bacteria can consume marble by either converting it into plaster or dissolving it. Other types of bacteria eat petroleum by-products, which makes them useful for cleaning up oil spills.

The Coming Plague, by Laurie Garrett (1994). This book covers many of the same topics as *The Hot Zone* but in a more straightforward and less sensationalist way.

The Hot Zone (1994), by Richard Preston. The deadly Ebola virus has gruesome effects on humans, like turning flesh and brains to mush. What would happen if it got loose in Virginia? This book is based on a true story.

Doomsday Book (1992), by Connie Willis. Historians of the future look to the Middle Ages—only to get an up-close-and-personal brush with the worst bacterial plague of all time, the Black Death.

A **bacterium** is a single-celled organism that is neither a plant nor an animal. Bacteria are all around you, and are found inside your body, too. Not all bacteria cause disease or are harmful to human beings. *E. coli* bacteria, in fact, serve as digestive aids from within the gastrointestinal tract. Such an arrangement, in which both host and guest organisms benefit from their association, is termed **mutualism**. However, introducing too many *E. coli* into your digestive system—for example, by eating contaminated, undercooked meat—can lead to serious health problems and even death.

Many bacteria cause disease. In order to combat diseases that are bacterial in origin, we use **antibiotics**. Antibiotics are drugs designed to take advantage of the differences between bacterial cells and human cells in such a way as to kill the bacteria without endangering the host (you). Examples of antibiotics include penicillin, sulfa drugs, streptomycin, and the tetracyclines. As technology has advanced, antibiotics have become plentiful—in fact, they have become too plentiful. The overprescription and overuse of antibiotics has led some bacteria to become evolutionary tricksters. The bacteria mutate over several generations, developing a resistance to the antibiotic. Additionally, since antibiotics have contained some of the more common and "tame" bacterial infections, more virulent strains no longer have to compete for resources. This leaves open the possibility of increasingly dangerous bacterial onslaughts. In response, even more potent antibiotics must be developed to kill off all but the strongest bacteria again—and so the cycle continues.

The most publicized recent "bacterial plague" has taken the form of the so-called flesh-eating bacteria. This bacteria is a mutated form of a **streptococcus**, the same bacteria that causes strep throat. At least seventy-five different bacteria belong to the family known as Group A streptococcus. The action these bacteria take against the human body ranges from none, to a sore throat, to scarlet fever, to necrotizing fasciitis—the form of rapidly spreading gangrene that caused the recent Strep-A scare (or, if you prefer the tabloid name, "The Killer Bug That Ate My Face"). Bacterial infections are not nearly as infectious as viral infections, but they can still be spread through prolonged direct contact with an infected individual.

8. The first vaccine was for

   (A) polio
   (B) smallpox
   (C) German measles
   (D) cholera

To treat a bacterial infection we use antibiotics. For a viral infection we only have two choices: immunization or the "wait and see" approach. Certain viral infections, such as chicken pox, cannot normally be caught more than once by an individual. This is because the body develops an **immunity** against this virus after the first time it is infected. In some cases, such as the viral infections of smallpox or tuberculosis, it is not prudent to wait for survival from an initial bout of symptoms, since there is not likely to be a second chance. In this case, we need to trigger the immune response of the body with vaccines.

There are two types of vaccines: active and inactive. In the active case, the person being immunized is actually injected with a small dosage of the disease-causing virus, or a much milder version of it. This dose is not enough to cause the disease in most people, although there are always exceptions. The body, recognizing the virus as a foreign material, develops an immune response to this small amount of virus and thus is able to fend off larger doses of the same virus should it attack later. Using this method, **Edward Jenner** (1749-1823) developed the first vaccine in 1796. The Jenner smallpox vaccine is an injection of a very similar virus, the cowpox. A second type of vaccination uses inactive virus cells. In this case, the cells with which you are injected can no longer cause infection, but they still fool your body into developing an immune response, so that it later recognizes and defends against active virus cells of the same type. Unfortunately, it is often found that inactive vaccines do not provide immunity against the active form, so an active vaccine must be employed.

Acquired immune deficiency syndrome (AIDS) is caused by the virus **HIV**. Research into a cure for AIDS—in other words, a vaccine for HIV—has been hampered by the ability of HIV to mutate itself into one of several different forms. This mutation occurs at a rate that is significant enough to allow the virus to escape human immune response. In effect, the virus incapacitates the immune system by infecting and destroying a crucial player in the fight against infections (helper T cells). Thus, otherwise rare diseases such as toxoplasmosis (a brain infection), cryptosporidium enterocolitis (an intestinal infection), and pneumocystis carinii pneumonia (a lung infection), are associated with AIDS (p. 203)

HEY GOOD LOOKIN', CAN I BUY YOU A MILK?

Edward Jenner's idea for vaccination came not from studies in the library or long hours in the lab, but rather from talking to girls. At the time, farm milkmaids often got cowpox. One such milkmaid told the nineteen-year-old Jenner that she believed her exposure to cowpox protected her from ever getting smallpox. By interviewing more milkmaids, Jenner confirmed this statement and began experiments on inoculating others with the cowpox virus.

9. **Which of the following is an example of a fungus?**

    (A) Baker's yeast
    (B) Truffles
    (C) The cause of athlete's foot
    (D) All of the above

Famine and Fungi

A single fungus (Phytophthora infestans) had a dramatic impact on the history of Ireland and the United States. This fungus caused the devastating Irish potato famine of 1845-1847 and the resulting immigration of thousands of Irish to America.

A **fungus** can be either a multicellular or a unicellular organism. Multicelled fungi are known as **molds**. Single-celled fungi are called **yeasts**. Fungi are neither plants nor animals. Thus, a mushroom is not a vegetable—in fact, it is not even a plant. By definition, a plant is able to manufacture its own food through the process of **photosynthesis**. Fungi lack chlorophyll, and thus, like animals, they must ingest their food. However, unlike animals, fungi are completely sedentary. They cannot ingest food that is not already in the form they require.

Fungi can spoil crops and foods, and they cause ringworm and athlete's foot. However, not all fungi are harmful. The entire world's supply of commercial penicillin is produced in pharmaceutical laboratories by the fungus *Penicillium chrysogenum*. Yeasts are used in the manufacture of alcoholic products, certain cheeses, and all risen breads. Mushrooms, and their expensive cousins, truffles, are types of fungi. Furthermore, fungi and bacteria work together to decompose vast quantities of dead organic matter that would otherwise rapidly accumulate and make the earth uninhabitable.

10. **Which of the following statements is true?**

    (A) The Salk vaccine is currently used to inoculate against polio.
    (B) Aspirin has no side effects.
    (C) Penicillin is a universal antibiotic.
    (D) Morphine, a derivative of opium, was once widely used as a pain reliever and sedative.

Thanks to a wide variety of medications, humans have gained an increased life expectancy, or at least a more comfortable lifespan. But can pharmaceutical "wonder drugs" live up to their advertisements? The **Salk vaccine** "cured" the incurable disease of polio, only to be supplanted in three years by the more effective Sabin vaccine. **Penicillin** once could stop bacterial infections dead in their tracks: soon it may prove ineffective for increasing numbers of rogue bacterial strains that are resistent to its action. Like many other products, most drugs have a limited lifespan. Nonetheless, some have been amazingly effective during that lifespan.

Listening to Prozac (1993), by Peter Kramer. This controversial book presents the mood-altering drug Prozac as a "good drug" that lacks significant side effects.

During the second half of the nineteenth century, **opiates** could be legally purchased and were easy to obtain. Since there were no laws governing disclosure of ingredients on patented medicines, many medications contained morphine, cocaine, and heroin. These opiates were prescribed for any ailment: as pain killers, as tranquilizers, for menstrual cramps, and for diabetes. It is estimated that by 1914, one out of every 400 Americans were addicted to opiates. Thus, **morphine**, once touted as a cure-all, suffered much the same fate as other "good"

Hold the cheese, please!

TAKE TWO MEADOWSWEETS AND CALL ME IN THE MORNING

The first aspirin was mass-produced from, and named for, the meadowsweet plant by the German company Bayer. In 1919, as part of the reparations it paid after World War I, Germany conceded Bayer's trademark for the name "Aspirin" to the Allies.

drugs: over-prescription by well-intentioned doctors led to a problem. In the case of morphine, the problem was addiction.

In the case of sulfa drugs and penicillin, the problem is ineffectiveness. Prontosil, the first "wonder drug" and a sulfa antibiotic, was introduced in 1932, and made widely available in 1935. It was advertised as a cure-all both to and by the medical profession. Not only did many people develop allergic reactions to sulfa drugs, but, by the mid-1950s, most sulfa drugs had lost their effectiveness.

11. **Which of the following statements is NOT true?**

    (A) Depo-Provera, once used a contraceptive, can cause birth defects.
    (B) All forms of thalidomide cause birth defects.
    (C) The insecticide DDT has been shown to affect the eggshells of birds.
    (D) It has been found that the toxic properties of Agent Orange were due to trace impurities.

False Prophets: Fraud, Error, and Misdemeanor in Science and Medicine (1987), by Alexander Kohn. Kohn describes the thalidomide tragedy and other instances of scientific misconduct, whether deliberate or accidental.

Some drugs that make it to the consumer market are later determined to do more harm than good, while other drugs are wrongfully accused. Either way, a chemical that was once loved by many becomes despised by all. The insecticide **DDT** was a big improvement over the highly poisonous arsenic compounds it replaced. Its inventor, Paul Müller, even won the Nobel Prize in 1948. However, the long-term effects of DDT, including thinning of the eggshells of birds, led to its disuse. **Depo-Provera** (a trademark name for medroxyprogesterone) was given the green light by the U.S. Food and Drug Administration (FDA) for use as a contraceptive. Soon afterwards, it was determined that this drug could also lead to birth defects. Also related to birth defects is the drug **thalidomide**. Thalidomide was prescribed to ease the discomforts of pregnancy and thought to be completely safe to the developing fetus. Thalidomide in one form is harmless, but it has an evil twin! Organic chemicals often have a "handedness" about them. **Nutrasweet** (aspartame) is the sweetest substance known. If we consider aspartame to be right-handed, somewhere there must be a left hand. The left hand of Nutrasweet is Bitrex, the bitterest substance known. You have heard of Nutrasweet because humans like sweetened food. The uses of Bitrex are undoubtedly more important. It is currently being added to an ever-growing number of household products that are not designed for human ingestion—one taste and little Billy won't be drinking the cool-looking green stuff anymore. Now, if we consider "good" thalidomide to be left-handed, then "evil" thalidomide is right-handed. It was trace amounts of the "right-handed" thalidomide that caused malformed limbs and other birth abnormalities. Even if you knew of a source of some pure "left-handed" thalidomide, would you buy it? Probably not.

12. **Members of different species**
    (A) cannot mate with one another
    (B) cannot mate to produce fertile offspring
    (C) may be designated by the same Latin name
    (D) do not live in the same geographical zones

In 1735, Swedish naturalist **Carolus Linnaeus** (1707-1778) classified all living things into general categories. From broadest to most specific, the categories are kingdom, phylum, class, order, family, genus, and species. Just as a person can be located by an address (planet, continent, country, state, county, city, street, number), any organism can be identified by its place in the Linnaeus classification. Moreover, the closer two

Five Kingdoms: An Illustrated Guide to the Phyla of Life on Earth (1988), by Lynn Margulis and Karlene V. Schwartz.

The mule, usually a hybrid betwen a male donkey and a mare, cannot reproduce.

organisms are placed within the classification, the more physically and genetically similar they will tend to be. Thus, at the most specialized level (species), two organisms are similar enough to mate and produce fertile offspring.

The five kingdoms are Plantae, Animalia, Fungi, Monera, and Protista. Plants are defined as organisms that manufacture their own food, while animals ingest particulate food. Fungi absorb their food in a ready-to-use form. The kingdom Monera, which includes all bacteria, is composed of single-celled organisms that do not have a true cellular nucleus. By contrast, Protista are single-celled organisms that do have a true nucleus.

The Linnaeus classification of human beings from kingdom to species goes like this: Animalia, Chordata, Mammalia, Primates, Hominidae, *Homo, sapiens*. Some prehistoric humans were of a different species or even a different genus, but still within the same family. Our closest living relatives are other members of the Primate order: the gibbons, orangutans, gorillas, and chimpanzees. All of these "great apes" are classified into the family Pongidae.

13. **Photosynthesis is**

    (A) the method by which the sun produces light
    (B) the method by which green plants convert sunlight to chemical energy
    (C) the method by which green plants convert carbon dioxide to oxygen
    (D) Both B and C

In the process of **photosynthesis**, green plants use sunlight, carbon dioxide, and water to produce oxygen and sugar molecules. The sugars are a form of stored chemical energy. It has been erroneously taught in high schools across America that photosynthesis allow plants to "convert" carbon dioxide to oxygen. The oxygen product actually comes from the water, not the carbon dioxide. This may seem like a picky detail, but it points out one of the basic tenets of survival: sharing. You cannot live

Almost two million species have been named. Many of these are now extinct, but new species are still being regularly discovered. Furthermore, some that were once considered close to extinction, including the bald eagle and the California gray whale, are now off the endangered species list.

WHY DO LEAVES TURN COLOR?

In the autumn, deciduous trees stop producing chlorophyll, so that other colors present in their leaves can be seen.
Photosynthesis cannot occur without green leaves, however, so the trees must survive off their stored energy during the fall and winter months.

LOOK MA, NO OXYGEN

Some photosynthesizers don't need water. Certain bacteria utilize hydrogen sulfide (H_2S) instead of water (H_2O) in photosynthesis. In this case, they give off sulfur gas, rather than oxygen gas as a product. Humans cannot use sulfur for the process of respiration. You wouldn't want to, even if you could—sulfur is the reason for the smell of rotten eggs.

without water and oxygen, while a plant cannot live without water and carbon dioxide. Let's pretend for a moment that you have been sentenced to be sealed in a container with a bucket of water and plants as your only oxygen source. The only way that you will survive is by sharing your water with the plants. Similarly, even if the plants could get up and get the water for themselves, they would be far better off giving some to you, too—you represent their only carbon dioxide source.

Plants produce not only oxygen, but sugar molecules as well. You are a sugar recycler. And what do you ultimately recycle sugar into? Carbon dioxide, of course, so that it can re-enter the plant, be re-converted into sugar, and begin the process again. This process is known as the **carbon cycle**.

A plant appears green because it absorbs all of the other colors of light that come from the sun, reflecting only the green portion. A substance in the plant called **chlorophyll** is responsible for both the green color and the process of photosynthesis. The sugars produced from this process are a type of food: that is, energy stored in chemical form. The plant carrying out photosynthesis can use this energy, as can the animals or people who come along and eat the plant.

14. **Animal testing**
    (A) is completely unnecessary
    (B) is absolutely necessary
    (C) can provide important medical information
    (D) is a twentieth-century invention

Without **animal testing** we would not have vaccines for such human life-threatening diseases as polio, hepatitus B, and rubella. We also would probably not have organ transplants, and might not even understand the principle of blood transfusion. Do these advances in human medicine warrant and justify the subjection of animals to sometimes cruel and often painful procedures? Decide for yourself. One thing about animal testing is certain: it is an extremely divisive issue.

The use of animals in medical experiments predates the birth of modern medicine. It was recognized early on that if you wanted to see if something worked, you could try it on the "guinea pig" first. As we have developed a greater understanding of the workings of the human body and its diseases, we have also developed a greater understanding of animals. We now understand that there is not much difference between humans and primates: therefore, whatever is done to a primate in the name of "research" ought to be something that we are willing to have done to ourselves. The perceived ignorance and/or arrogance of the stereotypical animal researcher is the lack of consideration displayed toward the animal test subjects. The perceived ignorance of the stereotypical animal rights activist is not "seeing the whole picture." If you listen carefully enough to proponents on both sides of this issue, you will find that there may be a middle ground between using animals in frivolous and cruel research and banning animal testing altogether.

Animal testing is but one issue in the wider arena of **medical ethics**. What action is justifiable to promote the survival of one human being? Are more drastic measures permissible when larger populations are involved? Who should receive what treatment? Who should decide what the right treatment is? Does a doctor have the right to assist in suicide? These questions have no easy answers; they may, in fact, have no correct answers. As medical technology has advanced, however, more of these difficult issues have surfaced for our contemplation.

15. Charles Darwin's *The Origin of Species*, published in 1859, introduced the concept of
   (A) a common ancestor of apes and humans ("the missing link")
   (B) survival of the fittest
   (C) mutations
   (D) heredity

Evolution is a name for the change in genetic makeup of a population over successive generations. Thus, an individual cannot evolve. In 1859, **Charles Darwin** (1809-1882) published the theory that evolution occurs by a process of **natural selection**, or survival of the fittest. When this theory was introduced, its primary competition was the concept of evolution by the inheritance of acquired characteristics, which was advanced by **Lamarck** (1744-1829). The Lamarckian theory proposed that physical changes in one generation are passed directly on to the next.

The limitations of Lamarck's theory are apparent if you apply it to the question of how zebras got their stripes. In Lamarck's version, zebras would have started out all white (or perhaps all black). Soon, however, they would realize that they stuck out like a sore thumb against the African grasslands, making easy marks for the marauding lions. Somehow, they would have willed themselves to develop camouflage. (Try harder! Harder! We're being eaten here!) A few perhaps succeeded,

Ancestors: The Search for Our Human Origins (1994), by Donald Johanson. This is a comprehensive and up-to-date summary of human evolution, by the paleoanthropologist who unearthed the famous fossil "Lucy."

No two zebras have the same pattern of stripes.

Doogie the spastic monkey is surprised to learn he has around 99% of the same genes as *Homo sapiens.*

and developed some streaky smudges. They passed on these smudges to their offspring, who added a few stripes of their own—and so on to the striped glory we see today. Darwin's explanation is much simpler and does not require zebra psychokinesis. Suppose that by random mutation, a striped zebra or two appeared. With their better camouflage, they would be far more likely to survive and reproduce than their buddies. In time, there would be a lot more stripy zebras than any other kind, because the plain ones had all been eaten before they could reproduce.

In 1871, Darwin explicitly presented the idea that humans had also evolved from other forms of life. His ideas were seen as heretical (p. 491), because they contradicted the literal Biblical version of human creation. However, it is possible simultaneously to accept the theory of evolution and to believe in a form of creationism, because evolution does not explain how life ultimately began on earth. It is much more difficult to reject evolution altogether, given the overwhelming evidence provided by the history of plant and animal domestication, the fossil record, genetics, and our own eyes.

16. **All of the following are true statements EXCEPT**

(A) DNA (deoxyribonucleic acid) is inherited
(B) DNA is only found in human beings
(C) DNA is different for every human being
(D) DNA is found in the form of a double helix

Rosalind Franklin and DNA (1975), by Anne Sayre. Sayre tells the story Franklin never could, and blasts Watson's chauvinistic account of the DNA breakthrough (*The Double Helix*, 1968) wide open.

Genetics is the study of heredity. Geneticists examine the similarities and differences observed in related organisms, which result from the interaction of inherited characteristics with the environment. The inherited traits are carried in **genes**, which are located within the **chromosomes** of all living organisms. Every cell in the human body, except eggs and sperm, contains an entire set (twenty-three pairs) of these chromosomes. Each gene is a segment of **deoxyribonucleic acid (DNA)** that "codes" for the synthesis of a particular protein. These proteins give rise to expressions of hereditary characteristics. The complete set of inheritable traits of an organism is termed its **genome.**

The DNA molecule has a double helix arrangement. For their elucidation of **Rosalind Franklin's** X-ray diffraction images, which revealed the helical structure of DNA, **Maurice Wilkins**, **James Watson** and

Francis Crick were awarded the Nobel Prize in 1962. Rosalind got bupkus (Nobel Prizes are not awarded posthumously).

Every individual, except an identical twin, has a distinct "DNA fingerprint." Identical twins, by the way, differ only in their actual fingerprints. It's true. A complete DNA fingerprint is the record of the entire genome of an individual. A DNA fingerprint is more incriminating than an actual fingerprint. First, there is no way for a criminal to remove his or her DNA fingerprint, but with a little concentrated acid and a high tolerance for pain, actual fingerprints are quite easily obliterated. Additionally, the odds against any two individuals having an identical DNA fingerprint is astronomical (less than one in eighty million millions, which is 200 times the number of humans that have ever lived).

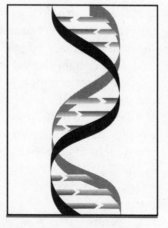

 The Fly (1986), with Jeff Goldblum and Geena Davis. Goldblum turns in a gruesomely funny performance as a scientist whose genes get swapped with a fly's.

17. **The human genome is**

    (A) a gene that only humans possess
    (B) the set of twenty-three chromosome pairs, each containing a collection of genes, of which all humans possess a version
    (C) a type of enzyme
    (D) a little guy that lives under a bridge

What the Manhattan Project did for physics, the **Human Genome Project** promises for biology, genetics, and medicine. The Human Genome Project, undertaken in 1990, is a fifteen-year, three-billion-dollar, government-funded effort to "map" the entire human genome. In other words, the result of the Human Genome Project will be the determination of the sequence of **base pairs** for all twenty-three chromosome pairs in the human body. In DNA, there are only four possible bases (also known as nucleotides): adenine, cytosine, guanine, and thymine. Each of these links up to a partner: adenine to thymine, cytosine to guanine. In the human genome there are over three billion base pairs.

Knowing the full sequence of base pairs may accelerate biomedical research into diseases that are currently known to be of genetic origin, as well as reveal other hereditary diseases. By determining the sequence of human DNA, it will also become possible to map the 10,000-plus genes

 So far, less than 5 percent of the human genome has been mapped out.

If the sequence of protein bases in the human genome were written out in full, the list would fill over five thousand books.

 Down's Syndrome occurs in individuals who possess an extra twenty-first chromosome.

YOU SAY TOMATO™

*Scientists can deliberately rearrange genes through a process known as **genetic engineering**. This technique can be used to modify bacteria, plants, and animals to have desired characteristics. The potential of the technique is enormous, but raises complex ethical and legal questions. Two controversial products now on the market are tomatoes genetically engineered to have a longer shelf life, and milk produced from cows given genetically engineered growth hormone.*

Book of Man (1995), by Walter Bodmer. This is a readable overview of the Human Genome Project, including a chapter on DNA fingerprinting.

that are responsible for human characteristics. If it is determined how certain diseases affect human DNA, it may be possible to develop treatments that prevent these effects. However, whether this massive effort will fulfill its potential is as yet unknown.

The determination of the entire human genome also has vast ethical consequences. If we are able to determine that criminality is gene-linked, should we institute laws that isolate humans with these genetic traits? Is the Human Genome Project thus a stepping stone to a totalitarian system in which the genetically favored rule? What will happen when genes can be first identified, then modified? If the results of the genome project are used judiciously, we all stand to benefit. However, if the results are used by factions to "prove" such things as supposed sexual or racial superiority, we all lose.

The human "G"nome

18. **Which of the following accurately describes the difference between identical and fraternal twins?**

(A) Identical twins—one egg and one sperm; fraternal twins—one egg and two sperms

(B) Identical twins—one egg and one sperm; fraternal twins—two eggs and two sperms

(C) Identical twins—two eggs and one sperm; fraternal twins—two eggs and two sperms

(D) Identical twins—one egg and two sperms; fraternal twins—two eggs and two sperms

In nature, there are many ways in which organisms reproduce themselves. All of these methods fall into one of two categories: sexual and asexual. In **asexual reproduction** there is no "female" or "male" distinction, and the cells produced are identical to the parent cells. By contrast, **sexual reproduction** makes genetic variation possible, because the male and female parent cells each contribute hereditary information. This explains why we aren't all clones of one another. For human sexual reproduction, genetic information is carried in the male sperm (produced in the testes) and the female ovum (produced in the ovaries).

Double the fun

ARTIFICIAL REPRODUCTION

*Various medical techniques are now available for couples who cannot conceive in the age-old manner. **Artificial insemination** with fresh or frozen sperm is the simplest technique. **In vitro fertilization** is also possible. In this method, an egg is extracted from the ovary, fertilized with sperm in a glass dish, and then reimplanted into the womb. The first such "test tube baby" was Louise Brown, born on July 25, 1978. In the future, reproduction may also be possible through cloning or egg fusion.*

Usually, a woman's ovaries produce only one ovum (egg) each month, but sometimes two are produced. If the two eggs are fertilized by two sperm, two individual **zygotes (embryos)** develop together in the womb. The result is fraternal (nonidentical) twins with different genetic information. Less frequently, a zygote that has been created from a single sperm and a single ovum spontaneously divides into two separate zygotes. The result is identical twins, each carrying the same genetic information.

During the first few weeks of pregnancy, the cells contained in the embryo begin to specialize into three layers: the ectoderm, which is the source of hair, nails, the brain, and the central nervous system; the mesoderm, from which muscles, bones, and blood are derived; and the endoderm, which later contributes to the respiratory and digestive systems. After eight weeks or so, the embryo becomes a **fetus**, a recognizably human organism, as opposed to the rather generic-looking embryo. This is also about when it starts kicking.

The Asian (Indian) elephant stays pregnant for as long as two years.

Twins (1988), with Danny DeVito and Arnold Schwarzenegger. This movie has an unlikely set of twins and an even more unlikely, but still entertaining, plot.

19. Which of the following connects bones to muscles?

(A) Cartilage
(B) Tendons
(C) Ligaments
(D) All of the above

A.D.A.M.: The Inside Story. A guided tour of human anatomy, this CD-ROM is used as a teaching tool in many American medical colleges today, but it's just as accessible to casual browsers.

THE NAVICULAR

The navicular bone in the hand is the only bone in the human body that does not have a direct blood supply. In many instances, if this bone is broken, it will not heal, leaving you with two naviculars (or three if you count the one in your other hand).

Lynn Swann risks life and ligaments to make this catch.

Having a skeleton is a very useful thing for a being that insists on walking upright. The human consists of over two hundred bones, but every human does not necessarily have the same number: you might have an extra rib or finger. Connecting your bones together, you have a series of joints which are either synovial (fluid), cartilaginous (made out of **cartilage**), or fibrous (made out of collagen fibers). Allowing motion of your bones is the job of your muscles. Muscles are connected to bones via **tendons**. **Ligaments** are fibrous attachments between two bones. The anterior cruciate ligament (ACL), the one that you really don't want to tear if you are a football player, connects the femur (thigh bone) to the tibia (big bone in the shin).

In order for your muscles to work, they usually must receive an electrical signal from the brain. These electrical signals are carried via the **central and peripheral nervous systems**. Your central nervous system is your brain and spinal cord, your peripheral nervous system is all the rest of your nerves. If you took your entire nervous system out and laid the nerves end to end they would cover a distance of over fifteen miles. If you didn't, they wouldn't.

20. Dentistry was first practiced

(A) before 2900 B.C.
(B) in the Middle Ages
(C) in the 1700s
(D) in the 1800s

Dentistry is the science of teeth, while **orthodontics** is the science of straightening teeth. If you don't have teeth, you can't chew; if your teeth aren't straight, you can't chew effectively. For these very good reasons, dentistry and orthodontics were developed long ago. At least as early as 2900 B.C., the first dental caries (cavities) were filled by the Sumerians. In 1790, the dental drill was invented. One hundred and sixty-seven years later the high-speed "painless" dental drill was developed.

For thousands of years dentistry consisted of removing rotten teeth, which could be done by anyone with a strong forearm and a pair of pliers, and making up false ones out of bones, ivory, or wood. The local barber often did double duty as a dentist. It was not until 1728 that dentistry was even regarded as a science, and the possibility of preventive dentistry was considered. During the westward expansion of the U.S., dentistry was a spectator sport. Tooth pulling was advertised, then performed on Saturday nights in the town square. Fifty years later, we finally classified teeth into molars, cuspids, bicuspids, and incisors. Another fifty years after that, nitrous oxide—laughing gas—was made available to the masses as a dental anesthetic. Today, the cause of dental cavities has been identified as a metabolic by-product of sugar produced by the bacteria that live in the mouth. Elimination of these bacteria, such as by fluoride treatment, can prevent tooth decay. In 1945, the first U.S. water supply was fluorinated in an effort to safeguard against tooth decay.

Little Shop of Horrors (1986), with Rick Moranis. Forget the plant. Steve Martin is the real star of the movie, as the most hilariously demented dentist-cum-Elvis ever to grace the silver screen.

McTeague (1899), by Frank Norris. Materialism and dentistry make for bad marriages and big trouble in this late-nineteenth-century classic.

21. Smoking is bad for you because

(A) it lengthens the healing time for bone fractures
(B) nicotine is addictive
(C) it impairs the normal functioning of your lungs and is a known risk factor for lung cancer
(D) All of the above

Respiration—the act of breathing—is an **involuntary** process. This is a good thing. Breathing is a combination of **inspiration** (breathing in) and **expiration** (breathing out). Inspiration is an active process—that is, it takes energy. When the body senses a need for oxygen, a signal is sent from the brain to the diaphragm telling it to contract (or flatten).

It is estimated that around thirty million Americans have dental phobia, which prevents them from seeking any dental treatments whatsoever.

"Smoker's cough" is caused by a buildup of mucus in the lungs. You may have noticed that smokers cough more in the morning than at any other time of the day. This is because as a smoker sleeps (and, therefore, does not smoke), the ciliated cells resume their appointed task of cleaning up the lungs—causing a buildup of mucus. When smokers awaken, their lungs send the message that they have extra mucus, and the hack commences.

This contraction causes a space to empty in the chest, giving the lungs space to expand. Seizing this opportunity, the lungs expand, and air rushes in to fill them. A bunch of little capillaries in contact with the lungs pick up the oxygen from the air and exchange it for carbon dioxide. The oxygen is then carried by the blood from the lungs to the rest of the body, where it is used to break down sugars into water and carbon dioxide. Taken as a whole, the series of chemical reactions by which this process occurs is essentially the opposite of photosynthesis (p. 217). The carbon dioxide product of these reactions is transferred back into the blood and returned to the lungs, where it is exchanged for new oxygen.

When the body senses that it has enough oxygen (or too much carbon dioxide), it stops sending a signal to the diaphragm. The diaphagm relaxes, forcing the air (which is now lower in oxygen and higher in carbon dioxide than when it came into the lungs) out of the lungs. This process of expiration is a passive process—it does not require energy.

Air is moved around in your lungs by little hairlike structures called **cilia**. These cilia also function to clean particulates out of the air, by producing mucus that traps the particles. When you smoke, you temporarily paralyze these cells so that they can no longer do their job. This leads to a diminished ability of your lungs to exchange oxygen for carbon dioxide, as well as to an incapacitation of the lung-cleaning system. Besides impeding your normal respiratory function and increasing your risk of lung cancer, smoking has been shown to lengthen the time for healing bone fractures. Broken bones take up to 50 percent longer to heal in smokers. Finally, tobacco contains **nicotine**, a physically and psychologically addictive drug. As the health risks to smokers and their associates have become better understood, the habit has become less socially acceptable. At one time 55 percent of Americans were smokers. Today, that figure is less than 20 percent and dropping.

Star Wars (1977), with Mark Hamill and Carrie Fisher. Arch-villain Darth Vader wears a respirator/vocal box that amplifies his every breath into hissing noises.

22. All of the following may be caused by nutritional deficiency EXCEPT

(A) anemia (low red blood cell count)
(B) a malformed skeleton and stunted growth
(C) disturbances in vision and brain functioning
(D) cancer

Humans are **omnivores**. This means that we have two choices for our meals: eat a food-maker (plant), or eat a food-eater (animal). Vegetarians recognize the foolishness of using a go-between, while the rest of us try not to think about it. When we eat, the useful chemicals from the food are separated out and categorized by our **digestive systems**. The rest, along with the chemical by-products of the useful stuff, are expelled from our systems. The four basic categories of useful chemicals are **carbohydrates** (sugars), **proteins**, lipids (**fats**), and **minerals** (dirt). Carbohydrates are complex sugars stored by the body for short-term use. As needed, they are broken down into simple sugars and used. Fats are longer-term energy storage systems. If you suddenly demand a lot of energy from your body, and it has exhausted its supply of simple sugars and carbohydrates, it will begin the conversion and breakdown processing of fats. The proteins that you eat fall into one of two categories: as-is or convertible. Some proteins, such as certain vitamins, are used by your body in the form in which they are ingested. Other proteins are broken down to supply the pieces for the proteins that your body wants to make for itself. The final chemical category, dirt, is the source of the majority of the inorganic chemicals that your body needs, such as minerals.

The lack of any of these four types of food in your diet can result in a **nutritional deficiency**. Deficiencies can cause health problems ranging from mild to fatal. Anemia is a result of low iron content. Stunted growth and skeletal deformities can be caused by rickets, a vitamin D deficiency. Lack of vitamin A may result in blindness or disturbances in brain functioning.

23. Anesthetics were first used during operations in the

(A) seventeenth century
(B) eighteenth century
(C) nineteenth century
(D) twentieth century

"Nutrition," by the Dead Milkmen on the album *Big Lizard in My Backyard* (1985). The rest of the album is equally educational.

People suffering from the psychological disorders of **bulimia** and **anorexia nervosa** deliberately deprive themselves of food and thus, essential nutrients. The resulting nutritional deficiencies can cause anemia, hypoglycemia, hormonal abnormalities, cardiovascular dysfunction, and death.

DON'T TRY THIS AT HOME

An early study of digestion was performed by William Beaumont in the 1800s. His patient and experimental subject, Alexis St. Martin, had been accidentally shot in the stomach. The wound healed, but left a hole through which the functioning of the stomach could be viewed. Beaumont's subsequent observations contributed to the modern understanding of the digestive process.

How would you like to undergo a surgical procedure without the aid of **anesthetics**? The invention of surgical anesthetics was the first major contribution that American medicine made to the world, but human surgical procedures predate anesthetics by several thousand years. Around 1700 B.C., the Code of Hammurabi specified a fair price for surgery (even then, controlling medical expenses must have been problematic), and an Egyptian medical papyrus from about the same time lays out procedures for many different operations. The great surgical advances of our times would not have been possible, however, without the development of anesthesia.

No gloves, no masks, no mercy

Sixteenth-century doctors poured boiling oil into gunshot wounds (without anesthesia, mind you) in a futile—and often fatal—effort to clean them out. In 1537, the young French barber-surgeon Ambroise Paré ran out of oil during the siege of Turin by the French Army, and in desperation, made up a soothing potion of egg yolks, rose oil, and turpentine. To his astonishment, the patients receiving this new treatment fared far better than the unlucky ones who had been burned with oil. Texts written by this pioneering surgeon were used as medical standards for centuries to follow.

Ether was first synthesized in 1540, while **nitrous oxide** was invented in 1772. Both were popular recreational drugs of the times: laughing gas parties became common among students, and traveling quacks would let the local yokels sniff some ether in exchange for a few pennies. Curiously, not until 1842 did Crawford Williamson Long, a native of Georgia, became the first doctor to use ether as a general surgical anesthetic. Dentist Horace Wells noticed the anesthetic effects of laughing gas in 1844, but failed to convince anyone that it was effective, due to a bungled demonstration of a tooth extraction. It was Bostoner **William Morton**, in 1846, who was the first to publish an article about the effects of ether as a general anesthetic. As a consequence, he is often credited as the founder of the field of anesthesiology.

In the same year that Morton described ether, Scottish physician James Simpson discovered that chloroform was a better anesthetic than ether or nitrous oxide. However, ether was the "anesthetic of choice" until 1884, when facts already known to the population at large (that cocaine was an extremely good local anesthetic) were finally accepted by the medical community. By 1924, ether had largely been replaced by other drugs in the anesthetization of patients, and a system of controlled anesthesia was in place.

 Coma (1978), with Genevieve Bujold. A deranged doctor steals patients' organs by inducing comas with poison anesthesia in this creepy hospital thriller.

24. **The left hemisphere of the brain controls all of the following abilities EXCEPT**

    (A) speaking
    (B) spatial construction
    (C) reading and writing
    (D) calculating and analytical thinking

We all know that we have brains, but that is about the limit of our understanding of this little five-pound marvel. Here's what we have managed to figure out so far. This brain thing seems to use biochemistry in conjunction with electrical impulses in order to make its container (the organism) use the rest of its parts to interact with its environment.

In a human being, there are two sets of electrical impulse circuitries (nervous systems). These two are called the **central nervous system** and the **peripheral nervous system**. The peripheral nervous system controls two circuitry subsets: the autonomic and the somatic, or the involuntary and the voluntary, respectively. The **somatic** system controls voluntary actions. The **autonomic** system is further separated into two systems, labeled the sympathetic and the parasympathetic. These two systems work antagonistically to regulate the systems and organs of the body. A parasympathetic signal tells your heart to slow down, relax, take a load off. A sympathetic signal tells your heart to speed up, danger is

 Brainstorm (1983), with Christopher Walken and Natalie Wood. Recorded brainwave patterns are the ultimate "virtual reality." The high-tech visual effects in this film are pretty wild.

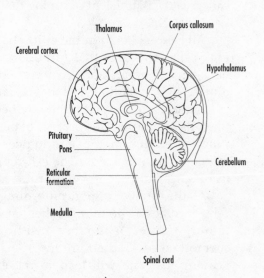

Thalamus
Corpus callosum
Cerebral cortex
Hypothalamus
Pituitary
Pons
Cerebellum
Reticular formation
Medulla
Spinal cord

Handedness appears to be unique to humans. Between 4 and 40 percent of all humans are left-handed: the exact figure is hard to determine, because the majority rule of the right-handers tends to suppress left-handed tendencies. The word "sinister" comes from the Latin for "left," while "right" is described by the more complimentary term "dextrous." The specialization of the brain hemispheres seems to differ between right- and left-handers.

everywhere, stay alert, watch out, run away. During those fight-or-flight situations it is important that your body accelerate its movement of blood, oxygen, and other nutrients throughout the body. However, it is not so important that your body finishes digesting the hoagie that you had for lunch. Therefore, while your sympathetic nervous system tells your heart to work harder, it tells your digestive system to slow down, or even to stop altogether.

The brain has two hemispheres: right and left. From direct experimentation, it has been found that areas in the right hemisphere influence spatial construction and recognition, while the left hemisphere contains centers involved in language processing and mathematics. The two hemispheres communicate through the **corpus callosum**.

25. Cancer is

(A) contagious
(B) incurable
(C) irreversible
(D) inevitable

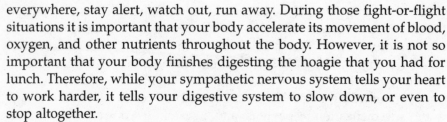

Medicine Man (1992), with Sean Connery. The lush and mysterious rainforest (p. 146) may well contain a cure for cancer.

Cancer is any **malignant** (harmful) and invasive growth or tumor in the body. This definition covers an extremely wide spectrum, so if you are holding your breath waiting for a cure for cancer, you can let the breath out right now. There is not one single kind, one single cause, nor one single treatment program for cancer. Thus, to claim that one is going to cure cancer is the equivalent of saying that one is going to cure all viral infections (p. 212).

All cancers begin in the **epithelial cells**. Epithelial cells are the "lining" cells—the cells that form a border between different organs or between an organ and a cavity. For some reason, these cells often mutate into cells that no longer play by the rules. In the normal circumstance, a cell is pressured into becoming a particular type of cell by the cells around it. This process of peer pressure is known as **induction**. When a cell does not give in to peer pressure and conform, it tends to forget where it belongs. The cell reproduces itself, as all cells do—but its offspring also do not conform.

As the number of nonconforming cells multiplies, a colony of these cells becomes a community, then an entire "nation"—in other words, a **tumor**. Cancer is doubly insidious. Removal methods (surgery, chemotherapy, radiation) must extract all of the cancerous cells. Leaving just one will lead to the eventual growth of a new tumor.

YES, CHEEZ-WHIZ

In laboratory tests on mice, certain fatty acids have been claimed to inhibit some forms of cancer. Good sources of these cancer-fighting chemicals include Cheez Whiz and grilled hamburgers.

Secondly, cancer cells do not seem to age. Therefore, you cannot rely upon the natural lifespan of a cell to eliminate the cancerous cells, as you can with many other diseases.

26. The "CAT" in "CAT scan" stands for
(A) cranial activity transmission
(B) cortical analysis test
(C) computerized axial tomography
(D) cerebral auditory topography

Medical techniques that do not require cutting open the body are favored by both doctors and patients. Several such **noninvasive** medical diagnostic techniques have been developed. Perhaps the most familiar is X-ray analysis. The short wavelength of an **X-ray** allows it to pass unaffected through human soft tissue. However, when it encounters dense material, such as a bone or a tooth, the X-ray is absorbed or reflected. A photographic film is placed on the opposite side of the patient and gets developed by the X-rays that pass through the less dense regions. The result is an X-ray photograph in which dark regions indicate dense materials and light regions indicate less dense materials. (The opposite is true in the negative, of course.) An extension of X-ray technology is the computerized axial tomography, or **CAT**, scan. In this X-ray method, the photographic film and the X-ray source are rotated about the patient in order to generate a 360-degree X-ray. This is particularly useful in the examination of skull and spinal injuries.

Ultrasound is another noninvasive procedure used for many diagnostic examinations. One application is to examine fetal development within the womb. In this case, ultrasonic vibrations are sent into the abdomen of a pregnant woman. These vibrations are deflected by the fetus, and an oscilloscope or similar device is used to convert the distorted sound impulses into a picture.

Newer on the scene is the technique of **magnetic resonance imaging (MRI)**. This is a technique that uses an extremely large magnetic field to probe the differences in tiny magnetic fields of individual hydrogen atoms in the human body. By successively measuring individual magnetic properties in thin cross-sections, a three-dimensional map of the magnetic fields in the body is produced. This map will show any abnormalities indicative of a disease, tumor, or internal injury.

Total Recall (1990), with Arnold Schwarzenegger. The futuristic version of the X-ray airport scanner is a walk-through model that literally strips you to the bones.

27. Your immune system helps defend against
    (A) disease
    (B) infection
    (C) allergens
    (D) All of the above

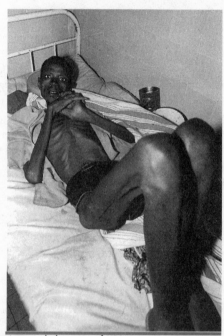

A man in the late stages of AIDS

I CAN'T GET OFF MY DUFF, I'M ALLERGIC

....

It is possible to be allergic to exercise! After strenuous exercise, some people show symptoms typical of severe allergic reactions, such as hives and choking.

The Boy in the Plastic Bubble (1976), with John Travolta. A boy must live inside an artificial immune system, i.e., a big plastic bag, but that's not the point. It stars John Travolta!

The human body is a remarkable machine with incredible recovery and recuperation abilities. The basis of these abilities is the **immune system**. This system is responsible for the production of the body's guardians: **antibodies**. When a foreign substance—an **antigen**—is detected by the body's immune system, the immune system responds by making antibodies for that antigen. What makes this system so remarkable is that for each different antigen, the body is able to produce a different antibody. Furthermore, if the antigen has not been exposed to the immune system before, the immune system can quickly learn to produce antibodies for this new antigen. The only times that the immune system is not successful in the production of antibodies is when the number of antigens is so great (or so varied) that the antibody production facilities are already operating at maximum capacity. This is the case with AIDS (p. 213). An infection can also become lethal if the infectious agent is toxic enough to cause nearly instant death, or if the infectious agent is able to mutate itself so rapidly that it is continually unrecognizable to the immune system. **HIV** is an example of the latter case.

In order for the immune system to operate effectively, it must not produce a response that damages the body (such as an allergy attack) and it must have a fine-tuned mechanism for determining what is "self" and what is foreign (antigenic). Occasionally, immune mechanisms go out of control, and the immune system comes to see things that are "self" as foreign. This is termed an **auto-immune** disease. Examples include rheumatoid arthritis, rheumatic fever, lupus, and ulcerative colitis. Auto-immune reactions have also been linked to the process of aging.

28. The amount of cholesterol in your blood

(A) affects the narrowing of coronary arteries
(B) may protect against diseases of the artery
(C) is solely related to what you eat
(D) Both A and B, depending on the kind of cholesterol

The body's **circulatory system** distributes blood to its furthest extremities, and cycles it through the lungs for oxygenation. The circulatory system relies primarily on two forces: gravity and the power of the body's internal flow pump, the heart. The heart is self-regulating, thanks to the sinoatrial (SA) node, or internal pacemaker. Without this pacemaker, the heart would operate at a higher speed, causing an increase in pulse and a cumulative increase in blood pressure. An artificial pacemaker simply does the job of a normally functioning SA node, providing a rhythm set to the metronome of the artificial pacemaker.

Veins carry blood to the heart, while **arteries** carry blood away from the heart. Most veins carry deoxygenated blood and most arteries carry oxygenated blood. In practical terms, this means that the heart pumps blood into the arteries and from there into the capillaries. Blood flows from capillaries into veins. But how does the blood find its way back to the heart? While the pressure created by a pumping heart is great enough to drive blood through the arteries, venal pressure is extremely low. Veins overcome this difficulty through the ingenous use of gates (valves). If you open a gate, people will rush through (until they meet the next gate). The same phenomenon allows veins to overcome the forces of gravity and return blood to the heart.

Cholesterol is a substance produced by the liver. The amount of cholesterol in your blood depends strongly on the kinds of foods you eat, but

French fries are a big hit on the Champs Elysees.

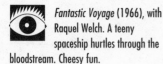

Fantastic Voyage (1966), with Raquel Welch. A teeny spaceship hurtles through the bloodstream. Cheesy fun.

may also be affected by heredity or disease. Too much cholesterol in the form of low-density lipoproteins (LDLs) can accumulate on the walls of your arteries, narrowing them so that blood pressure rises. However, high-density lipoprotein (HDL) cholesterol is thought to protect against arterial disease.

29. **Which of the following have been suggested as contributors to Alzheimer's disease?**
    (A) Eating from aluminum containers
    (B) Hereditary factors
    (C) Blows to the head
    (D) All of the above

"When I'm Sixty-Four" by the Beatles on the album *Sergeant Pepper's Lonely Heart's Club Band* (1967). Great song by the legendary band whose remaining members rapidly approach the swingin' sixties themselves.

Gerontology is the study of **aging**, the inevitable and irreversible process by which cells and organisms move toward death. Naturally, understanding the aging process—in order to be able to slow it down or prevent it altogether—is of great scientific interest. Unfortunately, this understanding is far from being achieved. Several theories have been proposed for why cells age. One is based on chemical arguments: over time, some toxic material may build up in the cell, or some essential chemical may be depleted. Genetic factors such as increasing errors in DNA replication or a preprogrammed "age gene" have also been implicated. Ironically, the "fountain of youth" may be discovered in cancer cells, which do not seem to age as other cells do.

PROGERIA

Progeria is a tragic illness. Children with this disease age much more rapidly than normal, coming to resemble very old men and women when they are not even to the normal age of puberty.

Former president Ronald Reagan was recently diagnosed with Alzheimer's disease.

In humans, aging makes people prone to **Alzheimer's disease**, a degenerative condition of the brain characterized by memory loss, disorientation, and changes in personality. Alzheimer's was virtually unknown a generation ago, for two possible reasons. Diseases that are curable today may have shortened the average lifespan such that

Blade Runner (1982), with Harrison Ford and Rutger Hauer. Ford chases soulless but way-cool artificial replicas of humans. See the director's cut if you have a chance.

Alzheimer's did not have a chance to announce itself. Contrarily, it is entirely conceivable that people have died of Alzheimer's disease for millenia, and we just didn't recognize it as such. Whichever is the case, Alzheimer's is now recognized as a serious affliction. In the United States, there are currently more Alzheimer's patients than there are AIDS and AIDS-related patients. Little is currently known about Alzheimer's disease, other than the fact that there are at least two forms—early onset, or hereditary Alzheimer's, and "normal" Alzheimer's. Researchers in this area have posited everything from the aluminum in the containers of TV dinners to blows to the head as causes of this disease. There is no known cure.

Cocoon (1985), with Don Ameche and Brian Dennehy. Aliens visit a Florida retirement community.

30. Medical technology has created viable artificial versions of all of the following EXCEPT the

(A) heart
(B) kidney
(C) knee
(D) brain

As we have become more knowledgeable and prosperous, we have found yet another way to stave off the Grim Reaper: artificial parts. At first, we ransacked the bodies of the dead for usable equipment. Now, in some cases, we have evolved from used-parts shoppers to buyers of factory knockoffs—given the scarcity of quality used parts that "fit."

The beginnings of the mechanization of the human body date back to 1667, when chemist Robert Boyle demonstrated that animals could be kept alive by artificial respiration. The application of this discovery came 260 years later, with the development of the **iron lung**—an external respiratory system. The first artificial parts implanted in the human body were those that did not utilize a blood supply: the artificial hip joint in 1905, followed by the first total artificial hip replacement in 1938. The first artificial organ, the kidney, was developed in 1913. The kidney dialysis machine was developed thirty years later, and home dialysis units were introduced in 1964. The **heart-lung machine** was developed in 1951 and used for the first time in 1953. In 1969, Cooley and Liotta implanted the first artificial heart into Haskell Karp. Mr. Karp lived almost three days. This was followed by William DeVries heading a team of surgeons to put the **Jarvik 7** heart into Barney Clark in 1982. Mr. Clark lived an additional 117 days.

Transplantation from other human bodies continues to be an alternative path for organ replacement. Most of the early success in organ transplantation is due to Alexis Carrel, who developed techniques for rejoining severed blood vessels in 1905 and performed the first successful heart surgery (on a dog) in 1914. In 1967, **Christian Barnard** (1923-) performed the first partially successful heart transplant operation. The patient, Louis Washkansky, lived for eighteen days. This was followed in 1968 by Barnard's second attempt—this time, the patient lived seventy-four days. **Rejection** of the foreign component by the body must be avoided for both transplanted and artificial organs. For transplanted organs, matching of blood groups and immunosuppressants are used. For artificial organs, special biocompatible materials are used.

31. **In the late 1800s, Sigmund Freud developed the theories of**

    (A) psychosis
    (B) psychoanalysis
    (C) psychiatry
    (D) psychology

"Sometimes a cigar is just a cigar."

What comes to mind when you think of a psychologist? A leather couch, inkblot tests, a Germanic voice murmuring "I see. Tell me more"? If so, you have **Sigmund Freud** (1856-1939) to thank for your caricature. Freud did not invent psychology. His contribution to psychology was the theory of **psychoanalysis**. Psychoanalysis holds that feelings and reactions that you have today are directly related to experiences that you have had earlier in life. Thus, all current psychological maladies have really been constructed over time. Much like Einstein, who is widely regarded as the "father of quantum mechanics," even though he spent much of his life trying to prove that quantum mechanics was a sham, Freud is often called the "father of psychology"—despite the fact that many modern psychological theories conflict with the psychoanalytic viewpoint.

Freud postulated three components of personality: the **id**, **ego**, and **superego**. The id is concerned solely with the gratification of basic desires like food and sex. The ego, however, realizes that reality sometimes gets in the way of gratification, and develops problem-solving techniques to deal with the environment. The superego impinges an additional restriction: moral considerations. By way of example, a baby's main concern is being fed by others; toddlers, on the other hand, become quite ingenious at getting what they want, regardless of the obstacles. Only later on in life (in some cases, never) do children listen to parental instructions about appropriate behavior and gain an understanding of punishment and guilt.

Freud also proposed stages of personality development. In the **oral stage**, pleasure is derived from the sensory stimulation of the mouth, such as in nursing or sucking one's thumb. The second stage is the **anal stage**, in which children are fascinated with "potty" products. During the **phallic stage**, pleasure becomes centered on the genitals. The next phase is the **Oedipal stage**, in which the child is hypothesized to form her first love relationship, with the parent of the opposite sex. Finally, adult personality should take hold, after a latency phase. However, traumatic events are thought to be able to "fix" or trap a person in a certain stage of development. Thus, we now freely use the term "anally fixated" to describe people who are metaphorically "unwilling to let go." Psychoanalytic therapy is intended to unearth these early events and work through the conflicts, so that development can continue normally.

32. **Which of the following describes the principles of behaviorism, or learning theory?**
    (A) Monkey see, monkey do.
    (B) If the carrot doesn't work, use the stick.
    (C) The squeaky wheel gets the grease.
    (D) All of the above

B.F. Skinner (1904-) advanced a model of human behavior that was quite different from the psychoanalytic model. While Freud sought to explain patterns of behavior by relating them to unconscious motivations and stages of psychosexual development, Skinner argued that behavior was due mostly to outside, or environmental, forces. To Skinner, and other proponents of **behaviorism**, or **learning theory**, behavior consists of a series of **responses** to environmental **stimuli**. Thus, a squeaky wheel (stimulus) can trigger one of several responses (grease the wheel, replace the wheel, complain about the wheel to someone nearby). Some stimulus-response pairs are **conditioned**: that is, we have learned to associate them together. This is why, for example, some people feel nervous or nauseous as soon as they enter an airport: from past experience, they associate

Equus (1977), with Richard Burton. Contains all the classic elements: repression, Oedipus complex, and psychologist-patient interaction. And just like psychoanalysis itself, it takes a long time to conclude.

"The End" by the Doors on their debut album, *The Doors* (1968). Jim Morrison erupts into an incomprehensible scream at mommy at the end of an Oedipal rant. Nice bass line too.

"Basket Case" by Green Day on their album *Dookie* (1994). Only a psychoanalyst would give an unqualified "yes" to the question "Do you have the time/To listen to me whine?"

CLEVER HANS

Clever Hans was a horse that supposedly knew how to count. When Hans was given a number, he would tap his hoof the appropriate number of times, with impressive accuracy. It was found, however, that the horse was actually responding to a slight, involuntary tension in the trainer's body. When the correct number was reached, the trainer would relax. So although Clever Hans couldn't really count, he was still quite clever to be able to pick up on this small stimulus and generate the appropriate response.

 In Japan, the saying about the squeaky wheel goes more like "The nail that sticks up gets hammered"—a rather different outlook on individualism versus conformity than that prevalent in the United States.

everything having to do with flying (stimuli) with physical discomfort (response).

When choices of responses are available, how do we learn which responses are socially acceptable? By the "monkey see, monkey do" principle, behavior is learned by **observation** of others, who act as **models** of correct behavior. Our earliest models are often our parents. Parents usually have an intuitive understanding of another behaviorist principle: that actions can be influenced by **positive reinforcement** (rewards) and **negative reinforcement** (punishments). Skinner showed that animal behavior could be easily modified by these techniques. Thus, he taught pigeons to "count" and "read" by

B.F. Skinner: "The real problem is not whether machines think, but whether men do."

rewarding appropriate responses with food. Another famous example was the dog experiments of Ivan Pavlov, in which Pavlov formed a conditioned response in the dogs, so that they salivated at the ring of a bell which was associated with a meal. However, behaviorist explanations do not fully explain the unique properties of the human mind—its abilities to learn and change.

33. **Which of the following statements about perception (the way people see the world) is most accurate?**

(A) Perception is a reflection of reality.
(B) Perception is affected by culture, experiences, emotions, and the environment around you.
(C) Perception is an innate, biologically inherited ability.
(D) Perception takes place only on a conscious level.

Cognitive psychology describes how humans acquire knowledge and put this knowledge into action. The basic theoretical construct of cognitive psychologists is **information-processing theory**, which, in its broadest sense, implies that all cognitive processes can be thought of as a series of sequential transformations of an abstract code, analogous to a computer program. The field of cognitive psychology is so new that the earliest cognitive psychologists were not psychologists at all, but rather linguists such as Noam Chomsky and computer scientists interested in artificial intelligence. **Perception** can be defined as the input in our brain's computer program. How we perceive things, however, is not necessarily how they really are. Perception is affected by culture, experiences, emotions, and your environment, and takes place on both conscious and subconscious levels.

Cognitive psychologists divide all knowledge into two types: declarative and procedural. **Declarative knowledge** refers to factual information that is somewhat static and inherently describable. The knowledge that George Washington was the first president of the United States is an example of declarative knowledge. You probably already knew this, you will probably know this until your death, and it is unlikely to change or become obsolete. Additionally, it is unlikely that any other pieces of information can be garnered that would improve your knowledge of this fact. **Procedural knowledge** refers to knowledge that is used to perform skillful actions. Whereas declarative knowledge tends to be static, procedural knowledge is dynamic and often indescribable.

34. **You are the proud parent of a seven-month-old baby boy whose favorite toy is a stuffed cow, "Osborne." He has not yet mastered the concept of object permanence, which means that**
    (A) he does not search for Osborne when the cow is out of view
    (B) he cries when Osborne is in another room
    (C) he sometimes mistakes another toy for Osborne
    (D) he is afraid of real cows

Observations of infant children by French psychologist Jean Piaget (p. life) did much to explain the development of thought processes, or **cognition**. Rejecting the strict behaviorist interpretation that the environment ultimately controls all actions, Piaget argued that it was an individual's **interaction** with the environment that was all-important. He used this

Subliminal perception is the term for observation without conscious awareness. Savvy advertising executives grabbed onto this idea immediately, and set out deliberately to send messages pitched just below our level of consciousness. Although subliminal advertising has been banned in broadcast media, it is still widely used in print media. For example, close inspection of a famous ad for an alcoholic beverage reveals the word "sex" in one of the ice cubes.

The Lawnmower Man (1992), with Pierce Brosnan, based on the book by Stephen King. Virtual reality and the manipulation of perception.

In a Different Voice (1982), by Carol Gilligan. From the viewpoint of developmental psychology, this influential book explores how gender may affect perceptions and personalities.

idea to propose stages of mental development in children. The first stage, from birth to about age two, is the **sensorimotor** stage. As the name suggests, most of the child's thoughts are concerned with sensory experiences and motor actions. Only toward the end of this stage do children master concepts such as object permanence (that objects do not cease to exist if hidden from view).

The second stage of mental development, from about age two to age seven, is **preoperational**. In this stage, children understand the use of symbols (words, toys standing for real-life objects) but maintain an egocentric view of the world.

In the third stage, the **concrete operational** stage from about age seven to age eleven, children can solve conceptual problems such as size relationships, conservation, and classification. Finally, in the fourth, **formal operational** stage of development from about age twelve to adulthood, abstract logic can be used to solve hypothetical problems.

35. **All of the following mental states can be influenced by medication EXCEPT**

    (A) clinical depression
    (B) hyperactivity
    (C) multiple personality disorder
    (D) mental retardation

The Madness of King George (1994), with Nigel Hawthorne. The perceived madness of George III (1760-1820) did much to heighten British public awareness of insanity. George may have suffered from porphyria, a rare disease which causes periodic episodes of mental dysfunction.

One Flew Over the Cuckoo's Nest (1975), with Jack Nicholson. Randall Patrick MacMurphy (check out the acronym) exerts much energy against evil Nurse Ratched and those who would remove from him his love of *fast living*.

Psychiatry involves the use of medical techniques to treat psychological problems. While psychiatrists are medical doctors (M.D.s), psychologists are Ph.D.s. This not only explains the variation in treatment practices between these two professions, but also the difference in bills—psychiatrists have to pay off their medical school loans.

The modern science of psychiatry originated in the asylums of Europe, when doctors began to classify and treat different types of mental illnesses. **Electroshock therapy** and **partial lobotomy** were two early biophysical methods of treatment. Today, however, psychiatry is associated mostly with chemical treatments, or drugs. The first successful drug treatment of a mental disorder was that of general paresis, a disease characterized by partial paralysis and progressive **dementia** (madness). This syndrome used to be quite common among elderly asylum patients in the U.S. Around the turn of the twentieth century, it became recognized that nearly all sufferers of general paresis were syphilitic. The first treatment for both syndromes was inoculation with malarial fever. It was the discovery and synthesis of penicillin, however, which provided a simple and effective chemical remedy.

There are many chemicals that are now known to be **psychotropic**: that is, they affect mental functioning. These include antipsychotic drugs such as Thorazine and Haldol, which are tranquilizers that reduce the severity of hallucinations; antianxiety drugs such as Valium; and antidepressant drugs. The beneficial effect of these medications can be obvious and immediate, but many also have serious side effects and require precise dosages to be effective. Since most drugs do not cure mental illness, but only treat their symptoms, psychiatry must continue to work hand-in-hand with psychology to gain maximum success.

36. **Which of the following is true about marijuana?**

   (A) It contains 50 percent more cancer-causing substances than tobacco.

   (B) It causes a decrease in male hormone and sperm production.

   (C) It causes temporary impairment of physical coordination, short-term memory, and learning ability.

   (D) All of the above

Using chemicals to attain altered states of consciousness is hardly original. Humans have been doing it for millennia, whether with Egyptian beer (3000 B.C.), Chinese marijuana (2700 B.C.), or Aztec peyote (A.D. 1330). Categories of these mind-altering or **psychoactive** drugs include **sedatives**, **stimulants**, **narcotics**, and **hallucinogens**. All of these can produce physical or psychological addiction (or both), and carry serious health consequences.

Alcohol and barbituates are examples of **sedatives**. Despite (or due to) its legal status, alcohol addiction is the most serious drug problem in the U.S., where over ten million people are classified as alcoholics. Alcoholism reduces the average life span by about twelve years, and is a leading cause of death, right up there with heart disease and cancer. Chronic alcoholism is associated with hypertension, cirrhosis of the liver, permanent kidney damage, and brain damage.

Amphetamines (speed) and cocaine are types of **stimulants**. Both cause strong psychological addiction, but little physical dependence. Chronic abuse of stimulants causes brain damage, in particular amphetamine or cocaine psychosis (a condition closely resembling **paranoid schizophrenia**). Opium derivatives such as morphine and heroin are **narcotics**, which have a tranquilizing and pain-relieving effect. The body can build up a high tolerance for these drugs, so that

LSD was not known as a psychoactive drug until the experience of Albert Hoffman, a Swedish chemist, in 1938. Hoffman was working on lysergic acid diethylamide as a possible headache remedy. After a long day in the lab he noticed strange symptoms, including dizziness and hallucinations. He experimented further by deliberately taking a small dose of the drug, and as a result, had the first really bad trip.

Still Smokin' (1983) and *Up in Smoke* (1978). The only good Cheech and Chong movies, and they're only good if you're, well . . . .

Brave New World (1932), by Aldous Huxley. The "happy drug" *soma* is used as a method of controlling the population.

larger and larger doses are required. Too large a dose, however, will result in coma or death.

Marijuana, peyote, LSD, and PCP are examples of **hallucinogens**. At one time or another, both marijuana and LSD have been claimed to be "safe" drugs with few side effects. Unfortunately, this is not the case. Long-term marijuana use has been associated with low sperm counts and a host of other ill effects, including "amotivational syndrome" (terminal slackeritis). Marijuana also contains 50 percent more cancer-causing substances than tobacco. And that's the *mild* drug: LSD is far worse. It can result in flashbacks, loss of memory and intelligence, and even psychosis.

37. **Intelligence is best defined as**

   (A) having a high I.Q.
   (B) being able to get good grades
   (C) a culturally and situationally specific concept
   (D) having a larger than average brain

In a 1921 report, the *Journal of Educational Psychology* asked fourteen well-known experts in the field of intelligence for a definition of this elusive concept. The result was fourteen rather different answers. All of the definitions, however, alluded in one way or another to (1) the capacity to learn from experience and (2) the capacity to adapt to one's environment. From this statement, it is reasonable to conclude that intelligence is a culturally and situationally specific concept, since experiences and environments differ across cultures. What is seen as intelligence in the U.S. may not be worth much to an Australian Aborigine. In fact, what is seen as intelligence in one part of the United States may not get you very far in another part.

Edwin Boring gave us perhaps the best definition of intelligence in 1923 when he became the first "expert" to admit (in writing) that intelligence is

SIZE DOESN'T MATTER

The cranial capacity of the average Neanderthal was larger than that of the average person alive today. However, our brains function more efficiently.

whatever the test measures. No two tests of intelligence measure the same thing, so we are left with as many definitions of intelligence as there are tests . . . certainly a far greater number than the number of experts in the field. Intelligence tests evolved in the early twentieth century in an attempt by some extremely insecure people to feel superior to others. To some it was important to prove that they alone possessed intelligence, while to others, it was important to advance a particular race or nationality. To most, it sucked. It still does.

Assume that you are the most intelligent person in the world and that we have developed an intelligence test. If you are the most intelligent person in the world, why would you want to take a test that we—at best, the second most intelligent folks in the world—have constructed? As the most intelligent person in the world, you would certainly recognize your prowess and would need to have it verified by an inferior about as much as Shaquille O'Neal needs you to tell him that he is taller than you.

MENSA is an organization that purports that all of its members are "genuises." The founder of MENSA, Sir Cyril Lodowic Burt, was so convinced that intelligence is genetically inherited that he made up data to support his claim. If you're so smart, why do you need anyone else to tell you so—and why would you pay for this privilege?

Flowers for Algernon (1966), by Daniel Keyes. An unforgettable and moving tale of a mentally challenged man who is suddenly made into a genius.

38. **Deviant behavior is**

   (A) a sign of debilitating mental illness
   (B) harmful to others
   (C) not always maladaptive
   (D) criminal

What constitutes **deviant behavior**? A male wearing a skirt in the United States may be considered to be acting like a deviant, but if that skirt is printed in a swell tartan plaid, you will be almost universally recognized as a descendant of the Scottish Highlanders. In fact, those in the know will be able to identify the clan of which you are a member. Is wearing a kilt deviant behavior? Certainly it is, in some parts of the U.S.

Rain Man (1988), with Dustin Hoffman and Tom Cruise. Dustin's autistic and Tom is his groovy, gambling brother in this Academy Award-winning movie.

The Man Who Mistook His Wife for a Hat (1970), by Oliver Sacks. Sacks offers fascinating clinical case studies of neurological disorders.

HOMOSEXUALITY

Many homophobes would assert that homosexuality is the ultimate example of deviant behavior. They would be wrong. At other times and in other places, homosexuality has been accepted as normal behavior: our own society is gradually moving toward this viewpoint as well. There is currently an intense controversy about whether homosexuality is a result of biological or psychological factors, or both. Finding a biological explanation for homosexuality might tempt researchers to label it as a disease requiring a cure, rather than an expression of the natural variability of the human species. Similarly, the attribution of homosexuality to psychological factors might imply that all homosexuals should be in therapy to be "fixed." One might as well be treated for having blue eyes or for liking country music (p. 318).

Boston Tea Party: did mob mentality launch a country?

In the ancient world, abnormal behavior was often thought to result from possession by demons, and was treated by exorcism. The vile potions, verbal abuse, starvation, and beatings used in exorcisms were not likely to improve anyone's outlook, however.

The Silence of the Lambs (1991), with Anthony Hopkins and Jodie Foster. Hopkins plays a sociopath and Jodie's an FBI agent in this chilling Academy Award-winning account of a serial killer.

Is wearing a kilt a sign of mental illness, a criminal activity, or harmful to others? Certainly not. Deviant behavior, then, is defined only by society's rules and customs. Some deviant behavior is maladaptive and harmful to the individual or to society. However, even the most criminal and maladaptive behaviors, such as murder, may be permissible in certain societal contexts like war or legal execution.

Mental illnesses leading to truly maladaptive behavior—the focus of **abnormal psychology**—can be loosely classified into categories that include **anxiety-based disorders (neuroses)** such as phobias, **personality disorders** such as psychopathy, and **affective (mood) disorders** such as clinical depression. Maladaptive behavior can be studied either as a biophysical phenomenon, a psychological phenomenon, or a sociological phenomenon. As researchers approach behavior from these three viewpoints, we will begin to understand what are now largely mysterious ailments, such as schizophrenia.

39. Group psychology differs from individual psychology in that

   (A) people may behave differently in groups than as individuals
   (B) counseling takes place in groups instead of individually
   (C) theories are developed by groups instead of individuals
   (D) in group psychology, individual viewpoints are not considered

Sociology is the study of the psychology and structure of groups. The development of the modern field of sociology is attributed in large part to **Emile Durkheim** (1858-1917). He regarded modern society as an organic unit analogous to a living organism, and spoke of society as being held together by an organic solidarity, in contrast to the more mechanical solidarity of primitive societies. Durkheim also introduced the concept of "anomie," a syndrome of alienation from society that can result in psychological unease, maladaptive behavior, or even suicide.

People often behave differently in a group than they would as individuals. This explains terms such as "mob mentality" and "mass hysteria." The relative anonymity granted by crowds can result in more uninhibited behavior, like dancing naked at Woodstock (p. 327). More disturbingly, a group context can even override individual reality. Psychological experiments in the 1950s and 1960s showed that people will give answers based on peer pressure, not on the evidence of their own eyes; that people can be induced to torture others just because an authority figure instructs them to; and that the mere assignment of roles like "prisoner" and "warden" can turn normal college students into sadists. This ability of society to impose its rules over individuals can lead to totalitarianism, in which deviation from the majority opinion is made to seem impossible.

Yet, the group can also be larger than the sum of its parts. Formal groups such as governments and businesses rely on many people working together to achieve a common goal. Informal associations, such as families and clubs, help integrate an individual into society and give a sense of belonging. It is a sociological fact that people need other people around to be truly satisfied—no matter how you might sometimes feel.

Ten (1991), by Pearl Jam. The rage and alienation expressed in grunge music (p. 329.) is a perfect expression of Durkheim's concept of anomie.

1984 (1948), by George Orwell. This is the classic denunciation of "groupthink."

Brazil (1985), directed by Terry Gilliam. The plot is derived from Orwell's *1984*, but the strange setting—a weird, old-fashioned future—and nightmare/dream sequences make the film highly original.

Karl Marx (p. 400), the influential communist thinker, also made important contributions to the field of sociology. Marx is credited with the **sociological conflict theory**—the argument that all history is the record of class struggle, and in particular, the struggle between the working class and their capitalist (p. 79) employers. This recognition of the importance of class and other group identifications in society is key to modern sociological thought.

ANSWERS

1. C	2. A	3. C	4. C	5. C	6. D	7. B	8. B	9. D	10. D
11. B	12. B	13. B	14. C	15. B	16. B	17. B	18. B	19. B	20. A
21. D	22. D	23. C	24. B	25. C	26. C	27. D	28. D	29. D	30. D
31. B	32. D	33. B	34. A	35. D	36. D	37. C	38. C	39. A	

Literature

From prevailing philosophies to social upheavals to scientific discoveries, the forces that act upon a culture shape the literature that culture produces. But literature itself is also one of the forces acting upon a culture. This duality is one of the things that makes literature dynamic, important, and always worthy of study. To understand the development of American literature—and the traditions within and against which it grew—is to have significant insight into American culture. But literature is also important because it allows us to get out of ourselves for a while. When we read, we enter into the mind of another human being, which often means confronting another time, another place, another way of experiencing the world.

1. The events related in the *Iliad* and the *Odyssey* took place

   (A) around the time the stories were written down
   (B) fifty years before the stories were written down
   (C) five centuries before the stories were written down
   (D) in the future

The sirens tempt Odysseus on his way home.

Like so much else, the roots of Western literary traditions lie in ancient Greece. Many literary genres were invented or at least formalized by the ancient Greeks, starting with the **epic**, a long verse narrative that relates an exalted, heroic story from the nation's past. **Homer's** (c.800 B.C.) *Iliad*, which tells of an episode in the Trojan War, and the *Odyssey*, which tells of Odysseus's return home to the island of Ithaca after the war, were written down around 750 B.C. but look back five centuries to a time of larger-than-life heroes. The two epics provided the Greeks with a moral code and source of practical wisdom during the **Classical Age**. Actually, it's not certain that someone named Homer, reputed to be blind, wrote the poems, or even that only one person was responsible for writing them. They had existed as part of an oral tradition for several centuries.

Lyric poetry encompasses shorter, personal poems of praise, celebration, or complaint that are often based on the sound patterns of music (the word comes from "lyre"). Some of the most compelling lyric poetry ever written is by **Sappho** (610-580 B.C.), a Greek noblewoman who lived most of her life on the island of Lesbos. In concise, direct, emotionally charged language, Sappho's poems tell of her intense relationships with a close circle of women. The genres of **elegy**, poetry composed to mourn the death of a loved one, and **pastoral**, poetry that praises the simple life of the countryside, were also developed in ancient Greece. The Greeks originated theater (p. 542) as we know it; they also created the disciplines of **rhetoric**, the art of speaking or writing persuasively, and philosophy. Plato's dialogues, which set forth the philosophy of his teacher, Socrates, are among the most influential literary and philosophic documents in Western history. The dialogues employ a question-and-answer approach to teaching known as the **Socratic method**. They are admired as much for their poetic refinement as for the high level of their philosophic content. In the *Republic*, for example, Socrates describes an ideal state, ruled by philosopher-kings (p. 385). Plato's student **Aristotle** is also a significant figure in literary history. He created an entire vocabulary for **literary criticism**, and codified aspects of philosophic and scientific thought.

The literature of ancient Rome reached its peak during the **Augustan Age** (43 B.C.-17 A.D.). The orator Cicero, also known for his essays, lived at this time. His contemporary **Horace** wrote patriotic poetry that included lyric and **satire**—ironic, witty attacks on human foibles. The one great Latin epic is the *Aeneid* (c. 29-19 B.C.) by **Virgil**, which recounts Aeneas's wanderings after the sack of Troy. Younger poets included the iconoclastic **Ovid**, author of *Metamorphoses* (8 A.D.), a long poem that assembles various mythological and legendary stories of transformation.

2. Dante is considered a major literary figure of which of the following periods?
   (A) Medieval
   (B) Renaissance
   (C) Gothic
   (D) Enlightenment

The **Medieval period** in Europe lasted for about eight hundred years, from the seventh to the sixteenth century. Historians used to call the first four hundred years of the Middle Ages the "**Dark Ages**," but this term has fallen out of favor. In the early Middle Ages, the church practically monopolized literacy as well as book production (books were still laboriously handwritten by **scribes**) and ownership. Most people who could read had learned it while studying to be clerics, and most books in existence were kept in monastery libraries. All cultural documents were written in Latin. Secular works were often kept alive orally, by storytellers, and only eventually written down. One way around church censors was through **allegory**, in which the characters and events of a story represent religious and moral principles. **Dante Alighieri** (1265-1321), who was exiled from his native Florence for political reasons, argued for the viability of literature written in **vernacular** languages, and boldly broke with tradition to write his *Divine Comedy* (1310-1314) in the Florentine Italian he loved. Full of unforgettable images and stories, the three-part poem records Dante's journey, guided first by the Latin poet Virgil, then by his beloved Beatrice, through *Inferno* (Hell), *Purgatorio* (Purgatory), and *Paradiso* (Heaven).

In medieval England, a linguistic shift from **Old English** to **Middle English** occurred around 1066, when the Norman duke **William the Conqueror** (1027-1087) invaded. Old English, also called **Anglo-Saxon**, is completely different from modern English. The main Anglo-Saxon text read today is the epic poem *Beowulf* (c. 700-750), which was originally part of an oral tradition. Written down sometime between the eighth and tenth centuries, the poem records the heroism of Beowulf, leader of the Danes, a Germanic tribe that were forebears of the English. Closer to modern English is Middle English, the language **Geoffrey Chaucer** (1340-1400) wrote in; with some coaching most of us can make out a lot of his clever, funny, and deep *Canterbury Tales* (c. 1387-1400). The rise of literary patronage by the wealthy at the end of the fourteenth century, as well as the influence of Dante and other vernacular writers, contributed to a flowering of secular authors such as Chaucer and the anonymous author of the most famous medieval romance, *Sir Gawayne and the Grene Knight* (c. 1375).

William the Conqueror

3. **Humanism is based on**

    (A) a rejection of the material world
    (B) an embrace of family and communal values
    (C) an emphasis on imagination and spirit over reason
    (D) a combination of Christian morality and classical learning

The outpouring of creativity in fifteenth-century Italy known as the **Renaissance** ("rebirth"), attributed to the rediscovery of the traditions and texts of ancient Greece and Rome, had as its intellectual base the idea of **humanism**. Departing from the communal and otherwordly values of the Middle Ages, humanism sought to combine Christianity and classical traditions by emphasizing the dignity and worth of the individual and of the life of this world. In England, the most prominent humanists included **Sir Thomas More** (1478-1535), author of *Utopia* (1516), a critique of European social, political, and religious institutions and practices. Influenced strongly both by Plato's *Republic* and by explorers' accounts of the new and strange societies of the New World, *Utopia* sets out More's

Humanist More

blueprint for a just and prosperous society. More's friend **Erasmus** (1467-1536), author of *Praise of Folly* (c. 1511), also criticized prevailing institutions and practices from a humanist perspective.

In Renaissance Italy, France, and Spain, writers experimented with developing and building on classical genres in the vernacular languages. **Ludovico Ariosto** created the epic *Orlando Furioso* (1516) out of the chivalric legends of Charlemagne (p. 389). **Marguerite de Navarre's** *Heptameron* is a series of tales connected by a humorous **frame story** that dramatizes the war between the sexes. In Spain, **Miguel de Cervantes** (1547-1616) revolutionized prose narrative with *Don*

Gutenberg's printing press

Quixote de la Mancha (1605-1615), the story of Don Quixote and his sidekick, Sancho Panza, and their humorous quest to revive the age of chivalry. In *The Courtier* (1528), **Baldassare Castiglione** (1478-1529) set down the etiquette of the ideal **courtier**, a member of one of the many courts of Europe. The key was to do everything with **sprezzatura**, a sort of studied nonchalance.

Queen Elizabeth I ruled England from 1558 to 1603, and under her shrewd eye that country became politically strong and united. During the **Elizabethan Age**, the court and the nobility provided would-be writers with their only real chance for financial survival. The idea of literature as an independent profession was unthinkable, and writers eagerly sought patronage in the form of direct financial support from particular nobles or appointments to bureaucratic positions within the court or universities. The sixteenth century was the first century to see books in print, but there was no such thing as copyright or royalties—writers sold their books outright to printers or booksellers for practically nothing. Even after the invention of the **printing press**, however, books were still circulated in manuscript, especially among the nobility.

MOVABLE TYPE

*The **Gutenberg Bible**, named after **Johannes Gutenberg**, inventor of the printing press, was the first book printed with "movable type"—one piece of type for each letter, which meant that the type could be reused.*

4. **A sonnet consists of**

    (A)   fourteen lines of blank verse
    (B)   fourteen lines of rhyming iambic pentameter
    (C)   sixteen lines of rhyming couplets
    (D)   sixteen lines of blank verse with a couplet at the end

> ❝
>
> *Poetry is simply Literature reduced to the essence of it's active principle."*
>
> ——PAUL VALÉRY
>
> ❞

Befitting a court society, in literature Elizabethans were big on structure, hierarchy, tradition, and conventions. Poetry was written in several classical forms. Elizabethans considered the epic, exemplified by **Edmund Spenser's** (1552-1599) interminable *Faerie Queen* (published c. 1590-1609), to be the highest literary form, promoting as it did the values of honor, heroism, loyalty, and national glory.

The **sonnet**, a type of lyric poetry originally invented by Dante's contemporary, **Petrarch**, flourished in Elizabethan England. With its strict structure of fourteen lines of iambic pentameter (ten beats, with an emphasis on every sec-

The Virgin Queen, Elizabeth I

ond beat), and rhymed according to one of several schemes, the sonnet was often written as part of a sequence, or series. Most, like the *Astrophil and Stella* (1582) sequence by Sir Philip Sidney (1554-1586), explored the highs and lows, hope and despair, of a lover yearning for an unattainable beloved. Eventually, the sonneteers' exaggerated metaphors reached the point of cliché: the "fire of my love, the ice of her heart, the roses in her cheeks," etc. Shakespeare (p. 547) wrote a famous sonnet sequence that tried to avoid the worn-out language of the **"Petrarchan lover."** His sequence, about a love triangle between a speaker named "Will," a beautiful young man, and a **"dark lady,"** used a rhyme scheme different from Petrarch's that has come to be called the Shakespearean or Elizabethan sonnet form. Sonnets were also written on religious themes, most notably by **John Donne** (1572-1631) in his *Holy Sonnets* (1633). Donne, who is called the first **metaphysical poet** (though he didn't use the term), moved beyond Elizabethan cleverness, decorativeness, and floweriness toward starker, more intellectualized images and symbols.

Nothing Like the Sun (1987) by Sting. The jazzy album's title takes its cue from Shakespeare's sonnet #130: "My mistress' eyes are nothing like the sun."

5. *Paradise Lost* was written by

   (A) John Milton
   (B) Sir Philip Sidney
   (C) William Shakespeare
   (D) Andrew Marvell

In the seventeenth century **John Milton** (1608-1674), author of the epic *Paradise Lost* (1667), combined the intellectual rigor and formal complexity of Renaissance writing with a brand of Christianity influenced by the Reformation (p. 494). After going blind in middle age, Milton wrote *Paradise Lost* to "justify the ways of God to men" through the story of the fall of Adam and Eve. Milton's Satan is one of the most compelling characters in all of literature. Readers are almost seduced by his energy and glamour until the poem moves to Paradise, and Satan is revealed not only as destructive but as a sort of one-note Johnny.

The young Milton

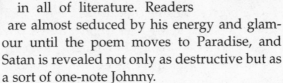

THE VOICE OF SATAN, FROM *PARADISE LOST*

To me shall be the glory sole among
The infernal Powers, in one day to have marred
What he, Almighty styled, six nights and days
Continued making, and who knows how long
Before had been contriving; though perhaps
Not longer than since I in one night freed
From servitude inglorious well nigh half
The angelic name, and thinner left the throng
Of his adorers

——John Milton

6. The first American poet to be published was

   (A) Edward Taylor
   (B) Jonathan Edwards
   (C) Walt Whitman
   (D) Anne Bradstreet

While European literature was being shaped by the Renaissance and the Reformation, Europeans who migrated to America in search of religious freedom, money, and a new start found a completely different environment to respond to. Early American writers imitated the European styles, but also came up with their own in response to radically new experiences. Sermons, histories, poetry, diaries, travel narratives, accounts of spiritual

Although the novel as we now know it—a long fictional prose narrative with a plot that unfolds through the actions, thoughts, and speech of its characters—didn't become popular until the eighteenth century, there are many precursors to the form. For example, the Roman writer Petronius's ribald Satyricon *uses prose and poetry to tell a story. During the Renaissance, "frame stories" were often used to link together several short tales into a unified work, such as in Marguerite de Navarre's* Heptameron *and Boccaccio's* Decameron, *in which a group of Florentines escaping the bubonic plague take turns telling stories to pass the time. The Arabic classic* The Thousand and One Nights *does this too.*

conversion, accounts of captivity by Indians—all reveal a culture still profoundly uncertain of itself. Many early American writers were influenced by Puritan doctrine (p. 500), although it never had a stranglehold on thought and expression. And even Puritan writings can be subtle and sophisticated,

PHILLIS WHEATLEY

Phillis Wheatley (1753-1854) was the first African American poet. Kidnapped from Africa at the age of seven, Wheatley was bought by a Massachusetts family, who reared her and encouraged her precocious intellect. The thirteen-year-old Wheatley became a sensation when she published her first poems in 1766 in London: no American publisher would publish a black writer—and a woman to boot! In 1773, her Poems on Various Subjects, Religious and Moral *was published and her reputation spread in Europe as well as in America (she was twenty).*

like the poetry of **Anne Bradstreet**, the first published American poet. Like **Edward Taylor** and **Michael Wigglesworth**, Bradstreet wrote verse shaped by the Puritan aesthetic of plainness, modesty, and submission to God's will, but she could also convey deep emotion, a surprisingly sexual passion for her husband, as well as a respect for classical traditions.

Puritan or not, writings from the colonial period reveal a people steeped in conflict, not just with the Indian tribes who lived around them but also among themselves. **William Bradford's** *Of Plymouth Plantation* (1646), for example, attempts to see God's divine plan at work in the early history of Plymouth, but must also come to terms with the very human imperfection of the community. **Cotton Mather's** *Magnalia Christi Americana*, or the *Ecclesiastical History of New England from its First Planting in the New Year 1620, unto the year our Lord 1698* (1702), likewise turns the religious history of New England into the mythical story of a chosen people. But Mather wrote his opus at a time when the religious fervor and unity of purpose of the original group of Puritans had begun to dissolve into a more diverse, mercantile society, and his nostalgia for the past comes through clearly.

7. In early America, the popular genre of the captivity narrative consisted of

(A) accounts of possession by the devil or witches
(B) accounts of the experiences of Africans brought to the New World as slaves
(C) accounts of the experiences of whites held as war hostages by Indians
(D) accounts of forbidden romance among the Puritans

Indian **captivity narratives**, true stories of whites, usually women, being held as war hostages by Indians, were wildly popular in the seventeenth century, both in America and England. The most famous of these, *A Narrative of the Captivity and Restoration of Mrs. Mary Rowlandson* (1682), provided an exciting package of adventure, violence, heroism, inside descriptions of the exotic ways of dark-skinned "savages," and faith in God and Christianity. Even after captivity by Indians no longer presented a threat (and secret thrill?) to white Americans, the genre of the captivity narrative continued to hold a central place in the American literary consciousness. This was reflected in fiction like **James Fenimore Cooper's** *The Last of the Mohicans* (1836) and **William Faulkner's** *Sanctuary* (1931). It continues in our own times, in the popular fascination with the kidnapping of white heiress **Patty Hearst** by the dark-skinned members of the Simbionese Liberation Army.

White settlement of the South yielded writings like *The Secret Diary of William Byrd of Westover*, *1709-1712*, that tell a different story of America, less influenced by the severe weather and religious struggles of New England, but shaped just as much by the conflicting cultures of the New World. **John Smith's** *The General History of Virginia, New England, and the Summer Isles* (1624), for example, includes the story of **Pocahontas**, the Indian maiden who saved his life at the moment of his execution and who

---

FROM *A NARRATIVE OF THE CAPTIVITY AND RESTORATION OF MRS. MARY ROWLANDSON*

Oh the doleful sight that now was to behold at this house! . . . Of thirty-seven persons who were in this one house, none escaped either present death, or a bitter captivity, save only one, who might say as he, "And I only am escaped to tell the News" (Job 1.15). There were twelve killed, some shot, some stabbed with their spears, some knocked down with their hatchets. When we are in prosperity, oh the little we think of such dreadful sights, and to see our dear friends and relations lie bleeding out their heart-blood upon the ground. There was one who was chopped into the head with a hatchet, and stripped naked, yet he was crawling up and down. It is a solemn sight to see so many Christians lying in their blood, some here, and some there, like a company of sheep torn by wolves, all of them stripped naked by a company of hell-hounds, roaring, singing, ranting, and insulting, as if they would have torn our very hearts out; yet the Lord by his Almighty power preserved a number of us from death, for there were twenty-four of us taken alive and carried captive.

later married another Englishman, John Rolfe. This story, which achieved the status of legend and was interpreted over and over in plays and novels throughout the nineteenth century, sets forth an enduring fantasy of white America: the willing submission by Native Americans to the irresistable force of the superior white culture.

8. An epistolary novel is
   (A) written in the form of letters
   (B) written only in dialogue
   (C) based on a true story
   (D) a thinly disguised autobiography

In Europe the novel began to evolve into its modern form in the early eighteenth century with such works as the adventurous *Robinson Crusoe* (1719) by **Daniel Defoe** (1660-1731) and even the pious, allegorical *The Pilgrim's Progress* (1698) by **John Bunyan** (1628-1688), which whetted the public's appetite for a new kind of fiction. But it was an **epistolary novel**, called *Pamela; or, Virtue Rewarded* (1740) by **Samuel Richardson** (1689-1761), that kindled the rage for reading novels when it was published in 1740. Written in the form of letters by an attractive servant girl as she struggles against the increasingly insistent advances of her employer, Mr. B, the novel follows the poor but virtuous Pamela's agonies until Mr. B. finally asks her to marry him. Although its silliness and excess—cleverly parodied by **Henry Fielding** in *Shamela (1741)*—are obvious, *Pamela* begins the modern novelistic tradition of psychological probing and character development. Richardson's next novel, *Clarissa* (1748), one of the longest ever written, introduces another helpless heroine, but this one falls into some wild adventures after she is seduced by a rake named **Lovelace**, who eventually deposits her in a brothel where she is drugged and raped. The manipulative, violent Lovelace was the inspiration for **Valmont,** the rakish villain of the well-known French epistolary novel by Choderlos de Laclos, *Les Liaisons Dangereuses (Dangerous Liaisons)* (1782).

The eighteenth century also saw a rebirth of satire influenced by **John Dryden** (1631-1700). The **Scriblerus Club**, which was expressly formed (in 1714) to "ridicule false tastes in learning," included **Alexander Pope** (1688-1744) and **Jonathan Swift** (1667-1745). Pope published translations of the *Iliad* and the *Odyssey*, a number of satiric, **mock-heroic** poems such as "The Rape of the Lock" (1712), and more serious philosophical verses like "An Essay on Man" (1733-1734).

Swift was born in Dublin and became a minister, a novelist, and, less famously, a poet. His best-known work is the novel *Gulliver's Travels*

(1726), in which he creates three fantasy societies in order to satirize the political and social pieties of his day. Swift also published pamphlets on English politics and on questions of theology. His pamphlet "A Modest Proposal" (1729), which advocates eating children as the solution to Ireland's famine, became a classic of political satire.

In America, the novel as a literary form was slower to take hold than in Europe. William Hill Brown's *The Power of Sympathy* (1789), a sluggish imitation of the German Goethe's early novel, *The Sorrows of Young Werther* (1774), is considered the first North American novel. There are some interesting eighteenth-century American novels, however. Susanna Rowson's *Charlotte Temple: A Tale of Truth* (1791) was the best-selling American novel for fifty years. It tells the story of an innocent English girl seduced by a roguish British Lieutenant, brought to America, made pregnant, abandoned and left to die of the cold in New York City. The simple story captures in almost mythic form the many fears of citizens of the new Republic: anxiety about separation from England, uncertainty about what the "freedom" they'd fought for really meant, wariness about the urbanized, impersonal place America was already becoming. Other novels of the period worth noting are **Charles Brockden Brown's** spooky if disjointed *Wieland* (1798) and **Hannah Webster Foster's** epistolary novel *The Coquette* (1797), the latter being yet another seduction tale but with—finally—a heroine who seems not at all helpless, although she still doesn't come to a happy end.

The early nineteenth century in England saw the further development of the modern novel. With **Sir Walter Scott** (1771-1832) the historical novel was born in works such as *Ivanhoe* (1819), sweeping imaginative stories full of action and passion set at different times throughout British history. Scott's contemporary **Jane Austen** (1775-1817) chose an almost completely opposite tack, focusing with minute detail on the lives of provincial English gentlefolk. Austen's works, from *Sense and Sensibility* (1811) to *Pride and Prejudice* (1813), are **novels of manners**, in which an ironic, aloof narrator describes actions that happen within a closed social circle that has its own unwavering rules and decorum. **Gothic fiction**, also in vogue during this period, was so called because its stories were often (though not always) set in gloomy medieval castles. In the Gothic genre, mystery, terror, and supernatural happenings in old decaying mansions are perfect outward symbols of the demons *within* characters and within readers themselves—secrets, guilt, obsession, violence, and perversion, to name a few.

THE REAL CHARLOTTE

A tombstone at New York's Trinity Church supposedly marking the grave of the "real" Charlotte Temple was a place of pilgrimage for over a hundred years (it's still there, by the way).

Jane Austen

9. Which of the following writers created the character
   of Leather-Stocking, or Natty Bumppo?

   (A) Herman Melville
   (B) Bronson Alcott
   (C) Raymond Chandler
   (D) James Fenimore Cooper

James Fenimore Cooper (1789-1851), often called "the American Scott," wrote historical novels that dealt with the increasingly vital question of the shifting American frontier in the early nineteenth century. Cooper's Leather-Stocking Tales, including *The Pioneers* (1823), *The Last of the Mohicans* (1826), and *The Deerslayer* (1841) tell the story of white and Native American cultures struggling to coexist. Cooper's central character, Natty Bumppo, aka Hawkeye and Leather-Stocking, is a figure of mythical American maleness—a rugged loner, more at home in nature than society. In his close friendships with Indians, Natty presents an ideal of a cross-cultural society, but ultimately the Leather-Stocking Tales record the encroachment of white civilization into the frontier and the vanishing of Native American culture. In the decade after The Leather-Stocking novels appeared, the debate over "The Indian Question" culminated in the federal policy of Indian Removal (p. 176).

Last of the Mohicans (1992), starring Daniel Day-Lewis. This flashy screen version plays fast and loose with both the plot and the themes of Cooper's novel. A love plot turns iconoclastic loner Natty Bumppo into a romantic hero, and the conflict with the British (the bad guys in the film) deflects attention from the ongoing hostilities between whites and Native Americans that are central to the book.

10. Which of the following is true of nineteenth-century
    romantic literature?

    (A) It stressed emotion and imagination.
    (B) It advocated political involvement.
    (C) It dealt mainly with love and marriage plots.
    (D) It developed Utopian ideas of communal living.

The seeds of the nineteenth-century **Romantic movement** were sown in the late eighteenth century, as major changes in the world, from the American Revolution (p. 626) to the French Revolution (p. 83) to the Enlightenment (p. 396) to the Industrial Revolution (p. 81), created a new social, economic, and intellectual environment in Europe. Romanticism was born in the hope that a new era of freedom, equality, and individual rights (p. 394) was dawning, and the feeling of new beginnings guided the literature of the period. Declaring that poets of the past had set artificial restraints on poetry, **William Wordsworth** (1770-1850) and **Samuel Taylor Coleridge** (1772-1834) set out to revolutionize poetic theory and practice with their *Lyrical Ballads* (1798). They wanted poetry to be more emotional and imaginative, "the spontaneous overflow of powerful feelings," in a famous phrase. Since poetry should directly express the poet's own mind and feelings, lyric poetry was the major Romantic form, and the poet himself was the main subject. Thankfully, most of the Romantics were pretty interesting characters.

Wordsworth's lengthy major poem, *The Prelude* (1850), records the growth of his mind, in part through his experiences in Nature, the other central Romantic subject. Coleridge, who spent many years addicted to opium, added to the natural the supernatural as grist for the poet's mind, and wrote visionary poems like "Kubla Khan" (1816). The most wildly visionary Romantic poet was **William Blake** (1757-1827), who was also an accomplished artist. Struggling to find support from a public that mostly thought he was insane, Blake set out to create an entirely new mythological account of human experience in collections of poetry like *Songs of Innocence and Experience* (1794), which he illustrated himself with detailed designs that incorporated the text of the poems. George Gordon, **Lord Byron** (1788-1824), author of the epic *Don Juan* (c. 1819-1824), was the most outrageous of the Romantics. Byron gave to posterity the idea of the **"Byronic Hero"**: the dark, passionate, moody, remorseful but unrepentant sinner who stands boldly against all institutions. Byron's fascinating, unpredictable personality, as much as his writings, made him a compelling figure. The handsome Byron was reportedly besieged by women throughout his life and had scores of affairs including one with his half-sister, Augusta Leigh. As poetic craftsmen, **John Keats** and **Percy Bysshe Shelley** top the Romantic list, though both had short, tragic lives. Shelley, whose life was also full of scandal, left his first wife to marry **Mary Wollstonecraft**

> ### FROM "THE WORLD IS TOO MUCH WITH US"
>
> *The world is too much with us; late and soon,*
> *Getting and spending, we lay waste our powers;*
> *Little we see in Nature that is ours;*
> *We have given our hearts away, a sordid boon.*
>
> ——*William Wordsworth*

> ❝
>
> *I must Create a System or be enslaved by another Man's.*
>
> ——WILLIAM BLAKE
>
> ❞

William Blake, one-man band

Frankenstein (1931), starring Boris Karloff. Though it takes major liberties with the original story, this frightening film version of Mary Shelley's novel still reigns as the best cinematic adaptation. Boris Karloff's monster is terrifying yet sympathetic, and Colin Clive is the perfect Dr. Frankenstein. The most recent adaptation, *Mary Shelley's Frankenstein* (1994), directed by Kenneth Branagh and starring Robert DeNiro as the monster, is more faithful to the novel but less effective as a film.

Shelley (1797-1851). Mary Shelley, daughter of the pioneering feminist **Mary Wollstonecraft**, wrote *Frankenstein, or The Modern Prometheus* (1818), a Gothic novel about the destruction wrought by the idealistic Dr. Frankenstein's quasi-human creation. The story, regarded as the origin of modern **science fiction**, is also noteworthy for its treatment of the Romantic **"noble savage"** motif—the idea that essentially good, "primitive" natures were turned bad by the corruptions of civilization.

11. **Which of the following novels was written during the Victorian period in England?**
   (A) *Clarissa*, by Samuel Richardson
   (B) *Great Expectations*, by Charles Dickens
   (C) *Ulysses*, by James Joyce
   (D) *The House of Mirth*, by Edith Wharton

The reign of **Queen Victoria** from 1837 to 1901, the longest in the history of the English monarchy, was a time of feverish industrial and economic expansion, which also caused plenty of social ills. During the **Victorian period**, the appalling conditions of industrial workers, with children as young as five toiling away in coal mines and families living in abject poverty, inspired many writers to ask whether the machine was a blessing or a curse to English society. Along with famous essayists **John Ruskin** and **Thomas Carlyle**, the prolific **Charles Dickens** (1812-1870) found the machine age ugly and heartless. Without ever losing his famous wit, the indefatigable Dickens used his fourteen novels, including *Oliver Twist* (1838), *Great Expectations* (1861), and *David Copperfield* (1850), to protest causes ranging from poor schooling to the conditions in London slums. **Elizabeth Gaskell** (1810-1865) also wrote influential novels dealing with English social problems, including the growing division between the poor industrial north and the prosperous south, which she captures in *North and South* (1855).

Working like the Dickens

Hollywood produced *David Copperfield* (1935), directed by George Cukor, and starring Freddie Bartholomew, Frank Lawton, and W.C. Fields. A British version of *Oliver Twist* (1948), directed by David Lean, is the best take on that novel, but the musical *Oliver!* (1968), directed by Carol Read, is even more fun.

Victorian novelists tended to build on Romantic foundations to explore questions of the individual struggling to make her or his own way in society. Two **Brontë sisters**, **Charlotte** (1816-1855) and **Emily** (1818-1848), concerned themselves with the possibilities of self-determination and love for women. Charlotte Brontë's masterful *Jane Eyre* (1847) is the story of a clever and passionate but plain and poor governess who eventually wins self-sufficiency, as well as the heart of her dashing employer, Rochester—but not before he is blinded and maimed in a fire. Emily Brontë's strange *Wuthering Heights* (1847) evokes an even more passionate, destructive force in the love between Catherine and Heathcliff.

FROM JANE EYRE

Mr. Rochester continued blind the first two years of our union: perhaps it was that circumstance that drew us so very near—that knit us so very close: for I was then his vision, as I am still his right hand . . . . He saw nature—he saw books through me; and I never did weary of gazing for his behalf, and of putting into words the effect of field, tree, town, river, cloud, sunbeam—of the landscape before us; of the weather round us—and impressing by sound on his ear what light could no longer stamp on his eye.

——*Charlotte Brontë*

Later in the century, **Thomas Hardy** (1840-1928), author of *Tess of the D'Urbervilles* (1891), added a tragic and religious angle to these same themes. **George Eliot** (1819-1880)—actually the pen name of Mary Ann Evans—took the Victorian novel to its highest level in complex, intellectually ambitious works like *Middlemarch* (1871-1872) that blended faithfulness to everyday life with the full development of her characters' inner lives.

George Eliot

WOMEN NAMED GEORGE

In picking "George" as her pen name, George Eliot was following in the footsteps of the free-spirited French writer Georges Sand (Aurore Dupin).

12. *Madame Bovary* **was written by**

    (A) Honoré de Balzac
    (B) Gustave Flaubert
    (C) Fyodor Dostoyevsky
    (D) Leo Tolstoy

The concern for faithfulness to reality that inspired realist literature also reflects society's growing confidence in science and the newly invented fields of the social sciences, as methods of arriving at some definitive truth about the way the world *is*. By the same token, it's no coincidence that the rise of realism in literature came at the same time as developments in the technology of photography (p. 612).

In nineteenth-century France, the novel developed along these same lines of psychological analysis, motive, and character development. The prodigious **Honoré de Balzac** (1799-1850), author of over ninety novels and tales, set the stage for the rise of **Realism** in the second half of the century. Realists saw the aim of literature not as "liberty," the Romantic credo, but "sincerity," including the scrupulous documentation of the everyday life of ordinary, often poor, people. **Gustave Flaubert** (1821-1880) wrote the quintessential realist novel, *Madame Bovary* (1857), the story of a provincial farmer's daughter, full of romantic illusions of luxury and Byronic lovers, who marries a buffoonish country doctor and embarks on a series of ill-starred adulterous affairs before poisoning herself. After the novel was published Flaubert was prosecuted, though later acquitted, for offenses against public morals. His famous words *"Madame Bovary, c'est moi"* reflect his deep investment in his heroine. The French novel reached its apotheosis at the beginning of the twentieth century in **Marcel Proust's** massive *Remembrance of Things Past* (1913-1927).

In nineteenth-century Russia, realist writers grappled with weighty intellectual and moral questions as much as they sought to reflect life around them. **Leo Tolstoy** (1828-1910) wrote the enormous *War and Peace* (1865-1869), which details events surrounding Napoleon's invasion of Russia in 1812. Tolstoy's astounding novel brought to life hundreds of characters, some actual historical figures. His *Anna Karenina* (1875-1877), a penetrating love story, was equally celebrated. **Fyodor Dostoyevsky** (1821-1881) aimed to transcend Russian reality and achieve universal significance in works such as *Crime and Punishment* (1866) and *The Brothers Karamazov* (1879-1880) Dostoyevsky presents a slightly abstract view of the world in order to zero in on questions of conscience and morality.

Russian novelist Leo Tolstoy

13. **The central figure of American transcendentalism was**

(A) Ralph Waldo Emerson
(B) William Wordsworth
(C) Edgar Allan Poe
(D) Henry James

Despite the success of Cooper and of **Washington Irving** (1783-1859), author of *The Sketch-Book of Geoffrey Crayon, Gent.* (1819-1820), by the 1840s it had become a commonplace that America still lacked truly original, independent, literary voices. **Ralph Waldo Emerson** (1803-1882), a Unitarian minister, lecturer, and philosopher, spearheaded the call for a new American literature. Emerson and his followers are often called American Romantics, because they adapted to their American experience European Romantic ideas. The eclectic philosophy Emerson (along with others such as **Margaret Fuller**) developed, called **transcendentalism**, saw the unity of the world and God, and approached nature as a divine revelation available for the artist to transform into Art and Truth. Transcendentalists stressed the power of the individual to know the universe through direct experience, and encouraged "**Self-Reliance**," as Emerson's most famous essay is called. Emerson's powerful personality, his bold ideas about the necessity of American intellectual independence from Europe, and his willingness to support unknown writers made him the central figure of a flowering of literary creativity in the 1850s, which is sometimes referred to as the **American Renaissance**.

The Concord sage, Ralph Waldo Emerson

Emerson's circle included **Nathaniel Hawthorne** (1804-1864), best known for his first novel, that warhorse of high school English reading lists, *The Scarlet Letter* (1850). Hawthorne wrote novels and short stories tackling big romantic themes like Good and Evil, Science and Nature, the Individual and Society.

FROM "SELF-RELIANCE"

Whoso would be a man must be a nonconformist. He who would gather immortal palms must not be hindered by the name of goodness, but must explore if it be goodness. Nothing is at last sacred but the integrity of your own mind . . . A foolish consistency is the hobgoblin of little minds, adored by little statesmen and philosophers and divines. With consistency a great soul has simply nothing to do. He may as well concern himself with his shadow on the wall. Speak what you think now in hard words, and to-morrow speak what to-morrow thinks in hard words again, though it contradict everything you said to-day. '—Ah, so you shall be misunderstood.'—Is it so bad to be misunderstood? Pythagoras was misunderstood, and Socrates, and Jesus, and Luther, and Copernicus, and Galileo, and Newton, and every pure and wise spirit that ever took flesh. To be great is to be misunderstood.

——Ralph Waldo Emerson

The most popular American writers of the nineteenth century were actually women, much to the chagrin of male writers like Hawthorne, who complained about the "damned mob of scribbling women" he saw as his competitors. Modern critics have denigrated the **domestic novels** written by nineteenth-century American women as sentimental, unsophisticated, and narrow—often a code for "about women." The question of why nineteenth-century America, however, produced no woman novelist on the level of Jane Austen, George Eliot, or Charlotte Brontë is one worth pondering.

Moby Dick (1956), directed by John Huston. Gregory Peck is fantastic as the deranged, heroic Captain Ahab and Orson Welles stands out as Father Mapple in this stark, atmospheric film.

Emerson's closest disciple, **Henry David Thoreau** (1817-1862), who never in his life ventured far from his native Concord, Massachusetts, developed a unique philosophy of life and a quirky literary style. In the classic *Walden, or Life in the Woods* (1854), the account of his two-year stay alone in the woods by **Walden Pond**, Thoreau created a pastiche of his observations of the natural world and his thoughts on subjects like "reading," "sounds," and "solitude." Thoreau's essay **"Civil Disobedience"** (1848) also set a standard of nonviolent protest later picked up by Martin Luther King, Jr., (p. 197), among others. Emerson's influence also extended to **Herman Melville**, though Melville ultimately challenged Emerson's optimistic views of human possibility and progress. Though today he's a big literary name, Melville was largely unappreciated in his own time, known if at all as "the man who lived among the cannibals," a reference to his first novel, *Typee* (1846), a fictionalized account of his adventures in the South Seas after jumping ship. Readers quickly rejected Melville when he turned to the philosophical topics and open-ended, experimental literary forms that really interested him. His loosely structured, metaphorical book of whaling and life, *Moby-Dick* (1851), was a crashing commercial failure that left Melville disillusioned and in debt to his publishers.

Edgar Allan Poe (1809-1849) charted his own course through the first half of the nineteenth century, pushing the boundaries of acceptable subjects and styles. Unlike Melville and Hawthorne, Poe actually made a living as a writer and editor. Poe's poem "The Raven" (1845) became instantly recognizable; you've probably heard it before ("Once upon a midnight dreary, while I pondered weak and weary . . . "). Poe is best known, however, for bizarre, **grotesque** tales like "The Tell-Tale Heart," (1843) and "The Fall of the House of Usher" (1839) that perfected the literary use of terror; they can still send a chill up the spine. Drugs and alcohol clearly helped Poe come up with the dream-like states and altered consciousness that add to the scariness of his stories. Nonetheless he was a dis-

Edgar Allan Poe: a Raven madman?

ciplined writer; the stories work because they are so polished and tightly constructed.

A vision of a slave being beaten to death inspired **Harriet Beecher Stowe** (1811-1896) to write *Uncle Tom's Cabin* (1852), a phenomenon of a novel that sold over a million copies and provided a needed push to the cause after the passage of the notorious Fugitive Slave Law (p. 181) in 1850. *Uncle Tom's Cabin* took the most cherished beliefs of nineteenth-century America—the sanctity of motherhood and the family and the Christian idea of redemption—and turned them into a pointed attack on the social system of slavery. Slavery breaks up families and denies that slaves have souls to save, was the novel's simple message, and it worked. As Lincoln reportedly said when he met Stowe during the Civil War, "So you're the little woman who wrote the book that started this war?"

14. **Which of the following figures wrote a famous slave narrative?**

   (A) Frederick Douglass
   (B) William Wells Johnson
   (C) Harriet Beecher Stowe
   (D) Harriet Tubman

One of the most fascinating, moving genres of American literature is the **slave narrative**, made up of autobiographical accounts by former slaves of their ordeals during slavery (p. 178), their escapes to freedom, and the new lives they struggled to build. But slave narratives are more than just straightforward histories; they are often rhetorically sophisticated, and consciously shaped to produce the greatest persuasive effect. Skillful writers exploited the built-in dramatic structure in these stories of suffering, flight, and redemption through freedom to produce compelling literature. Perhaps the most brilliant slave narrative—and indeed one of the most influential autobiographies in all of American literature—is the *Narrative of the Life of Frederick Douglass, an American Slave* (1845). Frederick Douglass writes with vivid detail but calm control, forcing his potentially hostile audience to see him as a full human being and a formidable intellect. **Harriet Jacobs's** *Incidents in the Life of a Slave Girl, Written by Herself* (1861) is similarly powerful. Jacobs's story contrasts with Douglass's work in ways that reflect the different experiences of men and women under slavery, as well

Frederick Douglass

as the separate literary cultures of nineteenth-century men and women. While Douglass is influenced by Thomas Jefferson (p. 405) and Emerson, Jacobs responds to the female tradition of writers like Harriet Beecher Stowe. The slave narrative influenced later African American literature as well, and continues to be honored by contemporary writers like **Toni Morrison** and **Ishmael Reed**.

FROM *NARRATIVE OF THE LIFE OF FREDERICK DOUGLASS, AN AMERICAN SLAVE*

It was this everlasting thinking of my condition that tormented me. There was no getting rid of it. It was pressed upon me by every object within sight or hearing, animate or inanimate. The silver trump of freedom had roused my soul to eternal wakefulness. Freedom now appeared, to disappear no more forever. It was heard in every sound, and seen in every thing. It was ever present to torment me with a sense of my wretched condition. I saw nothing without seeing it, I heard nothing without hearing it, and felt nothing without feeling it. It looked from every star, it smiled in every calm, breathed in every wind, and moved in every storm.

15. Walt Whitman's first collection of poems, *Leaves of Grass*, was considered shocking because

   (A) it was written in an original, free-flowing form
   (B) it dealt openly with sexuality
   (C) it made fun of Lincoln and other popular figures
   (D) both A and B

Walt Whitman (1819-1892) is best known for his collection of poems, *Leaves of Grass* (1855), which created a mild scandal when it was published, with Whitman's own money, in 1855. Almost completely ignoring conventional schemes of rhyme and meter, Whitman's debut exploded the controlled, regular form of poetry then being written. Even more outrageously, he wrote frankly about sexuality, and even hinted at his own sexual desire for other men.

With her wonderfully strange language, **Emily Dickinson** also revolutionized American poetry during the nineteenth century, though she published only seven poems in her lifetime, leaving over a thousand more behind in neat bundles at her death. Dickinson's poetic innovations are as radical as Whitman's, but move in an opposite direction: where Whitman is expansive, direct, and celebratory, Dickinson is condensed, indirect, and subtle. In their different ways, Whitman and Dickinson set a standard for all American poets who followed.

Robert Browning (1812-1889) had a productive literary union with Elizabeth Barrett until her death in 1861. He perfected the **dramatic monologue** form, in which a poem is "spoken" entirely by a particular character. Read by almost every literate person in both England and America, the poet **Alfred Lord Tennyson** (1809-1892) was called "the spokesman of the Victorian Age"—a label that proved disastrous to his reputation in the twentieth century, when everything about Victorianism came to be seen as stodgy and mannered. Poet and critic **Matthew Arnold** (1822-1888) is more to the taste of a modern audience, perhaps because he represents the subtle shift from *isolation*, characteristic of the nineteenth century, to *alienation*, the hallmark of the twentieth. Two poets in particular mark the turn into the twentieth century in literature: the English Jesuit priest **Gerard Manley Hopkins** (1844-1889) and the Irish nationalist

CONRAD AND LAWRENCE

*Two important English writers of the turn of the century are Conrad and Lawrence. **D. H. Lawrence** (1885-1930) grew up in poverty and became a teacher, poet, short story writer, and novelist. Frequently banned by authorities, his work dealt frankly with human sexuality and passion. Three important and controversial novels are* The Rainbow *(1915),* Women in Love *(1920, a sequel to* The Rainbow*), and* Lady Chatterley's Lover *(1928). The first two have been adapted by film director Ken Russell. **Joseph Conrad** (1857-1924) was born to Polish parents (his full name was Teodor Josef Konrad Korzeniowsky) in the Ukraine. He went to sea at seventeen on a French ship—much of his work is set at sea—and published his first novel at thirty-eight. Conrad was largely concerned with the issues of human vulnerability and corruptibility, which he explored most disturbingly in* Lord Jim *(1900) and in his famous long short story "Heart of Darkness" (1902), adapted and reset during the Vietnam War as* Apocalypse Now *(1979) by director Francis Ford Coppola (p. 124). Conrad's status as one of the most effective writers in English is remarkable given that it was his third language.*

William Butler Yeats (1865-1939), whose poem "The Second Coming" (1921) ends with a question that captures the existential dread of modernity: "And what rough beast, its hour come round at last / Slouches toward Bethlehem to be born?"

16. The rise of realism in American literature in the late nineteenth century can be seen as

   (A) a reaction against European-influenced styles of literature
   (B) a protest against the greed and scandals of the post-Civil War period
   (C) a response to a sharp decline in sales of novels
   (D) a reflection of the faster, more chaotic pace of life after the Civil War

   The rise of realism in American literature reflected the profound transformation of everyday life and national culture in the post-Civil War period. On the most basic level, realism responded to the changes in the

There have been three film versions of Louisa May Alcott's 1873 classic *Little Women*. The 1933 film, directed by George Cukor, stars a riveting Katharine Hepburn as Jo, the rambunctious budding writer. In 1949, under Mervyn Leroy's direction, the domestic angle is emphasized as June Allyson brings more polish, less grit to the role of Jo. And in 1994, Australian director Jane Campion pulled off a stunning new version that highlights the story's progressive and feminist messages.

tempo of American life: no more leisurely, thoughtful narrators, no more subtly developed allegory and symbolism. Realism aimed to reflect life as it was now lived—speeded-up, bustling with events, crowded with all types of people jostling for position. At the same time, realism sought to be an authentic record of the increasingly complex American social reality. Difficult subjects that were previously ignored by literature came to light, like the harsh lives of industrial workers in **Rebecca Harding Davis's** groundbreaking story "Life in the Iron Mills" (1861). Realists developed literary techniques that conveyed fidelity to how life really happens, like using regional dialects or mir-

W.D. Howells

roring the pace of events in the pace of their writing. Accuracy was the goal, whether in transforming spoken dialect into the written word or transporting the middle-class reader to scenes of urban ghettos. The champion of the movement toward realism in American literature was **William Dean Howells**. A novelist and editor of two still-lively and influential magazines that began in the nineteenth century, *The Atlantic Monthly* and *Harper's Monthly*, Howells captured the social confusion of urbanizing America in novels like *The Rise of Silas Lapham* (1885).

Not all realism was concerned with urbanization, though. Some of the most interesting works of the late nineteenth century are set in out-of-the-way places, and record the distinct habits of the rural population which seemed to be slowly disappearing. **Regionalism,** as this type of realism is called, sought to capture the unique ways of life of people in remote areas, from northern New England in the work of **Sarah Orne Jewett** and **Mary Wilkins Freeman** to **Hamlin Garland**'s rural midwest, just as regional differences began to be ironed out. Yet even regionalism had its urban interpreters: the Jewish writer **Abraham Cahan** (1860-1951) rose to popularity at the turn of the century with a volume of "regionalist" short stories called *The Imported Bridegroom and Other Stories of the New York Ghetto.*

The writings of **Mark Twain**, the pen name of **Samuel Clemens** (1835-1910), brought the status of "classic American literature" to realist, regional works. The novels *The Adventures of Tom Sawyer* (1876) and the even better *The Adventures of Huckleberry Finn* (1884) are often seen as children's literature, but they are in fact sophisticated takes on American culture. Huck's story is hugely entertaining, but is also a critique of the racist and conformist world around him. In his lifetime, Twain was a popular personality, known as a satirist, humorist, and lecturer, but his humor was always grounded in keen social observation. Twain's eye for what was happening in American culture is reflected in his novel (co-written with Charles Warner) *The Gilded Age* (1873), which coined the term still used to describe the post-Civil War period of ostentation and greed.

Mark Twain took his pseudonym from a riverboat captain's terminology.

17. **Which of the following writers is considered a naturalist?**

(A) Theodore Dreiser
(B) Mark Twain
(C) T.S. Eliot
(D) Ernest Hemingway

Another strain of realism that developed in America at the turn of the century was **naturalism.** Naturalist writers, influenced by European writers like the Frenchman **Emile Zola,** saw the world as full of forces, from nature to society to technology, that determine the fate of individuals. The naturalist world is essentially a hostile place, one where the idea that you are in charge of your own destiny is revealed as a cruel hoax. Most often, naturalist fiction uses urban settings to reveal the forces people must struggle against, as in *Maggie: A Girl of the Streets* (1893), **Stephen Crane's** novel of an impoverished, uneducated girl's seemingly inevitable fall into prostitution in an Irish ghetto of New York City. But the hard-living **Jack London** (1876-1916) used the force of the sea in *The Sea Wolf* (1904), or the extreme climate of the Far North in several works, to the same effect. Naturalist **Theodore Dreiser** (1871-1945) emphasizes in controversial novels like *Sister Carrie* (1900) and the monumental *An American Tragedy* (1925) that accident, timing, and chance are at the root of all success or failure, happiness or misery. Naturalist writers are often accused

The rugged Jack London

by belleletristic types of being journalistic and unliterary. Some naturalists did begin their careers as journalists, but their straightforward styles also reflect their belief that literature should be accessible and absorbing to the ordinary person.

Not considered a naturalist but concerned with similar themes, **Kate Chopin** (1851-1904) wrote moody, evocative fiction set in the **French-Creole** culture of Louisiana, and often provocatively explored charged subjects like sex and race. Chopin's *The Awakening* (1899) stirred controversy for its nonjudgmental, lyrical treatment of its heroine's casting off of a bland, entrapping marriage in order to experience her own sexual and spiritual awakening. Yet Chopin was ever the realist, and the novel ends with the idea that there is no place in society as Chopin knew it for a truly "awakened" woman. **Willa Cather's** (1876-1947) subjects were the northern European immigrants and the transplanted easterners of the western prairie states. Novels like *O Pioneers!* (1913) and *My Antonia* (1918) use a realist lens to view familiar American themes: the experience of starting over in a new place, and the relation of human beings to nature and the land.

> ## DIALECTIBLE
>
> *During Reconstruction (p. 183) African American writers had to deal with some significant intellectual issues—for example, whether they should have their characters speak in black dialect. While dialect would be more true to the experience of black life, it was also associated in many people's minds with mental inferiority and the racist stereotypes of blacks left over from the days of slavery ("Mammy," the loyal, self-sacrificing domestic servant; "Sambo," the happy-go-lucky but shiftless field hand; "Jezebel," the promiscuous temptress; etc.). The poet **Paul Laurence Dunbar** used both dialect and more formal language in his writings, playing the two off against each other.*

Henry James (1843-1916) and **Edith Wharton** (1862-1937), two of the most gifted and prolific American writers, are often considered apart from their American peers because they lived most of their adult lives in Europe. Yet both were obsessed by American culture and the American character—it's just that James and Wharton often chose to get at the essence of Americans by revealing the striking differences between Americans and Europeans. Both writers like to set naïve Americans loose in Europe. The misunderstandings are sometimes funny, and often poignant, as in James's *The Portrait of a Lady* (1881), in which Isabel Archer, the prototypical free-spirited "American girl," realizes that her European husband has married her for her money and has no intention of making her happy. James's ponderous writing style—long, long sentences, lots of big words, and convoluted phrases—is often parodied and makes his writing heavy going. Most of the time his sheer intelligence repays the close attention he requires. Though they were close friends and the

The Age of Innocence (1993), directed by Martin Scorsese. Scorsese, best known for gangster flicks like *Goodfellas*, captures well the mid-nineteenth-century New York upper-class milieu of Wharton's 1925 novel.

younger Wharton is often called a disciple of James, their styles are actually quite different—Wharton writes in a clear, direct, penetrating voice.

18. **Which of the following statements best captures the aesthetic philosophy of modernism?**

    (A) It celebrates the integrity of the individual consciousness.
    (B) It is indebted to classical ideas of proportion and beauty.
    (C) It favors open-endedness, fragmentation, and multiple perspective.
    (D) It finds beauty in the small, homely details of everyday life.

The major movement of the first half of the twentieth century, in literature as well as the other arts, is known as **modernism**. Like modernist artists, modernist writers wanted to break with what they saw as the constricted, conventional ways of the nineteenth century. They rejected the old fundamental aesthetic values like unity and coherence, daring instead to create new ideas of beauty in fragmentation, open-endedness, and multiplicity of perspective. Modernist literature like the Irish writer **James Joyce's** *Ulysses* (1922), with its disrupted syntax and disorienting, **stream-of-consciousness** style, expresses the sense that the modern world is a chaotic, de-centered place, and that the modern individual doesn't necessarily have a stable, unified essence. Rejecting the stifling, hidebound, middle-class world, modernists saw themselves as the **avant-garde** ("advance guard"), enlightened free spirits who questioned the established order. They wanted their art to help liberate society from the narrowness and ugliness of the bourgeois world. Many American modernists ended up living in Europe, a culture historically more open-minded and receptive to artists.

The development of feminism (p. 200), which brought together the political agenda of women's suffrage (p. 188) and the social agenda of women's right to personal and sexual autonomy, had a major influence on modernism. In the forefront of modernism on both sides of the Atlantic were outspoken women writers like **Virginia Woolf** (1882-1941), the English author of stunning experimental novels like *To The Lighthouse* (1927) and *Mrs. Dalloway* (1925). Among Americans, **Gertrude Stein** (1874-1946), who never hid her lesbianism, represented the cutting edge in literature and private life. Another expatriate fascinated by the American character—*The Making of Americans* (1925) told the history of one German-Jewish immigrant family as the representative American

Novelist **Charles Chesnutt**, a lawyer, drew upon the rich African American oral tradition in *The Conjure Woman and Other Stories* (1899) but also wrote realist novels like *The Marrow of Tradition* (1901) that explored the plight of educated blacks and the possibility of a multiracial society.

The Dead (1987), directed by John Huston. This faithful adaptation of James Joyce's subtle, melancholy short story of the same name (from *Dubliners*) is the last film directed by Huston and stars his daughter Anjelica. The story delivers two of Joyce's specialties: a clever dissection of Irish society and a moment of epiphany that changes the protagonist's life by revealing the dark truths he's turned away from.

Virginia Woolf

Often the modernists sought and celebrated freedom from the sexual repression of the Victorian era, sometimes called "Comstockery" after the Comstock Act of 1873, which prohibited the distribution of birth-control devices and even sending information about birth control through the U.S. mail. The popularization of the work of Sigmund Freud (p. 236) at the turn of the century went a long way toward changing the way people thought about sexuality. Freud's ideas had perhaps the most profound impact for women, who were suddenly acknowledged to be sexual beings in the same way men were.

story—Stein boldly declared herself the major literary thinker of her era. She broke new literary ground in complex, elliptic works like *The Autobiography of Alice B. Toklas* (1933), narrated in the voice of Toklas, her lover, but is perhaps even more famous for the *salons,* well-attended by a varying cast of luminaries from the literary and artistic worlds, which she hosted in her Paris apartment. While Stein's Jewishness was overshadowed by her other identities, another Jewish American woman writer, **Anzia Yezierska,** made a name for herself in the 1920s with powerful, raw fiction evoking the realities of Lower East Side Jewish life. Yezierska's novels and stories won wide popular acclaim that culminated in a brief career as a screenwriter in Hollywood.

World War I (p. 413) also determined the course of modernism, solidifying the sense that the old literary forms were not adequate to express the complex reality of modern life. The men who fought in the war, especially, emerged spiritually wounded and disillusioned, making them prime candidates to record the grim experiences and pessimistic world view of their so-called **Lost Generation. Ernest Hemingway** (1899-1961), for example, who was wounded while working for an Allied ambulance corps, captured the post-war themes of alienation and disillusionment after coming home to a provincial midwestern America under the grip of prohibition (see 418). Hemingway's friend and fellow heavy drinker **F. Scott Fitzgerald** (1896-1940) took as his subject the glittery side of America in the 1920s, which he christened the **Jazz Age.** Francis Scott Key Fitzgerald (the author of the national anthem was his forebear) and his equally famous wife, **Zelda**, lived a notorious life of hard partying and generally scandalous behavior, yet Fitzgerald also managed to sit down and document this flashy world of flappers and cocktail parties in fiction like *The Great Gatsby* (1925), which explores the promise—and the potential hollowness—of the "American dream."

Another stylistic innovator of the 1920s and 1930s, **William Faulkner** (1897-1962), captured the decline of the culture of the South, the twisted racial legacies of slavery, and the complexity of family feeling in novels set in the fictional Yoknapatawpha County (based on Faulkner's childhood home of Oxford, Mississippi). In works including *The Sound and the Fury* (1929) and *Absalom, Absalom!* (1936), Faulkner created an entire mythical world on what he called "my own little postage stamp of native soil," exploring themes of obsession, incest,

The Fitzgerald clan does a jig.

racism, and forbidden interracial love through the intertwined history of whites, blacks, and Indians in the South. Texas-born **Katherine Anne Porter** (1890-1980) wrote about her "native soil" and the history of southern families from a distinctly feminine perspective, captured in story collections like *Pale Horse, Pale Rider* (1939). The 1930s also marked the beginning of **John Steinbeck's** (1902-1968) long career. A good example of an extremely popular writer who never achieved wide critical acceptance, Steinbeck wrote novels like *Of Mice and Men* (1937), *The Grapes of Wrath* (1939), and *Cannery Row* (1945), grounded in the realities of the down-and-out, yet also full of symbolism, that critics have called heavy-handed and sentimental.

Mrs. Parker and the Vicious Circle (1994), directed by Alan Rudolph. Jennifer Jason Leigh stars as **Dorothy Parker** (1893-1967), the journalist, reviewer, poet, short story writer, and screenwriter known for her biting aphoristic wit, talent for satire, and darkly melancholic sensibility. The film dramatizes Parker's well-known lunches (called the Algonquin Round Table) at the Algonquin Hotel, at which Parker and her friends set the tone for much literary and journalistic discourse of the 1920s.

19. **Of the following writers, which is a modernist poet?**

(A) T.S. Eliot
(B) William Faulkner
(C) Zora Neale Hurston
(D) Adrienne Rich

Though nineteenth-century poets like Whitman and Dickinson had begun to stretch the boundaries of poetry, modernism was a wellspring of poetic experimentation and innovation. **Ezra Pound** (1885-1972), along with **T.S. Eliot** (1888-1965), the central figure of the modernist school, led the exhortation to poets to "make it new." Eliot's "The Love Song of J. Alfred Prufrock" (1910) is considered the first truly modernist poem, full of dense, allusive, often stark and disturbing images, tied together by the shifting consciousness of a defeated, isolated, middle-aged man. Eliot's great achievement, however, was *The Waste Land* (1922). This poem, a long, intricately worked collage of images, symbols, and allusions exploring the emptiness and waste inherent to modernity, nonetheless plays out the classic literary motifs of the quest or journey, renewal and rebirth. As a critic, Eliot was

T. S. Eliot writes in his lucky three-piece suit

PENNY WISE, POUND FOOLISH

Ezra Pound wanted his poetry to be in the service of political life and history, and it is for his politics that he has stirred the most controversy. After WWI, Pound espoused radical right-wing views that he broadcast on his own radio show from Rome. The shows were full of anti-Semitic tirades, support for the Italian Fascist Mussolini, condemnations of Roosevelt, and theories about international finance conspiracies. All the while, Pound produced startling, learned poetry, including the first parts of his projected life's work, the epic Cantos. *Arrested for treason in 1945 and incarcerated in an outdoor wire cage in Pisa before being brought back to the U.S. to stand trial, Pound was committed to a psychiatric hospital. Critics are unsure how to handle Pound: Do you focus on the poetic brilliance and bracket the politics? Or do you reject the poetry of someone whose politics are so horrendous, and are indeed tied to and expressed in his literary work? On a dramatic scale, the problem of what to do with Ezra Pound attests to the inseparability of art, culture, and history.*

also influential in defining an agenda, now considered by many literary scholars to be reactionary, that sought to divide works of literature into the "great" and the "marginal," and that celebrated the essential unity of the tradition of Western literature.

Hilda Doolittle, known as **H. D.** (1886-1961), perfected the Modernist school of poetry known as **imagism**, which sought to be objective and concise, yet rhythmically flowing, in order to get at the essence of "things in themselves." Poets indebted to H. D. include **Marianne Moore** (1887-1972), **Elizabeth Bishop** (1911-1979), and **William Carlos Williams** (1883-1963). Williams, who was a practicing physician in Rutherford, New Jersey for most of his life, was a masterful stylist, among the first poets to incorporate a visual level of meaning through the arrangement of words on the page. Influenced as much by modernism as by his New England upbringing, **Robert Frost** (1874-1963) had a dark sensibility discernible even in such classics as "Stopping By Woods on a Snowy Evening," yet he was also heir to a nineteenth-century romantic faith in the individual. **Free verse** as we know it, however—poetry absolutely unfettered by the need to use rhyme, meter, or any convention whatsoever—probably owes the most to the iconoclastic **e.e. cummings** (1894-1962), who invented a kind of poetic cubism (p. 604), breaking up his words and ideas in radical ways, and making up his own rules of punctuation, capitalization, and grammar.

FROM "THE LOVE SONG OF J. ALFRED PRUFROCK"

Let us go, through certain half-deserted streets,

The muttering retreats

Of restless nights in one-night cheap hotels

And sawdust restaurants with oyster shells

—*T.S. Eliot*

Twentieth-century poetry took off in all directions from modernism. Freedom is the key, but freedom doesn't mean simply rejecting old themes and styles—twentieth-century poets range through literary history to help define their own individual voices. In the postwar period, a return to traditional forms was discernible in poets like the hugely influential **W.H. Auden** (1907-1973), while the **Black Mountain Poets**, including **Robert Creeley**, **Charles Olson**, and **Denise Levertov**, worked in their own deliberately iconoclastic styles. Since the 1950s, an "old guard" of poets like **Anthony Hecht** and **John Hollander** have argued vociferously for a return to formalism, but appear to be waging a losing battle. The most compelling poets of the second half of the century, like **Robert Lowell** and **Anne Sexton**, gravitated away from structure toward an unpredictable, eclectic style. The personal voice, and the personal as poetic subject matter, has been another stage for battle among poetry theorists. Feminist poets like **Adrienne Rich** and **Nikki Giovanni** have often met with tense resistance as they openly explore their own identities, communities, and political investments, in their poetry.

FROM *THE PARIS REVIEW* INTERVIEW

I can't understand—strictly from a hedonistic point of view—how one can enjoy writing with no form at all. If one plays a game, one needs rules, otherwise there is no fun. The wildest poem has to have a firm basis in common sense, and this, I think, is the advantage of formal verse . . . Formal verse frees one from the fetters of one's ego.

——*W. H. Auden*

FROM *BLOOD, BREAD AND POETRY*

To write directly and overtly as a woman, out of a woman's body and experience, to take women's existence seriously as theme and source for art, was something I had been hungering to do, needing to do, all my writing life. It placed me nakedly face-to-face with both terror and anger . . .

——*Adrienne Rich*

20. The Harlem Renaissance occurred during

- (A) The 1920s
- (B) The 1930s
- (C) The 1940s
- (D) The 1950s

The Paris Review literary quarterly, edited by George Plimpton. Still going strong after over thirty years of almost-quarterly publications, *The Paris Review* contains some of the best fiction, poetry, and writer interviews you'll find anywhere. Pay special attention at used bookshops for old issues of *The Paris Review*, and also *The Evergreen Review*, a now-defunct quarterly that focuses on American poets and authors.

After the broken promise of Reconstruction (p. 183), the migration of large numbers of African Americans to the North made Harlem a mecca for ambitious and talented black artists, musicians, and writers. A heady climate of intellectual support and experimentation emerged there in the 1920s, and came to be known as the **Harlem Renaissance**. The growing appreciation and patronage of black culture by whites, as well, contributed to the public awareness of a new era of self-respect and self-determination for the "**New Negro.**" Yet "New Negro" writers like **Arna Bontemps** and **Jean Toomer** wanted not to break from African American cultural history but to build on it, incorporating elements of black folk culture and music into their writings in striking, original ways that reflect a modernist spirit of experimentation. **Langston Hughes** (1902-1967), perhaps the foremost Harlem Renaissance figure, wrote poetry grounded in the rhythms, styles, and themes of black musical innovations like spirituals (p. 505), jazz (p. 307), and blues (p. 307). The prolific Hughes expressed humor, warmth, and deep emotion as well as a sophisticated political awareness, and besides poetry wrote fiction, drama, essays, and historical accounts.

The onset of the Depression (p. 87) and the explosion of radical political movements that followed had a significant effect on blacks in the U.S., and is often seen by historians as causing the end of the Harlem Renaissance. A growing engagement in political and social issues marks African American writing from the 1930s to the 1970s. **Richard Wright** (1908-1960), author of *Native Son* (1940) and the autobiographical *Black Boy* (1945), brought a politicized yet subtle and sensitive point of view to his fiction, which explored the injustices of American racial practices and their effects on the African American psyche. Less overtly political black writers, like **Ralph Ellison** (1914-1994), author of *Invisible Man* (1952) and **Zora Neale Hurston** (1903-1960), author of *Their Eyes Were Watching God* (1937), often found themselves criticized by Wright and others for understating the problem of racial oppression and seeming to seek conciliation or integration with white society. Ellison unapologetically saw his art as African American and at the same time engaged in universal themes. Hurston, who wrote of a black culture largely indifferent to white society,

Terrible Honesty: Mongrel Manhattan in the 1920s (1995), by Ann Douglas. This huge study of the intertwined black and white cultures of New York in the twenties dazzles the reader with insights into the lives of dozens of literary, musical, and show-biz biggies.

challenged the idea that "black lives are only defensive reactions to white actions," and incorporated her anthropologic research into black folk culture in her work. Recently, Hurston has been rediscovered by a new generation of African American women writers like **Alice Walker** and **Toni Morrison,** who are indebted to Hurston's lyrical celebration of black identity and the innovative narrative strategies she developed.

The clear, forceful, sophisticated voice of **James Baldwin** (1924-1987) also emerged in the 1950s. Novels like *Go Tell It on the Mountain* (1953) and *Giovanni's Room* (1956) treat Baldwin's main concerns of homosexuality and race relations. Baldwin's skills as an essayist were also unsurpassed. Though he died in 1987, Baldwin's best work is still surprisingly fresh. In the 1960s Baldwin and other African American writers addressed political and social issues with a new vigor. The **Black arts movement,** with its emphasis on black cultural nationalism, flourished in the work of the poet **LeRoi Jones (Amiri Baraka)** and others.

The irrepressible James Baldwin

21. **Who invented detective fiction?**

(A) Edgar Allan Poe
(B) Raymond Chandler
(C) Mickey Spillane
(D) Sir Arthur Conan Doyle

It was the unpredictable Edgar Allan Poe, way back in the 1840s, who wrote the first modern **detective fiction.** Poe's "*The Murders in the Rue Morgue*" (1841) and "*The Purloined Letter*" (1845) introduced C. Auguste Dupin, master of **ratiocination** and the prototype of all fictional detectives. The classic detective story reverses the usual narrative sequence of events: the reader learns of the central event, some catastrophe (usually a murder), right at the beginning of the story. The suspects are then introduced, and the reader follows the detective as he pieces together what happened. The story ends in a climactic revelation of whodunnit, why, and how.

Dashing Dashiell Hammett

Detective fiction became one of the most popular twentieth-century genres, taken to new places beginning in the 1920s by writers like **Dashiell Hammett** (1894-1961) and his disciple, **Raymond Chandler** (1888-1959). While Poe and followers like **Sir Arthur Conan Doyle**, creator of **Sherlock Holmes**, had made their detectives genteel, high-brow types and set their murders in polite society, Hammett and Chandler moved the scene to a gritty urban environment, and introduced the cynical, tough, hardened sleuth embodied by Hammett's Sam Spade in classics like *The Maltese Falcon* (1930). Chandler's Philip Marlowe also captured fans of hardboiled detective fiction in works like *The Big Sleep* (1939) that were later turned into successful movies. Detective fiction has always been a good gauge of what's going on behind the face our society shows the world, and today's detective fiction reflects the multicultural reality of American life. The contemporary sleuth is as likely to be black (in the work of **Walter Mosley**) or Native American (in **Tony Hillerman**) as white, female (**P.D. James** and hundreds of others) as male, etc. She might even be gay (**Sandra Scoppettone**).

22. **Which of the following was a movement in post-World War II literature?**

   (A) Neoclassicism
   (B) Neoromanticism
   (C) Postmodernism
   (D) Post-traditionalism

The French Lieutenant's Woman (1981), starring Jeremy Irons and Meryl Streep. How do you adapt a postmodern novel, full of authorial self-awareness, to the screen? This movie takes **John Fowles's** novel and adds a postmodern cinematic twist: a film is being made within the film.

The literature produced after World War II (p. 650) is sometimes called **postmodern**. A response to the almost unthinkable evil and destruction the world had witnessed during World War II, postmodernism continues the questioning, anti-establishment intellectual tradition of modernism. But postmodernism also differs significantly from modernism. Modernism was in many ways an elitist movement that placed art in a privileged realm; modernists rejected the average, common, and ordinary. Postmodernists, in contrast, attempt to incorporate **mass culture**—television, cartoons, popular music, advertising—into their art. A central technique of postmodernist literature, obvious in the work of **Thomas Pynchon** (1937-), for example, is to freely blend genres, styles, and attitudes into a pastiche that defies easy classification. The postmodern writer also tends to be highly self-conscious about his own role as author and about the reader's expectations when she sits down to read a book. Postmodernists like the Frenchman **Roland Barthes,** the naturalized American **Vladimir Nabokov**, and the Czech **Milan Kundera** call attention to their work as a constructed, indeterminate *text*, not a transparent reflection of some outside "reality." In the postmodernist **antinovel** and the **new novel,** which originated in France, all the reader's expectations, such as for plot or a description of setting, can be left out. And like postmodernist developments in other fields—pop art (p. 615) or the music of John Cage (p. 304), for example—postmodern literature has a playful side.

These aspects of postmodernism, associated also with the school of linguistic and literary theory called **poststructuralism**, present a point of view about the nature of not only literature and art but of human existence. Postmodernists challenge the humanist (p. 250) assumption that human beings are coherent, purposeful essences and that the world is centered and knowable. The "decentered" literary works of postmodernism call into question the author's authority and the ability of language to communicate reality. This idea gave rise in the 1970s to the school of literary criticism known as **deconstruction**, brought to the spotlight by critics and theorists such as **Jacques Derrida** and **Michel Foucault**. Deconstructionists highlight the ways in which literary texts inevitably contradict themselves, and in so doing, expose the author's underlying ideological agendas. Deconstructionists herald the **death of the author**—seeking not to uncover an author's intentions, but instead examining the text as a cultural artifact.

While postmodernism was germinating, the "mainstream" of American literature in the 1950s was made up of a group of writers—mostly well educated, white, and male—who wrote literate, traditional fiction that was published in magazines such as *The New Yorker*: **John Updike, John Barth,** and **John Cheever,** among others. A few women

---

WHEN IS A NOVEL NOT A NOVEL?

Some contemporary writers continue to blur the line between fiction and nonfiction. Documentary fiction, such as E.L. Doctorow's Ragtime (1975), goes beyond historical fiction to incorporate not only characters and events from the past but also actual news reports. The (oxymoronic?) nonfiction novel is even more daring: Truman Capote's In Cold Blood (1966) and Norman Mailer's The Executioner's Song (1979), both stories of convicted murderers, are based on detailed interviews with the murderers themselves, purporting to offer "inside" fiction.

FROM *THE ART OF THE NOVEL*

You know, the novel took the particular historic path it took. It could just as easily have taken a completely different one. Throughout its history, the novel hasn't much taken advantage of that. It has missed out on that freedom. It has left unexplored many formal possibilities.

——Milan Kundera

writers, like **Mary McCarthy** and **Grace Paley**, achieved the same kind of status. The popularity of similarly traditional writers who also were Jewish, like **Saul Bellow**, **Bernard Malamud**, **Isaac Bashevis Singer**, and **Philip Roth**, during this time attests to the mainstreaming of Jewish-American culture by the 1950s. Another *New Yorker* writer, **J.D. Salinger** (1919-), also appeared—and disappeared—in the 1950s and early 1960s, publishing the immortal novel of adolescence *Catcher in the Rye* (1951) and several other novels and stories before retreating from the public altogether in 1965.

A saturnine Salinger

23. **The Beat Generation writers were influenced by**

    (A) drugs, Buddhism, and jazz
    (B) technology and science fiction
    (C) natural healing, vegetarianism, and mysticism
    (D) dadaism and surrealism

Would you have Naked Lunch with this man?

While the 1950s are looked back on as a stiff, establishment decade, actually a lot of innovation and rebellion existed right alongside the mainstream. The **Beats** were a loosely organized group of anti-establishment writers and poets centered in New York City and San Francisco during the 1950s and 1960s. The so-called **Beat Generation** lifestyle was created around a loose amalgam of bebop (p. 311), drugs, and Buddhist (p. 479) musings and a rejection of crass, commercialized American society. As writers, the Beats were strongly influenced by **Henry Miller** (1891-1980), whose energetic, sexually charged fiction (including the autobiographical novels *Tropic of Cancer* (1934) and *Tropic of Capricorn* (1939) celebrates intense individualism and the search for a free, natural, expressive way of life.

John Clellon Holmes's *Go* (1952) is often considered the first Beat work. **William S. Burroughs** (1914-) was the most outrageous and drugged-out Beat, famous for *Naked Lunch* (1962), a surreal account of the horrors of the addict's life. The poets **Gregory Corso** and **Allen Ginsberg** recorded the poetry of protest, writing intense, often bitter denunciations of the corrupt society around them. **Lawrence Ferlinghetti,** founder of the City Lights Bookshop in San Francisco and publisher of Ginsberg's *Howl* (1956), for which Ferlinghetti was arrested on obscenity charges, wrote accessible poetry concerned with political issues in popular collections like *A Coney Island of the Mind* (1958). **Jack Kerouac's** (1923-1969) *On the Road* (1957), a free-wheeling account of

Hit the road, Jack

THE PARIS REVIEW INTERVIEW

Oh the beat generation was just a phrase I used in the 1951 written manuscript of On the Road *to describe guys like Moriarty who run around the country in cars looking for odd jobs, girlfriends, kicks. It was thereafter picked up by West Coast leftist groups and turned into a meaning like "beat mutiny" and "beat insurrection" and all that nonsense; they just wanted some youth movement to grab onto for their own political and social purposes. I had nothing to do with any of that.*

——*Jack Kerouac*

Beats on the road, looking for fulfillment and adventure, is another classic of the Beat movement.

24. **Which of the following is a characteristic of the Native American oral literary tradition?**

(A) Repetition is emphasized.
(B) Imagery is more important than plot.
(C) There is interaction between listener and speaker.
(D) All of the above

The process of recording the long and varied traditions of **Native American oral literature** did not begin until the nineteenth century, the time when many Native American communities were on the brink of annihilation. Besides the difficulty of preserving a cultural tradition whose practitioners are often fighting for survival, writing down oral texts is tricky because it changes their very nature. Essential aspects are lost, such as changes in the teller's tone of voice, the use of song, facial expressions, and the use of the space of the audience to represent places in the story. Interaction between speaker and audience, an important aspect of the oral tradition, is also impossible. Other qualities that enliven oral literature, like repetition and striking imagery that often overshadows plot, don't translate well to the written page. Nonetheless, traditional Native American oral narratives continue to be read and spoken today for their great beauty and the access they offer to the Native American cultural perspective.

The 1970s marked the emergence of a new vitality in Native American literature, sometimes called the **Native American Renaissance**. N. Scott Momaday's *House Made of Dawn* (1968), which won a Pulitzer prize, provided a huge source of inspiration. Contemporary Native American writers, some whom have never participated in tribal life, continue to draw from the rich sources of the oral tradition, often blending them with modern and postmodern literary themes and techniques.

A ZUNI CREATION MYTH

Yes, indeed. In this world there was no one at all. Always the sun came up; always he went in. No one in the morning gave him sacred meal; no one gave him prayer sticks; it was very lonely. He said to his two children: "You will go into the fourth womb. Your fathers, your mothers, ka-eto-we, tcu-eto we-mu-eto we-le-eto* we, all the society priests, society pekwins, society bow priests, you will bring out yonder into the light of your sun father." Thus he said to them. They said, "But how shall we go in?" "That will be all right." Laying their lightning arrow across their rainbow bow, they drew it. Drawing it and shooting down, they entered.

*The-eto-we are fetishes that represent the force, found deep in the earth, that is behind each society. The pekwin priest keeps the ritual calendar, and bow priests are elders who govern war and social life.

Two well-known writers who do this particularly well are **James Welsh** and **Louise Erdrich**. Novels like **Leslie Marmon Silko's** *Ceremony* (1977) have explored the relationship of Indian writers to their traditional culture and to other crucial issues: people of mixed blood contending with different traditions, the tenacity of popular stereotypes of Indians, and the question of how to tell Native American history.

Other ethnic American literatures have continued to flourish as well in the last few decades, reminding us once again that America has always been a place of diverse, sometimes conflicting voices. **Maxine Hong Kingston**, **Amy Tan**, and **Bharati Mukherjee** have brought **Asian American literature** into the mainstream in novels like Kingston's *The Woman Warrior* (1976) that evoke the immigrant experience while also broadening the definition of American identity. Gay and lesbian writers such as **Edmund White** and **Dorothy Allison** have gained wide readerships and critical acclaim with novels exploring gay identity. African American literature and intellectual life hasn't been more vibrant since the Harlem Renaissance: along with Walker and Morrison, **Charles Johnson** and **John Edgar Wideman**, among others, produce sophisticated,

> "
>
> *Literature becomes the living memory of a nation.*
>
> ——ALEXANDER SOLZHENITSYN
>
> "

eagerly awaited novels and stories. The opening up of the category of mainstream literature to previously marginalized voices—and the new critical methods that have developed in response to the new face of literature—have been perhaps the most significant literary trends of the past few decades.

25. **Which of the following is true of "hard" science fiction?**

(A) Unlike most science fiction, it is based upon known scientific fact.
(B) The story is always set in space.
(C) Time travel is a key element for plot development.
(D) While it flourished in the nineteenth century, it is rarely written by contemporary authors.

The first thing to know about science fiction is that the initiated call it **sf**, *not* sci-fi.

Mary Shelley's *Frankenstein* (1818) established a central theme for sf—the possibilities of destruction and havoc that follow from technology's challenge to nature. Two magazines, **Hugo Gernsback's** *Amazing Stories*, founded in 1926, followed by the rival *Astounding Stories*, founded in 1930, were instrumental in defining the genre. Beginning in the 1950s, a lot of sf has been concerned with the threat of nuclear annihilation, but sf fans emphasize that the genre is mostly optimistic—interested not so much in warning about inevitable futures as in speculating about possible futures. **Isaac Asimov**, **Frank Herbert** (author of *Dune* [1965]), and **Ursula K. Le Guin** all fall into this category. Often there is no "science" per se in sf novels—many address cultural growth rather than scientific development. Most frequently, the authors imagine reconstructed social orders rather than the status quo recast in space.

Science fiction that deals specifically with science is a different ball of wax. "Hard" science fiction is the product of a careful extrapolation of known scientific facts into unheard-of situations. **Michael Crichton**, author of *The Andromeda Strain* (1969) and *Jurassic Park* (1993), has gotten rich on this formula.

Ursula K. LeGuin

Just as Shelley built Frankenstein out of the burgeoning medical knowledge of the time, so too have recent discoveries in the world of computers given rise to the genre of **cyberpunk**. The cyberpunk genre relates the stories of people whose explorations of electronically constructed worlds are just as fraught with danger as Buck Rogers's battles in space. The cyberpunk novelists make adventure out of information; the space ships of the past have turned into fileservers. The latest in cultural rebellions, cyberpunk goes where most rebels are loathe to go—techno.

William Gibson has been called the father of cyberpunk. He may have coined the term "cyberspace," calling it a "consensual hallucination," but he didn't invent the concepts. Writers like Thomas Pynchon and William S. Burroughs were onto the ideas behind cyberpunk way back in the 1950s and 1960s.

26. **Does the computer age mean the end of literature?**
    (A) Yes
    (B) No
    (C) Maybe
    (D) Of course not

Contemporary literature students can't help but confront the dawn of the computer age, with **interactive books**, books on **CD-ROM**, and a thousand other alternatives to reading that the computer seems to present. Does the rise of computers mean the end of books? Will we all end up "reading" everything on CD-ROM? Will reading be obsolete in a future of endless online entertainment possibilities? In a word: *no*. Maybe it's the smell and feel of books. People are still reading, arguably more now than at any time since the advent of television. The rise of computers is not the end of literature, but rather a new phase in literary history. New literary forms are emerging that simply broaden the possibilities of literature, such as **cyberpunk fiction** and novels composed of E-mail (p. 348) correspondence. And interactive computer literature, **hypertext**, in which readers can choose from among several plot possibilities at crucial points, in some ways brings us back to the very roots of literature—the oral tradition, with its possibilities for variation and a more active role for the reader.

In this light, one recent development worth noting is a rebirth of poetry as a vital part of our culture. Bookstores report increased sales of books of poetry, and small poetry magazines flourish. **MTV** airs segments called

"The Spoken Word," in which trendy young poets read lines influenced by hip-hop (p. 329) and grunge (p. 329). In New York, the **Nuyorican Poets Cafe** hosts **poetry slams**, competitions in which poets are scored by a panel of judges while a raucous crowd shouts insults and encouragement. Most major cities have **open-mike poetry readings** in coffee bars and cafes, democratic forums for poets, from the inspired to the aspiring, from the obnoxious to the jewel-in-the-rough, to take turns reading their latest stuff. Poetry, with its sound-bite potential, seems to fit right into the fast and fragmented spirit of the age. But there are also reports from around the country of outcrops of **literary salons**, held in ordinary urban—and even suburban—households. People are actually gathering after work to discuss Jane Austen or the latest from **Jane Smiley**. We're here to tell you that reports of the demise of literature, to borrow a well-worn phrase from Mark Twain, have been greatly exaggerated.

TEN AMERICAN AUTHORS WORTH READING

Paul Bowles (1910-). Paul Bowles left America to settle in Morocco after World War II and became a famous expatriate, consulted regularly by American writers traveling through the area. Also an accomplished composer, Bowles captured the despair of the immediate post-World War II period in his daring, original *The Sheltering Sky* (1948), which was made into a so-so movie by Bernardo Bertolucci. Expatriates always have incisive views of the American character, and Bowles is up there with the best of them.

In addition to *The Sheltering Sky*, *Let it Come Down* (1952) and *The Spider's House* (1955) offer his original brand of observation about what makes Americans tick, especially compared to Arabs. His wife, Jane Bowles, who died in 1973, was also a fascinating, quirky writer, who left one novel, two plays, and several stories.

Emily Dickinson (1830-1886). While she spent most of her life at her home in Amherst, Massachusetts, the image of Emily Dickinson as an eccentric recluse is exaggerated. Dickinson had passionate attachments to family and friends, read widely, and followed the events of her day. Despite her delicate looks, she was a strong-willed, emotional person, impatient with the status quo in social as well as intellectual life, and her decisions not to publish, not to marry, and not to venture much into the world at large reflect the sophisticated philosophy she developed in her poetry and letters. Dickinson packed emotion into her language, often by using words in startling ways: "I can wade Grief— / Whole Pools of it— / I'm used to that— / But the least push of Joy / Breaks up my feet / And I tip, drunken..." In contrast to her contemporary, Walt Whitman, who preferred bigness ("I skirt the sierras . . . my palms cover continents"), Dickinson found great meaning in smallness: "It would have starved a Gnat— / To live so small as I— / And yet I was a living Child— / With Food's necessity . . . " Even a quick glance at Dickinson's poems is enough to convince you that she had a brilliant, unique mind worth spending some time with.

Ernest Hemingway (1898-1961). His style is easy to parody—the annual "imitation Hemingway" contest continues to draw hundreds of often hilarious entries—but its revolutionary quality, and the work that went into creating it, shouldn't be overlooked. The short and clipped—or long and unmodulated—sentences, the understatement and seemingly flat tone, are meant to convey turbulent depths beneath the controlled surface of his characters' lives. A dull reader will see Hemingway's writing as emotionless; a subtle one will discern the enormous, complex feelings behind everything. Start with *In Our Time* (1925), a collection of linked short stories that take place in the aftermath of World War I, which introduce Nick Adams, Hemingway's alter-ego. Later novels like *The Sun Also Rises* (1926) and *A Farewell to Arms* (1929) further Hemingway's exploration of the masculine American character: the conflict between emotional repression and the need for love, the difficult place of his brand of rugged masculinity in genteel American culture, and the missed communication between men and women.

Langston Hughes (1902-1967). The writing of Hughes, the major figure of the Harlem Renaissance, still seems innovative—and fun—today. Hughes had a playful, sneaky sense of humor and a strong, emotional understanding of human problems in general and the African American ordeal in particular. His use of jazz and blues rhythms and themes in his poetry is astounding. A huge volume of his collected works has just come out, but if you want to start small, try *The Weary Blues* (1926), his first collection of poetry. "Droning a drowsy syncopated tune / Rocking back and forth to a mellow croon, / I heard a Negro play, / Down on Lenox Avenue the other night / By the pale dull pallor of an old gas light . . . "

Herman Melville (1819-1891). If you never got through *Moby-Dick* (1851) in school, it's never too late to go back to it. Though he was an astute observer of his own culture, Melville's outlook and talents were ahead of his time. He failed to earn a living as a writer, ending his days as an inspector at New York's Custom House, composing poetry and his spare, wistful final novel, *Billy Budd, Sailor* (1891), without the hopes of an audience. Melville is a supremely undisciplined writer—he breaks all the rules, he rambles exuberantly, he introduces characters, then forgets them, he favors strange and outrageous comparisons. For all these things modern audiences have loved him. *Moby-Dick* is simply a ton of fun. But if you're not up for the length of it, some of Melville's stories pack an equal punch in a much smaller space. No indictment of slavery is as sly, smart, and terrifying as "Benito Cereno." No story captures the dawning strangeness of modern urban life as well as "Bartleby the Scrivener."

Toni Morrison (1931-). Winner of the 1994 Nobel Prize for literature, the first black woman to have won this highest award, Toni Morrison is at the center of the American literary scene right now. Her early novels, like *The Bluest Eye* (1970), *Song of Solomon* (1977), and *Sula* (1973), are joyful and heartbreaking at the same time, steeped in emotion but never sentimental, held together with a no-nonsense, clear-eyed vision. Even these early works, however, won't prepare you for *Beloved* (1987). This complex, lyrical novel about Sethe, who murders her baby rather than give her up to slavery, is mind-blowing. Morrison makes all of African American history come together seamlessly; in her hands the historical novel appeals directly to today.

Flannery O'Connor (1925-1964). O'Connor whipped up a strange, heady brew of Catholic, Southern, Grotesque, and Gothic fiction. She wanted to shock her readers into seeing mystery, the extraordinary, in everyday life. Her stories of poor Southern whites are funny, sad, macabre, and finally horrifying. Suffering from lupus erythematosus, a debilitating disease of the immune system, O'Connor died at thirty-nine after over a decade of struggling with intense pain, walking only with canes and crutches, but continuing to write two or three hours a day. Her two novels, *Wise Blood* (1952) and *The Violent Bear It Away* (1960), are memorable, but her real forte was the short story. The collections *A Good Man Is Hard to Find* (1955) and *Everything That Rises Must Converge* (1965) give you the full range of her powers.

Adrienne Rich (1929-). She started her career writing precise, formal poetry, which was praised by Auden himself. But after coming out as a lesbian and becoming involved in the feminist movement, Adrienne Rich moved her poetry toward the freely structured, personal, politically aware mode she has become acclaimed for. Her intellectual rigor and flair for the perfect word and the perfect image make even her open-ended poetry seem somehow tight and disciplined. Reading poems from her early collections, like *A Change of World* (1951) to later ones like *Diving Into the Wreck* (1973) and *A Wild Patience Has Taken Me This Far* (1981), lets you chart the course of a woman's mind coming into awareness of itself and a sad but strong confidence of its place in the world.

Edith Wharton (1826-1937). Wharton was an upper-class snob and an anti-Semite, but she is a fascinating writer who has a lot to say about the society she lived in and about human experience in general. The place to start is *The House of Mirth* (1905), the story of the demise of the beautiful Lily Bart. Published in 1905, the novel captures with stunning clarity the unjust situation of society women who must marry to make a living. Lily is a compelling heroine, plucky and honorable but never idealized, and the forces that combine to bring her down—the hypocrisy of upper-class East Coast society, the precarious position of upper-class women with no skills except looking good, the power over women's lives invested in the hands of men—come through with a subtle force. The irony of Wharton's life is that she helped bring about the downfall of a society that she came to value in some ways over what replaced it. In *The Age of Innocence*, published in 1920 after World War I and wrenching social changes, a nostalgic Wharton looks back fifty years to a time of social obligations and a touching, if repressive, gentility.

Walt Whitman (1819-1892) Walt Whitman sought to create a new, genuinely American style of poetry, and his work is still startling and energizing today. His lines are loosely structured, rambling, passionate, anti-elitist, fiercely democratic. His central subject was often himself, but he spoke always as one of the people. He was the great equalizer—no subject was too delicate for him to broach, from masturbation to homosexual love. In the central poem of *Leaves of Grass*, "Song of Myself," Whitman names himself: "Walt Whitman, an American, one of the roughs, a kosmos / Disorderly fleshy and sensual . . . eating and drinking and breeding / No sentimentalist . . . no stander above men and women or apart from them . . . " Whitman took genuine delight in the hodgepodge of American life, and his poetry still stands as a testament to the possibilities of democracy and equality.

ANSWERS

1. C	2. A	3. D	4. B	5. A	6. D	7. C	8. A	9. D	10. A
11. B	12. B	13. A	14. A	15. D	16. D	17. A	18. C	19. A	20. A
21. A	22. C	23. A	24. D	25. A	26. B				

Over time, the function of music in Western culture has changed. Music has gone from being a key element of social, spiritual, and political rituals to being primarily a form of entertainment. The tight control over music exercised by the Church beginning in the Middle Ages led to the eventual division of music into written, "high" art forms and oral, "low," or folk, traditions. This bifurcation continues today, with entire musical traditions evolving within each category. The rise of popular music as a fundamental element of twentieth-century mass culture seems to indicate the triumph of "the people's music." Yet the continuing vitality of the classical canon and the success of forms, like jazz, that bridge the gap between the two attest to the dynamic and always unpredictable role of music in our culture.

1. The lyre, an ancient instrument, is the origin of which of the following?

   (A) Lyra, the constellation
   (B) Lira, Italian money
   (C) Liar, as in one who tells untruths
   (D) Laryngitis, as in losing one's voice

Music in the Roman Empire was, to put it bluntly, stolen Greek music. Other than some brass instruments, Roman culture contributed little to the music of its time. The old adage has it that Nero fiddled while Rome burned. More likely, he was plucking on a Greek *kithara*.

Like virtually every other Western artistic tradition, Western music finds its roots in Greek and Roman culture. However, because of music's performative nature and the relatively late development of a standardized system of musical notation, we have a far less detailed understanding of what music was like in classical culture than we do of literature and the visual arts. The spread of Christianity in Europe from the fifth to ninth centuries also had a lot to do with the disappearance of the music of antiquity. Christians believed the music of the Greeks and Romans was related to pagan ritual, and they therefore sought to erase all evidence of ancient musical practices.

The Greeks believed that music possessed **ethos**—the ability to affect the emotion and behavior of the listener. They also believed it was a gift from the gods, so music plays a big part in Greek mythology. **Apollo**, god of music, prophecy, and healing, is often depicted in Greek art holding a **lyre**, a guitar-like instrument made of a tortoise shell and two wooden shafts with strings stretched between them. According to Greek mythology, Apollo was the father of **Orpheus**, a Thracian poet and the greatest

Orpheus soothes the savage beasts.

mortal musician. The lyre, in this case, was passed from father to son. On the day that Orpheus was to marry his beloved **Eurydice**, she was killed by a poisonous snake. Heartbroken, Orpheus decided to seek her out in the realm of the dead. When he arrived in the underworld, Orpheus sang so tenderly for his lost bride that it is said that tears streamed down the **Furies'** cheeks and **Sysiphus** sat on his rock to listen. Also moved by this lament was Pluto, god of the underworld, who in turn allowed Orpheus to lead Eurydice back to the world of the living, but only on the condition that he never look back to see if his bride was following. Orpheus couldn't bear the suspense. He looked back to check on Eurydice, and immediately she was dragged back to the underworld. Again, Orpheus turned to his music, playing a lament so sad it caused Thracian maidens, in a fit of passion, to tear him into a million pieces and throw his head and lyre into the river Hebrus. Oops. Out of sympathy, Jupiter, king of the gods, picked the lyre out of the river and placed it among the stars. To this day, you can see that instrument in the constellation **Lyra**.

L'Orfeo, by Claudio Monteverdi. Many early operas and operettas looked to classical culture for material.

Almost no actual written music remains from ancient Greek culture, but Greek painting, sculpture, and literature show us that music, in addition to being associated with religious ritual and storytelling, was an important social activity and source of entertainment. In addition to the lyre, the *aulos* (a primitive type of flute), and *kithara* (a forerunner of the guitar) were the principal instruments used (though all three originally came from Asia). Music at this point in Western history was exclusively **monophonic**, which means it consisted of a single melodic line. The move from monophony to **polyphony**—music with more than one melodic line—was a critical musical innovation of the Middle Ages.

The Lyre of Orpheus (1990), by Robertson Davies. This is a brilliant, clever book—a love of music and mythology play out in a gripping contemporary novel.

2. **When was Gregorian Chant developed?**

   (A) The seventh century
   (B) The ninth century
   (C) The eleventh century
   (D) The thirteenth century

A chorus of medieval monks

From the fifth to the fifteenth centuries of the Middle Ages, the codification and technological development of music was overseen by the Christian church. Meanwhile, a great deal of secular folk music and musical storytelling was performed by travelling entertainment troupes. Within the church, the principal musical form was **plainchant**, or plainsong—a monophonic, chant-like vocal music that evolved from Hebrew cantillation and the Greek **chorus**. In the ninth century, plainchant came to be known as **Gregorian chant**, named after St. Gregory, the reformer of liturgical music who sought to unify the Christian church "by means of a common music." Texts for Gregorian chant were taken from the Mass, the Bible, and the Psalms.

TASTY TUNES

"The delight of melody He mingled with the doctrines so that by the pleasantness and softness of the sound heard we might receive without perceiving it the benefit of the words, just as wise physicians who, when giving the fastidious rather bitter drugs to drink, frequently smear the cup with honey."

3. When are vespers supposed to be recited?

   (A) Sunrise
   (B) Sunset
   (C) During the Mass
   (D) At noon

Through the twelfth, thirteenth, and fourteenth centuries, a "science" of music—a systematic codification of its component parts—was developed by the Church. Along with this deeper analysis came the gradual development of **polyphony**. The two broadest categories of church music in the Middle Ages were the **Mass** and the **Offices**. The standard Mass consisted of five sung parts, to be recited in the following order:

1. *Kyrie eleison*   "Lord have mercy upon us"
2. *Gloria in excelsis deo* "Glory be to God on high"
3. *Credo in unum deum*   "I believe in one God"
4. *Sanctus/Benedictus*   "Holy, holy, holy"/"Blessed is he
                               that cometh"
5. *Agnus Dei*   "Lamb of God"

The Offices were to be recited in the following order, from dawn till late in the evening:

1. Matins   Before daybreak
2. Lauds   At sunrise
3. Prime   6:00 AM
4. Terce   9:00 AM
5. Sext   Noon
6. Nones   3:00 PM
7. Vespers   At sunset
8. Compline   Immediately following vespers

4. Which one of the following types of performers was NOT a product of secular music in the Middle Ages?

   (A) Troubadores
   (B) Castrati
   (C) Meistersingers
   (D) Jongleurs

In sharp contrast to the ever more formulaic and disciplined music of the medieval church, medieval secular music thrived on entertainment,

Die Meistersinger von Nürberg, by Richard Wagner and *Il Trovatore* by Giuseppe Verdi. These operas, both written in the nineteenth century, are about the medieval minstrels of Germany and Spain. Both are among the most popular and widely performed today.

humor, and improvisation. So, while the church was endeavoring to unify Europe spiritually with "Christian music," wandering poet-composers were uniting smaller regional groups through tales of love, war, heroism, and chivalry. Among these secular minstrels were Spanish and Italian *troubadores*, German *meistersingers* (literally, "master singers"), and French *jongleurs* (from "jugglers," who also traveled with musical entertainment troupes).

5. **Who was known in the Renaissance as "The Prince of Music?"**

   (A) Mozart
   (B) Apollo
   (C) Dionysius
   (D) Palestrina

Renaissance composer *Giovanni Pierluigi da Palestrina* (1524-1594), composer of 104 Masses, 250 **motets** (complex unaccompanied vocal pieces on sacred themes), and numerous **madrigals** (the same idea but on secular themes), was instrumental in loosening up church music from the extreme strictures of the Middle Ages. The Masses he wrote were so original that a "Palestrinian Style" of Mass writing became popular. Known as "The Prince of Music," Palestrina is said to have singlehandedly saved polyphony in church music. There's a story behind this: on September 10, 1562, the Church Council of Trent decided that church music had to allow for the words of the Mass to be understood clearly by the listener, and that **counterpoint**—the combination of two or more melodic lines (a.k.a. polyphony)— made the words incomprehensible. What's more, the council held that the "mixing" inherent to

In the thirteenth century, at the time of its invention, the motet was for three voices. In the Renaissance, motets were written for six voices. The madrigal, first developed in the fourteenth century, is often written in five parts. Its chief musical characteristic is the close reflection of the words in the sound of the music. For example, if the text describes someone running down a hill, the accompanying music might quickly descend down a scale.

Anne, if you screw that chord up *one more time* . . .

counterpoint was just too risqué for church: they proclaimed that "all music in which anything lascivious or impure is mixed, whether for the organ or for voices, is to be kept out of the churches . . . ." In response, Palestrina presented the Council with his *Missa Papae Marcelli*, or *Pope Marcellus Mass*. The counterpoint in this Mass was so clean, the words so clear, and the music so moving, that the Council rescinded its restriction of counterpoint, and Palestrina earned a place in Western history as the savior of church music.

Missa Papae Marcelli, by Palestrina. If possible, get the recording of the Tallis Scholars singing this Mass. It's one of the most magical pieces of music you will ever hear.

6. **A string quartet consists of**
   (A) two violins, one viola, and one victrola
   (B) two violins, one cello, and one viola
   (C) two violins, one viola, and one bassoon
   (D) two violas, one violin, and one cello

The **baroque** period in music, roughly spanning the years 1600 to 1750, was characterized by the development of the *stile moderno*, or "modern style," which arose in reaction to the *stile antico*, the "old style" church music. A number of new musical forms were created in the *stile moderno*, the most important being the "*drama per musica*."

Generally, in the baroque period, oratorios were based on biblical stories, while operas dealt with mythology.

The invention of the **violin** and the **harpsichord**, as well as big advances in the quality of instrument manufacturing, were vital to the development of the *stile moderno*. Composers quickly discovered that violins could be played at tempos and pitches that were impossible for the human voice to reach. This led to the development of **chamber music**—music for small instrumental ensembles. With all these innovations, music was becoming an appreciable form of art in itself, and not just a tool for religious worship.

"Opera" is short for the Latin *opera per musica,* or "musical work." An oratorio, on the other hand, is a dramatic poem set to music for soloists and orchestra, to be performed without costumes or staging.

BLIND PASSION

While the stile moderno was developing throughout the 1600s, 1685, the year both Bach and Handel were born, is known as the true birth of the modern era in music. Bach and Handel never met. However, toward the end of their lives they both had similar eye problems and were both operated on by the same doctor who may have had the distinction of blinding the two greatest composers of the Baroque era.

7. Which two Gospels did Bach put to music in his
   Passions?

   (A) Matthew
   (B) Mark
   (C) Luke
   (D) John

GREAT BAROQUE MUSIC

Bach's Mass in B minor *and his*
    Brandenburg Concertos
Handel's Messiah
Vivaldi's The Four Seasons

Johann Sebastian Bach (1685-1750)
was diligent, religious, and, in his time,
relatively unappreciated for his
extraordinary composing abilities.
Staggeringly prolific, he is remembered as the greatest composer of
the baroque period: he wrote
over 200 cantatas, 170 chorales,
forty-eight preludes and fugues,
three passions (one of which is
lost—we still have John and
Matthew), the monumental *Mass
in B minor*, and a long list of
sonatas, concertos, partitas, suites,
airs, preludes, fantasies, and toc-
catas. Bach worked his entire life as a
humble organist and music director for
various courts in Germany. While Bach
claimed that he wrote music exclusively

Johann Sebastian Bach

to please God, his countryman **George Frederick Handel** (1685-1759)
openly admitted that he wrote simply to please the public. Not surprisingly, Handel became rich and famous while Bach did not. Handel is
remembered principally as the composer of *Messiah*, an **oratorio** that is
still ubiquitous around Christmas time. Handel also wrote over forty
operas and many other musical works.

8. Which of the following is NOT a musical form
   characteristic of the Classical period?

   (A) Symphony
   (B) Sonata
   (C) Tone Poem
   (D) String Quartet

In the **Classical period** of classical music (a strange distinction to make), music began to break with the aesthetic principle of representation that was originally established by the Greek philosophers. In other words, up until the late 1700s, music was supposed to be an artistic imitation of reality. But gradually music began to be seen as expressive rather than representational, meaning a melody could be appreciated as a thing in itself, unconnected to any earthly object or action.

 How can music imitate reality? Does it make sense to call music a representative, or **mimetic** art form? This question has been debated—and has remained unresolved—since the time of Plato and Aristotle.

9. What are the three steps, in order, that a theme takes in a classical sonata?

(A) Recapitulation, Development, Exposition
(B) Development, Exposition, Recapitulation
(C) Exposition, Development, Recapitulation
(D) Exposition, Recapitulation, Development

The musical forms introduced in the Baroque period became firmly established in the Classical period. The major types of classical pieces are:

 Symphony #88 in G major by Josef Haydn. Now that's a symphony!

Sonata
> A specific musical structure in which a theme goes through:
> > 1. Exposition
> > 2. Development
> > 3. Recapitulation

Symphony
> A sonata written for full orchestra.

String Quartet
> A chamber ensemble of two violins, a cello, and a viola.

Concerto
> A piece written to showcase a particular instrument or group of instruments against the backdrop of an orchestra.

Opera
> An old format that began to embrace subjects other than myth and religion.

> "
> *What passion cannot Music raise and quell?*
>
> —— JOHN DRYDEN
> "

10. **Mozart wrote which of the following?**

    (A) *The Marriage of Figaro*
    (B) *The Barber of Seville*
    (C) *William Tell*
    (D) *Carmen*

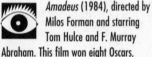

Mozart (1991), by Wolfgang Hildesheimer. This is a fascinating biography that reads like a novel.

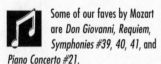

Amadeus (1984), directed by Milos Forman and starring Tom Hulce and F. Murray Abraham. This film won eight Oscars, including Best Picture. It's really good, especially Abraham's role as the doomed-to-mediocrity composer Salieri.

Some of our faves by Mozart are *Don Giovanni, Requiem, Symphonies #39, 40, 41,* and *Piano Concerto #21.*

Calling **Wolfgang Amadeus Mozart** (1756-1791) the greatest composer of the Classical period may be selling him short. In most people's estimation, he is the greatest composer in all of Western music, and one of the most magical artists of any kind the world has ever known. As a child prodigy, Mozart was paraded around Europe by his father, Leopold, performing for royalty in every European country. At one point, a British scientist conducted a study of the extraordinary young Mozart's genius, and in the process insisted on having a copy of Mozart's birth certificate sent to him as proof that Mozart wasn't just a phenomenally talented midget. By the time he was ten, Mozart was writing music of a simple and effortless sophistication that many of the greatest composers in history couldn't equal even in their prime.

Wolfgang Amadeus Mozart

While Mozart perfected the various types of composition taught to him, **Franz Joseph Haydn** (1732-1809) was the great structural innovator of his day. He was to the music of his time what Miles Davis (p. 312) was to the structure of jazz in this century.

11. **Who wrote the quintet known as *The Trout*?**

    (A) Gustav Mahler
    (B) Ludwig van Beethoven
    (C) Robert Schumann
    (D) Franz Schubert

In the nineteenth-century romantic period (p. 258), music turned away from the structure and rationality of the Classical period and back toward nature. Medieval heroism and mythology were once again revered, as artists began to let their imaginations run wild and their human sensibilities dictate the form of their work. This philosophical shift gave rise to music guided more by emotion than format. The strict structural guidelines of classical symphonies and string quartets were shattered in the wake of the artist's passion. Musical movements previously named only by the Italian term that dictated their pace (allegro, andante, etc.) were instead given titles that described the objects and events that inspired them. The blasphemy! In a celebration of nature and simplicity, composers wrote melodies based on folk tunes, children's songs, and regional dances. **Robert Schumann** (1810-1856) based a piano quintet on a folk tune called "The Trout" and gave it the same name. **Gustav Mahler** (1860-1911) shifted the children's song "Frere Jacques" into a minor mode and made it a funeral-like **dirge** in his first symphony, the *Titan*.

Robert Schumann was well known for his musical criticism. Oddly, however, his critical writing often took the form of a dialogue between two imaginary friends named Florestan and Eusebeus. Most people thought he was joking around with these alter egos but, apparently, Schumann actually believed these two to be real people.

12. **Beethoven wrote his Eroica, or heroic symphony, about which of the following people?**

(A) Goethe
(B) Napoleon
(C) Kant
(D) Pope Pius VII

More than any other composer, **Ludwig van Beethoven** (1770-1827) embodied the transition from classical to romantic music. His first symphony is regular, formulaic, resolved—typical of the classical method. His third symphony, the *Eroica*, expands in size and grandeur. His sixth symphony, the *Pastoral*, has five movements with **programmatic** titles such as "Scene by the brook" and "Merry gathering of country folk." His ninth symphony completely breaks with tradition, as the final movement, the famous *Ode to Joy*, is a choral piece set to a poem by German poet and dramatist **Friedrich Schiller** (1759-1805).

Ludwig van Beethoven

Listen to all of Beethoven's symphonies and all of his string quartets. It doesn't get any better than this.

Immortal Beloved (1995), starring Gary Oldman. Factually iffy, but the movie captures the mad composer's fits of passion and his anger at becoming deaf.

Beethoven named his third symphony the *Eroica*, or "heroic symphony." He had intended that it be dedicated to Napoleon, but when Napoleon began to cross over the line from freedom fighter to maniacal conqueror, Beethoven scratched his name out and instead dedicated the symphony "to a great man."

13. Who wrote the William Tell Overture?

(A) Mozart
(B) Rossini
(C) Beethoven
(D) Wagner

14. Who wrote Die Zauberflöte?

(A) Richard Strauss
(B) Wolfgang Amadeus Mozart
(C) Richard Wagner
(D) Franz Schubert

Opera does not belong to any particular period of musical history, and it's hard to pinpoint the exact tradition from which it emerged. Some possibilities are the choruses in Greek drama, the musical dramas of the medieval church, and (more locally) the oratorios of Bach and Handel. When we think of opera today, we normally think of **"grand opera,"** opera written to appeal to the European populace in the eighteenth and nineteenth centuries. The best-known opera composers of the last 300 years are:

Wolfgang Amadeus Mozart. Once again, the Shakespeare (p. 547) of music. Many drama critics claim that Mozart's operas are as valuable to the history of drama as they are to the history of music. Though all of his operas demonstrate his extraordinary creativity and are performed worldwide, the four biggies are *Die Zauberflöte* (*The Magic Flute*), *Le Nozze di Figaro* (*The Marriage of Figaro*), *Cosi Fan Tutte* (just call it by name!), and *Don Giovanni* (that is a name).

Giuseppe Verdi (1813-1901). Verdi was the pop stylist of his day. He wrote tunes for the opera that he knew he would hear people whistling the day after the show. He wrote twenty-six operas, none of them particularly innovative. The Italian Verdi believed that an Italian composer should devote himself entirely to Italian music, and this showed in the subject matter of his operas. Verdi imposed strict structural limitations on his work, but within those boundaries he painted extraordinary psychological portraits. It's hard to narrow down his operas to the most beloved, but *Otello*, *La Traviata*, *Aida*, *Rigoletto*, and *Il Trovatore* are certainly on any list of his best.

Richard Wagner (1813-1883). The brooding philosopher's composer. Deeply embedded in his comprehensive aesthetic and moral philosophy,

DON'T FORGET ROSSINI

Between the ages of eighteen and thirty, Gioacchino Rossini (1792-1868) wrote thirty-two operas, most notably The Barber of Seville *and* William Tell.

One of opera's most enduring classics is Giacomo Puccini's *Madame Butterfly* (1904), the story of an Asian woman's love affair with an American naval officer.

Wagner's operas (*Tristan und Isolde, Parsifal, Die Meistersinger von Nürnberg, The Ring Cycle*), were, in his words, *Gesamtkunstwerke*—"total works of art." Believing that music could be used as the ultimate expression of dramatic emotion, Wagner took the well-established European tradition of romantic opera and combined it with mythological symbolism and German nationalism (p. 393). In the process, he took the conventional tonal nature of Western music and foreshadowed *atonality*—music not based on the harmonic scale that had been the basis of Western music since ancient Greece. To the ear of the Westerner, he essentially said that 2+2=5. Wagner was convinced that he had discovered the future direction of musical composition, and he was right.

> " *Wagner's music is better than it sounds.*
>
> ——Edgar Wilson Nye
>
> "

15. Whose ballet, *The Rite of Spring*, incited a riot at its debut in Paris on May 29, 1913?

(A) Samuel Linsky
(B) Igor Stravinsky
(C) Fyodor Dostoyevsky
(D) Peter Tchaikovsky

With his pioneering use of atonality, Wagner ushered in the twentieth century. Classical music since Wagner has seen a number of very different phases, but through them all it's fair to say that music in the twentieth century has effectively shattered all the assumptions that had been the underpinnings of Western music since Gregorian chant. Between 1900 and 1930, European music was characterized by shocking tonal and performative experimentation. This was known as the period of **new music**. Much as in modernist art (p. 271) and modernist literature, no artistic convention was safe from the fervor of the composer caught up in the icon-smashing culture of the early twentieth century.

But all was not avant-garde experimentation in the early-twentieth-century musical world. The nationalism brought on by disintegrating national boundaries inspired a return to folk tunes as themes in order to celebrate national identity. **Leos Janácek** (1854-1928) and **Béla Bartok** (1881-1945) were instrumental in cultivating classical pieces out of folk traditions. From 1930 to about 1950 a resurgence of interest in classical composition occurred called the **neoclassical** period. **Igor Stravinsky** (1882-1971) was deeply involved in neo-classicism. Besides composing in the neoclassical style, Stravinsky also wrote the music for the wildly controversial ballet *Le Sacre du Printemps*, or *The Rite of Spring* (p. 559). With its unorthodox rhythms and harmonies, *Le Sacre du Printemps* caused a riot when it opened in Paris in 1913.

Other notable twentieth-century composers include **John Cage** (1912-1992), known for his instrumental innovations and daring iconoclasm. In his piece 4'33", Cage has his performers sit silently on stage for four minutes and thirty-three seconds. The music, he claims, is the rustling of the audience. **Phillip Glass** (1937-), though best known for his three operas *Einstein on the Beach*, *Satyagraha*, and *Akhnaten*, has written a good deal of gorgeous piano music, including *Solo Piano* based on Franz Kafka's short story "The Metamorphosis" (the story in which Gregor Samsa turns into an insect—either a cockroach or a dung beetle, depending on whom you talk to).

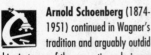

Arnold Schoenberg (1874-1951) continued in Wagner's tradition and arguably outdid him in terms of the romantic explosiveness and jarring pathos of his music. He referred to his music as "expressionistic," and claimed that it sought to represent the inner world, rather than the outer world.

16. Who wrote *Porgy and Bess*?
    (A) Ira and George Gershwin
    (B) Leonard Bernstein
    (C) Rogers and Hammerstein
    (D) Gilbert and Sullivan

Derived from the tradition of European opera and American vaudeville (p.554), the phenomenon of the American musical originated around the turn of the century and had its heyday in the twenties and thirties. Musicals are made up of songs stitched together with dialogue in order to tell a story, often about some aspect of American culture. Two of the greatest writers of musicals were **George Gershwin** (1898-1937) and the team of **Richard Rodgers** (1902-1979) and **Oscar Hammerstein** (1895-1960). Gershwin wrote *Rhapsody in Blue* (1924) and a great deal of popular American music in the early twentieth century. With his brother, Ira, George wrote the great folk opera *Porgy and Bess* (1935). Rogers and Hammerstein were the creators of *Oklahoma!* (1943), *Carousel* (1945), *South Pacific* (1949), *The King and I* (1951), and *The Sound of Music* (1959).

George and Ira Gershwin teamed up to write the first musical ever to win a Pulitzer Prize. *Of Thee I Sing* won the award in 1931.

Leonard Bernstein (1918-1990) is one of the great musical geniuses of our century. He is also one of the rare composers in whose work classical and popular music come together. During his illustrious career Bernstein performed, composed, directed, wrote books, and taught. By the time he was fourteen, he was directing and producing musicals in his high school. As a youth, he had a musical memory so powerful that (rumor has it) after seeing a performance of Cole Porter's *Kiss Me Kate*, he and some friends gathered around a piano and sang back all seventeen songs from memory. Bernstein is best known for musicals such as *Wonderful Town* (1953) and *West Side Story* (1957), though he also wrote symphonies (*Jeremiah* [1944]), movie scores (*On the Waterfront* [p.131]), and books (*The Joy of Music* [1959]).

Bernstein rehearsing for a performance (the piece he wrote had a kazoo part).

17. **The hit musical *Cats* is based on the poetry of which of the following American poets?**
    (A) Wallace Stevens
    (B) T.S. Eliot
    (C) Ezra Pound
    (D) Robert Lowell

Though the musical is past its prime, new and elaborately staged musicals continue to be produced on Broadway. Contemporary musicals draw on a number of diverse themes and are no longer restricted to the standard flag-waving fare of the art form's early days. Modern musicals include *Hair*, about the Vietnam war and antiestablishment sixties youth, *Jesus Christ Superstar*, a retelling of the Gospel, *Cats*, based on the poetry of T.S. Eliot (p. 273), and *Tommy*, the rock opera written by The Who (p. 325) that was recently staged on Broadway.

Groovy, a musical about *hair*, man. Far out.

18. **What musical tradition did NOT contribute to the creation of jazz?**
    (A) "Field hollers"
    (B) The Vienna Waltz
    (C) The blues
    (D) American popular song

Several traditions came together in African American culture at the end of the nineteenth century to form **jazz** music. Some of these were the "call and response" of West African tribal ritual music, the "field hollers" and work songs of southern plantation slaves (p. 504), the church music of hymns and spirituals, and the early, co-evolving, phenomenon of the **blues**.

The first jazz style was **ragtime**, an up-tempo syncopated piano music with "raggy rhyhms" that enjoyed tremendous popularity at the turn of the century. Pioneered by legendary Midwestern composer and pianist **Scott Joplin** (1868-1917), ragtime took off when Joplin's "Maple Leaf Rag" (1899) became a nationwide hit. Ragtime was the soundtrack for urban living in America: at dances and concerts, private parties, as stage music for variety theater, and later as the live accompaniment played in the dark houses of that new art form, the cinema.

Joplin's fame as a ragtime master was nearly outdone by Los Angeles composer and piano man Ferdinand Joseph LaMenthe **"Jelly Roll" Morton** (1885-1941). Unlike Joplin, Morton had the good fortune to play

Scott Joplin

 Scott Joplin's ragtime hits were in such demand that they helped to popularize a new invention marketed at the end of the nineteenth century—**the player piano**. While Edison's phonograph had started to appear in the homes of many people, no recording industry yet existed and Marconi's invention of the radio (p.514) was still years away.

GREAT RAGTIME AND EARLY JAZZ RECORDS

Scott Joplin: King of the Ragtime Players *(Biograph). This is a recording of rare piano rolls.*

Jelly Roll Morton:

      Volume 1: 1923-24 Masters of Jazz *(import)*

      Volume 2: 1924-26 Masters of Jazz

      Volume 4: 1925-28 Masters of Jazz *(JSP import)*

Sidney Bechet (1937-38) *(Classics)*

Bix Beiderbecke and the Wolverines *(Starline)*

New Orleans Rhythm Kings and Jelly Roll Morton *(Milestone Records)*

Louis Armstrong: Jazz Collection Disc *(The Collection)*

 Ragtime's last great period, from the end of WWI to the early 1920s, saw some of its finest performers in the composer/pianists **"Fats" Waller** and **Joe Turner**, the singer-composer **Eubie Blake**, and the great saxophonist **Sidney Bechet**.

his compositions at a time when the fledgling recording industry had developed into a thriving business. His tunes found great popularity as **phonograph records**, and cheered untold thousands of Americans weary from the dark days of World War I (p. 643).

19. **What is improvisation in jazz music?**

   (A) Making up notes to fit a tune
   (B) Composing on the spot
   (C) Following a written score when playing a solo
   (D) Both A and B

CUTTING UP IN NEW ORLEANS

*The New Orleans street tradition of marching brass bands was perhaps the earliest manifestation of improvisation in jazz music, in informal competitions known as **cutting sessions**. When two brass bands would meet each other in the street, the best hornmen in each band would try to outdo one another with improvised playing that showed off their talents. This form of musical combat survives in **jam sessions** to this day.*

While the brevity and quickness of jazz music distinguished it from the European classical tradition and surely led to its mass popularity among Americans in the Roaring Twenties, what made jazz different musically from the compositions played by European philharmonic orchestras were two things: **improvisation** and **syncopation**. Improvisation in music—the spontaneous, on-the-spot creation of melodies or the unrehearsed elaboration on a composition—was part of the tradition of many other immigrant cultures in the New World; it's likely that the instrumental improvising of Irish and Scottish jigs and reels—dance music—influenced jazz in its earliest stages. But what made jazz music unique was that the freedom of improvisation found new expression through the slightly modified classical European orchestra, and against the constraining framework of traditional European musical composition. In Western classical music, syncopation—the stressing of a weak or unstressed beat in a regular phrase of music—is always a regular pattern, occurring on the same beat or beats in each bar, and usually only in the melody or the harmony. In jazz music, syncopation is fluid and dynamic, and it happens all the time—on the melody line, in thematic phrases, in the bass line, *everywhere*.

ALMOST BLUE

*The most important experiment of early jazz performers had a permanent influence not just on jazz but on music in general: the development of new principles of harmony that departed from the traditional Western emphasis on the tonic or dominant notes in the major scale. Instead, the new jazz music emphasized an altered tonality that used partially flattened intervals in the scale, striking the note between the flat and the natural, creating a "bent" or **"blue"** sound. When this diminishing of the interval was applied particularly to the natural third and natural seventh, **"the blue note"** was said to be played.*

20. Prohibition was enacted in

- (A) 1917
- (B) 1919
- (C) 1920
- (D) 1923

After prohibition (p. 418) was enacted in 1920, the new **hot jazz** quickly developed in the speakeasies and gin-joints of America's cities. This new style was best exemplified by **King Oliver's Creole Band** in Chicago, with a newcomer named **Louis "Satchmo" Armstrong** (1901-1971) on backup cornet. Armstrong soon switched bands to become musical director of the famous **Fletcher Henderson Orchestra** in Chicago, which became the first **big band** to gain national fame as a touring road act. By 1925, the great era of the jazz band was in full flower. Bands all over the country showcased talented young musicians, many of whom would go on to forge the continually evolving language of jazz. **Benny Moten's** band based in Kansas City, Jelly Roll Morton's **Red Hot Peppers** on the West Coast, Louis Armstrong's **Hot Five** and **Hot Seven** in New York and later Paris, **Duke Ellington's** early band from St. Louis and later New York, and many others made the twenties an exciting time for jazz enthusiasts. These early jazz bands formed a sort of perpetually evolving sound laboratory, working out in their performances and recordings the rules and conventions that would form the basis of all ensemble jazz playing for the next thirty to forty years.

> ❝
>
> *Man, if you gotta ask, you'll never know.*
>
> ——Louis Armstrong, when asked to define jazz
>
> ❞

James P. Johnson, the greatest of the pianists known for playing a late form of ragtime known as **"stride"** piano, also composed the tune that more than any other came to symbolize the frantic, careless feel of the Roaring Twenties— "The Charleston."

Louis Armstrong

21. **What instrumental sections are generally NOT found in a swing orchestra?**

(A) Brass and reeds
(B) Woodwinds and strings
(C) Rhythm and percussion
(D) None of the above

The stock market crash of 1929 (p. 87) ushered out the Roaring Twenties, and the era of hot jazz gave way to the ascendancy of **swing**. Swing music got its name from the way that its syncopated playing seemed alternately to push and pull the beat along, emphasizing a stronger, more confident rhythmic element for jazz band playing. Composers like **Edward Kennedy "Duke" Ellington** (1899-1974), who played piano, envisioned an expanded instrumentation modelled after the classical **philharmonic orchestra**, only built for swing. Working from this model, he quickly adapted the concept of sections, only instead of filling them out with different string and woodwind voicings, he used brass and reeds. In an era that didn't know amplifiers, these bands were loud!

Duke Ellington

When swing bands slowed down long enough to play a ballad, they were the tunes the country fell in love to: clarinetist **Artie Shaw's** band playing "Stardust" (1939), the **Glen Miller Band** playing "Sentimental Journey" (1940), or the Basie band's "Body and Soul" (1939).

William "Count" Basie (1904-1984) and **Cabell "Cab" Calloway** (1907-1994) led two of the most popular swing bands of the thirties. With the **Benny Goodman** (1909-1986) and **Dorsey Brothers** bands also vying for attention, the field of competitors was crowded. If ragtime and early jazz gave birth to the record business, swing can likewise claim credit for much of the

GREAT BIG BAND AND SWING RECORDS

Ellington is Forever Vol. 1 (Fantasy Records)

Ellington is Forever Vol. 2 (Fantasy Records)

Benny Goodman and his Orchestra (Radiola)

Best of Louis Armstrong (MCA Jazz)

Fletcher Henderson: A Study in Frustration (Columbia)

Duke Ellington and Count Basie: First Time (OOY)

Count Basie

success of radio from the late 1920s through World War II. Nightly broadcasts from the **Cotton Club** in Harlem, **Symphony Sid's Royal Roost** all-swing show, the regular live appearances of the Goodman and Basie bands on the NBC and CBS radio networks, and the many famous broadcasts of concerts from New York's Town Hall made swing music the most popular form of entertainment during the Depression. Swing also united the country with dance fads like "jitterbugging" and the "lindy hop."

 Both blues and ensemble jazz use a structural element called the **"break,"** in which instrumentalists could show off their talents in improvised solos. These impromptu displays were highly competitive, and helped to shift the musical influence in jazz from composer to performer.

22. Which of these jazz musicians did NOT directly contribute to the creation of the bebop style?
    (A) "Dizzy" Gillespie
    (B) "Yardbird" Parker
    (C) "Bud" Powell
    (D) "Satchmo" Armstrong

During World War II, the cost of maintaining large, travelling swing bands became too prohibitive for all but the most popular acts; the mobilization of the war effort took away not just audiences but many of the players, too. Jazz ensembles underwent a downsizing for practicality's sake, and created the new sound called **bebop**. Alto saxophonist **Charlie "Bird" Parker** (1920-1955) and trumpeter **John Birks "Dizzy" Gillespie** (1923-1994) met in 1943 while both had jobs with the **Earl Hines Orchestra**. Parker had grown up in the Kansas City area and was influenced most by the bluesy, cool voicings of Lester Young. Gillespie broke from the trumpet tradition of Armstrong and instead forged a new

 How fast was the fastest bebop? Swing music, not known for being particularly slow itself, generally played note values of around 100 quarter notes to the minute. When Bird and Diz played their famous "Cherokee," the tempo typically went up to over 300 quarter notes per minute.

LADY DAY

Jazz vocalist Billie Holiday (1915-1959), also known as "Lady Day," was beloved for the completely original phrasing she brought to jazz and is best known for the classics "Stormy Weather" and "Strange Fruit," a haunting song about a lynching she witnessed as a child in the south.

style partly indebted to Roy Eldridge's fast lines. Gillespie had his own quintet playing on New York's famed 52nd Street when Parker joined him, and together they created the new sound—complex, high-speed passages played in unison by sax and trumpet, with astonishing back-to-back solos. The numbers were quick and full of energy, and the result was pure genius. Bebop was born.

23. **Which of the following were fundamental techniques of bebop improvisation?**

   (A) Following a written score
   (B) "Quoting" a short musical phrase from a popular song or an ad jingle
   (C) Playing scales derived from the chords in the tune
   (D) Both B and C

MONK

Thelonious Monk (1917-1982) brought an entirely new approach to playing piano that dispensed with most of the rules of classical and jazz traditions. Though in his day his music was sometimes denigrated as atonal, non-rhythmic playing, his achievement as a composer is now widely praised, and many credit him with being significant in the creation of a jazz modernism.

With his seminal quintet of 1947—featuring **Bud Powell** on piano, **Max Roach** on drums, **Tommy Potter** on bass and the newcomer **Miles Davis** (1926-1991) on trumpet—Bird wrote a veritable textbook on how to play bebop. Beboppers used several different modes of improvising on a theme. Some of these were: substitution of different phrases or notes; "quoting" from popular sources in the middle of a phrase; paraphrasing the melody in a slightly altered form; mode-based phrasings and chord-based phrasings; and free improvisation, which dispensed with tonality and harmony altogether.

GREAT BEBOP, HARD BOP, AND COOL JAZZ RECORDS

Charlie Parker: Bird's Best Bop on Verve *(Verve)*

Miles Davis, Milestones *(Columbia Jazz Masterpieces)*

John Coltrane: Blue Train *(Blue Note)*

Charles Mingus: Mingus Ah Um *(Columbia)*

24. Which of the following statements about Miles Davis is true?

(A) He was a poor musician from the deep South.
(B) He learned music solely by ear.
(C) He was classically trained at a music conservatory.
(D) He pioneered "swing" music.

The most famous young bebop musician to play with Parker was the conservatory-trained son of a midwestern doctor. Miles Davis, an untested twenty-one-year-old trumpet player, was asked to join Parker's group in 1947 after Gillespie and Bird split up. Though he was initially criticized for playing cracked notes, Davis went on to become the single most influential performer and composer in jazz, leading the vanguard of stylistic change that kept the music fresh for the next forty years. Virtually every kind of popular jazz was pioneered by Davis—**hard bop**, **cool jazz**, **modal jazz**, and **fusion**. During Davis's peak years of the 1950s, it was difficult for jazz affi-cionados to keep up with him.

Kind of Blue (1959), by Miles Davis. This may be the single most famous jazz album ever, with a band that reads like a *Who's Who* of bebop.

While hard bop and the cool sound prevailed in New York and Chicago, the West Coast sound took wing in the 1950s under the leadership of **Charles Mingus** (1922-1979), a brilliant bassist and composer. Mingus was renowned for his workshops, extended jam sessions intended to explore jazz composition as a collective act.

GIANT STEPS

Davis protégé John Coltrane (1926-1968) was a brilliant tenor saxophonist who revitalized the saxophone tradition at the end of the 1950s. His first great record as a band leader, Giant Steps *(1960), influenced a new generation of players, and along with Sonny Rollins, Cannonball Adderley, Stan Getz, and Dave Brubeck, Coltrane's playing increasingly went beyond the confines of the ensemble tradition. By the end of the decade Coltrane had come to influence yet another stylistic development—free jazz, led by the brilliant and iconoclastic Texas saxophonist Ornette Coleman.*

25. Who led the "Tonight Show" band when Jay Leno took over?

(A) Wynton Marsalis
(B) Branford Marsalis
(C) Paul Schaffer
(D) Doc Severenson

In the 1960s, under the growing influence of **funk** and **rock** music, **fusion jazz** became popular. Fusion unites the strong rhythmic element of the popular forms with large-scale jazz instrumentation. Miles Davis led

Working with the orchestral arranger **Gil Evans**, Miles Davis created two famous albums in the "cool" jazz style that also explored another of Davis's great innovations, **modal jazz**. *Sketches of Spain* (1959-1960) is an exploration of Spanish-flavored themes, and *Porgy and Bess* (1959) is an instrumental recording of Gershwin music from the famous Broadway musical.

the way with his 1967 album *Bitches' Brew*. Many jazz critics and fans date the increasingly diffuse trends in jazz music to the rise of fusion in the 1960s. Jazz had always been diverse, but never before had it seemed so fragmented into discrete tastes and styles. After fusion, in the 1970s and 1980s jazz forces diverged into **Afro-Cuban jazz**, **funk-jazz**, **electronic jazz**, and many other varied sounds.

Today, there's a return to bebop and "traditional" jazz music underway, led in part by the conservatory-trained trumpeter **Wynton Marsalis** and his saxophonist brother **Branford Marsalis** (who led the "Tonight Show" (p. 534) band for two years). Other newcomers like Wallace Roney, a gifted young trumpeter, have made playing swing and bebop fashionable again.

GREAT FREE JAZZ, FUSION, AND AVANT-GARDE RECORDS

Ornette Coleman: Free Jazz *(Atlantic)*

Ornette Coleman: Shape of Jazz to Come *(Atlantic)*

Miles Davis: Bitches' Brew *(Columbia Jazz Masterpieces)*

The Art Ensemble of Chicago: Complete Live in Japan 1984 *(DIW)*

26. **What is "race music"?**

(A) Music inspired by athletic events
(B) Sexually suggestive music
(C) A term for African-American music once used by white record-sellers
(D) The music played at the Kentucky Derby

White-owned record companies stopped using the term "race music" in the fifties after they became aware that its pejorative connotation was offensive to the increasing numbers of African American consumers who bought recordings. Not surprisingly, the term was equally ineffective in marketing the records to white consumers.

Over the years, the term **rhythm and blues** has been used to mean any popular music made by African Americans for African Americans that was not jazz. A huge range of music has been classified this way: early Chicago "boogie" blues in the 1940s, doo-wop and early rock and roll in the 1950s, vocal groups, soul music and Motown in the 1960s, funk and disco in the 1970s, and rap and house music in the 1980s and 1990s have all been labelled or marketed to some degree as "R & B." The term actually goes back to what was known as **"race music"** in the period following World War II. Race music was a term used by the record industry to market records by black performers to their largely black audiences, and it included a wide range of musical styles, including gospel, some

The Temptations were one of the first R & B bands that recorded with the now-legendary R & B label Motown.

country-blues and jazz, and a new species of popular, dance-oriented music later known as R & B.

While R & B had its roots in the blues, it was distinct from the **country-** and **delta-blues** music of bluesmen such as **Robert Johnson** and **Lightnin' Hopkins**, who played in the folk tradition. R & B was ensemble music, with instrumentation influenced by bebop and swing, but with the emphasis on strongly accented, simple dance rhythms.

27. **What instrument absent from 1930s swing bands was first established in R & B rhythm sections?**
    (A) Mandolin
    (B) Electric guitar
    (C) Cello
    (D) Bassoon

R & B used standard 12-bar and 16-bar blues forms, with some variations, and the rhythmic component relied mostly on the standard 4/4 time. But the instrumentation had been influenced by small jazz combos and orchestras. At the bottom of the R & B sound was the **rhythm section**,

 Louis Jordan scored big hits during wartime with his novelty records "G.I. Jive," "Choo Choo Ch' Boogie," and "Ain't Nobody Here But Us Chickens."

comprising a trap set of drums, a stand-up or "slap" bass, and by the end of WWII, the newly popular electric guitar. The melody duties usually fell to the piano, which was played in a style derived largely from the **stride playing** of the 1920s and the **boogie-woogie** style popular during the Depression (p. 87). Sometimes an organ would substitute, with a saxophone or a fuller horn section to round out the sound. Finally, in the tradition of blues and ballads, the R & B singing style emphasized feeling over virtuosity.

28. Sonny Boy Williamson and Little Walter both played
    (A) electric guitar
    (B) "slap" bass
    (C) saxophone
    (D) blues harmonica

The first R & B bands were really small jazz combos called **"jump bands."** They played in the swing style popularized by **Louis Jordan** (1908-1975) and others, and they were influenced by the blues that always lay at the heart of jazz music. Jordan's down-and-dirty horn phrasings and jive-peppered vocals fronted the **Tympany Five**, a fast and bluesy ensemble that was popular on the radio well into the 1950s. In the 1940s, some of the first great acts to establish R & B as a form distinct from jazz music were the Texas blues guitarist and vocalist Aaron **"T-Bone" Walker**, the booming "shouter" **Joe Turner**, and the legendary Chicago blues harmonica players **Sonny Boy Williamson** and **Little Walter**.

29. Masses of southern blacks moved to northern cities
    during World War II because
    (A) slavery had finally ended
    (B) locusts destroyed the cotton fields
    (C) they feared a German invasion
    (D) high-paying industrial jobs were plentiful

Radio in the early 1950s spread the driving new sound of rhythm and blues across the heartland of America, broadcasting such R & B shows as the "Jockey Jack Gibson Show" from Atlanta and "Ol' Swingmaster Benson" from Chicago.

During WWII, with most of the American population mobilized by the war effort, industrial jobs were available for African Americans for the first time ever, offering them a chance to break the cycle of tenant-farmer poverty that went back to slavery days. While it came with a sense of liberation from the oppression of the old South and the stifling reality of Jim Crow (p. 185), the mass movement of this essentially agrarian people north to an alien industrial environment presented new problems. Much of the R & B music created after the war filled a social need: bringing black

Chicago was a veritable Mecca for southern Blacks, with a plentitude of relatively well-paying jobs in factories and meat-packing plants.

THE GREAT GLOVED ONE

Rhythm and blues and pop music coalesced in one man: Michael Jackson (1958-). A child star in the 1970s with his brothers in the Jackson Five, Jackson belted out R & B like a miniature James Brown. Jackson went solo in his twenties and reached his pop music peak in 1982 with the best-selling album in history, Thriller. Jackson gained a world-wide popularity not seen since the Beatlemania days, but recently the focus has been more on Jackson's troubled personal life than his music.

people together for good times and dancing, allowing them to forget for a moment their homesickness. If much of the early R & B sounds like good-time music, that's because it is; in the words of a big hit by Louis Jordan, R & B aimed to "Let the Good Times Roll" (1946).

By the 1950s, R & B had begun to reach a larger audience, through the success of small, independent record labels often owned by African American businessmen and through radio broadcasts. Many of the famous R & B musicians of this period are also associated with the birth of rock and roll, such as **Fats Domino**, **Ray Charles** and **Etta James**. But R & B had come to encompass varied styles of popular music. The early vocal and doo-wop groups such as **The Platters** and **Frankie Lymon and the Teenagers** brought the street-corner New York and Philadelphia traditions of close harmonizing to a wide audience. R & B even began to attract white listeners. The efforts of white musicians to reproduce what they heard from African Americans created what came to be known as rock and roll (p.322).

GREAT R & B RECORDS

Sonny Boy Williamson: The Real Folk Blues *(Chess Records Originals)*
Louis Jordan and the Tympany Five *(BMG Video)*
The Best of Smokey Robinson and the Miracles *(Motown)*
Prince: The Hits, I & II *(Paisley Park/Warner Bros)*

30. Which of the following musical traditions did NOT contribute to the development of country music?

    (A) Celtic folk music
    (B) The blues
    (C) Gospel church hymns
    (D) Sonata form

American country music sells more records worldwide than any other single kind of recorded music, and in this respect it probably forms many people's first cultural impressions of America. It's easy to see the mass appeal of country's sentimental ballads, accessible melodies, and romantic depiction of a mythic Western way of life. But as commercially successful as country music is today, its roots are in the humble folk traditions of early America. These multi-ethnic traditions brought together disparate elements of oral cultures—British and Celtic balladry, Scottish and Irish instrumental dance music, the blues, work songs, early "string band" music, church hymns, cowboy songs, "mountain music," German polkas, and Mexican folk music, to name some.

While many of these strands have traditions extending over centuries, they came together to make what we know as country music sometime in the second half of the nineteenth century, mostly in the South and on the western frontier of the evolving republic. Early country music was practical—a single voice accompanied by Spanish guitar, employed to keep cowboys entertained on cattle drives; or a fiddle, mandolin, and guitar folk-ensemble providing dance music at a prairie wedding. Country music became "entertainment" after its first recordings won popularity in the early part of this century.

In bluegrass music a type of fast-paced, improvised instrumental tune known as a **"breakdown"** came to symbolize the music's wild energy. Perhaps the most famous of all the traditional breakdowns was by the Bluegrass Boys, called "Foggy Mountain Breakdown."

31. Bluegrass music came from what geographic region?

    (A) California
    (B) The Appalachian Mountains
    (C) New England
    (D) The Canadian Rockies

In the early days of country, the folk traditions that contributed to country's popularity were still mostly unassimilated within the music. **Bluegrass** music arrived from the culture of the Appalachian Mountains (p. 157) in the eastern United States, especially the Blue Ridge coal mining country in West Virginia, North Carolina, Tennessee, and Kentucky. Bluegrass traced its genealogy to the Irish and Scottish immigrants who

The **pedal steel guitar** gave many country dance tunes and ballads a distinctive voice, with its high, clear vibrato. The pedal steel consists of two or more horizontally mounted fret boards, with different stringing and tuning arrangements, played with a steel or glass tube laid across the strings that the picker slides up and down the octaves to achieve the famous sound.

came to work the coal mines and brought their music with them. In the cauldron of their mutual work experience, these immigrants and working-class Americans transformed the jigs and reels of Celtic folk music into a vital tradition of lightning-fast mandolin, banjo, and fiddle picking, which soon won popularity on recordings and radio. During the Depression, **Bill Monroe and his Bluegrass Boys** became the first bluegrass act to sell records nationally. Monroe is still active and touring today at almost ninety years old. That mountain music is tough to kill.

32. The Grand Ol' Opry began as
    (A) a television comedy show in the 1950s
    (B) a distinguished Italian opera company
    (C) an amusement park
    (D) a weekly live country-music radio show

To the east of the Cumberland Gap in Tennessee, the small city of Nashville became the mecca of country music, mostly due to the enormous success of a Saturday-night radio show based in Nashville and broadcast over a vast region stretching from Texas to the Great Lakes. This live show was billed as **"The Grand Ol' Opry,"** and it offered thousands of hungry country fans a changing roster of guests from all over the nation. Over the 1930s and 1940s, the show was central in the development of **"the Nashville Sound."** Any country act that wanted to succeed in the recording business first had to succeed on the Opry Night stage. Many of the great names of country got their break by auditioning as unknowns for the Opry, then pleasing the audience so much they won recording contracts. **Ernest Tubb**, **Lefty Frizzell**, **Earl Scruggs** and **Loretta Lynn** all became country legends on the strength of their Opry performances.

Hank Williams (1923-1953), perhaps the greatest of all the stars from country's golden era, left behind dozens of great songs and the legend of

. . . IF IT AIN'T GOT THAT TEXAS SWING

During the Depression, a unique form of country string-band music, influenced by the jazz big bands of the day, found acclaim: Texas Swing made a kind of jazz out of country, with its emphasis on virtuoso banjo, mandolin and guitar picking, improvised steel guitar and fiddle solos, and a rhythmic side that made listeners want to dance.

GREAT COUNTRY RECORDS

Bob Wills and the Texas Playboys: Anthology *(1935-1973) (Rhino)*

Bill Monroe and the Bluegrass Boys: The Essential Bill Monroe & His Bluegrass Boys *(Legacy Records)*

Johnny Cash: Johnny Cash at San Quentin *(Columbia)*

Hank Williams: Greatest *(Polydor)*

Patsy Cline: Walkin' After Midnight *(Rhino)*

Willie Nelson: Nite Life—Greatest Hits and Rare Tracks 1959-1971 *(Rhino)*

k.d. lang: Absolute Torch and Twang *(Sire/Warner Brothers)*

the tough-luck, hard-drinking, honky-tonkin' man of the road, an image embraced ever since by musicians of all genres. The list of Williams' hit songs is long indeed— "Your Cheatin' Heart," "Jambalaya," "Move It On Over," and many others. While Williams first gained fame traveling the honky-tonk and county fair circuit of Texas and Oklahoma, he eventually appeared on the Grand Ol' Opry and was a sensation with his high, lonesome ballad voice and his rowdy, bluesy, up-tempo singing. Hank Williams had bad luck in love and life, and his unhappiness kept him a lonely man. Touring constantly in the 1950s, Williams abused amphetamines and alcohol until his body gave out at the age of twenty-nine.

Hank Williams Jr., our first country superstar

Patsy Cline (1932-1963), the undisputed queen of country music, had a clear, strong voice capable of both heart-rending balladeering and foot-stomping honky-tonking that brought country recordings to a new level of sophistication in the 1950s. Through the careful selection of songs, Cline shifted some of the industry's emphasis from pickers to the songwriter, and the search was suddenly on for great songwriters to supply the stars with good material. Several hits made Cline country's

THE MAN IN BLACK

Johnny Cash (1932-) became a country music legend with hit records like "Folsom Prison Blues," "Ring of Fire," and, with his wife June Carter Cash (from the famous bluegrass clan, The Carter Family), "Will the Circle Be Unbroken." Cash has always brought outside influences to country to keep it fresh, and in 1995, forty years after his first recording, he had yet another hit record with American Recordings, which won new fans among the teenage audience of MTV (p. 536).

first bona fide international star: "Crazy," "Walkin' After Midnight," and "I've Loved and Lost Again" were some of the incredibly personal songs that made her fans so loyal. There was an outburst of grief when Patsy Cline died in an airplane crash on her way to a performance.

One of the singer-songwriters who wrote some of Patsy Cline's best numbers was a Texan who couldn't convince record companies to let him sing his own songs because his soft, bluesy voice didn't conform to the style of the day. **Willie Nelson's** (1933-) distinctive blend of blues, jazz, and Texas Swing stylings made it hard for him to establish a career as a performer, and instead for twenty years he watched songs he sold to publishers for as little as fifty dollars (like "Crazy") became international hits. Eventually Willie's outsider status in Nashville helped establish a fresh, new approach that carried country music into the 1970s.

33. **Alan Freed used what medium to popularize R & B?**

    (A) Radio
    (B) Television
    (C) Books and magazines
    (D) None of the above

The confluence of two great streams of popular American music—the blues traditions of African-Americans and the country and popular song traditions of white Americans—creates the river of **rock and roll**. As the folk-blues and rhythm and blues of the 1940s and 1950s grew in popularity, white performers increasingly adapted the new sounds to music for white audiences, and the result was yet another hybrid musical form, emphasizing a strong beat for dancing, standard blues and ballad song structure, and using small combo instrumentation.

Much of the credit for exposing white listeners to the vibrant music of rhythm and blues, and hence the credit for helping to "create" rock and roll itself, falls to the Cleveland disc jockey **Alan Freed** (1922-1965), who as early as 1951 spun "race" records for teenaged white listeners. The acts he popularized included **Fats Domino**, whose New Orleans boogie-woogie piano sound had direct antecedents in the stride jazz-piano men of the 1920s; **Nat "King" Cole**, with his sophisticated jazz vocal stylings and piano playing;

Alan Freed chatting with Frankie Avalon and a few one-hit wonders.

and **Eartha Kitt**, whose recordings relied on fast rocking electric music. Freed is credited with coining the term "rock and roll," though it may have already been in use among black radio announcers.

34. Who was the first white rock and roll performer to "sing black"?

(A) Eddie Cochran
(B) Pat Boone
(C) Perry Como
(D) Elvis Presley

Elvis Presley (1935-1977) was the first white performer who, in the words of alarmed cultural observers of the day, "sang black." While today it's difficult to understand these strict racial categories, in the context of the music available to white pop fans in the 1950s—typified by such bland, clean-cut performers as **Pat Boone**, **Dean Martin**, and **Connie Francis**—any white singer who would get up on a stage and sing sexually suggestive lyrics in a loose, slurring and moaning voice while shaking his hips had clearly crossed over the "color line" in American society.

The King

HE WAS ALWAYS SUCH A SWEET BOY

Elvis Presley was a truck driver when he cut his first record using a popular attraction of the day, an instant record booth, where for a few dollars a customer could sing into a microphone, wait a few minutes, and have a freshly-cut wax record as a keepsake. Elvis's first recording was a birthday song for his mother, Gladys.

Presley's singing offended many older white listeners, but to their children, the sound he made was amazingly liberating. Presley's early hits, such as "Heartbreak Hotel," "Hound Dog," and "Don't Be Cruel," were equally popular with white and black audiences.

While the spectacle of Elvis Presley's sensational popularity represented, in part, a new generation of white Americans accepting and enjoying what were essentially black cultural forms, the conflicts inherent in the new music made the racism of

American culture in the fifties plain. For while Elvis consciously modelled his sound on the great early African American rock legends **Little Richard**, **Bo Diddley**, and **Chuck Berry**, the lucrative demand for product on the part of huge white audiences that he set in motion never really translated into success for the black performers of the day. Only those white acts expert enough to capture the black sound profited. **Bill Haley and the Comets** had a hugely popular hit in 1955 with "Rock Around the Clock"; **Jerry Lee Lewis** struck big with many hits, including "Great Balls of Fire"; **Eddie Cochran's** "Twenty-Flight Rock" was a hit; and even Pat Boone attempted to copy the black sound and popular rock and roll songs, to his great personal enrichment. In this respect, rock and roll captured in its early years one of the prevailing themes of the country as a whole: it was simultaneously a point of cultural community and conflict.

35. **The people buying rock and roll records were**

   (A) college professors
   (B) music critics
   (C) teenagers
   (D) parents

While Elvis Presley was the first true rock star, his years as a rock and roller were short-lived. When he received his draft notice for military service, fans all over the country thought the new sound had no chance of surviving Presley's departure for Germany. Cultural critics dismissed the past three years of frenzied teenage adulation as nothing more than a fad. But these observers underestimated the enormous force of the new youth culture growing daily in every corner of American life. By the end of the 1950s, the postwar baby boom had produced its first wave of teenagers crazy for their own culture. Rock and roll was their music, and its development over the next decade went hand-in-hand with the growing social, political, and moral influence of youth culture. The early heroes created by the new culture of youth included the great Texas songwriter and rocker **Buddy Holly**, the Chicano star **Richie Valens** (who died in the same plane crash as Buddy Holly), and the New York City Italian-American idol **Dion DiMucci**. For every segment of young people, there was a rock and roller to worship.

TWISTIN' THE NIGHT AWAY

The early rock and roll dance craze "the Twist" was inspired by the song of the same name by **Chubby Checker**, *a Philadelphia chicken-plucker who wanted to sing rock and roll.*

WHEN THE CAT'S AWAY

Elvis's first real recording session at the legendary **Sun Records** *was not going well: they had spent the afternoon trying various Perry Como-type vocal covers. When the producer and owner* **Sam Phillips** *left the studio for a moment, Elvis and the band fooled around with some R & B stylings. He sang a popular "black" song "That's Alright Mama," and the rest is history.*

36. The Detroit sound was called

(A) jump music
(B) swing music
(C) Motown
(D) jive music

In Detroit, the beginning of the 1960s saw the development of a new form of R & B music that many white rock and roll fans embraced as their own—the **Motown** sound, so-called after the black-owned record label founded by the legendary **Berry Gordy Jr**. (1929-). Motown's first great star was the group **Martha and the Vandellas**, led by a young black singer named Martha Reeves, and produced by a brilliant artist of the new medium of the recording studio, **Phil Spector** (1940-). Their hits "Heatwave" and "Dancing in the Street" marked the signature Motown sound: saturated reverb, horns, and a driving beat behind a "wall of sound." Following quickly on Martha and the Vandellas' success, a parade of great Motown acts bridged the gap from the early rock and roll to the English pop bands and beyond to the Vietnam years: **the Supremes**, **the Ronettes**, **Smokey Robinson and the Miracles**, and **Marvin Gaye** (1939-1984), among others. The Supremes, led by their glamorous lead singer **Diana Ross** (1944-), created the trend of the all-girl singing group, which can still be seen today in the success of such acts as Salt n' Pepa and En Vogue.

By 1964, rock and roll began to lose steam as the first wave of rock and rollers died (Buddy Holly and Richie Valens), left for Hollywood (Elvis), or were driven from the music business for morals violations (Jerry Lee Lewis). A new crop of talent, however, was growing in England, absorbing every note of American music played over Armed Forces Radio or Radio Free Europe. These English teenagers, like their American counterparts, were looking for a culture of their own, and found it in rock and roll. In the industrial city of Liverpool, a rhythmic, folk guitar-based

GODFATHER OF SOUL

James Brown, the Godfather of Soul, the Hardest Working Man in Show Business, Soul Brother Number One, basically invented funk. After playing fairly standard R&B for a few years, rhythm became everything to Brown, who fired drummers for missing a beat and levied fines on players for hitting wrong notes. He's still performing regularly today, and the drum beats from his hits are the most-sampled tracks in rap (p. 329).

music called **skiffle** had captivated dance-hall teens in 1959 and 1960, and a small scene of pop music fans devoted to the American sound were busy grafting onto skiffle the sounds of Motown and Chuck Berry. Out of this scene came a group called **the Beatles**.

37. **Which early rocker was an influence on the Beatles?**

 (A) Chuck Berry
 (B) Little Richard
 (C) Jerry Lee Lewis
 (D) All of the above

The Beatles had been playing covers of Little Richard and Chuck Berry tunes to packed houses in the dark dance clubs of Hamburg, Germany. Soon after, they began writing their own tunes and had a string of hits in England with "Love Me Do," "I Want to Hold Your Hand," and "I Saw Her Standing There." These records made their way onto American top-40 radio stations, and in early 1964 the Beatles made their first trip to New York City to play on national television, on the most popular variety show of the day, The Ed Sullivan Show (p. 522). From the airport arrival through the broadcast, the result was pandemonium, as tens of thousands of teenage American girls and boys tried to see the Beatles, touch the Beatles, and be the Beatles. The **British Invasion** was on, and **Beatlemania** was born.

The Beatles used careful song-crafting in the ballad, music-hall, R & B, and folk traditions to create a repertoire of original songs written by one

John, Paul, George, and Ringo receiving the Most Likely To Become Cool Hippies Award.

of the most successful songwriting partnerships ever— **John Lennon and Paul McCartney**. But their songs and their sound were not all they brought—the Beatles looked different, with longish hair (for the time), Mod clothes, and style to spare. Youth culture now had a music and a look to emulate; the political consciousness came later.

MM MM MMY JJJJENNERRAYSHUN!

The Who, one of the most successful British Invasion groups, had an early hit with a song called "My Generation" (1965), in which the singer purposefully stutters the words, and sings the immortal rock and roll refrain, "I hope I die before I get old."

The Beatles' 1967 album *Sergeant Pepper's Lonely Hearts Club Band* is considered by many pop critics to be the greatest studio album ever made—utilizing full string and horn sections, concept songs, and revolutionary studio techniques invented spontaneously by producer **George Martin**.

38. Many of the British Invasion bands drew on what kind of American music?

(A) Swing music
(B) Country music
(C) Chicago and Delta blues
(D) Zydeco music

Gimme Shelter (1970), directed by David Maysles. This is an incredible documentary of the Rolling Stones' free concert at Altamont Speedway in California in 1969. Four people were killed, one right in front of the stage. The Rolling Stones have never looked so stoned.

Following the Beatles were a plane-load of British rock bands who all used Chicago and Delta blues music as their springboard. Chief among them were **The Rolling Stones**, who idolized American blues masters such as **Muddy Waters** and **Howlin' Wolf**, and brought a darker, rootsier sound to the new pop music; blues rockers **The Yardbirds**, with **Eric Clapton** and then **Jimmy Page** on guitar; **The Kinks**, with hard-edged songs like "You Really Got Me"; and **The Animals**, who played rock versions of such traditional blues tunes as "House of the Rising Sun." The excitement and mutual influence of these years was a watershed period in popular music.

39. The protest song was a popular kind of what music?

(A) Broadway musical show tunes
(B) Folk music
(C) Jump band music
(D) None of the above

This Is Spinal Tap (1984), directed by Rob Reiner. This *faux* documentary follows the aging British rock group Spinal Tap on its latest comeback tour. The satire is brilliant, the largely improvised performances are a riot.

While the British Invasion was in full flowering, a grassroots American folk music revival, begun in the 1950s, had reached its apotheosis with the music of a young Minnesotan named **Bob Dylan** (1941-), who idolized the dust-bowl era folksinger and social activist **Woody Guthrie** (1912-1967). Dylan settled in New York City's Greenwich Village, where a lively folk music scene thrived, populated by many purists who eschewed the new rock and roll music as vulgar. Dylan, with just his guitar and harmonica and a growing body of songs, was an instant success with the folk crowd, and soon had a recording contract with Columbia Records. His early albums are great artifacts of American culture, and his popularization of the **protest song** had an enduring effect on songwriting and popular dissent.

Dylan wrote songs of social protest that spoke to the great fermenting turmoil of the civil rights movement (p. 197). Songs like "The Ballad Of Hattie Carrol," "The Ballad of Hollis Brown," and "Only a Pawn in Their

Game" told stories of men and women victimized by social hypocrisy, poverty, and racism. As the Vietnam War (p. 659) gained momentum from 1964 to 1965 with an escalation of U.S. involvement and a greater commitment of young American men, Dylan's protest songs became cornerstones of the growing anti-war movement. He toured and recorded almost non-stop during these years, and his concerts in England and Australia made him an international star. Feeling the pressure of continually writing about social problems, Dylan turned to more interior subjects. Surrealism, adult treatments of love and desire, and pure poetry found their ways into his songs, with recordings like "Tambourine Man" and "Desolation Row" showing the way to a new kind of popular songwriting that could tackle complex and profound subject matter.

Bob Dylan

As Dylan himself became influenced by the rock and roll sound in America and Britain, he began to electrify his music, playing a new sound called **folk rock**, which infuriated the folk purists. Undeterred, Dylan continued to embrace change, absorbing country sounds, hard rock, and reggae over the years.

The British acts that dominated the top-40 charts during the middle sixties, to the exclusion of all but a few American pop bands, eventually gave way to regional explosions of talent, with different identifiable sounds. By 1967, rock music had developed a drug-oriented **psychedelic** sound centered around several San Francisco bands such as **The Grateful Dead** and **Jefferson Airplane**. In Los Angeles, a vital scene also bloomed

BY THE TIME WE GOT TO WOODSTOCK . . .

The sixties' hippie/drug/protest music scene culminated in the now-legendary three-day Woodstock festival in August of 1969. Headlined by Jimi Hendrix, the festival included most of the popular bands and singers of the time, including Country Joe and the Fish, The Who (the only British band to play), Richie Havens, and Joe Cocker. In 1994 a second Woodstock was held to commemorate the first, with the Red Hot Chili Peppers, Nine Inch Nails, and Aerosmith headlining (and lots of commercial tie-ins). The times, they have a-changed.

with popular bands, **The Doors**, led by **Jim Morrison**, and **Frank Zappa's Mothers of Invention** leading the charge. In New York City, an obscure art-rock scene connected to pop artist Andy Warhol (p. 615) spawned the legendary **Velvet Underground**, led by **Lou Reed** (1942-). By the end of the 1960s, country music also began to exert a great influence on rock in California bands **The Byrds** and **The Flying Burrito Brothers**.

> ## KEEP ON TRUCKIN'
>
> *The Grateful Dead have gone from being a rock and roll band to being a rock and roll phenomenon. With legions of Deadheads who follow the band across the globe, the Dead have turned into a traveling party. If you ask a devoted Head why she follows a band of graying hippies, she is likely to answer, "It's all about the music, man."*

In the 1970s, an increasingly commercial rock music scene seemed to lose its central place in the youth culture. The vibrant regional scenes of the sixties gave way to a corporate rock culture, typified by giant stadium concerts and expensively produced recordings. Rock had become a decadent spectacle, with the exception of some obscure bands, such as **The Stooges** and **MC5**, and iconoclasts such as the androgynous glam-rocker **David Bowie**. The popularity of the exuberant R & B dance music known as **disco** was one innovation in a largely enervated pop music scene.

40. **What is "D.I.Y."?**
    (A) A punk rock "philosophy"
    (B) "Do it yourself"
    (C) An excuse for bad musicianship
    (D) All of the above

At the end of the 1970s, rock music managed to re-invent itself in another great burst of energy known as **punk rock**. Begun in New York with bands who played at the night club **CBGB's**, punk rock caught fire when bands such as **The Ramones** and **The New York Dolls** travelled to England where they, in turn, influenced a whole generation of angry young Brits caught up in the rigid atmosphere of England under Prime Minister Margaret Thatcher. **The Clash**, **The Sex Pistols**, and **The Damned** burst out in a fury of primitive vocals and instrumental energy. The punk aesthetic rejected virtuosity in favor of a philosophy known as **D.I.Y.**—short for "do it yourself." Instead of paying your hard-earned wages to listen to millionaire rock stars who had nothing to say, why not start your own band, and entertain yourself? The Sex Pistols, led by the

Sid Vicious looking better than ususal on the Pistols' first and only tour of the U.S. (they disbanded after six dates in the states).

skulking "singer" **Johnny Rotten**, was the band that launched a thousand acts. If a group of self-destructive lunatics who could barely play their instruments could make a statement, and a damn good album, with *Never Mind the Bollocks, Here's the Sex Pistols (1977)*, anyone could.

The punk explosion, with its 1980s spin-offs of **hard-core, industrial noise** and **new wave**, brought pop music back to its rebellious origins. At the end of the 1980s, a punk revival re-emphasized the D.I.Y. philosophy for a new generation of teenagers, who formed a clutch of new, angry, punk bands with a sound known as **"grunge"** led by **Kurt Cobain's** short-lived **Nirvana**.

Sid and Nancy (1986), directed by Alex Cox and starring Gary Oldman. Oldman's resemblance to Sid Vicious is eerie, and the movie itself captures the putrid glory of the first English punk scene. If you like *Sid and Nancy*, you'll love Cox's better movie, *Repo Man* (1984) starring Emilio Estevez as a confused L.A. punk caught in the middle of an extraterrestrial scandal.

41. **A beat box is**

   (A) the box you beat on during the space jam at a Grateful Dead concert
   (B) the turntable or system of turntables used by a DJ to "make the music" in rap music
   (C) slang for "accordion"
   (D) another term for a pianist's metronome

In 1979, **rap** and **hip hop** (musical styles so similar the terms are now almost synonymous) made it to the big time with the Sugar Hill Gang's "Rapper's Delight," the first hip hop single to make the Top 40. Using a **DJ** who spins and **samples** one or two records on a **beat box** to create much of a song's rhythm and music, and an **MC** who "raps" over this music, rap was an amazing Postmodern departure from, and hybrid of, preceding musical styles. Roland Barthes (p.279) would have been impressed!

After the success of "Rapper's Delight," hip hop maintained a steady popularity in urban centers across the U.S. In 1984, the **Def Jam** label was founded by co-owners Russell Simmons and Rick Rubin, and rap music would never be the same. Def Jam's first single was "I Need a Beat" by

Run DMC wore Adidas tennis shoes. At the height of Run DMC's popularity, the Adidas sportswear company manufactured four Run DMC styles of sneakers, an unheard-of marketing ploy considering the guys were non-athletes.

"Yo! MTV Raps" (MTV). One of MTV's highest-rated shows, this daily program spins the latest in mainstream rap, with a few not-so-well known groups thrown in.

sixteen-year old future rap superstar **L.L. Cool J**. Mainstream rap (i.e., white people like it, too) was off and running. Def Jam bands **The Beastie Boys** and **Run DMC** enjoyed enormous success during the 1980s. Run DMC scored the first gold rap album, the first multi-platinum rap album (the seminal *Raising Hell*), and became the first hip hop band to appear on the cover of the white rhythm-and-blues-lovin' magazine *Rolling Stone*.

42. What does the acronym NWA stand for?

(A) Nice White Anglo-Saxons
(B) New Wave Albums
(C) National Woodworker's Association
(D) Niggaz With Attitude

It Takes a Nation of Millions to Hold Us Back (Def Jam), by Public Enemy. A full-frontal attack on hypocrisy, greed, and all that is evil in the world. We're not kidding.

As the Def Jam-is-rap era waned, their traditional "partying all night" themes got a couple of new neighbors. **KRS One**, known as "the teacher" within the hip hop community, set the stage for self-empowering hip hop with lyrics promoting black uplift. In 1988, the Black Panthers (p. 200) of rap, **Public Enemy**, released *It Takes A Nation of Millions* to huge critical and commercial success. Public Enemy repre-

Chuck D and Flavor Flav get the message out at a raucous Public Enemy concert.

The powerful **Queen Latifah**, dubbed the "Queen of Royal Badness," raps against the rampant sexism in male rap and speaks for education and revolution from a woman's point of view. Her best song is probably "Wrath of My Madness" from the album *All Hail the Queen* (1989).

sented the radical political left wing of hip hop, with their unique hard-edged sound and warnings to the black community to "**Fight The Power**."

Gangsta rap was the other new sound in rap. Originating in the gang culture of urban Los Angeles, gangsta rap takes as its theme violence and the grim reality of ghetto life. Acts like **NWA** (Niggaz With Attitude) and **Ice-T** glorify street violence and sexism in the name of artistic integrity: after all, they are telling the truth about *their* world as they see it. The success of the West Coast sound, however, brought numerous poseurs and gangsta wannabes, who cashed in on the violent and sexist stances of their more talented predecessors. Unintimidated, female rappers like **Queen Latifah** and **Sister Souljah**, among others, fought right back.

CB4 (1993), starring Chris Rock. A bunch of middle-class guys pose as gangsta rappers. Kind of like a rap *This Is Spinal Tap.*

43. Where did reggae develop?

(A) Haiti
(B) Cuba
(C) Puerto Rico
(D) Jamaica

Among the most vibrant and popular music worldwide, Caribbean music is actually not indigenously Caribbean. Rather, it's derived from the rhythms brought there by West African slaves and the harmony and lyricism brought by the European colonizers. Much of the liveliness of Caribbean music stems from the era of colonization that brought so many different influences together in such a small area.

Cuba is the home of *sol*, and out of *sol* sprouted **salsa**, the most popular and best known Caribbean dance music. Not far behind salsa, however, comes **reggae** from Jamaica. There are many more Caribbean styles, but salsa and reggae most successfully moved out of the Caribbean and into the popular world market. In fact, salsa developed in the Latin communities of Miami and New York in 1940s and 1950s, during the big band (p. 309) era, and Latin American culture kept right in step with stars such as **Tito Puente**, who is also known as **"El Rey"** or **"The King"** of Mambo. Reggae owes its world appeal almost entirely to the late, great **Bob Marley** (1949-1981).

Bob Marley

 Almost every Caribbean nation has its own particular national music: Trinidad has **calypso**, the Dominican Republic has **merengue**, Haiti a slowed variant called **maringue**.

44. In which city did bossa nova originate?

(A) Santiago
(B) Caracas
(C) Rio de Janeiro
(D) Buenos Aires

Much like the music of the Caribbean, South American music is also wildly popular all over the world. It has achieved its popularity through a quirky and complex composite of European colonial, African-injected, and indigenous Indian influences. Latin American music is the world's choice of dance music; among the favorites are Brazilian **samba**, Colombian **cumbia**, and Argentinian **tango**. Brazil, South America's largest country, and Rio, Brazil's hippest city, boast **samba**, **bossa nova**, and **lambada.** Bossa nova was invented by two men; **Joao Gilberto** and **Antonio Carlos Jobim**. Their hip, sexy new dance was so popular in America that some say it would have defined late sixties music had Beatles (p. 325) not come along.

 Zydeco is the music of the black French-Creole culture located mainly in Louisiana. Driven by accordions and fiddles, zydeco combines upbeat, spicy dance music with an undercurrent of sadness stemming from an awareness of the reality of poverty. **Boozoo Chavis, Rockin' Dopsie**, and **Buckwheat Zydeco** are among the greatest Zydeco performers.

ANSWERS

1. A	2. B	3. B	4. B	5. D	6. B	7. A,D	8. C	9. C	10. A
11. C	12. B	13. B	14. B	15. B	16. A	17. B	18. B	19. D	20. C
21. B	22. D	23. D	24. C	25. B	26. C	27. B	28. D	29. D	30. D
31. B	32. D	33. A	34. D	35. C	36. C	37. D	38. C	39. B	40. D
41. B	42. D	43. D	44. C						

Physical Sciences & Technology

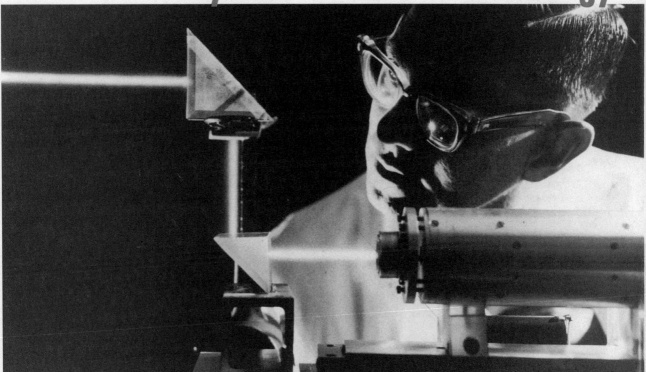

From the subatomic to the interplanetary, the physical sciences—astronomy, mathematics, physics, chemistry, and earth science—study everything inanimate. These disciplines depend heavily on technology. Technology is sometimes seen as merely an application of the principles of science to a practical end. Often, however, a technology predates understanding of the scientific laws it embodies. Fire, for example, was used to give heat and cook food long before the chemical principles of chemical combustion, thermodynamics, and microbiology were elucidated. Technology is better defined as a collection of tools that solves some problems and creates new ones to work on.

1. **What is the Big Bang?**

    (A) The explanation of how life originated on Earth
    (B) The name of the first observed supernova
    (C) The theory of how the universe originated
    (D) The method by which black holes are formed

Our galaxy, the Milky Way

Chaos (1987), by James Gleick. This is a good discussion of the scientific and philosophical ramifications of a universe ruled by entropy.

Most astronomers now agree with the theory that the universe was created approximately fifteen billion years ago through a process known as the **Big Bang**. The term "Big Bang" was originally coined as a term of derision by **Fred Hoyle** (1915-), who promoted the rival "steady state theory." To speak of events "prior to the Big Bang" is meaningless: at that point, the universe was infinitely small (in fact, it had no size at all), and a meaningful discussion of time requires a measurable space (just ask your neighborhood astrophysicist).

How do we know the age of the universe? Why, the **anthropic cosmological principle**, of course. This principle basically states that in order for us to be here observing the universe, which we are a part of, enough time in the history of the universe must have elapsed to permit the creation of such "observers." We will leave the calculations to the physicists, who tell us that a universe any younger than fifteen billion years would not permit our existence as observers, nor would it permit the current size of our ever expanding universe.

The Big Bang is not an event of which we have *direct* physical evidence, although Penzias and Wilson's report of radio-wave remnants of the Big Bang in 1965 is enough to convince most astronomers. According to Big Bang theory, the universe just prior to "the event" was completely ordered (in other words, it had a vanishingly low **entropy**). Since then, the universe has expanded by getting messier. In order for the universe to increase its entropy (messiness), parts of the universe must also increase their entropy. If you are like most people, you are probably mimicking the universe—and thus, in a sense, helping it to expand—as you read this.

2. **Which planet has (i) the longest year, (ii) the longest day?**

   (A) (i) Mercury, (ii) Pluto
   (B) (i) Pluto, (ii) Mercury
   (C) (i) Neptune, (ii) Venus
   (D) (i) Earth, (ii) Mars

Scientists now believe that the Earth shares its sun with eight other planets: **Mercury** and **Venus**, which are closer than our Earth to the sun; and **Mars**, **Jupiter**, **Saturn**, **Uranus**, **Neptune** and **Pluto**, which are all further than Earth to the sun. Four of the planets are larger than the Earth (Uranus, Neptune, Saturn, and Jupiter) and four planets are smaller than the Earth (Venus, Pluto, Mars, and Mercury). Four planets have longer days than Earth (Mars, Pluto, Mercury, and Venus) and four planets have shorter days than Earth (Neptune, Uranus, Saturn, and Jupiter). In other words, maybe humanity should stop assuming that it is so damned superior—we live on an awfully average planet!

Our current view of a **solar system** was proposed by **Nicholas Copernicus** (1473-1543), and goes like this: a central star (sun) with orbiting satellites (planets) which have their own orbiting satellites (moons).

WHAT HAPPENS NEXT?

We now have a theory on how the universe was born, but how will it die? There are several options. The expansion that began from the Big Bang might go on forever, until the universe becomes more and more empty and dead. Or, everything might collapse together again in a "Big Crunch." The third possibility is that the universe can be born, die, and reborn over and over again.

The Martian Chronicles (1950), by Ray Bradbury; and *To Open the Sky* (1967), by Robert Silverberg. Two great science fiction writers explore the possibility of human colonization of our neighboring planets, Mars and Venus.

Martin Luther, a contemporary of Copernicus, did not believe that the Earth moved. The publication of Copernicus' work was overseen by a Lutheran minister, Andreas Osiander, who added a preface stating in effect that the Earth did not really move—but that assuming that it did made Copernicus's calculations easier. This preface made Copernicus the laughingstock of the literate population, but underground organizations of astronomers realized the importance of the work and continued to refine the Copernican doctrine.

WHERE NO ONE HAS GONE BEFO . . .

Evidence is mounting that there may be a black hole right here in our own galaxy, the Milky Way.

This is a **heliocentric** (sun-centered) model. This model, when first presented, was not easy for many people to swallow, since it eliminated Earth as the center of the universe . . . the model put forth in the **Ptolemaic system**. Many people were put to death or worse for espousing the heliocentric model. Copernicus waited until he was near death to publish *De revolutionibus orbium coelestium*, which states that the planets travel around the sun. Copernicus' work, first published in 1543, was banned by the Church from 1616 until 1835, and the Roman Catholic Church continued to deny the Copernican theory until 1922. Yes, 1922. **Galileo** (1564-1642) became the chief advocate of the Copernican system in the early seventeenth century, and thus he also became Public Enemy Number One to the Roman Catholic Inquisition (p. 491). In 1633, Galileo was forced to recant his Copernican view before the Inquisition. It is said that at the end of his recantation, Galileo was heard to mutter *"e pur se muove"* (nevertheless, it moves).

3. A black hole is

   (A) a source of energy to the universe
   (B) completely empty
   (C) an intense gravitational field
   (D) an inexplicable anomaly in the space-time continuum

In 1703, sixteen years after he had originally published his theory, **Sir Isaac Newton** (1642-1727) first told a story about observing an apple fall from a tree in his yard and becoming inspired to develop the **law of universal gravitation**. This has been dismissed by many as the ramblings of an old man (the apple part, not the gravity part). Time has now bent this story into an apple conking Newton on the head. Did the apple actually fall? Probably. Did Newton see it fall? Maybe. Did it hit Newton on the head? Probably not.

Galileo studied the properties of free fall. However, Newton did originate the concept that *any* two things exert a gravitational force upon one another and that the size of this force is related to

Newton's hair proves gravity.

the mass of each object and the distance between them. Therefore, no matter who you are, everyone in the world is naturally attracted to you, by your gravitational field.

Just as your gravitational field—the amount of pull that you can exert on objects—is tiny compared to the gravitational field of the planets or sun, there are areas in the universe where the local gravitational field is enormous relative to the gravitational fields of the planets. These areas are referred to as **black holes**. An astronomical black hole derives its name from the idea of a gravitational field so intense that no light would be able to escape. Black holes are purely theoretical constructs, since if anyone ever has observed a black hole, up-close-and-personal, they haven't as yet gotten free to tell about it. Astronomers postulate the existence of black holes in order to help explain the beginning of the universe (Big Bang) and to explain the mess left behind in the wake of the gravitational collapse of a star exploding as a **supernova**.

"Supernova," by Liz Phair from her album *Whip Smart* (1994). This is a much cheerier take on the subject of black holes.

"Black Hole Sun," Soundgarden from the album *Superunknown* (1994). Sometimes life sucks so bad, don't you just wish the sun would instantly age, get very dense, and implode, taking the Earth and the rest of the solar system with it into the soothing nothingness of a black hole?

4. **How might "warp speed" (faster-than-light travel) be possible?**
    (A) Through a nuclear reaction in a material such as a dilithium crystal
    (B) Through the generation of antigravitational forces
    (C) Gaining acceleration from the sun via a "slingshot" effect
    (D) It has been proven to be impossible

Many people bandy about **Einstein's** famous $E = mc^2$ equation as a proof of faster-than-light travel being an impossibility. In fact, it is precisely this equation, and its descendants, that show that faster-than-light travel is theoretically possible. By definition, however, traveling faster than the speed of light assumes that you are also traveling backwards in time. It has to do with that whole **space-time continuum** thing. In order to travel forward in time, you would have to travel slower than the speed of light. If your major goal in life has always been to time-travel into the future, consider that goal accomplished. That is exactly what you are doing right now!

As far as this "warp" thing goes, a **time warp** is a hypothetical eccentricity in the fabric of time postulated in the 1950s (mostly by science fiction writers) that would somehow allow you to jump either forward or backward in time, or that could somehow halt the progression of time. If a spaceship's "warp drive" could artificially generate such a region (while managing to remain unaffected itself), faster-than-light travel might be

Faster-Than-Light (1988), by Nick Herbert. The physics of FTL are explored in this preliminary foray.

DIDN'T YOU GET MY MESSAGE?

Without faster-than-light travel, we are faced with the somewhat depressing fact that communication is also limited to light speed. Therefore, any alien messages from afar, whether friendly or threatening, would be many thousands of years late. Nor would there be any hope of sending a timely reply. Thus, actual communication with aliens would require that they show up right on our doorstep.

possible. For example, the warp drive might produce a form of **antigravity** to expand the space-time continuum. However, the difficulties in testing such theories, let alone putting them into practice, make "warp speed" more of a pleasant thought than a topic of actual research. And by the way, there is no such thing as a dilithium crystal.

A relatively relaxed Einstein

5. What event in space exploration took place on July 20, 1969?

    (A) First unmanned satellite in Earth orbit (*Sputnik*)
    (B) First man to orbit Earth
    (C) First man in space
    (D) First man on the moon

BEEN THERE, DONE THAT—WHAT'S NEXT?

Will there be another American triumph in space? The National Aeronautics and Space Administration (NASA) has plans for a manned space station, but is finding that ballooning costs and decreasing public interest are not conducive to jump-starting new technologies. Ironically, a joint mission with the Russians may be the best solution.

Can you name the astronaut who stayed aboard Apollo 11 that day in July? Most people know that **Neil Armstrong** (1930-) was the first human being to stand on the moon and that **Buzz Aldrin** (1930-) was quick to follow, but how many of us remember poor **Michael Collins**, who had to stay behind? Why all the fuss anyway? On October 4, 1957, the **space race** was initiated by the Soviet launching of the first artificial satellite, *Sputnik I*. Schoolchildren across America were stunned and amazed, and the U.S. government recognized a great marketing opportunity. Here was a chance to kick some Soviet butt. All we had to do was get a man to the moon faster than they did. By 1959, the Soviets had upped the ante. *Lunik I*, aimed at the moon, missed and became the first artificial planet by going into an orbit around the sun; *Lunik II* reached the moon, but unfortunately was not equipped with landing gear. No word yet from the Americans. In 1961, the Soviet cosmonaut **Yuri Gagarin** (1934-1968) became the first human to orbit Earth. Americans apparently were having difficulty getting off the ground, as scientist Melvin Calvin won the Nobel Prize working on theories of photosynthesis not propulsion.

In 1963, the United States began to catch up with the successful launch of *Syncom 2*, the first satellite in **geosynchronous orbit**—an orbit matched to Earth's rotation so that the satellite always remains directly over one location on Earth. In 1965, the Soviets made **A. Leonov** get out and walk (in only a space suit) for twenty minutes before he was let back in for the long ride home. The United States countered with the first two- and three-person crews and the first space rendezvous. In 1966, the Soviet Union seemed poised to capture the ultimate prize when they completed the first soft landing on the moon four months before the U.S. Surveyor I. This made the "one small step" that much sweeter for the United States.

 "Space Oddity," by David Bowie from the album *Man of Words, Man of Music* (1969); and "Rocket Man," by Elton John, from the album *Honkey Chateau* (1972). These two songs attempt to express the combination of awe and loneliness an astronaut might feel in space.

How 'bout taking one of them giant leaps over here and helpin' me with this flag.

 The Right Stuff, by Thomas Wolfe (1979). The men and women behind the *Apollo* missions paid a price to get to the moon.

6. **Triangulation is**

   (A) a useful mapping technique
   (B) a means of plotting the location of a point using two known points
   (C) a practical application of the Pythagorean theorum
   (D) All of the above

Exactly when humans began to graph things is not clear. Were there blueprints for the first wheel? Presumably, the idea of graphical representation evolved from the need to explain exact directions to someone, as in,

 "World Atlas 5.0" (The Software Toolworks, Inc.). Take a trip through the beautiful high-resolution full-color maps and up-to-date travel information.

The Travels of Marco Polo (c. 1300; Penguin edition, 1958), by Marco Polo and Rustichello. One of the world's great explorers chronicles his travels.

meet me behind the third bush after the fourth tree over the second hill, I've got something to show you. Oh hell, do you want me to draw you a picture?

The oldest known map was made on a bone about 15,000 years ago. As mathematics and travel became more advanced, maps became more and more reliable. The first map using the modern techniques of **triangulation** was undertaken in 1744. Triangulation is the method of using two known points to plot the exact location of a third point. At the time of the great explorers, maps of the "known world" could be off by as much as five hundred miles!

Graph theory is closely related to the human interests of exploring new places and building better mousetraps. In order to explore a new place, most people would like to have a map (or, at least, be able to make a crude one so that they can find their way back from whence they came.) In order to build a better mousetrap, you need to be able to draw up blueprints for your mousetrap. Graph theory is also critically enmeshed in our desire to relate things to one another. We have observed many relationships between various phenomena that can be represented by mathematical equations. For example, we now understand that the uptake of oxygen by hemoglobin in the blood at first approximates an exponential growth curve, but as more and more oxygen is taken up, this curve begins to flatten as the hemoglobin becomes saturated in oxygen. The curve is also affected by carbon monoxide concentration and blood acidity. Oh hell, do you want us to draw you a picture?

7. Assume that you are the architect placed in charge of building the Great Pyramid of Giza. The Pythagorean theorem would be most useful in calculating

    (A) the amount of materials that will be needed to complete the job

    (B) the complete ridiculousness of such a monumental undertaking

    (C) the slope of the sides of the pyramid

    (D) the number of hours of slave labor that will be required

During the nineteenth century B.C., what is now known as the **Pythagorean theorem** was formulated by Mesopotamian (p. 154) mathematicians (right before they worked out the first multiplication tables.) **Pythagoras** (c. 580 - 500 B.C.) himself was not born for another 1300 years. This theorem states that the square of the hypotenuse of a right triangle is

"Bizarre Love Triangle," by New Order from the album *Brotherhood* (1986). Remember, the Pythagorean theorem only applies to right triangles.

equal to the sum of the squares of the other two sides. Without this handy little piece of information, it would be impossible to determine the distance required to enclose a triangular space of which two sides already exist without actually measuring the distance of the third side. While on a household scale, this may not pose much of a problem, it can pose tremendous difficulty on a global or astronomical scale.

So how does the Pythagorean theorem relate to the Great Pyramids (p. 34)? By using this simple relationship between the sides of a right triangle, you can easily calculate the required length of the sides of the pyramid, which in turn will allow you to calculate the volume of the enclosed space and therefore the amount of materials required to complete the job. The slope of the sides of a pyramid does not require the use of the Pythagorean theorem, since a "perfect" pyramid rises at a slope of 45 degrees. Fortunately for you, the architect, the Pythagorean theorem will not be worked out for another one thousand years—so you can mathematically calculate neither the ridiculousness of such a monumental undertaking nor the number of slave labor hours (and slave deaths) that the Pyramids will require. Just be glad that you weren't one of the slave laborers . . . the wheel was not known in Egypt at that time, either.

Even though Pythagoreas didn't discover the relationship named after him, he was no dummy. Around 525 B.C. he founded the Pythagorean Brotherhood, a school dedicated first and foremost to mathematics. Students of this school later discovered the dodecahedron (a regular 12-sided figure) and irrational numbers.

Pythagoras would have been proud.

8. **Considering a circle circumscribed by a square, π is the ratio of**

   (A) the area of the circle to the area of the square
   (B) the circumference of the circle to the perimeter of the square
   (C) the diameter of the circle to the side of the square
   (D) the circumference of the circle to the side of the square

Right now, in several dimly lit rooms scattered about the United States, several people (who need to get lives), are busy attempting to calculate the exact value of π (pi). What is π, and why does anyone care? First, π is the ratio of the circumference of a circle to the length of the side of a square which perfectly circumscribes it. This

The Phantom Tollbooth (1961), by Norton Juster. The coolest number book around, this is not just for kids.

HAVE YOUR π AND COUNT IT TOO

Before computers were invented, Englishman Williams Shanks calculated out pi to over 700 places. Unfortunately, it was later discovered that the 528th place—and thus, every digit after it—was incorrect. Mathematician Martin Gardner predicted in 1966 that the millionth digit of π was 5. He was found to be correct, eight years later. Today, supercomputers have calculated π to over 200 million places.

value is approximately 3.14. This number is interesting in that it is a **universal constant**: it holds for any circle. Second, this simple number, as it turns out, it not so simple after all; it is the first known example of an **irrational number**—that is, a number that does not terminate and does not repeat. A **rational number** either terminates or repeats its digits in order. The only way to prove that a number is not rational but irrational is to show conclusively that it never repeats its digits—thus, the π-counters.

Mathematicians like to put things into nice neat "boxes" that they alternatively call **equations**, **theorems**, **axioms**, or the like. If you can prove that pi is actually a rational number, then you may have begun the first proof that **all** numbers are rational (which is currently disputed by the numbers π, e, and e^2). This proof would make mathematicians very happy, because then they could all throw out their "irrational numbers" boxes. It may not bother math-types so much that irrational numbers exist, but it just doesn't seem right that they went to all this trouble to develop a system of numbers and a bunch of stuff you can do with them, only to find out that perhaps the most important number of all, π, doesn't play by the rules—kind of the same way that water doesn't play by chemistry's rules.

9. **Exit polling, an application of statistics, relies on**
   (A) the assumption that the views of the people being polled reflect the entire population
   (B) interviewing almost every member of the population
   (C) the assumption of a normal distribution (bell curve)
   (D) nonscientific principles

The field of **statistics** uses mathematical relationships to predict the characteristics of a population from a sample. In many areas of interest, it is impossible to survey an entire population, but the use of a **random sample**, or subset of the population, can give information about the whole. It is important to remember that the accuracy and reliability of this information is only as good as the sampling and predictive techniques that are used.

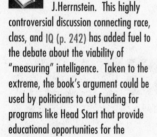

The Bell Curve (1994), by Charles Murray and Richard J.Herrnstein. This highly controversial discussion connecting race, class, and IQ (p. 242) has added fuel to the debate about the viability of "measuring" intelligence. Taken to the extreme, the book's argument could be used by politicians to cut funding for programs like Head Start that provide educational opportunities for the underprivileged.

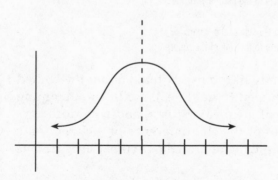

POLLS HAVE HOLES

Opinion polls predicted a landslide for Dewey in the 1948 Presidential election—but they had neglected the rural voters, whom Truman wooed during his famous "whistle-stop" campaign. Truman 1, Statisticians 0

Don't count your chickens before they're polled.

Innumeracy: Mathematical Illiteracy and Its Consequences (1988), by John Allen Paulos. Statistics and other mathematical concepts can be applied every day.

A common statistical distribution is the **normal distribution**, or **bell curve**. The bell curve describes a set of continuous random values such as the heights, weights, or shoe sizes of a given adult population. In such a set, there will be a central, or average, value "μ." Most people will measure fairly close to the average, while relatively few will show a large variation from the center. The difference from the average value is called deviation; a **standard deviation** s is defined such that for the normal distribution, the values between μ – s and μ + s will account for about 68 percent of the population. Moreover, about 95 percent of the population will fall between μ – 2s and μ + 2s. Thus, the normal distribution gives us a mathematical way to describe many naturally occurring variables.

However, some variables are not continuous, but **discrete**—that is, they can only take on certain fixed values. For example, rolling a pair of dice will always give a number between one and twelve. Election polling also provides discrete values—you can indicate a vote for the Republican, Democratic, or independent candidate, but write-ins are generally not tabulated.

> "*There are three kinds of lies: lies, damned lies, and statistics.*"
>
> — BENJAMIN DISRAELI

10. Which has a lowest probability of occurring?

(A) Being struck by lightning
(B) Being struck by lightning twice
(C) Winning a multi-state lottery
(D) Being born

The **actuarial tables** used in life insurance represent probabilities—for example, how much sooner can a smoker be expected to die, compared to a nonsmoker? (And therefore, how much more can the smoker be charged in premiums?) The first such mortality table was compiled by John Graunt, an English cloth merchant, in 1662. Using church records, Graunt compiled data that showed that women tend to live longer than men, but that more boys were born than girls. His information soon led to the founding of the first life insurance company in 1699.

Congo (1980), by Michael Crichton. Character Karen Ross uses space-age computers to evaluate the probabilities of success for all possible circumstances and all possible actions that her expedition might take. Made into a lousy movie in 1995.

The above question is, in some ways, a trick question, since obviously you must first be born in order for any of the other occurrences to *happen to you*. The field of probability was developed by, among others, mathematicians **Blaise Pascal** (1623-1662) and **Pierre de Fermat** (1601-1665) during the 1650s. Shakespeare's *Hamlet* (p. 547) was written some fifty years earlier, and provided the inspiration for the Tom Stoppard play, *Rosencrantz and Guildenstern are Dead*. The fact that the science of probability had not yet been invented makes the coin flipping scene in the movie all that much more enjoyable. So, was it easier to beat people at card games and in coin flips prior to the 1650s? No, we just didn't have a bunch of math to explain complex probabilities, so we relied on religion, magic forces, and witchcraft. Now that we do have a mathematical construct to explain probabilities, we have slot machines, casinos (p. 466), lotteries, lightning rods, and life insurance.

The study of **probability** attempts to explain the likelihood of occurrences. While statistics uses a **sample** to make inferences about a **population**, probability works in reverse. Probability reasons from the population to the sample. Considering a normal six-sided die, it is a simple matter to determine that each side has an equal probability of landing face up (assuming the roll is fair and the die is equally balanced). We can therefore say that the probability of rolling a three is equal to the probability of rolling a four: they are both one-sixth. What we have done, in effect, is to rationalize that if the die were rolled an infinite number of times (population = infinity), we would record the same number of threes as fours, which would in turn also equal the number of ones, twos, fives, and sixes. In this population, one-sixth of the time we would expect to record a three. Therefore, in a sample of one (one roll), we can say that the probability of rolling a three is one-sixth. If we did not apply the laws of probability, and rolled the die one time and got a three, all we could say was that every time we roll this die we will get a three—that would be statistics.

PLATE 3
PORTRAIT OF THE DAUGHTER OF ROBERTO STROZZI
OIL ON CANVAS, 1.5 × .98 M
ARTIST: TITIAN (TIZIANO VECELLIO)(1487-1576)
1542

PLATE
RAPE OF EUROP
OIL ON CANVAS, 6'1" × 6'
ARTIST: TITIAN (TIZIANO VECELLIO)(1487-157
156

PLATE 6
ARTIST IN HIS STUDIO
OIL ON CANVAS, 51.5' x 43.25 '
ARTIST: JAN VERMEER (1632-1675)
1666

PLATE 8
DONA MARIA SOLIDAD
OIL, 105.3 x 84.4 CM
ARTIST: FRANSISCO GOYA (1746-1828)
1807

PLATE 9
BISHOP DON FRAY MIGUEL
OIL, 78.5″ x 41.5″
ARTIST: FRANSISCO GOYA (1746-1828)
1800

PLATE 7
ODALISK WITH A SLAVE
OIL ON PANEL, 28.5″ x 39.5″
ARTIST: JEAN AUGUSTE DOMINIQUE INGRES
(1780-1867)
1840

PLATE 10
THE BALCONY
OIL ON CANVAS, 66.5 x 49.5"
ARTIST: EDOUARD MANET (1832-1883)
1868

PLATE 11
THE MONET FAMILY
OIL ON CANVAS, 24" x 39.25"
ARTIST: EDOUARD MANET (1832-1883)
1874

PLATE 12
DANCERS PRACTICING AT THE BARRE
OIL ON CANVAS, COLORS FREELY MIXED WITH TURPENTINE
29 3/4" x 32" (75.6 x 81.3 CM)
ARTIST: EDGAR DEGAS (1834-1917)
1876
THE METROPOLITAN MUSEUM OF ART, BEQUEST OF MRS. H.O. HAVEMEYER, 1929.
THE H.O. HAVEMEYER COLLECTION (29.100.34)

PLATE 13
WATER LILIES, GIVERNY
OIL ON CANVAS, 6'6 1/2" x 19'7 1/2" (2 x 6 M)
ARTIST: CLAUDE MONET (1840-1926)
1907
MUSEUM OF MODERN ART, NY. MRS. SIMON GUGGENHEIM FUND.
PHOTOGRAPH © 1994 THE MUSEUM OF MODERN ART, NY

PLATE 14
ARRANGEMENT IN BLACK AND GRAY: THE ARTIST'S MOTHER
OIL ON CANVAS, 57" x 64 ¹/₂" (144.6 x 163.8 CM)
ARTIST: JAMES MCNEILL WHISTLER (1834-1904)
1871
SCALA/ART RESOURCE, NY

PLATE 15
BOYS IN PASTURE
OIL, 15.5 x 22.5 "
ARTIST: WINSLOW HOMER (1836-1910)
1874

PLATE 17
NATURE MORTE A LA COMODE
OIL ON CANVAS, 28 7/8 x 36 3/8"
ARTIST: PAUL CEZANNE (1839-1906)
1887

PLATE 16
SUNFLOWERS
OIL ON CANVAS, 17" x 24" (43.2 x 61 CM)
ARTIST: VINCENT VAN GOGH (1853-1890)
1887

PLATE 18
THE DANCE
OIL ON CANVAS, 8'5 3/4" x12'9 1/2" (2.59 x 3.9M)
ARTIST: HENRI MATISSE (1869-1954)
1910

PLATE 20
LES DEMOISELLES D'AVIGNON
OIL ON CANVAS, 8' x 7'8" (2.43 x 2.33 M)
ARTIST: PABLO PICASSO (1881-1974)
1906-7
MUSEUM OF MODERN ART, NY. ACQUIRED THROUGH THE LILLIE P. BLISS BEQUEST. PHOTOGRAPH
© 1994, THE MUSEUM OF MODERN ART, NY.

PLATE 19
FEMME A LA MANDOLINE
OIL ON CANVAS, 51.25 x 38.25 "
ARTIST: GEORGES BRAQUE (1882-1963)
1937

PLATE 21
THE PERSISTENCE OF MEMORY
OIL ON CANVAS, 9 ¹/₂" x 13" (24 x 33 CM)
ARTIST: SALVADOR DALI (1904-1989)
1931
MUSEUM OF MODERN ART, NY. GIVEN ANONYMOUSLY. PHOTOGRAPH © 1994,
THE MUSEUM OF MODERN ART, NY.

PLATE 23
THE GRAND TENOCHTITLAN
FRESCO, 4.92 x 9.71 M
ARTIST: DIEGO RIVERA (1886-1957)
1943

PLATE 22
THE STRUGGLE OF THE CLASSES
FRESCO, 7.49 x 8.85 M
ARTIST: DIEGO RIVERA (1886-1957)
1929-1930

PLATE 27
ONE (#31)
OIL AND ENAMEL ON UNPRIMED CANVAS, 8'10" X 17'5 ⁵/₈" (2,69 X 5.32 M)
ARTIST: JACKSON POLLOCK (1912-1956)
1950
MUSEUM OF MODERN ART, NY. SIDNEY AND HARRIET JANNIS COLLECTION. PHOTOGRAPH © 1994,
THE MUSEUM OF MODERN ART, NY.

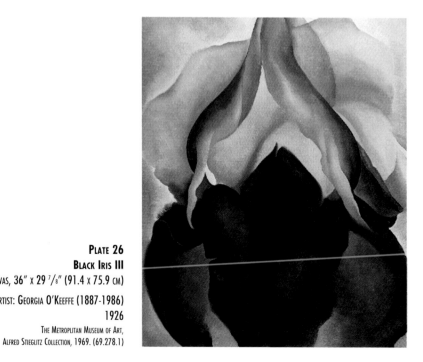

PLATE 26
BLACK IRIS III
OIL ON CANVAS, 36" X 29 ⁷/₈" (91.4 X 75.9 CM)
ARTIST: GEORGIA O'KEEFFE (1887-1986)
1926
THE METROPLITAN MUSEUM OF ART,
ALFRED STIEGLITZ COLLECTION, 1969. (69.278.1)

PLATE 28
THREE FLAGS
ENCAUSTIC ON CANVAS, 30 ⁷/₈" x 45 ¹/₂" x 5" (78.4 x 115.6 x 12.7 CM)
ARTIST: JASPER JOHNS (1930-)
1958
COLLECTION OF WHITNEY MUSEUM OF AMERICAN ART, NY.
PHOTOGRAPH BY GEOFFREY CLEMENTS, NY.

PLATE 29
CAMPBELL'S SOUP
OIL SILK SCREEN ON CANVAS, 36 ¹/₈" x 24"
(91.7 x 60.9 CM)
ARTIST: ANDY WARHOL (1928-1987)
1965
MUSEUM OF MODERN ART, NY. ELIZABETH BLISS PARKINSON FUND.
PHOTOGRAPH © 1994, THE MUSEUM OF MODERN ART, NY.

11. You are a professor questioning three students: Brandon, Dylan, and Kelly. You know that each student always tells the truth or always lies. Brandon says, "Exactly two of us tell the truth." Dylan says, "No way, dude, only one of us tells the truth." Kelly says, "Exactly two of us lie. Now can we go to the beach?" Which students are truthful, which are liars?

(A) Brandon is truthful; Dylan and Kelly are liars.
(B) Brandon, Dylan, and Kelly all lie.
(C) Brandon, Dylan, and Kelly are all telling the truth.
(D) Kelly is truthful; Brandon and Dylan are liars.

In order to solve this problem, we have to use **logic**. We have to consider each piece of information separately and then consider all of the pieces simultaneously to see if we can make a conclusion. We know that each student either tells the truth or lies. In order to start this problem, we will have to make an **assumption**. First, let us assume that Brandon is truthful. In that case, only one of Dylan and Kelly is a liar. This would mean that Brandon and one other student tell the truth, therefore, Dylan must be a liar. But, Kelly cannot be truthful if Brandon is truthful, so Kelly must also be a liar. If Kelly is a liar, there are not two truthful students, and therefore Brandon's statement is a lie. We now adopt this as our new assumption (Brandon is a liar), and work the whole process over again. If Brandon is a liar, then we can say that exactly two students do not tell the truth—therefore, three do, one does, or none do. We already know that Brandon is a liar, so we can eliminate three truth-tellers. If one tells the truth, it has to be Dylan or Kelly. If Dylan is truthful, then he is the only truthful one (given his statement), and therefore Kelly is a liar. If Kelly is a liar then exactly two of the students are not liars, which invalidates Dylan's truthfulness. We now know that Dylan is a liar and that Brandon is a liar. What about Kelly? If Dylan is a liar then there cannot be exactly one truth-teller. There must be none. Brandon, Dylan and Kelly all lie! Of course, if you have ever watched "Beverly Hills 90210" you already knew that without the logic exercise.

The logic process we have been through—making assumptions, testing them for their validity, and either accepting or rejecting them—is fundamental to both mathematics and all other scientific endeavors. Computers use **binary logic** (in which every bit of information is assigned either a true or false value) to operate and perform calculations.

Gödel, Escher, Bach: An Eternal Golden Braid (1979), by Douglas R. Hofstadter. Take a lesson in formal logic, paradoxes, recursion, and computer algorithms—enjoy the numerous detours into music, fantasy, and games.

Frenchman **Pierre de Fermat** (1601-1665) was a brilliant mathematician whose ideas led to the development of analytical geometry. He is perhaps best known for work he never published, however. In the margin of one of his math books, Fermat scribbled down a new theorem, and then a note stating only: "I have discovered a truly remarkable proof which this margin is too small to contain." The proof was never found, and ever since, mathematicians have struggled to logically prove "Fermat's last theorem."

12. Which is the largest number?

(A) The number of atoms in the head of a pin
(B) The number of feet from the Earth to the sun
(C) The number of nucleotides in the human genome
(D) The number of times the quartz crystal in a wristwatch vibrates in one year

Honey, I Shrunk the Kids (1989), starring Rick Moranis. Plucky youngsters encounter life on a micron scale.

CHIPCHAT

Hardware: *the physical equipment that makes up a computer, including the computer chips, the disk drive, the monitor, et cetera.*

Remember when you took high school chemistry and you were asked to remember **Avogadro's number?** Avogadro's number is simply the number of atoms that it takes to make up a "**mole**" of atoms. This number is 6.02×10^{23}—or if you prefer, 602,000,000,000,000,000,000,000. A "mole" is nothing more than a convenient packaging unit, like a "dozen." A dozen means twelve of anything; similarly, a mole is 6.02×10^{23} of anything.

Often in science, the numbers to be dealt with are either extremely big or extremely small. Given the natural laziness of humankind, we have developed a shorthand for representing these numbers. This shorthand is called **scientific notation**. Scientific notation is nothing more than the rewriting of a number as (1) a number between one and ten, and (2) a note of how many times you need to move the decimal point (i.e., how many times you would have to multiply or divide your new one digit number by ten to get your original number). Let's illustrate this using an example from the above question.

A quartz crystal vibrates 32,768 times each second. There are sixty seconds in a minute, sixty minutes in a hour, twenty-four hours in a day, and 365.25 days in a year (don't forget leap years). Therefore, $32,768 \times 60 \times 60 \times 24 \times 365.25 = 1,034,070,436,800$. This is just over a million millions—rounding off, 1,000,000,000,000. We can now simply move the decimal point over twelve places to the left and rewrite this as 1.0×10^{12}. Since we moved the decimal to the left, we get a positive power of ten. Had we moved the decimal to the right, we would get a negative power of ten. You may also see this number written as $1.0E^{12}$ (especially on computers): it means the same thing.

There are also approximately 1.0×10^{12} atoms in the head of a pin. The distance from the Earth to the sun is about 5.0×10^{11} feet, and there are approximately 3.0×10^{12} nucleotides in the human genome (p. 221). Therefore, the answer to the question is C.

13. When was the first fully assembled, mass-marketed personal computer introduced?

(A) 1945
(B) 1981
(C) 1965
(D) 1977

In 1823, Englishman Charles Babbage persuaded the British government to finance his "Difference Engine." This was to be a machine that could undertake any kind of calculation by resorting to an entire program of operations stored on a punched tape. Babbage's machine was never completed. But thanks to his work and that of British mathematician Alan Turing, Max Newman was able to formulate the first electronic programmable computer in 1943: the **Colossus**. This machine was designed to crack secret German military codes.

The first multi-purpose, fully operational large-scale electronic digital computer, **ENIAC** (electronic numerical integrator and computer) was built at the University of Pennsylvania between 1943 and 1946. ENIAC launched the modern era of the computer. During the next three

Friendly Users

decades, the computer slowly began to gain a foothold in the business world, but was confined mostly to computational tasks that could not be handled by a human being. It was not until **Steve Jobs** and **Steve Wozniak** introduced the Apple II **personal computer** in 1977 that computers began to become a way of life in the United States. The Apple II was the first computer designed for home use and mass-marketed to the consumer. Four years later, IBM—the leader in the business market—introduced its first home computer, the IBM PC.

Today, increasingly easy-to-use home computers have nearly replaced typewriters, adding machines, accounting ledgers, and drafting tables. Computing power enables high-quality desktop publishing, detailed mathematical calculations, and rapid communication. It is not so difficult anymore to visualize a future in which we carry portable computers around with us everywhere—a task which would have been quite impossible with the room-sized ENIAC.

14. Which of the following people might find something of interest on the Internet?

    (A) A computer hacker
    (B) A homemaker
    (C) A home wrecker
    (D) All of the above

Where can you exchange messages with the president, find ten people interested in full-body tattoos, or assume an entirely new personality? Yes, it's the **Internet**. Unless you happen to have just emerged from a

USEFUL INTERNET ADDRESSES

The Princeton Review: e-mail books.tpr@review.com;

InterNIC (Network Information Center): WWW http://www.internic.net/

Library of Congress: gopher marvel.loc.gov

The President of the United States: e-mail president@whitehouse.gov

HOLD STILL, MAC, THIS WILL HURT A LITTLE

With so many computers now communicating with one another, the danger of spreading programs that intentionally cause disruption or damage—viruses—is increasing. A computer virus works a little like a biological one. It attaches itself to an existing program and changes it, so that memory and data are adversely affected. Moreover, computer viruses can replicate themselves and spread to "infect" other computers, either by Internet or via infected disks. "Vaccines" and virus detection programs are now an essential part of any computer user's toolkit.

years-long stay in a cave, you have probably at least heard of this network of computers and their users, but you may not be aware of the wealth of information that it can provide *anyone*. The Internet was born in U.S. government laboratories about twenty years ago, as ARPAnet. The purpose of ARPAnet was originally to connect all of the U.S. military research laboratories in the world via a computer network that could withstand partial power outages (read "war"). Once the network was in place, however, it was also made available to universities. Soon, people realized that the net was just about the only way to enable computers of different manufacturers to "talk" to one another. The convenience of this service led to the exponential expansion of the Internet.

What can you do with the net? Just about anything! The most basic Internet service is electronic mail, or **E-mail**. This service allows you to contact any other Internet user at their Internet address. Simply type your letter into your computer, then instead of printing it out and mailing it, click a few buttons and it's sent on to your long-lost cousin living in Tibet. Next up the line in netdom is the **newsgroup**, a computerized discussion group. The Internet is currently running over 5000 newsgroups on just about every imaginable topic, from the keeping of tropical fish to linguistics theory. Any net client can join any newsgroup (although some newsgroups have strict admissions policies). Similarly, any client could conceivably start a newsgroup. Many newsgroups include regular postings of FAQs, which are the answers to frequently asked questions in the area of interest to the newsgroup. Similar to the newsgroup is the **mailing list**. However, whereas a newsgroup is not "owned" or managed by any particular user, a mailing list is. In order to get information from a mailing list, you must first subscribe by sending an E-mail message to the list manager. The manager then e-mails you the contents of the list on a regular basis.

Now you know how to send and receive messages, but what about loading up free data and software for your own computer from the Internet? To do this, you need an **FTP**—a file transfer protocol. In order to FTP something, you have to know where to FTP it from. That's where search engines and browsers come in. Using a **search engine** (such as *Gopher* or *Archie*), you can find the location of information on almost any topic and then FTP it to your computer. *World Wide Web* (WWW) is a **browser**. A browser allows you to "take a walk" around the Internet to find out what is available or seek additional information. Finally, the software **Telnet** allows you to log on to one computer from a second remote computer. Telnet access to an on-line service, such as America Online or CompuServe, allows you to log onto the Internet without the use of a modem.

Sounds great, you say, but how do I get on? More and more companies are hooking up to the net, but for home access, you will have to pay for an account. The basic requirements for Internet access are a modem, communications software, and an account with an Internet service provider or a commmercial on-line service. Of these, **America Online** provides the most comprehensive services with no extra Internet charge. Some of the other services, such as Prodigy, offer only e-mail services without an additional charge. Whichever you choose, you are guaranteed to find something of interest to you—literally, a whole world of information and people await you.

The Whole Internet: User's Guide & Catalog, 2nd Ed. (1994), by Ed Krol. This is a comprehensive guide to the ins and outs of the Internet.

New Rider's Official Internet Yellow Pages, 2nd. Ed. (1994), by Christine Maxwell and Czeslaw Jan Grycz. This is a handy directory of addresses and services.

15. **Simple machines are useful because they**

   (A) reduce the amount of work needed to complete a task
   (B) reduce the amount of force needed to complete a task
   (C) reduce both the amount of work and the amount of force needed
   (D) require the consumption of fewer calories by the people doing the work

Despite how you may feel when faced with a complicated machine, particularly if you have just broken it, the basic principles of mechanical machinery are just that—basic. It turns out there are actually only six manmade machines on the entire planet, and these machines are very simple. In fact, they are so simple that they are called the **simple machines**. The simple machines are: the **pulley**, the **lever**, the **ramp**, the **screw**, the **wedge**, and everyone's favorite, the **wheel** and **axle**. If you understand these six items, you understand the fundamental basis of anything mechanical, because anything that is not a simple machine is merely a combination of simple machines. Want to be rich beyond your wildest estimations? You need only to invent a seventh simple machine.

Now, let's clear up some common misconceptions about machines and what they can do for us. It does not take less work to

> " *"Give me a lever and a place to stand, and I will move the earth."*
>
> —ARCHIMEDES
> "

CULTURESCOPE

DON'T SWEAT IT

Calories are a unit of work. When you exercise to "burn off calories" the amount of work that you do equates with the amount of calories burned. Simply in terms of calories burned, it is not important that you sweat, raise your pulse, or pant like a dog. A slow and steady pace is sufficient for calorie burning. Breaking a sweat, bringing up your heart rate, and breathing harder are all parts of cardiovascular fitness, however.

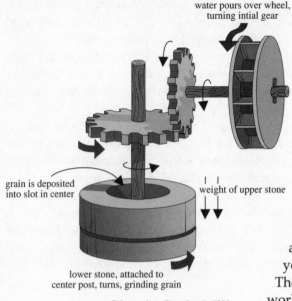

water pours over wheel, turning intial gear

grain is deposited into slot in center

weight of upper stone

lower stone, attached to center post, turns, grinding grain

Simple Grain Mill

carry a box of books up a ramp and into a moving van than in does to lift the books straight up. It seems like you are doing less work because you are exerting less force. However, the amount of the decrease in force that you must exert is exactly countered by the additional distance that you have to travel. Therefore, the amount of work that you have done is identical. In fact, the amount of work that is done by pushing a hand cart up the same ramp with the same box of books is equal to the amount of work that is done by carrying the box up the ramp or by lifting the box from the ground into the truck.

16. You have a ball attached to a string, which you are whirling above your head. The direction of the spin is clockwise (north to east to south to west). If you release the ball when it reaches due north, which direction will the ball fly at the instant you let it go?

(A) East
(B) Northeast
(C) Southeast
(D) Down

CHIPCHAT

Bug: *an error in a program which causes it to work incorrectly. The term perhaps came from a real bug (a moth) which caused a malfunction in an early computer at Harvard.*

Philosophiae Naturalis Principia Mathematica (1687), usually just called the *Principia*, is arguably the most important work ever written in the field of physics. Here, for the first time, **Sir Isaac Newton** (1642-1727) not only elaborated the law of universal gravitation but also presented his three laws of motion. The above question is an application of **Newton's first law:** "Every body persists in its state of rest or of uniform motion in a straight line unless it is compelled to change that state by forces impressed on it." In other words, once you remove the force of the string, the ball will travel in a straight line (that is, east). This law is also called the **law of inertia**.

Newton's second law of motion was probably the first equation that you learned in physics (if you took physics): $F = ma$. The acceleration of an object is simply the force upon that object divided by the object's mass. **Newton's third law of motion** states: "To every action there is always opposed an equal reaction; or, the mutual actions of two bodies upon each other are always equal, and directed to contrary parts." This law basically says that if you kick open a heavy door your foot will hurt (since the door is exerting a force back on your foot). Combining this law with Newton's second law, we can rationalize why your foot hurts more if you kick a heavy door than it does if you kick a light door. However, only you can explain why you kicked the door in the first place.

Your **mass** in kilograms is just that, a mass. Your **weight** is measured in pounds or in newtons. If you have a mass of 50 kilograms, you weigh 490 newtons (or 110 pounds). If, however, you take a trip to the moon, where gravity is one-sixth the gravity of Earth, you still have a mass of 50 kilograms but, you now weigh 81.7 newtons (or 18.3 pounds)!

17. **Which of the following best describes the energy conversions in a flashlight?**

(A) Kinetic to electrical to chemical and light energy
(B) Chemical to electrical to light and heat
(C) Heat to kinetic to chemical and heat
(D) Electrical to kinetic to potential and heat

Energy conservation as the term is used today does not refer to the laws of conservation of energy. The "energy conservation program" is an attempt to get people to use less energy and therefore use up less of the dwindling supplies of chemical energy from fossil fuels.

Energy can neither be created nor destroyed. This is a statement of the **law of conservation of energy**. In a chemical or physical process, such as the flashlight discussed above, energy is not consumed—it is merely converted from one form to another. In the case of the flashlight, chemical energy stored in the batteries is first converted into electrical energy. This

$E = mc^2$

······································

The law of conservation of energy is actually the laws of conservation of mass and energy. Quantum physics allows for the interconversion of mass and energy. Einstein used this idea to demonstrate the wave-particle duality of light. Although mass and energy can be interconverted, the sum of the two must always remain constant.

Newton was so important in the field of mechanics that the unit of force is named after him. A newton (N) is approximately the amount of force that a magazine feels as it is dropped to the floor.

The resistance of some materials approaches zero as they are cooled to near absolute zero. This phenomenon is known as **superconductivity**. In the late 1980s, materials were discovered which exhibited superconductivity at much higher temperatures than previously achieved. These "warm" superconductors were much more economically and technologically viable than their predecessors, and immediately generated a great deal of scientific and public excitement.

electrical energy is then used to heat the filament of the light bulb (heat energy) and to cause the filament to glow (light energy). While we may speak of the battery being "drained of energy," we are not destroying the energy, but rather converting it into the more useful form of light energy (assuming we are looking for something in the dark). Presumably, we have not turned on the flashlight as a source of heat, so the energy in the form of heat is "wasted." However, this heat is not destroyed, either—it is simply transferred to the surroundings, where it adds to the entropy (p. 335) of the universe.

There are actually only two forms of energy: **kinetic energy** (the energy of motion) and **potential energy** (stored energy). When we speak of the energy stored in macroscopic particles or the motion of these particles, we are speaking of mechanical potential energy and mechanical kinetic energy, respectively. All other energies are the so-called "nonmechanical" energies: heat, electrical, light, sound, magnetic, and chemical. The first four of these are the result of motion of submicroscopic particles and are therefore forms of kinetic energy. The latter two energies are atomic scale potential energies, since they do not involve movement.

18. Which of these four elements is the best conductor of electricity?

(A) Aluminum
(B) Silver
(C) Gold
(D) Copper

Electricity is defined as the flow of electrons. A material through which electrons can flow easily is said to have a low resistance and is called a good **conductor**. A material through which electrons have an extremely difficult time flowing is said to have a high resistance and is called an **insulator**. In the above question, all four elements are metals and good conductors. Since you probably have copper wire running throughout the walls of your house, you may have been inclined to choose copper as the best conductor. However, silver is actually the best conductor of the four. So why do we use copper? Copper has advantages other than its electrical performance. Silver and gold are both too expensive to use in household wiring (or, for that matter, household anything). Aluminum, on the other hand, is cheaper than copper, but it is not as good a conductor of electricity. Copper is used for wiring because it wins the battle of conductance versus price, hands down.

Some materials, called **semiconductors**, have properties intermediate between conductors and resistors. Thus, current can flow through semiconductor materials, but it encounters a significant resistance. (Even in good conductors, a finite resistance to current flow exists—this is low and can approach zero, as in the materials known as **superconductors**). Semiconductors are used in integrated circuits (ICs), the computer chips that go into everything from automobiles to washing machines. They can also be used to make light-emitting diodes (LEDs), lasers, and solar cells.

 Electrical conduction and insulation are not the same as **thermal conduction** and **thermal insulation**. A material can be a lame electrical insulator but an excellent conductor of heat: diamond is one example. Similarly, some electrical conductors are rather poor thermal conductors, like stainless steel.

19. **Jumper cables have two red and two black ends. What is the best method of hooking up a dead battery to a live battery?**

(A) Black to negative terminal of dead battery and engine block of the car with the live battery, both red to positive terminals

(B) Red to positive terminal of live battery and engine block of the car with the dead battery, both black to negative terminals

(C) Red to positive of live battery and negative of dead one; black to negative of live battery and positive of dead one

(D) Black to positive of live battery and negative of dead one; red to negative of live battery and positive of dead one

It is extremely convenient to know how to use jumper cables. The principle of these cables is quite simple: use the "juice" from a live battery to rejuvenate a dead battery. In order to make this concept work, you need to create a complete electrical **circuit**—a continuous loop of flowing current. When your battery is attached just to your car, electrons flow out of the negative terminal of your battery through the electrical system of your car and back to the positive terminal of your battery. These electrons are provided by a chemical reaction between lead and sulfuric acid. As the battery operates, it becomes less efficient at provid-

Everybody loves jumper cables.

ing the electrons, and drains its charge. In this way, the battery would die very quickly, except that your car engine is also producing energy as it runs. The energy that your car produces continually recharges the battery. But leaving the engine off, running your car radio for too long, or leaving your lights on will completely deplete the battery.

In order to bring a dead battery back to life, you need to reverse its chemical reaction to recharge it, and to do this, you need to provide its negative terminal with some spare electrons. The best way to do this is by method "A" above. The metal engine block of the car with the live battery acts as an electron source, because metals are good conductors and readily give up electrons. The electrons run into the negative terminal of the dead battery, and out its positive terminal (since it is running backwards). From here, they return to the positive terminal of the live battery, and out its negative terminal to the running engine, as usual. In a short time, the chemical reaction is sufficiently reversed to recharge the battery. However, a battery can only be recharged a limited number of times, because the reversal is not complete.

20. **The black strips on the back of credit cards are**
   (A) decoded by lasers
   (B) magnetized
   (C) similar to one-way glass
   (D) vulnerable to erasal by random forces

Magnets are all around us. We may not consider magnets to be useful for much more than holding notes to the refrigerator door, but they serve many other purposes. A magnetic material is a material in which there is an alignment of electrons within the individual atoms to create an overall magnetic field. For a variety of reasons, some materials can align their electrons better than other materials can—so some materials are magnetic, and others are not.

The little black strips on the back of your credit cards are magnetized. The strip is not uni-

formly magnetized, and thus, there are slight fluctuations in the local magnetic field from one region of the

The **maglev** (magnetic levitation) trains now built in Japan can attain speeds over 300 miles per hour. The trains literally float on a layer of air some four inches thick. The air gap is produced by the repulsion of strong magnetic fields.

strip to another. As the card is run through a scanner, devices within the scanner detect these differences in magnetic field and recognize certain magnetic field strengths as different numbers, much the same way as the infrared scanner at the supermarket detects the distance between lines in a bar code. This same principle is used in computer **floppy disks**, which also rely on magnetic fields to store information.

Because the strips on your cards are magnetized, they are subject to erasure by other magnetic fields. If you put a weak magnetic field in the presence of a strong magnetic field, the strong field will tend to attract the weak field. As a result, weak magnetic fields set up to represent a series of numbers, as on your credit cards, may become scrambled after being exposed to a strong magnetic field. It is a common misconception that airport X-ray scanners will distort the magnetic field on credit cards and computer disks. While X-ray machines do generate a weak magnetic field, airport scanners are tuned to a low enough level that your credit cards and disks will not be affected.

The **northern lights (aurora borealis)** appear in the night sky at northern latitudes. They occur because the Earth's magnetic field concentrates charged particles from the sun in these regions. The charged particles interact with molecules in the upper atmosphere to produce the spectacular light displays.

21. You have just returned from a long day at the office. All you want to do is slip into your hot tub with a nice cup of tea. Your hot tub has a volume of 500 liters and your tea cup has a volume of 250 milliliters. You want to raise the temperature in the hot tub from 39°C (102°F) to 40°C (104°F). In order to make your tea, you need to raise the temperature of the tea water from 20°C (room temperature) to 100°C (boiling). Which of the following statements is true if each process takes five minutes?

(A) It is more expensive to heat the hot tub one degree than to heat the tea water eighty degrees.

(B) It is more expensive to heat the tea water eighty degrees than it is to heat the hot tub water a single degree.

(C) The two processes will cost approximately the same amount of money.

(D) Money is entirely unimportant, I am tired and I want my tea and hot tub!

Heat and **temperature** are not the same thing. The temperature of an object is a measure of the "hotness" of that object. Heat is a form of energy. The heat contained by two different objects may be equal without the temperatures of these two objects being equal. Every substance has a particular **specific heat**. This specific heat is defined as the amount of heat

Fahrenheit 451 (1953), by Ray Bradbury. 451°F is the temperature at which books burn. A great novel that is more social commentary than science fiction.

CULTURESCOPE

energy that must be added to this material in order to raise the temperature of one gram of this material one degree Celsius. Since different materials have different specific heats, materials will increase in temperature at different rates. Metals tend to have low specific heats. Therefore, while cooking, you are more likely to burn your hand on the metal pot in which you are heating water than with the water itself, which has a relatively high specific heat. Specific heat is synonymous with **heat capacity**. The heat capacity of a material is a measure of how well that material "holds" heat. Materials with high heat capacities, like fiberglass insulation, hold heat well, so they make good heat insulators.

A material that holds heat well (has a high heat capacity) will require the input of more energy for the same temperature increase to be realized as for a low heat capacity material. But in the question above, rather than considering substances with different heat capacities, we are considering differing amounts of the same substance (water). In this case, it is clear that we must add much more heat to the hot tub water to raise the temperature one degree than the amount of heat that must be added to the relatively small volume of tea water to effect a raise in temperature of eighty degrees.

22. **If you are standing at a train station and an approaching train blows its whistle, you will hear**
    (A) the sound of the whistle go up in pitch as the train approaches and down in pitch as the train speeds by (it wasn't your train)
    (B) the sound of the whistle will appear to go down as the train approaches and up as the train recedes
    (C) the sound of the whistle will appear to go up in pitch as long as the train is within hearing distance
    (D) the sound of the whistle will appear to go down in pitch as long as the train is within hearing distance

Sound travels in waves similar to the waves in the ocean. The waves in the ocean do not permanently bring the water of the ocean with them into shore. Likewise, sound does not permanently bring the medium within which it is travelling with it. Rather, a wave travels through a medium by temporarily disrupting that medium in the direction of the wave's travel.

Bearing this in mind, it is evident that if a hypothetical giant could push the shore closer to the ocean wave, the wave would hit the shore sooner. Similarly, if we now consider any two objects—a wave source and a wave receiver—we will find that if the two objects are closer together, the wave will travel from source to receiver faster than if the objects

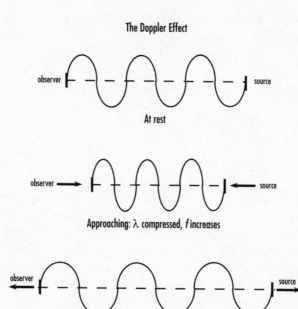

The Doppler Effect

observer ⊢ — — — — ⊣ source

At rest

observer → ⊢ — — — — ⊣ ← source

Approaching: λ compressed, *f* increases

observer ← ⊢ — — — — ⊣ → source

Receding: λ expanded, *f* decreases

Mach 1 is equivalent to the speed of sound (340 m/s). Thus, Mach 2 is twice the speed of sound, Mach 3, thrice, and so on. As an airplane flies through the air, it causes turbulence. While the plane is traveling slower than Mach 1, the air turbulence remains well ahead of the plane. However, when the plane reaches Mach 1, it catches up to (and passes) the disturbed region of air. When this happens, a "sonic boom" is heard as the pressure in front of the plane drastically rises and the air impacts the plane all at once.

RESONANT FREQUENCY

*Many objects have a natural **resonant frequency**. Application of a small force can create a relatively large vibration at this frequency. This is the principle by which stringed instruments work, and also explains why a wineglass might shatter from a soprano's voice (the frequency of the note would match that of the glass). In 1940, winds triggered the natural frequency of the Tacoma Narrows Bridge: the ensuing vibrations caused the bridge to tear itself apart.*

are further apart. It is in the nature of waves that if the objects are moved during the "transmission," the wave will also "move" in a similar direction. That is, if a wave source is moving towards a wave receiver as the wave is being sent, the wave will "recognize" the shortening of the distance and will compensate by shortening its **wavelength**. A decrease in wavelength is accompanied by an increase in **frequency** (or pitch). Wavelength is the length required for a wave to complete a cycle, while frequency is the number of cycles that can be completed in a second. Thus, if the wavelength increases, the frequency must decrease.

Consider a train that is moving through a train station blowing its whistle. As the train comes closer to the stationary observer at the station, the observer will notice a rise in the apparent pitch of the whistle. As the train passes the station, the distance between the train and the observer is increased, and therefore, a lower pitch will be heard. This effect is called the **Doppler effect**.

23. What is the correct order of invention?

    I. Color television

    II. Home satellite dishes

    III. Fiber optic cables

    IV. Closed captioning for the hearing impaired

    (A) I, II, III, IV

    (B) IV, II, III, I

    (C) I, IV, II, III

    (D) I, IV, III, II

The increasing ease and speed of global communication is one of the distinctive features of modern society. Long ago, it was possible to spend a lifetime blissfully unaware of people and events outside your immediate vicinity. Oh, you might hear some fanciful stories of far-off lands, but these were better suited for children than sober-thinking adults. This began to change with the development of movable type and printing presses, first by the Chinese around 1041 and then, four hundred years later, by **Johann Gutenberg** (1400-1468). Previously, books had been rare, hand-produced items too precious for mass consumption. However, written communication still had to be somehow carried from place to place, and its speed was thus inherently limited. The invention of the **telegraph** in 1833 changed all that, by enabling communication over electrical lines. Soon thereafter, in 1876, **Alexander Graham Bell** (1847-1922) invented the **telephone**. This device made possible communication at the speed of the spoken word, over longer distances than were possible with the telegraph. However, telephones still required

I'M CALLING FROM THE SUMMIT OF MT. EVEREST!

Telephones are overcoming their earlier limitations by going wireless. Mobile, or cellular, telephones work by transmission of microwaves through the air. Currently, the signals are generated at transmitters on the ground, but soon orbiting satellites may be used to enable phone calls to and from anywhere on Earth.

Alexander Graham Bell opening the New York/Chicago telephone line

wiring, and the more efficient fiber-optic cables were not developed until 1977. In 1895, Italian engineer **Marconi** developed wireless communication—the first radio (p. 514).

The invention of the television (p. 517) in the 1930s, and its commercialization after 1941, was another leap in communications technology because it enabled the transmission of much more information than was previously possible. Color television broadcasts soon followed (1950). In 1976, closed captioning was initiated by PBS, so that hearing-impaired viewers could have the same access to television. Finally, in the 1980s, increasing numbers of orbiting communications satellites and better receiver technology enabled the proliferation of the **home satellite dish**.

Videodrome (1982), directed by David Cronenberg. The film depicts a murky future in which televisions are an instrument of destruction. Long live the new flesh!

24. Why does the sky appear blue?

(A) Air is naturally light blue, and when you look at a lot of it you see a darker blue.

(B) The atmosphere is reflecting the color of the ocean.

(C) Blue light is the shortest wavelength of visible light that is radiated from the sun, therefore blue light is scattered more by the atmosphere.

(D) Most people on Earth prefer the color blue to the alternative—chartreuse.

Waves travel with a specific **wavelength** and **frequency**. The waves that are visible to the human eye are but a small part of the entire **electromagnetic spectrum**. Extremely small wavelength (high frequency) waves are used to investigate the interior of the human body (X-rays), whereas large wavelength (low frequency) waves are used to transmit television and radio signals over long distances. Somewhere in the middle are the waves that we see as colors—the **visible spectrum**. The wavelengths of the colors, from shortest to longest, exactly corresponds to the order of the colors from the inside to the outside of a rainbow. Thus, blue (or violet) waves have the shortest

"This most excellent canopy the air"—Hamlet

Unlike the sun, which gives forth light with all visible wavelengths, **lasers** produce intense light with one specific wavelength and color—that is, **monochromatic** light. The process by which this works is described in the word "laser"—it was originally an acronym for light amplification by stimulated emission of radiation.

WHY'S YOUR FISH LOOKING AT ME THAT WAY?

Humans can only see light within the visible spectrum, but other living creatures have different abilities. Some insects can see ultraviolet light, while dark-dwelling snakes sense infrared radiation. A goldfish can see infrared, ultraviolet, and everything in between.

wavelength and the highest frequency, and red waves have the longest wavelength and the lowest frequency.

The light that travels from sun to the Earth is white light. This means that by definition, it contains light of every wavelength and frequency (and thus every color) in the visible spectrum. As that light strikes the Earth's atmosphere it interacts with the molecules of the atmosphere. Since blue light has the shortest wavelength, it is scattered more by the atmosphere because it hits more atmospheric gas molecules. The larger wavelength colors, such as red, do not collide as often with these molecules. This is what makes the sky appear blue.

As the sun sets, we often notice yellows, oranges and reds. This phenomenon is due mostly to pollution created during the day. When we see the sun low on the horizon, we are viewing its light through the lower atmosphere. This is full of so many particles that even the orange and red wavelengths are scattered. The next time you see a movie in which a cowboy rides off into a beautiful sunset, remember that during the 1800s, there may not have been enough pollutants in the air to produce such a lovely backdrop.

25. **Which of the following is true about a near-sighted person?**
    (A) She will have a positive power prescription with concave lenses in her glasses.
    (B) She will have a negative power prescription with concave lenses in her glasses.
    (C) She will have a positive power prescription with convex lenses in her glasses.
    (D) She will have a negative power prescription with convex lenses in her glasses.

Just try going through an entire day without utilizing the power of **optics**. We can consider optics as falling into two major groups: **lenses** and **mirrors**. Most of us have at one time or another used lenses to correct our vision or to enlarge small objects, while mirrors let you be the first to greet yourself in the morning—as well as ensure your safety on the drive to work.

Perhaps you have noticed the trick, often used in hotel lobbies and restaurants, of using mirrors to make a room "feel" larger than it is. Mirrors make a room seem larger by reflecting light, while lenses can seem to enlarge or reduce objects by transmitting light. Your car probably has at least one mirror that makes objects appear farther away than they

"I Can See for Miles" (1967), by The Who from their album *The Who Sell Out*. You don't need glasses when there's magic in your eyes.

are. If you looked closely at this mirror, you would observe that this mirror is **convex**, or curved out. It is this convexity that demagnifies objects and makes them look more distant than they actually are. If we made the mirror **concave** (curved in) instead, objects would appear to be closer than they actually were.

Exactly the opposite holds for lenses. If you have perfect vision, an object in your field of vision is properly focused by the lenses of your eyes, so that the image appears directly upon your retinas. If you are near-sighted, objects are focused by your lenses in front of your retinas. If you are far-sighted, the object is focused behind your retinas. Another way to say this is that the lenses in the eyes of a near-sighted person are too convex, or too **converging**, and that the lenses in the eyes of a far-sighted person are too concave, or **diverging**. In order to correct either of these problems, we simply supply the person with a set of artificial lenses that correct the focus in the opposite direction. Thus, a near-sighted person gets diverging lenses and a far-sighted person gets converging lenses. A negative power prescription for your glasses is an indication to the manufacturer of your glasses how much to make the lenses thinner in the middle (thus, diverging), while a positive power prescription tells how much to make the middle of the lenses thicker than the edges (thus, converging).

"Without my glasses, I couldn't have won the Nobel Prize. Thanks, glasses!"

26. The "inventor" of quantum mechanics, who won the Nobel Prize for his quantum theory of light, was

(A) Werner Heisenberg
(B) Erwin Schrödinger
(C) Albert Einstein
(D) Max Planck

In the early part of the twentieth century, people began to realize that classical or "Newtonian" physics could not explain things that physically occur on either an extremely small scale (subatomic) or an extremely large scale (astronomical). A new theory was developed to help clarify certain of these otherwise inexplicable observations. This theory is known as **quantum mechanics**.

In 1900, **Max Planck** (1858-1947) proposed that light was made up of "packets" of fixed energy values, or quanta. This theory was considered unorthodox and was not accepted for many years. However, in 1918, Planck won the Nobel Prize for this insight. In 1905, **Albert Einstein** (1879-1955), then twenty-six years old, used Planck's quantum theory to suggest that light acted like particles, called photons. Einstein won the

The earliest mirror was no doubt a reflective surface of water. Next, polished surfaces of metal were used. The first glass mirrors were made in Venice, around the year 1300. They were hand-poured from molten glass, and were so expensive that the wealthy wore them on neck chains as jewelry. Yet these first mirrors more often than not produced poor quality, distorted reflections. Not until glass sheet technology was improved, more than three hundred years later, could perfectly reflecting mirrors be produced.

Parallel Universes (1988), by Fred Alan Wolf and *Quantum Reality* (1985), by Nick Herbert. The authors present some of the mindbending implications of the "new physics" in (thankfully) nonmathematical language.

The word "lens" comes from the Italian word *lenticchie*, for lentil. Glassworkers noticed that convex lenses bore a resemblance to the circular bean.

Nobel Prize in 1921 for this work. 1927 saw the introduction of the **Heisenberg uncertainty principle**. This states that the position and speed of a particle cannot be simultaneously measured to absolute accuracy. Rather, only the probability of position or momentum can be calculated. These calculations are most commonly done using the **Schrödinger wave equation**.

Nobel Prize winners Ivan Bunnin, Erwin Schroedinger (with his favorite glasses), Paul Dirac, and Werner Heisenberger

Heisenberg's uncertainty principle and the other concepts fundamental to quantum mechanics have raised philosophical questions about the nature of the universe. Physicist **Niels Bohr** (1885-1962) suggested that "there is no deep reality"—that is, it is impossible to provide a concrete, unambiguous description of phenomena. Worse, the "reality" we see may be our own creation, and not exist at all outside our observations. (If a tree falls in the forest . . .) Another possibility that has been raised is that of parallel universes: given that events have finite probabilities of occurring, any event must have occurred somewhere in a universe.

BEAM ME UP, HEISENBERG

*Physicists exploring the possibility of **teleportation** use quantum mechanical arguments to rationalize their work. The concept relies on "entangled" particles (photons, electrons, or protons). These particles are sometimes produced in pairs, and by the rules of quantum mechanics, each member of the pair "knows" what the other is doing and assumes an opposite polarization. If we separate the pair and react one member with a third particle, it is possible to recreate the third particle at the location of the second member of the pair—the fundamental requirement of teleportation.*

27. Which of the following does NOT depend on the use
of a region of the electromagnetic spectrum to work?

(A) Your microwave oven
(B) Your television remote control
(C) Your cellular phone
(D) Your computer printer

If you are presently on Earth (if not, send us a postcard), you are being bombarded by an enormous amount of **electromagnetic radiation** (EMR) at this moment. The **electromagnetic spectrum** is a construct by which scientists can classify all forms of radiation in terms of **frequency** and **wavelength**. Since frequency and wavelength are inversely related, a high frequency implies a low wavelength, and vice versa. **Radio waves**, with low frequency and high wavelength, are found at one end of the electromagnetic spectrum. This region of the spectrum is used to transmit radio and television broadcast waves. Within this range, the shortest frequency waves are used for AM radio broadcasts, then U.S. television channels two through six, followed by FM radio broadcasts and television channels seven through thirteen. The designation **UHF** stands for ultra high frequency, while **VHF** means very high frequency. From this, we can determine that UHF channels (channels above thirteen) must have a higher frequency than VHF channels.

Microwaves have frequencies just higher than the radio and television broadcast waves. This portion of the electromagnetic spectrum is now used to cook food in almost every kitchen in America. Following the microwave region is the **infrared**, or IR, region. IR radiation is used in television remote controls and home security devices, among other things. Next higher in frequency is the **visible** region of light (colors) from red to violet, followed by the **ultraviolet**, or UV, region. The UV region is

My three-inch pumps give me a better view of my browning bird.

UHF (1988), with Weird Al Yankovic. This is the kind of supremely silly movie that you laugh at, then wonder why you're laughing.

How Much For That Air?

Radio, television, and cellular phone signals are transmitted through the air at different frequencies. With the explosion in demand for these services, the number of available frequencies is dwindling, and "frequency allocation" is a hot commodity. In the United States, the Federal Communications Commission (FCC) controls the usage of the regions of the spectrum.

used in such devices as "invisible ink" detectors of hand stamps at some nightclubs and bars. At an even higher frequency is X-rays, followed by gamma rays. The wavelength of a typical AM radio wave is 300 meters (or 1000 feet). The wavelength of a typical microwave is 3 cm (or just over an inch). The wavelength of an X-ray is approximately 3 angstroms (or $3E^{10}$ meters, or one hundred-millionth of an inch).

28. **In an atom, where are electrons located?**

   (A) In the nucleus
   (B) In a circular orbit around the nucleus
   (C) In a spherical shell around the nucleus
   (D) Only the probability of the electrons' locations can be determined

Isotopes are atoms of the same element that have different numbers of neutrons, but the same number of electrons and protons. The **carbon-14** isotope has two more neutrons than the most common form, carbon-12. This isotope radioactively decays at a constant rate with a **half-life** of 5730 years—that is, half the original amount will remain at this time. Thus, carbon-14 can be used in **radiocarbon dating** to accurately measure the age of a fossil or artifact.

To a chemist, the simplest form of matter is the **atom**. An atom is comprised of a central **nucleus** surrounded by an **electron cloud**. The nucleus contains subatomic particles called **protons** and **neutrons**. The electron cloud is, you guessed it, a cloud containing electrons . . . somewhere. Where exactly, it is impossible to know, according to the Heisenberg uncertainty principle (p. 362). The whole thing is held together by the attraction between positively charged protons and negatively charged electrons.

The idea that the world is composed of indivisible pieces called atoms is attributed to **Democritus** (who was actually taught this by Leucippus in the fourth century B.C.). Democritus believed that change is the nature of all things. To him, change was manifest in the local motion of atoms: the indivisible components of all matter. Anything not composed of atoms is void. This is basically a statement of the tenets of modern chemistry. Unfortunately, **Aristotle** and **Plato** rejected these concepts, so these ideas remained around only in jokes until the seventeenth century. In fact, seventeen hundred years after his death, Democritus was provided one of the lowest places in hell by **Dante** (and it wasn't because Dante hated chemistry—chemistry hadn't even been invented yet). Plato and Aristotle were from the KISS (keep it simple, stupid) school of chemistry. They eliminated the idea of atoms and posited the five elements: earth, fire, water, air and ether. Who's laughing now?

29. By definition, a chemical compound always

(A) contains more than one element

(B) contains more than one molecule

(C) is synthesized, or artificially manufactured, in a laboratory

(D) is a potential health or ecological hazard

Chemists classify all matter into the categories of **atom, molecule, element**, and **compound**. An atom is considered to be the smallest indivisible particle, although we now understand that the atom itself is also divisible (p. 365) . A molecule is a group of two or more atoms held together by strong forces called chemical bonds.

In order to consider the definitions of element and compound, we must first consider the term **matter**. All things are composed of matter. Further, matter may be broken down into the two general categories of **mixtures** and **pure substances**. An element is a pure substance in which every atom is chemically the same. In order for atoms to be chemically the same, each must contain the same number of **protons**. A compound is a pure substance in which every atom is not chemically the same. A mixture is a combination of two or more pure substances—whether these substances are elements or compounds is not important.

The category "mixture" may be further divided into the categories of **homogeneous** mixture, also called **solution**, and **heterogeneous** mixture. We can distinguish a homogeneous mixture from a heterogeneous mixture by considering a bucket of each. If we take a spoonful of the homogeneous mixture, the resulting mixture in our spoon would have the same characteristics as the mixture as a whole, regardless of where our "spoonful" came from within the bucket. On the other hand, in the case of a heterogeneous mixture, our "spoonful" would not necessarily be identical to the bucket contents as a whole, nor would we anticipate that any two "spoonfuls" would be identical. An example of a homogeneous mixture is apple juice. An example of a heterogenous mixture is sand mixed with water.

Superman I (1978) and *II* (1981), with Christopher Reeve and Margot Kidder. The mythical element kryptonite affects Superman in strange ways, but you just know he's going to get the bad guys in the end.

BUCKY WOULD HAVE BEEN PROUD

*Discovered in 1985, **buckminsterfullerene** is a molecule containing sixty carbon atoms arranged in a structure like the surface of a soccer ball— or like the geodesic domes designed by American architect* R. Buckminster Fuller (p. 60) *The discovery of this molecule led to the finding of other, similar structures which are now lumped together as **fullerenes**.*

30. Why does ice float in pure water but sink in a strong gin and tonic?
    (A) Ice is less dense than water.
    (B) The alcohol in the gin makes the resultant gin and tonic less dense than the ice.
    (C) Both A and B are true.
    (D) A is true, B is false.

Cat's Cradle (1963), by Kurt Vonnegut. The king of science fiction hypothesizes about a form of water with a melting point above room temperature . . . the dreaded "ice-nine."

I'LL HAVE A GLASS OF GLASS, PLEASE

Glass is a solid—or is it? Actually, glass is a very, very thick (or viscous) liquid. Thus, in old buildings, you might notice that the windows appear thicker on the bottom. The glass has actually flowed downward over the years, at an extremely slow rate. It may be hundreds of years before the effect can be noticed.

All materials can exist in one of three states: **gas**, **liquid**, or **solid**. (There is also a fourth state of matter known as the **plasma state**, but we need not concern ourselves with that here.) Each of these states is accessible from each of the other states by altering the temperature or the pressure of the material. Pressure has the same effect as temperature, so we will limit our consideration to temperature changes.

At the coldest temperatures, all materials exist as solids. As we raise the temperature, each material will reach its melting point and begin to convert from the solid state to the liquid state. As we further increase the temperature, each liquid will eventually reach its boiling point and begin to convert into the gas state. Going from a solid to a liquid is termed **melting**, and the opposite process is called **freezing**. Similarly, the opposite of **boiling** is **condensation**. Under appropriate conditions (such as dry ice at room temperature) it is possible for materials to go directly from the solid state to the gas state. This is termed **sublimation**. The opposite of sublimation is **deposition**.

Density is the measure of mass per unit volume. Thus, material A is more dense than material B if a volume of A has a greater mass than an equal volume of B. Most materials are densest in the solid state, intermediate in the liquid state, and least dense in the gas state. Fortunately for life on Earth, water is a material that is an exception to this statement. Liquid water is more dense than solid water, so ice floats in water. However, if we reduce the density of the liquid water by adding another liquid (such as gin) that is not as dense, we can make the resultant liquid less dense than the ice. When this happens, the ice sinks. If ice were denser than water, the ice formed on lakes and rivers would sink to the bottom, eventually freezing them solid in winter so that little or no life could survive there.

31. **Which of the following events occurred first in history?**

    (A) The development of the Periodic Table of Elements
    (B) The invention of the stock ticker
    (C) The development of the first artificial plastic
    (D) The completion of the U.S. transcontinental railroad (with the driving of the golden spike at Promontory Point, UT)
    (E) The first chain drive bicycle
    (F) Publication of the first issue of the scientific journal *Nature*
    (G) Opening of the Suez Canal linking the Mediterranean and Red Seas
    (H) The opening of the first railroad tunnel through the German Alps
    (I) They all occurred in 1869

In 1869, the same year as the opening of the Suez Canal and Thomas Edison's invention of the stock ticker, **Dmitri Mendeleyev** (1834-1907) developed the first periodic table of the elements. Ever since, the **Periodic Table**, in one form or another, has adorned classroom walls throughout the world. The Periodic Table allows us to classify an element based on its similarities to other elements. Using it, we can predict that sulfur should have similar chemical properties to oxygen, because sulfur is arranged directly below oxygen in the table. The columns of the Periodic Table are called **groups**, or families. Each member of a group will have similar chemical properties to other members of the group. The rows of the table are called **periods**. Members of the same period have the same number of filled electron shells, but they are not necessarily expected to behave in chemically similar manners. This is because chemical behavior is primarily determined by the number of electrons that are in the shell that is not full—the **valence shell**. All members of the same group have the same number of electrons in their valence shells: therefore, they are chemically similar.

Periodic Table of the Elements

1 H 1.0																	2 He 4.0
3 Li 6.9	4 Be 9.0											5 B 10.8	6 C 12.0	7 N 14.0	8 O 16.0	9 F 19.0	10 Ne 20.0
11 Na 23.0	12 Mg 24.3			Transition Elements								13 Al 27.0	14 Si 28.1	15 P 31.0	16 S 32.1	17 Cl 35.5	18 Ar 39.9
19 K 39.1	20 Ca 40.1	21 Sc 45.0	22 Ti 47.9	23 V 50.9	24 Cr 52.0	25 Mn 54.9	26 Fe 55.8	27 Co 58.9	28 Ni 58.7	29 Cu 63.5	30 Zn 65.4	31 Ga 69.7	32 Ge 72.6	33 As 74.9	34 Se 79.0	35 Br 79.9	36 Kr 83.8
37 Rb 85.5	38 Sr 87.6	39 Y 88.9	40 Zr 91.2	41 Nb 92.9	42 Mo 95.9	43 Tc (98)	44 Ru 101.1	45 Rh 102.9	46 Pd 106.4	47 Ag 107.9	48 Cd 112.4	49 In 114.8	50 Sn 118.7	51 Sb 121.8	52 Te 127.6	53 I 126.9	54 Xe 131.3
55 Cs 132.9	56 Ba 137.3	57 La 138.9	72 Hf 178.5	73 Ta 180.9	74 W 183.9	75 Re 186.2	76 Os 190.2	77 Ir 192.2	78 Pt 195.1	79 Au 197.0	80 Hg 200.6	81 Tl 204.4	82 Pb 207.2	83 Bi 209.0	84 Po 209.0	85 At 210.0	86 Rn 222.0
87 Fr 223.0	88 Ra 226.0	89 Ac 227.0															

Lanthanum Series

58 Ce 140.1	59 Pr 140.9	60 Nd 144.2	61 Pm 145.0	62 Sm 150.4	63 Eu 152.0	64 Gd 157.3	65 Tb 158.9	66 Dy 162.5	67 Ho 164.9	68 Er 167.3	69 Tm 168.9	70 Yb 173.0	71 Lu 175.0

Actinium Series

90 Th 232.0	91 Pa 231.0	92 U 238.0	93 Np 237.0	94 Pu (244)	95 Am (243)	96 Cm (247)	97 Bk (247)	98 Cf (251)	99 Es (254)	100 Fm (253)	101 Md (256)	102 No (253)	103 Lr (257)

"The Elements" (1959), by Tom Lehrer. The 102 elements known in 1959 are all named in this little ditty. Since that time, seven more have been discovered. Time for another verse.

Members of the same period do not have the same number of electrons in their valence shells and are thus chemically dissimilar. Each member of a period has one more electron in its valence shell than the element directly to its left and one less electron in its valence shell than the element directly to its right. Because of this, we might expect that elements that are close together in the same period would have somewhat similar chemical properties, since they would vary in only one or two valence shell electrons. This is another truth that was elucidated by Mendeleev's organization of the elements into the periodic table.

32. The history of materials used by humans shows that first ceramics, then metals, then plastics were implemented. What statement best explains this progression?

(A) The Earth is made mostly of ceramic materials, which are readily accessible.

(B) Metals can be formed into intricate shapes more easily than ceramics.

(C) Plastics are lighter and more varied in properties than metals.

(D) All of the above

The role of materials in the progress of civilization has been sufficiently important that anthropologists and historians have identified early cultures by the material of greatest significance at that time. The earliest known human artifacts, from the **Stone Age**, are made of natural materials (bone, skin) and **ceramics**—both abundant and readily accessible. Later, the developement of metallurgy, during the **Bronze Age** and the **Iron Age**, enabled complex shapes to be formed from the more workable **metals**. Many would label post-1950 as the **Plastic Age**. **Plastics**, with their wide variation in properties, have now replaced many former applications of ceramics and metals.

The discovery and use of new materials by artisans and technologists enables better products and quality of life. Thus, clothing evolved to become more protective against the environment or more attractive; tools were made more widely available and less expensive; homes were designed for greater comfort; vehicles achieved longer ranges and greater speeds, giving greater access to food, supplies, and enjoyment; and weapons became more destructive and lethal in an effort to obtain security against the opponent's advanced weapons. Similarly, the arts and crafts were influenced by the artisans' abilities to process materials into desirable objects.

The materials of choice in a culture can have other effects as well. For example, the transition from the Bronze Age into the Iron Age introduced fundamental societal changes. Iron was readily abundant . . . the first "democratic material." Thus, for the first time, wealth and station did not determine material availability. The number of users increased exponentially in the shift to iron, causing an increased demand for skilled craftspeople in the materials trades and beginning the shift from an agrarian to an industrial economy, although this was not realized for almost three millenia.

33. Salsa, which according to George Castanza on "Seinfeld" is now the second most popular condiment in the United States,

   (A) causes heartburn because it is acidic
   (B) causes heartburn because it is basic
   (C) acts as an excellent cleanser of pennies
   (D) Both A and C

Salsa and other "hot" foods taste hot because of the irritation that we feel in our digestive tracts and nasal passages from these **acids** in these foods. What we experience as **heartburn** is the buildup of excess stomach acid. If a food is basic, it might taste soapy or chalky. Both soap and chalk are **bases**. The 14-point **pH scale** is used to classify something as either an acid or a base. The scale uses pure water as a standard. Water is termed neutral, and has a pH of 7. Anything with a pH below 7 is termed acidic, while anything with a pH above 7 is termed basic. The further away from 7 a substance's pH is, is the more acidic or basic it is. Thus, materials with extreme pH values are called strong acids and bases, while those with pH values closer to 7 are called weak acids and bases.

This suit was a steel

The Graduate (1967), directed by Mike Nichols, starring Dustin Hoffman. The old guy was right: plastics were the future. If only Dustin had taken his advice, he might have ended up comfortably wealthy, instead of on the run with some girl he hardly knew.

OUT OF THE FRYING PAN

*In 1938, young chemist Roy Plunkett became puzzled when no gas came out of his tank of tetrafluoroethylene. He sawed it open to find a curious, waxy white material inside. The TFE had **polymerized** to PTFE. Ta da . . . Teflon! DuPont scientists found that this material was uniquely slippery and resistant to chemical degradation. However, they thought its cost was too high for useful applications. Along came World War II, and the need for very rugged gaskets and valves for use in the atomic bomb: a timely justification for the mass production of Teflon.*

Batman (1989), starring Michael Keaton and Jack Nicholson. Jack falls into a pool of acid and comes out as the Joker. Holy transmogrification!

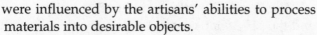

The pH of mild salsa is about 4.5, the pH of medium salsa is about 3.2, and the pH of hot salsa is 1.7. The people who suffer the most from eating hot foods are people with ulcers. An ulcer is a hole in the digestive tract. These holes can be caused by a variety of things, but they are perhaps most aggravated by acidic foods. People with ulcers are often told to eat dairy products or even to drink milk of magnesia to ease symptoms. Dairy products and milk of magnesia are basic foods that can counteract the acids produced in the digestive tract, which are elevated by stress. If an acid and a base are placed together, they will tend to react with, or **neutralize**, one another to bring the pH back toward seven.

Strong acids and bases are common components of household cleaners. Tarnish removers and products that remove mineral deposits are usually acidic; bleach and drain openers are basic. The violence of a reaction between a strong acid and a strong base can be enough to liberate a lot of heat and gas—in other words, to cause an explosion. It is more than prudent to read labels and avoid mixing combinations of different products.

34. **Why was gunpowder invented?**

    (A) Accidentally in Chinese alchemy experiments (trying to make gold)
    (B) For mining and civil engineering applications
    (C) For the purposes of warfare
    (D) For use in pyrotechnic displays (fireworks)

Many college students view thermodynamics as one of the most challenging of science courses. However, the study of thermodynamics, as it applies to everyday life, is not at all complex. Basically, we only have to consider two things: **enthalpy** and **entropy**. While these names, in and of themselves, are enough to send many running for the exits, there is really nothing to fear. Entropy is simply a measure of "messiness." If the amount of "messiness" increases, you have increased entropy. Enthalpy is a measure of how much heat is being stored in our system. If we have more heat stored in our system after an event than we had stored in our system before that event, we have an increase in enthalpy.

Let's focus on enthalpy. An event that occurs with an increase in enthalpy (more heat stored after than before) is termed an **endothermic** (heat storing) event. An event that occurs with a decrease in enthalpy (less heat stored after than before) is termed an **exothermic** (heat releasing) event. Any event that goes "bang" or makes a huge light display out of a small container (gunpowder, fireworks, other explosives) is an example of a highly exothermic event. Recall that heat is a kind of energy. If we release a bunch of heat, we are releasing a bunch of energy. Sound and light are also forms of energy. Thus, some of the heat energy released was simply converted to light, and some was converted to sound. Imagine what a surprise that Chinese alchemist had when he got a huge explosion instead of a nice pot of gold.

Fireworks over Victoria Harbor in Hong Kong

35. Why do cars in snowy climates rust faster than in warm climates?

   (A) Metal rusts faster in the cold.
   (B) Salt and sand used on snowy roads promote rusting.
   (C) Snowy climates are more humid.
   (D) People in warm climates better maintain their cars.

The process of rusting is a form of **corrosion**. Corrosion is a form of **oxidation**. No oxidation reaction can occur without an accompanying reduction reaction. Therefore, the term reduction-oxidation reaction, or redox reaction, is sometimes used to describe this chemical process. A material that gives up, or loses, its electrons is said to be oxidized. In order for this to happen, a second material must be available to accept, or gain, these electrons. This second material is said to be reduced. In the process of rusting, iron (Fe) is oxidized to rust, or iron (III) oxide (Fe_2O_3). The material that gives up electrons is the iron. The material that gains electrons is oxygen—from the air. This process would proceed at a pretty

Galvanic coatings protect against corrosion by providing a sacrificial metal surface layer. Even if the underlying metal is exposed, it will not corrode, because the surface layer is more easily attacked. Galvanic coatings are named for **Luigi Galvani** (1737-1798), whose discoveries led to the invention of the battery.

good clip even without sand or salt from wintery roads, but these substances speed up the rusting process.

Sand is an abrasive. As such, it will not only remove the paint, which acts as a protectant, from the iron in the body of your car, but it also serves to rub off the rust layers that have already formed. This leaves clean, uncorroded iron vulnerable to the atmospheric oxygen. Road salt (potassium chloride, KCl) is even more insidious. It works not only as an abrasive, but also as an accelerant, or **catalyst**. Since the chloride atom in road salt has an extra electron, it is more than happy to temporarily donate this electron to the oxidation process. It will get an electron back when the iron gives one up.

HOW COME ALUMINUM DOESN'T RUST?

It does. The surface of aluminum is coated with a monolayer of aluminum (III) oxide—the corrosion product of aluminum metal. However, unlike iron oxide, which forms in clusters, aluminum oxide forms a nice, clean monolayer that prevents the aluminum atoms underneath it from being exposed to atmospheric oxygen. This thin layer is transparent, not "rust-colored." If you were to continually scratch the surface of an aluminum can to rub off the aluminum oxide protective layer, it would eventually all turn to aluminum oxide. If you were to do so, however, you would simply end up with a small pile of talcum powder, since that is what aluminum oxide is.

36. **Organic chemistry is**

    (A) the study of the chemicals found in living organisms
    (B) the study of bodily organs
    (C) the study of the chemicals found in living or formerly
        living organisms
    (D) the study of chemicals containing carbon

Marie Curie was a doctoral student of **Antoine Henri Becquerel** (1852-1908), the first scientist to identify the phenomenon of natural radioactivity. He stumbled upon this by accident during an experiment to measure phosphorescence caused by sunlight. Becquerel, no doubt a bit annoyed by several cloudy days in a row, had to postpone his work and packed away a photographic plate with a (radioactive) uranium crystal. When he developed the plate, he was surprised to find a clear image. He assigned Marie Curie the task of identifying the material responsible for forming these dark images—and shared her first Nobel Prize.

Organic chemistry is the study of chemicals that contain the element carbon. The term **organic** means alive, and almost all sources of carbon on our planet either are, or were once, living. Here in the twentieth century, a great many of the products and processes we take for granted are the result of organic chemistry. Without organic chemistry you would not be able to wash your clothes in a washing machine (inorganic detergents are too harsh and would cause the machinery to rust), and these clothes would not contain any nylon, polyester, acrylic, Spandex, Lycra, or Velcro. Nor would you would also not be able to drive to work: the gasoline that you put in your car is processed by organic chemists. The cosmetics and perfume industries would not exist without organic chemistry—not to mention the organic chemicals that go into almost every over-the-counter drug and prescription drug that has ever been taken. Furthermore, every time you cook a meal, you have chemically altered your food (organically) so that it is more palatable to you.

Despite the many real benefits that organic chemistry has given us, it has become associated in conventional wisdom with health and environmental hazards. The **Dow Chemical Company** of Midland, Michigan originally ran advertisements with the slogan "better things for better living through chemistry." After a short period of time, market analysis showed that some less-than-scientific Americans were afraid to buy anything with the Dow label since their products contained "chemicals." Dow quickly truncated their slogan to "better things for better living." True, there have been a few colossal blunders in the attempt to use synthetic chemicals to improve peoples' lives. Many natural chemicals are also harmful to your health, or even fatal. However, how many of you are willing to give up organic chemistry completely and forego cooked food, modern medicines, gasoline, and plastics?

The makers of **Velcro** are now researching a quieter version for military applications.

37. **Radioactivity is**
    (A) a naturally occurring event observed in most chemical systems
    (B) evil
    (C) a phenomenon observed in certain high atomic weight elements
    (D) dangerous because no barriers can effectively stop the radioactive particles

Radioactivity is not evil! Unfortunately, the average person's acquaintance with radioactivity is confined to the horror stories of the evening news and bad science fiction or horror movies. It is true that very intense irradiation, or high doses accumulated over time, have been linked to cancer and genetic mutations. Yet radioactive material is commonly used in medical diagnoses, archaeology, and even smoke alarms with no ill effects.

Uneasy Careers and Intimate Lives: Women in Science, 1789-1979 (1987), by Pnina G. Abir-Am and Dorinda Outram. This work profiles Marie Curie and other women in science, with special attention to the challenges of balancing personal and professional demands.

Radioactivity is the tendency of an atom to stabilize itself by emitting subatomic particles. Some of these particles, at high dosage, are extremely dangerous. Others of these particles, regardless of the dosage, can be stopped by an ordinary piece of notebook paper! Radioactivity was discovered by **Marie Curie** (1867-1934), in her studies of pitchblende. Madame Curie, one of the first women to be acknowledged as a scientist, did not "invent" radioactivity, nor did she invent pitchblende. She simply recognized the fact that the radium in the pitchblende would develop photographic plates all by itself. For this and related work, she won two separate Nobel Prizes.

While many are still amazed by the accomplishments of Marie Curie, they remain horrified by the term "radioactivity." This is, as Mr. Spock would say, highly illogical. As discussed earlier, an atom is composed of electrons, neutrons, and protons. Like most things, an atom seeks its most stable state. Sometimes an atom feels that it is just too heavy, so it ejects two protons and two neutrons—in a process called **alpha decay**. Sometimes an atom feels that it has too many neutrons, so it converts one to a proton—this is called **beta decay**. The opposite (conversion of a proton to a neutron) is termed either **positron emission** or **electron capture**. A final form of radioactivity is the emission of electromagnetic radiation, the feared **gamma rays**.

Alpha particles, as well as positrons, will be stopped by a piece of paper or your own skin: they can only harm you when ingested or inhaled at high levels. **Beta particles** are equivalent to electrons, while gamma rays are the same as light with very short wavelengths. While beta and gamma rays are more penetrating, they are less damaging to the body than alpha particles. Finally, natural sources, especially sunlight, account for more of a person's typical radiation exposure than do man-made sources such as X-rays and TVs.

38. Which of the following events occurred first in 1945?

(A) The bombing of Hiroshima with a uranium-235 atomic bomb

(B) The bombing of Nagasaki with a plutonium-based atomic bomb

(C) Japan's surrender in World War II

(D) Germany's surrender in World War II

WHAT IS IT GOOD FOR?

War-driven funding has also led to some important advances in the field of medicine. The Penicillin Project, which ran concurrently with the Manhattan Project, was designed to isolate, purify, and make available large quantities of penicillin for the Allied war effort. This was the first project to mass-produce lifesaving drugs.

Science and technology do not exist apart from economics, history, sociology, or any other aspect of culture. It has always been true that without adequate funding, the advance of science is slowed or halted. Given the accelerating pace of technological development, financial entities on the governmental scale are required to bankroll many scientific advances. As a result, much technological progress has been intimately tied to warfare and weapons development. The development of the computer is one such example. ENIAC (p. 347) was developed at the request of the U.S. War Department for assistance in ballistics calculations. This is not to say that the now-omnipresent computer would not have come into existence were it not for World War II, but doubtless, it would have taken a much longer period of time to do so.

Surprisingly, many of the devices that are routinely used today are in some way related to the **Manhattan Project**. The Manhattan Project is the most impressive scientific collaboration that has yet been achieved. Hundreds of American and Allied scientists from around the globe worked together, in an effort to produce an atomic bomb before the Axis forces were able to do so. Had they not been successful, and had sabotage efforts of the Axis' project not been *remarkably* successful, it is possible that you would be reading this in German. At one time during World War II, the Germans were up to two years ahead of the Allies in atomic technology. The scientists working on the Manhattan Project were by no means unaware of or indifferent to the thorny questions raised by their work. Several became anti-war, or even anti-nuclear power, after realizing the full impact of the bombs.

The Making of the Atomic Bomb (1986), by Richard Rhodes. A Pulitzer Prize-winning account of the Manhattan Project tells a story of personalities and politics, as well as technology.

Bikini Atoll: This is only a test . . .

39. Why do clocks run clockwise?

(A) Civilization developed in the northern hemisphere.
(B) The geographic poles and the magnetic poles are misaligned.
(C) The Earth's gravitational field makes clockwise mechanisms run more efficiently than counter-clockwise mechanisms.
(D) It is entirely arbitrary.

Civilization arose from the five great rivers of the world: the **Nile**, the **Yellow** (Hwang), the **Indus**, and the Tigris and Euphrates. Did you ever notice that these rivers have one other thing in common? They are all located in the **northern hemisphere**! If you are presently in the northern

Empires of Time: Calendars, Clocks, and Cultures (1989), by Anthony Aveni. The anthropologist-astronomer explores how concepts of time influence society and worldviews.

hemisphere, you have probably noticed that the sun rises in the east and sets in the west, or travels from the right to the left as you are facing north. This means that the shadow of the sun on a sundial in the northern hemisphere moves from west to north to east to south to west—**clockwise**. Had civilization developed in the southern hemisphere, we would probably consider the other direction "clockwise," since the shadow of the sun on a sundial in the southern hemisphere would travel in the opposite direction.

Related to this is the **Coriolis effect**, first postulated in 1835 by Gaspard Coriolis (also the originator of the term "kinetic energy"). Because Earth spins to the east, all moving objects in the northern hemisphere turn somewhat clockwise of a straight line, while objects in the southern hemisphere turn somewhat counterclockwise. This effect explains not only the direction of the tradewinds, but also why the water in your toilet flushes in a counterclockwise direction. In the southern hemisphere water should flush in a clockwise direction, and a toilet placed directly on the equator should flush water straight down. However, for such a small volume of fluid, these effects are seldom realized—so toilet water, alas, still flushes counterclockwise (more due to engineering than to the Coriolis effect). But, if you had a really big toilet…

40. **The hole in the ozone layer was first discovered in**

    (A) 1985
    (B) 1956
    (C) 1948
    (D) 1929

Ozone is the name for a molecule of oxygen containing three atoms, instead of two found in "regular" oxygen molecules. This form of oxygen is created from the decomposition of two-atom oxygen molecules by sunlight. The **ozone layer** is a region of the upper atmosphere in which ozone is most likely to be found. This layer absorbs ultraviolet (UV) radiation. Without it, high levels of UV radiation from the sun cause an increase in skin cancers and cataracts, as well as disrupt plant and animal ecology.

A hole in the ozone layer, in the region of the South Pole, was discovered in 1985. The hole appears to be growing. However, because of the recency of this discovery, it cannot be established whether the hole was there before, nor whether it naturally shrinks and expands in cycles. Scientists *have* proposed a cause for the hole. They implicate **chlorofluorocarbons** (CFCs), chemicals once widely used in foams, aerosols, refrigerants, and air conditioners. CFCs build up in the upper atmosphere, and are decomposed to produce chlorine gas in the ozone layer. The chlorine acts as a **catalyst** in an ozone destruction reaction: it breaks down ozone again and again, without being affected itself.

Today, the industrialized nations are moving toward elimination of CFCs. In the agreement known as the **Montreal Protocol**, 128 countries committed to gradually stopping production of the two main CFCs. Now, other materials, such as butane, are used as the propellants in spray cans, and alternative refrigerants to replace **freon** are being developed.

 You have probably sniffed ozone without knowing it. The bright light of a photocopier causes an electrostatic discharge of the oxygen molecules found in air, and some ozone is produced. With its strong characteristic odor, ozone is easily detected by the human nose. Perhaps you would like to reconsider before you try copying your face again?

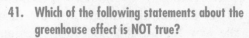

41. Which of the following statements about the greenhouse effect is NOT true?

(A) The greenhouse effect is only observed on the planet Earth.

(B) The excessive amounts of carbon dioxide and other gases in the atmosphere can trap the sun's radiation, causing warming of the Earth's surface.

(C) Deforestation, cement production, flatulent cows, and the burning of fossil fuels can all contribute to excessive carbon dioxide in the atmosphere.

(D) The world's oceans currently absorb 50 percent of carbon dioxide produced by humans.

The **greenhouse effect** is a name for what could happen if excessive carbon dioxide and other gases built up in the Earth's atmosphere. These gases can act like the roof of a greenhouse, letting in the sun's light but trapping its heat inside the atmosphere. If the effect were severe enough, significant **global warming** would result. A warmer climate might be appreciated in Alaska, but would have serious ecological consequences elsewhere. California would become a large desert; the oceans would rise to flood the coasts; and the polar ice caps would begin to melt. The heat near the equators might be unbearable for human inhabitants. For a further warning, we need only look to Venus, our sister planet. Scientists believe that a "runaway" greenhouse effect on Venus contributes to its

AND NOW FOR SOME REALLY GOOD NEWS

Ironically, the global efforts to reduce or reverse the damage to the ozone layer may worsen the greenhouse effect. Ozone itself acts as a greenhouse gas, as do the chemicals being developed as replacements for the ozone-eating chlorofluorocarbons.

Some of the greenhouse gases pouring into the atmosphere come from lesser-known sources. The periodic climate shift known as El Niño causes droughts in tropical regions: when the plants there die from the heat, they give off a large amount of carbon dioxide. Meanwhile, a major source of methane gas is the world cattle population. Specifically, the cows' belches during digestion send up to 400 liters of methane gas per cow per day into the sky.

The Man Who Fell to Earth (1976), starring David Bowie. An asexual stranger seeks water for a desertlike planet of the future (you'll never guess which planet it really is). This cult classic is an imaginative movie with some great photography.

The acids found in acid rain are the same ones that are synthesized in mass quantities for industrial applications. More pounds of sulfuric acid are made in the U.S. than of any other chemical; nitric acid is eleventh on the list. The acids are used in fertilizers, explosives, plastics, dyes, petroleum refining, and metal and ceramic manufacturing.

ragingly hot surface (over 800 degrees Fahrenheit) and high atmospheric pressure (almost ninety times that of Earth).

Carbon dioxide is the most important of the "greenhouse gases": others include methane, nitrous oxide (also implicated in **acid rain**) and chlorofluorocarbons (also implicated in the destruction of the ozone layer). Carbon dioxide is another byproduct of the burning of fossil fuels. Levels of carbon dioxide are also increased when forests are leveled to make way for humans, because trees and plants consume carbon dioxide to produce oxygen. The oceans currently absorb around half of the carbon dioxide produced on Earth, but it is unclear how much more capacity they have, and what effect any increased absorption might have. Experts disagree on how rapid the global warming rate is, but most agree that the long-term trend towards a warmer climate is there. Humanity has made this happen, and for better or for worse, we will all have to live with the consequences.

42. **What is acid rain?**

   (A) Rain with a pH value significantly above 7
   (B) Rain with a pH value significantly below 7
   (C) Rain containing chlorofluorocarbons (CFCs)
   (D) Rain containing lysergic acid diethylamide (LSD)

Rain is naturally somewhat acidic, with a pH of 5.6. However, rain containing unusually high amounts of sulfuric and nitric acid can have pH values below 5 (the acidity of coffee) and sometimes as low as 2 (the acidity of lemon juice). The term "acid rain" encompasses all rain with a pH below 5. How do the

acids get in the rain? The falling water picks up gaseous sulfuric dioxide and nitrogen oxides in the atmosphere. Most of these gases are produced from the burning of fossil fuels, in our power plants, automobiles, and industrial factories.

Life on Earth has been affected in many ways by increasingly acidic rainfall. Some North American and European lakes have become so acidic that no fish can survive there. Acid rain can eat away materials like marble and limestone, which are bases. (Naturally acidic pigeon droppings have a similar effect.) Forests and crops have also suffered. Acid rain is becoming a political issue as well. For example, Canada and the former West Germany do not appreciate the acid rain caused by their polluting neighbors, the United States and the former East Germany. Their governments have lobbied for stricter legislation or reparations from the guilty parties to alleviate the problem. The best remedy would be to reduce the emissions from coal-burning power plants, perhaps by exploiting another source of energy.

43. **What do the letters in the word "scuba" stand for?**

(A) Self-Contained Underwater Breathing Apparatus
(B) System for Controlled Underwater Biological Analysis
(C) SCientific Underwater BAthysphere
(D) Nothing; the word was coined by Jacques Cousteau

The vast oceans cover two-thirds of the Earth's surface, and are in a sense the "final frontier" of unexplored territory on the planet. Only in the twentieth century have the ocean depths been explored, and a wondrous picture of strange life forms, dramatic scenery, and incredible variation has emerged. Though modern oceanography is often dated to the voyages of the British **HMS Challenger**, from 1872 to 1876, the French seem to have had an especial

Say "anemone"!

 Deep-sea divers must be careful of the increasing water pressure in the ocean depths, which can lead to a syndrome known as **the bends**. The increased pressure forces gases to be absorbed into the diver's body. If the diver comes up to the surface too quickly, the gases can form bubbles in the blood and in body tissue, with painful or even fatal consequences. A related effect is narcosis (literally "sleepiness"), a loss of alertness associated with absorbed nitrogen in the blood.

20,000 Leagues Under the Sea (1870), by Jules Verne. Verne predicts deep-sea observation ports, incandescent lighting, and oxygen synthesis for his imaginary submarine, the *Nautilus*.

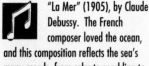

"La Mer" (1905), by Claude Debussy. The French composer loved the ocean, and this composition reflects the sea's many moods, from calm to sparkling to splendidly violent.

affinity for deep-sea exploration. In 1943 **Jacques Cousteau** invented an improved diving suit, which he called the Aqualung, that enabled divers to descend up to 500 feet below the surface. Today Cousteau's invention is more commonly referred to as the **scuba** suit, for self-contained underwater breathing apparatus. Cousteau's countryman, **Auguste Piccard**, designed and built a bathyscaphe (Greek for "deep boat") that in 1960 successfully dove to the deepest point on Earth, 35,800 feet down to the bottom of the Mariana Trench. In 1973, the French Navy bathyscaphe *Archimede* began the first scientific survey of the region known as the Mid-Atlantic Ridge.

The ocean floor has active volcanoes, deep chasms, and slow, cold currents. Over 200,000 species of animals live in the ocean, including the largest known living creature, the 100-ton blue whale. Oceans also provide valuable resources to humanity—not only food, but oil trapped below the sea floor, hydroelectric energy from the motion of the tides and waves, and rich mineral deposits.

44. All of the following methods of energy production use renewable resources EXCEPT

   (A) solar power
   (B) hydroelectric power
   (C) geothermal energy
   (D) burning of coal and oil

Burning of fossil fuels (p. 144) like coal and oil uses up nonrenewable resources, and is also implicated in acid rain and the destruction of the ozone layer. Moreover, the United States, and other countries such as Japan, are very concerned about the political consequences of excessive dependence on foreign oil sources. So why on Earth do we use fossil fuels? Alternative, nondestructive sources of energy—such as **solar power**, **hydroelectric power**, and **geothermal energy**—exist. Unfortunately, solar cells are currently too inefficient to generate sufficient power, and are thus impractical. Hydroelectric power, which gets energy from flowing water, has the disadvantage of requiring significant environmental changes, damming a river on one side and flooding land on the other. Geothermal energy refers to heat from the Earth's core. Such heat cannot be easily tapped, except in certain areas. Thus, fossil fuels remain the most efficient and inexpensive source of energy known.

There are two ways to address the "energy problem." The first is simply to improve efficiency. You do this the same way you would budget money (for some, this is another example of a nonrenewable resource). That is, you "spend" less energy, and when you must spend it, make good use of it through economical tricks like insulation, efficient lighting, and fuel-conserving

COLD FUSION

In 1989, professors B. Stanley Pons and Martin Fleischmann announced the creation of "cold fusion" in a room-temperature beaker of water. The announcement was made at a press conference (prior to publication of the work) and scientists and media alike immediately seized on its potential to provide an unlimited, inexpensive energy source. It sounded too good to be true, and perhaps it was. Several years and millions of dollars in research later, Pons' and Fleischmann's findings have yet to be conclusively duplicated, and most scientists have discredited the work. However, a small minority continues to pursue the technology in the hopes of a breakthrough.

transportation. The second alternative is to find another source of energy. Perhaps the best candidate is nuclear power (p. 170). In a modern nuclear reactor, atomic nuclei undergo "splitting," or **fission**, with an accompanying release of heat energy. This heat is used to drive steam turbines. However, fission reactors produce radioactive waste, which must be safely disposed of. If nuclei could be combined in a **fusion** process, even more energy could be produced, with relatively little radioactive byproducts.

ANSWERS

1. C	2. B	3. C	4. B	5. D	6. D	7. A	8. D	9. A	10. B
11. B	12. C	13. D	14. D	15. B	16. A	17. B	18. B	19. A	20. B
21. A	22. A	23. D	24. C	25. B	26. D	27. D	28. D	29. A	30. C
31. I	32. D	33. D	34. A	35. B	36. D	37. A	38. D	39. A	40. A
41. A	42. B	43. A	44. D						

Government is an inescapable fact of our existence, and it's important to have some understanding of what governments—especially our own relatively young one—have stood for and accomplished over the centuries. Politics and political ideology have always suffused American culture; after all, we are a nation founded by a group of lawyers who knew the political theory of the time inside out. To know political history is to have insight into the culture we've created and an informed view of the possibilities for the future.

1. **All states must possess which of the following characteristics?**

    I. **Bounded territory**

    II. **A population**

    III. **A government**

    (A) I only
    (B) II only
    (C) II and III only
    (D) I, II, and III

In the lingo of political science, a state is a defined physical locus inhabited by a group of human beings, the bulk of whom willfully submit to the binding political decisions of a centralized institution. For everybody else, a state is any place where some people live and a common government exists whose authority is recognized by most of the people.

The oldest view concerning the origin of the state is the **divine theory**, which asserts that the state was a premeditated plot devised by a local deity. The early Hebrews (p. 485) and most other ancient peoples subscribed to this theory. According to the Hebrews and, later, the Christians (p. 488) and the Muslims (p. 495) God created the state to bring order out of the chaos created by humanity, and to allow individuals to atone for their own sins (p. 493) through obedience to the laws. Right or wrong, persuading people to buy into this idea yielded obvious benefits to religious and political leaders alike; if God created the state, it followed that God decided who should govern it.

Attila the Hun invades Italy

A second and more secular notion maintains that a few extraordinary individuals or groups of individuals created the state by compelling previously free people to submit to their will. According to this **charismatic theory**, these rare individuals unified entire groups of people for their own purposes using psychological force or, if that didn't work, threats of physical harm. History is certainly full of charismatic leaders who have shaped nations and empires through sheer force of will. Most of them, though, like Adolf Hitler (p. 649) and Attila the Hun (p. 72) have tended to embrace remarkably pinheaded convictions.

Political philosophers have suggested countless other theories regarding the origin of the state. The **natural theory**, for example, contends that the state evolved because the process of civilization necessitated more and

BEASTLY BLONDES

German philosopher **Friedrich Nietzsche (p. 507)** *suggested that a mysterious people known only as the Blonde Beasts brought about government by forcing their will upon all primitive societies. Once the blonde beasts came, everybody else found their freedoms severely restricted. As a result, individuals had to reach within themselves to find pleasure and happiness. The consequence of this "inwardness" was the generation of the human soul which, Nietzsche maintains, has plagued humanity with problems ever since.*

more order. Basically, somebody had to provide some organization in an increasingly complicated society, so somebody did. The **sportive theory** of Spanish philosopher Jose Ortega y Gasset speculates that the male adolescent instinct for adventure and sexual conquest caused young men in primitive tribes to bond together to fulfill their biological desires. In response, older tribe members organized their own groups to coerce the miscreants into behaving. The cumulative effect of these primitive social structures formed the first tribal states.

2. **Where was Plato from?**
   - (A) Syracuse
   - (B) Sparta
   - (C) Athens
   - (D) Cleveland

The word "politics" comes from the ancient Greek word *polis*, or **city-state**, and the Greeks not only closely identified with the polis of which they were part but also spent a lot of time theorizing about different kinds of governments. One of the most famous of these Greek political philosphers was **Plato** (427-347 B.C.). Plato held that the material reality we humans perceive is only a shoddy copy of an unconditionally perfect reality that mere mortals can never know through sensory experience. He maintained, however, that some people (especially philosophers like himself) can comprehend the other, ultimate reality by meticulously engaging in pure thought processes. If, as Plato concluded, perfection is better than imperfection, humanity would benefit by allowing these sages to mold material reality after the ultimate reality as much as possible. In the *Republic*, a series of dialogues starring **Socrates**, Plato conceived of his version of an ideal political state. Probably a bit disillusioned by totalitarian Sparta's conquest of his native **Athens** in the Peloponnesian War, Plato put into his ideal political system decidedly few traces of the democracy enjoyed by the Athenians. In order to obtain the maximum amount of justice, Plato's ideal government would require all members of society to do what they are best suited to do. Individuals best suited for agricultural production would become farmers while individuals best suited to fight wars would become soldiers, and so on. The most rational and intelligent members of society—regardless of their original social station—would be hand-picked, rigorously educated, and judiciously reared to one day become **Philosopher Kings**. These erudite social engineers would dish out wisdom for the betterment of society; their purpose in life would be to settle disputes among the masses and rule for the good of all.

Athenian democracy under the great ruler **Pericles** (c. 490-429 B.C.) is considered the most enlightened of ancient governments, but still the economy was supported by slave labor, and slaves (most of whom were war prisoners), women, and foreign-born residents were not considered citizens and had no say in the running of the polis. Most polises had fewer than 20,000 citizens, who were vitally involved in public affairs as a point of honor.

3. Who is famous for saying "man is by nature a political animal"?

(A) Heraclitus
(B) Aristotle
(C) Cicero
(D) Socrates

Though he may not have been the first person to realize it, **Aristotle** (384-322 B.C.)—a student of Plato's—gets the historical credit for noting that, indeed, man is a political animal. Had he not been a creature of his times, Aristotle might have added that women are also political animals. In fact, had Aristotle ever sat in a barnyard for a while, he might have noticed that even chickens—what with their pecking orders—seem to possess inherently political instincts.

Aristotle

With an eye toward ultimately determining what sort of government would most benefit humanity, Aristotle sought first to classify the kinds of governments in the world. He decided that there are only three fundamentally different types available to a society: government ruled by one person, government ruled by a few people, or government ruled by many people. Aristotle argued that a state ruled by a single individual can be either a **monarchy** or a **tyranny**. Under a monarchy, a just ruler seeks to attain fairness and order. A tyrant, on the other hand, governs for the sake of getting rich and gratifying a lust for power. Aristotle classified rule by a few people as either an **aristocracy** or an **oligarchy**. Within an aristocracy, a handful of wise and just individuals rule by committee for the benefit of the populace. An oligarchy occurs if these same people use their power to accumulate wealth and make impartial laws. A **polity** results when all qualified citizens cooperate in the affairs of the state through open discussion and general compromise. If, instead of attempting to achieve maximum public satisfaction through reasonable compromise, the participating multitudes seek simply to satisfy their own desires without regard to the welfare of others, the mob rule of a **democracy** ensues.

So, according to Aristotle, government can be a solution to problems or a problem in itself. Depending upon the character of the leaders within a state, each type of government can lead either to general happiness among the people or to discontent and, eventually, societal collapse. Aristotle liked the idea of a polity, but he feared that a state with too much decentralized power would easily yield to the precarious nature of a democracy. With a nod to his mentor, Aristotle concluded that a system combining the best elements of an aristocracy and a polity would most benefit everyone. In his final assessment, Aristotle suggested a state in which the masses could vote representative Philosopher Kings into and out of political power.

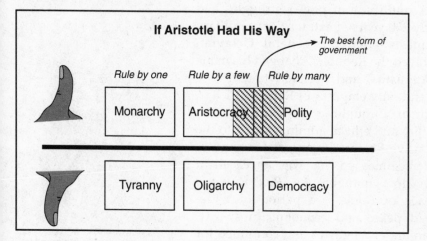

If Aristotle Had His Way

> *Politics n. A strife of interests masquerading as a contest of principles. The conduct of public affairs for private advantage.*
>
> ——AMBROSE BIERCE,
> The Devil's Dictionary, 1906.

4. **Which of the following ancient empires did the Romans defeat to achieve independence?**

(A) The Macedonians
(B) The Etruscans
(C) The Athenians
(D) The Carthaginians

In 509 B.C., the Romans, then a small and simple agrarian people, successfully revolted against the **Etruscans**, a prosperous and powerful empire with a strong navy. Wary of the tyranny the Etruscans had imposed, the designers of the resulting **Roman Republic** created a government in which officials elected by wealthy, landowning **patricians** held power for short periods of time. Early Roman government consisted of a large legislative body called the **Senate** and an executive branch of two **consuls** who could only serve one term each. Eventually, the lower classes, or **plebeians**, started demanding some measure of political representation for themselves and, in what may have been a historical first,

Spartacus (1960), directed by Stanley Kubrick. This first-rate epic film tells the story of an enslaved gladiator who leads a revolt against the Romans. Don't miss the fully restored 1991 version, with an erotic bathing scene between Laurence Olivier [dubbed by Anthony Hopkins] and Tony Curtis put back in.

they actually got it. After nearly a century of considerable quarreling between the patricians and the plebeians, the Senate passed a series of measures granting a host of political rights to poor folks. The Senate decreed the creation of the **Tribal Assembly**, a forum for political debate, and the **tribune**, an executive agency with the power to veto any Senate legislation it considered detrimental to the masses. By 287 B.C., the Tribal Assembly had assumed an amount of legislative authority similar to the power held by the Senate.

A multitude of power struggles and nearly 250 years of extraordinary military conquests later, the general **Octavian** dissolved the Republic, changed his name to **Augustus**, and declared himself the one and only **emperor** of Rome in 31 B.C. Augustus brought a sense of political stability and ethical administration to the expansive Roman Empire; as far as autocratic regimes go, his was an excellent one. Most notably, the *Pax Romana* ("Peace of Rome"), a period of widespread peace and economic prosperity, began under Augustus and continued for over 200 years.

Hey, can someone get this little guy off me?

The Roman Republic and the subsequent Roman Empire endured for over a thousand years. Politically and culturally, the Romans tended to hold pragmatic views. Because they sought to expand their empire and to increase their personal wealth, the Roman leadership and its citizenry rarely got caught up in ideological debates. Roman leaders traditionally allowed conquered peoples to go about their business and their religions as usual, as long as they paid their taxes and swore their allegiance to Rome.

OF PLOUGHSHARES AND SWORDS

According to Roman legend, the popularly elected Senate of the fledgling Republic found itself staring down a pressing military threat. A worried Senate delegation traveled to the farm of Cinncinatus, a venerable retired general who was busy ploughing his fields at the time, and asked him to become the dictator of the Roman Republic during the crisis. Cincinnatus accepted and headed to the city immediately, leaving his plough in the fields. The new dictator quickly attacked the enemy and, sixteen days later, returned to Rome victorious. The elated Senate decreed that Cincinnatus should remain the dictator of Rome. Wanting no part of absolute power, Cincinnatus went back to his fields, picked up his plough where he had left it, and returned to his normal, boring life. The moral to the story: political power should be used only to further the interests of the people, not to further self-interest.

But while the Romans were busy establishing their Republic, several relatively uncivilized tribes from the remote regions of northern Europe began a slow migration south in search of better land and warmer temperatures. About 800 years later, they found what they were looking for at the western edge of the Roman Empire. As Rome gradually grew politically weak and because the militaristic Huns (p. 72) kept attacking their new turf, these peoples (known collectively in history books as the **Germanic tribes**) started trickling into the Roman Empire itself. Ruling a crumbling empire and trying to control a wave of immigrants proved to be more than the Romans could handle and, by 500 A.D., their once great empire had completely collapsed.

5. For about how long did the feudal state remain the dominant social system in western Europe?

(A) 17 years
(B) 300 years
(C) 600 years
(D) 900 years

The virtual anarchy that prevailed throughout most of Europe after the fall of the Roman Empire provided a regular breeding ground for would-be political leaders. For the next two centuries, any shrewd and enterprising male with an interest in despotism and the ability to raise an army could try his hand at starting a state. Those leaders who could defend an area for any length of time were able to establish tiny protectorates. In exchange for the military security provided by these political chiefs, the grateful people within each protectorate gave their leader a portion of their annual agricultural production. This simple societal scheme eventually evolved into feudalism (p. 74), an only slightly more complicated political system that dominated Europe and much of Asia for approximately the next 900 years.

CHARLEMAGNE

*The Frankish **Carolingian Dynasty** provided the longest period of political stability during the early Middle Ages. Led by **Charlemagne** (a.k.a. **Charles the Great**), the Carolingian Empire encompassed most of western Europe at its height. Although he was no less ruthless or barbaric than his peers, Charlemagne was a great military leader and, because he effectively navigated the treacherous relationship between church and state, an extraordinary statesman. A brief surge of scholarly and artistic achievement, known as the Carolingian Renaissance, occurred during Charlemagne's reign (768-814). Alas, when Charlemagne died in 841, the Carolingian Dynasty and the Carolingian Renaissance quickly disintegrated. In 843, three of Charlemagne's grandsons established the **Treaty of Verdun** and split the Empire into three parts: **Charles the Bald** got the area that is now France, **Louis the German** got the western part of present-day Germany, and poor **Lothair** got the ill-fated area between the two that is northern Italy and the **Rhineland**. The Treaty of Verdun started the process that would ultimately produce the **nation-states** of Europe.*

The Princess Bride (1987), directed by Rob Reiner. Set in the early Middle Ages, this classic love story has heroes, villains, dastardly deeds, romance, and political intrigue. On top of all that, the characters are hilarious. **Andre the Giant** was robbed for not even being nominated for an Academy Award. If you don't get all sappy watching the climactic finish, there's something wrong with you.

A Distant Mirror (1979), by Barbara Tuchman. The eminently readable and popular historian Tuchman sheds fascinating light on the Middle Ages.

Once the leaders of these tiny protectorates got their own territories in order, many of them set out to expand their domains. Eventually, as they were able to consolidate more land, amass wealth, and develop more sophisticated weaponry, the most competent feudal leaders became very powerful. In response to the need for more government in their growing provinces, feudal leaders delegated a limited degree of power to a few loyal individuals who governed parts of each kingdom. These less powerful leaders, or vassals (p. 73), gave themselves titles like **baron**, **duke**, and **earl**, and the supreme leader called himself the king (p. 322—Elvis). Lest their families lose any clout, members of the feudal ruling class designated their children the heirs to their positions. As a result, the bulk of people in feudal society found themselves completely out of the political loop after a few generations.

One group that desperately needed military protection and didn't care to be out of the political loop was the Christian church (p. 488), an institution that had gained widespread European acceptance during the twilight years of the Roman Empire. As the kings of feudal states became more powerful, church leaders sought to forge alliances with them. While kings provided for the protection of church property, financing, and the safeguarding of priests and religious leaders, the church preached that kings and vassals ruled by **divine right**, or as a direct result of God's will. This mutual insurance policy provided the framework for the long and tenuous relationship between church and state that would last until the late 1600s.

Although the church fulfilled its part of the bargain by paying lip service to the idea that kings ruled by divine right, it constantly meddled in the affairs of the state. By the late **Middle Ages**, tension between kings and church leaders had grown into genuine conflict. Essentially both institutions wanted absolute power over society, and neither was willing to share it.

6. **What revolutionary episode caused the European Christian church to divide into two factions?**

    (A) The Glorious Revolution
    (B) The Council of Trent
    (C) The Reformation
    (D) The Enlightenment

Beginning in the early 1600s, Martin Luther (p. 494), a pious German friar, sparked the Reformation (p. 494). By 1618, this ideological argument had become a wholesale military battle centered in Germany. Hoping to strengthen the Catholic church, religious and political leaders in the southern regions of Germany started the hideous Thirty Years' War by attacking the Protestant German kingdom to the north. Several other kingdoms intervened in the long and bitter struggle and, three decades later, no clear winner emerged.

What did emerge was a very exhausted group of European political leaders. In 1648 most of the major political players of western

One Night Only at the Hollywood Bowl: Martin Luther Solo Tour— with very special guest The Doors!

Europe met in a small German town to iron out their differences and somehow end the conflict between Protestants and Catholics. Their resulting agreement, the **Treaty of Westphalia**, shaped a fundamentally new world order. Under the treaty, each king would decide whether the Protestant or Catholic version of Christianity should prevail within his dominion. In a brilliant strategic maneuver, the European monarchs effectively empowered themselves to limit the activities of the church because, henceforth, the church would need the state's permission to sustain itself. The new agreement also put religious leaders in an inferior position because, after all, if a spiritual change of heart suddenly seized the king, everyone working for the authorized church would just as suddenly be seized by unemployment.

NOT QUITE MACHIAVELLIAN

*The name **Niccolo Machiavelli** (1469-1527) has become synonymous with political cunning due to his treatise* The Prince *(1513), in which he used the ruthless but politically skilled Florentine ruler **Cesare Borgia** (1476-1507) as a model of a politician who is able to consolidate power and get things done. Actually, Machiavelli himself was a sensitive and learned guy; he also wrote a history of Florence and two comedies.*

7. Which of the following political concepts emerged as a result of the Treaty of Westphalia?

(A) Total democracy
(B) Absolute monarchy
(C) Total plutocracy
(D) Absolute meritocracy

The Romans and the Greeks had historically restrained themselves with the concept of a natural order of the universe; these self-imposed limitations prevented political leaders of yore from completely subjugating society to their will. Later, feudal leaders had to contend for power with the ubiquitous Christian church. With the church divided by the events of the Reformation, however, European rulers could, for the first time ever, legitimately claim unadulterated rule over their territory. All this power certainly had its perks. Kings could have as much money as they wanted, as many wars as they wanted, and whatever kind of social order they wanted. The kings of Europe emerged from the Thirty Years' War as **absolute monarchs**. By 1650, the feudal state had been transformed into the **nation-state**, a social institution of such brazen scope that it eclipsed all previous ones.

In addition to having geographic boundaries, a population, and a formal government, the absolute monarchy of the European nation-state also possessed a new element of **absolute sovereignty**, the idea that no force on Earth is superior to the government of the state. In the eighteenth and nineteenth centuries, democratic movements gradually weakened the unchecked power of kings. Despite the gradual shift to more **parliamentary systems**, in which a group of popularly elected representatives shared power with the king, the concept of absolute sovereignty remained dear to the political heart of Western civilization. Although the power of monarchs gradually diminished, the absolute sovereignty of the state did not. Instead, it just shifted to the newly created parliaments.

I am the state.

——LOUIS XIV,
KING OF FRANCE 1643-1715

NATIONAL GEOGRAPHIC

The geography of Europe played an enormous role in defining the territories of nation-states and curbing the expansionist tendencies of European leaders. The British, for example, were held in check by the English Channel. The French were separated from other kingdoms by several mountain ranges, and the Scandinavian monarchs had the Baltic Sea isolating them from the rest of Europe. These bodies of water and mountainous regions that stood in the way of further conquest also protected existing nation-states from encroachment.

8. **Which of the following is NOT a historical cause of nationalism?**

   (A) The development of different languages
   (B) The religion advocated by the state
   (C) The emergence of distinct national cultures
   (D) The proliferation of international commerce

As sovereign nation-states slowly evolved in Europe, common bonds developed between monarchs and their subjects and a unique culture emerged within each kingdom. As different groups of people came to share a common language, and as each national version of Christianity grew more distinct, members of individual nation-states began to feel quite similar to their fellow citizens and a lot different from everybody else. By the early nineteenth century, the concept of a sovereign nation complete with its own cultural heritage was entrenched throughout Europe and much of Asia.

This notion of **nationalism** had tremendous effects on the course of human history. The advent of the nation-state irrevocably divided a generally homogenous bunch of Europeans according solely to where they lived. Although the resulting diversity bore immense fruits for Western civilization, it also provided the structure for many of the political conflicts that continue to this day. The ugly side of nationalism rears its head whenever two culturally unified groups of people lay claim to the same chunk of land. Most of the wars and political calamities of the last two centuries, like the two World Wars for instance, have been sparked by nationalistic movements.

9. **How did Thomas Hobbes characterize the quality of human life in primitive society?**

   (A) "Nasty, brutish, and short"
   (B) "Indecent, swinish, and brief"
   (C) "Gnarly, twisted, and bogus"
   (D) "Perilous, harsh, and fleeting"

In an attempt to justify the absolute sovereignty of the English monarchy, British philosopher and royal crony **Thomas Hobbes** (1588-1679) asserted that, without an authoritarian leader preserving civilized society, the state would degenerate back into **"the state of nature"** that characterized society before government existed. According to Hobbes, the state of nature was an extremely unpleasant situation. Everyone was at war with

Hobbes's allegorical figure of a commonwealth

everyone else, life tended to be "nasty, brutish and short" and, with no hope for stability, general despair prevailed. Eventually some of the more reasonable individuals of primitive society cooked up a plan to improve the overall quality of life for everyone. In an agreement Hobbes called the **social contract**, all members of society pledged to obey the will of one lucky ruler. Forever. In exchange, the ruler agreed to maintain sufficient order and resolve disputes. Hobbes contended, of course, that society really had no choice but to waive its collective rights to an absolute ruler; it was the only way to make life tolerable.

Hobbes ultimately hoped to convince factions of the British upper classes who were calling for a more representational government that people just like them created the state and, by implication, the monarchy. Fooling with the social contract after it had worked so well for so long would just be asking for trouble.

The English monarchy so cherished by Hobbes came out on the losing end of a long and complicated civil war which ended in 1688 with the **Glorious Revolution**. With virtually universal public support, the upper-class leaders of the English parliament were able to force tax-happy James II to abdicate the throne. To replace the deposed monarch, parliament imported his Dutch relatives **William** and **Mary**, on the condition that they accept a more restricted role in the affairs of the state.

Using the social contract as his foundation, **John Locke** (1632-1704) embarked on an intellectual quest to explain this new and bizarre concept of **limited sovereignty**. Locke stipulated that the state of nature had its disadvantages to be sure, but it wasn't the hellhole imagined by Hobbes. The reasonable people who created the social contract in Locke's version of the story simply realized that everyone would be better off if a central authority figure—a monarch—could engender a little more order and organization in society by monopolizing power. Locke regarded the social contract as a more mutual agreement. In exchange for obeying the law, paying taxes, and respecting the rights of others, members of society could expect the monarch to respect and protect their fundamental rights of **life**, **liberty**, and **property**. If members of society failed to hold up their

 A quick glance at the American Declaration of Independence illustrates just how profoundly John Locke's version of the social contract and his theory of natural rights influenced Western history. Whereas Locke championed "unalienable rights" such as "Life, Liberty, and Property" the Declaration cites "Life, Liberty, and the pursuit of Happiness." Inspired by Locke's proposition that members of society could rebel against a monarch who failed to respect these rights, the signers of the Declaration decided to start their own country.

end of the bargain, the monarch could punish them. Likewise, if the monarch attempted to unreasonably usurp any life, liberty, or property, the people had the right and the responsibility to overthrow the weasel.

According to Locke, then, the principal function of government is to protect the natural, inalienable rights of individual members of society. Like Aristotle, Locke mistrusted the political discretion of the masses and advocated restricting government participation to the landed upper classes. Unlike Aristotle, he believed that combining a monarchy and an aristocracy would produce the best kind of government. Locke's political convictions helped shape the profoundly influential notion that at least some individuals outside of the monarchy are necessarily entitled to government representation.

John Locke

10. **How did French philosopher Jean-Jacques Rousseau characterize life in the state of nature?**

(A) As more favorable than life under the social contract
(B) As not much different than it is now
(C) As like a box of chocolates
(D) As very complex

Jean-Jacques Rousseau (1712-1778) added an interesting twist to the social contract theory by asserting that life in the state of nature was far more pleasant than life in the modern world. Instead of the perpetual anarchy described by Hobbes, Rousseau's version of the state of nature resembled the Garden of Eden, except without the part about **God**. According to Rousseau, the advent of government and the growth of civilization created social inequality, which in turn spawned greed, lust, violence and all manner of social malaise. The time had come, he said, to establish a new social contract that would foster equality. In the society Rousseau envisioned, all male citizens would freely participate in a general discussion of public problems. Out of this discussion would arise the **General Will**, a common agreement concerning the way society ought to be governed. Once established, the General Will itself would become

> 66
>
> *All men are born free, yet everywhere they are in chains.*
>
> ——*Jean-Jacques Rousseau*
>
> 99

Rousseau models the prune danish wig.

the instrument of sovereignty, and community leaders would be entitled to enforce its directives upon dissident individuals.

Rousseau's interpretation of history brought the ironic evolution of the social contract to an end. With some generous modifications, the same basic argument Hobbes advanced in an effort to defend the king of England wound up completely undermining the concept of a monarchy in most Western nations. A profusion of revolutions—most notably in France and the American colonies—ultimately resulted from this shift in the political climate. By the end of the eighteenth century, the idea that a monarchy is the best form of government had only a few royal voices in the wilderness to defend it.

The late-eighteenth century, the period known as the **Enlightenment**, was an unpleasant time for anyone holding out hope to preserve the status quo of Western civilization. While the European kings and queens were reveling in their power, two centuries of extraordinary intellectual advancement and spiritual transformation had gradually undermined the beliefs that had perpetuated the absolute monarchies of Europe and the dominance of the church. Reformation leader John Calvin (p. 500), although he was certainly no tolerant lover of freedom, had further weakened the Catholic church by convincing millions of Protestants that they didn't need the assistance of priests to attain eternal salvation. The social contract theorists had destroyed the previously accepted notion of rule by divine right. Nicolaus Copernicus (1473-1543) (p. 335), Isaac Newton (p. 350), and a host of other scientists had completely discredited the dogmatic beliefs of the church concerning the nature of the universe. The merchants in the North American colonies were becoming more and more bent on achieving independence. The eccentric Scottish economist

Adam Smith (p. 80) was even suggesting that people don't really need much government to prosper in life, and people were actually taking him seriously.

The effects of the revolutionary ideas spawned during the Renaissance (p. 579) and the Reformation (p. 494) and nurtured during the Enlightenment ultimately culminated in a new political world order. New nations were born in the New World. Slowly and often chaotically, the monarchies of Europe crumbled and power shifted into the hands of popularly elected **parliaments**. The leaders of these new political institutions hoped to create new social contracts based on individual freedom, equality, and natural rights instead of the absolute sovereignty of a few special people and their children.

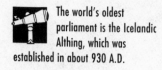
The world's oldest parliament is the Icelandic Althing, which was established in about 930 A.D.

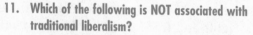

11. Which of the following is NOT associated with traditional liberalism?
    (A) Individual freedom
    (B) A classless society
    (C) Limited government
    (D) A capitalist economic system

Liberalism is an "ism" that has become wholly unmoored from its original meaning. During the Enlightenment, **traditional liberalism** developed from Locke's contention that human beings necessarily have rights, and that no institution, regardless of its absolute power, good intentions, or ties with the supernatural, should be allowed to infringe upon those rights. Expounding upon these **natural rights** theories advanced by Locke, Adam Smith developed liberalism into a practical body of thought. Smith was a die-hard capitalist (p. 79) who believed strongly in the concept of private property and thought a limited government would best serve the interests of society. He contended that individuals left to their own devices would meet or exceed the needs of the people within each nation-state. According to Smith and the early liberals, the natural desire to accumulate and spend money not only increases national wealth, it benefits humanity.

The storm of new ideas that raged in the eighteenth century had been brewing since the 1500s, when the invention of moveable type had made literacy more common among the well-to-do.

The belief that individuals are entitled to the amount of wealth they are able to create naturally lends itself to a society divided by class differences. Since limited resources exist on Earth, those people blessed with access to more available resources will necessarily thrive economically and end up with more political clout. Ultimately, critics of traditional liberalism have charged, the minimal state advocated by

John Stuart Mill

traditional liberals allows the rich to get richer while the poor will, at best, maintain their position.

Later liberal theorists, like **John Stuart Mill**, became increasingly more concerned about the plight of the less prosperous members of society. Mill and many other utilitarians expanded the concept of natural rights to include the poorer classes and proposed that everyone (even women!) should have a voice in a representational government. They also stressed the notion that society should aim to maximize economic and political freedoms. Because they advocated granting the broadest liberties to as many people as possible, and because they perceived the state as the only mechanism that could guarantee rights and freedoms, later liberals tended to favor expanding the scope of the state instead of narrowing it.

12. **Who was the original leader of the conservative movement?**
    (A) Edmund Burke
    (B) Charles Dickens
    (C) Otto von Bismarck
    (D) Rush Limbaugh

Anarchy, State, and Utopia (1977), Robert Nozick. Libertarian political philosopher Nozick seeks to justify the institution of government by imagining how it was originally formed and asking what limits ought to be placed on it.

Conservatism is a strange animal. Of all political ideologies, it offers the least guidance in the way of governing or economics in its original form. In historical terms, it is the bastard child of the secular reason and intellectual influence of the Enlightenment and the **French Revolution** with some resentment toward the new class structure caused by the fledgling Industrial Revolution (p. 81) thrown into the mix. Its father was an Englishman, **Edmund Burke** (1729-1797), who outlined a criticism of liberalism in light of the atrocities of the French Revolution and the headlong changes being produced by the flood of new industry and technology. In essence, conservatism began as a philosophy calling for a little more tradition and a little less chaotic flux. Whereas the leaders of the French Revolution were calling for "Liberty, Equality, and Fraternity" and, later, Marx and Engels (p. 84) encouraged all working people of the world to unite, the unofficial slogan of the early conservative movement went something like: "Hey! Wait a Minute."

Burke argued that the history of society ought to be one of long, slow progress. By trying to change the structure of society suddenly, or by allowing rapid and perpetual change to occur, society itself ends up damaged; revolutions, regardless of their nature, usually cause more harm than good in society. Burke also believed in the ultimate authority of God, and he believed that human beings are far from being imminently reasonable creatures. Thus, he proposed a society governed by an elite few who would keep the passions of the masses in check using a combination of state-supported religion and raw physical force. These modern Philosopher Kings would control change in society and provide for the slow and orderly evolution of society.

Modern conservatism, especially the kind espoused by the religious right (p. 509) in the United States, owes a debt to Edmund Burke. Just like all other ideologies, though, conservatism has experienced incredible growth and change; its advocates are far from being a unified group bent on making the world go to church on Sundays and putting everyone in their place. Many people who call themselves conservative today might more aptly call themselves liberals because they basically agree with Adam Smith and the traditional liberals. But such a moniker would muck things up because another political group has already laid claim to this name. Of these modern liberals, many of them believe strongly in a centralized government, which isn't what the original liberals wanted at all. It's all very confusing.

Edmund "Baby Face" Burke

13. What is the fundamental principle underlying socialism?
    (A) Liberty
    (B) Fraternity
    (C) Equality
    (D) Absurdity

While Locke, Smith, and Mill were espousing the benefits of liberty, and while the Americans were busy getting a country started, a relatively obscure group of seventeenth- and eighteenth-century political thinkers including Robert Owen (p. 83), Claude Henri, and Comte de Saint-Simon was busy dreaming of a classless society based primarily on the principle of **equality**. Drawing largely on the works of Plato and

SAINT SAINT-SIMON

French social scientist Claude Henri, Comte de Saint-Simon led an interesting life. He fought in the American Revolution and was later imprisoned for his activities during the French Revolution. In his spare time, Saint-Simon advocated a socialist system similar to Plato's Republic, in which a corps of social engineers would rule industrial states in everyone's best interests. Saint-Simon also had a few personality quirks. For instance, he occasionally claimed to be a reincarnation of Jesus Christ.

Sir Thomas More (p. 250), these socialists (p. 79) believed that a truly humane and peaceful world could be created through the collective ownership of property, industry, and wealth. Although early socialists had little if any influence on the political climate of the immediate period, their vision of a society in which industry would be used to eradicate poverty and self-interest would be replaced by universal cooperation eventually gained intellectual support and, more importantly, the endorsement of the industrial working classes.

With varying degrees of success, several varieties of socialism have been attempted all over the world since the late 1700s. In practice, socialist leaders had to gain control of farm lands and the major industries within each society to get their movement off the ground. With the factors of production (p. 80) under their control, they could work toward providing a subsistent amount of food, clothing, and shelter to all members of society. Ultimately, socialist leaders hoped to create a society that could provide free education, free medical treatment, and a high-quality standard of living to everyone, regardless of their social station.

14. **Which of the following thinkers had the greatest effect on the philosophy of Karl Marx?**
   (A) Georg Wilhelm Friedrich Hegel
   (B) Johann Wolfgang von Goethe
   (C) Claude Henri, Comte de Saint-Simon
   (D) the artist formerly known as Prince

Karl Marx and Friedrich Engels based their socialist doctrines largely on the philosophical ideas of the eminent eighteenth century German philosopher **G.W.F. Hegel** (1770-1831), who believed that human history consists of a perpetual series of struggles between old ideas and new, better ones. Inevitably, as civilizations grow fond of peace and, thus, stagnant in the absence of strife and flux, these ideological conflicts manifest themselves as turbulent revolutionary clashes within and among societies. They also serve to intellectually reinvigorate society and pump fresh energy into civilization. According to Hegel, the most recent of these historical transformations had occurred during the Reformation and the Thirty Years' War. These military and ideological battles produced the nation-state, which he held to be the highest political achievement humankind could possibly attain.

Already leaning toward radical socialism, Marx and Engels applied Hegel's complicated **dialectical** concepts of constant ideological struggle and positive progression to the history of economic systems (p. 66). They contended that the unrestrained capitalism (p. 79) made possible by the technological advances of the Industrial Revolution had allowed a few greedy factory owners to enslave the proletariat (p. 84), the masses of poor people who lived in the industrialized nations of nineteenth-century Europe. Marx and Engels wanted to produce a revolution to liberate the proletariat from their socioeconomic circumstances. They hoped to seize control of the factories to exploit technologies for the benefit of all. A new system called **communism** would follow, creating a global harmony and equality that would indeed be humanity's highest social achievement.

The **Marxists** were confident that, beginning in the most industrialized European nations, popular proletariat revolutions would soon overthrow the capitalists. Marx had his heart particularly set on France or Germany. However, communist movements in western Europe fizzled, and the revolution that Marx predicted would sweep the modern world began in 1917 in **Russia**, arguably the most backward Western nation in existence at that time.

Shiny, happy Hegel

15. **When was the Constitution of the United States of America ratified?**

   (A) 1778
   (B) 1781
   (C) 1788
   (D) 1791

Once they achieved independence from England, the leaders of the American Revolution (p. 626) attempted to create a radically liberal government based on the concept of the social contract. Unfortunately, their new nation and its **Articles of Confederation** was floundering. There were bills to pay, an economy to take care of, and a national defense that really didn't exist. With a unique combination of virtuous wisdom and keen intelligence, our forefathers convened in Philadelphia to revise their imperfect

TEN FACTS ABOUT THE FRAMERS OF THE CONSTITUTION

Oldest delegate: Benjamin Franklin (81)

Youngest delegate: Jonathan Dayton (27)

Approximate number of slaves owned by framers: 1,400

Number with college degrees: 31

Number with law degrees: 31

Total number of delegates: 55

Number of blacks, women, and small farmers present at the convention: 0

Number of delegates sent by Rhode Island: 0

First state to ratify: Delaware (December, 1787)

Last state to ratify: Rhode Island (May, 1790)

THE BILL OF RIGHTS IN A NUTSHELL

1st Amendment: guarantees freedom of speech, the press, peaceful assembly, and the right to petition government; restricts the state from meddling in religious affairs.

2nd Amendment: a triumph of ambiguity which provides for a "well-regulated militia"; either insures the right of citizens to have guns or it doesn't, depending on who you talk to.

3rd Amendment: prevents soldiers from sleeping at your house unless a war is going on.

4th Amendment: keeps the cops from snooping around your stuff without first obtaining a search warrant.

5th Amendment: gives you the right to "take the fifth" or not incriminate yourself; requires Grand Jury indictments for criminal cases; prohibits the government from putting people on trial twice for the same offense; requires the government to pay you what your property is worth if they decide to take it.

6th Amendment: a mouthful that provides for a speedy and public trial by an impartial jury near the crime scene; requires the government to tell people why they are on trial; guarantees the right to legal counsel; requires the state to present witnesses in front of the person on trial; allows accused persons to call witnesses in their defense.

7th Amendment: guarantees the right to trail by jury in civil cases, and the right to trial by jury in general.

8th Amendment: prevents the state from imposing excessive bail and prohibits cruel and unusual punishment.

9th Amendment: points out that there are rights not listed in the first ten amendments, and that government cannot infringe upon those rights, either.

10th Amendment: drives the 9th Amendment home; federal powers not mentioned in the Constitution and the subsequent amendments are powers the federal government does not have.

The Constitutional Convention was called after a series of localized uprisings by farmers and working-class men, many of whom had fought in the Revolution and were outraged to find that they could not represent themselves under the Articles of Confederation. Economic chaos and high taxes levied by the new and broke government didn't help things, nor did the government's policy of seizing debtors' property to raise cash. In 1786, **Shays' Rebellion**, led by Massachussetts army veteran **Daniel Shays**, shook the feds up enough to inspire real changes in the system.

system, and thus provided the structure for the flawless utopia that is the United States today.

Well, not exactly. The creators of the **Constitution** were all wealthy and powerful white guys who believed their new nation could not survive without a more powerful central government. Most of them were lawyers. Their document was curiously self-serving, politically expedient, and vague in its highfalutin' prose. Furthermore, far from being based firmly on a foundation of principled liberalism, it was filled with compromises between slave owners and those opposed to slavery, North and South, urban and rural interests, advocates of big and small government, and all the other special interests of the day. However, the framers of the Constitution were also brilliant and educated men. The document they created contains many of the best elements of thousands of years of political thought, and it represents the triumph of enlightened philosophy. Many constitutions have come and gone since the U.S. Constitution was officially ratified in 1788, yet the U.S. Constitution remains relatively unchanged.

16. How many amendments to the Constitution did the
    Bill of Rights originally contain?

    (A) Ten
    (B) Twelve
    (C) Thirteen
    (D) Sixteen

Ultimately, the Constitution is a gigantic compromise that was hammered out over four long months and more than 600 tedious votes. It is a blueprint for government containing a system of checks and balances designed to satisfy the diverse interests of many people by not allowing any one particular person or group of people to do too much. The branches of the **legislature** (Congress), the **judiciary** (the Supreme Court), and the **executive** (the president) all have authority to check each other, thus leading to a **balance of power** (see chart).

Although the majority of Americans rank the Constitution somewhere near the Ten Commandments (p. 492) in their list of wise and perfect documents, nobody really knew whether the thing would actually get ratified. Many political leaders feared that the new Constitution would produce a ubiquitous central government. They foresaw a government no better than the monarchies of Europe that would trample on individual rights and render the power of the states meaningless. To soothe these anxieties, the framers sweetened the Constitution by promising to change it a bit. In September of 1789, **James Madison** submitted a list of twelve amendments to the Constitution designed to restrict the power of the central government. The ten of these amendments that made it into the Constitution are known as the **Bill of Rights**.

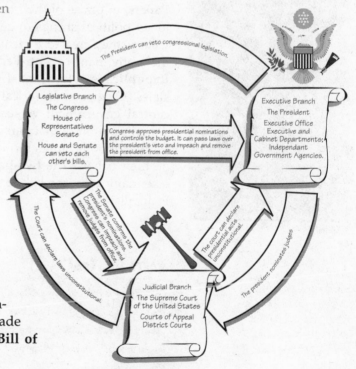

Legislative Branch
The Congress
House of
Representatives
Senate
House and Senate
can veto each
other's bills.

The President can veto congressional legislation.

Executive Branch
The President
Executive Office
Executive and
Cabinet Departments;
Independant
Government Agencies.

Congress approves presidential nominations and controls the budget. It can pass laws over the president's veto and impeach and remove the president from office.

The Senate confirms the President's nominations. Congress can impeach and remove judges from office.

The court can declare presidential acts unconstitutional.

The Court can declare laws unconstitutional.

The president nominates judges

Judicial Branch
The Supreme Court
of the United States
Courts of Appeal
District Courts

The balance of power

17. **Which of the following people was a Federalist?**

   (A) George Clinton
   (B) Patrick Henry
   (C) Judd Hirsch
   (D) John Jay

Many of the people who didn't like the Constitution were perfectly happy with the Articles of Confederation. They favored a loosely knit union of states and a weak central government, and no one was going to convince them to fix something they didn't think was broken. The **Federalists** who supported the Constitution, such as **James Madison**, **Alexander Hamilton**, and **John Jay**, saw a strong, centralized government as the only way to save their fledgling nation from either collapsing into several sovereign states or, worse, being overrun by the armies of the British, French, or Spanish, all of whom still maintained a strong presence in North America.

In addition to writing over eighty-five essays, called the **Federalist Papers**, in praise of their cause, the Federalists pulled a lot of old-fashioned political strings to get their Constitution ratified. On the way to victory, they created a great deal of animosity between themselves and the aptly named **Anti-Federalists**, also known as the **Democratic-Republicans**, who wanted more power in the hands of the individual states. Of greater historical consequence, the argument over a **strong central government** versus **states' rights** drew a line in the sand of American politics that persists to this day. The debate raged on as supporters of both causes formed strong political groups, or **parties**, based on their beliefs. The **two-party system** of modern American politics is essentially a direct result of this argument between Federalists and Anti-Federalists.

John Jay

PARTY ON, TOM!

"Men by their constitutions are naturally divided into two parties: 1. Those who fear and distrust the people, and wish to draw all powers from them into the hands of the higher classes. 2. Those who identify themselves with the people, have confidence in them, cherish and consider them as the most honest and safe, although not the most wise, depository of the public interests. In every country these two parties exist . . ."

——*Thomas Jefferson*

18. Which Supreme Court justice wrote the majority
    opinion in the landmark *Marbury v. Madison* case?

    (A) John Marshall
    (B) John Jay
    (C) John Rutledge
    (D) Earl Warren

As the nineteenth century dawned, the ruling Federalist Party and its president, **John Adams** (1735-1826), **George Washington's** (1732-1799) successor, dug its own grave with the infamous **Alien and Sedition Acts** of 1798. Aimed at the increasing support of the Anti-Federalists by newly arrived immigrants, the Alien Act increased the residency requirement for citizenship (from five to fourteen years) and made immigrants from "enemy" nations ineligible for citizen status. The Sedition Act prohibited any assembly intended to oppose the government and outlawed any "false, scandalous, or malicious" speech or writing against the government. Public outcry over the unconstitutional nature of these Acts led to the demise of the Federalist Party, and helped **Thomas Jefferson** (1743-1826) capture the presidency under the Democratic-Republican banner.

The Adams administration did leave Jefferson and the opposition with a nasty parting gift, though. In the eleventh hour, Adams and his pals in Congress created federal judgeships galore and filled them with loyal Federalists. None too pleased, Jefferson

Thomas Jefferson

responded by refusing to give official commissions to several of the judges, including one named **William Marbury**. Marbury sued, and the 1803 decision *Marbury v. Madison*, written by the eloquent and charismatic **Chief Justice John Marshall** (1755-1835), declared the law establishing the judgeships void. This decision established the precedent of **judicial review**, the idea that the Supreme Court is authorized to overturn any law passed by

LEAVE IT AT THE OFFICE

After a lifetime of resounding military and political successes, a somewhat discouraged George Washington retired to Mount Vernon, his Virginia planatation. Washington did not see the need for political parties, and was dismayed by the burgeoning Federalist/Democratic-Republican split.

Jefferson in Paris (1995), starring Nick Nolte. This Merchant/Ivory production has reignited an old controversy: did Jefferson have a long love affair with Sally Hemings, one of his slaves? The film makes the alleged affair central to Jefferson's years as an Ambassador in Paris. Some historians argue, however, that the affair was merely a silly rumor started by a detractor after Jefferson's death and given strangely wide currency.

The election of Thomas Jefferson to the U.S. presidency marked the first peaceful transfer of power from one party to another in modern history.

Congress it deems unconstitutional. *Marbury v. Madison* established judicial review as the central role of the Supreme Court.

Jefferson's presidency represented a shift away from the economic policies espoused by the Federalists, who had favored the financial and manufacturing interests of the Northeastern states. Jefferson opposed the elitism of the previous administrations, and **Jeffersonian Democracy** appealed to independent farmers, artisans and workers through an Enlightenment faith in human reason and the will of the majority. Yet Jefferson's belief in majority rule also included the crucial caveat that the majority's will must not prevail at the expense of the rights of the minority. Protection of minority interests has become a fundamental tenet of the American political system.

19. **Why did the political opponents of President Andrew Jackson call themselves the Whigs?**

    (A) Jackson once called his opponents "whigmongers" in a fit of rage, and the name stuck.
    (B) Their most prominent leader was New York Senator Leland Clinton Whig.
    (C) The American patriots who opposed the British called themselves "Whigs."
    (D) Most of them were bald, and they couldn't spell very well.

After losing the bitterly contested presidential election of 1824 to **John Quincy Adams** (1767-1848), Tennessee Senator **Andrew Jackson** (1767-1848) cruised to victory in 1828. Jackson's victory symbolized a major transformation of the American political landscape. By 1820, the effects of the Industrial Revolution were beginning to cause a profound metamorphosis in the United States. The intellectually static, agriculture-based agenda of Jeffersonian Democracy could no longer satisfy the public urge for economic growth and westward expansion. Jackson blazed the trail for a new political era, **Jacksonian Democracy**, that was less of a political agenda and more of an attitude. For the whiskey-drinking, frontier-loving white crowd, Jackson embodied a new American spirit. Politically, Jackson advocated slavery, national expansion, the elimination of Native American tribes, and a strong executive branch. His administration also extended voting rights to include poor white men as well as wealthy ones, and he strived to provide more economic opportunity for common (white) people. Although Jackson captured an overwhelming 77 percent of the popular vote in the presidential election of 1832, he was not universally admired by his political peers, or by the electorate. Federalists—their party comatose but not dead—refused to support Jackson because he opposed the centralized **Bank of the United States**. Many states' rights advocates from the South became increasingly disenchanted with "King Andrew" because they thought he was hoarding entirely too much power for the executive branch, and for the federal government in general. And several members of Congress just didn't like Jackson's roguish style of leadership.

Andrew Jackson

These strange political bedfellows gradually formed a coalition based almost exclusively on their opposition to Jackson and his newly abbreviated **Democratic** party. Led by Congressional heavyweights **Daniel Webster** (1782-1852) and **Henry Clay** (1777-1852), this new political party, the **Whigs**, borrowed their name from the pre-Revolutionary patriots who had opposed the British. Despite the fact that they never really developed a platform, the Whigs managed to put two war heroes, **William Henry Harrison** (1773-1841) and **Zachary Taylor** (1784-1850), in the White House. Both Whig presidents died in office and were succeeded by their vice presidents, **John Tyler** (1790-1862) and **Millard Filmore** (1800-1874), respectively. None of the Whig presidents did much worth writing home about, and the lack of a coherent program eventually caused the demise of the party. Without Jackson to rally against or Webster and Clay to provide Congressional leadership, the Whigs had all but disintegrated by the 1850s. In 1854, both remaining Whigs forged an alliance with Northern Democrats who had become frustrated with their party's pro-slavery stance, and members of this new party began calling themselves **Republicans**.

General Jackson is the majority's slave; he yields to its intentions, desires, and half-revealed instincts, or rather he anticipates and forestalls them.

——*Alexis de Tocqueville, 1836*

20. Which of the following was NOT a federal attempt to find a compromise between slave states and free states?

(A) The 3/5 Compromise
(B) The Arkansas Acts
(C) The Compromise of 1850
(D) The Kansas-Nebraska Act

Since the days of the Constitutional Convention, slavery had been a charged and divisive issue in the United States. The **3/5 Compromise** of the Constitution, which allowed slaveowners to count each of their slaves as 60 percent of a person for purposes of representation and taxation, only perpetuated the fundamental social and economic differences between the northern and southern states of the union. Southern states favored slavery because they needed it; it was the lifeblood of their entire economy. Northerners opposed slavery on moral grounds and because they believed slave labor gave the agrarian South an unfair economic advantage. The economic impact of slavery caused the southern and northern states to disagree on just about every national issue. About the only thing the North and South could agree on was that land held by Native Americans and neighboring nations ought to be appropriated. As the nation expanded westward, whether or not these new territories would allow slavery became the overriding issue in the public mind, since new **slave states** would presumably vote with the South and new **free states** would vote with the North in Congress.

Both sides offered lofty arguments for their causes. Southern leaders, who saw nothing wrong with owning slaves, contended that prohibiting slavery anywhere infringed upon the natural property rights guaranteed by the Constitution. They maintained that the new territories should allow slavery in case any plantation owners got the urge to relocate. Northern leaders countered that allowing slaves in the new territories would discourage free labor and business interests from moving west. Furthermore, they pointed out that owning other human beings presented somewhat of a moral predicament for a nation supposedly founded on principles like freedom and justice.

By the middle of the 1800s, the debate over slavery had grown altogether hostile. Many attempts by Congress to appease both sides, like the Compromise of 1850 (p. 181), did nothing to quell the sectional animosities. Tensions rose and blood boiled for a decade. Clashes between northern and southern interests became increasingly violent, from fist fights on

WHICH WAY TO UTOPIA?

Nineteenth-century Americans were remarkably willing to search for Utopia right here at home. More than a hundred experimental communities were formed before 1861, including the Shakers and three communities loosely based on the socialist ideas of **Robert Owen** *(p. 83): New Harmony in Indiana; Nashoba, a community for freed slaves, in Tennessee; and the* **Transcendentalists'** *(p. 263) Brook Farm in Massachusetts.*

the floors of Congress to a series of stormy confrontations known collectively as **Bleeding Kansas,** the fallout from the 1854 **Kansas-Nebraska Act,** which put the question of slavery in Kansas to a popular vote. In that neophyte state, armed factions of abolitionists, including John Brown (p. 183), and pro-slavery

LINCOLN AND DOUGLAS GO AT IT

The 1858 debates between Democrat Stephen Douglas and Republican Abraham Lincoln, vying for an Illinois Senate seat, had an immense impact on history. Lincoln opened the debates with his famous "House Divided" speech, declaring that "a house divided cannot stand." Douglas, a master of compromise, championed states' rights and charged Lincoln with trying to foist "one consolidated empire" on the states. Although Lincoln lost the Illinois election, he was propelled to national prominence.

forces established rival governments, backed by militias, and fought to hold sway. In Kansas and elsewhere, sporadic violence continued well into 1861; the chasm between North and South had grown to hopeless proportions.

21. **Whom did Abraham Lincoln defeat in the 1860 presidential election?**
    (A) Jefferson Davis
    (B) Henry Clay
    (C) Stephen Douglas
    (D) John Brown

In the presidential election of 1860, Republican **Abraham Lincoln** (1809-1865) defeated compromise-seeking Democrat **Stephen A. Douglas** (1813-1861), further galvanizing the southern states. A few days later, South Carolina decided to take its ball home and **secede** from the union. In short order, the political leaders of Alabama, Florida, Georgia, Louisiana, and Mississippi followed suit and the **Confederate States of America** was born, with Mississippi Senator **Jefferson Davis** as its president. Eventually, five more states—Texas, Virginia, Arkansas, North Carolina, and Tennessee—joined the Confederacy.

After the Civil War, the once-again-United States had to heal. Reconstruction (p. 183), the attempt by the federal government following the war to reconcile differences with the South and rebuild the war-torn Union following the war, was largely unsuccessful. The United States was united again, but the essential economic and political differences between North and South persisted. The North remained a bastion of industry, commerce, and progressive agriculture; the South was still essentially one big farm. Not surprisingly, the South and the North still found plenty to disagree about politically, and congressional votes

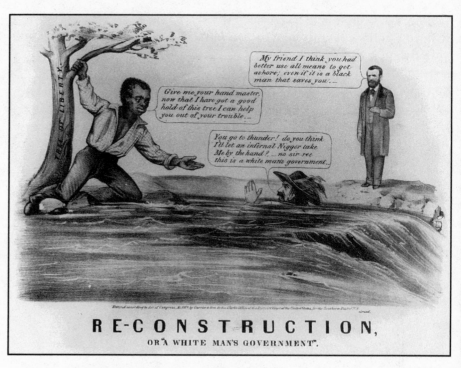

RE-CONSTRUCTION,
OR "A WHITE MAN'S GOVERNMENT".

continued to split right down the Mason-Dixon line. In the era of Reconstruction, the North became the bulwark of the Republican party and, pretty much by default, the South turned into a stomping ground for the Democrats.

22. Between 1860 and 1900, which of the following groups made the greatest social and political gains?

   (A) Women
   (B) Leaders of the Confederacy
   (C) The Communist party
   (D) Organized labor

With extraordinary resilience, the United States picked itself up from the Civil War, dusted itself off, and, over the next fifty years, matured into a dynamic global power. Industrialists (popularly known as the **"robber barons"**) like steel magnate **Andrew Carnegie** (1835-1919), oil baron **John D. Rockefeller** (1839-1937), and railroad tycoon **Cornelius Vanderbilt** (1794-1877) molded the United States into a burgeoning mecca of industry and technology, creating enormous wealth for the nation and vast fortunes for themselves along the way. A string of presidents running the gamut from pathetic to dimwitted to moderately subpar, coupled with a succession of pro-business Congresses, provided a laissez-faire (p. 81) atmosphere that allowed a huge gulf to develop between the rich and powerful and everybody else. For the wealthy few reveling in unadulterated economic freedom, it was a great era to be alive. The periodic depressions they themselves caused through speculation and attempts to **corner** (buy up all the stuff in) certain commodities markets were not so severe as to affect their fortunes, although these economic downswings certainly victimized the increasingly disenfranchised poor. Millions of American laborers saw some room for improvement.

From 1860 to 1900, organized labor (p. 190) made creeping—and sometimes violent—inroads into the American political system. As they slowly gained political influence, many moderate union supporters in the Northeast found a comfortable home in the Democratic party, which already had a stranglehold on the South. The Republican party, on the other hand, became increasingly viewed as the party of big business interests by many poor and middle class Americans, especially in the budding Western and Midwestern states. Both parties shared in the graft and corruption that characterized the period. With labor unions in their pockets and the nearly universal support of newly arriving immigrants, corrupt Democratic politicians built huge **political machines** like **Tammany Hall** in New York that controlled entire urban governments largely for their own personal enrichment. Meanwhile, propped up by the millionaire industrial and banking industries, dishonest Republicans concentrated on bilking the country as a whole.

23. **What is the historical significance of the Monroe Doctrine?**
    (A) It established the first serious foreign policy of the United States.
    (B) It created peace treaties with several Native American tribes west of the Mississippi.
    (C) It recognized Canada and Mexico as sovereign nations.
    (D) It prohibited interstate trade.

For all intents and purposes, the United States did not have a foreign policy until President **James Monroe** (1758-1831) proposed one in an 1823 speech to Congress. In the speech, Monroe promised that the United

THE BOSS MAN

*In the 1860s, a New York election supervisor named **Boss Tweed** (1823-1878) brought corrupt city government to new heights. Tweed masterminded a network of city officials, Democratic Party workers, and contractors, known as the **Tweed Ring**, who controlled New York's budget through kickback schemes in which they got a cut of all city contracts. Eventually these shenanigans brought the ciy to its knees financially, and Tweed was convicted and imprisoned.*

States would not meddle in the affairs of the nations of Europe or their existing colonies as long as the Europeans did not interfere, militarily or otherwise, with political affairs in the western hemisphere. The **Monroe Doctrine**, as it came to be called, effectively isolated the United States by declaring neutrality toward European politics. At the same time, it justified the growing American penchant for westward expansion. Regarding extant European nations, the Monroe Doctrine was as much a statement of American political philosophy as it was a foreign policy: you don't bother us, we won't bother you. It was also a savvy political strategy because, by the 1820s, European nations didn't have many existing colonies *left* in the Americas. The British had given up on colonial ventures in North America; the once-mighty Spanish empire had mostly crumbled into several weak, independent nations in South America; the French had sold most of their North American territory to the United States in 1803 in the **Louisiana Purchase**.

The 1803 Louisiana Purchase included about 828,000 square miles, doubling the size of the nation for about four cents an acre.

For the better part of the nineteenth century, American leaders remained mostly faithful to the central tenets of the Monroe Doctrine, steering clear of the European powers both at home and abroad and slowly pushing toward the Pacific coast. Manifest Destiny (p. 176), the concept that the United States was on a mission from God to occupy North America from sea to shining sea, provided moral ammunition for the drive westward. In a series of skirmishes, the Native Americans and Mexicans who also claimed western lands fell to the increasingly strapping United States military forces.

Eventually, the West was won and American politicians and business leaders began itching to throw around some military muscle on the international scene. Thus began the **big stick** era of American foreign policy, a term made

Teddy and his Rough Riders atop San Juan Hill

famous by President **Theodore Roosevelt** (1858-1919). In the "splendid little" Spanish-American War (p. 641) of 1898, the United States bullied its unwilling Spanish sparring partners into "liberating" Cuba, Puerto Rico, Wake Island, Guam, and the Philippines. Once these colonies were successfully delivered from Spanish domination, the U.S. proceeded to occupy them. In that same year, the U.S. also decided to annex Hawaii in order to gain a foothold in the Pacific. By 1900, the United States had grown into a political and geographic superpower complete with a modest empire of islands in the Caribbean and the Pacific.

Although the isolationist sentiment of the Monroe Doctrine continued to prevail in the hearts and minds of many Americans, the United States had graduated to big boy status among the nations of the earth, and early-twentieth-century foreign policy reflected the new **world cop** role of the U.S. Whereas the Monroe Doctrine had said "don't mess with us and we won't mess with you," big stick foreign policy went something like "don't mess with us unless we mess with you first." The political and commercial interests of the United States stretched as far west as China and as far South as the **Panama Canal**, which was finally completed in 1914. Because of the influx of immigrants (p. 194) in the late 1800s, the United States had become increasingly linked in spirit to all the folks back home in Italy, Germany, Ireland, and a host of other European nations. And with international trade and communication increasing at a rapid pace, the affairs of the rest of the Western world were necessarily the affairs of the United States. If a huge conflict occurred in Europe or Asia, the Americans would have no recourse but to choose sides.

Speak softly and carry a big stick.

——*AFRICAN PROVERB AND ROOSEVELT'S FAMOUS PHRASE*

24. **What was World War I originally called?**

   (A) The Global Conflict
   (B) The Great War
   (C) The Ultimate War
   (D) The Very Large Skirmish

After the final defeat of **Napoleon** in 1815, Europe enjoyed a relatively long period of peace. During the respite from major warfare, nationalist tendencies swelled to a feverish pitch, Western nations entangled themselves in a Rube Goldberg scheme of complicated alliances and extended colonial empires, and, thanks to the technological advances of the

Woodrow Wilson

Industrial Revolution, the nations of Europe spent the early twentieth century arming themselves to the gills with new-fangled killing machines—just in case. All of these elements boiled over in 1914 in World War I (p. 643).

Initially, most Americans tried to be content letting the Europeans kill each other. U.S. business interests stood to make a lot of money selling armaments and supplies to countries on both sides of the **"Great War"** and the melting pot of American immigrants would have trouble supporting any aggression against their native lands. However, neither the **Allied Powers** (Britain, France, Russia, and Italy) whose navies controlled the surface of the seas nor the **Central Powers** (Germany, Austria-Hungary, and the Ottoman Empire) who wreaked havoc below it with their submarines wanted American goods supporting the enemy, and both sides did plenty to obstruct American shipping. Moreover, as casualties mounted and the war dragged on without either side gaining a clear advantage, both sides stepped up their appeals for American intervention. A number of diplomatic blunders hindered German attempts to court the United States, and the Central Powers certainly didn't help their cause by sinking numerous American commercial vessels during the course of the war.

On the eve of the presidential election of 1916, the neutrality of the United States was seriously wavering toward the Allied camp. Democratic President **Woodrow Wilson** (1856-1924) asked Congress to declare war

CONVENTIONAL WISDOM

*The American **"party convention,"** originated by the short-lived Anti-Mason Party in 1827, is an institution not found in any other Western Democracy. Originally, delegates met in the proverbial smoke-filled rooms to choose their party's candidates to statewide office. Soon the national convention evolved to nominate presidential candidates and running mates. Rituals such as a ballyhooed **keynote address** and the hammering out of an official **party platform** were in place by the twentieth century. Since the 1950s, with the convention's decision-making role practically gone, the event has been adapted to the Television Age as a spectacle of party unity staged to appeal to prime-time audiences.*

on Germany in the spring of 1917. And so began a massive domestic propaganda campaign to ensure sufficient ill will against the Central Powers. Once trained, our boys were sent across the Atlantic to fight for the preservation of noble ideals like democracy, the liberties of small

A LEAGUE OF THEIR OWN

*During negotiations for the Treaty of Versailles, President Wilson pressed European leaders to form the **League of Nations**, an organization of world leaders that would try to prevent future wars through communication and compromise. But the Republican-controlled U.S. Senate balked at American membership into the League of Nations because Wilson hadn't bothered to consult them. The American people, appalled by the war, wanted no part of international politics. As a result, the United States never joined the organization that its president had basically created. Although it paved the way for the more successful **United Nations**, the League of Nations quickly turned into a joke without American involvement.*

nations, and American shipping interests. If only due to sheer force of numbers, the entrance of the United States and all of its fresh, young bodies turned the tide of the war in favor of the Allies.

World War I was a truly tragic event that caused the deaths of 28 million soldiers and civilians over the course of five dreadful years. Not surprisingly, the victorious Allies were not ready to forgive and forget when the Central Powers surrendered in 1919. Under the **Treaty of Versailles**, the Allies carved Austria-Hungary into several brand new countries while the British and French divvied up the oil-rich **Ottoman Empire** among themselves. These penalties were as nothing, though, compared to the cruel manner in which the Allies treated Germany. In an outrageously boneheaded move, the Allies not only enraged the Germans by forcing them to give up an incredible amount of land, they wrecked their already war-torn economy by demanding impossible monetary reparations. With their tails between their legs and visions of sweet revenge dancing in their heads, German leaders had no real choice but to sign the agreement. The impoverished German people would be left licking their wounds and looking for somebody to blame. World War II (p. 650), anyone?

25. Which of the following twentieth-century leaders did
    NOT subscribe to fascism?

    (A) Benito Mussolini
    (B) Adolf Hitler
    (C) Francisco Franco
    (D) Neville Chamberlain

During the long, worldwide depressions (p. 87) of the 1920s and 1930s, leaders espousing the political ideology of **fascism** gained power in many European nations. The first of these leaders, **Benito Mussolini**

Mussolini: newspaper editor, fascist dictator, hat wearer

(1883-1945), a socialist newspaper editor who thought Italy got a raw deal under the Treaty of Versailles, came to power in Italy in 1922. Nazi (p. 649) leader Adolf Hitler (p. 649) became the dictator of Germany in 1933. In Spain, the fascist forces of **General Francisco Franco** (1892-1975) came out on the winning end of a bloody civil war. These magnetic leaders were able to capitalize on the general prevalence of pessimism and global disillusionment that followed World War I.

Fascist regimes have generally ascended to power by using propaganda and pageantry to stir up nationalist fervor. Once in control, they create a mystique around the institutions of the state. As a political philosophy, fascism is like an explosive combination of socialism and nationalism, all rolled up into a big autocracy. The defining characteristic of the fascist state is a bureaucratic corporate structure, ultimately headed by the leader of the country, that makes the production decisions for all major factories. Fascist states have a rigid and distinct class structure that classify members of society according to race, gender, and ability. Fascists also wholly reject the freedoms and rights of the individual so cherished by liberals; citizens with a claim against the fascist state have no judicial recourse and secret police maintain the political order. Finally, once they gain power, fascist leaders seem to have a lust for attacking neighboring nations.

The pinnacle of fascist philosophy was reached in *Mein Kampf* (*My Struggle*), which Hitler wrote from 1925-1927 while in prison for leading an unsuccessful uprising. This rambling treatise lambasts "international Jewry" as the cause of the world's problems. Disturbingly, it also spells out Hitler's plans for the "final solution" (p. 649)—was anyone listening?

26. **What catchy phrase was the centerpiece of Warren G. Harding's presidential campaign?**

    (A) "Let Freedom Ring"
    (B) "Return to Normalcy"
    (C) "Isolation and Independence"
    (D) "Tippecanoe and Harding, too"

Members of the Ku Klux Klan

In 1920, sick of war and generally tired of international affairs, the United States turned to the Republican party and **Warren G. Harding** (1865-1923) for, according to Harding's vague campaign slogan, a "return to normalcy." Amidst a number of scandals involving his cabinet, Harding died in office and was succeed by **Calvin Coolidge** (1872-1933). "Silent Cal" and the Republicans shunned international affairs, curbed immigration, and renewed the hands-off economic policies that had been abandoned to finance the war effort. In these respects, the **Roaring Twenties** saw a "return to normalcy" indeed; the national economy boomed, isolationist sentiment prevailed, and the popularity of racist groups like the Ku Klux Klan (p. 184) experienced a violent resurgence. However, Americans had also built up an incredible amount of repressed energy during World War I and, over the next decade, they unleashed it with a fury. To the chagrin of many political and religious leaders, many Americans threw conventional Puritan (p. 500) morality out the window in favor of short skirts, the Cotton Club, fast cars, and the Charleston.

27. What did the Volstead Act prohibit?

(A) "The manufacture, sale, or transportation of intoxicating liquors"

(B) "The abridgment of the privileges or immunities of citizens of the United States"

(C) "Election to the office of the President more than twice"

(D) "The power to lay and collect taxes on incomes"

The Godfather (1972), directed by Francis Ford Coppola, starring Marlon Brando, Al Pacino, Robert Duvall. The Godfather of all organized crime movies, it is an absolute must-see, as is *The Godfather Part II* (1974).

The Public Enemy (1931), starring James Cagney. This movie about the rise and fall of a gangster during prohibition made Cagney's career.

The **temperance movement**, which saw the consumption of alcoholic beverages as the source of a host of "moral delinquencies" and a scourge on the U.S., had been gaining political ground since the turn of the century. Looking for the government to provide the moral guidance the churches no longer could, the temperance crowd had gained sufficient political support by the end of World War I for a Constitutional amendment prohibiting "the manufacture, sale, or transportation of intoxicating liquors." In 1920, Congress passed the **Volstead Act** to enforce the **18th amendment**, and the era of **prohibition** began. However, the Volstead Act proved completely unenforceable from just about day one. You can take a lot of things away from the average American without a fuss, but beer is not one of them. Instead of ushering a new morality into the United States, prohibition basically dared normally obedient Americans to break the law, thus producing a general demise in moral conduct.

Because of Prohibition, **organized crime**, which had been a nuisance in the United States since the first wave of immigrants in the 1880s, exploded into a massive problem in urban areas. Gangsters like **Al Capone** (1898-1947) made millions by smuggling and selling alcoholic beverages to anybody with the money and connections to buy them. A new kind of private saloon—the **speakeasy**—became a fixture of American life. Poor people liked their liquor, too, and they made **moonshine** in their backyards and, using rubbing alcohol, "bathtub gin" in their homes. Despite prohibition, a lot of people still managed to get rollicking drunk in the 1920s. By 1933, the "great social experiment" of prohibition had very little popular support and—for the first and only time in American history—ratifying conventions in the states voted to repeal an amendment. The **21st amendment** re-legalized intoxicating beverages.

28. Which of the following federal programs was part of
    FDR's "alphabet soup" of federal programs?

    (A) The FERA
    (B) The HMO
    (C) The NSTM
    (D) The RASB

Feeling pretty good about themselves and their leaders, Americans elected Republican **Herbert Hoover** (1874-1964) by a comfortable margin in the presidential election of 1928. A year later, the Great Depression (p. 87) set in, and Americans responded to the economic catastrophe by putting **Franklin D. Roosevelt** (1882-1945) in the White House in 1932. Roosevelt promised Americans a New Deal and his programs provided one of the most important turning points in American political history. The New Deal was made up of various efforts to combat the Great Depression and in the process remake the nation's economy by enlarging the scope of the federal government. The philosophy reflected in the New Deal was drawn largely from progressive ideas that had been circulating since the turn of the century.

Progressivism was a catch-all term for several popular schemes for reform. In the 1912 elections, Theodore Roosevelt had called his short-lived breakaway party the **Progressive party**, but people who ended up calling themselves progressives came from all the parties and ideologies on the political map. They were unified only in the desire to reform the U.S. political and economic system to make it more just. Reforms embraced by early-twentieth-century progressives included attempts at the local level to restructure city governments and end the era of back-room deals and widespread corruption. On the national front progressives were fiercely anti-monopoly and broadly populist, supporting measures such as anti-trust laws and the direct election of Senators by the people. Many progressives also dabbled in moral reform issues such as outlawing alcohol. But rather than being a particular political philosophy, progressivism can be seen as an ethos, a warm and fuzzy feeling among the middle class that a sense of moral purpose and Protestant values should guide national politics. The Progressive umbrella provided a safe haven for a dizzying number of completely contradictory political agendas and, in this slightly chaotic form, progressivism found its way into the New Deal.

Ragtime (1981), directed by Milos Forman. Adapted from the semi-fictional novel by E.L. Doctorow (p. 279), this film gives a wild panorama of the early-twentieth-century American scene.

The Untouchables (1987), directed by Brian DePalma. Kevin Costner stars as a naive federal agent dealing with the prohibition underworld, with an excellent star-studded supporting cast, good script, and great action.

After suffering a bout of polio (p. 214) in 1921, FDR lost the use of his legs. But using braces and a cane—and with cooperation from the press that today's politicians would kill for—he managed to conceal his predicament from the public; in any televised appearance he would purposefully take the few steps he was able.

Initially, during the first-ever **first 100 days**, Roosevelt leaped out of the gate by proposing a series of bold measures, sometimes called his **"Alphabet Soup."** Among them: the Federal Deposit Insurance Corporation (FDIC), designed to shore up the sagging banking system; the Agricultural Adjustment Agency (AAA), aimed at helping out troubled farmers; the Securities and Exchange Commission (SEC), intended to clean up the stock market; and several poverty-relief measures such as the Federal Emergency Relief Administration (FERA).

29. **Why did the Supreme Court invalidate many New Deal programs?**

   (A) They ruled that the programs infringed on the power of the states as outlined in the Constitution.
   (B) They ruled that the programs trampled on individual rights.
   (C) They ruled that the programs interpreted the interstate commerce clause of the Constitution too broadly.
   (D) They ruled that the programs did not promote the "general welfare."

All this legislating increased Roosevelt's popularity and helped the nation's financial infrastructure, but did nothing to end the Great Depression. More than anything, it greatly expanded the federal government, and the Supreme Court questioned the constitutionality of many of Roosevelt's programs. Dominated by Republican appointees at the time, the court invalidated several of the acts on the grounds that the New Dealers had interpreted the **interstate commerce clause** of the Constitution, which gives the federal government the power to regulate interstate commerce, too broadly. As a result, some of the acts were redrawn to pass muster, and Roosevelt came up with several others, such as the famous **Works Projects Administration** (WPA), which created truckloads of jobs for the unemployed. The **Social Security Act** of 1935 was perhaps the most far-reaching aspect of the New Deal, providing for the first time in American history a "safety net" for the elderly, children, and the poor.

These were salad days for the Democratic party. Americans re-elected Roosevelt by a landslide in 1936, and both houses of Congress gained huge Democratic majorities. The lone holdout against the New Deal was

FRANKLIN AND ELEANOR

*The marriage of **Eleanor Roosevelt** (1884-1962) to her first cousin FDR represents one of the most fruitful political partnerships in American history. Eleanor redefined the role of First Lady, becoming not just an advisor to her husband but also an outspoken, influential advocate for causes ranging from civil rights and women's rights to international cooperation. The latest biography of Eleanor, No Ordinary Time (1994), by D. Goodwin, fills in the details of a fascinating life.*

FDR signs the Social Security Bill in 1935 (when the average lifespan of an American was sixty-two).

the Supreme Court, which continued to rain on Roosevelt's parade. In 1937, Roosevelt came up with his **"court-packing"** plan, a blunderous scheme to expand the number of Supreme Court justices so he could appoint some new, more ideologically congenial ones. Congress rejected it. Unfazed, the Roosevelt administration embarked on a successful campaign against monopolies, and passed legislation establishing for the first time a federal **minimum wage**.

But for all the displays of federal firepower, in the end the New Deal did not end the Great Depression or obliterate poverty, nor did it significantly alter the structure of American business. In the face of waning public support for the New Deal, the last two of Roosevelt's unprecedented four terms as President were spent focused mainly on foreign affairs. The New Deal's main legacy was the philosophy of an **activist government** that would buttress the liberalism of the Democratic party for the rest of the century.

30. **What was the U.S. foreign policy designed to stop the spread of communism called?**

    (A) Neo-isolationism
    (B) Deliverance
    (C) Marshallism
    (D) Containment

With the American entrance into World War II (p. 650) in 1941, the United States finally had itself a war to feel good about. The bad guys were really bad and, because the Japanese had attacked a naval base in American territory, it even appeared that the nation might be in some actual danger. World War II also provided the boon the American economy needed to completely escape the Great Depression. When the war ended in 1945, the United States found itself staring down a new enemy it could feel really bad about: the dastardly **Soviet Union**. After 1945, American foreign policy shifted from general isolationism to constant interventionism in the hopes of stopping the spread of communism. With the Truman Doctrine (p. 655) and a theory called **containment**, the United States plunged headlong into the ensuing Cold War (p. 656). The idea was simple: prop up non-communist nations with lots of money, keep the Russians from trading with these nations and, at all costs, prevent all communist revolutions (p. 656). The effects were not so simple: the Korean War (p. 656) and the Vietnam War (p. 659) resulted from this new American foreign policy.

The seemingly overwhelming Russian threat seriously affected domestic policy as well. Responding to anti-communist zeal, President Harry S Truman instituted **loyalty boards** to search for communist sympathizers in the federal government. Nothing much came of these investigations except a few tarred reputations and ruined careers, but the **Red Scare** refused to die. By 1950, an attempt to weed out members of the Communist party from positions of power had taken on the characteristics of a witch hunt. Led by **Joseph McCarthy** (1909-1957), an opportunistic, heavy-drinking freshman senator from Wisconsin, the Senate began to hold committee hearings to investigate communist infiltration of the government, the movie industry, and even the venerable ranks of the armed forces. Between 1950 and 1954, McCarthy managed to remain one of the most powerful people in the country, providing the press with new and more sweeping accusations against innocent, law-abiding, red-blood-ed Americans almost daily. McCarthy finally overstepped even his bounds, though, when he questioned the patriotism of **Secretary of Defense George C. Marshall** (1880-1959), not a smart move considering the president at the time was **Dwight Eisenhower** (1890-1969), a retired general. With Eisenhower pulling political strings behind the scenes, Congress convened a special committee to investigate an attempt by McCarthy to win special treatment for one of his aides who had been drafted into the army. The hearings, which were televised nationally, exposed McCarthy as a crude thug. In December of 1954, the Senate voted to censure McCarthy, essentially ending his political career.

The Manchurian Candidate (1962), starring ol' Blue Eyes. This is a riveting take on the paranoid political atmosphere of the McCarthy era.

31. **Whom did John Kennedy defeat in the presidential election of 1960?**
   (A) Richard Nixon
   (B) Hubert Humphrey
   (C) Barry Goldwater
   (D) Henry Cabot Lodge, Jr.

With Roosevelt's New Deal programs firmly entrenched, the United States had made an unusually smooth transition from a state of war to a state of peace after World War II. The Cold War and the new interventionist American mindset kept international tensions high, but plenty of Americans were employed in the defense industry. A few minor recessions slowed the national economy in the 1940s but the United States plugged along as the world's foremost superpower throughout the supposedly idyllic 1950s. Americans bought television sets and washing machines, went to the movies, listened to Perry Como and Elvis Presley, and flocked in their shiny new automobiles to new homes in the suburbs—bought thanks to generous government programs such as the **G.I. Bill**. Between 1946 and 1964, American G.I.s showed how glad they were to be home by helping to create over 76 million **baby boomers**.

In 1960, with the space race (p. 338) beginning and the communist threat still in high gear, Americans elected **John F. Kennedy** (1917-1963), a young, attractive, Roman Catholic senator from Massachusetts, over his untelegenic Republican rival, **Richard Nixon** (1913-1993), in the hotly

Libra (1988), by Don DeLillo. One of our best fiction writers takes on the JFK assassination case from a postmodern perspective, showing how the case captures the darkest aspects of the national psyche.

The nation was glued to the television throughout the Cuban Missile Crisis.

contested presidential election of 1960. Kennedy lowered taxes, fought organized crime, created the **Peace Corps**, and tried his darndest to rid the world of communism. He sent 40,000 "military advisors" into politically unstable Vietnam and, in an attempt to overthrow the Castro regime (p. 86) in Cuba, he approved a disastrous U.S.-sponsored invasion on the beach at the Bay of Pigs (p. 658). Luckily, Kennedy got a second chance to be tough on communism during the Cuban Missile Crisis (p. 658) by successfully convincing the Russians to remove nuclear missile sites from America's backyard.

When Kennedy travelled to Dallas in 1963 to shore up waning Texas support for his re-election bid, he was assassinated by either **Lee Harvey Oswald**, angry Cubans, angry anti-Cubans, Mafia hitmen, disgruntled CIA agents, extraterrestrials, or some odd combination of the above. Whoever killed Kennedy certainly could not have been pleased at the outcome of the deed, though. After his assassination, the press and an anguished American public turned him into a martyr.

32. Which of the following federal programs was NOT a part of Lyndon Johnson's Great Society?

(A) Medicare
(B) Medicaid
(C) The Environmental Protection Agency
(D) The Department of Housing and Urban Development

The politically ruthless Texan **Lyndon B. Johnson** (1908-1973) succeeded Kennedy as president. On the domestic front, Johnson initiated several massive programs designed to combat the growing problem of poverty in the United States by increasing the economic role of the federal government. Known collectively as the **Great Society**, these programs constituted the most consequential expansion of the federal government since the Roosevelt administration. The Great Society was a two-pronged effort with the lofty goals of achieving civil rights (p. 197) for all Americans and waging a **"war on poverty."** Numerous civil rights acts made job and housing discrimination illegal, guaranteed voting rights for blacks, and granted the full protections of the Constitution to Native Americans on reservations (p. 177). Johnson's Great Society also expanded the social welfare system by creating **Medicare** and **Medicaid** to ensure federal funding for the medical costs of the elderly and the poor, and the **Food Stamps** program to provide grocery vouchers to the poor. The Great Society also included educational programs like **Head Start**, job training programs like **Job Corps**, and numerous programs that dramatically expanded housing subsidies. In addition, Johnson expanded the federal government into new areas of public life with the creation of such agencies as the department of Housing and Urban Development (HUD), the National Endowment for the Humanities (NEH), and the Corporation for Public Broadcasting (PBS). But, not unlike the New Deal, from which it drew inspiration, the Great Society fell far short of expectations and left a mixed legacy. Poverty did not disappear and in fact became even more entrenched in the inner cities and rural areas. Medicare and Medicaid turned out to be administrative nightmares that remain among the highest-costing items in the federal budget. The role of the federal government in the arts, education, and the lives of the disadvantaged was expanded in ways many feel were crucial, but conservatives continue to argue that the Great Society stretched the reach of the federal government too far.

Meanwhile, Johnson was getting the United States more and more entangled in the increasingly unpopular Vietnam War (p. 659). Television brought the horrific reality of war home to Americans for the first time, and the acrimony of the protest movement caused a deep wound in the national psyche that still has not healed. Johnson's inability to end the war led to a grave loss of credibility that was the most significant factor in his decision not to seek a second term as President. Richard Nixon was elected in 1968 (over Vice-President Hubert Humphrey) largely on a promise to end the war. It dragged on for five more years.

The Other America (1962), by Michael Harrington. Calling attention to the fact that "somewhere between 20 and 25 percent of the American people" were living below the poverty line, Harrington's book had a big influence on the War on Poverty.

33. Who were Woodward and Bernstein?

(A) A comedy team that ruthlessly made fun of Nixon during the Watergate scandal
(B) The reporters who uncovered the Watergate scandal
(C) Author and composer of the musical *Tricky Dick*
(D) The attorneys who argued against Nixon in the Watergate hearings

All the President's Men (1976), directed by Alan J. Pakula. Robert Redford and Dustin Hoffman star as Woodward and Bernstein in this first-rate political thriller/detective story about Watergate.

Although he was overwhelmingly re-elected in 1972, Nixon sowed the seeds of his own downfall with his paranoid fear of political enemies. On June 17, 1972, responding to a routine burglary tip, Washington, D.C. police officers arrested seven people employed by the **Committee to Re-Elect the President** (CREEP) attempting to break into the headquarters of the **Democratic National Committee** in the Watergate Apartment Complex. If not for the investigative tenacity of **Bob Woodward** and **Carl Bernstein**, two reporters for the *Washington Post* who exposed the facts of the **Watergate Scandal** to the American public, the whole thing might have blown over. As the story unfolded, Americans learned that their president had conspired with his aides to sabotage the campaign of **Senator George McGovern** (1922-), Nixon's opponent in the 1972 presidential race, then had tried to hinder Congressional investigations of the misdeed. The attempted cover-up, which included Nixon's refusal to turn over tape recordings of conversations in the Oval Office, was where Nixon really dug his grave; some Nixon supporters argue that the dirty campaign tactics were nothing out of the ordinary. When the Supreme Court rejected Nixon's claim of executive privilege, he was forced to turn over some of the tapes (though there was a large section erased) and Congress began **impeachment** proceedings. With a trial looming and the case against him seemingly airtight, Nixon resigned in 1974, making him the first president ever to step down from office. Gerald Ford (1913-), Nixon's successor, granted him an unconditional pardon a month later, but his name remained symbolic of dishonesty and corruption for many years.

Check out the sign in the foreground: no short cuts.

But wait! A dogged Nixon sprang back to public life in the 1980s and 1990s, largely rebuilding his reputation as an elder statesman with a spate of books and lectures on foreign policy, an area in which he had always been considered an expert.

34. **What was George Bush calling Michael Dukakis when he invoked the "L-word" during the 1988 Presidential campaign?**

   (A) Luscious
   (B) Lilliputian
   (C) Lily-livered
   (D) Liberal

The Democratic party was the dominant political party for most of the twentieth century, with a virtual lock on elections in the South and in Northern industrial states like Wisconsin, Illinois, and New York. But the party foundered in the 1970s and 1980s. Part of the problem was what **George Bush** (1924-) in the 1988 Presidential election called the **"L word"**—liberalism. As a political philosophy, liberalism came into disrepute as faith in the power of government to improve the lives of the disadvantaged, the basis of much twentieth-century liberal policy, was shaken. Economic stagnation in the industrial states following the Vietnam War hit working-class whites hard, and Republicans blamed the state of the economy on the programs of the Great Society. Right or wrong, the strategy worked. Former-B-movie-actor-turned-Governor-of-California **Ronald Reagan** (1911-) was most successful at pitting disaffected white voters against the "liberal agenda," which was held to be composed of intellectuals who wanted to tax the middle-class to death to support programs like Affirmative Action and Welfare. Reaganites also held liberalism responsible for the spread of what was characterized as "moral decay" in American society—the increase of teenage pregnancy, drug abuse, and violence. Partly by stressing these themes Reagan built a coalition of working-class whites, evangelical Christians, and wealthy corporate interests that was referred to by pundits as the **Reagan Revolution**. Bush, Reagan's successor, had brief success with the anti-liberal strategy but was driven from office after one term by a deep economic recession, an unusal three-way race, and an opponent, **Bill Clinton** (1946-), who managed to present himself as a **"New Democrat,"** an activist with a moderate social agenda.

President Bill Clinton

CULTURESCOPE

 After 1865, the South remained a lock for the Democratic party, largely because Southern voters couldn't bear the thought of supporting the party of Lincoln. Over the past twenty years, however, the South has become a Republican stronghold.

Bill Clinton's election in 1992 seemed to herald new life for the Democratic party, but efforts to agree on legislation for **universal health care coverage** were stymied, and this failure, along with other policy crises, left the party in limbo. Republicans parlayed Democratic floundering and continuing hard times into a historic series of victories in the 1994 congressional elections that gave them control of both houses of Congress for the first time in forty-six years. With the New Deal principles of activist government currently under attack again, liberalism in general and the Democratic party in particular are in a state of crisis. Only a few Democratic victories, mostly on social issues such as abortion rights (p. 201), seem secure.

But though it is currently in ascendence the American political right has certainly been forced to take its lumps in the second half of the twentieth century, partly because history has shown it to be wrong on so many issues: dragging its feet (at best) on Civil Rights, for example, and a penchant for high tariffs (p. 94) are just two examples of Republican missteps. Even today, with lunatics who blow up federal buildings claiming to be in league with the growing movement called **neoconservatism**, the right is stigmatized as fanatic, not to mention heedless of the realities of poverty and **downward mobility**. Nonetheless, and to the confused chagrin of liberals, the neoconservatism espoused by the Republican party appears to have stolen the political spotlight, although—as always—the current shifts in political power may or may not signal long-term changes in the shape of our political system.

STAY *AU COURANT* WITH THESE POLITICAL MAGS

The Left	The Right	You Make the Call
The Nation	National Review	The New Republic
Harper's	Reason	Atlantic Monthly
Utne Reader	Commentary	Tikkun
Mother Jones	American Spectator	
Flush Rush	The Limbaugh Letter	

35. Since World War II, which of the following has occurred?

(A) The establishment of postcolonial governments in the Third World
(B) The emergence of South America as an economic powerhouse
(C) Peace on Earth and goodwill to men
(D) A nationalistic fervor among Scandinavian nations

After World War II, the political atmosphere of Europe remained relatively stable despite a few failed revolutions (Hungary, 1956, for instance) and continual posturing on both sides of the **Berlin Wall**. Weary of war, the leaders of Europe concentrated on rebuilding their economies and infrastructures via monetary aid from the USSR or the U.S., depending on which side of the Cold War fence each nation's political leaders sat. The occasional peasant uprisings in underdeveloped colonial regions that had previously been crushed now grew into multiple revolutions as the tired nations of Europe allowed the last remnants of colonialism to disappear. In place of the colonial powers, a **Third World** of fledgling **post-colonial** nations struggled into being around the globe. Indeed, by 1980, the world order had the Soviet Union and the United States jockeying at the top; aging contenders like France, Great Britain, and a divided Germany hung tough in the middle; and newly free nations like India, Angola, and Taiwan striving for respect in the lower echelon.

The real political action of the post-war world has been in the East. After being kicked around a little too long and colonized a little too much by Europe, China went communist and reasserted itself on the world stage under the leadership of **Mao Zedong** and his successors. With an uncanny resilience and a little help from the United States, Japan (p. 82) turned its devastated economy around and, with miraculous speed, became one of the world's foremost economic powers. Meanwhile, in the areas of Korea and Southeast Asia, the United States and the Soviet Union (and China and Japan) gave money, armaments, and lives to the various political factions battling for control of these Asian outposts throughout the 1950s and 1960s.

For nearly four decades after World War II, it appeared that the communist Soviet Union and the democratic capitalist U.S. would fight an epic and final battle. But with the Cold War over (and the communists all but finished), the **New World Order** is yet to be firmly established.

P.C. NATION

In recent years, the rise of "political correctness" or "p.c.," especially on college campuses, has sparked a huge debate: Does p.c. culture stifle free thought or promote a more just and caring society? The term "p.c." sprung up among the politically liberal to describe a cluster of positions and attitudes, including support for the broadest possible rights for minorities, and, most notoriously, sensitivity to language that potentially offends or belittles minority groups and women (er, womyn).

Wars and problems still persist, and the international political atmosphere seems more complicated than ever. Dogmatic religious movements—which caused so much bloodshed for so many hundreds of years—appear to be taking hold throughout the world once again, as Fundamentalist Muslims, Christians, and Hindus, among others, all insist that theirs is the cause to die for. On the economic front, nearly seventy years after the Hawley-Smoot tariff (p. 95) sparked a trade war that devastated the American economy, trade wars among all nations continue to simmer and loom perpetually on the horizon. And the Balkans—that troubled region where World War I started—is at it again; warring Serbs and Croats have stirred nationalist fervor into a long and bloody war that has included accusations of genocide.

Answers

1. D	2. C	3. B	4. B	5. D	6. C	7. B	8. D	9. A	10. A
11. B	12. A	13. C	14. A	15. C	16. B	17. D	18. A	19. C	20. B
21. C	22. D	23. A	24. B	25. D	26. B	27. A	28. A	29. C	30. D
31. A	32. C	33. B	34. D	35. A					

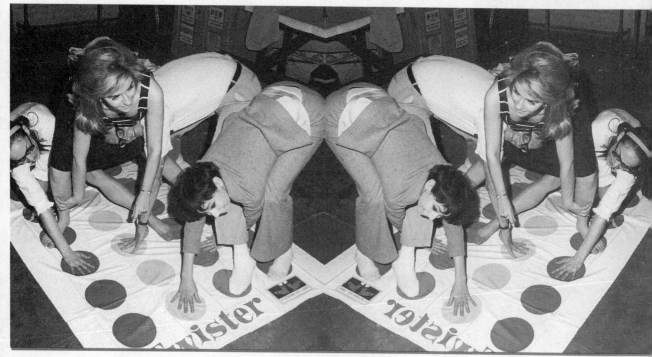

People have always invented tests of speed, strength, and skill, at first mainly to prepare them for the physical demands of combat and the hunt. Eventually, organized games took on religious significance and were seen as a way to gain access to the divine. In the eighteenth and nineteenth centuries, organized athletics were revived on college and prep school campuses, with the idea—harking back to antiquity—of promoting excellence in the mind and body. Then came industrialization and the labor movement and with them the growth of free time among all social classes, and suddenly both amateur and professional sports, along with less physical forms of competition such as chess and billiards, had a newly important role to play in Western society. Today, sports stars are revered—you might even say worshiped—in ways that remind us of the surprisingly integral place of athletics in our cultural imagination.

1. **What is the official game of Canada?**
   (A) Hockey
   (B) Football
   (C) Shinty
   (D) Lacrosse

Lacrosse is believed to have been invented as *baggataway* around A.D. 900 by the Iroquois tribes, in the northeastern part of what is now the United States. The modern name was coined by French settlers, who thought the netted stick used to fling the ball into the goal looked like the staff a bishop holds during a mass. They called the stick *la crosse* (which is also the French name for a hockey stick). Among some tribes, each player held two sticks, but most played with just one. Either a piece of deer hide stuffed with deer hair or a knot cut from a dead tree served as the ball. Teams had to be even but their sizes could vary from a dozen to several hundred players, with the dimensions of the field changing accordingly. The highly organized games, judged by a panel of elders, were part of several days of prayer and dancing related to the contestants' hopes for the crops, climate, or good fortune in some other realm of tribal or individual affairs. Athleticism was considered a method of communicating with a higher spirit. Players prayed before a big game to be able to play well and the judges prayed that they might judge fairly. Players generally wore nothing except a loincloth and a modicum of religious adornment. Among some tribes, a shaman (p. 471) would scratch each player twenty-eight times on each arm and the same number on each leg, just deeply enough to break the skin. It must have been quite painful, but the running blood was thought to increase speed and agility.

Today, lacrosse is popular all over North America. The Montreal Canada Club established the first modern rules in 1867, around the same time that lacrosse was named Canada's official game (ice hockey is the official *sport*).

Shinny is another Native American game that may be the forerunner to both field and ice hockey—tribes have played it on both surfaces for centuries. As in hockey, the objective is to put a ball into a goal by moving it along the ground with a stick. Native American sticks were stylized and, as in lacrosse, neither team nor field size was standardized. One recorded shinny game had a field whose goals were seven and a half miles apart.

Mesoamerican tribes played a now-lost game called *pok-ta-pok* (the Mayan name) or *tlachtli* (the Aztec name) on courts built as part of temple complexes (p. 34), reflecting the games' profound religious significance. The game was nearly universal in the Americas—courts have been found as far north as southern Arizona and as far south as Guatemala and Honduras. Only aristocrats were allowed to play. There were usually five players per team and each player wore padding for protection against the ball, which was solid rubber. The stone court was usually I-shaped, about fifty feet-by-100 feet, with sheer walls and a stone ring extending perpendicular to each long wall about fifteen feet above the floor. A team propelling the ball through the opponents' ring

Aztec nobles enjoy a rousing game of *tlachtli.*

won the game outright. This was no mean feat, as the players could not touch the ball with their hands or feet, but could only use their thighs, hips, shoulders, and heads. Points were also scored by keeping the ball in the air, and players often injured themselves diving for the ball on the stone floor. The winners were entitled to the clothes and jewelry worn by the losing team's supporters, who were often injured as well trying to flee the stadium with the winning team's henchmen on their heels. The game was banned by the Spanish clergy in the sixteenth century.

2. **What is another name for the Colosseum?**
   (A) The Circus Maximus
   (B) The Acropolis
   (C) The Flavian Ampitheatre
   (D) The Parthenon

Roman **gladiatorial combat** began as the simple sacrifice of slaves or prisoners of war at the graves of the dead, who it was thought could be appeased by human blood. Later, in the interest of sport, the doomed men were made to fight at the gravesides, and gradually the battles were moved to the **Circus Maximus** and the **Flavian Ampitheatre,** aka the Colosseum (p. 37). The Colosseum was four stories tall, had eighty arches

Blood, sweat, and cheers: a Roman amphitheatre

and a seating capacity of 50,000. Contemporary accounts report that Thracians, Egyptians, Sabean Arabs, Cilicians, Sugambrians, and Ethiopians flocked to Rome to witness mortal combat between two or several men, or between one man and several animals. Men (and sometimes women) fought to the death with swords, tridents and spears. There was Greek-style **boxing**, too, with the Roman innovation of the *cestus* (sharp metal studs bound to the knuckles). One *cestus* champion was said to have killed 1,425 opponents.

Most gladiators were slaves or condemned criminals who hoped to prolong their lives or even secure their freedom through valor in the ring. But impoverished freemen also fought, as victory could be financially rewarding. Winners were paid in gold, with the spectators calling the price and the festival promoter required to meet it. Champions commanded the largest treasures. For a time, even Roman aristocrats fought, in matches both fixed and fair, until the Emperor Augustus (p. 388) forbade it. A whole subculture sprang up around the slaughter, with schools

The gladiator's oath, according to Petronius: "We swear, after the dictation of Eumolpus, to suffer death by fire, bonds, stripes, and the sword; and whatever else Eumolpus may command; as true gladiators we bind ourselves body and mind to our master's service."

of gladiatorial combat and medical specialists in sword and trident wounds.

Roman politicians used the contests as political and military celebrations, but also as diversions intended to prevent the citizenry from responding in an organized way to the realities of a vast, inequitable imperial state. As the mime Pylades supposedly said to his employer, "It is to your advantage, Caesar, that we keep the public occupied." Social critics today make similar points about modern spectator sports: today's "violent" sports, they suggest, provide a safe outlet for the aggressive impulses of the fans, who might otherwise take their frustrations out on the powers that be.

3. **When were the original Olympic Games held?**
   - (A)   776 B.C.
   - (B)   394 A.D.
   - (C)   1896
   - (D)   1936

The first officially documented **Olympic Games** were held in 776 B.C. at Olympia, near Elis, in ancient Greece, although legend suggests that the Greeks held similar festivals at the site, in honor of Zeus (p. 472). In 884 B.C. the legendary King Iphitos of Elis arranged a treaty between **Sparta** and Pisatis that established *ekecheiria*, the sacredness of Olympia, rendering the site immune to military

MARATHON MAN

The marathon takes its name from the story of Pheidippides, a Greek soldier who ran approximately twenty-four miles from the city of Marathon to Athens carrying the news of the Greek victory over the Persians in the Battle of Marathon in 490 B.C. He is said to have dropped dead after delivering his message. Current marathons are a grueling 26.6 miles.

aggression. The original games featured only one event, a foot race from one end of the stadium to the other, a distance of 192.27 meters, ending at the altar of Zeus. Eventually, longer races were added to the program, races around the stadium eight, ten, twelve and twenty-four times. In 520 B.C. a more grueling foot race was added—two 192-meter lengths of the stadium in full armor, including helmet and shield. Training for such events is considered one of the primary reasons the Greeks defeated the Persians in the Persian Wars, fought between 500 and 440 B.C. With the Olympic Games at their peak, fostering athleticism was the civic duty of every Greek citizen. All young men looked forward to competing in the *agon*, or contest, and acquiring the virtues of *arete*, the aristocratic manly

WHERE ARE ALL THE WILD THINGS?

At the Emperor Trajan's games, in 107 B.C., 11,000 wild animals were slaughtered: rhinoceri, bulls, tigers, lions, panthers, bears, apes, gazelles, and elephants.

ideal, and **kalokagathia**, a perfect harmony between body and spirit. Many city-states (p. 385) of the thriving Greek world sent competitors to Olympia. The athletes served as cultural representatives, much as they do today.

The decline of the ancient Games began in 440 B.C., as the slave-driven economy stagnated and the twenty-seven-year Peloponnesian War (431-404 B.C.) between Athens and Sparta accelerated the break-up of the city-states. The following century saw a number of violations of the *ekecheiria*, first by Sparta in attacking Elis, then by the Arcadians, who went so far as to attack the temples at Olympia and seize treasures from them to pay their soldiers. These violations were not the only sign of a decline in the spiritual nature of the games. During the fourth and third centuries, B.C., the most violent events, like wrestling, boxing, and the **pancratium**,

The Pugilist at Rest, Greek statue

gradually became the most popular. Chariot races, introduced to the games in 680 B.C., became more and more spectacular, the charioteers driven to ever more thrilling and dangerous feats.

In 146 B.C., Roman conquest ended the pan-Hellenic character of the games for good. The last Olympic Games of ancient times were held in A.D. 393. When Christianity became the Roman state religion, the Games were forbidden as a pagan festival. Plundered by various Roman emperors, the once-sacred temples at Olympia were finally razed. What was left collapsed in the earthquakes of A.D. 522 and 551 and was buried by a change in the course of the river Cladeus.

The hugely popular **pancratium**, first fought in Olympic competition at the 33rd Olypiad in 648 B.C., was down and dirty, hand-to-hand combat with unprotected knuckles in which nearly anything went, including the deliberate breaking of fingers, kicking and punching below the belt, and strangleholds. The signal for giving up was a quick tap on one's opponent's torso. The barbarity of the sport increased to the point where even very young boys were allowed into the ring to beat each other senseless in front of large, cheering crowds.

4. **Who is considered the father of the modern Olympics?**
   (A) Woodrow Wilson
   (B) Otto von Bismarck
   (C) Baron Pierre de Coubertin
   (D) Jean-Jacques Rousseau

In 1835, Greece won its independence from the Turks, sparking a renewed interest in antiquity across Europe. The archeological expedition to unearth the treasures buried at Olympia began in 1875. In 1892, a French professor named **Baron Pierre de Coubertin** (1863-1937) proposed that the Games be revived on an international scale. He then spent two years organizing a conference to discuss the idea, and the **International Olympic Committee** was founded in 1894.

During his thirty-year tenure as president of the IOC, Baron de Coubertin tried to get all participating nations to embrace the Olympic ideal of peaceful competition, stressing the significance of the Games as an expression of human potential. However, if the competitors saw themselves as athletes first and foremost, on the whole their governments and countrymen considered them representatives of national character, of race, or of ethnic identity. Nationalism (p. 393) was a staple of the Olympics from the first modern Olympiad and has remained a tenacious presence.

Inevitably, the choice of a host city has become a politically charged issue, despite the IOC's desire to keep politics out. For the host country, the games are a financial and public relations bonanza. As hosts of the **1936 Games**, the Germans spared no expense in giving their visitors a dose of Nazi pomp and circumstance. The Deutsches Stadion was enlarged to hold 110,000 spectators.

Baron de Coubertin: sportsman, humanitarian, champion of the moustache

Although Coubertin stressed internationalism and peace, the conference was not without rancor. The delegation from Germany declined to attend after the French, still smarting from their defeat in the Franco-Prussian War twenty-four years earlier, announced that they would not sit at the same table with the German enemy.

CROSS-DRESSING SPRINTER

Olympic history is full of challenges to athletes' eligibility on charges of professionalism, drug use, even sexual identity. When six-foot American Helen Stephens beat out Polish world champion sprinter Stella Walsh at the 1936 Berlin Games, a Polish journalist accused Stephens of being a man. In 1980, Stella Walsh was killed during a robbery, and when her body was undressed for the autopsy, it was discovered that she had male sex organs.

Carl Diem, one of the German organizers, came up with the idea of having the Olympic torch brought by relay from the Greek town of Marathon to light the fire in the arena, a tradition that continues to this day. Athletes and dignitaries praised the accommodations in the Olympic village. But the United States team almost didn't go to the Games at all, as Jewish groups and others had urged a boycott on moral grounds.

Not surprisingly, 1968, a year of tumult around the world including student uprisings in Paris, the Tet Offensive (p. 660), and the murders of Martin Luther King, Jr., and Robert F. Kennedy (p. 200), saw an especially volatile political atmosphere surrounding the Games. Less than a month before the games were scheduled to begin in **Mexico City**, Mexican troops advancing on students protesting the government's alleged betrayal of the Mexican Revolution shot and killed dozens, perhaps hundreds, of protesters. In November of 1967, black sociologist Harry Edwards had tried to organize a boycott of the Games by African American athletes angry at continuing discrimination in the U.S. In the end, the athletes competed, but when two of the medal-winners, Tommy Smith and John Carlos, raised black-gloved fists—the Black Power (p. 200) salute—on the victory stand, they were suspended from the U.S. team and ordered to leave Mexico within forty-eight hours.

The German organizers of the 1972 Munich Games wanted to erase memories of the ugly mentality that had marked the "Nazi Olympics." Unfortunately, Munich was to be remembered for a horrifying act of political terror: six Palestinian terrorists climbed the fence at the Olympic village and found the quarters of the Israeli team. A few of the athletes escaped, but nine were taken hostage. Two were killed soon after, when they managed to grab knives and wound two of their captors. The terrorists demanded the release of Palestinian prisoners held in Israel and West Germany and safe passage to an Arab destination. After hours of tense negotiation, they were allowed to take the hostages to Furstenfeldbruck airfield, where the German police opened fire. Three of the terrorists and all of the hostages were killed.

5. Which of these countries *did not* join the U.S. boycott of the 1980 Moscow Games?

(A) West Germany
(B) Great Britain
(C) Japan
(D) Israel

On December 28th, 1979, at the height of the Cold War, Radio Moscow announced that the USSR would intervene in the civil war in Afghanistan at the request of the Kabul government. President **Jimmy Carter** (1924-) had to respond or risk appearing weak on the eve of a re-election campaign. He chose the relatively ineffectual method of a boycott of the upcoming 1980 Moscow Olympics because economic sanctions were likely to be too costly to the United States.

In 1984, the USSR retaliated with a boycott of the Los Angeles Games, though they claimed that the boycott was based on fears for the Eastern-bloc athletes' safety. One hundred teams, including China and Romania, attended the 1984 Games, but the dominance of the U.S. team, which won eighty-three gold medals, and the chants of "USA! USA!" that shook the stadium were embarrassing to some American and foreign observers. The 1984 Games were further criticized for their rampant commercialism. The chairman of the Los Angeles Olympic Organizing Committee, Peter Ueberroth, had ensured that the Games would not lose money, as every Olympiad but one had since 1932, by selling $258 million in television rights and getting an

> *Sports don't build character, they reveal it.*
>
> — HEYWOOD BROUN

Jackie Joyner-Kersee stood out in the Olympic heptathlon, added in 1981 as a women's version of the men's decathlon.

additional $130 million out of corporate sponsors. To many television viewers, it seemed that the Olympics had become more about selling hamburgers than about athletics. But the LAOOC emerged with a surplus of more than $200 million.

6. **Who did an Associated Press Poll name the greatest athlete of the first half of the twentieth century in 1950?**
   (A) Lou Gehrig
   (B) Jim Thorpe
   (C) Jesse Owens
   (D) Babe Ruth

Jim Thorpe All-American (1951), starring Burt Lancaster. Thorpe was paid a measly $1,500 for his life story.

Part-Native American **Jim Thorpe** (1888-1953), named the greatest athlete of the first half of this century, won gold medals in both the **pentathlon** and **decathlon** at the Stockholm Olympics in 1912. Months later, it came to light that Thorpe had once been paid to play semi-pro baseball, and his medals were rescinded. Later, Thorpe played both professional football and professional baseball, excelling especially in the former. Years of litigation to have his medals returned finally ended in success in 1982, twenty-nine years after his death. Disqualification from the Olympics for professionalism has become extinct in the past twenty years, as the concept of pure amateurism has come to seem old-fashioned, unrealistic, and elitist.

Mildred "Babe" Didriksen (1914-1956) won three track and field medals at the 1932 Games (two golds and a silver), then turned to professional golf and won fourteen tournaments in one year. She also excelled at basketball. An Associated Press poll voted her the greatest female athlete of the first half of the twentieth century in 1950.

Sonja Henie (1912-1969), a Norwegian who was the most

Jim Thorpe, All-American

famous figure skater of all time, brought the sport to new levels of athleticism and grace. She won gold medals at the 1928, 1932, and 1936 Winter Games and went on to star in ten Hollywood vehicles.

Jesse Owens (1918-1980) was the star of the 1936 Games and was favorably portrayed in the both the German press of the time and Leni Riefenstahl's documentary of the Games, *Olympia* (p. 111). Owens, an African American, broke records in the 100 and 200-meter dash, and showed-up Nazi propagandists, who had trumpeted the superiority of the Aryan athlete. Yet upon his return from Berlin Jesse Owens could find no more rewarding job than that of a janitor. He performed in exhibitions in which he raced horses and cars for money, and even appeared with the Harlem Globetrotters. Later, he became a professional banquet speaker, giving talks on the themes of clean living and patriotism. He tried to mediate in the 1968 boycott dispute, and was excoriated as an Uncle Tom. He later wrote two books about the experience: *Blackthink* (1970) and *I Have Changed* (1972).

An airborne Jesse Owens

Johnny Weissmuller (1904-1984) was a strapping Austrian immigrant to the United States who won gold medals in swimming at the 1924 and 1928 Games. In training for the 1932 Games, he was cast as Tarzan in *Tarzan, the Ape Man*, and eventually starred in twelve Tarzan movies.

Mark Spitz (1950-) was an American swimmer who set a record by winning seven gold medals at the 1972 Games in Munich.

Recent Olympiads have seen multiple gold medals won by Americans like hurdler Edwin Moses, diver Greg Louganis, gymnast Mary Lou Retton,

Belts are back: Johnny Weissmuller models the latest in swimwear

 Competing in a celebrity golf tournament in Cuba in 1959, Weissmuller and his friends were held up by a band of Castro's guerillas en route to the golf course. Taking stock of the situation, Weissmuller began beating his chest and bellowing his Tarzan yell. Recognizing him, the rebels dropped their guns and gave him an escort to the golf course.

sprinter and long-jumper Carl Lewis, heptathelete Jackie Joyner-Kersee, and sprinter Florence Griffith-Joyner.

7. Who invented baseball?
(A) Abner Doubleday
(B) Alexander Cartwright
(C) A.G. Spalding
(D) Cy Young

Baseball (1994), by Ken Burns. This is a typically exhaustive and engrossing documentary. Burns effectively weaves many cultural and historical elements in his chronicle of America's pastime.

THE LAST FIVE WORLD SERIES CHAMPIONS
••••••••••••••••••••••••••••••••

1994 *(No series due to strike)*
1993 *Toronto Blue Jays*
1992 *Toronto Blue Jays*
1991 *Minnesota Twins*
1990 *Cincinnati Reds*

Baseball's origins go back to a seventeenth-century British children's game called **rounders**. Unlike baseball, however, in rounders the bases were not uniformly spaced and the fielders put runners out by throwing the ball at them, presumably as hard as they could. In 1905, **A.G. Spalding** (1850-1915), a former pitcher and sporting goods dealer, suggested that a commission be appointed to find out who invented baseball. The group's report, which established **Abner Doubleday** (1819-1893) as the founder of the game, was discounted by historians as early as 1939, when the Baseball Hall of Fame was opened in **Cooperstown**, New York. The experts maintain that **Alexander Cartwright** (1820-1892), who founded the Knickerbocker Base Ball Club in 1845, also set down the original standard rules. It is Cartwright who is enshrined at Cooperstown.

Early baseball clubs were just that. Players were not paid and matches were social affairs, with parties afterward. Membership in the clubs was based on class—no laborers allowed. The Civil War (p. 633), which brought a huge range of men into close contact, expanded the game's inter-class appeal. The first openly professional team, the **Cincinnati Red Stockings**, was founded in 1869. The ball was pitched underhand, no gloves were used, and final scores regularly recorded dozens of runs.

Until the 1880s, some black players performed in the major leagues, but they were few and far between, and all were soon forced out by an increasingly racist atmosphere. For several decades thereafter, African American entrepeneurs organized ball clubs that eventually came together under the aegis of Andrew "Rube" Foster as the **National Negro League** in 1920. The Negro League teams played many more games a season than the major leagues, and some of the greatest players of all time graced their rosters. The Negro League flourished for almost thirty years, until the sublimely talented **Jackie Robinson** (1919-1972) was recruited to play for the Brooklyn Dodgers in 1947, paving the way for the gradual integration of the sport and the demise of the Negro League.

After pitchers started throwing overhand hits were hard to come by,

Jackie Robinson sneaks home.

and baseball remained a pitcher's and runner's game for many years. In 1920, the cover of the ball was sewn tighter, making the ball "livelier" and crowd-pleasing home runs more common. Early baseball aficionados were as displeased with this innovation as later fans were with the introduction of **AstroTurf** and the **designated hitter**. But it helped to make baseball the most popular spectator sport in the nation for decades, until television conferred that honor upon another, faster-moving and more violent game: football.

The Bad News Bears (1976), starring Walter Matthau and Tatum O'Neal. A team of bumbling little-leaguers turns their season around with a beer-swigging gruff for a coach.

8. **Who is second on baseball's list of all-time leaders in number of hits?**

   (A) Ty Cobb
   (B) Lou Gehrig
   (C) Pete Rose
   (D) Cal Ripken

Ty Cobb (1886-1961) was nicknamed the "Georgia Peach" by a sportswriter who was no doubt referring more to his playing than to his personality. Cobb, a fast runner and one of the best hitters of all-time, won twelve batting championships. Only two people have stolen more bases and only one person has gotten more hits since Cobb's retirement in 1928. But for all these heroics, Cobb was a difficult man who got into fist fights with players and umpires and on one occasion even climbed into the stands to brawl with a heckler.

Lou Gehrig (1903-1941) was a Yankee first baseman nicknamed "the Iron Horse" because he never sat out a game. From 1925 until 1939 he played in 2,130 consecutive games, which is still a record. A power hitter who had

The Georgia Peach rounds third.

Hank Aaron (1934-) is best-known for breaking Babe Ruth's career home run record of 714. Aaron finished his career with 755 home runs.

twelve straight .300 seasons (most power hitters don't hit .300), Gehrig played somewhat in the enormous shadow of his teammate **Babe Ruth**, and died in 1941 of amyotrophic lateral sclerosis, a hardening of the spinal cord that has ever since been referred to as **Lou Gehrig's Disease**.

A dignified, reserved centerfielder for the New York Yankees for thirteen years, **Joe DiMaggio** (1914-) still holds the record for hitting safely in the most consecutive games: fifty-six. He played in ten World Series and had an outstanding career batting average of .325. After his retirement he married a Hollywood icon, Marilyn Monroe and was immortalized in two songs, *Joltin' Joe DiMaggio* and Simon and Garfunkel's *Mrs. Robinson*.

Gibson eludes the tag.

Josh Gibson (1910-1947) may have been the greatest baseball player in the Negro Leagues, and perhaps in any league. A catcher and power-hitter, Gibson hit seventy-five home runs for the Homestead Grays in 1931, and though records in the Negro Leagues were not reliably recorded, some fans insist that Gibson's record for a season was eighty-nine homers. The Major League record of sixty-one, by contrast, has stood for thirty-three seasons. Gibson died of a cerebral hemorrhage at the age of thirty-six, in 1947, four months before Jackie Robinson broke the color barrier in the majors.

THE SPORT THAT RUTH BUILT

Babe Ruth (1895-1948) was baseball's greatest star ever, and he is credited with saving the game—after the damage done its reputation by the 1919 scandal—with his power-hitting on the field and prurient exploits off. Raised in an orphanage, Ruth flouted every accepted rule of athletic conditioning (smoking, drinking, and wolfing hotdogs) while leading the league in home runs six years in a row. He appeared in movie shorts and even played himself in a film about the life of his teammate, Lou Gehrig. (Pride of the Yankees [1942]) is mainly worth seeing for Ruth's raucous performance.) He was only fifty-three when he died of cancer, so maybe he shouldn't have smoked so much.

Leroy "Satchel" Paige (1906-1982), who got his nickname as a seven-year-old baggage carrier at the Mobile, Alabama, railroad depot, went on to become what some consider the best pitcher who ever lived. Pitching most of his career in the Negro Leagues and on "barnstorming" tours around the country, Paige is said to have started around 2,500 games. He pitched 105 games in 1934, winning 104 of them. After he signed with the American League's Cleveland Indians at the age of forty-two, he drew 72,000 people to his second game.

Willie Mays (1931-) was a centerfielder for the New York Giants, San Francisco Giants, and New York Mets who is best-known for his patented underhand "basket" catch. He hit 660 home runs during twenty years in the majors, having missed two seasons to serve in the military. Some historians believe he would have passed Babe Ruth on the career home run list if he had played those seasons. Mays also made perhaps the most famous catch of all-time in the 1954 World Series on a long drive to deep centerfield, for which he ran at full speed toward the wall and, looking straight up into the sky for the ball, reached out and caught it as it sailed over his head. The play demoralized the heavily favored Cleveland Indians and the Giants went on to win the series.

Among today's players, **Barry Bonds** (1964-) of the San Francisco Giants (son of the great Bobby Bonds) and **Ken Griffey, Jr.**, (1969-) of the Seattle Mariners, stand out. Bonds is a great all-around player whose team is a perennial contender for the Western Division pennant. Griffey is a slugger who already has twenty more home runs at twenty-five than his father, Ken Griffey, Sr., hit in a nineteen-year career. When the 1994 player's strike was called in August, Griffey was only a few games off **Roger Maris's** 1961 pace and had a chance to break the single-season home run record. The Atlanta Braves's young pitcher, **Greg Maddux**, has won the National League's **Cy Young Award**, given annually to each league's top pitcher, three consecutive times.

Satchel winds up.

Eight Men Out (1988), starring John Cusack. With excellent baseball scenes and solid acting this movie covers all of the details surrounding the Black Sox scandal.

THE BLACK SOX SCANDAL

*Just before the 1919 World Series was to be played between the Cincinnati Reds and heavily-favored Chicago White Sox, White Sox first baseman **Chick Gandil** contacted a well-known gambler named Joseph Sullivan and promised he could get seven other Chicago players to help him throw the world series for $80,000. (In those days players had little power and were generally ill-paid. Corruption was a common if never-reported phenomenon, but it is unlikely that any team had ever thrown a World Series.) Sullivan brought in legendary fixer **Arnold Rothstein** and in the end eight players, including Gandil, pitcher **Eddie Cicotte**, and left fielder "**Shoeless**" Joe Jackson were paid for their part in the conspiracy. A year later the scandal broke and all eight players were banned from baseball for life.*

9. **Who is considered "the father of American football"?**

    (A) Walter Camp
    (B) Clark Shaughnessy
    (C) Knute Rockne
    (D) Jim Thorpe

American **football** developed at Harvard, Yale, and Rutgers in the mid-nineteenth century out of a number of different games similar to **rugby**. Rugby is a contact sport, invented in the early nineteenth century at the Rugby Boys' School in England, in which a team tries to move a ball into a goal area by running with it and "lateraling" it to teammates. In 1880, **Walter Camp** (1859-1925) suggested two rules that moved American football into its modern form: the number of players on each team was lowered to eleven and the offensive team retains possession of the ball after the runner is downed instead of both teams fighting for the ball after every tackle.

The game remained extremely violent. To move the ball, offenses used maneuvers like the bloody and crowd-pleasing **flying wedge**, in which a group of five or six blockers locked arms in front of the ballcarrier and stampeded any defender who strayed into their path. No pads or helmets were worn, and the game was often fatal—thirty-three college players were killed in 1909. The following year passing was legalized, although it was restricted to twenty yards. Offenses were required to have six men on the **line of scrimmage** and a neutral zone was established between the offensive and defensive lines. (Before the neutral zone, teams faced off

THE LAST FIVE SUPER BOWL CHAMPIONS

1995 *San Francisco Forty-Niners*

1994 *Dallas Cowboys*

1993 *Dallas Cowboys*

1992 *Washington Redskins*

1991 *New York Giants*

against each other shoulder to shoulder, much as they do in a rugby **scrum**.) In 1912, after many changes, the present scoring system (three points for a **field goal**, six for a **touchdown**, one or two points for a **conversion**) was adopted.

The **National Football League** was founded by thirteen teams in 1920, but college football remained much more popular. A number of offensive innovations had been made, all based on the **T-formation**, in which the linemen are the crossbeam of the T and the quarterback and running backs are the stem. The T-formation was perfected by Coach Clark Shaughnessy at Stanford in 1940. Shaughnessy split his linemen, forcing the defensive line to spread out, which developed holes in the defense that the backs could run through. Stanford's quarterbacks also began the practice of dropping back from the center to make or fake handoffs. If he faked, the quarterback was in a good position to throw the ball.

In 1960 the **American Football League** set up franchises in a number of cities, threatening the NFL's share of soon-to-be-very-lucrative television rights. The two leagues agreed to merge six years later, but were subject to anti-trust suits from their players associations. **Pete Rozelle** (1926-), the commissioner of the NFL, applied to have the merger exempted from anti-trust action. The exemption was granted by a Congressional vote and the two leagues merged in 1970.

Two of the exemption's chief sponsors were Senate Whip Russell Long, and House Whip Hale Boggs, both from Louisiana. Not long after the exemption was granted, New Orleans received the NFL's very first expansion franchise, the Saints, who began playing in 1967.

10. **Which of these stars popularized professional football in the 1920s?**
    (A) Y.A. Tittle
    (B) Frank Gifford
    (C) Vince Lombardi
    (D) Red Grange

George Gipp (1895-1920) was the star of the football powerhouse Notre Dame, which was undefeated with him at quarterback in 1919 and 1920. He scored at least one winning touchdown, in the final minutes against Indiana, after suffering a dislocated shoulder. Gipp died of pneumonia at the age of twenty-five. The story goes that in 1928, with Notre Dame tied with Army 0-0 at halftime, Coach Knute Rockne told his players that Gipp's deathbed wish was for them to "win just one for the Gipper." Inspired, the Notre Dame players went on to win, twelve to six.

Knute Rockne—All-American (1940), starring Pat O'Brien as Rockne and Ronald Reagan as George Gipp. This is the movie that dramatizes the "one for the Gipper" story. During Reagan's presidency, at least one satirist referred to the United States's attack on Grenada as "one for the Gipper."

Harold "Red" Grange (1903-1991) was already famous as a running back for the University of Illinois Fighting Illini when he signed with the Chicago Bears in 1925 for $100,000. In a game against Michigan, Grange had run for 263 yards and scored four touchdowns in twelve minutes. A tremendous star in his day, Grange was featured in a movie serial called *The Galloping Ghost* (one of his nicknames) and is credited with almost single-handedly popularizing professional football.

Don Hutson (1913-) was a receiver who played eleven years for the Green Bay Packers during the 1930s and 1940s, an era when only twelve games were played in a season (now it's sixteen) and passing was not emphasized. He still managed to set a number of records, the most impressive of which, his ninety-nine career touchdown receptions, was not broken until 1989 (by Steve Largent).

Knute Rockne (1888-1931) played for Notre Dame but was much more famous for his thirteen winning seasons as that team's head coach and his inspiring pep talks. Rockne also developed a number of offensive and defensive techniques such as the "balanced" T-formation, which made it difficult for defenses to see what was coming, and "stunting," in which defensive linemen charge diagonally instead of straight ahead. Rockne was an outstanding public speaker who gave motivational talks to salesmen, wrote three books, and appeared in movie shorts. He died in a plane crash in 1931, at the age of forty-three.

"The Galloping Ghost," Red Grange

North Dallas Forty (1979), starring Nick Nolte. This movie chronicles professional football teams' widespread and reckless use of painkillers to get seriously injured players numb enough to play.

An exultant Vince Lombardi

Vince Lombardi (1913-1970) was offensive coach of the New York Giants and helped them to win four division titles and the 1956 Championship of the National Football League. He took over as head coach of the losing Green Bay Packers in 1959 and coached them to three consecutive NFL championships in 1966-68. They also won the first two **Super Bowl** games in 1967 and 1968. Briefly retired, Lombardi returned to football to revive another losing team, the Washington Redskins, in 1970. They were on their way to a winning record when Lombardi was diagnosed with cancer, which killed him during the season. Lombardi is often (possibly apocryphally) quoted as saying, "Winning isn't everything, it's the only thing." The trophy given to the winner of the **Super Bowl** was renamed in his honor in 1972.

Jim Brown's (1936-) many records, set playing for the Cleveland Browns (among other teams) in the 1950s and 1960s, have been broken, but many still consider him the best running back ever, based on his flawless combination of power and speed. Brown led the NFL in rushing eight times in nine years. After retiring he became an actor and youth counsellor.

O.J. Simpson (1947-), a running back for the Buffalo Bills and San Francisco Forty-niners in the 1970s and 1980s, was not as powerful as Brown, but had moves that have to be seen to be believed. When "the Juice" got loose he had no equal. Simpson was the first player to gain 2,000 yards in one season. After his retirement his fame only increased with his many product endorsements and small acting roles in movies. Simpson's athletic excellence has been overshadowed by his recent murder trial.

Terry Bradshaw (1948-), who quarterbacked the Pittsburgh Steelers to four Super Bowl victories in the 1970s, had great receivers in Lynn Swann and John Stallworth, a tough offensive line, and a superstar running back in Franco Harris. Still, a lot of the credit for those Super Bowl victories should go to him.

Walter Payton (1954-), another Bears runner, missed only one game in thirteen seasons and rushed for 275 yards in one game (a record) on a day when he had the flu. Payton even quarterbacked a game in 1984 when all the Bears's passers were injured. He finished his career with 16,726 yards and 125 touchdowns.

Jerry Rice (1964-), of the San Francisco Forty-niners, has been called the best wide receiver of the last half-century. It only took him eight seasons to best a record (for career touchdown receptions) it took Don Hutson eleven years to set and Steve Largent fourteen years to break. He is sure-handed, fast, and able to pour on an extra burst of speed after catching the ball. Rice also holds the distinction of being the highest-paid non-quarterback in NFL history. It may be that playing with **Joe Montana** (1956-), one of the smartest quarterbacks of all time, made Rice unstoppable rather than just great.

Barry Sanders of the Detroit Lions and Emmitt Smith of the Dallas Cowboys are two of the best runners in the NFL today.

11. **Who invented basketball?**

   (A) Dr. Julius Erving
   (B) Dr. James Naismith
   (C) Marv Albert
   (D) Bill Walton

Hoop Dreams (1994), by Steve James, Frederick Marx, and Peter Gilbert. This stunning documentary follows two teenagers from the Chicago mean streets to college in their separate quests for careers in the NBA.

Basketball was created in 1891 by a Canadian named **Dr. James Naismith** (1861-1939), who worked as a youth instructor at the Springfield, Massachusetts, YMCA. Instructed to find an indoor sport to occupy his young charges during the winter months, Naismith nailed a half-bushel peach basket to the balcony ten feet above the floor at either end of the gymnasium. Two years later, one company marketed a pole that supported a metal ring with a netted bag attached. Until 1913, though, the bags had no holes in them. A chain had to be pulled to let the ball out after every basket.

A few years after the game's inception, a number of teams had been formed and began to play professionally. The courts in those days were enclosed in cages of steel mesh to protect the players from the fans and the fans from the ball. Balls that bounced off the cage were still in play and players learned to use the cage to change direction suddenly. But the metal caused a lot of injuries; the court was regularly covered with blood. One team addressed this problem by replacing the steel mesh with rope netting, but injuries continued to take their toll, many of them attributable to spectators, who liked to jam hatpins and lit cigarettes through the netting to arouse the players.

The National Basketball Association was founded in 1946 from a consolidation of early leagues and might have died an early death if not for the addition of the **twenty-four second rule** in 1954. Teams had been in the habit of passing and dribbling the ball for several minutes at a time without shooting, a practice that led to low-scoring games that were driving fans away. The league reviewed a number of games and surmised that the average time a team took to find an open shot was eighteen or twenty seconds. The league increased that figure to twenty-four seconds to give teams the benefit of the doubt, speeding up the game and granting spectators an extra measure of anxiety, adding yet another buzzer for a clutch-shooting player to beat.

THE LAST FIVE NBA CHAMPIONS

1995 Houston Rockets
1994 Houston Rockets
1993 Chicago Bulls
1992 Chicago Bulls
1991 Chicago Bulls

12. For what shot is Kareem Abdul-Jabbar known?

   (A) The slam dunk
   (B) The sky hook
   (C) The turnaround jumper
   (D) Whisky with a beer chaser

Kareem Abdul-Jabbar (1947-), born Lewis Alcindor, was College Player of the Year twice at **UCLA**. As a center for the Milwaukee Bucks and Los Angeles Lakers, he played on five championship teams. His trademark was the **sky hook**, in which Abdul-Jabbar, sideways to the basket, would shoot the ball over his head one-handed, his arm fully extended. He retired having played twenty seasons, and set scoring records for points (38,387) and field goals (15,837).

Arnold "Red" Auerbach (1917-) became coach and general manager of the **Boston Celtics** in 1950 and led them to nine championships. He retired with more than 1,000 victories, including ninety-nine in playoffs. In 1980 he was voted the greatest coach in NBA history by the Professional Basketball Writers Association.

Wilt Chamberlain (1936-), the 7'1" dominator of the NBA in the 1960s, averaged over fifty points per game during the 1961-62 season, scoring, in one game, 100 points. He also popularized the now-ubiquitous **slam dunk**.

Kareem on the way up

Bob Cousy (1928-) was a Boston Celtic for thirteen seasons during the league's infancy and attracted many new fans to the game. He played on seven championship teams and patented the "blind pass," which he could throw accurately, without looking, over his shoulder or behind his back, deceiving both his opponents and, until they learned to expect it, his teammates. The artistry of his passing and intricacy of his dribbling inspired one sportswriter to nickname him "the Houdini of the Hardwood."

Julius Erving, "Dr. J," (1950-) was the biggest draw in the NBA in the 1970s. He refined the slam dunk, performing it at the end of flying leaps that began near the foul line, presaging spectacular scorers like **Michael Jordan**.

Wilt the Stilt and his nemesis, "E"

In 1980, **Bill Russell** (1934-) was named the greatest player in NBA history, mainly in appreciation of his defensive skills and rebounding ability. The 6'10" center was a Celtic for thirteen seasons, played on eleven championship teams, and was the NBA's most valuable player five times. In 1966, he became the league's first African American coach, leading the Celtics to two more championships in 1968 and 1969.

The Celtics, having gone 29-53 the preceding year, signed **Larry Bird** (1956-) in 1979. That year they had a record of 61-21, and Bird was Rookie of the Year. Over the next eleven seasons, Bird averaged twenty-five points a game and led the Celtics to three championships.

Signed by the Los Angeles Lakers the same year as Bird, **Earvin "Magic" Johnson** (1959-) had a similar effect on his team, and even revitalized the game of his veteran teammate Kareem Abdul-Jabbar. The Lakers won the championship in Johnson's rookie season and went on to win four more titles with Johnson at guard.

An acrobatic inside shooter when he came to the Chicago Bulls in 1984, **Michael Jordan** (1963-) turned himself into a spectacular outside shooter midway through his career, becoming in the process the most famous athlete on the planet. Jordan led (some say carried) the Bulls to three consecutive championships and supplemented his basketball salary twenty-fold with product endorsements. He retired at the peak of his career to try his hand at professional baseball. Baseball proved more difficult to master than Jordan had thought, and he returned to the Bulls at the end of the 1994-95 season.

13. **What two hockey players were teammates on the Boston Bruins for many years?**
    (A) Gordie Howe and Bobby Hull
    (B) Mike Bossy and Guy Lefleur
    (C) Bobby Orr and Phil Esposito
    (D) Mark Messier and Wayne Gretzsky

Ice Hockey was supposedly first played by British troops in Ontario in 1855, although they used field hockey sticks with curled ends and a solid rubber ball. Some sources say they had brought the sport from England; others allege that it developed from shinny (p. 432) , played by North American Indian tribes for centuries. The first formal rules for hockey were written in 1879 by McGill University students. These called for nine players on each side and allowed for neither forward passing nor "body checking," clearly absurd restrictions. During the 1880s the stick's blade was modified for better ball-handling on the ice and the ball itself was changed to a puck, reportedly during a few minutes one day, using a pocket knife.

As was always the case with developing sports in the nineteenth century, the taint of "professionalism" threatened to break up the organized leagues that were forming. In 1917, the **National Hockey League** replaced the National Hockey Association and, in 1927, the NHL was split into two divisions, the American and the Canadian. (Now there are four divisions: the Atlantic, Northeast, Central, and Pacific.) Today, hockey is the least popular of the major professional sports played in America, a fact largely due to the difficulty of keeping track of the puck on television and the lack of national media coverage (p. 531) that baseball, basketball, and football enjoy.

Gordie Howe (1928-) was an outstanding stick handler with a strong shot who won the league's scoring title six times and was the most valuable player in the NHL six times in the 1950s and 1960s. He played for the Detroit Red Wings, the World Hockey Association's Houston Aeros, and the Hartford Whalers, retiring from professional hockey for good at the age of fifty-two.

THE LAST FIVE STANLEY CUP CHAMPIONS

1995 *New Jersey Devils*
1994 *New York Rangers*
1993 *Montreal Canadiens*
1992 *Pittsburgh Penguins*
1991 *Pittsburgh Penguins*

FATHER AND SON

Thirty-one-year-old Brett Hull, Bobby Hull's son, has been a right wing in the NHL since 1985, most recently for the St. Louis Blues. He has led the league in goals three times.

Bobby Hull (1939-) was the league's leading scorer three times and MVP twice for the Chicago Black Hawks and the Winnipeg Jets.

Bobby Orr (1948-) is thought by many fans and sportswriters to be the best player of all time. Joining the Boston Bruins at the age of eighteen, Orr was Rookie of the Year and later the only defenseman ever to lead the NHL in scoring, which he did twice. He averaged 1.393 points (goals or assists) per game over his career.

Wayne Gretzky (1961-) signed with the Edmonton Oilers at age

Bobby Orr takes a champagne shower.

eighteen and became as dominant a force in hockey as Michael Jordan has been in basketball. He was the NHL's Most Valuable Player nine times, broke every scoring record possible, and led the Oilers to four Stanley Cup championships. A national hero and omnipresent celebrity in Canada, Gretzky broke the hearts of millions of his countrymen in 1988 when he allowed himself to be traded to the Los Angeles Kings, where he now plays.

14. **Where was tennis invented?**
    (A) England
    (B) France
    (C) Spain
    (D) Portugal

Tennis originated in twelfth-century France as *jeu de paume*, in which players slapped the ball over the net with the palms of their hands. A modern version of the game called *sphairistike*—Greek for "playing ball"—was developed and patented in Wales four centuries later by **Major W.C. Wingfield**. His court was hourglass-shaped, narrower at the net than at the baselines, and the net was five feet high. The game spread to England where it was revised and became lawn tennis. The first tennis championship was played at **Wimbledon** in 1877.

An American sportswoman, **Mary Ewing Outerbridge**, imported the game to the United States in 1874. The first **Davis Cup**, a competition between teams from different countries, was played in 1900. The sport grew considerably during the 1920s, producing its first celebrities. The proliferation of sponsored events, younger, more famous players, and television coverage in the 1960s made tennis a mainstream recreational and competitive sport.

15. **Which company was the major sponsor of the women's tennis tour from 1995?**

    (A) Tampax
    (B) Chevrolet
    (C) Virginia Slims
    (D) Nike

"Big Bill" Tilden (1893-1953) became the first American man to win the singles title at Wimbledon in 1920, at the age of twenty-seven, and also won the United States title seven times. He was temperamental, and tended to glare at the official when he disagreed with a call, even if the call was in his favor. Often, after he finished glaring, Tilden would deliberately blow the next point. He became a professional in 1931, but his tours didn't consistently make money, partly due to the Depression (p. 87), partly to the fact that Tilden's opponents didn't present much of a challenge. Tilden is among the athletes, like boxer Jack Dempsey, the racehorse Man O'War, and the New York Yankees, bound in the public memory to the 1920s, the so-called Golden Era of Sports.

Helen Wills (1906-), a steady baseline player who rarely made an unforced error, dominated women's tennis in the 1920s. She won eight singles titles at Wimbledon from 1927 until 1938.

Maureen Connolly (1934-1969) was small (five feet, four inches, 130 pounds) but powerful and a precise shotmaker. In 1953, at age nineteen, she was the first woman to win the **Grand Slam** (the Australian, English, French, and United States titles). She retired the following year after a

Monica Seles (1973-), an immigrant to the United States from the former Yugoslav republic, won the French, Australian, and U.S. Opens in both 1991 and 1992. Seles also prevented Steffi Graf from breaking Martina Navratilova's record of seventy-four consecutive match wins in 1990. Seles was only nineteen years old when she was attacked by a deranged fan at the Citizen Cup Tournament in Hamburg, Germany on April 30, 1993. Gunter Parche, a forty-year-old German said to idolize Steffi Graf, stabbed Seles in the back of the neck with a nine-inch boning knife. Seles didn't return to competitive tennis until the summer of 1995, more than two years after the stabbing.

Virginia Slims has relinquished sponsorship of its tournament twice, first to Avon in 1978, after a dispute with the Women's Tennis Association over the structure of the circuit. Virginia Slims returned to sponsoring the tour in 1983 but was pressured to give it up again (this time to Kraft General Foods) in 1991, after years of controversy over the seeming contradiction inherent in allowing a tobacco company to publicize its product through the sanitizing filter of a youth-oriented professional sport.

Billie Jean King rules the court.

horseback riding accident in which she badly broke her leg. Thereafter she devoted herself to the support of young athletes. She died of cancer at the age of thirty-four.

Billie Jean King (1943-) transformed the image of female tennis players with vigorous, aggressive play. She also won more Wimbledon championships than any player ever, with a total of twenty (six singles, ten doubles, and four mixed doubles). King beat self-confessed male chauvinist **Bobby Riggs** in straight sets in a publicity match billed "The Battle of the Sexes" in 1973, but her more lasting achievements were her co-founding of the **Women's Tennis Association** (WTA) and the Virginia Slims Tournament Circuit. She was instrumental in the struggle to acquire equal prize money for female tennis players.

The most successful professional tennis stars of the 1970s and 1980s were Jimmy Connors, Bjorn Borg, John McEnroe, Ivan Lendl, Chris Evert Lloyd, and Martina Navratilova. More recently, tennis has come to be dominated by Boris Becker, Andre Agassi, Pete Sampras, Jim Courier, Steffi Graf, Arantxa Sanchez-Vicario, and Monica Seles.

16. **Who won the 1994 World Cup?**

    (A) United States
    (B) England
    (C) Colombia
    (D) Brazil

Soccer had several precursors. A soccer-like game called *tsu-ch'iu* was played in China 2,500 years ago. The Greeks' *hapraston* was adopted by the Romans, who spread it throughout their empire. The English street pastime of the Middle Ages was formalized by the Football Association, which established rules in 1863. Referred to as Association Football and then Association, the name was shortened to "assoc," which became soccer, a term that is only used in North America. The most popular game in the world is known as **football** everywhere else.

In the summer of 1994, the **World Cup**, soccer's championship tournament held every four years, was hosted by the United States for the first time. Two-and-a-half years earlier 143 nations had signed up to compete in the qualifying rounds, which took 491 matches to whittle the field down to two dozen teams. They played fifty-two games in nine American cities. **The Brazilian** team emerged triumphant, taking home its fourth World Cup, a record.

Although fourteen million American kids play soccer at various levels, the professional sport has never caught on here. A Harris poll taken in 1994 indicated that only 25 percent of the adults polled knew what sport the World Cup involved.

THE LAST FIVE WORLD CUP CHAMPIONS

1994 *Brazil*

1990 *West Germany*

1986 *Argentina*

1982 *Italy*

1978 *Argentina*

As a child, Pele practiced with grapefruits because his family couldn't afford a soccer ball.

 The North American Soccer League was formed in 1968 and popularity spread throughout the 1970s, when international superstar, **Pele**, the only soccer star widely known in the United States, played for the New York Cosmos. In 1979, stadium attendance and television ratings began to decline. The league folded after the 1984 season.

Unhappily, violent behavior has long been associated with soccer fans, particularly in Britain and Latin America, with stadium riots frequently in the news. In an unusual twist on such incidents, after the 1994 World Cup tournament a Colombian player, who had ruined his team's chances by kicking the ball into the wrong goal during a match with the U.S., returned to his country and was in a nightclub parking lot one evening when he was murdered by four gunmen. They shot him several times, yelling "Goal! Goal! Goal!"

The Brazilian World Cup soccer team after defeating Italy

17. What sport does Ernest Hemingway's *Death in the Afternoon* concern?

(A) Big game hunting
(B) Deep sea fishing
(C) Bullfighting
(D) *Pok-ta-pok*

The attitude of the fans at a Spanish or Mexican **bullfight** is often compared to that of the spectators at the Roman circuses, a comparison that is something of a stretch. After all, aficionados of the *fiesta de toros* are delighting in the slaughter of several large, brutish animals (six in a typical *corrida*) whereas the Romans flocked to the ampitheaters in the cheerful knowledge that they would witness the deliberate murder of fellow human beings. Still, critics accuse bullfight fans of secretly (or not so secretly) hoping that the matador will make some stupidly valorous gesture that will lead to a goring. Cowardice in the ring is treated harshly, with the

UH . . . RIGHT

"It is impossible to imagine that people could leave a good corrida de toros *with an inclination for political rallies or social disturbances; they have unburdened themselves, they have shouted, they have laughed, they come away happy!"*

——*Father Pareda*

Matador Manolete in the ring

throwing of trash, including bottles. In *Death in the Afternoon*, Ernest Hemingway (p. 286) condones the tyranny of the crowd, saying that throwing trash is all right, as long as the bottles are not aimed at the matador's head. Many matadors have confessed to fearing the wrath of the maniacal fans more than they do the charge of the bull, and some historians insist that the crowd's goading has indeed caused the deaths of a number of matadors, including Joselito, Manolete, and Paquirri.

18. **Which of these boxers was a Heavyweight Champion of the World?**

    (A) Jack Dempsey
    (B) Henry Armstrong
    (C) Jake La Motta
    (D) Rocky Graziano

Boxing, as noted earlier, dates back even before ancient Greece, but the modern sport developed in England, where bare-knuckled prize fighting was popular in the eighteenth century. The first American heavyweight champion was **John L. Sullivan** (1858-1918), whose reign spanned

The World Boxing Organization, World Boxing Council, and International Boxing Federation all hold title bouts and crown (or belt) champions. At certain times in boxing history, there have been three champions in each weight class.

both the end of the bare-knuckle days and the first years after the adoption of the **Marquis of Queensberry Rules**, which provided for gloves (to protect the knuckles, not the face) and the presence of a referee.

In December, 1984, the American Medical Association passed a resolution calling for the abolition of boxing, citing the fact that it is alone among dangerous sports in that the chief object of it is to cause bodily harm. From 1945 to 1985, at least 370 boxers died from injuries sustained in the ring. (In fact, boxing was somewhat safer before the gloves were adopted, as a man's fists will break sooner than his face will.) But most young boxers insist that they are safer in the ring than on the street, and even champions seem to get addicted to the adrenalin rush they experience before and during a fight. And perhaps surprisingly, boxing has become a favorite sport of intellectuals like Norman Mailer and Joyce Carol Oates, who are intrigued by the sport's combination of danger, beauty, instinct, and finesse.

19. **Who was the first black heavyweight champion?**

   (A) Joe Louis
   (B) Sugar Ray Robinson
   (C) Cassius Clay
   (D) Jack Johnson

BOXING WEIGHT CLASSES

Heavyweight—no limit

Cruiserweight—max. 195 lbs

Light Heavyweight—max. 175 lbs

Middleweight—max. 160 lbs

Junior Middleweight—max. 154 lbs

Welterweight—max. 147 lbs

Junior Welterweight—max. 140 lbs

Lightweight—max. 135 lbs

Junior Lightweight—max. 130 lbs

Featherweight—max. 126 lbs

Junior Featherweight—max. 122 lbs

Bantamweight—max. 118 lbs

Flyweight—max. 112 lbs

The Manassa Mauler

Henry Armstrong (1912-1988) was the only boxer to hold championship titles in three weight classes at the same time. He was champion as a featherweight, a welterweight, and a lightweight. Heavyweight **Jack Dempsey** (1895-1983), **"the Manassa Mauler,"** was one of the pre-eminent sports heroes of the 1920s. He drew the first million-dollar gate, fought in front of crowds of 100,000 people, and in retirement became a low-key, beloved restauranteur. Having learned his art in unrefereed bouts in western saloons at the age of sixteen, Dempsey was a savage and not very clean fighter. He was notorious for standing over his fallen opponent and slugging him as he attempted to rise, even when the "neutral corner" rule was in effect. He also refused to fight the best black heavyweights of his day, despite the urging of sportswriters and boxing enthusiasts.

Jack Johnson (1878-1946) was the first black heavyweight champion, a title he won from Tommy Burns, whom he had to chase to Australia before Burns would fight him.

Jake LaMotta (1921-) was a fierce, fearless brawler who was middleweight champion for a couple of years (1949-1951). He was a childhood friend and partner in juvenile delinquency of another middleweight champion, **Rocky Graziano** (1919-1990). Both men wrote autobiographies that were made into movies—*Raging Bull* and *Somebody Up There Likes Me*, respectively.

Raging Bull (1980), directed by Martin Scorsese and starring Robert De Niro. This is a brilliant film, and De Niro wins a much-deserved Oscar for his part. You should know, though, that Scorsese skips LaMotta's teenage years and doesn't explain one of the reasons for the guilt that drove him to take so much punishment in the ring. LaMotta believed for eleven years that he had once killed a man during a robbery. Once he found out that the man had lived, his interest in boxing waned.

Joe Louis (1914-1981), the second black heavyweight champion, was a fighter groomed by his black managers to be acceptable, unlike Johnson, to white fans. The rules were that Louis was never to exult in victory, enter a nightclub alone, or be seen in the company of a white woman. He held the title longer than any other fighter: twelve years, from 1937 to 1949. As with all

Joe Louis dispatches an opponent.

champions many of Louis's defenses were achieved against nobodies—his famous "Bum of the Month" tours. Fighting past his prime to earn money to allay income tax debts, he was unseated by Ezzard Charles and beaten in a comeback attempt by **Rocky Marciano** (1923-1969).

Muhammad Ali (1942-), born **Cassius Clay**, was an Olympic gold medalist at the 1960 games and the first defiantly black heavyweight champ since Jack Johnson. Known for his provocative pre-fight boasting and impromptu doggerel, Ali won the championship from **Sonny Liston** (1917-1970) in 1964. Three years later the World Boxing Association (later

The Pugilist at Rest, by Thom Jones. This is a grim and compelling account of an ex-Marine boxer afflicted with epilepsy and regret.

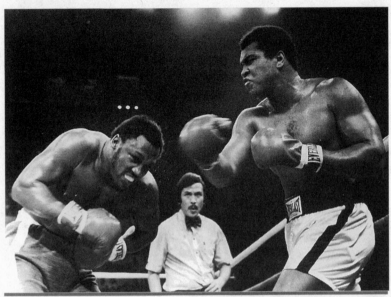

Ali pummels Joe Frazier as Sonny Bono referees.

AND THE WINNER IS . . .

Rocky Marciano (1923-1969) was the only heavyweight champion to retire undefeated.

called the World Boxing Organization) revoked his title and the New York Athletic Association rescinded his license when Ali refused to be drafted for the Vietnam War (p. 659). He did not box again professionally until 1970, and many observers thought that the lay-off cost him some speed. The young Ali had been so fast that opponents found it almost impossible to hit him, but Ali in the early 1970s developed a new style (**"rope-a-dope"**) in which he stood against the ropes with his gloves in front of his face and took an enormous amount of punishment with his body until his opponent wore himself out. Ali was named Fighter of the Year in 1974, lost and regained his title in 1978, retired, made a comeback, and quit for good in 1981. In recent years, Ali's speech and reactions have been slowed by Parkinson's disease, but the stature he acquired as a symbol of racial pride during the civil rights movement (p. 197) and his principled stand against the divisive Vietnam War have not been diminished.

20. **Who was a major star of professional golf in the 1920s?**
    (A) Sam Snead
    (B) Arnold Palmer
    (C) Lee Trevino
    (D) Walter Hagen

Historically among the most class-bound of all sports, golf was invented in Scotland and imported to the United States, where there were over 1,000 clubs by 1900. Professionals at the time were usually Scotsmen who repaired equipment for club members and were generally looked down upon. This state of affairs persisted even after 1913, the year a twenty-year-old former caddy named **Francis Ouimet** beat a famous English professional and made golf desirable to large numbers of middle-class people. **Walter Hagen** was the professional who broke the class barriers at country clubs where tournaments were played in the 1920s. A hard-drinking, irreverent friend of the Prince of Wales, Hagan simply ignored the rules that said professionals had to come and go by service entrances, and before long the rules went unobserved at tournaments everywhere.

After the Depression forced many courses to close, golf enjoyed a second boom in the years of postwar prosperity. Public courses and fee-for-a-day courses became common across the country. However, the game has never lost its perceived connection to the largely discriminatory country club circuit.

21. In which country did chess originate?

    (A) England
    (B) France
    (C) India
    (D) Syria

While some board games like **backgammon** may be older, and others, like **Monopoly** somewhat more evocative of modern life, **chess** is still the most popular strategic board game in the world. An early forerunner of it, *chaturanga*, made its first appearance in India in the sixth century A.D. It spread throughout Asia and was introduced to Europe by Muslim traders (Moors in Spain, Saracens in Italy) around A.D. 700. By the sixteenth century, the modern rules had been adopted, the first manuals had been published, and knowledge of chess had become a sign of nobility. Masters traveled around Europe taking on all comers for fun and profit. It was not uncommon for wealthy noblemen to patronize chess talent.

Today, tournaments are organized by **FIDE**, an international chess-promoting body that also ranks players by a scoring system both exacting and vague, as "masters" and "grandmasters." The youngest grandmaster of all-time was **Bobby Fischer** (1943-), an American who

Fischer busts a move.

Millions of people now play chess against their computers but the earliest "chess playing machine" was invented in 1769 by Baron Wolfgang von Kempelen. Called "The Turk," it was named after the lifesize, grinning, metal figure that stood over a chessboard mounted on a cabinet. Challengers "played against" the figure, whose moves were actually made by a small man hiding in the cabinet with powerful magnets.

Two sixteenth-century chess masters earned murderous envy by winning. Giovanni Leonardo di Bona and Paolo Boi both won a great deal of money, and each was killed by means of poison.

became a grandmaster at fifteen in 1958. Fourteen years later he beat **Boris Spassky** (1937-) in the most famous match of all-time, ending twenty-five years of Soviet dominance. Fischer retired in 1975 without defending his title, but in 1994 he came out of retirement to play a single, million-dollar match against Spassky. Fischer won again.

Some chess books still use descriptive notation to describe moves ("Queen's rook to Queen's rook six [QR-QR6]), but many have adopted **algebraic notation**, in which the horizontal ranks of the chess board are numbered one through eight (bottom to top—white lining up on ranks one and two; black lining up on ranks eight and seven) and the vertical rows are lettered a through h, so that each square on the board has its own designation, no matter which color is moving. Beginners may find all chess books baffling, however, as the books tend to skip language-based explanation of strategy and leap right into notation. The best way to improve your game is by playing a superior player or a computer.

22. The governing body of tournament billiards is the

   (A) Tournament Billiards Association
   (B) Straight Pool League
   (C) Pocket Billiards Association
   (D) Billiard Congress of America

Pool is the popular name for American pocket billiards, a game that developed from carom billiards and snooker during the nineteenth century. Becoming adept at pool is one of the most enjoyable ways to win friends, money, and beer. But, since hanging around pool halls to learn the game is not as atmospheric or inexpensive as it used to be, and barroom tables are notoriously tiny and beat-up, it's best to hunt down a friend's rec room with a regulation-size (9' long x 4.5' wide x 29" high) table and undamaged cuesticks.

In **straight pool**, two players compete to be the first to reach an agreed-upon number of points, usually 150, with each ball, called and pocketed, worth one point. In **eight ball**, two players or pairs compete to be the first to pocket all of the solid-colored balls, or all of the striped balls, followed by the eight ball. If the eight ball is sunk before a player's solids or stripes are sunk, that player loses. In **nine ball**, the balls numbered one through nine are racked in a diamond shape and two players compete to be the first to pocket the nine ball, which they can only do after pocketing the other balls in order first. Sometimes this game can be won early by using a low object ball in combination with the nine ball.

The name "pool" developed into a synonym for "pocket billiards" in the 1840s. At the time, bettors gathered in billiard parlors to place bets on horse races, and all bets were combined into a pool to pay those who bet on the winning horse. The billiard parlors came to be referred to as "pool halls" and the game as "pool."

23. An early form of bowling was called

(A) snooker
(B) skittles
(C) alley
(D) ten pins

Bowling's early incarnations were the English pub game **"skittles"** and the Dutch game "nine pins," which in turn were derived from a German religious ceremony in which a parishioner proved his faith by rolling a stone down the aisle of the church to knock over a club called "the heathen." The game had a sordid reputation until the 1890s, when it moved out of the taverns and billiard halls into its own spaces and women got involved. The **American Bowling Congress** was formed in 1895 and peaked in 1979 at almost five million members. It has since experienced a slight decline. (The amateur leagues formed under its auspices, however, continue to feed a vital tributary into the fickle current of American fashion: the gaudy and glorious Bowling Shirt.)

The photographer is still in critical condition.

The **Professional Bowlers' Tour** debuted in 1958 and has come to sponsor several tournaments, each worth around $200,000 in prize money. The Ladies Professional Bowlers Tour offers comparatively puny purses due to a lack of television coverage. Bowling is not too exciting to watch on television, anyway, in part because the pros refuse to wear interesting shirts.

24. Gambling was _____ in Native American societies before Europeans arrived.

(A) unknown
(B) forbidden
(C) somewhat common
(D) universal

There is famous story of two men in medieval China who bet each other their ears on which side a falling leaf would come to rest. Serious

Both Harvard and Yale were constructed in part with the proceeds from lotteries.

gamblers have even been known to bet outrageous sums of money on which raindrop would reach the bottom of a window pane first. **Gambling** may be one of the most "animalistic" of urges, in that the same adrenaline rush that a rabbit gets running across the road in front of a speeding car can be experienced by a human being without physical exertion, simply by betting more than she can afford to lose on the outcome of a football game or the spin of a roulette wheel.

North American tribes bet on games of lacrosse and shinny for centuries before Europeans settled here. Participants in the games as well as spectators laid clothing, jewelry, and weapons on two piles indicating which team they thought would prevail. Winners got their wager back with something of equal value from the other team's pile. The Aztecs, who were moralistic about sex and alcohol, still embraced gambling, both on the *tlachtli* contests and in games of dice.

Casino gambling was prevalent in London in the eighteenth century and cropped up again on about 500 river boats that trolled the Mississippi in the 1850s. But it really came into its own in the next decade, when Charles III of France annexed Monaco and turned the casino **Monte Carlo** over to Francois Blanc. A financial genius who had served a prison sentence for stock fraud but had somehow managed to retain 100,000 francs of his profits, Blanc turned Monte Carlo into the premier gambling house on the continent. The place catered to the crowned heads of Europe, the

Vegas basks in its own glow.

Aga Khan, and American millionaires like W.K. Vanderbilt and J.P. Morgan. After the 1920s, Monte Carlo lost its luster, although it got a slight boost in publicity when Monaco's Prince Rainier married Hollywood actress Grace Kelly.

Gambling was legalized in Nevada in 1931, but wasn't exploited there until 1947 by the gangster **Bugsy Siegel** (1906-1947), who went over budget on his construction of the **Flamingo Hotel** and was murdered by his associates before he could real-

Dapper casino owner and felon Bugsy Siegel

ize his dream. In less than fifty years, Las Vegas has become synonymous with gambling. New Jersey legalized casino gambling in 1978. Advocates promised that the casinos's profits would rejuvenate the rundown **Atlantic City** community surrounding the boardwalk, but while the profits have been huge, the community remains rundown. Today, most casinos have **blackjack** tables, **roulette** wheels, **craps**, **baccarat**, **keno**, and **slot machines**. Some have private rooms for games of **poker**. Few have clocks, windows, or any other reminders of the outside world, and a gambler can usually drink for free as long as he's at the tables.

Horse racing has been popular in the United States since the late eighteenth century. The most famous races in the U.S. consist of three-year-old thoroughbred horses bidding for the elusive **Triple Crown**,

The Gambler, by Fyodor Dostoevsky. Dostoevsky was a compulsive gambler who claimed to have once had an orgasm at the moment he lost a huge amount of money at roulette.

FROM THE HORSE'S MOUTH

Dam: *horse's mother*

Sire: *horse's father*

Gelding: *castrated horse*

The Call: *description of the race to the audience through a public address system*

Oatburner: *a chronic loser*

A Horse is a Horse

All modern racehorses are thoroughbred descendants of three stallions: the Beyerly Turk, the Darley Arabian, and the Godolphin Arabian.

which is obtained by winning the Kentucky Derby, the Preakness, and the Belmont Stakes. The last time this was accomplished was in 1978 by Affirmed. Secretariat and Seattle Slew were also Triple Crown winners in the seventies. A majority of the races run in the U.S. are sprints (less than a mile) with the most popular distance being six furlongs (1 furlong = 220 yards). Thoroughbred racing definitely qualifies as a sport, but not too many people enjoy the horses for long without placing bets. You can put money "on the nose" (money on the horse to win) or place an "exotic" wager such as an exacta (picking, in order, the position of the first two horses) or trifecta (picking 1, 2, 3).

ANSWERS

1. D	2. C	3. A	4. C	5. B	6. B	7. B	8. A	9. A	10. D
11. B	12. B	13. C	14. B	15. C	16. D	17. C	18. A	19. D	20. D
21. C	22. C	23. B	24. C						

Religion

It's not always clear what separates the religious from the political, social, or economic. Divergent as they are, the world's religions do have some things in common: they reach from the natural to the supernatural, and they deal with whatever is of ultimate or supreme concern to individuals or groups. Religion has a complicated legacy: it has been the source of an incredible amount of oppression and bloodshed as well as a wellspring of joy and community.

1. Which type of myth seeks to explain the beginning of existence?

    (A) Initiation myth
    (B) Sun myth
    (C) Creation myth
    (D) Death myth

The Power of Myth (1988), by Joseph Campbell, with Bill Moyers. This book presents an interesting cross-cultural analysis of the world's myths and religions.

The Navajo view creation as having evolved through the four worlds, in each of which humans and animals co-exist. Changing Woman, born of First Man and First Woman, appears in the fourth world, which is the one we are in now. The sun impregnates Changing Woman and she gives birth to twin sons: Child Born of Water and Monster Slayer, who create the good (the sun, the moon) and the evil (flies and monsters), respectively. The world emerges from the conflict between good and evil forces.

The sacred histories of the world's religions share the desire to explain the beginning of time and human existence. Who or what created the world? How did we get here? How did good and evil come to coexist? Narratives of the creation of the universe connect humans to their environment and to the divine. The expulsion of Adam and Eve from the Garden of Eden is a familiar version of a typical **creation myth**. Native American **Earth Diver** tales tell of a being that emerges from the water or the inner world and discovers and gives life to the earth. Among the Gikuya of Kenya, a tree grows during dark thunderstorms until it reaches light; beneath this tree of life the creator places Gikuya and Mumbi, the first human couple.

Creation myths also define the beginning of time. Before the creation of humans no consciousness existed to mark time. Some primal peoples viewed time as, paradoxically, atemporal. The Australian Aborigines, for example, use the term "the Dreaming" to refer to the "everywhen," the collapse of distinction between past, present, and future—the infinite now. Among some Native American nations, the power attributed to words allows the reenactment of creation as the teller tells the story. Time disappears as the teller breathes life into the beginning. For many Asian traditions, such as Hinduism, Buddhism, and Taoism, time is cyclical. Birth, death, and rebirth form the circle of life. Among the Western faiths—Judaism, Christianity, and Islam—time moves in a linear fashion, and the future and salvation are of utmost importance.

2. **The primitive kinship between an individual or group and an animal, plant, or natural object is known as**

   (A) animism
   (B) fetishism
   (C) shamanism
   (D) totemism

The Gods Must Be Crazy (1981), directed by Jamie Uys. The biggest foreign box office hit in history, this film is a wonderful slapstick comedy about the clash of European and native African cultures.

The term **animism** refers to the belief that inanimate objects have souls. Many tribal peoples do not make strong distinctions between humans, animals, vegetation, and objects. Life, many groups believe, goes beyond the flesh. The Navajo say that the outlines of the Macaw people's faces can be seen on rocks, and these images of the "rock people" indicate living spirits within. The **totem** serves as an emblem for the family clan or tribe and embodies the life force of the species. Tribal peoples believe the totem's vitality transfers to the health of their own clan. In exchange for the totem's protection, the clan promises not to harm the totem.

In addition, it provides a social system from which each family member gains an identity as well as a bond with the natural environment. The North American Ojibway, for example, created carvings—the **totem pole**—to represent their clan relationships. When representing ancestral lineage, the totem serves as an intercessor to the Other World. Ancestors might be present anywhere in the natural world. The Australian Aborigines believe their original ancestors emerged through the plains and left their spirits in water holes and caves.

Some tribal peoples believe spirits can be called on with the use of a **fetish**, or magical charm. Its powers are usually specific: a good hunt or successful trading, for example. For good fortune, the African Ba Teke placed an elder's hairs along with white chalk (a symbol of the bones of ancestors) in the belly of a carving. The **shaman**, a priest or medicine man, is endowed with the power to guide the souls of the dead, heal diseases, and mediate between good and evil spirits. Trances, altered states, possessions, cleansings, healings, and sometimes, sleight-of-hand tricks characterize shaman ceremonies.

ANCESTOR WORSHIP

Food offerings placed upon ancestral graves ensured safe passage to the Other World and expressed the hope that the dead would not trouble the living. The King of the Ashanti in Ghana possessed the "Golden Stool" or royal drum that embodied the spirit of the ancestors. Offerings were laid upon the stool. The revered and personified "Golden Stool" has its own umbrella and attendants. The Ugandan Ankole drum has its own wives.

3. **The Aztecs' preferred style for sacrificing humans to the gods was**
   (A) drowning children in sixty-foot-deep wells
   (B) tearing out their hearts with a stone dagger
   (C) boiling them in large vats of oil
   (D) stoning them at frenzied religious festivals

I left my heart in Mesoamerica.

At the core of the violent practices of some indigenous peoples of the Americas was the ideology that the universe needed balance. Fearing the impending violent end of the world, the Aztecs fed the sun human blood to keep it alive. The heart of the sacrificed person was the most precious offering to the gods. In the Great Temple, the priest stretched the victim across the sacrificial stone, then tore out his heart with a stone dagger. After the sacrifice the priest usually cast the body down the temple's stairs. According to tradition, the legs and arms of sacrificed enemies could be eaten afterward.

 The Golden Bough (1963), by Sir James Frazer. This must-read classic about magic and realism describes our ancestors' methods of worship, sex practices, strange rituals, and festivals.

Memory of Fire (1985), by Eduardo Galeano. This trilogy ("Genesis," "Faces and Masks," and "Century of the Wind") explores the history of the Americas in beautiful, prose poems filled with passion and anger.

CORTES AND MONTEZUMA

*In 1519 on the shores of Mexico, Spaniard Hernando Cortes emerged from a floating island (a ship) dressed in iron and followed by strange four-legged beasts (horses). According to Cortes, the Aztecs mistook him for the god **Quetzalcoatl**, the feathered serpent, a god of the air and earth who abhorred war and had promised to return after his death three hundred years earlier. Montezuma, ruler of the Aztecs, offered helmets full of gold to the risen god. Cortes accepted, then imprisoned Montezuma. The conquistadors razed the temples of the Aztecs and murdered their rulers.*

Every man on earth carries with him some conviction; but it is for a brief period only that flowers of happiness pass before our eyes

——AZTEC POEM

Religion pervaded almost every aspect of Mesoamerican life. Everyone from chiefs to slaves participated in the war, music, dance, ritual sacrifice, and games performed for the gods. The Aztecs constructed spectacular temples and pyramids (p. 34) dedicated to numerous deities, particularly those connected with war and agriculture. The concept of space and time play an integral role in the creation of these temples; the sloping stairs often mark the ascent and descent of the sun. The Aztecs believed the universe evolved through periods of successive suns. To prevent cataclysmic catastrophes when the suns changed over, cosmic order had to be maintained. Because **Huitzilopochtli**, the god of war, protected the Fifth Sun, the Aztecs determined that they had to take care of earthly matters during the fifth cosmic age. In order to harmonize the universe they needed to gather all others under their power; therefore, their urge to conquer was religious in nature.

4. **Whose poems have been called "the Bible of the Greeks"?**
   - (A) Hesiod
   - (B) Homer
   - (C) Sophocles
   - (D) Euripedes

The ancient Greeks left us no authoritative works of religious dogma. The story of the **pantheon** of Greek deities, however, unfolds in the two great Homeric epics, *The Iliad* and *The Odyssey* (p. 247), often called "the Bible of the Greeks." In these poems, the ruler of the gods and the universe, **Zeus**, lives on **Mount Olympus**. He and the other gods aid and interfere in Greek lives. These Olympian gods differ from many other deities in that they embody human qualities—losing self-control, for example, is one of their weaknesses. **Euhemerism**, named for

MORE PURE

The pursuit and practice of purification played a big role in ancient Greek religious life. Greek temples were often restricted to priests or veiled priestesses. Offending material objects did not escape purification. Once, after a formal sacrifice during the festival of Zeus, the ax used by the priest was tried, condemned, and hurled into the sea. On another occasion a rope and tree were banished after a suicide hanging.

the Greek mythographer Euhemerus, refers to the view that the gods are glorified humans who sustain their immortality by eating ambrosia and drinking nectar from their private stock. However, a strong belief in *moira*, or destiny, prevented the deities from having total control over the Greeks' lives. **Hesiod** attempted to find an order for the myriad Greek myths in his book *Theogeny*. In addition, he explained that the origins of the universe arise from four spirits: *Chaos* (Space), *Gaea* (Earth), *Tartarus* (Abyss), and *Eros* (Love).

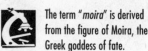 The term "*moira*" is derived from the figure of Moira, the Greek goddess of fate.

5. Which Greek philosopher viewed God as the Unmoved Mover?

   (A) Socrates
   (B) Plato
   (C) Aristotle
   (D) Plotinus

By the sixth century B.C., Greek philosophers began to challenge the belief that the universe originated from the Olympian gods. While they believed in the gods, they felt the myths were not adequate for understanding the origins of the material world. In their search for tangible explanations they turned first to their **four elements**—earth, air, fire, and water. The idea of the One, beyond thought and comprehension, then began to develop.

DON'T BELIEVE YOUR EYES

*The famous allegory of **Plato's Cave**, from the Republic (p. 385), goes like this: imagine being raised in a cave lit only by a flickering fire. Chained and unable to turn around, you see shadows dancing on the wall. The shadows are your reality, but this reality is only a pale copy of the original. This is the nature of human existence. The real world, what Plato calls the **World of Forms**, is the Ultimate Reality; everything there exists in an ideal version unperceivable by the human senses. Only the mind can comprehend the Ultimate Reality.*

The philosopher **Socrates** (470 - 399 B.C.) taught that reasoning revealed truth. His motto "know thyself," adopted from the Temple of Apollo, suggested that it was crucial to meditate upon human qualities

Socrates

first: contemplate "goodness" and "goodness" will result. Although he expressed belief in the gods, sometimes Socrates' rationalist approach mocked them, angering the Athenian elders. Socrates' student Plato (p. 385) who recorded his teacher's philosophy after Socrates was put to death, wrote that contemplation could lead to the discovery of abstract perfection. For Plato, thought led to transcendence of the material world. This **World of Matter** is a mere shadow, a cheap imitation of perfection. The blueprint for this world lies in the Other World, the **World of Forms** (the state of Being), where there is perfect piety, perfect justice, and perfect beauty. The World of Forms, according to Plato, is reality and therefore immortal and unchanging. The World of Matter, which we perceive through our bodily senses, is mortal and mutable.

We are so much at the mercy of Chance that Chance is our God.

—PLINY THE ELDER

Aristotle (384 - 322 B.C.), Plato's student, rejected Plato's theory of Forms and instead turned his attention to dissecting the material world as it exists. Justice, he said, is neither an idea or a "good" but a real operating system; every effect can be traced back to a cause. At some point, he reasoned, the **First Cause** must be reached. Aristotle claimed that God was the First Cause, the **Unmoved Mover**. According to Aristotle, God engages in constant self-contemplation, playing no active role in the material world. Instead, the material world responds to God. Aristotle's Great Chain of Being placed matter (mere potentiality) at the bottom, and God (the perfect actuality) at the top.

Greek philosophical theories profoundly affected Christianity. For centuries, the church accepted Plato's notion of God as immortal and perfect and suppressed Aristotle's teachings, which implied an uninvolved God. St. Thomas Aquinas made Aristotle's ideas palatable to Christians.

6. In order to augment his reputation as divine, an ancient Roman Emperor might

(A) commission an angelic self-portrait
(B) start a Punic War
(C) contact the Sibylline Oracle
(D) build temples to the gods

Ancient Roman religion inherited the polytheism of the Greeks—gods and goddesses were imported and adapted. Sacrifice, most often of a pig, nourished the hungry gods. Prayer and flattery were used to cajole the divinities to fufill human needs: a good harvest, a healthy child. An emphasis on the

performance of **rites** gave way to a state religion as the Roman empire grew. Good relations with the gods allowed the state to remain stable. The Romans developed a code of divine law that laid out the rules for worship. Various boards of priests oversaw the Roman state religion. The most important board, the **pontifices**, in particular the prestigious *pontifex maximus* (a term later adopted by the popes of the Roman Catholic Church), oversaw general public worship. Another board, the **augurs**, observed the flight of birds in an effort to translate the messages of the gods regarding the state's actions. By the sixth century B.C., many Romans were occupied with temple building, which was considered an honorable activity. The Pantheon (p. 38), one of the most famous Roman temples, was erected as an homage to numerous gods.

The political nature of Roman religion suggested that the emperor was a god who could unite the world empire. Cults sprang up surrounding these state leaders and deification often followed their deaths. **Emperor Augustus** (63 B.C. - 14 A.D.), an atheist but also a pragmatic politician, took over the pontificate and adopted religion as the foundation of his rule. With the help of slave labor, he built temples with abandon. The majestic Palatine of Apollo, the god of light and culture, emblematizes the image Augustus tried to project during the peaceful era of the *Pax Romana* (p. 388).

The Etruscans practiced astrology and divination. The Stoics and Platonists later encouraged astrology, while the Christians and Epicureans opposed its practice. **Hepatoscopy**, however, was one of the Etruscans most curious practices: they studied the livers of sacrifical victims for markings of good or bad fortune. Maps separated the liver into forty notable sections.

7. **What is the greatest historical significance of the Hindu spiritual poem the *Bhagavad Gita*?**

    (A)   Its sweeping epic dramatization of ancient Indian war
    (B)   Its pre-Freudian investigation of sibling rivalry
    (C)   Its promise of the coming of the messiah Gita
    (D)   Its endorsement of Bhakti Yoga, the path of love

The longest poem in the world, the massive ***Mahabharata***, describes a fratricidal struggle for power over the Delhi region of India. Contained within this epic is the ***Bhagavad Gita*** (*Song of the Blessed One*), one of the most influential Hindu scriptures. The *Bhagavad Gita* presents a dialogue between the god **Krishna** and **Arjuna**, one of the brothers involved in the

CULTURESCOPE

battle. Arjuna faces a dilemma of *dharma* (righteousness, religion, law, and duty). Because he is a member of the warrior caste he must fight in the war, but kinship forbids him from killing a family member. The dilemma symbolizes Arjuna's spiritual struggle. How can he free his soul from the battle of good and evil?

Hinduism recognizes that different types of people will follow different paths to God. Some people's lives are animated by action or work, some by introspection, and others by emotions. The practice of **yoga**, a dis-

This is a symbol for the Hindu mantric word "Om," a complete expression of Brahman.

ciplined training, leads to spiritual tranquility. In the *Bhagavad Gita*, Krishna describes three ways to liberation or God: action (*karma* yoga), enlightenment (*jnana* yoga), and devotion (*bhakti* yoga). All paths involve extinguishing the ego (p. 236).

Karma **yoga** is the path to God through work or action. People normally work either for psychological necessity or for personal reward. This inflates the ego, so the renouncing of the fruits of one's labor is crucial. This renunciation builds up good karma, for only karma, good or bad, brings one back to the wheel of rebirth. "He who does the task/Dictated by duty/Caring nothing for the fruit of the action/He is a yogi" (*Bhagavad Gita*, VI:I).

Jnana **yoga** is the path to God through knowledge. What you think you are is not all you are; people tend to mistake the surface personality

On July 16, 1945, as **Robert Oppenheimer**, director of the Los Alamos project (p. 651), watched the explosion of the first atomic bomb in the New Mexico desert, two lines from the *Bhagavad Gita* flashed through his mind. The speaker is God: "I am become death, the shatterer of worlds; Waiting that hour that ripens to their doom."

(self) for the whole Being (Self). In *jnana* yoga you renounce the self. The discovery of the *Atman* (God within) occurs after the layers of personality have been peeled away.

Bhakti **yoga** is the path to God through love. Everyone and everything you love contains the love of God, so you must direct all the love in your heart toward God for no other purpose than to love. Adoration of god is the ultimate goal. According to the *Bhagavad Gita*, love is the means of uniting the finite with the infinite, the **Brahman**. The *Bhagavad Gita's* strong endorsement of the *bhakti* way helped make this path the most popular in India. It is not unlike the **Song of Songs** in the Hebrew Bible (p. 485) or the basic tenets of Christianity, both of which require the same intensity of devotional love.

The form by which a Hindu chooses to view God doesn't matter. God may be personal, like the Judaic and Christian God, or transpersonal, a god without attributes. Hinduism does not bind God to one form, which accounts for the more than 330 million gods found in the Hindu tradition. They are all considered personal manifestations of Brahman.

8. **The Hindu term** *"moksha"* **means**

   (A) liberation
   (B) reincarnation
   (C) God
   (D) love

For many Hindus, **caste** determines a person's social and religious status upon entering this lifetime. People are born members of the top caste, the **Brahman** seers, or successively down the ladder as administrators, producers, servants, or "outcastes." Privileges in society are given out according to responsibility, with those at the top of the caste deemed the most responsible and therefore the most privileged.

Hindus believe in **reincarnation**, and someone's caste is believed to result from the *karma* he achieved in a previous life. Freedom from *samsara*, the grievous cycle of birth and rebirth, is the ultimate goal and principal preoccupation for the Hindu. To be liberated from this cycle is to achieve *moksha*. Your karma accrues from the acts you perform in your lifetimes and creates a mode of personal responsibility, since adhering to the principles of right living embodied in dharma increases your merits. *Dharma* differs from caste to caste, so as the proportions of responsibility change, so do the specific duties.

A Passage to India (1924), by E. M. Forster. This is a classic novel of the clash of cultures in British India after the turn of the century.

9. **Which is the most common expression for the Hindu supreme reality or god?**

   (A) *"Neti . . . neti"*
   (B) "Oh thou, before whom all words recoil"
   (C) Brahman
   (D) Nirvana

Among Western thinkers influenced by the *Upanishads* are Goethe, Schopenhauer, and Emerson (p. 263).

Another important sacred text of Hinduism is the ***Upanishads,*** a portion of the ***Vedas,*** India's oldest scriptures. "Upanishad" means both "sitting near devotedly" and "secret teaching." The doctrines of reincarnation, karma, and *moksha* first apppear in these writings, which focus on the mystical experience with the One, the quest for Brahman. The Upanishads refer to god as ***"neti . . . neti"*** ("not this . . . not this") with the idea that what remains after using this phrase is God. The South Indian philosopher Shankara addresses God in a prayer as "Oh thou, before whom all words recoil."

According to Hinduism, people want pleasure, success, and community. These wants evolve through three stages of life: **studenthood,** during which the prime responsibility is to learn and seek pleasure; **householder,** during which marriage, family, duty to community, and desire for success and pleasure prevail; and **retirement,** when one may withdraw from social obligations and begin delving into life's great mysteries. A fourth stage, *sannyasin,* allows one to cut free from all bonds to the world. The person in this stage usually adopts the life of the homeless mendicant who doesn't care about "being somebody." The *samskaras,* or initiation rites, celebrate the stages of the ascent to maturity.

A lavish Hindu temple.

THE MANY PATHS

"God has made different religions to suit different aspirations, times, and countries. All doctrines are only so many paths; but a path is by no means God Himself. Indeed, one can reach God if one follows any of the paths with whole-hearted devotion. One may eat a cake with icing either straight or sidewise. It will taste sweet either way."

——*Rama krishna Paramahamsa, Indian saint*

10. **Which of the following religions does not demand a belief in God?**

    (A) Buddhism
    (B) Roman Catholicism
    (C) Islam
    (D) Judaism

Buddhism sprang from Hinduism, but unlike Hinduism, it began with a founder, **Siddhartha Gautama** (c. 563 B.C. - c. 483 B.C.), who according to tradition, shook off the silk robes of his princely existence and went to the woods seeking enlightenment. Gautama's discontent followed his discovery of old age, disease, and death. "Where is the realm of life in which there is neither age nor death?" he asked, and the **Great Renunciation** was launched.

Gautama followed the leading Hindu masters of the day, then joined a band of ascetics. The experience of both extremes led to his development of the principle of the **Middle Way**. Neither extreme—**asceticism** (mortification) nor indulgence—would do. Gautama sat beneath the *bodhi* (enlightenment) tree, determined to remain immovable until enlightenment came to him. During a full-moon night, he thwarted a series of temptations involving desire and death. The *bodhi* tree rained red blossoms, and the **Great Awakening** arrived. For forty-nine days Gautama swam in rapture. He emerged as the **Buddha**, which means "enlightened one" or "awakened one." The Buddha did not claim to be divine: someone asked him, "Are you a god?" His answer was, "No, I am awake."

Original Buddhist teachings rejected the Hindu caste system. The Hindu Brahmins had exploited their position as guardians of religious secrets: "There is no such thing as close-fistedness in the Buddha." In addition, the

Shrines to Buddha like this one dot the landscape of Japan.

After the death of the Buddha, his followers separated into two main camps: *Mahayana* **Buddhism**, primarily for the lay person, focuses upon compassion and community as the path to enlightenment, while *Hinayana* **Buddhism**, primarily for monks and nuns, focuses upon wisdom with each individual responsible for his own enlightenment.

CULTURESCOPE

Buddha taught in the language of the people rather than the scholarly Sanskrit, thereby excluding no one—not even women.

11. **The Eightfold Path of Buddhism is designed to**
    (A) define existence
    (B) eliminate the suffering that flows from bondage to the wheel of rebirth
    (C) direct prayers
    (D) All of the above

Siddhartha (1922), by Herman Hesse. This is a brilliant, inspirational reimagining of the story of Siddhartha Gautama's life and spiritual journey.

The Buddha analyzed the human condition and offered a solution: "Work out your own salvation with diligence." The **Four Noble Truths** and the **Eightfold Path** outline the necessary journey for reaching **nirvana**, as proposed by the Buddha. Nirvana literally means "to be extinguished." Metaphorically it means eliminating the boundaries of the finite, or false, self. Nirvana, the state of eternal bliss, is not God. "One thing I teach," said the Buddha, "suffering and the end of suffering."

The Four Noble Truths of Buddhism define the basics.

1. All individual existence is filled with suffering (birth, sickness, decrepitude, fear of death, separation)
2. Suffering originates with desire; desire is the cause of suffering
3. Suffering can be dissolved through the annihilation of the self, the release from individual identity
4. This cessation of desire can be gained by following the Eightfold Path, which is designed to eliminate suffering

The Eightfold Path lays out an approach to awareness that involves the faculties of wisdom, faith, strength, mindfulness, and concentration.

1. Right belief: belief in the Four Noble Truths
2. Right intent: mental attitude of good will
3. Right speech: wise and truthful speech directed toward reconciliation—no gossiping; no lying
4. Right conduct: do not kill, lie, steal, drink intoxicants or be unchaste (for monks—celibacy; for the married, fidelity)
5. Right livelihood: one's occupation is a means, not an end, and should complement spiritual progress if possible

6. Right effort: an arduous path requires strength of will
7. Right mindfulness: observe your thoughts; maintain an attitude of goodness and peaceableness
8. Right concentration: meditation leads you further along the path to enlightenment

In the 1950s and1960s, the Beats (p. 280), including Jack Kerouac, Allen Ginsberg, and William Burroughs, took much inspiration from Buddhism and helped bring it to mainstream American youth culture.

The Buddha also put forth the doctrine of *anatta* (soul): the human self has no permanent soul, no identifiable substance, and is impermanent. Existence is transitory: "Regard this phantom world/As a star at dawn, a bubble in a stream/a flash of lightning in a summer cloud/a flickering lamp—a phantom—and a dream."

12. **How does Tibetan Buddhism differ from the Mahayana and Thervarla schools of Buddhism?**

    (A) It has experienced attempted genocide by the Chinese republic.
    (B) It incorporates pre-Buddhist tantric traditions with Buddhist dharma.
    (C) It claims the Dalai Lama as its central incarnation of the compassion principle.
    (D) All of the above

According to Tibetan tradition, in the seventh century B.C., King Srong Tsan Gam Po's two wives introduced Buddhism to Tibet. **Indra**, the Indian Thunder God, blended with the Buddha and his thunderbolt became the Buddha's diamond scepter. The merging of Indra with the Buddha symbolized the incorporation of pre-Buddhist traditions into essential Buddhist teachings. Tibetan Buddhism is called *Vajrayana*, or the **Diamond Way**, for nature's hardest and most transparent stone.

Tantras, the texts that are central to Tibetan Buddhism, originated with Hinduism and were "extended" (one interpretation of the Sanskrit word "tantra") with Tibetan Buddhism. They emphasize the "weaving" (a second interpretation) or interconnectedness of all things, and teach that enlightenment may be achieved by utilizing all body-based and latent energies in ritualized practices. Tibetan Buddhism claims that enlightenment is possible in one lifetime.

Mantras are deep-throated chants woven together with *madras*, or hand dances. Monotonal sounds escalate into harmonic chords, and gesticulations help bring about the desired state of consciousness. *Mandalas* involve visualizing gods or holy icons; one appropriates particular powers

> **"**
>
> *Be lamps unto yourselves.*
>
> ——THE BUDDHA
>
> **"**

Following an ancient custom intended to indicate faithfulness to the peaceful Buddhist tradition, a Buddhist monk burned himself to death in 1963 to protest the Vietnam War.

The Tibetan Book of the Dead (1960), compiled by W. Y. Evans White. Recited on the occasion of death, this book serves as a guide for the dying, dead, and living.

by merging identities with a particular god. This animated form of meditation contrasts sharply with most forms of silent, immobile meditation. Tantric sexual practice, under the direction of *gura*, cultivates sex as a "spiritual ally." The goal of all these practices is to transform physical energy into spiritual energy.

13. **Zen Buddhism utilizes which unusual exercise during meditation?**

   (A) Call and response, the sound of ducks quacking
   (B) Tethers, repetitive ball bouncing
   (C) Koans, paradoxical word problems
   (D) None of the above

The Buddha's **flower sermon** marked the beginning of **Zen Buddhism**, which took root in Japan and incorporated features of Chinese Taoism (p. 484). The Buddha stands on a mountain, surrounded by his disciples, and utters only silence; then he raises a golden lotus flower. No one understands, but Mahakasyapa quietly smiles. The Buddha designates him his successor because he understood.

Breaking the language barrier, as in the Buddha's flower sermon, is essential to Zen, which defies verbal definition at every turn. According to Zen, words intrude by replacing realizations. Once when a Zen master was asked the meaning of Zen, he lifted his index finger. Another responded by kicking a ball. Paradox, contradiction, and conundrums are crucial to the unorthodox style of Zen.

Zen and the Art of Motorcycle Maintenance (1974), by Robert M. Pirsig. Pirsig and his son take a cross-country motorcycle trip on which Pirsig muses upon his personal quest for *quality*. This is a beautiful and harrowing tale.

> "
>
> *Cicada—did it chirp till it knew nothing else?*
>
> —BASHO, ZEN POET
>
> "

With Zen, a primary feature of study is meditation. *Zazen*, seated meditation, lasts for many hours and often takes place in huge halls. One of Zen's most unusual techniques for spiritual training involves a question, or a *koan*: "What was the appearance of your face before your ancestors were born?" or the more well-known riddle, "What is the sound of one hand clapping?" Contrary to the Western reliance on reason, Zen states that another type of knowing must go beyond the limits of rationality. One may meditate for years on one

The Wisdom of Insecurity: A Message for an Age of Anxiety (1951), by Alan Watts. Watts, known for his writings on Zen, sees an awareness of impermanence as spiritual insight.

koan before such "knowing" comes. Zen strives to turn the mind upside down, forcing reason to confront absurdity. The student presents answers to the Zen master each day. Until *satori* (enlightenment or break-through) the master helps the student stay enthused. After *satori*, the real training begins, the goal of which is full awareness—introducing the eternal into the now.

Everyone please please help us find the Dalai Lama's contact lens.

14. **The Analects of Confucius use anecdotes to prescribe which of the following ideas regarding civilization?**

(A) Humor is necessary to maintain a moral and therefore content society.

(B) Government must impose force on people to keep society good.

(C) Universal love engenders a good society.

(D) Well-formed character engenders a good society.

Confucianism represents the practical side of Chinese religion, while **Taoism** represents the mystical side. **Confucius** (c. 551 - 479 B.C.), the Honorable Master K'ung, revived and reformulated the "way of the former kings." Believing that the Period of the Warring States in China had caused the disintegration of chivalric behavior, Confucius reinstituted "correct attitudes" based on ancient teachings. In his dialogues, collected in the *Analects*, Confucius created a prototype of character that, when taught generation after generation, eventually established itself as second nature. Tradition begot behavior and, under Confucius, a sort of collective national ethos grew.

> "
>
> *By poetry the mind is aroused; from music the finish is received. The odes stimulate the mind. They induce self-contemplation. They teach the art of sensibility. They help restrain resentment.*
>
> ——CONFUCIUS
>
> "

Since 1949, under the Communist domination of China, religion has been repressed. Marxist philosophy precludes a formal state religion or adherence to the idea of God. In the 1970s, Mao Tse-tung's cultural revolution incited Chinese youth to overturn established teachers and long-existing authority structures, including religion.

According to Confucius, human relationships are more important than individualism, and group attitudes shape individual minds. Central to his teachings is the cultivation of virtue. *Jen*—essential goodness—includes empathy, sympathy, and courtesy. *Li*, respect, and *hsiao*, family love, place mutual reciprocity and respect among family and friends at the heart of Chinese culture. For Confucius, a healthy family is the foundation for a healthy society. One can draw strength from *te*, moral example or power, which is provided by the family as well as the government. *Chung* is loyalty to the state. Finally, *wen*, the arts, transform and exalt a culture. By maintaining social harmony, Confucius sought to unite Heaven and Earth.

Confucius enjoying a cold popsicle on a hot summer day

15. **Which phrase best articulates Taoism?**

(A) Two ships pass in the night.
(B) To speak of the way is to not speak of it at all.
(C) Silence is a friend who will never betray.
(D) Ride a rollercoaster ride through a tiger's mouth.

Chinese Religion (1989), by Laurence G. Thompson. Thompson's book is a good overview of the complex religious history of China.

According to **Taoist** tradition, **Lao Tzu** rode a water buffalo out of China. A border guard stopped the Ancient Master and asked him to write down his teachings. He agreed, wrote the *Tao Te Ching*, then disappeared. Historians date the event between the sixth and third centuries B.C.; others say Lao Tzu never existed. But the *Tao Te Ching* exists and, along with the *Chuang Tzu* and the *Lieh Tzu*, forms the core of philosophical and religious Taoism.

NEOTAOISM

*Born from Confucianism and bred in Chinese folk religion, **Neotaoism** developed in China toward the end of the second century A.D. Neotaoism sought physical immortality by practicing breathing techniques, selective diet, sexual practice that avoided the loss of vital energy, the use of charms, and drinking an alchemically processed "elixir of life." This cosmic physiology of the human body and the experiments with extending physical life profoundly influenced Chinese medicine.*

The Tao of Pooh (1983), by Benjamin Hoff. Pooh just *is* in this Taoist revision of the classic children's book character.

Like its younger cousin, Zen, Taoism defies language. "To speak of the Tao is to not speak of it at all," as one phrase maintains. The two-volume *Tao Te Ching* is paradoxical and enigmatic. It's also short—you can read it in thirty minutes, then again and again for the rest of your life. Unlike its practical sibling, Confucianism, Taoism prefers spontaneity to order, non-action to action. According to Taoism, "The best way to govern is not to govern."

Taoism does not, however, mean chaos and slothfulness. *Tao* roughly means "the way." *Te* means "power": "The way to do is to be." In other words, reducing friction and conflict to a minimum will increase your energy. Rather than wasting energy on pomp, aggression, and violence, you are able to move into the empty spaces in life the way water finds its way through crowded caverns. Meditation, increasing *ch'i* (energy), divination (The *I Ching, The Book of Changes*), and faith healing are all part of the Taoist Way.

The Chinese **Yin/Yang** symbol sums up the complementary nature of Taoism and Confucianism—passive/active, female/male, Taoism's spontaneity/Confucianism's formalism.

> "
>
> *Nothing in the world is as soft and yielding as water.*
>
> *Yet for dissolving the hard and inflexible, nothing can surpass it.*
>
> ——LAO TZU
>
> "

16. The first five books of the Hebrew Bible are called
    (A) The Talmud
    (B) The Torah
    (C) The Prophets
    (D) The Cabala

Genesis, Exodus, Leviticus, Numbers, and Deuteronomy comprise the first five books, known as the **Torah**, or the Pentateuch, of the **Hebrew Bible**. The Torah contains the covenant between the **Jews** and their God, **Yahweh**. Yahweh (which in English translates to "I am that which I am") is revealed as powerful, loving, righteous, and concerned with human affairs, and Jews are urged to have the same compassionate spirit.

Back to the Sources (1986), edited by Barry W. Holz. This is a good introduction to many original Jewish texts.

KOSHER CUISINE

The Book of Leviticus outlines the dietary and cleanliness laws of Judaism. Kosher food includes the following: animals that both chew cud and have cloven hooves (cattle, sheep, and goats, but not pigs, camels, or rabbits); fish that have both fins and scales (no lobsters, crabs, or oysters); and fowl (chicken, turkey, ducks, and geese are okay—no birds of prey). The manner of slaughter is crucial. Animals are slaughtered by a Shochet, who kills the animal at the jugular vein, which is considered less painful. All blood must be removed, which means taking out the veins and arteries. Meat must be soaked in water and salted. Meat and dairy must not be served together. This extends to the dishes and utensils on which they are served.

For example, the Torah says, "You will not oppress the stranger; you know the heart of a stranger, seeing you were strangers in the land of Egypt" (Exodus 23:9). According to tradition, **Moses** (c. thirteenth century B.C.) penned the five books during a period of divine inspiration atop Mt. Sinai. The Torah includes narratives of **Noah** and the flood, **Abraham**, the first Patriarch who crossed the river Euphrates to the Promised Land, **Joseph** and the Pharoah's dreams, and Moses wandering in the desert with the Jews. Dietary and cleanliness laws follow the narratives.

Obedience to the Torah plays a central role in the lives of observant Jewish people. Jews believe that fulfilling the divine law of the Torah will lead to the future establishment of God's kingdom on Earth. The Torah encourages the recognition of the holiness of ordinary life, and suggests that the conditions of life improve. Interpretations and commentaries on the "Written Law" of the Torah are found in the "Spoken Law" of the **Talmud**. The Talmud introduces an intellectual dimension to Judaism in which study, questioning, and logic supplement worship.

Passover commemorates the exodus of Jews from Egypt.

17. **What is the most important day in the Jewish calendar?**
    (A) The Sabbath
    (B) *Rosh-ha-Shanah*
    (C) *Yom Kippur*
    (D) Passover

Judaism emphasizes its fundamental beliefs through the practice of ritual and the observance of the 613 *mitzvot* contained in the Torah.

The **Sabbath** begins at sundown on Friday and lasts until sundown on Saturday. It is the most important day in the Jewish calendar because it commemorates God's completion of the creation of the universe. According to the Book of **Genesis**, the first book of the Hebrew Bible, God created the world in six days and rested on the seventh. The Sabbath is considered a day of abstention from work to which Jewish people adhere in varying degrees.

BLAME IT ON THE MOON

Based on computations culled from happenings recorded in the Bible, twelfth-century Jewish scholars calculated the year one, Creation, to have taken place 3761 years before Christ was born. The Jewish calendar is lunar, not solar, so months don't correspond with the traditional American calendar. In any given Western year the lunar calendar overlaps two solar years.

18. **What was the only formal movement of Judaism until the nineteenth century?**

    (A) Conservative
    (B) Halacha
    (C) Orthodox
    (D) Reform

The Hebrew language, an emphasis on family-centered rituals, and dedication to the study of the Torah held a dispersed people together for 2,000 years—a unique situation in the history of religion. The Hebrew **diaspora**, the breaking up and scattering of the people, lasted until the establishment of the State of Israel in 1948, following the genocidal Nazi slaughter of some six million Jews in the Holocaust (p. 649) during World War II.

Until the nineteenth century, **Orthodox Judaism** was the only formal movement of the Jewish religion. Orthodox Jews accept without question that the Torah is God's word as revealed to Moses. Strict observance of the Jewish Sabbath, **kosher** dietary laws, and holy days characterize their worship. During Orthodox services, males and females are segregated and the proceedings are conducted primarily in Hebrew; no musical

Hasidic children caught cutting class

HASIDISM

*At the end of the eighteenth century, the **Hasidim** emerged from Poland. Originally steeped in the mystical tradition of Judaism, Hasidism preaches joyous communion with God through the experience of prayer, study and the natural world. Today the Hasidim are a strict sect and follow a philosophy of modesty. Men dress in long black coats and wide-brimmed hats as worn by Polish gentry when the sect began. Women's dress features long sleeves and long hemlines.*

Daniel Deronda (1876), by George Eliot. This novel explores Jewish identity in Christian-dominated nineteenth-century England.

accompaniment is permitted. Authority comes from the *Halacha*, or rabbinic law. Orthodox men generally keep their heads covered as sign of respect for the presence of God, and Orthodox women cover their heads after marriage.

Reform Judaism originated in Germany in the early 1800s. It rejects the authority of the *Halacha* as well as the dietary laws. Services are conducted primarily in the vernacular, and organ music is permitted. Women have full rights and may become Reform rabbis. **Conservative Judaism** began in the late nineteenth century. It accepts Halacha and the dietary laws, although the movement reinterprets tradition in the light of modernity. Services allow for mixed seating, and women are able to participate fully in synagogue rituals, as well as to become rabbis.

19. The main conflict at the beginning of Christianity between Jewish Christians and Gentile Christians was about

 (A) who would spread the good news to Rome
 (B) the ruler of Jerusalem
 (C) how to convert the pagans
 (D) the maintenance of Jewish law

Jesus, whom Christians believe to be the **Messiah**, was Jewish, as were the **twelve apostles**. They knew the teachings of the Hebrew Bible and adhered to Jewish law. **Gentiles** did not maintain Jewish dietary rules and did not practice circumcision, and were therefore considered unclean. Upon the **crucifixion** and **resurrection** of Jesus Christ, the apostles continued to spread his teachings to both Jews and Gentiles. **Peter**, designated "the rock" and inheritor of the keys to the kingdom of heaven, assumed leadership. As the number of followers of Jesus' teachings increased, the issue of maintaining Jewish law became paramount. Two camps formed—the

"Judas, stop poking Peter with that stick."

Jewish-Christians and the Gentile-Christians. Both groups believed Jesus Christ was the Messiah, but one group maintained Jewish law and one didn't. A power struggle emerged between Peter, James (the "brother" of Jesus and leader of the Jerusalem Church), and Paul (the "apostle to the Gentiles"). Peter's leniency about circumcision for Gentiles angered many Jewish-Christians. James insisted that Gentile-Christians convert to Judaism, and thereby submit to Jewish law. Paul thought this was unnecessary because although the Gentiles didn't want to be Jewish, they did want to be followers of Christ. In Paul's view, faith superseded tradition.

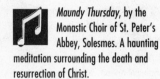

Maundy Thursday, by the Monastic Choir of St. Peter's Abbey, Solesmes. A haunting meditation surrounding the death and resurrection of Christ.

20. **Which gospel is not considered a *synoptic* gospel?**

   (A) Mark
   (B) John
   (C) Luke
   (D) Matthew

The four canonical **gospels** ("good news") relate Jesus' teachings and the events of his life. They comprise the first four books of the **New Testament**, all of which were anonymously written at least fifty years after the end of Jesus' life. Dates of origin are based on the gospel's apparent knowledge or ignorance of the destruction of the Temple of Jerusalem, which took place in 70 B.C.

Matthew, Mark, and Luke are called the **synoptic** ("seen together") gospels because their general viewpoint and arrangement are similar. "The Johannine problem" occurs because John differs sharply from the other three in style, structure, and theological emphasis.

Mark, generally considered to have been written first (c. 65 - 70 B.C.), is the most blunt, primitive, and perhaps closest in style to oral history. Scholars believe Mark's gospel may originate from a follower of Peter, which suggests historical plausibility. It's also postulated that this gospel was written for Gentiles living outside Palestine who had limited knowledge of Palestinian geography. Mark's emphasis on the inevitable suffering of Jesus' followers perhaps coincides with the widespread persecution of Christians at that time.

The Gnostic Gospels

In 1945, an Egyptian peasant unearthed what proved to be the **Gnostic Gospels**, *the sacred books of one of the earliest Christian sects. The writings suggest a number of contradictions regarding the beliefs established by Judaic and Christian traditions. First, God is not "Other" but rather identical with the Self; and second, Jesus preaches enlightenment, not repentance for sin. Scholars note a distinctly Eastern sensibility among these early writings, perhaps Buddhist or Hindu.*

The Gospel According to Woman (1987), by Karen Armstrong. This provocative interpretation of the history of women in Christianity reveals attitudes toward women that have shaped Christianity and Western society as a whole.

The Grand Inquisitor (1880), by Fyodor Dostoevsky. In this separately published episode from *The Brothers Karamazov*, Ivan imagines Jesus returning to a sixteenth-century Spain in the throes of the Inquisition.

Scholars believe the author of **Matthew** (c. 80 - 90 B.C.) wrote primarily for Jewish-Christians. Matthew emphasizes the mandate to convert all people to Christianity and stresses that the aim of Christian worship is salvation. In Matthew, Jesus' teachings take precedence over the stories.

Luke (c. 80 - 90 B.C.) omits semitic words and Jewish preoccupations, like cleanliness, which indicates that this author's audience was predominantly Greek-speaking Gentile-Christians. Luke stresses Jesus' role as teacher, as well as his concern for women and the poor. The author of Luke is considered the most literary writer of the group. Acts of the Apostles, the sequel to Luke, seems to have been penned by the same hand. Matthew and Luke are generally believed to have been based on Mark and a second source known as "Q."

John (c. 85 - 95 B.C.), distinctly different from the first three gospels, presents a more sublime Jesus. In this text the emphasis on spirituality provides a more mystical and theological version of the "good news." Eyewitness details and an understanding of the issues that developed between Judaism and the new religion have led scholars to believe the author is John, one of the twelve apostles.

21. **What atrocious religious event set the stage for European expansion?**

    (A)   The Black Death
    (B)   The Miracle on Thirty-Fourth Street
    (C)   The Crusades
    (D)   The Inquisition

In the eleventh century, Muslim Turks conquered Jerusalem, and **Pope Urban II** (1042 - 1099) sanctioned the first Christian "holy war." Pope Urban envisioned a united Christendom, and the recovery of holy places such as Jerusalem for Christianity became the goal of the early crusaders. Thousands of Christian peasants to whom religion was all-important marched East and were massacred. The **First Crusade** (1095-1099) ended with Christian soldiers storming and retaking Jerusalem.

FROM *THE BROTHERS KARAMAZOV*

"I don't accept this world of God's, and although I know it exists, I don't accept it at all. It's not that I don't accept God, you must understand, it's the world created by Him I don't and cannot accept."

——*Fyodor Dostoevsky*

I love a crusade.

By the Fourth Crusade (1202-1204), the combination of bloodthirstiness and piety had led to pillaging and destruction in the name of God. Papal sanction helped transform the idea of war into a religious experience. The slaughter of the "enemies of Christ" gained holy merit for commoners as well as knights: one could show love for God by killing off non-Christians, and to many, this was probably more attractive than becoming a monk. But the Turks took back the Holy Land piece by piece, and by the Eighth and final crusade, which ended in 1270, it was obvious that at least as far as religion was concerned, the Crusades had been futile. Politically, they had, however, expanded Europe far beyond its original borders.

Persecution of the Church's "enemies" continued into the **Inquisition**, which began in 1233 with the establishment of a tribunal of the Roman Catholic Church. This time, Christians began fighting Christians. Supposedly designed to root out **heretics**, the Inquisition abused both religion and state power. Condemned heretics, the majority of them women accused of being "witches," were handed over to the state and sentenced to death during a religious ceremony called an *auto-da-fe*. In this way, responsibility for countless executions was deflected away from the church. To uphold the motto *ecclesia abhorret a sanguine* (the Church shrinks from blood), victims were burned at the stake.

SAINT JOAN

*In 1429, **Joan of Arc**, the daughter of a French farmer, claimed that heavenly voices had ordered her to take up arms and defend France from the invading English. This was during the bloody **Hundred Years' War**. Joan persuaded a panel of theologians and then Charles VII himself, who vacillated while the infant Henry VI of England was crowned King of France, that her sacred mission was legitimate. Clad in armor, the intrepid Joan successfully led the French troops in the Siege of Orleans. She was later captured by forces loyal to the English, tried Inquisition-style, found guilty of witchcraft and heresy, and burned at the stake, still sporting her masculine garb, in 1431. In 1920 she was canonized.*

22. The central importance of the sacrament of the Holy Eucharist characterizes which Christian Church?

(A) Roman Catholic
(B) Eastern Orthodox
(C) Protestant
(D) All of the above

With over one billion followers worldwide, Christianity is full of both major and miniscule differences. The **Roman Catholic Church**, centered at the Vatican in Rome, dominates Central and Southern Europe, Ireland, and South America. The **Eastern Orthodox Church** oversees the Greek, Russian, Slavic, and Baltic churches. The **Protestant Church** dominates Northern Europe, England, Scotland, and North America. Since early in the church's history, ecumenical councils, theologians, kitchen philosophers, and street corner preachers have decided, reformed, and debated the essence of Christian beliefs. What can be agreed on are three cornerstone beliefs that unite most Christians: Christ was simultaneously both fully God and fully human (the doctrine of Incarnation); Christ released humanity from the bondage of sin (the doctrine of Atonement); and the reality of the **Trinity,** which states that while God is fully one, God is also three: God the Father, God the Son, God the Holy Spirit.

The **Roman Catholic Church** views the church as a community of celebrants who realize God through participation in the seven **sacraments**. Five of these take place at pivotal moments in life. Baptism introduces grace into the soul of a child, and parents and godparents take responsibility for guiding the child's spiritual life. Confirmation offers an older child strength as he acknowledges his ability to discern responsible action. Holy Matrimony unites adult companions in marriage. Those who choose the vocation of holy life—becoming priests, nuns, or monks—receive the Sacrament of Holy Orders.

The Sacrament of Reconciliation, or confession, received frequently throughout life, gives a Catholic the opportunity to receive forgiveness for falling into sin, that is, breaching the **Ten Commandments**. Confessions are made to priests, and **penance**, usually prayer, is recommended in order to receive absolution from God. The **Holy Eucharist**, also called Holy Communion and the Lord's Supper, is the main Sacrament of the Catholic Church. Catholics believe that God is present in the consecrated Eucharist. During **Mass**, the priest recites the words Jesus said during the **Last Supper** before he vas betrayed and crucified: "This is my body . . . this is my blood . . ." and transforms bread and wine into

Monty Python and the Holy Grail (1975), starring the Monty Python players. Your favorite religious history turned on its ear by the irrepressible band of bawdy Brits.

Christ's human body and blood. This does not mean the actual elements of bread and wine change but that the perception of God's presence enters the celebrants.

The **Eastern Orthodox Church** is quite similar to the Roman Catholic Church in that it celebrates the seven Sacraments, called "mysteries." An encouragement of mystical union with God characterizes the Eastern Church. Rather than leadership under the authority of the Roman Catholic Pope, councils, led by the **Patriarch of Constantinople**, form the decision-making body of the Eastern Church. The **Protestant Church**, like the Eastern Orthodox Church, does not ascribe to the leadership of the Pope, and numbers approximately nine hundred denominations with diverse leadership.

23. **Christianity's doctrine of Original Sin was first articulated by which philosopher?**

    (A) St. Augustine
    (B) St. Thomas Aquinas
    (C) Pascal
    (D) Descartes

The **doctrine of original sin**, unique to Christianity, explains evil through the Biblical story of Adam and Eve. **St. Augustine** (354 - 430 B.C.) offered an influential interpretation of the Biblical story, emphasizing that the original man, **Adam**, influenced by the original woman, **Eve**, chose to sin against God and eat from the **Tree of Knowledge**. As a result, humanity—Adam's progeny— receives original sin at the moment of conception. Only God's grace ensures salvation. Faith overrules reason, according to Augustinian philosophy. Throughout the Middle Ages Augustine's views dominated church thinking. His best known works are the autobiographical *Confessions* and *The City of God*.

Saint Augustine

St. Thomas Aquinas (1225-1274) carried the issue of original sin into medieval scholasticism. Aquinas postulated the **theory of natural law**, which states that a person can discern between right and wrong through reason, without divine revelation. He used his theory to define sins against nature (masturbation, bestiality, and homosexuality, for example) and sins of lust (fornication, adultery, seduction, and rape). Aquinas' best known works are *Summa Theologica* and *Summa Contra*

Gentiles. Aquinas' doctrines profoundly shaped Western views toward women, sexuality, and salvation. For many Christians, religion became a battle with guilt, spurred on by a fear of ending up in hell.

24. **What was a major cause of the spread of the Protestant Reformation?**

 (A) An overabundance of living saints
 (B) A revival of paganism
 (C) The printing press
 (D) A conflict regarding celibacy

The Bible-publishing industry claims at least 2,500 English-language versions of the Bible. The perennial best-seller rings up an estimated $180 million in sales each year.

Martin Luther (1483-1546) vowed to become "really Christian" when lightning uprooted a tree near where he stood, so he became an Augustinian friar. After the anxious friar reread the Scriptures, the cruel truth that one might live as God commanded and still not know if this would bring salvation brought Luther to the brink of madness. He meditated on the lines, "Anyone who is righteous by faith will live" (Romans 1:17), and came up with an answer: "Salvation through grace alone." This became the basis of his teaching—faith alone, grace alone, scripture alone.

Songs of Innocence and Experience (1789-1794), by William Blake. A Romantic, Blake trains his visionary stare on the hell his early-industrial Earth has become in the *Experience* poems, and outlines his version of Utopia in the *Innocence* poems.

Luther posted his **Ninety-five Theses**, which lambasted the church for selling indulgences in exchange for remission of sins. Luther's intention was to encourage reform, not to break away, but when he contested the Pope's infallibility, the church excommunicated him and the **Reformation** was begun. Luther translated the Bible into German, and the new **printing press** facilitated their mass production and permitted the spread of Luther's ideas on a grand scale. Prior to the invention of the press, only the clergy and a few wealthy citizens had direct access to the Bible's teachings.

25. **The Five Pillars of Islam provide Muslims with which body of guidance?**

 (A) The blueprint for building a mosque
 (B) The etiquette surrounding the pilgrimage to Mecca
 (C) Details of the way to live in accordance with Allah
 (D) A history of Muhammad and the Quran

In the sixth century B.C. an orphaned camel driver named **Muhammad** (c. 570 - 632 B.C.), esteemed for his gentleness and compassion, went to a cave on the outskirts of Mecca to escape the licentiousness of the city. His electrifying cry from the cave, "La ilaha illa 'llah!" ("There is no God but God!") laid the foundation for a third major monotheistic religion—**Islam**, meaning "surrender," as in surrender to God. Forced to migrate to Medina to avoid persecution, Muhammad eventually succeeded in uniting the vast territory of Arabia and inspiring mass conversion to Islam.

Islam proclaims belief in one God, **Allah**, as well as his prophets, the angels, and the Last Day, on which one's actions send one's soul to heaven or hell. According to Islam, as successor to the prophets Moses and Jesus, Muhammad fulfilled God's prescriptions for living life, as set down in the **Quran**. Permeating every aspect of **Muslim** life, the Quran ("recitation") is believed to be the materialization of God's words, and teaches "the straight path" to which one must ahdere to live in accordance with Allah.

The Autobiography of Malcolm X (1965), by Malcom X with Alex Haley. Published the year Malcom X was assassinated, the book covers Malcom's journey from street hustler to prison inmate to the most recognized Black Muslim in the nation.

Mecca, with Muhammad's tomb in the foreground.

The Five Pillars form the core of the Quran's teachings. The first pillar, *Shahadah*, or confession of faith, asks that a Muslim proclaim from the heart, at least once in life, his love for Allah. In reality, the phrase "There is no god but God" will be heard frequently throughout a Muslim's life. The second pillar, *Salat*, or ritual prayer, stipulates that one must pray five times a day, at the sun's ascent, peak, decline, and setting, and before sleep. The third pillar is *Zakat*, or almsgiving. Two-and-a-half percent of one's income must be given each year for the benefit of the less fortunate (this has changed somewhat with the advent of the modern tax system). The fourth pillar requires daytime fasting during the month of *Ramadan*, which commemorates Muhammad's migration and revelations. The purpose of fasting is to inspire thought, teach self-discipline, help people to appreciate dependence on God, and engender compassion for the hungry. Finally, at least once during a Muslim's lifetime, if she has the means and health, she must make a *Hajj* or pilgrimage to Mecca.

26. What ancient division among Muslims has been revived in the twentieth century?

(A) The mathematicians against the astronomers
(B) The Sunni against the Shi'a
(C) The Caliph against the Ayatollah
(D) The Bedouins against the camel drivers

 One of the notorious *fatwas* (death warrants) issued by Khomeini is for writer Salman Rushdie. Rushdie's *Satanic Verses* infuriated fundamentalists who believed the word of God had been blasphemed in the novel. In 1993, a Japanese translator of the *Satanic Verses* was murdered. Although Khomeini died in 1989, Rushdie remains in hiding to this day.

When Muhammad died suddenly in 632 B.C., war broke out. **Abu Bakr** was elected as *Caliph*, or successor, and his followers were called the **Sunni**. The Bedouin tribes defected from Islam, and Abu Bakr launched campaigns to bring them back into the Islamic fold. From there, Arabian forces spread into Syria, Palestine, Damascus, Iraq, Egypt, Iran, North Africa, Spain, and France, where Muslim expansion was brought to a halt at the **Battle of Tours** in 732 B.C. These conquests proved to be remarkably permanent: today Islam remains dominant in all these territories except Spain, where the **Moors** were exiled, converted, or massacred by Christians in 1492. Regarding war, the Quran says, "Defend yourself against your enemies, but do not attack them first: God hates the aggressor" (2:190). As for the idea of conversion by the sword, it says, "Let there be no compulsion in religion" (2:257). Adherence to these principles seems to have eluded most religions with the exception, perhaps, of Buddhism.

By the third century of its existence, Islam had developed a sophisticated culture synthesizing Eastern and Western ideas. Islamic advances in medicine, physics, astronomy, and architecture, along with systems such as algebra and the Arabic numerals, and the concept of zero (vital to mathematics) were transmitted to medieval Europe. Ironically, the European Renaissance (p. 579) which was due at least in part to such advances, eventually led to the stagnation of Islam and the defeat, by the mid-nineteenth century, of the Ottomans in Turkey, the Mughal in India, and the Persian in Iran.

In the twentieth century, Islam experienced a new awakening as Muslims adapted to modern life. This revival, however, renewed tensions between two divisions of Islam: The Sunni, who make up 90 percent of the Islamic population, and the **Shi'a**, who make up the remaining minority (but who receive plenty of media attention due to their fanaticism as embodied by **Ayatollah Ruholla Khomeini** in the 1970s and

Ayatollah Khomeini

1980s). The Sunni consider Abu Bakr the first legitimate *kalifah* while the Shi'a believe Muhammad's son-in-law, Ali, was the true successor.

Shi'a fundamentalists believe Western culture is decadent, irreligious, and irreverent to God. Western individuality is the cause of moral decay; the Muslim way of life is superior. Iranian Fundamentalists call the United States "The Great Satan." In contrast, the nation of Saudi Arabia exemplifies the Sunni moderate stance of adapting Islam to the modern age. Many Sunni are embarrassed by the antics of the Shi'a, which have given Islam a negative image in the West.

PLATO IN IRAN?

*Shi'a **Ayatollah Ruholla Khomeini** (1900-1989) called for a return to the Islamic republic based upon the ideas of Plato's* Republic, *which advocates the rule of many by the ideal man—meaning Khomeini. In 1979, after fifteen years in exile, Khomeini returned to Iran to fill the deposed Shah's empty space. His anti-West sermons were sold in the markets. He spoke of the "joy" of dying a martyr, especially in a war with the United States.*

27. Which of the following is an element found in all religions?
    (A) Mysticism
    (B) Tithing
    (C) Sacrifical rites
    (D) Opulence

Transcending rationality, mysticism breaks the barriers of human existence. It is union with One and denial of self. This experience— sometimes lasting, sometimes fleeting—follows a long inward journey. Hinduism and Buddhism do not separate the mystical experience from religion; the aim of divine fusion with Brahman or Nirvana pervade all their teachings. Western mystics, on the other hand, have often been ostracized. Buddha, Moses, Jesus, and Muhammad all experienced mysticism.

Ramakrishna (1838-1866), a Hindu mystic, said, "To be able to hear the divine calling, for grace to flow abundantly, it is enough to love something dearly, music, the sun, or a little child." His teachings were based on

SCIENCE AND RELIGION

"The most beautiful emotion we can experience is the mystical. It is the sower of all true art and science. He to whom this emotion is a stranger . . . is as good as dead. To know that what is impenetrable to us really exists, manifesting itself to us as the highest wisdom and the most radiant beauty, which our dull faculties can comprehend only in their most primitive forms—this knowledge, this feeling, is at the center of all true religiousness. In this sense, and in this sense only, I belong to the ranks of devoutly religious men."

——*Albert Einstein*

years of study at the feet of Hindu gurus, Muslim Sufis, and Christian mystics. He believed suffering was caused by humankind's refusal to live in God: "Name God with any name and worship God in any form you like best, you are sure to reach God." The *Arahant,* or Buddhist holy person, breaks all bindings to the Wheel of Karma. Through deep meditation, the *Arahant* attains the Buddha-nature. Some gifts that may follow include the power to discern the minds of others and psychokinetic activity, for example, walking on water.

Sufism is the mystical branch of Islam. Sufis, like Buddhists and Hindus, teach that suppression of the ego leads to union with God. An unbroken chain from Muhammad to Sufi followers has imparted the knowledge of mysticism. According to Sufism, mystical intoxication with divine love results from years of study and may lead to special powers, which should be concealed. Perhaps the most famous of the Sufi mystics are the **whirling dervishes** of Turkey, whose whirling dance is a form of meditation.

Sufi whirling dervishes

The Jewish **Kabbalah** also seeks a personal union with God through spiritual exercises, meditation, and contemplation. Origins of Jewish mysticism go back to the story of creation, in which an incorporeal God creates a temporal world. The *Zohar* (book of splendor), developed in the mid-thirteenth century, teaches that nothing exists unless it participates in the divinity.

Salvation is generally more of a concern to Christians than is mysticism. Christian mystics, however, describe how the soul can achieve union with God. The mystic **St. Teresa of Avila** (1515-1582) outlined her spiritual path in the *Interior Castle* and *The Way of Perfection.* After undergoing conversion and a long spiritual journey to free her mind from vanities and distractions, she reportedly could go into ecstasy just as easily while frying eggs as while praying. **Meister Eckhart** (1260-1327) advocated the need to get out of the self in order to become one with eternity. He was accused of pantheism and was only recently recognized as a universal teacher with a particular affinity to Zen Buddhism.

28. **What is the result of the combination of Native American religion and Christianity?**
    (A) Wounded Knee
    (B) Smallpox
    (C) The Native American Church
    (D) The American Indian Movement

The tragedy of European and Native American relations is minimized only slightly by religion. Although the missionaries, both Protestant and Catholic, set out to convert, not exterminate, tragic misunderstandings were common. Moved by a love of nature, self (they would die martyrs), and God (they would populate heaven with the baptized), missionaries zealously set out to convert Native Americans. What they found were a people understandably mistrustful of the white man and his religion. While one missionary would find he could arouse curiosity with his crucifixes and statues of Mary, another would have to leave town quickly when a child died after being christened with holy water.

The ghost dance of the Oglala Sioux

After the murder of **Crazy Horse** and the exile of Sitting Bull (p. 640), a messianic faith developed among a number of Native American tribes. **Wovoka** (1858-1932), the son of a Paiute shaman, had been adopted by a California family. Establishing himself as a wonderworker, he began preaching of an impending paradise in which no whites existed. He taught Native Americans to live in peace with the white man and to celebrate the coming of paradise with a dance, later called the **Ghost Dance** by whites. As the promise of a return to paradise gathered speed, so did the frequency of the dance. The white government, fearing rebellion, moved to stop it. At the same time, Sitting Bull took up the dance. When the military ordered the **Sioux** to Wounded Knee (p. 641), they complied, having been taught by Wovoka not to resist. A medicine man threw dust in the air to signal the arrival of the millennium, and the Ghost Dance began. In the confusion, a shot was fired, and the military opened fire on the Indians. Over 150 Native Americans were killed. Wovoka, disconsolate, withdrew to the mountains, and the movement died out.

The **Native American Church** developed as a result of accommodations between Christian and Native American traditions. In 1964, the church offered the first glimmer of religious freedom for Native Americans, when the California Supreme Court ruled in favor of the use of **peyote** as a form of religious expression. The Native American Church combines certain Christian teachings with the belief that peyote embodies the Holy Spirit and that taking the drug helps lead to communion with God. This did not, however, signal an end to traditional Indian forms of worship untouched by Christianity.

In 1970, President Richard Nixon, in another important move for traditional Native American religions, returned the sacred Blue Lake to the Taos Pueblo Indians. In 1978, the U.S. Congress passed the **American Indian Religious Freedom Act**. Official U.S. policy is now "to protect and preserve for American Indians their inherent right of freedom to believe, express, and exercise the traditional religions of the American Indian . . . including, but not limited to, access to sites, use and possession of sacred objects, and the freedom to worship through ceremonials and traditional rites." Burial sites, sacred relics, and access to ancestral sacred places are beginning to be reclaimed by Native Americans all over the nation.

29. **The Pilgrims and Puritans emigrated to America primarily for what reason?**

    (A) Desire for purification of worship
    (B) Desire for land and gold
    (C) Desire for religious tolerance of all faiths
    (D) Desire for improved economic situation

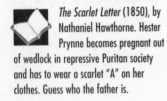

The Scarlet Letter (1850), by Nathaniel Hawthorne. Hester Prynne becomes pregnant out of wedlock in repressive Puritan society and has to wear a scarlet "A" on her clothes. Guess who the father is.

Reformation fervor struck England with the advent of **Calvinism**. On the heels of Martin Luther, **John Calvin** (1509-1564) sought the purification of the church and the creation of a new Christian city. Rule by the Bible, not the Bishop, became the call. Calvin preached a **doctrine of predestination** that held that the mass of sinners would be tortured in hell for all eternity while the "elect" would enjoy eternal bliss. The tricky thing was that no one could be certain to which group she belonged.

In England, the Calvinist **Puritans** became impatient with the Church of England, and argued in particular that religion should be separate from politics. Harassed and labeled "non-conformists," worthy of social disgrace and/or prison, the Puritans left for Holland and eventually for

Virginia in 1620 on the *Mayflower*. They landed in Plymouth Bay determined to create the ideal Christian town in America. An initial partnership between the **Pilgrims** and the Native Indians led to the **First Thanksgiving**, in which God was thanked for the Pilgrims' survival and prosperity. The term Pilgrims was applied to this group in the nineteenth century, but they themselves didn't use the name.

The Puritans who left England for the New World in 1629 were a group of middle-class, educated seekers of "pure" religious worship; they brought the Church of England with them, establishing the Massachusetts Bay Colony, where Governor John Winthrop declared that taking Indian land was in accordance with a mandate from God. He cited the Bible: "Whosoever therefore resisteth the power, resisteth the ordinance of God: and they that resist shall receive to themselves damnation" (Romans 13:2). The subsequent massacre of the Pequot Indians was similarly justified.

The Puritans did not come to America in search of religious freedom for all. They came to establish their own "pure" form of worship, and all dissenters would be **exiled** or **ostracized**. Puritan worship was simple and austere. Puritans argued that a careful reading of the New Testament eliminated the need for a bishop and all but two of the sacraments: baptism and communion. According to the Puritans, no ministers or saints acted as intermediaries to God. Only male members of the Puritan church could vote although all people were taxed in accordance with "God's laws." The Puritans later evolved into the **Congregationalists.**

30. Separation of church and state began as a reaction to
    (A) Puritan demand for conformity
    (B) taxation without representation
    (C) mandatory oaths of Puritan beliefs
    (D) All of the above

Religious conformity among the Puritan colonies claimed a high price: intolerance, punishment, and exile. The Massachusetts Bay colony banished clergyman **Roger Williams** (1603-1682) for disseminating "news and dangerous opinions." His alarming proposals included the defense of American Indians' claim to the land and complete separation of church and state. In 1636, Williams fled to Rhode Island, dubbed by the Puritan clergy "Rogues Island" and the "sewer in which the Lord's debris collects." At Providence (named for "God's merciful providence unto me in my distress") he bought land from the local Indians and helped build an

THE TWELVE RULES OF PURITAN BEHAVIOR

Profane no Divine ordinance

Touch no state matters

Urge no healths

Pick no quarrels

Encourage no vice

Repeat no grievances

Reveal no secrets

Maintain no ill opinions

Make no comparisons

Keep no bad company

Make no long meals

Lay no wagers

 Puritan "blue laws" that required rigid observance of the Sabbath and restricted kissing among unmarried couples, among many other things, led to a repressive atmosphere from which the hysterical Salem witch trials resulted. In 1692, nineteen persons and two dogs were convicted and hanged as witches; one accused person was pressed to death.

early **Baptist** church. Williams stated that "civil magistrates have no business meddling in matters of conscience and religion." In Providence, no religious oaths—litmus tests to weed out Roman Catholics—mandatory worship, or taxes were demanded of denizens. Squatters, malcontents, and exiles formed an independent and individualistic home in this early experiment in religious liberty.

Anne Hutchinson (1591-1643), who had been banished after a farcical trial for misinterpreting the sermons of the Puritan clergy and holding religious meetings for women in her home, ended up in Providence. Hutchinson had threatened the Puritan social fabric by daring to bypass the clergy and "enthusiastically" declaring interpretations based on her reading of the Bible. The fact that Hutchinson was a woman made the situation that much more grave.

Another group of dissenters, the **Society of Friends** or **Quakers**, enraged civil and religious authorities by refusing to pay taxes to support the Church of England, by refusing to take oaths, and, as advocates of passive resistence, by refusing to take part in military service. **William Penn** (1644-1718) argued for religious tolerance in England long before establishing **Pennsylvania** ("Penn's Woods") in 1681. After receiving a deed to the land from the King of England, Penn sent word ahead to the Delaware Indians that he wished to occupy the land "with your love and consent."

William Penn

Philadelphia ("the city of brotherly love") was planned as a "holy experiment" in civil justice and religious tolerance. London, however, pressured Penn to prevent Catholics and Jews from voting or holding office, though they were free to worship. Philadelphia attracted richly mixed ethnic groups: Irish, Scottish, Swedish, German, Welsh, and free Africans. The city flourished, but not without much quarrelling and eventually the mismanagement of funds by Penn's deputies. "Liberty without obedience is confusion," said Penn, "and obedience without liberty is slavery." Penn died disappointed with the moral anarchy that had taken hold, but left behind a noble monument to freedom of conscience and worship.

31. The Great Awakening was sparked by

(A) Benjamin Franklin
(B) George Whitefield
(C) John Calvin
(D) Samuel Davis

After generations of declining participation in religion, a religious revival in the 1730s and 1740s laid the seeds of the American Revolution (p. 626). "New Light" preachers roamed the colonies arousing passionate conversions, challenging "Old Light" ministers in a competition for souls and, ultimately, political power. **George Whitefield** (1714-1770), a cross-eyed English alehouse attendant, really sparked what has come to be known as the **Great Awakening**. Armed with a magnificent voice and the desire to convert the masses, Whitefield gave open-air sermons famous for their tumbling "sinners," shrieking and rolling on the ground. Thousands came to hear him, including Benjamin Franklin, who was so moved that the notoriously frugal statesman offered a donation. There was lots of fire-and-brimstone rhetoric urging the faithful to examine their consciences closely. Theologian **Jonathan Edwards** (1703-1758) who came to be called "the Artist of Damnation," declared that religion "is not a thing that belongs to reason . . . it is not a speculative thing, but depends on the sense of the heart."

The public nature of the Great Awakening meant that Church order was undermined by these ministers who arrived in towns unannounced and challenged the reigning pulpit masters. Denominations split as **Baptists** and **Presbyterians** increased their membership and weakened the control of Puritan-Congregationalists and Anglicans. Perhaps most attractive to converts to these new denominations was that good works

> 66
>
> *Serving God is doing good to man, but praying is thought an easier service, and therefore more generally chosen.*
>
> —BENJAMIN FRANKLIN
>
> 99

PUBLICK RELIGION

....

Benjamin Franklin, influenced by the Enlightenment (p. 396), fashioned a new idea of American religion. "Publick Religion" promoted "the excellency of Christian religion" by respecting the Bible and Jesus without the miracles and superstitions. Reason counted more than faith, morals more than grace. God was spoken of as an abtraction, not a person, and Jesus, recognized as a great human, was not considered the divine Son of God. Franklin, along with Jefferson and Madison, demanded that churches call on God and the congregations to support themselves, not rely on the government. Thus separation of church and state became a part of the Constitution (p. 402).

could save a sinner, a direct challenge to the Calvinism of Puritan-Congregationalists who believed in predestination. But the spiritual arrogance of all this wrangling led one preacher, Samuel Davis, to say, "To be a Christian is not enough now-a-days, but a man must also be something more and better, that is, he must be a strenuous bigot to this or that particular church."

32. **Gospel music originated**
    (A) with the career of Mahalia Jackson
    (B) at spirituals
    (C) during the Enlightenment
    (D) in 1923

As the institution of slavery (p. 178) attacked Africans' family bonds and cultural heritage, religion offered some sense of community and hope. Though literacy was prohibited for slaves, some slaves learned to read the Bible. Many were attracted to the Biblical message that the poor and oppressed would be saved. Slaves and ex-slaves found solace in the biblical stories of Moses, Joshua, and David, which described the lowly becoming conquerors. White owners, meanwhile, often told blacks that they were descended from Ham, Noah's wicked son, and therefore must accept their lot in life. The Bible was used as a proslavery tract—"there are masters and there are slaves"—but also by those opposed to slavery —"do unto others as you would have done to you." The pacifist Quakers were the first white religious group to argue publicly that slavery was anti-Christian.

Frederick Douglass

Slave preachers, especially, were crafty interpreters of the Bible. Under the watchful eye of whites, black preachers

Their Eyes Were Watching God (1990), by Zora Neale Hurston. Hurston writes a beautiful, bluesy narrative about an African American woman's spiritual and sexual awakening.

GULLAH RELIGIOUS CULTURE

*The spirituals sung by the **Gullah** people (who live on the Sea Islands along the coast of South Carolina and Georgia in relative isolation from whites) reveal an amazing preservation of their native African traditions. Christian ideology pervades the songs, but the "shout songs" that accompany the dancing have traditional African religious roots. Scholars have found that many "nonsense" words sung for generations are actually African words.*

led the **spirituals**, or "shout songs," which were sometimes accompanied by ecstatic dancing. The singing of spirituals gave slaves messages of hope, offered them a place to express repressed emotions, and provided cryptic information about the underground railroad (p. 181) and other paths to freedom. At such times a disenfranchised slave could feel part of a "family." Spirituals gave rise to **Gospel music**, which in turn inspired rhythm and blues (p. 314) and rock and roll (p. 322).

The **Great Awakening** had inspired a revival of Black American Christianity, as evangelists seemed to bridge the gap between whites and blacks by abandoning the lofty rhetoric of establishment preachers. In 1816, ex-slave Richard Allen organized the **African Methodist Episcopal Church**, and Absalom Jones organized the **Protestant Episcopal Church.** For the first time institutional structure was brought to bear on the chaos of life wrought by slavery. Meanwhile, as the Abolitionist (p. 181) movement gathered momentum, criticism of the churches' role in slavery came to the forefront. Frederick Douglass declared, "The church and the slave prison stand next to each other . . . We have men sold to build churches, women sold to support missionaries, and babies sold to buy Bibles and communion services."

After slavery, African American religious groups flourished. In 1895 the **National Baptist Convention** created a black-run institution that later created a publishing house, a missionary system, and a lobbying machine. By 1900 it was two million strong. At the same time, African Americans galvanized the **Pentecostal** movement (based on the Book of Acts and characterized by the the full touch of the Holy Spirit, which results in phenomena such as speaking in tongues and faith healing). **The Church of God in Christ**, founded in 1897 in Mississippi, became the largest black Pentecostal church in the world. Today, the Pentecostal movement continues to grow vigorously.

33. **Which leader did an angel lead to the golden plates, resulting in the start of a major new American religion?**
    (A) Joseph Smith and the Mormons
    (B) William Miller and the Adventists
    (C) Mary Baker Eddy and the Christian Scientists
    (D) Baha'u'llah and the Bahai'i

After receiving visitations from an angel telling him that existing churches were in error and that the true gospel would be restored, **Joseph**

Mama, I Want to Sing, by Vy Higginsen. The longest running black off-Broadway musical in history is about the role of gospel and pop music in the African American church.

Smith (1805-1844) found the golden plates buried beneath a hill in upstate New York. He translated the ancient hieroglyphs incribed on the plates into *The Book Of Mormon*, a supplement to the Bible. In 1830, the **Church of Jesus Christ of Latter-Day Saints**, also known as the Mormon Church, was launched. Forced by hostility to move from Ohio to Missouri to Illinois, this home-grown religion increased quickly in size and encountered opposition at every turn. "Outsiders" objected to the Mormons' additional scriptures and to practices such as polygamy and holding property in common. Joseph

Brigham Young

Smith was eventually arrested and murdered in jail. **Brigham Young** (1801-1877) moved the Saints, as Mormons called themselves, to the Utah desert. The appeal of the Mormon religion seemed to lie in its newness (it did not spring from Protestantism), as well as its close community, promise of purity, and the Second Coming it was said to be helping to bring about.

The Varieties of Religious Experience (1993), by William James. Philosopher and psychologist (and brother of Henry), James explores humanity's response to conversion, repentance, and mysticism.

Today, the vast majority of Mormons no longer practice polygamy. Mormons abstain from tobacco and alcohol. Youths must spend two years proselytizing, and all members offer one-tenth of their income to the church. With a high birth rate and active proselytizing, the self-sustaining Mormons have increased their numbers to almost four million and now rank as the seventh-largest denomination in the United States.

Belief in the Second Coming also inspired William Miller and his **Millennialists**. Based on a reading of Daniel 8:13, Miller calculated that the Second Coming would occur in 1843. This aroused great expectations among followers, and Christ's

FROM "MY LIFE CLOSED TWICE"

My life closed twice before its close—
It yet remains to see
If Immortality unveil
A third Event to me

So huge, so hopeless to conceive
As these that twice befell.
Parting is all we know of heaven,
And all we need of hell.

——*Emily Dickinson*

failure to appear led to disenchantment and despondency. **Ellen G. White** (1827-1915) rejuvenated the dismayed believers with the notion that the vision was correct and only the date wrong. The **Adventists** (from Advent, meaning coming or arrival) followed Mrs. White and imposed restrictions on tobacco, alcohol, and meat.

 Baha'u'llah (1817-1892), a Persian prophet, advocated one world faith that embraced Jesus, Moses, Muhammad, Krishna, Buddha, and Zoroaster as messengers of one God. In 1912, his son founded the first **Baha'i** house of worship in Wilmette, Illinois. There is no clergy, ritual, or traditional rites. It is believed that each seeker will find spirit without ecclesiatical assistance.

Mary Baker Eddy (1821-1910) believed "the Principle of all harmonious Mind-action to be God." Eddy's book, *Science and Health with Key to the Scriptures,* "reinstates primitive Christianity with its lost element of healing." In 1892, Eddy established the **Church of Christ, Scientist**. The premise of Christian Science is that bodily ills are mental in origin; false belief leads to ill health. Health comes from spiritual understanding and prayers, and God's powers surpass all human skills. Today the Christian Science Publishing Society includes the highly praised *Christian Science Monitor* newspaper and provides numerous reading rooms around the country.

34. Which philosopher's struggle with Christianity laid the foundation for existentialism?

   (A) Friedrich Nietzsche
   (B) Ralph Waldo Emerson
   (C) Soren Kierkegaard
   (D) Henry David Thoreau

Becoming a Christian is a lifelong struggle, or so said the Danish philosopher **Soren Kierkegaard** (1813-1855). "Just think what it means to live in a Christian state, a Christian nation, where everything is Christian, and we are all Christians, where, however a man twists and turns, he sees nothing but Christianty and Christendom, the truth and witnesses to the truth . . . ." Kierkegaard posed the idea that enlightenment was only possible by committing oneself to God, but that God might never respond. This idea, the absurdity of Christianity, was a precursor to the philosophy of **existentialism**. Existentialism says that existence is unexplainable and that an excruciating freedom of choice plays a critical role in our lives. Kierkegaard's best-known works include *Either/Or*, *Fear and Trembling*, and *Sickness Unto Death*.

Following in Kierkegaard's existential footsteps, **Friedrich Nietzsche** (1844-1900) announced the demise of God: "All religions are at the deepest level systems of cruelties." According to Nietzsche,

Soren Kierkegaard

Existentialism from Dostoevsky to Sartre (1975), by Walter Kaufmann. This is a good introduction to a bunch of those wacky existentialists.

meaning and memory come only from suffering; Christianity's "truth" is that meaning begins from the suffering of Jesus Christ. Nietzsche posited the "will of power" as the primary human drive and advocated "transvaluation of values" in which the feminine aspects of Christianity (submission and compassion) join a masculine set of virtues (courage and toughness) to form a morality that strives to greatness rather than goodness. His best known works include *Thus Spoke Zarathustra, The Will to Power, Twilight of the Idols*, and *Ecce Homo* (his autobiography).

35. **Which controversial book cast serious doubt on a literal interpretation of the Bible?**

(A) *The Adventures of Huckleberry Finn*
(B) *The Fall of the House of Usher*
(C) *On the Origin of Species*
(D) *Leaves of Grass*

In the nineteenth century, science and the Christian faith clashed. In 1859, **Charles Darwin** (1809-1882) shook conventional religious beliefs when he published *On the Origin of Species* (p. 219), in which he postulated that humans evolved from lower forms of life. Evolution undermined the literal interpretation of the Old Testament by challenging the Genesis story of the simultaneous creation of all living things. "Modernist" clergy and teachers who embraced the theory of evolution were dismissed from their posts. "Fundamentalists" insisted on the truth of the Bible. Some took the middle road, like theologian **Henry Ward Beecher** (1813-1887), who said that evolution was just another example of "the diversified unfolding of God's plans on earth."

The 1925 trial of **John Thomas Scopes** (1900-1970), a biology teacher who taught evolution, epitomized the modernist/fundamentalist conflict. Teaching evolutionism was prohibited in Tennessee public schools. Scopes was arrested, and **William Jennings Bryan**, a Presbyterian Fundamentalist and three-time candidate for the presidency, prosecuted Scopes. **Clarence Darrow**, a famed criminal lawyer, defended the teacher. On trial with Scopes was the authority of the Bible. Scopes was fined, but it was a hollow victory for fundamentalists.

Inherit the Wind (1960), starring Spencer Tracy and Gene Kelly. See this fictionalized version of the Scopes Monkey Trial. (Bad-TV buffs: look for a youngish Norman Fell—that's right, Mr. Roper from "Three's Company.")

In 1961, a district judge in Arkansas declared unconstitutional the "Balanced Treatment for Creation-Science and Evolution Science Act" since it would amount to government sponsorship of a particular religious view. "No group, no matter how large or small, may use the organs of the government, of which the public schools are the most conspicuous and influential, to foist its religious beliefs on others." Today the battle over creationism versus evolutionism continues.

AN EXCERPT FROM THE SCOPES MONKEY TRIAL

Darrow: But what do you think that the Bible itself says? Don't you know how it [the date of Noah's flood] was arrived at?

Bryan: I never made a calculation.

Darrow: A calculation from what?

Bryan: I could not say.

Darrow: From the generations of man?

Bryan: I would not want to say that.

Darrow: What do you think?

Bryan: I do not think about things I don't think about.

Darrow: Do you think about things you do think about?

Bryan: Well, sometimes.

---

36. Televangelist Jim Bakker was incarcerated for which of the following crimes?

(A) Indecent exposure
(B) Grand larceny
(C) Fraud and conspiracy
(D) All of the above

In the late 1970s, one-third of the adult American population claimed to have had a **"born again"** experience. In 1976, **Jimmy Carter** (1924-), an avowed "born again," ascended to the presidency, and *Time* magazine declared 1976 "The Year of Evangelicals." **Fundamentalist Christianity**, a subset of Evangelism militantly opposed to modernity, reared its head and looked toward political offices as a way to promote the Bible and have conservative Christian views dominate American life. Overturning *Roe v. Wade* (p. 201), authorizing prayer in public schools, and increasing the defense budget are some of the major issues fundamentalists rally around. When President Carter turned out to be too "liberal," fundamentalists ushered in **Ronald Reagan** (1911-). The ideas of the **"Religious Right"** were propagated by the charismatic televangelists and the newly elected President Reagan.

Marion Gordon "Pat" Robertson (1930-) founded the first U.S. Christian television station in 1960, which eventually evolved into **CBN** (Christian Broadcasting Network), which, by 1986, was the largest cable network. Robertson, the host of "The 700 Club" unsuccessfully sought a presidential bid in 1988. The "electronic church" has amassed financial

---

MAN AND SUPERMAN

"Yes, it is mere talk. But why is it mere talk? Because my friend, beauty, purity, respectability, religion, morality, art, patriotism, bravery, and the rest are nothing but words which I or anyone else can turn inside out like a glove."

——*George Bernard Shaw*

Wise Blood (1976), by Flannery O'Connor. Revivalist preacher Hazel Moats founds The Church of God Without Christ.

Oral Roberts describes how big an ass he was to starve himself for $4.5 million.

contributions totaling about one billion dollars. In a relatively short period of time, others such as Jerry Falwell, Oral Roberts, and Jim and Tammy Bakker gained talking-head fame and huge followings. Networks were set up, universities built, lobbies fortified, and theme parks planned.

Jim and Tammy Faye Bakker founded the **PTL** (Praise the Lord) television network in 1973. At its peak the show reached 13,000,000 viewers. Bakker was defrocked by the Assemblies of God and convicted of fraud and conspiracy following a sex scandal in 1989, though he vehemently denied the charges. **Oral Roberts** fell from grace and into ridicule after claiming to have seen a ninety-foot vision of Jesus and then climbing a tower to fast until contributions to his church increased. Jerry Falwell organized the **"Moral Majority"** in 1979; he identified with right-wing political causes and used a technologically advanced system of mail-order solicitation to inspire voter registration and votes for conservative Republicans.

37. **Mass suicide of which cult fired debate about the limitations of freedom of religion?**

(A) The Unification Church
(B) The Peoples' Temple
(C) The Church of Scientology
(D) The Church of the Immortal Saints

The U.S. District Court of California denied tax-exempt status to the Neo-American Church in 1965. The court had problems with its leader, Chief Boo Hoo; its three-eyed-toad symbol, its sacred songs "Puff, the Magic Dragon" and "Row, Row, Row Your Boat," and its slogan "Victory over Horseshit."

On November 18, 1978, 900 followers of **James (Jim) Warren Jones** drank poisoned Kool-Aid and died. Not surprisingly, the mass suicide of the **Peoples' Temple** in Jonestown, Guyana shook up all the old arguments for religious tolerance. People wanted to know whether or not the government could have done anything to prevent it. Many people felt the limits of tolerance had been reached. The Peoples' Temple originated as a mainline congregation of the Disciples of Christ, which is a member of the mainstream National Council of Churches. The degeneration of the Peoples' Temple into a bizarre cult of personality, however, went unnoticed by leaders.

The difficulty of defining a "cult" was also highlighted by the Jonestown case. The term "cult" refers primarily to groups outside mainstream Western religion. Most experts agree that cults possess several destructive features, including the discouragement of rational thought, the requirement that members swear total allegience to an all-powerful leader, deceptive recruitment techniques, the psychological weakening of members and manipulation of their guilt, and the taking over of members' personal decisions by leaders.

The Church of Scientology was founded by **L. Ron Hubbard**, author of *Dianetics*: *The Modern Science of Mental Health*. Members practice a series of exercises designed to eliminate the "reactive" mind so that the true, or "Thetan," self can be revealed. One of the biggest battles the Church of Scientology has faced has been with the IRS over its tax-exempt status.

Pre-Guyana Jim Jones and his wife, Marcelline

 *Rosemary's Baby* (1968), directed by Roman Polanski, starring Mia Farrow and John Cassavetes. Unsuspecting wife's husband joins a witches' coven operating in their apartment building, and guess what the witches want—her unborn baby! AAHHHGGG!!!

The **Unification Church**, led by the **Reverend Sun Myung Moon**, began when he received a vision in his native Korea of victory over Satanic forces. Now based in the U.S., Moon believes Jesus failed to accomplish his mission by not marrying and can therefore offer believers only spiritual salvation, while Moon offers physical salvation. He instituted a period of sacrificial work and celibacy for his followers, which takes place prior to an arranged marriage, usually across racial and cultural lines. Many family members of those who are "Moonies" feel the church is a cult and uses brainwashing techniques on its followers, but Moon works doggedly to maintain a respectable image for his church, for example by publishing the conservative *Washington Times* and *Insight* magazine.

SAKI ON THE HALF-SHELL

"Oysters are more beautiful than any religion. . . . There's nothing in Christianity or Buddhism that quite matches the sympathetic unselfishness of an oyster."

——*Saki*

ANSWERS

1. C	2. D	3. B	4. B	5. C	6. D	7. D	8. A	9. A	10. A
11. D	12. D	13. C	14. D	15. B	16. B	17. A	18. C	19. D	20. B
21. C	22. D	23. A	24. C	25. C	26. B	27. A	28. C	29. A	30. D
31. B	32. B	33. A	34. C	35. C	36. C	37. B			

Television programming is a product of the top one hundred corporate advertisers in the country. These companies are run mostly by old, white, upper-class Protestant men who dictate what the rest of us watch by which programs they decide to sponsor. Advertisers support shows that appeal to the masses, avoiding programs that deal with difficult racial or political issues and supporting shows that are in line with an American moral standard that they determine. TV certainly does not represent an accurate cross-section of our society. The premise of all television programming is to bombard the viewer with so much information and advice that the viewer lets television think for him.

Or . . .

TV is the most public art gallery in the world. The medium requires artists to create hourly, daily, or weekly pieces of art under the condition that each creation attract the largest possible audience and engage that audience so strongly that it stays until the piece is completed, despite the

 Mediaspeak; How Television Makes Up Your Mind (1983), by Donna Woolfolk Cross. This is a scathing read about the influence of television on politics, news, children and just about everything else in our lives.

Teleliteracy: Taking Television Seriously (1992), by David Bianculli. This book provides insight and interviews with some of the most respected minds in television about the positive influence TV has had on our culture.

fact that there are annoying interruptions and over fifty other programs competing for their attention. From a cultural standpoint, television is our shared language. It has become our most popular pastime and a common point of reference, and has played a decisive role in monitoring our government. TV has saved lives, exposed wrongdoing, brought us tears of joy and sadness, and opened our lives to the farthest reaches of our planet and universe.

You decide.

1. **Who invented radio?**
   - (A) Thomas Edison
   - (B) Alexander Graham Bell
   - (C) Albert Einstein
   - (D) Guglielmo Marconi

When Gugliemo Marconi and his mother reached England, customs officials were suspicious of the black box that housed his radio because two years earlier the French president had been killed by an Italian anarchist's bomb. They opened the box, saw all these wires and tubes that they had never seen before, and smashed the box to pieces. Marconi's mother, who was Irish, had relatives who put him in touch with Britain's chief telegraph operator who had done some wireless experiments of his own and together they built a new black box.

In 1895, twenty-year-old **Guglielmo Marconi** (1874-1937) sent audible signals via radio waves across his bedroom. Breaking the wave into short dots and dashes using a Morse telegraph key, Marconi successfully transmitted information from one end of a room to the other, marking the birth of **wireless communication**. He moved his experiments outdoors but ran into trouble maintaining signals over hills and through trees, so he invented an **antenna** and placed it on top of the highest hill, enabling him to send signals over greater distances. In 1896 Marconi headed for England to exhibit his invention to the British Empire. In 1897 Marconi established the British wireless manufacturing company, British Marconi, and outfitted the Royal Navy fleet with wireless receivers. In 1899 Marconi took his company to America, arriving on the eve of Admiral George Dewey's triumphant return from the Spanish-American War (p. 641).

Radio Days (1987), directed by Woody Allen. This film offers a nostalgic look back at American life before and during World War II when people's lives revolved around what was on the radio.

Marconi's receiving set

Dewey complained about the poor communication between the army, navy, and Washington. British Intelligence often knew American war strategies before the American military did. Marconi's wireless changed all of that.

2. During World War I, who took over control of radio?

   (A) General Electric
   (B) The navy
   (C) Westinghouse
   (D) The army

In 1907 **Lee de Forest** created the **audion tube**, a glass bulb capable of generating and amplifying radio waves in clear frequencies. Radio operators began popping up all over the country. Amateurs, called "hams," cluttered the airwaves sending messages back and forth, tuning in to police and fire emergencies and all too often intercepting military communications. As a result of the unregulated chaos on the airwaves, the U.S. Navy took control of radio during World War I (p. 643). All non-military radio operators were banned from the airwaves for the duration of the war. The navy was so pleased by the clarity of their wireless operations during the war that at its end they declared that the navy would permanently control radio communications. Ham operators, who had been eager to get back to the airwaves after the war, protested the government's decision and a compromise was reached. On October 17, 1919, the navy and General Electric, the second largest manufacturer of wireless equipment after British-owned American Marconi, established the **Radio Corporation of America (RCA).** Essentially a private monopoly, RCA was the government's way of controlling radio and forcing foreign interests out of the American communications business. American Marconi was taken over by RCA within the year.

3. Who was the first president to have election results broadcast on radio?

   (A) Herbert Hoover
   (B) Warren G. Harding
   (C) Franklin D. Roosevelt
   (D) Harry S Truman

In 1920 **Frank Conrad** began playing his favorite records through his radio amplifier on Saturday evenings from his home in Wilkinsburg,

David Sarnoff was twenty years old when he worked for American Marconi as a radio operator. In 1912 Sarnoff faintly made out the signal: "S.S. Titanic ran into iceberg. Sinking fast." He alerted rescue ships in the area and broadcast casualty reports to relatives in the U.S. American Marconi received worldwide attention and Sarnoff became a hero. Fourteen years later he founded NBC in order to create a programming schedule to help stimulate the sale of radios. In 1947 Sarnoff was responsible for creating RCA's color television system, and by the 1950s he made NBC the first network to broadcast completely in color in order to sell RCA color TVs.

Tube Of Plenty: The Evolution of American Television (1990), by Erik Barnouw. Barnouw gives a concise, thorough, and insightful account of the history of radio and television.

In 1922, RCA sold $11,000,000's worth of radios sets. By 1924, they had sold over $50,000,000's worth.

Pennsylvania. Other radio operators enjoyed the music as a relaxing break from the chatter on the airwaves and began to tune in to listen. Conrad, who worked for **Westinghouse**, one of the leading radio manufacturers, recognized the potential for radio as a source for entertainment as well as information. He convinced Westinghouse to let him build a shack on top of their factory to begin broadcasting concerts, dramatic readings, and news. On November 2, 1920, Westinghouse broadcast the first presidential election results, declaring Warren G. Harding the winner over James M. Cox.

4. **Which was the first company to establish the concept of radio advertising?**

   (A) Coca Cola
   (B) AT&T
   (C) Ford Motor Co.
   (D) McDonald's

The Sponsored Life: Ads, TV, and American Culture (1995), by Leslie Savan. Hundreds of commercials from 1985-1993 are dissected in this funny, scary study of what commercials are trying to do to your brain.

In the early days of radio people would read newspapers, play records, and perform entire plays over the air without any concern for copyrights. By 1923 artists and the corporations who produced their work threatened lawsuits that would put radio out of business. Broadcasters needed to devise a way to profit (p. 80) from their programming. Four suggestions were offered—one, an "endowment" to be established by wealthy donors to stations. Philanthropists were not interested. The second was to have radio fall under the auspices of local government. The third was to levy a tax on each set ($2 per tube), and the fourth was a plan put forth by **AT&T** called **toll broadcasting.** The idea was to create toll booths in thirty-eight stations around the country in which people could pay to broadcast their messages over the airwaves. No one showed up. At 5:00 p.m. August 28, 1922, on WEAF in New York, the owners of a brand-new Long Island apartment complex purchased time to broadcast a commercial message to potential buyers. Apartments sold. In January, 1923, actress Marion Davies was paid by a cosmetics company to go on the air for an informal chat and a promise to autograph photos for people who wrote in. Letters flooded in, other advertising companies caught wind of it, and commercially sponsored broadcasting was born.

5. **What famous TV show did NOT get its start on radio?**

(A) "Amos 'n' Andy"
(B) "Howdy Doody"
(C) "Marx Brothers"
(D) "The Perry Como Show"

In 1928, two white men, **Freeman Fisher Gosden** and **Charles J. Correll,** created **"Amos 'n' Andy,"** an instantly popular situation comedy in which they told stories and jokes in "Negro" dialect. Families began

In 1907, the word "television" was first used in an article in *Scientific American.* The first TV station in the U.S. was WRNY in Coatsville, NY.

FDR reaches out to a depressed country.

huddling around their radios each night to listen to programs that were often more entertaining than anything at the theater or the movies, and it was free! Programming for the whole family followed with "The George Burns and Gracie Allen Show" and the "Marx Brothers" for adults, "Howdy Doody" for kids, and "The Romance of Helen Trent" for women. It was 1932, the middle of the Great Depression (p. 87) and President Franklin Delano Roosevelt used the communal power of radio to broadcast inspiring "fireside chats" from the White House to living rooms across the nation.

6. **When was television invented?**

(A) 1920s
(B) 1930s
(C) 1940s
(D) 1950s

Experiments with the concept of sending pictures over the airwaves began in 1912. However, it was not until the 1930s that television sets as we know them today were invented. RCA, Westinghouse, General Electric, and AT&T battled to be the first to produce an affordable prototype. World War II (p. 650) brought the impending development of

When the British Broadcasting Corporation (BBC) began their service, the 10" x 12" pictures were received on sets that amateurs built themselves.

television to a halt as all electronics materials were put toward the war effort. By 1936 the **BBC** had begun broadcasting the world's first regular service, three times a day for three hours. In 1939 President Roosevelt became the first U.S. president to appear on television during an RCA experimental television exhibit at the New York World's Fair. In 1941 WNBC New York began the first commercial broadcast. Television premiered with a whimper, offering only four hours of programming a day in only three cities (New York, Los Angeles, Chicago) causing skeptics to proclaim TV to be an expensive passing fad.

In 1947 television manufacturing exploded. The end of World War II meant the rebirth of American mass production. Returning servicemen filled factory vacancies, ex-military wireless operators were hired to run TV stations, and military technicians began developing the latest technological advancements for television manufacturers. The demand quickly outnumbered the supply (p. 66) as Americans began spending their wartime savings on TVs.

7. ABC was once a part of which network?

(A) Fox
(B) NBC
(C) DuMont
(D) CBS

The **National Broadcasting Company (NBC)** was created by RCA in the 1920s to sell radios and the broadcasting equipment that RCA manufactured. NBC became the broadcasting arm of RCA when television emerged in the 1940s. NBC was originally composed of two networks,

THE SEVEN RULES OF PROGRAMMING (ACCORDING TO MICHAEL DANN, HEAD OF CBS PROGRAMMING IN THE 1970S)

1. In any given time period, the success of a show depends solely on its competition.
2. More than three-quarters of new programming will fail.
3. Never reschedule a whole night.
4. Never schedule one comedy by itself.
5. Never start feature movies at the beginning of the evening, especially because so many of them do not appeal to younger people.
6. Try to protect a new program by scheduling it between established shows.
7. Remember, the position a program is assigned is far more important than the content of the program itself.

Red and Blue, but in 1943, with only one other radio network in operation, the **Federal Communications Commission (FCC)** ruled that NBC's two networks constituted a monopoly. The Blue Network was sold to

"All in the Family"

Edward J. Noble, the owner of Lifesaver Candy, and became the **American Broadcasting Company (ABC)** in 1943. CBS started in 1927 as the United Independent Broadcasters. The company did not have the finances to make it on the air so they took on the Columbia Phonograph and Records Company as a partner and became the **Columbia Broadcasting System (CBS)**. In 1946 Allen B. DuMont created the **DuMont Television Network,** which folded in 1955.

The **Big Three** networks have always struggled to define themselves through their programming lineups, technological breakthroughs, exclusive "moments," and stars. CBS, known as the "Tiffany Network" because of the quality of its programming, was the number-one network until 1976. CBS defined itself with an all-star lineup of entertainers like Lucille Ball ("I Love Lucy" [1951-1957]), Jackie Gleason ("The Honeymooners" [1955-1956]; [1971]), Dick Van Dyke ("The Dick Van Dyke Show" [1961-1966]), Carroll O'Connor ("All In The Family" [1971-1983]), Mary Tyler Moore ("The Mary Tyler Moore Show" [1970-1977]), Telly Savalas ("Kojak" [1973-1978]), and Alan Alda ("M*A*S*H" [1972-1983]). In the transition years between radio and television' CBS bought many of NBC's biggest talents, including Amos 'n' Andy, Jack Benny, and Red Skelton. CBS was the first to recognize the significance of a network's channel placement on the dial and immediately set out to secure the first channel, number two, as their home on the television dial in major markets. The prime channel placement established

Rob and Laura Petrie have phone trouble in the suburbs.

CBS as both the channel most viewers would start watching and the network with the strongest signal frequency. In addition to its powerful entertainment roster, the network also built a reputation for news, based on the journalistic integrity of Edward R. Murrow, Walter Cronkite, and "60 Minutes."

NBC vs. CBS vs. ABC

The competition between the networks to broadcast news footage first became so fierce that in 1953 the coronation of Elizabeth II of England became a historic television event. NBC was determined to air footage of the event within hours to beat CBS's coverage. NBC sought help from scientists at the Massachusetts Institute of Technology and Eastman Kodak to devise a means of developing film on location. They devised a box able to develop 100 feet of film in twenty-five minutes. The developer was a secret formula that had to be mixed moments before developing. An NBC technician carried the secret formula in his wallet. The event was shot, the film was developed and put on board a chartered DC-6 from which NBC had removed the seats to make room for editing equipment. The footage was edited en route and ready for air by the time they landed in Boston. NBC beat CBS but, ironically, ABC, which did not participate in the race, received pictures of the event via BBC footage that arrived in Canada before NBC reached Boston. ABC took the Canadian Broadcasting Corporation signal and beat both CBS and NBC.

NBC could not compete with the star power of CBS, so they built a reputation as the network of innovation. NBC programming was built on the premise of mass appeal. The network concentrated on creating television formats that would attract the broadest possible audience. NBC is responsible for a number of TV firsts: talk show ("Broadway Open House" [1950]), morning talk ("Today" [1952-]), Sunday panel show ("Meet The Press" [1947-]), one-minute newscast ("Update" [1961-1963]), dual-anchor newscast ("The Huntley-Brinkley Report"), made-for-TV-movie, ensemble comedy show ("Rowan and Martin's Laugh-In" [1968-1973]), late-night programming ("Saturday Night Live" [1975-]), specials, one-hour soap operas, and full-color programming. NBC's star lineup included some of the most versatile entertainers in television history: Bob Hope, Groucho Marx, Sid Caesar, Jimmy Durante, Jack Paar, Johnny Carson, and David Letterman.

ABC was the youngest and the weakest of the networks. Finding it almost impossible to compete in original programming and unable to sign big stars, the network turned to movie studios like Disney and Warner Bros. for television production. The "Wonderful World Of Disney" went on to become a huge hit. The expense of converting to color in the 1960s almost destroyed ABC and left it vulnerable to takeovers by the likes of billionaire Howard Hughes. Throughout the difficult financial times the network concentrated on building its reputation in a single genre and established itself as the leader in sports television by its coverage of the Olympic Games, the creation of "Wide World Of Sports," and "Monday Night Football." In the 1970s and 1980s, ABC produced three of the most successful mini-seies of all time: "Roots" (1977), "The Thornbirds" (1983), and "Winds Of War" (1983).

Fox Broadcasting Co., whose name is taken from 20th Century-Fox studios, became the fourth network in 1986. The network premiered with a single program, "The Joan Rivers Show" (1986-1987). The show only lasted a year, calling into question the viability of a fourth network. Backed by the fortune of media mogul Rupert Murdoch, Fox began offering limited programming on Sunday. Instead of producing programming competitive with the other three networks, Fox established itself as a risk-taker by offering totally new concepts in television with the first prime-time animated series ("The Simpsons" [1989-]); the first tabloid news show ("A Current Affair" [1986-]); the first "reality-based" program ("America's Most Wanted" [1988-]); and a crude new image of the all-American family ("Married . . . with Children" [1987-]). By 1991 Fox's lineup was consistently placing shows in the top ten and they successfully attracted the audience most valuable to advertisers, fifteen- to thirty-five-year-olds.

The success of Fox brought two other Hollywood studios to television in 1994. Warner Bros. (WB) and Paramount (UPN) launched their own networks a few weeks apart to showcase their extensive movie libraries and establish prime locations on the dial before the expected channel explosion of the twenty-first century.

The spectacle of the Olympic games is well-suited to television's multimedia capabilities.

8. **The "Golden Years" of television refer to what time period?**

    (A) 1927-1937
    (B) 1937-1947
    (C) 1947-1957
    (D) 1957-1967

The years between 1947-1957 are generally regarded as the **"Golden Years"** of television. These were the gestation years for the medium, when popular radio programs switched to TV and listeners became watchers. The visual translation of some of these programs was crude and often

TUBETALK

....

Hammock Hit: a show that becomes popular because it's placed between two hit shows.

In 1946, there were 7,000 TV sets in existence; by 1992, there were over 900 million sets worldwide.

During the live tapings of "The Honeymooners," Jackie Gleason often forgot his lines. Rubbing his belly was the signal for Art Carney and Audrey Meadows to help him out.

Future big-time movie directors Woody Allen, Mel Brooks, and Carl Reiner all wrote for "Your Show Of Shows."

Television performers have to join the Screen Actors Guild (SAG) or AFTRA (American Federation of Television and Radio Artists). People in the audience of a show like "The Late Show with David Letterman" who read scripted material get paid SAG minimum—a couple hundred bucks.

uncomfortable because the wall between performer and audience had suddenly been erased. By 1947 the networks began developing ways to create more visually entertaining shows by finding talent whose looks and versatility could capture an audience's attention. These were the days of live television, in which everything was shot on film; studio shoots began using three cameras; dress rehearsals "wrapped" just prior to air time; the exact timing of shows varied due to differences between rehearsals and performances; the studio audience was established; sets created the bare minimum in atmosphere; and programs used film clips of street traffic or weather changes to give actors enough time to change wardrobes or run to the next location. When disaster struck, producers flashed amusing trouble cards on screen until the situation was restored and the show continued. Without the aid of editing or fancy graphics, television was honest, spontaneous, and highly addicting.

9. **Who was the host of "Your Show Of Shows"?**
   - (A) Ed Sullivan
   - (B) Milton Berle
   - (C) Groucho Marx
   - (D) Sid Caesar

"Your Show of Shows" (1950-1954) took over Saturday night entertainment. Hosted by **Sid Caesar** and **Imogene Coca,** the ninety-minute variety show featured everything from circus acts to comedy skits. On Saturday nights movie theaters in major television markets like New York City experienced a 20 to 40 percent drop in attendance, restaurants were empty, and taxicab receipts were down.

Popular radio **variety shows** soon became television's biggest sensation. **Milton Berle** hosted NBC's hit Tuesday night variety show "The Texaco Star Theater" (1948-1956). Berle started on radio without much success, but he was a physical comedian and TV captured all of his outrageousness, making him an instant star. "The Ed Sullivan Show" (1948-1971), originally called "Toast of the Town" (until 1955), did for Sunday nights what Sid Caesar did for Saturdays. Sullivan, nicknamed "The Great Stoneface," was an anomaly on TV with his lanky features, his obvious nervousness, and his odd way of speaking (". . . really big shew"), but he was a master at booking guests who were both topical and about to hit it big. Jack Benny, Jackie Gleason, Dean Martin, Jerry Lewis, Dinah Shore, the Beatles and Elvis Presley all made their TV debuts on the show.

Ed Sullivan gets satisfaction from Mick and the Stones.

Elvis made three apearances on "The Ed Sullivan Show." On his third appearance in 1956, Sullivan (who had allowed Elvis's prior appearances to be shot wide) instructed cameramen to shoot Elvis only from the waist up because he thought his suggestive hip movements corrupted the morals of American youth.

10. Walter Cronkite interrupted which program to report that President John F. Kennedy had been shot?

(A) "The $64,000 Question"
(B) "Leave It To Beaver"
(C) "As The World Turns"
(D) "What's My Line?"

During World War II (p. 650) Americans relied on the uncompromising integrity of **Edward R. Murrow's** radio newscasts for their information. He set the standards for tough, eloquent, and candid newscasting, and established CBS as *the* news network. Murrow is best remembered for a series of interviews on the TV's first documentary series "See It Now" (1952-1955), in which he confronted Senator Joseph McCarthy (p. 422) at the height of his power. The program made a hero out of Murrow and sowed the seeds of McCarthy's swift demise.

Walter Cronkite (1916-) followed Murrow at CBS news in 1962 and by the 1970s had garnered the label "the most trusted man in television." On November 22, 1963, Walter Cronkite interrupted "As the World Turns" to report: "In Dallas, Texas, three shots were

"

And that's the way it is.

—— WALTER CRONKITE'S SIGN-OFF

"

ANCHORS AWAY

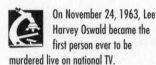 On November 24, 1963, Lee Harvey Oswald became the first person ever to be murdered live on national TV.

IMAGE IS EVERYTHING

 Broadcast News (1987), starring Holly Hunter and William Hurt. This film is a behind-the-scenes look at the madcap world of network news and the people who rise and fall according to looks rather than brains.

fired at President Kennedy's (p. 423) motorcade. The first reports say that the president was 'seriously wounded.' " Moments later, Cronkite wept openly as he announced the death of the president. For three days the nation was riveted to television sets as the networks offered around-the-clock coverage of the events unfolding in Dallas. The Kennedy assassination still stands as television's defining moment, prompting President Lyndon B. Johnson (p. 424) to issue this statement in its aftermath:

"Television's remarkable performance in communicating news of President John F. Kennedy's assassination and the events that followed was a source of sober satisfaction to all Americans. It acted swiftly. It acted surely. It acted intelligently and in impeccable taste. On that unforgettable weekend in November 1963, television provided a personal experience which all could share, a vast religious service which all could attend, a unifying bond which all could feel. I take this opportunity to add my voice to those who already have recognized television's historic contribution."

11. **How many women have anchored a weekday nightly news show on their own?**

   (A) None
   (B) One
   (C) Three
   (D) Five

The unspoken rule in television programming is that a woman cannot carry a show on her own. As of 1995 there has not been an evening weekday news show anchored solely by a woman. Television programming caters to advertising dollars and the audience most sought after by advertisers is young males, which explains why such a large proportion of television programming is centered around that population's tastes.

The role of women on television has changed very little over the years despite a significant increase in the number of women who work in the medium since the 1970s. Television derives most of its drama and humor through stereotypes. Women are invariably cast into one of four roles: the dimwit, Gracie Allen ("The George Burns and Gracie Allen Show" [1950-1958]) and Lucille Ball ("I Love Lucy" [1951-1957]); the matron, Barbara Billingsley ("Leave It To Beaver" [1957-1963]) and Florence Henderson ("Brady Bunch" [1969-1974]); the bombshell, Tina Louise ("Gilligan's Island" [1964-1967]) and Pamela Dean Anderson ("Baywatch" [1989-1990]); or the romantically desperate, Mary Tyler Moore ("The Mary Tyler Moore Show" [1970-1977]) and Kirstie Alley ("Cheers" [1982-1993]).

Phyllis, Mary, and Rhoda yuk it up on the "Mary Tyler Moore Show."

"I Love Lucy" Firsts

1. *First show filmed in front of a live audience*
2. *First show shot with three cameras*
3. *First show produced by an outside production company (Desilu)*
4. *First show filmed on the West Coast*
5. *First show to use actual pregnant woman on TV (Lucille Ball with Desi Arnaz Jr.)*

Notable exceptions include shows like "Roseanne" (1988-), "Murder She Wrote" (1984-), and "Murphy Brown" (1988-), all of which feature strong, independent women.

12. **What year did all three networks begin broadcasting in color?**
    (A) 1950
    (B) 1955
    (C) 1960
    (D) 1965

From the inception of television, manufacturers were developing the technology to broadcast in color. CBS was the first to create a full-color picture in 1946, but it operated on a rotating wheel that could not be viewed on the existing black-and-white sets. Six months later, RCA developed a shaky but compatible color system for black-and-white sets and the FCC awarded them the license to develop color TVs.

NBC was the first network to offer color programming in the 1950s, but the transition was slow and few shows were willing to go to the expense of switching to color film when advertisers were not being charged for the difference and the great majority of homes could only receive black-and-white images. It was not until 1965 that all three networks began broadcasting in color.

Tubetalk

Piggy back: *In order to keep the large audience of a previous show, the following show will start immediately, without a commercial break.*

 In 1955, 7.4 million TV sets were sold in U.S—forty-to-fifty thousand were color TVs.

13. Which opponent did Jimmy Carter defeat in a nationally televised presidential debate?

(A) Ronald Reagan
(B) Richard Nixon
(C) Gerald Ford
(D) George Bush

Political campaigns spend millions on commercial television time to create a positive image of their candidate or paint a derogatory picture of an opponent. In 1991, billionaire businessman Ross Perot spent millions to purchase half-hour prime-time slots on national stations to expound his political ideology in his bid for the presidency.

Bob Roberts (1992), starring Tim Robbins. This mock documentary takes a satirical look at a senatorial campaign—poking fun at the media, politics, and the American political climate.

One-time movie and television actor President Ronald Reagan was called "the great communicator" for the way in which he used television appearances to manipulate lawmakers and sway public opinion in his favor.

In 1960 the first presidential debate was televised. Since then every "winner" of televised debates has gone on to capture the presidency. Television has changed the course of American politics. TV's first debate featured the young, handsome John Kennedy versus the stern Richard Nixon (p. 425). Kennedy was tan, having just returned from campaigning in California, and Nixon looked pale, apparently fighting a cold. Both candidates were asked if they wanted makeup. Kennedy was the first to say no, and then Nixon declined. Nixon's advisors were worried about his appearance and applied Lazy-Shave, a product that was supposed to hide five-o'clock shadow. It didn't work. Radio listeners scored the debate even, but the seventy million television viewers declared Kennedy the overwhelming winner. Nixon learned a valuable lesson about the power of the medium and never accepted another invitation for a televised debate during his presidency.

Television and politics have shared a tenuous relationship since the medium's emergence in the 1940s. It can elevate a politician to the godlike idolatry President Kennedy enjoyed during much of his term in office. It can also expose skeletons and improprieties from which presidents never recover as Nixon discovered with Watergate and Reagan, to a lesser extent, with the Iran-Contra affair (p. 663). Presidents have been forced to learn how to use the medium to their advantage by staging made-for-TV "photo opportunities" in strategic locations and addressing the nation with carefully scripted speeches, wardrobes, and gestures.

14. How many American households have Nielsen boxes on their television sets?

(A) One million
(B) 650,000
(C) 125,000
(D) 4,000

In 1923 **Arthur C. Nielsen** established a company that would tabulate the radio audience's numbers for radio stations so that stations could set

Radar's bear will be the only one with dry eyes after this final scene from M*A*S*H.

TUBETALK

Sweeps: *February and November are the months advertisers look at to set their rates. Shows try to attract viewers by airing titillating or controversial programs or big Hollywood movies.*

their advertising rates according to the popularity of different programs. Today the **Nielsen rating system** tabulates the same thing for television. Four thousand television households in two hundred markets across the country have been selected through census data to be Nielsen families. Every TV set in these households is hooked up with a Nielsen box that records the shows that are watched, how long the viewer stays tuned, whether channels are switched to avoid commercials, and who is watching.

The Nielsen ratings determine the percentage of the population that is watching a particular show. For example, a rating of twenty means that 20 percent of the television households in that market watched that show. Advertisers are also interested in a show's **share numbers**, which indicate how many people watched a particular show out of all the households watching TV at the same time. Share numbers indicate how well a show is doing compared to all the other shows in the same time period, ranking a show in its time slot for advertising dollars.

Ten Top-Rated Programs of All Time

Rank	Show	Rating
1.	"M*A*S*H" (last episode)	60.2
2.	"Dallas" (Who Shot J.R.)	53.3
3.	Roots (part 8)	51.1
4.	Super Bowl XVI	49.1
5.	Super Bowl XVII	48.6
6.	Winter Olympics '94	48.5
7.	Gone With The Wind (Part 1)	47.7
8.	Super Bowl XX	48.3
9.	Gone With The Wind (Part 2)	47.4
10.	Super Bowl XII	47.2

15. Match the show with the television genre:

(A)	"Wonder Woman"	_____	Soap Opera
(B)	"Falcon Crest"	_____	Talk Show
(C)	"Lifeline"	_____	Police Show
(D)	"Little House on the Prairie"	_____	Sci Fi/Fantasy
(E)	"Adam-12"	_____	Sitcom
(F)	"Seinfeld"	_____	Medical Drama
(G)	"Remote Control"	_____	Western
(H)	"Today"	_____	Detective Show
(I)	"Ironside"	_____	Game Show

Television's most popular genre is the **situation comedy**. The name derives from the format's dependence on an incident or device that activates the comedy element. Episodes usually begin with a familiar set of characters in normal situations. Inevitably something out of the ordinary occurs to one or more of the characters which sets up a series of funny lines and scenarios before resolving itself in a hilarious climax. The essential element of a **sitcom** is to establish a consistency in its main characters because it is the predictableness with which they approach each new situation that elicits the huge laugh . . . from the laugh track.

The **soap opera** got its name from the soap companies like Procter & Gamble, which sponsored the early shows. Shown in the daytime hours to an almost exclusively female audience, the soap opera has not changed significantly from its beginnings on radio in the 1930s to today. The premise of a soap is that through a large and ever-changing cast, complex stories between characters can overlap, slowly evolve, and resolve themselves as new plot-lines develop in an unending cycle. Themes center predominantly around troubled human relationships, moral and legal dilemmas, and popular issues of the day. Soaps are infamous for addressing cases of adultery, nymphomania, murder, impotence, and fortuitously timed amnesia.

Soaps generate a fanatically loyal following, making the popular shows like "All My Children" (1970-) and "General Hospital" (1963-) two of the longest-running shows on TV, and the chances of starting a successful new one almost impossible. In the late 1970s the networks tried replicating some of that fierce daytime loyalty in prime time and had enormous success with shows like "Dallas" (1978-1991) and "Dynasty" (1981-1989) and again in the 1990s with "Beverly Hills 90210" (1990-) and "Melrose Place" (1991-).

Due to their popularity at the movies, **westerns** made an easy transition to TV. Two different types of westerns appeared on TV. The first were

FAMOUS ONE-TIME SOAP OPERA ACTORS

Susan Sarandon

Marisa Tomei

Christian Slater

Alec Baldwin

Demi Moore

Tony Randall

horse operas featuring horse and rope tricks performed by polished cowboys like Hopalong Cassidy (1949-1951) and The Lone Ranger (1949-1957). The second were the adult westerns in which grungy cowboys fought over good and evil in shows like "Gunsmoke" (1955-1975), "Wyatt Earp" (1955-1961), and "Bonanza" (1959-1973). In 1959 there were thirty-two westerns on television, but by 1975 there were none, as police and detective shows took over the reins.

The police show, TV's second most-popular genre of all time, premiered in 1951 with "Dragnet" (1951-1959; 1967-1970). The police show brought realistic suspense and no-nonsense dialogue to TV. Some of the greatest programs include "The Mod Squad" (1968-1973), "The Streets Of San Francisco" (1972-1977), and "Hill Street Blues" (1981-1987).

SPIN-OFFS	
Original	*Spin-Off(s)*
"All In The Family"	"Maude"/"The Jeffersons"/"Gloria"
"The Andy Griffith Show"	"Gomer Pyle, U.S.M.C."/"Mayberry, R.F.D."
"Happy Days"	"Laverne & Shirley"/"Mork & Mindy"/ "Joannie Loves Chachi"
"The Mary Tyler Moore Show"	"Rhoda"/"Phyllis"/"Lou Grant"
"M*A*S*H"	"Trapper John, M.D."/After M*A*S*H
"The Tracey Ullman Show"	"The Simpsons"

Out of the police show came the detective show. The scenario changed from episode-to-episode but the result was always the same. These shows are almost always built around the eccentricities of the detectives who lend the shows their character. Some of the most memorable are "77 Sunset Strip" (1958-1964), "Columbo" (1971-1978) "The Rockford Files" (1974-1980), "Charlie's Angels" (1976-1981), and "Magnum P.I." (1980-1988).

Medical shows have been around since 1954's "Medic" (1954-1956) and have provided endless hours of life-or-death drama. These shows often play to the deepest fears of their audience by enacting believable accidents and realistic medical emergency procedures. The most inspiring include "Marcus Welby M.D." (1969-1976), "Emergency" (1972-1977), "St. Elsewhere" (1982-1988), and "ER" (1994-).

Since 1949's "Captain Video And His Video Rangers" (1949-1955) there have been sci-fi and fantasy shows on the air playing with our notion of

"Drive! She said."

outer space, superhuman capabilities, the supernatural, and the future. Many of the programs served as showcases for the latest in gadgetry, special effects and computer-generated images. Shows like "Buck Rogers in the 25th Century" (1979-1981) and "Star Trek" (1966-1969) take weird looks at the future. "The Twilight Zone" (1959-1964) featured big-name actors like Robert Redford ("Nothing In The Dark") and Burgess Meredith ("Time Enough at Last") to propel the viewer into another realm, a "fifth dimension," that gave television the sense of being a window into a different reality. Don't miss these other classics: "Lost In Space" (1965-1968), "Battlestar Galactica" (1978-1979), "Dark Shadows" (1966-1971), and "The Six Million Dollar Man" (1974-1978).

The talk show made its debut in 1950 with the unscripted "Broadway Open House" (1950-1951). The talk show has evolved in different directions over the years, from comedy, "The Steve Allen Show" (1951-1957), current events, "The Today Show" (1952-); celebrity brownnosing, "The Merv Griffin Show" (1962-1963), comfortable personalities, "The Oprah Winfrey Show" (1986-), and late-night, "The Tonight Show" (1957-) and "The Late Show with David Letterman" (1993-). All of these constitute talk shows in one form or another and all capitalize on the fact that television is, at its base, a personality medium. It seems like each of us will have a chance to host a talk show some day, at the rate these shows come and go each year. Talk shows are extremely cheap to produce compared to a half-hour sitcom and can generate tremendous revenue for a network or syndicator if, for some intangible reason, people want to hear you talk.

Over 400 **game shows** have come and gone on TV since its inception. Starting on radio, the game show has held a firm place in daytime and early evening network lineups ever since. The basic elements in all the shows are virtually identical: a lively host, a studio audience, "real people contestants," a game, and prizes of cash or merchandise. Only the game element differs among shows. Starting on radio with programs like the "$64 Question," games have included matched wits, "The College Bowl" (1959-1970, 1987); dating, "The Dating Game" (1965-1974, 1978-1980, 1986); talent, "The Gong Show" (1976-1980); pricing, "The Price is Right" (1956-); lying, "Truth or Consequences" (1950-1978); and music, "Remote Control" (1987-1990). The chance to win an easy fortune coupled with suspense and surprises all add up to an encapsulation of the American Dream.

On "Star Trek," Captain Kirk and Officer Uhuru shared TV's first interracial kiss (if you don't count Spock kissing Nurse Chapel, which happens a few seconds earlier in the same episode).

Quiz Show (1994), starring Robert Redford. This is an enthralling look into the quiz show scandal and its permanent effect on the trust between the public and TV.

16. How much was CBS's record-breaking contract with major league baseball worth?

(A) $6.24 Billion
(B) $1.08 Billion
(C) $817 million
(D) $378 million

In 1921, experimental radio aired a prizefight. In 1939 experimental television broadcast a Princeton vs. Columbia baseball game (p. 442). Athletic competition offers live unscripted action, suspense, unpredictability, heroes, and villains while delivering the almighty young male audience advertisers drool over. Television offers unrivaled insight and perspective on games and events, from the locker room to the blimp and everywhere in between, that can sometimes even beat being at the event itself. It's the ideal marriage. Television and sports have become enmeshed to the extent that sporting events are now created for television, rules are changed to allow for commercial interruptions and more scoring opportunities, locations are determined by the TV market size, and starting times are adjusted to maximize national and international viewing potential. Both pro and college sports have become products of television, using it to market their players, schools, and merchandise while allegedly upholding the integrity of real competition between teams.

This marriage has led to outrageous sums of money changing hands between networks and leagues, and leagues and players. Every few years new television contracts are offered to the highest bidder for exclusive coverage of games and events and new records are set, like the $1.08 billion CBS paid in 1990 for the rights to major league baseball coverage or the $1.58 billion Fox paid in 1994 for the television rights to NFL games.

The 1980s saw the emergence of the superstar sports figure. Athletes like Magic Johnson, Michael Jordan, Joe Montana, Wayne Gretzky, and Roger Clemens became symbols of their respective leagues. These players

TUBETALK

PSA: Public Service Announcement aired for free by stations to promote a moral or informational cause.

THE HEIDI INCIDENT

On November 17, 1968, the New York Jets were leading the Oakland Raiders in Oakland 32 to 29 with 1:05 left in the game. NBC executives felt it was obvious who was going to win the game and switched to the made-for-TV children's classic, "Heidi," after a commercial. What football fans did not witness was an amazing last-minute comeback by the Raiders, as running back Daryl Smith scored on a 43-yard run and scored again nine seconds later when the Raiders recovered a Jets kickoff return fumble on the two-yard line and returned it for a touchdown. The Raiders had won 43 to 32. Now almost all live sporting events are shown in their entirety, even if they run a little long.

Superstar, celebrity, and multi-millionaire: it's Magic!

not only elevated their teams' standings but created a personal marketability that generated hundreds of millions of dollars for the league, the teams, the networks, and, of course, themselves. No longer did superstar athletes see themselves as players on a team within a league. They were now celebrity entertainers worthy of multi-million-dollar, multi-year contracts, and often earned twice their salaries in advertising endorsement deals. The whole mentality of team sports changed, forcing wealthy teams to acquire one or two "marquee players" to draw crowds and, poorer teams to pray for miracles.

Cable television further expanded the relationship between sports and TV with the wildly successful twenty-four-hour sports channel ESPN as well as pay-per-view events, HBO SPORTS, ESPN2, and MTV Sports.

17. You've got a video tape of Madonna "doin' the nasty" with Michael Jackson and you want some cash for it; who do you call?

(A) Madonna
(B) A bodyguard
(C) A tabloid TV show
(D) Michael

You're in the check-out line at the supermarket scanning the magazines, your eye catches an outrageous headline with a shocking picture of a celebrity, you look both ways, grab the rag, and the next thing you know you're flipping through as many pages as you can before the guy ahead of you finishes bagging. You get home, flip through channels and see the same story you were reading about on TV. If any of this sounds familiar, count yourself a victim of **tabloid journalism,** one of the fastest growing genres in media.

"A Current Affair" (1986-) was launched by Fox, the only network without a national news show. Critics were outraged that this type of sensational journalism was brought to television, threatening decades of journalistic integrity the other networks had battled to uphold. By 1994 every news show on television was competing with tabloid shows like "Hard Copy" (1989-) and "Inside Edition" (1990-) for stories.

These shows often pay up to several hundred thousand dollars for exclusive interviews and footage, not questioning the veracity of the source and often discounting key witnesses' testimony in the case of a trial. Bidding wars between shows for exclusive rights surround even the most obscure cases, calling into question the perpetrators' motives for some widely publicized criminal acts.

ADDING INSULT TO INJURY

"A Current Affair" gained national exposure in 1988 during the Robert Chambers "preppy murder" trial when it aired an exclusive home video of Chambers laughing and joking with scantily clad women and apparently reenacting with a doll his crime of killing a woman.

18. **Which sitcom inspired "The Flintstones," "The Jetsons," and "The Simpsons"?**
    (A) "All in the Family"
    (B) "Happy Days"
    (C) "The Honeymooners"
    (D) "Father Knows Best"

In the early years, TV manufacturers highlighted television's appeal to children in order to sell sets. In the 1950s when most households had one set, programs were often targeted to children in the late afternoon and early evening hours because networks believed children controlled the TV viewing in a household until they went to bed. Today networks still put a priority on attracting young audiences in hopes they will lure adult viewers to their network. Until the 1960s children were not considered a lucrative market-

"One of these days, Alice!"

CULTURESCOPE

WATCH ME, LOVE ME, BUY ME

Shows like "The Smurfs," "Teenage Mutant Ninja Turtles," and "Mighty Morphin Power Rangers" have all generated millions of dollars in profits for merchandisers and networks and have spawned a Saturday morning marketing frenzy.

 On New Year's Day, 1965, comedian Soupy Sales jokingly told kids watching his show to get their fathers' wallets and take out "those little green pieces of paper with pictures of George Washington, Benjamin Franklin, Lincoln, and Jefferson on them. Send them to me." The letters came in, parents were outraged, and Soupy was suspended from the show for a week.

ing group for advertisers because advertising was still so expensive that most products were geared toward adults. In 1965 children's programming began to change for two reasons. First, a significant number of homes became dual set owners, freeing up one set for kids to select their own shows. Second, networks discovered that they made a big profit off their cheap Saturday morning time slots by offering advertisers a solely children's audience during those hours.

During the 1960s animated cartoons arrived on Saturday mornings with the adventures of Rocky and Bullwinkle in "Rocky and His Friends" (1959-1961), a cartoon parody of "The Honeymooners" called "The Flintstones" (1960-1966), and later a space-age parody called "The Jetsons" (1962-1983). The Television Code restricted networks to nine and a half minutes of commercials per hour in prime time but there were no rules for Saturday mornings and networks sold advertisers as much as sixteen minutes per hour. Nobody seemed to notice the abuses until networks began trying to attract kids by producing gratuitously violent cartoons in the 1970s. Parents eventually objected and watchdog groups were established to monitor children's programming and advertising.

In 1969 public television launched the revolutionary concept that TV could provide programs for kids that both taught and entertained. Shows like "Mr. Rogers' Neighborhood" (1967-1975; 1979-) "Sesame Street" (1969-) and "The Electric Company" (1971-1976) led the commercial networks to develop a few educational programs of their own, but nothing has compared to the success of PBS's children's programming.

19. **Whose gap tooth is wider?**
    (A) Lauren Hutton
    (B) Alfred E. Newman
    (C) Dave Letterman
    (D) Ollie North

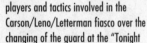 *The Late Shift* (1994), by Bill Carter. Carter gives us a behind-the-scenes look at the players and tactics involved in the Carson/Leno/Letterman fiasco over the changing of the guard at the "Tonight Show" in 1992.

There are only three names you need to know in the pantheon of late-night television—Ed Sullivan, Johnny Carson, and David Letterman. Ed Sullivan helped transfer the format from radio to television and created a place on TV to showcase talent. Carson brought a middle-American sensibility to it, polished it, and peppered it with off-color

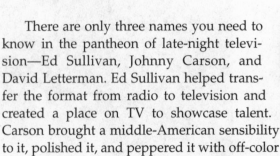

"What, me worry?"

humor. Letterman has combined the best of both predecessors and added his own signature sense of unpredictability, irreverence, and fun. Letterman is a fitting king of late-night, having guest-hosted for Johnny Carson on the "The Tonight Show" and renovated Ed Sullivan's old theater in New York City when he switched networks in 1993.

20. **When was cable television introduced?**
     (A) 1950s
     (B) 1960s
     (C) 1970s
     (D) 1980s

Cable television was introduced in the late 1970s as a means of transmitting a larger number of channels through coaxial cable as well as improving network television reception. Its impact has brought the most significant change to television to date. Pioneered as a pay service by **Home Box Office (HBO)** in 1975, cable TV offered uncut, uncensored, commercial-free movies and sports events for a monthly fee.

By 1980 cable TV exploded and everyone wanted a piece of it. Specialized channels for news (CNN), sports (ESPN), music (MTV), politics (C-SPAN), sex (Playboy Channel), kids (Nickelodeon), and culture (Arts & Entertainment Network) emerged and attracted large audiences. The networks were blindsided by the cable invasion and totally missed the boat on creating their own channels with which to market their existing programs and re-broadcast shows from their libraries. Advertisers suddenly had fifty additional channels to place their commercials on, which forced ad rates to come down and opened the television market to smaller companies that once could not afford to advertise in the medium.

21. **Which one of these TV attachments was introduced in 1975?**
     (A) Atari game system
     (B) Sony Betamax
     (C) VHS recorder
     (D) Pong

In 1975 Sony introduced a technological breakthrough in home entertainment, capable of recording and playing video cassettes on television. **Betamax** attracted a lot of attention, but the units were expensive and the tapes only offered 100 minutes of recording time. Before you could say **"video cassette recorder,"** Matsushita introduced **VHS**-format cassettes and VCRs at half the price and twice the recording time as the Betamax. Matsushita had wisely enlisted the U.S. electronics giant, RCA, to market its new VCR in the United States. RCA staged an aggressive marketing campaign that established VHS as the wave of the future despite the fact that Betamax offered both better-quality picture and sound.

The VCR brought a revolution to television viewing at the same time that cable television was catching fire. Movie classics and recently released films saw a rejuvenation in the video market and Hollywood studios that were at first wary of the VCR's impact on first-run movie releases recognized the immense revenue they could garner by turning their film libraries over to the rental market. The rental market has put pressure on film studios to create "blockbuster" hits accompanied by promotional blitzes to convince audiences to see a film in the theater instead of waiting for it to come out on video. Television manufacturers have developed larger-format TV screens and stereo sound systems as televisions started evolving into home movie theaters.

TUBETALK

Back-End: income created by a show after its original run, usually in syndication, foreign market, licensing, video, etc.

22. **What was the first music video ever played on MTV?**
    (A) "Video Killed the Radio Star" (The Buggles)
    (B) "Paradise By the Dashboard Lights" (Meatloaf)
    (C) "Candy O'" (The Cars)
    (D) "Rebel, Rebel" (David Bowie)

In 1980 The Buggles' song "Video Killed The Radio Star" ironically launched the **Music Television Channel (MTV)**. MTV (p. 320) was originally formatted like a radio station, employing knowledgeable music buffs as video jockeys (VJs) to introduce music videos and offer commentary in between. The aim was to create a captive audience while playing music from a wide variety of different musical genres. The channel began developing original programming that mirrored the traditional network lineup of news, sports, game shows, dramas, cartoons and specials, and structured them loosely around music themes. The mixture of the familiar format and the latest music instantly set MTV apart from everything else on the dial.

The competition between record labels to get their artists' videos aired on MTV is fierce. Having a video played on MTV means the difference between success

Anchorwoman Tabitha Soren of MTV

and failure for many artists. Practically every top-100 artist on the pop and rock charts has at least one video from their latest release playing on MTV. The virtual monopoly MTV holds on the recording industry has led many artists and labels to call into question their criteria for selecting videos and artists, and the conflict of interest inherent when MTV plays music videos that promote their own projects like the "Unplugged" series. MTV has created a home for the music industry and cultivated its stars in a way that rivals the movie industry in prominence.

At the same time that music videos were becoming more sophisticated, so were the advertisers who chose to run their commercials on MTV. Advertisers started incorporating an "MTV style" of fast cutting, skewed camera angles, and "in your face" promotion so that their ads wouldn't pale in comparison to music videos. Today the MTV style is everywhere, from feature films to network shows. MTV's manic style caters to a new generation of television viewers whose familiarity with the medium allows information to be broken into smaller and faster pieces with the same amount of information retention. Essentially, MTV is responsible for cultivating a new television language.

23. **How much money did Rev. Oral Roberts claim he needed to raise from his television ministry before God would take his life?**

   (A) $1,000,000
   (B) $2,300,000
   (C) $4,500,000
   (D) $12,000,000

During the seventies and eighties, fundamentalist (p. 509) preachers bought up air time on Sunday mornings that local stations once gave as a public service to local religious programming, and created television ministries. Televangelists (p. 509) preach salvation and solicit financial contributions from their viewers. Televangelists like Jim Bakker (p. 510) and Jimmy Swaggert not only raked in hundreds of millions of dollars in "donations" but their loyal adherents helped form the base of what was to be called the religious right (p. 399). Widespread scandal and corruption led to the demise of televangelism in the late 1980s. Oral Roberts reached a low point when he told listeners that God would take his life if he did not raise $4.5 million. Oral did not attain his goal, but another message from God offered a reprieve. Hallelujah!

INFOMERCIALS

Another television marketing phenomenom to come out of the 1980s is the commercial masquerading in the form of a program, the infomercial. "Great Looking Hair #9," "The Flowbee," "The Vegematic," "Psychic Friends," and "The Abdominizer" are all products being offered after midnight on television channels that don't have enough programming to fill a twenty-four-hour schedule.

24. In 1994 what was the most watched show in the world?

(A) "The Simpsons"
(B) "Beverly Hills 90210"
(C) "Baywatch"
(D) "Murder She Wrote"

Ever wonder why the rest of the world looks at Americans funny? The answer might be in our old TV shows. Italians still watch "Baretta," and Turks still dig "Kojak." Swedes love "Beverly Hills 90210," Brazilians get a kick out of "The Simpsons," and in 1994 "Baywatch" was the world's most popular program. The world television market has opened up in the 1990s as television sales continue to rise and cable TV spreads through Europe and Asia. The United States produces more programming and exports more of our old and current shows than any other country. Kids in parts of Asia are imitating the Fonz from "Happy Days" and dressing like Daisy Duke from the "Dukes Of Hazard," though they can't speak a word of English nor do they realize that those shows were cancelled years ago.

Syndication, the marketing of programming to local and international stations, is where the big money in television production lies these days. Shows like "M*A*S*H," "The Cosby Show," and "Cheers" will live on forever in the syndication market, earning millions for their producers and stars years after they are off the air. The trend in both film and television production is to create movies and programs that attract a worldwide audience. Blockbuster action films like *Terminator* and "all-American" TV

The Fonz with Richie and Ralph Malph at Arnold's

shows like "Baywatch" promote a stereotypical view of American life—gun-wielding villains and babes in bikinis double or triple the revenue in the foreign market.

25. Which of these companies is NOT yet involved in the future of television?
    (A) TCI
    (B) FMCI
    (C) REI
    (D) IBM

Five hundred channels, two-way video telephones, video on command, interactive programming, high-definition images, banking, taxes, shopping, voting, school, libraries, business, and dating will all be available through our television sets in the near future. Since its inception people have recognized the enormous potential for the future of television. Computer giants like **IBM**, telephone companies like **MCI**, and cable television conglomerates like **TCI** are merging and competing for a piece of the information superhighway. Whatever hardware is produced will combine the elements of a telephone, personal computer, and television. At this point, the future is mostly conjecture but it is certain that there will be an enormous demand for programming to fill the world's insatiable appetite for new information and entertainment. Television has introduced us visually to different parts of the world, the Internet (p. 347) has opened up the means of communication, and the future will combine the two, making each of our homes television studios and all of us hosts of our own adventures. Stay tuned.

Answers

1. D	2. B	3. B	4. B	5. D	6. B	7. B	8. C	9. D	10. C
11. A	12. D	13. C	14. D	15. From top to bottom: B,H,E,A,F,C,D,I,G					16. B
17. C	18. C	19. How the hell should we know?			20. C	21. B	22. A	23. C	
24. C	25. C								

Theater, like history, tends to repeat itself. The stories we tell of betrayal, love, ambition, and rotten families have been around since before the ancient Greeks, and we continue to retell these stories, with a modern twist, in current theater, television, and movies. When we study theater, older cultures become more accessible and more understandable.

The development of theater also reflects political and social pressures as they act on culture. Generally speaking, periods of serious drama decline into those of decadence, featuring sex, spectacle, and pure entertainment rather than insight and ideas. What follows, then, is a reaction by the dominant religious or ideological group, which denounces theater as dangerous and immoral, and things quiet down, until the whole process starts back up again. You just can't keep a good playwright down, and you can't keep the urge to write and perform out of any civilization that takes itself seriously.

The Greek Way (1930), by Edith Hamilton. Scholarly and easy to read, Hamilton's books on the Greeks and Romans are the way to go if you want to understand the context of the culture, including theater.

1. **Match the Greek to his play:**

   (A) Aeschylus   ___*Frogs*
   (B) Euripides   ___*Antigone*
   (C) Sophocles   ___*Medea*
   (D) Aristophanes   ___*Oresteia*

The stories and gods of Greek tragedy came from earlier civilizations, mostly the Minoan, Mycenean, and Trojan. Using the Phoenician alphabet, the Greeks began writing around 700 B.C. In 508 B.C. the Athenians started the first democracy and became the artistic center of Greece.

Oresteia (458 B.C.), by Aeschylus. This trilogy of tragic dramas consists of *Agamemnon*, *Choëphori*, and the *Eumenides*. It has all of the elements of classic mythology: grisly murders, the Furies, fallen royalty, dramatic irony. It's better than "Melrose Place."

Ancient Greeks are more or less credited with the invention of Western European drama, which evolved from religious festivals, rituals, and celebrations. Chants to **Dionysus**, the god of fertility, wine, and drama, evolved into tragedy, definitely a Greek invention.

Greek tragedies began as plays for only one actor (although he played more than one part) and a chorus, and followed a set of dramatic conventions: the *prologue*, which explains the situation about to unfold; the *parados*, in which the chorus enters; a number of episodes of action; and finally the *exodus*, which wraps up the story.

Aeschylus (c. 525-456 B.C.), sometimes called the father of Western drama (playwrights of nearly every age since have stolen shamelessly from his trilogy, the *Oresteia* [458 B.C.]), is said to have written his plays while drunk. One of his innovations was to add another actor to the stage, which gave dramatists more flexibility in telling a complicated story. One advantage the Greek tragedians had was that their audiences knew the stories in advance. Everybody knew about the curse on the **House of Atreus** and other standard Greek plots, so the writers were free to interpret these legends rather than having to come up with their own material.

Sophocles (496 - 406 B.C.) was a big winner in the prize competitions that brought a flurry of writers to Athens. He further developed dramatic structure by adding a third actor and emphasized psychological motivation in his complex characterizations. Both his *Antigone* (440 B.C.) and *Oedipus Rex* (424 B.C.) are still frequently performed and reinterpreted.

Euripides (485-406 B.C.) was not particularly popular with Athenians of his time, partly because his plots were considered unacceptably racy and did not support the prevailing family values. His **Medea** killed her own children, and, in other plays, his characters get mixed up in bestiality

FROM POETICS

Tragedy, then, is an imitation of an action that is serious, complete, and of a certain magnitude; in language embellished with each kind of artistic ornament, the several kinds being found in separate parts of the play; in the form of action, not of narrative; through pity and fear effecting the proper purgation of these and similar emotions.

——*Aristotle*

The exact circumstances of Sophocles' death are not known and have been the subject of some improbable conjecture. One of the stories the ancient Greeks circulated about the great poet is that he died while trying to recite a particularly long line from *Antigone* without taking a breath.

and incest. Euripides's imagination, coupled with his questioning of the gods, was thought dangerous, and this most skeptical and angry of the Greek tragedians would receive his full due only from later generations.

About a hundred years after Aeschylus, **Aristophanes** (450-388 B.C.) wrote comedic plays that satirized contemporary society, full of sex, overeating, and drinking. In *Frogs* (405 B.C.), the characters are his rivals, Aeschylus, Sophocles, and Euripides, who are engaged in a contest in Hades, arguing over literary matters. Other well-known works include *Lysistrata* (411 B.C.) and *Clouds* (423 B.C.).

In 404 B.C. Athens lost the **Peloponnesian War** and that was pretty much the end of their domination of theater art.

2. **The Roman dramatist known for his plots of mistaken identity and long-lost twins is**

   (A) Seneca
   (B) Tertullian
   (C) Plautus
   (D) Terence

Romans enjoyed a great variety of entertainment: jugglers, sporting events, chariot races, music, and dance. A favorite of the Romans was gladiatorial combat (p. 433). Romans were generally more interested in military matters than in philosophy, and this difference from the more philosophical Greek character shows in their art.

Plautus (251-184 B.C.) and **Seneca** (4 B.C.-65 A.D.) are the two major Roman dramatists whose work is still studied. **Plautus** (254 B.C.-184 B.C.) gave familiar Greek plots his own bizarre spin, so much so that the adjective "plautine" refers to the zany Roman's peculiar brand of farcical illogic. The stories tended to fall apart, but the comic effect was tremendous. A hundred years after his death Romans still flocked to see Plautus's weird brand of unreality.

Plautus

Andrew Lloyd Webber's theatrical excitements are puny compared to the Romans' *Naumachiae*. Julius Caesar ordered his slaves to dig a lake and fill it with water. Add 2,000 marines, and 6,000 oarsmen and, *voilà*, a sea battle for a day's entertainment!

A Funny Thing Happened On the Way to the Forum (1966), based on Stephen Sondheim's Broadway musical. In this film you get to see Zero Mostel and Phil Silvers in togas!

CULTURESCOPE

Seneca pushed the extremes as well, but in the other direction. He specialized in stories of depravity that always featured plenty of gore (think *Friday the 13th* in togas). It's unclear whether the Romans ever actually staged any of Seneca's tragedies—they were probably only read by the jaded upper crust. Yet Seneca's influence on theater has been considerable. He was the first to divide plays into **five acts**, and the Elizabethan tragedians studied Seneca and copied many of his effects, like leaving the fifth act's stage strewn with fresh corpses.

Theater began to dwindle at the end of the Roman Empire, mostly because the Empire itself was falling apart, and partly because the Christians opposed it, understandable given that theatrical subjects tended toward adultery, paganism, and violence, with jokes about Christian sacraments applied liberally throughout.

 Satyricon (1970), by Federico Fellini. This cinematic adaptation of the one Roman novel extant (although it is not complete) is insane, confusing, and bizarre—the one movie that shows the freaky Rome that, in all probability, really existed.

3. Which one of the following was NOT developed in the thirteenth and fourteenth centuries?

   (A) Passion plays
   (B) Morality plays
   (C) Sanskrit plays
   (D) Mummer's plays

When the Roman Empire fell, it fell hard. The accumulated learning and artistic sophistication of centuries of Mediterranean culture were almost entirely lost. The Catholic Church (p. 492) became the supreme cultural force, and, not surprisingly, new theater centered around the church. Enactments of the last days of Christ, called **passion plays**, were popular, and later, a kind of theater emerged which dramatized the soul's struggle through earthly life toward the ultimate goal of salvation. **Miracle plays**, which were purely Biblical, evolved into **morality plays**, which were still allegorical but dramatized the Devil and his various temptations, to the delight of audiences. *Everyman* (1510) is the most famous of these.

In medieval times, **Dances of Death** were performed throughout Europe. The dancing got particularly frenzied when the **bubonic plague** hit and death was everywhere. Less macabre forms of dance took place during pageants on Saint's Days, at tournaments, and during seasonal festivals.

The Far East—especially India—maintained a relative social continuity in the first millennium. Indian theater enjoyed an evolving tradition that was already many centuries old. Indeed, Hindu legend has the lesser gods staging a spectacle for the Great God Brahma (p. 477) himself.

Classical Indian theater, also called **Sanskrit theater**, is difficult for Western civilization to comprehend fully. Where in the West dance has long had a problematic relationship to drama, in India the two have always been inextricably linked. Along with the close relationship of theater and dance in Sanskrit plays, one finds a very different sense of how a story should be told. Narration, poetry, dance, mime, music, and dramatic performance were combined fluidly; this was necessary because the language could get so bombastic that much of the audience wouldn't know quite what the characters were saying to each other. As for the plots, the Sanskrit authors played fast and loose with reality, leaping from place to place and time to time at the blink of a metaphor. The heros sometimes disappear for an act or two, and whole plot lines are abandoned. But all this mayhem, besides being delightfully entertaining (which, after all, is the point), obeyed carefully conceived rules. Indian classical theater was based on the sophisticated notion of *rasa*, a highly developed sense of harmony drawn from a religious world-view that sees the universe as intricately and divinely ordered. As a result of this complex aesthetic sense, classical Indian theater shows a world in which chaos and imbalance threaten to take over, but ultimately bliss is restored.

DANSOMANIA

Around 1530, Paracelsus tried to cure "dansomania," in which whole towns at a time would be caught up in day-long wild dancing, fall down, and get trampled. The Italians believed such dancing was brought on by the bite of a tarantula, and that people would die from the poison if they stopped dancing. The folk dance that came from this is called the tarantella.

4. **What is considered the classic theater of Japan?**
   (A) *Kabuki*
   (B) *Kyogen*
   (C) *Bunraku*
   (D) *Noh*

Japanese culture's exquisite refinements, such as the **tea ceremony**, in which tea is slowly and painstakingly prepared, or *ikebana* (the highly codified art of Japanese flower arranging), can easily confound the uninitiated. *Noh*, the classic theater of Japan, is one such acquired taste. With scripts that typically run only a few pages long, one might think *Noh* is for those with short attention spans. Think again. One actor's entrance might take several minutes. The pace is *slow*. But every step and movement, down to the tiniest gesture, conveys meaning. *Noh*, when properly understood, has a heartbreaking subtlety. The earliest *Noh* plays date from the form's origins in the fourteenth century and are still performed to enthusiastic audiences today.

The Japanese do lighten things up a bit though; between "acts" in *Noh* plays come **Kyogen** performances. These are essentially clown

The tightly organized feudal system in Japan contributed to the development of native theater. From the fourteenth to the sixteenth century, Japan was isolated from the rest of the world, so Japanese artists had time to develop their own work without outside influence. And the shoguns—the big cheeses—acted as patrons of all the arts.

Kabuki began when a female performer made a splash with the public, poking fun at Buddhist religious rites. She formed an all-female troop. Later, young men and boys performed Kabuki. The effect of handsome and young, cross-dressed Japanese in wild outfits and makeup was just too kinky, so the authorities outlawed it. Kabuki eventually rose to respectability (damn!) with casts made up exclusively of adult males.

shows, full of broad humor, puns, and shenanigans. Two other significant, popular, and for the Westerner, more accessible Japanese theater forms, are *Kabuki* and *Bunraku*. In traditional *Kabuki* both male and female roles are performed entirely by men. Like *Noh*, *Kabuki* is highly conventionalized, but it features incredible costumes and make-up, dancing, spectacle, and a strong undertone of the erotic. *Bunraku* is puppet theater taken to the level of fine art. Each skillfully made puppet is nearly life-size and manipulated by a team of three or four puppeteers, who remain in full view of the audience. Stories of star-crossed lovers, spirits, and heroes are narrated in song to the accompaniment of music.

5. **The sixteenth-century neoclassical dramatists depended on which of the following for guidance?**
   (A) Aristotle's *The Poetics*
   (B) Horace's *The Art of Poetry*
   (C) John Rastell's *The Four Elements*
   (D) *Théâtre du Marais*

Cardinal Richelieu

Sixteenth-century Italians were crazy for anything classical. They first imitated the Romans, Plautus and Seneca in particular. The fall of Constantinople meant that Greek plays became available as well. Unfortunately, during the Dark Ages one of the lights that went out was the ancient Greek language. Renaissance translations from the Greek were typically shabby. Out of a weakly translated and comprehended version of Aristotle's *The Poetics* came sixteenth-century Italy's notion of the **three unities**: there should be one consistent locale (no "meanwhile, back at the farm"), one consistent story (no subplots), and one consistent time (no "ten years later" stuff). These limitations put a crimp in nearly everyone's style, but nevertheless the idea caught on and the **neoclassical theater** was born. Though not particularly good, its influence was felt for centuries, particularly in France.

In the seventeenth century, playwright **Pierre Corneille** (1606-1684) struck a blow against the unities with *Le Cid* (1637). Corneille's rivals went into a tizzy and the powerful Cardinal Richelieu ordered the newly formed *L'Académie Française* to criticize the upstart playwright for violating the unities; this it did with ferocity, but to almost no effect. *Le Cid* was a hit. Just when it seemed neoclassicism might be cast aside, the form found its one playwright of real genius, **Jean Racine** (1639-1699). With subtle poetic gifts, and a strong sense of what makes humans tick, Racine revived the moribund neoclassical school of theater. Because the poetic language of such great plays as *Andromaque* (1667), *Bérénice* (1671), *Iphigénie* (1674), and *Athalie* (1691) is difficult to translate, Racine is seldom performed in English. The French, however, consider Racine their Shakespeare.

 The plot of Racine's *Phèdre* was taken from Euripides. First, Phèdre falls in love with her stepson. While her husband Theseus is away on business, she confesses her love to the stepson, who angrily rejects her. When Theseus gets back, a servant accuses the stepson of trying to seduce Phèdre. That's the end of the stepson, so Phèdre kills herself. Racine said that he wrote the play to show that "a good poet could get the greatest crimes excused and even inspire compassion for the criminals."

6. Match the Shakespearean quotation with the character who said it:

    (A) "Brevity is the soul of wit"   ___Polonius
    (B) "I have come to bury Caesar,
         not to praise him"   ___Mark Antony
    (C) "Hath not a Jew eyes?"   ___Shylock
    (D) "Now is the winter of our discontent   ___Richard III
         made glorious summer by this sun
         of York"

William Shakespeare (1564-1616) is widely considered the greatest writer the West has ever produced. While this view shouldn't be news to anyone, it is remarkable that such a consensus has been reached. Try to get even five or six people to agree on the greatest-ever artist, or architect, or tennis player, and it becomes obvious that the level of agreement on Shakespeare's pre-eminence is unique.

 New York City sponsors free outdoor performances in its "Shakespeare in the Park" series every summer. Maybe you can catch Michelle Pfeiffer as Rosalind in *As You Like It*.

THE SHAKESPEARE CHART

The Histories

Henry VI, Parts I, II, and III; Richard III; King John; Richard II; Henry IV, Parts I and II; Henry V; Henry VIII.

The Comedies

Twelfth Night, The Comedy of Errors, The Two Gentlemen of Verona, Love's Labours Lost, The Taming of the Shrew, A Midsummer Night's Dream, The Merchant of Venice, Much Ado About Nothing, As You Like It, The Merry Wives of Windsor, Troilus and Cressida, All's Well That Ends Well, Measure for Measure.

The Tragedies

King Lear, Titus Andronicus, Romeo and Juliet, Julius Caesar, Hamlet, Othello, Macbeth, Antony and Cleopatra, Timon of Athens, Coriolanus.

 There are bunches of films based on Shakespeare plays. These are some of the best: *Much Ado About Nothing* (1993) and *Henry V* (1989), both directed by and starring Kenneth Branagh; *Romeo and Juliet* (1968), directed by Franco Zefferelli; *Hamlet* (1948), *Richard III* (1955), and *Henry V* (1944), all directed by and starring Laurence Olivier; and *Othello* (1952), directed by and starring Orson Welles.

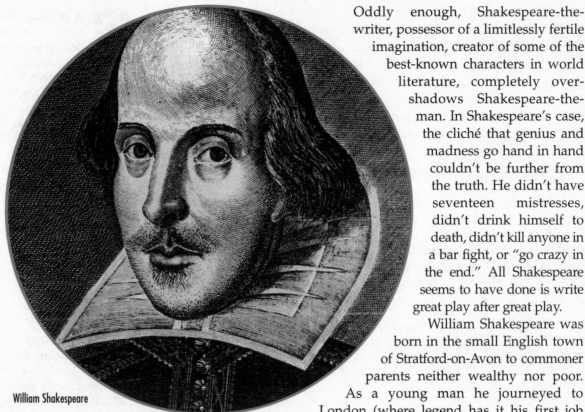

William Shakespeare

Oddly enough, Shakespeare-the-writer, possessor of a limitlessly fertile imagination, creator of some of the best-known characters in world literature, completely overshadows Shakespeare-the-man. In Shakespeare's case, the cliché that genius and madness go hand in hand couldn't be further from the truth. He didn't have seventeen mistresses, didn't drink himself to death, didn't kill anyone in a bar fight, or "go crazy in the end." All Shakespeare seems to have done is write great play after great play.

William Shakespeare was born in the small English town of Stratford-on-Avon to commoner parents neither wealthy nor poor. As a young man he journeyed to London (where legend has it his first job was to hold the reins of well-to-do patron's horses outside the theater he would make famous, the Globe), becoming first an actor, and subsequently a playwright. But very little substantial biographical data exists about Shakespeare, even the order in which he wrote his plays is not firmly established. This relative lack of information (coupled with the snobbish view that no low-born man could possess the talent and education necessary to write so much great stuff), has led a few scholars to suggest that some, or even all, of Shakespeare's plays were the creation of other writers. Philosopher of science and aristocrat **Francis Bacon** and gifted playwright **Christopher Marlowe** (who also happened to be a homosexual playboy and spy,) are the two most frequently cited ghostwriters. Our opinion is that these "Shakespeare-didn't-exist" theories are about as plausible as the "single-bullet theory" of the JFK assassination (p. 423).

If you've got some time on your hands, try reading all of Shakespeare's plays in the order in which he wrote them (we're not kidding). You'll see how his learning progresses. If you want to read the best from each category, try *Richard III*, *As You Like It*, and *King Lear*. You'll laugh, you'll cry, you'll understand what all the fuss is about.

7. **The term "bowdlerization" refers to**

(A) the censorship of foul language from a great literary work, as was done to Shakespeare's works in the late eighteenth century by Thomas Bowdler

(B) the imitation of the manner and dress of Shakespeare's Hamlet, as made popular by eccentric English aristocrat Thomas Bowdler

(C) too harshly criticizing the structure and content of a great play, as Thomas Bowdler did of Shakespeare's *The Taming of the Shrew*

(D) the disastrous removal of all subplots from what one believes is too complex a play, as Thomas Bowdler did to Shakespeare's *A Midsummer Night's Dream*

So staggering has Shakespeare's achievement been that it is impossible to isolate any one element on which his literary value ultimately depends. In creating Hamlet, or King Lear (to name just two of a vast gallery of indelible creations), Shakespeare wrote into being characters with a psychological depth centuries in advance of the creations of other writers. He wrote light-hearted romantic fantasies like *A Midsummer Night's Dream* (1595), historical dramas like *Henry IV* (1597-1598), and dark tragedies like *Macbeth* (1606), and *Othello* (1603). (In all, he wrote ten histories, seventeen comedies, and ten tragedies.) Line by line and speech by speech, the language with which Shakespeare breathes life into his characters is as varied and brilliant as the plays themselves.

But Shakespeare hasn't always been quite so universally praised. In the eighteenth century Thomas Bowdler felt that the sex and vulgarity in Shakespeare's works was completely out of hand, and might shock the delicate sensibilities of ladies or children attending the theater. They decided to issue "bowdlerized" versions of the plays. This endeavor was the literary equivalent of insisting the Venus de Milo wear a bra, and the Bowdler name has since become synonymous with texts that have been over-edited, censored, or watered-down.

But Bowdler was not exactly wrong: Shakespeare could become quite crude when the situation demanded it. For example, when Hamlet yells at Ophelia "get thee to a nunnery" this is slang for "go to work at a whore-house." This example also brings up the biggest problem for contemporary

> ## FROM *RICHARD III*
>
> Was ever woman in this humor wooed?
> Was ever woman in this humor won?
> I'll have her, but I will not keep her long.
> What? I that killed her husband and her father
> To take her in her heart's extremest hate,
> With curses in her mouth, tears in her eyes,
> The bleeding witness of my hatred by,
> Having God, her conscience, and these bars against me,
> And I no friends to back my suit at all
> But the plain devil and dissembling looks?
> And yet to win her! All the world to nothing!
> Ha!
>
> ——William Shakespeare

During Shakespeare's time, Rosalind was played by a boy, which meant that a boy played a girl who pretended to be a boy. Olivier outdid himself as Kate in *The Taming of the Shrew*. Cross-dressing by actors hasn't been limited to men dressing as women, however; Julia Glover and Sarah Bernhardt both played Hamlet.

readers. Because our present modern English has evolved quite far from the Elizabethan English of Shakespeare's day, modern readers often find the bard's writing tough to decipher. But it is well worth the effort. Shakepeare makes use of every weapon in the linguistic arsenal, from sweeping lyric in strict iambic pentameter and rhymed couplets, to coarse and drunken punning slang, from the smooth cadences of lust to the clipped phrases of barely suppressed rage or the sibilant hissings of plotted vengeance. An intelligent reading of Shakespeare is perhaps the best education in poetry one can have. There are at least two good ways to study Shakespeare. The hard way is to read a good, thoroughly annotated edition of any of the plays. Read slowly, read the notes, and tough it out— you'll find that after an act or two, after you have a handle on the characters and the plot, the language begins to make a lot more sense. The easy way is to see good professional stage productions (or films) of the plays. With any luck the director and actors have done the interpretative work necessary to make the play accessible.

> ❝
>
> *How sharper than a serpent's tooth it is*
>
> *To have a thankless child!*
>
> ——*King Lear*
>
> ❞

8. **What European playwright first published his plays as "collected works"?**

   (A) Molière
   (B) Webster
   (C) Jonson
   (D) Wycherly

Molière's best works are *Tartuffe* and *Le Misanthrope*. Look for productions done by regional or college theater companies or even *La Comédie Française*, when they go on tour.

In seventeenth century, European playwrights were pretty far down on the literary pecking order; publishing one's plays was thought pretentious, and calling them "works" would be an act of unheard-of pomposity. Who better then to do it first than **Ben Jonson** (1572-1637), a great playwright with an even greater ego. He stirred up trouble wherever he went, bounced in and out of jail (usually for political crimes that never amounted to anything), killed a man in a duel, came within a hair's breadth of being executed, drank far too much, talked about himself incessantly to a crowd of young worshippers, and managed to write some very funny comedies about how stupid and foolish most other people were (the most famous of which is *Volpone* [1606]). Jonson lacked the imagination of some of his contemporaries but he made up for it with his gift for sharp observation. His satires took everyone down a peg with biting accuracy. The joke was ultimately on Jonson though, as even he could see that Shakespeare was the greatest playwright of the day.

In France, a few decades later, another satirical playwright, **Molière** (1622-1673) caused a stir. After some lean years, Molière hit it big, winning the favor of both the French public and King Louis XIV. Molière's witty, sexy comedies, such as *The School for Wives* (1662), *The Doctor In Spite of Himself* (1666), *The Misanthrope* (1666), and *Tartuffe* (1669), are still performed. He also had a hand in the new art form—ballet—which was developing at the king's court.

Molière

9. **In which play does the protagonist tell people he is impotent so that he can get away with sexual shenanigans?**
   (A) *The Country Wife*
   (B) *The Plain Dealer*
   (C) *The Way of the World*
   (D) *London Cuckolds*

In England, the seventeenth century brought difficult times for the theater. Similar to what happened during the last days of the Roman Empire, religious groups—largely the Puritans (p. 500)—proclaimed theater immoral and succeeded in having theater declared illegal. In 1649 Charles I of England lost his fight for absolute political control and the Puritans chopped off his head. Eventually Oliver Cromwell took over and grabbed all the power for himself.

Restoration theater takes its name from the restoration of the monarchy in 1660, when Charles II

FROM *THE SCHOOL FOR SCANDAL*

Sir Peter:

Hey! What the plague! Are you ashamed of having done a right thing once in your life?

Snake:

Ah, sir, consider I live by the badness of my character! I have nothing but my infamy to depend on, and, if it were once known that I had been betrayed into an honest action, I should lose every friend I have in the world.

——*Richard Sheridan*

In England, Tom Stoppard has been writing what you might call the modern version of Restoration comedies. Unlike most of his contemporaries, Stoppard is more excited by satire and sophisticated jokes than anything else. If you get the chance, see *Jumpers* (1972) or *Rosencrantz and Guildenstern Are Dead* (1966).

hopped on the throne, and the power of the Puritans diminished, allowing theater to flourish again and, of course, to swing in the opposite direction of decorum and virtue. The Restoration comedy of manners, as written by dramatists such as Sir George Etherege, William Wycherley (*The Country Wife* [1675]), William Congreve, and others, did away with the serious treatment of weighty topics. Restoration comedy is about seduction, sex, rotten morals, and cute remarks.

10. **What is the name of the first homegrown American play on record?**

   (A) *Pocahontas*
   (B) *Hiawatha*
   (C) *Ye Bare and Ye Cubb*
   (D) *Shoot the Redcoat*

Seventeenth-century colonial Americans, isolated from the rest of the world, hadn't had enough time to develop their own culture, but some communities had their own playhouses, and local actors might perform works written by other colonists, including the first American play, *Ye Bare and Ye Cubb* (1655). By the eighteenth century, even politi-

THE BOOTH FAMILY

Junius Booth, a big star from England, came to America in 1821. He popularized the tragic acting style and founded one of the first American acting families. Although Junius ran into some problems due to his unpredictable behavior, his son Edwin was an acclaimed Shakespearean actor, known for his dedication to high standards and the extravagant productions mounted at the Booth Theater. Junius's other son, John Wilkes Booth . . . well, you know the rest.

cians were getting into the act. The first published American play was written in 1715 by New York State Governor Robert Hunter.

American theater wasn't helped by the decision of the Continental Congress in 1774 that forbade all stage entertainment. Those damn Puritans! Theater was made legal again after the Revolution, when everybody was in the mood for some light entertainment. Comedies abounded, and theater began to take on a true American aspect. **Royall Tyler** (1757-1826), in *The Contrast* (1787), introduced the Yankee, the first "American type" to appear on stage.

Flexibility is a requirement of the burlesque dancer.

11. **The origin of American musical theater is credited to**
    (A) the expansion of the railroad
    (B) a French ballet company stranded in New York
    (C) Lydia Thompson
    (D) Gypsy Rose Lee

The ballet-opera, with its English and French influences, was packing the houses in post-Revolutionary America. Initially performed by English actors, these musical comedies were soon written by American composers and playwrights for a population increasingly on the move, staking out claims in the territory west of the original thirteen colonies.

In 1866 a French ballet troupe was scheduled to open at the New York Academy of Music, but the theater burned down. The manager of Niblo's Garden Theater, his own play struggling, hired the ballet dancers, dressed them in skimpy costumes, and put them into *The Black Crook* (1866), which was supposed to be a Faustian melodrama. Considered the first American musical, *The Black Crook* made over a million dollars and had a run of 474 performances, making it the most successful American production of the nineteenth century. Not surprisingly, members of the clergy denounced the scantily-clad dancers, giving the production even more publicity.

 An American burlesque in the 1840s parodied *Macbeth*. It was called *Bad Breath, the Crane of Chowder*.

The Night They Raided Minsky's (1968), directed by William Friedkin. Britt Eckland, playing an Amish woman, comes to New York and gets tangled up with Jason Robards, a burlesque comic, and accidentally invents the strip-tease.

The sight of women's legs was quite a draw in those days. **Burlesque**, which had been a form of topical satire popular in the early eighteenth century, evolved into revues displaying "feminine charms," that is, the female performers were good-looking and didn't wear much. Lydia Thompson's "British Blondes" were an especially big hit. The parody of the older burlesques disappeared, and by the 1920s, with striptease, so did the performers' clothes.

12. **What pair of friends was associated with the "Storm and Stress" movement?**
    (A) Kierkegaard and Nietzsche
    (B) Fran and Ollie
    (C) Lerner and Lowe
    (D) Goethe and Schiller

The early decades of the eighteenth century were characterized by rationality, earning them the moniker **The Age of Reason**. The end of the century saw Robespierre guillotine the nobles of France during "the terror" and Napoleon begin his epic and bloody conquest of Europe. Not surprisingly the arts, especially theater, reflected these dramatic changes.

In the first half of the nineteenth century, English theater took a nosedive. Nobody was doing "serious" theater; the popular forms were pantomime, burlesque, and musical entertainment.

Before electricity, theater lighting was a big problem. By 1840 some theaters were using gas, but it smelled terrible, made everybody too hot, and was a serious fire hazard. Further inventions, the gas table and the fishtail burner, allowed the light man to control the lights individually and helped to get rid of the fumes. Limelight, made by heating oxygen and hydrogen with lime, was a kind of primitive spotlight.

Goethe getting rid of some of that storm and stress.

The early part of the eighteenth century was not one of the golden ages of theater, though some good work, especially comedy, was produced. Neoclassicism (p. 44), which emphasizes controlled purity and simplicity, was being given its last rites. In the 1770s a new German aesthetic called *"Sturm und Drang"* (in English, "storm and stress") breathed renewed life into European theater. The principal dramatists of this movement were **Johann Goethe** (1749-1832) and **Friedrich Schiller** (1759-1805). Both were awesomely gifted artists, and Goethe, a true genius, was accomplished not only as a poet but also as a philosopher, mathematician, and scientist. Both would eventually turn to more disciplined forms in later life (you grow up and you calm down) but in their works as young men they championed passion, grandeur, and nobility of spirit. Their enthusiasm coupled with their talent rocked Europe.

Typically, a Sturm und Drang play features a young male hot-head who follows his impulses with reckless courage, and whose intensity and truth to his own passions highlight the weak, hypocritical values of those around him. Sometimes he loves a married woman (who loves him back but can't abandon conventional morality), sometimes he hates his father, sometimes both. In the end the hero dies, tragically and beautifully. It's all society's fault. If this all sounds a little ridiculous, it wasn't, *at first*. The plays Goethe and Schiller wrote as young men were fresh and the passions were genuine. The Sturm und Drang movement was so sensational that it didn't last long in any real sense. Every third rate hack who fancied himself a playwright or poet tried writing in a similar vein and what had been Sturm und Drang became melodrama.

13. **Who is Woyzeck?**
     (A) A pagan god
     (B) A polish nobleman
     (C) A revolutionary
     (D) An illiterate soldier

Georg Buchner's *Woyzeck* (1879), the story of an illiterate soldier's last miserable days, is one of the first serious works of theater to center around a man of the lower classes. But subject matter is by no means the most remarkable thing about *Woyzeck*. Though incomplete, and not produced until long after Buchner's death, *Woyzeck* is considered one of the most important works of nineteenth-century theater because with it **Buchner** (1813-1837) single-handedly invented a bold new theatrical idiom. *Woyzeck* is the first example (and a powerful one) of expressionism (p. 607). While

Immanuel Kant (1724-1804), writing in Germany at the end of the eighteenth century, claimed that the existence of the world originates in the human mind. He discounted objectivity in favor of subjectivity, which was music to the ears of the Romantics, Goethe included.

Bedazzled (1967), starring Peter Cook, Dudley Moore, and Raquel Welch. It tells the story of Faust with a lot more humor and in a lot less time than Goethe.

the Western theater world was just beginning to grapple with styles that would make the representations of the stage more true to life, Buchner leapt into the next century and dramatized subjective reality. He brought the inner life of man to the forefront, portraying not how Woyzeck's life looked from the outside but rather showing somehow what it might look like from inside Woyzeck himself, how it might *feel* to be a poor illiterate soldier driven to murder his wife after she prostitutes herself. Buchner's tremendous poetic gifts were coupled with a truly bleak view of existence. His pessimism may have been justified. Buchner died of typhoid at the age of twenty-three. His early death, like that of poet John Keats, must be considered one of the great losses to world literature.

14. **Chekhov's plays required a new style of acting developed by**

    (A)   Igor Stravinsky
    (B)   Konstantin Stanislavski
    (C)   Lee Strasberg
    (D)   Vladimir Nemirovich-Danchenko

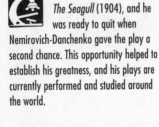

Chekhov initially failed with *The Seagull* (1904), and he was ready to quit when Nemirovich-Danchenko gave the play a second chance. This opportunity helped to establish his greatness, and his plays are currently performed and studied around the world.

The Three Sisters (1970), starring Laurence Olivier, Joan Plowright, and Alan Bates. This is the definitive screen adaption of a Chekhov classic.

Because some of the plays written in the second half of the nineteenth century did not occur in a milieu of grand language and exalted deed (as plays had for centuries) but in provincial households among more-or-less ordinary people, the old declamatory style (formulated in England by **John Philip Kemble** (1721-1802), which amounted to facing the audience and formally reciting one's lines, wouldn't do. Actors needed an entirely new approach to performance. They found that approach in the theories of Russian **Konstantin Stanislavski** (1863-1938). A member of the **Moscow Art Theater**, Stanislavski originated what is known in the United States as **the method**, or **method acting**, a discipline in which the actor uses memory and experience to understand the inner state—the motivations, fears, and desires—of the character she seeks to portray. The basic

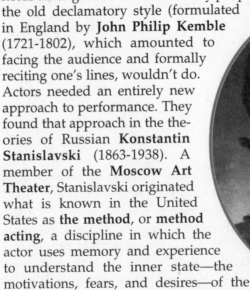

Konstantin Stanislavski

idea is that if the actor can reproduce the interior of a character thoroughly enough, the outside will take care of itself. This important and influential style was popularized in the United States through the efforts of **Lee Strasberg** (1901-1982), of the prestigious Actors' Studio in New York City. Strasberg's pupils read like a Who's who of American theater and film. Marlon Brando, Dustin Hoffman, Geraldine Page, and Robert DeNiro are just a few of the actors who have studied under Strasberg. Ironically, Strasberg was more of a method purist than Stanislavski himself, who never intended to completely replace the more standard techniques of acting (like discretely pulling out nostril hairs in order to cry), but only to augment them.

The story goes that in New York City, during the filming of *The Marathon Man*, Laurence Olivier and Dustin Hoffman had to do a scene together in which both should look utterly exhausted and bedraggled. Hoffman sprinted twice around the Central Park reservoir and came crawling back to the set only to find Olivier calmly looking over the script. "How are you going to do the scene?" Hoffman inquired. Olivier replied, "My good man, I intend to act."

15. **What is THE question in ballet that has surfaced time and again since the seventeenth century?**

(A) Who was the better dancer, Taglioni or Pavlova?
(B) Should a short stiff tutu be worn, or long and flowing chitons?
(C) Should the raw athletic ability of the dancers or the emotional expressiveness of the dance itself be emphasized?
(D) Is there a way to record dance on paper?

Ballet has origins in the social dances of aristocracy in the royal courts of Europe. It truly came into its own, though, in seventeenth-century France. Louis the XIV had a passion for dance. His nickname, the "Sun King," came from the role he danced in a ballet at the court when he was fifteen. In pursuit of more and better dancing, Louis brought to his palace at Versailles some of the best and most innovative artistic talents of the nation, such as the dancing master **Beauchamps** (1636-1705), the composer **Lully** (1632-1687), and the playwright Molière (p. 551). Under Louis the ballet rapidly became it's own distinct art-form, danced by professional dancers (Louis couldn't stand to see noblemen bumble about amateurishly on stage). As with so many theatrical arts, when ballet became professional it also, for a short time, became all male, but some noblewomen of Louis's court quickly put a stop to that by simply showing the men up, and dancing beautifully.

Dance, like music, can be written. The first to systematize the notation of dance was Pierre Beauchamps, the dancing master of Louis XIV's court. His disciple, Raoul Feuillet, recorded and helped popularize the system in *Chorégraphie L'Art D'Écrire la Danse*. It's pretty to look at, but terribly hard to master, and nevertheless incomplete. Better systems, like Labanotation have since been devised, but none are entirely adequate.

At the beginning, under Louis, the ballet was still a kind of "pure" dance. The object was to appear as graceful, beautiful, and skilled as possible. Leaps, turns, complicated steps, these were the dancer's bread and butter. But some artists quickly saw, and seized upon, the expressive possibilities of dance. The man credited with first grasping ballet's narrative

Court dancing was such a big deal in eighteenth-century France that men sometimes wore falsies to accentuate their calves.

The French writer Théophile Gautier called prima ballerina Maria Taglioni "a madrigal in a word," "a poetic personification," and "an opalescent mist seen against the green obscurity of an enchanted forest." We bet he said that to all the girls.

Dance, A Short History of Classic Theatrical Dancing (1987), by Lincoln Kirstein. Erudite and thorough; if you want one book on dance, this is it.

Anna Pavlova, a major ballet star in Russia, was the Madonna of her day. Her fans were so crazy about her they baked her toe shoes and ate them.

The Magic of Dance (1979), by Margot Fonteyn. This is an insider's history of dance with terrific illustrations and photographs.

and expressive potential was **Noverre** (1727-1810). His theories, like the incorporation of mime into dance, and the demand that dancers act as well as move, were far ahead of his time. Noverre's theories were by and large neglected in his own day and had to be re-discovered by later innovators in the nineteenth century. Eventually Noverre's ideas would become part of the backbone of what we call classical dance. But in important ways the debate is not over but has only been extended. When Nijinsky leapt skyward from the stage of the Ballets Russes, his grace and athleticism thrilled the audience regardless of the story, regardless of whether that audience understood what the leap meant. Some say that in the magic of just this kind of physical display is truly the essence of dance. At the other end of the spectrum are some of today's radical choreographers who create emotionally effective works of art using untrained performers.

16. **Who started Ballets Russes?**

   (A) Nureyev
   (B) Diaghilev
   (C) Nijinsky
   (D) Petipa

   Although ballet started in France, some of its highest achievements have been Russian. With the support of the Czar, **Marius Petipa** (1818-1910) choreographed *Sleeping Beauty* (1890) and *Swan Lake* (1895) while he was ballet master of the Imperial Ballet. The man who should have succeeded him, **Michel Fokine** (1880-1942), ended up with **Diaghilev** (1872-1929) in Paris, where interest in ballet exploded.

   Diaghilev was neither a dancer, a musician, nor an artist. He was the man who stirred the cocktail. For his extravagant productions he gathered together the cutting-edge artists of his day including **Fokine** (1880-1942) as choreographer, **Igor Stravinsky** (1882-1971) as composer, and **Nijinsky** (1890-1950) as an amazing principal dancer. Diaghilev even persuad-

Nijinsky cutting the hardwood with Tamara Karasavin

ed Picasso (p. 604) to design some scenery for the Ballets Russes.

Not merely a legendary dancer, Nijinsky also possessed genius as a choreographer. In *The Rite of Spring* (1913), Nijinsky, who as a choreographer had already declared himself sick of grace and beauty, created a choreography based on primitive gestures, awkward movements that were sometimes tense, sometimes frankly ugly. It was bold; it was original; it was unpopular. Faced not only with Nijinsky's choreography, but also a Stravinsky (p. 304) score that used sharp dissonances and abrupt rhythmic transitions, the opening night audience of *The Rite of Spring* rioted. At one point Nijinsky had to stand on a chair in the wings and shout out instructions to the dancers, who couldn't hear the orchestra over the mayhem in the audience as the cream of Parisian society brawled in the aisles.

Diaghilev's shocking, grand, audacious Ballets Russes was one of the most productive moments in the history of theater. From out of his hand-picked cast of geniuses came groundbreaking works such as *Scheherezade* (1910), *The Firebird* (1910), *Petrouchka* (1911), *The Afternoon of a Faun* (1912), and *The Rite of Spring*, to name just a few. Nijinsky became a household word and toured Europe, the United States, and South America. For many people, Nijinsky was ballet. Tragically though, in 1919 Nijinsky had a nervous breakdown and left dancing forever.

The dashing
Sergei Diaghilev

17. Who led one of the first dance movements to represent a break with ballet?
(A) Ted Shawn
(B) Merce Cunningham
(C) Isadora Duncan
(D) George Balanchine

The turn of the century was a time of revolt against the restrictive Victorian Age, just as the free-love, bra-burning sixties were a reaction to the staid, conformist fifties. Corsets were out. Women's suffrage was in. And for **Isadora Duncan** (1878-1927), the first modern dancer, toe shoes and ballet were emblematic of the old order that needed to be overthrown.

Dancing barefoot, she took Europe by storm, filling concert halls wherever she went, and inspiring other artists of the day who sought liberation from the restrictions of outmoded artistic codes. (Fokine, among

The seductive, free-spirited Isadora Duncan

others, credited Duncan with opening his eyes to the potential of dance.) And Duncan lived as she danced. She espoused free-love and bore children out of wedlock by two different men. Those who were close to her testify to Duncan's rare, radiant spirit. But after her initial successes tragedy hounded her. Her two young children were accidentally drowned. When she married a Russian poet in 1922, much of the American public reviled her as a communist and she went into self-imposed exile from the United States. (Her husband, Sergei Esenin, eventually went mad and killed himself.) Duncan herself died in one of the most famous accidents in all of theater: she was strangled when one of the long scarves that were her trademark became entangled in the wheels of a car she was riding.

FROM MY LIFE

I was seeking and finally discovered the central spring of all movement . . . the mirror of vision for the creation of the dance . . . . The Ballet school taught the pupils that this spring was found at the center of the back at the base of the spine. From this axis, says the ballet master, arms, legs, and trunk must move freely, giving the result of an articulated puppet. This method produces an artificial mechanical movement not worthy of the soul.

———*Isadora Duncan*

18. Who invented the problem play?

(A) Henrik Ibsen
(B) George Bernard Shaw
(C) August Strindberg
(D) Anton Chekov

Norwegian **Henrik Ibsen** (1828-1906) was interested in such naturalistic subjects as municipal corruption, marriage, and venereal disease. His work follows the course from romanticism to realism and then to symbolism, and the power of his best plays—*Peer Gynt* (1867), *An Enemy of the People* (1882), *The Doll's House* (1879), and *Hedda Gabler* (1890)—comes from a mix of all three.

> ### FROM *THE DOLL'S HOUSE*
>
> *Nora:*
>
> *When I was at home with papa, he told me his opinion about everything, and so I had the same opinions; and if I differed from him I concealed the fact, because he would not have liked it. He called me his doll-child, and he played with me just as I used to play with my dolls. And when I came to live with you . . .*
>
> *Helmer:*
>
> *What sort of an expression is that to use about our marriage?*
>
> *Nora (undisturbed):*
>
> *I mean that I was simply transferred from papa's hands into yours.*
>
> ——Henrik Ibsen

In his choice of subject matter, Ibsen deliberately embroiled himself in controversy; he often chose a social ill around which to write a play. Marriage and, in particular, the subservient role of women, was a favorite topic for attack. In the prefeminist *The Doll's House*, Nora ditches her husband after realizing she has been treated like a doll. In *Ghosts* (1881), the wife stays with her errant husband but her son goes insane from the syphilis he has inherited from his father.

Because Ibsen got rid of such conventions as **soliloquies** and **asides** and used scenes primarily as a way to develop character, he is, with Chekov, considered an early proponent of realism. Believing that the purpose of theater went beyond simple entertainment, he aimed for insight and ideas as well as poetic expression.

A big fan of Ibsen's, **George Bernard Shaw** (1856-1950) was a drama critic for years before his comedies were staged. Shaw has much in common with Ibsen: an intellectual's preoccupation with ideas, a certain delight in controversial subjects, and a concern with social politics. An

Henrik Ibsen shortly after being exposed to static electricity

incredibly prolific writer, some of his major plays include *Arms and the Man* (1898), *Mrs. Warren's Profession* (1898), *Major Barbara* (1907), *Man and Superman* (1903), and *Pygmalion* (1914).

19. Which of the following had the greatest influence on Strindberg?

(A) Freud
(B) Molière
(C) Zola
(D) Proust

Take your Prozac before going near **Strindberg** (1849-1912). This nutty Swede was obsessed with his own subjective reality, which was not exactly a day at the beach, especially after the breakdown. Freud's (p. 236) writing on the unconscious finds its dramatic equivalent in Strindberg's work. Taking the realism of Ibsen as his starting point, Strindberg wrote bitter plays about pleasure-seeking, controlling women (*Miss Julie* [1888]) and the workings of his own personality (*A Dream Play* [1902]). The influence of Freud shows both in the themes of Strindberg's work—the sex drive and aggression—and in the structure, which attempts to imitate the actual disconnections and ramblings of the human mind.

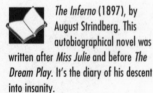

The Inferno (1897), by August Strindberg. This autobiographical novel was written after *Miss Julie* and before *The Dream Play*. It's the diary of his descent into insanity.

August Strindberg

As August himself wrote: "I have rather broken with tradition in not making my characters catechists who sit asking foolish questions in order to elicit a smart reply. I have avoided the mathematically symmetrical construction of French dialogue and let people's brains work irregularly, as they do in actual life, where no topic of conversation is drained to the dregs, but one brain receives haphazard from the other a cog to engage with."

WILDE AND WOOLLY

As an antidote for Strindberg, take some Oscar Wilde, an Irish playwright working at about the same time. Wilde is best-known play is The Importance of Being Earnest.

Some of his remarks:

"A little sincerity is a dangerous thing, and a great deal of it is absolutely fatal."

"In married life three is company and two none."

"It is very vulgar to talk like a dentist when one isn't a dentist. It creates a false impression."

"It is better to be beautiful than to be good . . . but it is better to be good than to be ugly."

"I couldn't help it. I can resist everything except temptation."

20. Which of the following O'Neill plays was not performed until after Eugene O'Neill's death?

(A) *Mourning Becomes Electra*
(B) *The Iceman Cometh*
(C) *Desire Under The Elms*
(D) *Long Day's Journey Into Night*

Eugene O'Neill (1888-1953) was a great shaggy monster of a writer. His plays are long sprawling affairs notoriously difficult to stage. He wrote in almost every style: expressionism, realism, romanticism, and symbolism. He didn't inspire imitators, at least none who were successful. O'Neill was simply O'Neill. Though his plays are often faulted for a myriad of technical inadequacies, O'Neill's achievement in the theater was awesome. In Europe, Shaw and Ibsen had tackled intellectual themes. But O'Neill, taking Strindberg as his principal inspiration, went even further, sounding spiritual and philosophical depths

A scene from the film based on
Eugene O'Neil's *Long Day's Journey Into Night*

Long Day's Journey into Night (1962), starring Katharine Hepburn and Jason Robards. This movie is faithful to the original O'Neill play, and you shouldn't miss a doped-up Katharine Hepburn.

Mourning Becomes Electra (1931), by Eugene O'Neill. This wild ride in New England is based on the story of Orestes from Greek mythology.

CULTURESCOPE

At What Price, Genius?

O'Neill's father was a hard-drinking, unsuccessful actor. His mother was a morphine addict, and his brother an alcoholic wastrel. Eugene, too, had alcohol problems. In his twenties he attempted suicide and contracted tuberculosis. As an adult, O'Neill was still tormented by family life. His three marriages were unhappy. One of his sons killed himself, and Oona, his daughter, married Charlie Chaplin (O'Neill disapproved). At the height of his powers, illness prevented him from writing (he couldn't even hold a pen). The last ten years of his life were spent in a hotel room, waiting, and wishing, to die.

 Reds (1980), directed by and starring Warren Beatty. The movie is an aspiring look at the journalist John Reed's involvement with Communism. Jack Nicholson plays an alcoholic O'Neill who sleeps with Reed's wife.

that hadn't been reached since Shakespeare. He created characters simultaneously real and larger than life. In an O'Neill play, when the passions crescendo, the language can reach an almost religious intensity. His brand of realism is not the "slice-of-life" kind that attempts to depict the everyday problems of everyday people, nor does O'Neill ever stoop to triviality.

One of O'Neill's masterpieces is the autobiographical *Long Day's Journey Into Night* (1956). Because of the play's painful content, in accordance with O'Neill's wishes, it was not produced until after the playwright's death. Other important works by O'Neill include *Desire Under the Elms* (1925), *Anna Christie* (1922), *The Hairy Ape* (1923), *The Emperor Jones* (1921), *Mourning Becomes Electra* (1931), *Ah, Wilderness* (1933), *The Iceman Cometh* (1946), and *A Moon for the Misbegotten* (1947).

21. Jerome Kern and Oscar Hammerstein's _____ was an early example of the transition from the revues of Ziegfeld to musical theater based on narrative.

   (A) *Oklahoma!*
   (B) *Showboat*
   (C) *Anything Goes*
   (D) *Carousel*

 Cabaret (1972), directed by Bob Fosse and starring Liza Minelli and Joel Grey. The classic musical (eight Academy awards) set in prewar Berlin features Minelli's huge voice.

 West Side Story (1961), directed by Robert Wise and Jerome Robbins. This Romeo and Juliet adaptation is set in the streets of New York in the fifties with Leonard Bernstein and Stephen Sondheim providing the tunes.

Everybody knows somebody who insists on listening to show tunes. Be patient. Maybe they're not trying to torture you, maybe they're just patriotic. For many, the musical *is* American theater. Although its roots are partly European (the comic opera, burlesque, and the operetta, American musical theater also drew from American forms such as the minstrel show to become what it is today.

Unfortunately, the **minstrel show** is a pretty embarrassing part of American theater history. White actors put on

George and Ira Gershwin

Richard Rodgers and Oscar Hammerstein's *Oklahoma*

blackface, danced jigs, and imitated African-American speech to the great amusement of audiences. Minstrel shows were so popular in the second half of the nineteenth century that black performers did them too, wearing the same makeup. *Showboat*, in 1928, was the first musical entertainment to use the songs as a means to advance the story rather than simply as an interlude. *Oklahoma!*, in 1943, integrated music, dance, and story. Although the out-of-town reviews said "No legs, no jokes, no chance," the show was a huge hit. The form certainly attracted major talents, such as composers and lyricists Irving Berlin, Cole Porter, George Gershwin, Rodgers and Hammerstein, Lerner and Loewe, Leonard Bernstein, and Stephen Sondheim.

The plots of musicals have come from diverse sources. Shakespeare (*Kiss Me Kate* [1948]), Dickens (*Oliver!* [1960]), sports (*Damn Yankees* [1955]) and God (*Godspell* [1971] and *Jesus Christ Superstar* [1971]) have all provided inspiration to the playwrights. Although the majority of musicals tend to be upbeat and somewhat nostalgic, there have been some anomalies. *Hair* (1967) is a counter-culture rock musical; Stephen Sondheim's acid *Sweeney Todd* (1979) involves murder and cannibalism.

66

It seems that the moment anyone gets hold of an exclamation point these days, he promptly sits down and writes a musical around it.

—GEORGE JEAN NATHAN,
DRAMA CRITIC

99

The American musical is known for featuring songs you can hum yourself, big casts, impressive dance numbers, and titles that end in exclamation points. The name of the game is spectacle, which Aristotle called the puniest, least important element in drama.

22. **Who is known as the First Lady of American Dance?**
   (A) Anna Pavlova
   (B) Ruth St. Denis
   (C) Margot Fonteyn
   (D) Martha Graham

Ruth St. Denis (1879-1968), the First Lady of American Dance, began her serious artistic career when a poster for a brand of Egyptian cigarettes so fascinated her that she was drawn to study Far Eastern art and philosophy. These in turn led her toward dance, and with her husband **Ted Shawn** (1891-1972) she founded the **Denishawn school**. The Denishawn school was known for its radical eclecticism, treating folk, Native American, Middle-Eastern, and above all, Asian dance with a seriousness and respect previously only accorded ballet.

The Denishawn school's most famous pupil was the pioneering modern dancer and prolific choreographer **Martha Graham** (1894-1991), who over her long and distinguished career would apply the Denishawn principles, repudiate them, and eventually fuse them with her own daring, jagged, and sexual style. Though Isadora Duncan may have been the first modern dancer, and St. Denis and Shawn the founders of the

Doris Humphrey of the Denishawn School

first significant modern dance school, Graham can be credited with bringing modern dance into its own as a truly distinct art form. Known for her intellectual approach, she choreographed pieces based on the work of Emily Dickinson (p. 285) and Walt Whitman (p. 289).

As modern dance became more sure of itself, classical ballet, under choreographers like **George Balanchine** (1904-1983), stuck to its guns, honed its techniques to a gleaming edge, and did what it did best: present breathtakingly talented performers dancing to gorgeous music. The Russian Anna Pavlova, and Englishwoman Margot Fonteyn are two of classical dance's most famous virtuoso *prima ballarinas*. Both combined physical perfection with true interpretive artistry, and both are legends.

Martha Graham swirling in
Letter to the World

23. One of Bertoldt Brecht's main themes is

(A) the struggle between good and evil
(B) socialist politics
(C) universality
(D) the emptiness of modern life

REVIEW OF *NELL* STARRING JODIE FOSTER

"As you watch her swaying and gyrating sensuously to the rhythms of nature, you can't help wondering how this backwoods hermit managed to pick up all that classy Martha Graham technique."

——*Terence Rafferty,*
in The New Yorker

Bertoldt Brecht (1898-1956), an ardent and unorthodox Marxist, transformed John Gay's melodrama *The Beggar's Opera* (1728) into a musical (*The Three Penny Opera* [1928]) whose main theme was socialism. Brecht was a serious fellow, known for his intellectualism, avant-gardism, and passion for social change. He took on Fascism, the Nazis, the plight of women, and the cruelty of war. In his best works, *Mother Courage*, *The Good Woman of Sezuan*, and *The Caucasian Chalk Circle*, strong characterization and politics are mixed in complementary parts, so that the plays are not simply treatises, but powerful dramas.

Much of the last ten years of Brecht's life was devoted to theoretical writing, and it is this writing, as much as his plays, that has influenced theater, television, and film. Brecht did not want the audience's "willing suspension of disbelief"; he wanted the audience to watch objectively, aware that what they were seeing was a performance. To accomplish this, he exposed the artifice of theater, allowing the lighting to show, and making no effort to hide the work of stagehands. "It's Gary Shandling's Show," a television show on the Fox network (p. 521) in the 1980s, used similar effects; Gary spoke to the audience directly, and talked about what the actors were doing as they were doing it.

WHAT ARE WE WAITING FOR?

Clifford Odets, writing in 1930s and 1940s, attempted to do his part for socialism by inspiring the working class through such plays as Awake and Sing *and* Waiting for Lefty. *In the realistic style, they dramatize complicated family relationships. In Odets's* Waiting for Lefty, *Lefty never shows up. In Beckett's* Waiting for Godot, *Godot never shows up. This must mean something— you figure it out.*

---

24. In Ionesco's *Rhinoceros*, the characters turn into

    (A) nuns
    (B) flies
    (C) rhinoceroses
    (D) cats

In France during the 1940s, **existentialism** made a big splash. Although the term "existentialism" brings to mind an image of an angst-ridden person sitting in a café smoking cigarettes, the philosophy as described by **Sartre** (1905-1980) demands that individuals set high personal standards, resisting conformity at all costs, and that they become politically *engagé*. In the theater Sartre put his theories forward in *Les Mouches* (*The Flies* [1943]) and *Huis Clos* (*No Exit* [1945]). Both plays work as philosophical explorations as well as drama.

Existentialism led to the **theater of the absurd**, which rests on the belief that what truth there is to life can best be grasped in those unsettling moments when suddenly the world (and oneself) appears hopeless,

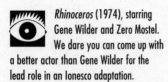

Rhinoceros (1974), starring Gene Wilder and Zero Mostel. We dare you can come up with a better actor than Gene Wilder for the lead role in an Ionesco adaptation.

stupid, and funny—in a word, absurd. **Eugène Ionesco** (1912-1994), a Rumanian, operated on the same assumption that life is irrational, but made no attempt to fashion any kind of order out of the chaos of modern life. He was living in Paris and teaching himself English. If you've ever studied a foreign language you know how goofy the sentences in the textbooks are—"Give me the pen of my aunt"—and these sentences inspired Ionesco to write *The Bald Soprano* (1950), which he called an "anti-play" about the "tragedy of language." Ionesco went beyond Brecht, wanting the audience not only to fail to make an emotional connection with the play, but to be alienated from it, to be shocked by it. Like Sartre, he was horrified by the prospect of conformity; in *Rhinoceros* (1959), every character is able to turn into a rhinoceros but him. In his other work he typically presents the themes of man's isolation and the numbing effects of bourgeois life.

Jean Genet (1910-1986), though sometimes considered an absurdist as well, was a true original whose work isn't easily categorized. Genet, writing in prison for much of his career, lived in revolt against what he believed was a completely arbitrary social value system. Obsessed with crime, homosexuality, and the social outcast, Genet wrote with daring and passion. Though it is easy to be overwhelmed by the shocking elements of his writing, Genet's novels, memoirs, and plays contain much tenderness, pity, and beauty as well. His ritualistic work attempted to demonstrate the necessity of acknowledging both sides of humanity: the lawful and the criminal, love and hate, the straight and the not-so-straight. The two characters in *The Maids* (1947) act out a ritualized murder—one maid pretends to be the mistress, and the other maid pretends to kill her. The setting for *The Balcony* (1956) is a brothel where anything goes, no matter how kinky. Needless to say, the subjects of Genet's work shocked audiences of the 1950s; he managed to break down even further the limits on what was acceptable for public view.

 The break between the realism of prewar theater and the absurdity of postwar theater was caused by at least several things: the scope and horror of World War II, the invention and deployment of the atom bomb, and the total domination of bourgeois values (especially in Europe and America). To take a semi-Marxist view, industrialism had begun to separate man from meaningful work, and by the postwar period, people no longer had any sense of their place in the world or in society. Artists did not search for meaning—they believed there was no meaning.

25. The two main characters in *Waiting for Godot* are
   (A) Rosencrantz and Guildenstern
   (B) Vladimir and Estragon
   (C) Gilbert and Sullivan
   (D) Porgy and Bess

Absurdism was probably made most famous by **Samuel Beckett** (1906-1986) and his play *Waiting for Godot* (1952). Although Beckett was always a determined avant-gardist, the play was a popular success in

WAITING FOR BECKETT

Samuel Beckett was nearly as bizarre as the characters he wrote about. Beckett and Peggy Guggenheim, the famous art patron, were lovers briefly in Paris in the twenties. In her memoirs Guggenheim describes Beckett as sometimes getting into bed with her in his clothes (shoes and all). He would abruptly leave every now and then to pace up and down a traffic island in the middle of the street.

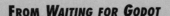

FROM *WAITING FOR GODOT*

Vladimir: We'll hang ourselves to-morrow. (Pause.) Unless Godot comes.

Estragon: And if he comes?

Vladimir: We'll be saved.

Estragon: Well? Shall we go?

Vladimir: Pull on your trousers.

Estragon: What?

Vladimir: Pull on your trousers.

Estragon: You want me to pull off my trousers?

Vladimir: Pull ON your trousers.

Estragon: (realizing his trousers are down) True. He pulls up his trousers.

Vladimir: Well? Shall we go?

Estragon: Yes, let's go.

They do not move.

——Samuel Beckett

Beckett to Pinter: "If you insist on finding form, I'll describe it for you. I was in a hospital once. There was a man in another ward, dying of throat cancer. In the silence, I could hear his screams continually. That's the only kind of form my work has."

Paris when it was first produced in 1953. Unlike Ionesco, who was concerned with social relationships, Beckett writes about man's relationship to the world, to existence itself. He does not reach happy conclusions. His characters are typically impotent, spiritually lost, old, crippled, lame, blind, and unable to make sense of themselves or their lives.

The action of *Godot* revolves around two tramps, Vladimir and Estragon, who are waiting for someone named Godot to show up. He never does. Though another pair of bums, Lucky and Pozzo, do intervene briefly, raving. In spite of its depressing themes, the play contains much of Beckett's trademark bleak humor.

26. Which play features "the no-neck monsters"?

(A) *A Streetcar Named Desire*
(B) *Cat on a Hot Tin Roof*
(C) *Who's Afraid of Virginia Woolf?*
(D) *Zoo Story*

Ah, the decadence and faded glamour of the South. **Tennessee Williams's** (1911-1983) plays are laden with the sultry heat of his hometown, New Orleans. Sexual desire—forbidden or unsatisfied—is often the overt theme as well as the subtext of his work, although Williams takes a very different approach than that of either Genet or O'Neill. He uses a poetic and realistic style, full of dramatic, often violent action. Usually an

Marlon Brando and Jessica Tandy in *A Streetcar Named Desire*: no one else comes close.

older woman is featured, desperate, even deranged, who struggles with a young stud, like Marlon Brando. In both *The Glass Menagerie* (1945) and *A Streetcar Named Desire* (1947), the older woman is attempting to cling to a version of her younger self against the countervailing forces of age, society, and loss.

From 1945 to 1960, Williams was the most popular playwright in America. He appeared on numerous television talk shows, and several of his plays were successfully adapted for the movies. Hollywood actors

Cat on a Hot Tin Roof (1958), starring Elizabeth Taylor and Paul Newman. Set in the South, a dying patriarch fends off money-grubbing suck-ups. There's a great cast of actors and actresses in this film adaptation of the Williams's classic.

FROM *CAT ON A HOT TIN ROOF*

Maggie: One of those no-neck monsters hit me with a hot buttered biscuit so I have to change!

Brick: Why d'ya call Gooper's kiddies no-neck monsters?

Maggie: Because they've got no necks! Isn't that a good enough reason?

Brick: Don't they have any necks?

Maggie: None visible. Their fat little heads are set on their fat little bodies without a bit of connection.

Brick: That's too bad.

Maggie: Yes, it's too bad because you can't wring their necks if they've got no necks to wring!

——Tennessee Williams

loved the well-made dialogue and rich characterizations of his scripts. Some of Williams's lines have become part of the American idiom: "gentleman caller" from *The Glass Menagerie*; "no-neck monsters" from *Cat on a Hot Tin Roof* (1955); and, of course, "Stell-aaa!" from *A Streetcar Named Desire*. Both *Cat on a Hot Tin Roof* and *A Streetcar Named Desire* won Pulitzer prizes.

27. **Arthur Miller was married to**

    (A) Elizabeth Taylor
    (B) Vanessa Redgrave
    (C) Marilyn Monroe
    (D) Lillian Hellman

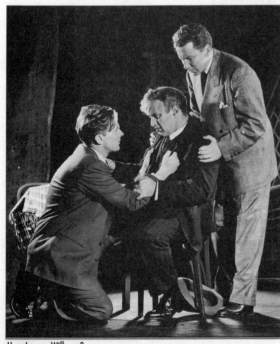

How Lo can Willy go?

The international relief brought by the end of World War II (p. 650) didn't last long. American playwrights, like their European counterparts, were soon writing of disillusionment. In the plays of **Arthur Miller** (1915-), that disillusionment took the form of psychological realism. His first success, *All My Sons* (1947), is about the deaths that resulted from a sleazy airplane manufacturer's lust for profit. The theme of material success, or lack of it, runs through several of his plays, most notably *Death of a Salesman* (1949).

When a person reaches a certain age, he is likely to look back on his life and measure it. Unfortunately for Willy Loman, the main character in *Death of a Salesman*, the view isn't pretty. In society's terms, he is a loser, but he has the courage to confront this reality and to try, before his death, to do something for his family. Miller's combination of realistic techniques, fantasy, and memory results in a finely-drawn psychological portrait of a man gripped with the fear of living a life that comes to nothing.

28. Who wrote *The Birthday Party?*

(A) Tom Stoppard
(B) Edward Albee
(C) Arthur Miller
(D) Harold Pinter

The setting is indoors, a living room usually, and a few characters are talking . . . or not talking, as the case may be. **Harold Pinter** (1930-), like Chekov before him, is the master of the pause. The silences in Pinter's dialogue are part of the tight architecture of the play, and can be more telling than the long speeches of some other dramatists.

Although the plays appear to be set realistically, once things start to roll it is clear why Pinter is considered the English absurdist. Unknown forces begin to threaten the characters, who behave defensively and evasively to the world, to each other, and to themselves.

In American literature, Pinter is somewhat like American writer Raymond Carver. For both, the world is a menacing place, and language is employed by characters in a strategic and defensive manner. The dialogue seems effortless, natural, even poetic. Pinter's plays *The Birthday Party* (1958), *The Caretaker* (1960), *The Homecoming* (1965), and *No Man's Land* (1975) are terrific to read, and even better onstage.

WHO'S AFRAID OF ANOTHER DRINK?

Edward Albee's brilliant Who's Afraid of Virginia Woolf? *takes place during a night of unrestrained drinking that gradually peels away every layer of civility from the characters on stage. If you can, check out the incomparable movie version (1966), directed by Mike Nichols and starring Richard Burton and Liz Taylor. But don't watch it if you're already depressed.*

 Betrayal (1983), with Jeremy Irons and Ben Kingsley. The story, based on Pinter's play of the same name, depicts a love triangle progressing backward in time. The plot opens with the couple breaking up and ends with their first encounter.

29. Which play did Sam Shepard NOT write?

(A) *Curse of the Starving Class*
(B) *Burn This*
(C) *Tooth of Crime*
(D) *Fool For Love*

In almost all of the plays by **Sam Shepard** (1943-), the male characters are trying to figure out what it means to be a man, and how to go about acting on whatever that meaning is. But Shepard hardly limits himself to one particular theme or type of hero. He writes about the American West, about the battlefield of the family, and the human struggle to come to grips with the past as well as the present. Comic elements may come into the plays, but more often the action combines violence and lyricism to startling effect. Although, as in *True West* (1981), the characters may be hanging out in the kitchen playing with a toaster, the plays are not exactly naturalistic. There is an epic quality to Shepard's work, because of the

FROM *THE TOOTH OF CRIME*

Hoss: Yeah. Look at me now. Impotent. Can't strike a kill unless the charts are right. Stuck in my image. Stuck in a mansion. Waiting. Waiting for a kid who's probably just like me. Just like I was then. A young blood. And I gotta off him. I gotta roll him or he'll roll me. We're fightin' ourselves. Just like turnin' the blade on ourselves. Suicide, man. Maybe Little Willard was right. Blow your fuckin' brains out. The whole thing's a joke. Stick a gun in your fucking mouth and pull the trigger. That's what it's all about. That's what we're doin'. He's my brother and I gotta kill him. He's gotta kill me.

——*Sam Shepard*

RENAISSANCE SAM

Aside from writing Pulitzer Prize-winning theater, Sam Shepard has also had a successful career as a rock musician, and his rugged good looks have made him something of a film star. His romantic alliances have included poet/rocker Patti Smith and actress Jessica Lange (his wife).

way he uses language and because the characters appear to be archetypes drawn from American popular fantasy.

Considered by many to be the most talented playwright of his generation, Shepard got his start in **off-off-Broadway**, and has since won a Pulitzer Prize and written, directed, and starred in films. His long list of plays includes *Chicago* (1965), *Icarus's Mother* (1972), *Mad Dog Blues* (1971), *The Tooth of Crime* (1967), *Curse of the Starving Class* (1977), *Buried Child* (1979), and *True West* (1981). *Tooth of Crime* is a good example of early Shepard at his best. In an impossible, dream-like future, Rock-and-Roll stars Hoss and Crow stake out territory and stalk each other like gunfighters, duelling to the kill. The weapon they use is language.

30. **Whose idea was "the theater of cruelty"?**

(A) Jerzy Grotowski
(B) Julian Beck and Judith Malina
(C) Lee Breuer
(D) Antonin Artaud

In the United States, with the social upheavals sixties and seventies came the growth of small avant-garde theaters. Oddly enough, one of the most profound influences on the American experimental theater movement was Frenchman **Antonin Artaud** (1896-1948), who developed his theories of the theater of cruelty in the thirties and forties. Throughout his life Artaud sought an art that might viscerally connect the individual human life and spirit to the greater community. He eventually conceived of theater as the vehicle for his project. It would be called the theater of cruelty: poetic, anti-rational, ritualistic, and centered around performers who would in some sense martyr themselves for the audience. Though incontestably brilliant, Artaud, haunted by drug-addiction and mental illness, was unable to realize his grand schemes. His manifestos, written with visionary intensity, reached later generations who put them into action. In one famous formulation, Artaud wrote that an actor should be like a man being burned at the stake "signaling through the flames." Many of today's performance artists, like Karen Finley (known to smear her naked body with gooey foods while shouting obscenties at the audience), Chris Burden (who has dragged himself over broken glass, had himself shot, and risked electrocution, all in the name of art), and Stellarc (who suspends himself from hooks sunk into his flesh), can perhaps be best understood in the context of Artaud's theories (though none of these artists would want to be called an actor).

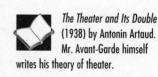

The Theater and Its Double (1938) by Antonin Artaud. Mr. Avant-Garde himself writes his theory of theater.

31. **Actors Spaulding Gray and Willem Dafoe first worked together in which theater?**
    (A) La Mama ETC
    (B) The Performing Garage
    (C) The Open Theater
    (D) The Poor Theater

Today, contemporary theater strives to carve a niche for itself against the competition of television, cinema, and video. The means of survival undertaken by theater artists are various, and often challenging (and sometimes incomprehensible). From out of the ranks of perfomers, playwrights, and directors struggling in urban artistic centers like New York, Paris, London, and Prague, come artists and ideas that continue to rejuvenate the mass media. Comic actress Whoopi Goldberg gave some of her first performances at New York's legendary **La Mama Experimental Theater Club**. Actor Willem Dafoe, and actor/writer Spaulding Gray both began their careers in a tiny theater in New York called **The Performing Garage**. As founding members of the **Wooster Group**, both continue to perform there, Dafoe especially, in the difficult and brilliant collagist pieces of Wooster Group director Elizabeth LeCompte.

Artists like Peter Brook, Robert Wilson, Ping Chong, Meredith Monk, Philip Glass, Laurie Andersen (p. 617), Peter Sellars, Pina Bausch, and Mark Morris continue to push the boundaries of art. In quest of new forms and horizons, many of these artists have become uncategorizable, breaking down the traditional barriers between theater, dance, music, and the other visual arts. Meredith Monk, Philip Glass, and Laurie Andersen both come from a music background, while Pina Bausch's background is in modern dance. LeCompte of the Wooster Group originally trained as a painter. All are undeniably a part of theater.

Of course in the arts the "cutting edge" is a ragged edge and most of this work will pass into oblivion as has so much that came before it. However, we can be certain too, that some will survive. That radiant quality that can only come from a flesh-and-blood performer before us on the stage continues to draw audiences to the theater as it draws artists both to the backstage and the limelight. Theater's power to unite, to heal, and to speak for entire communities was known to the ancient Greeks, and can be seen in our own day.

Answers

1. DCBA	2. C	3. D	4. D	5. A	6. ABCD	7. A	8. C	9. A	10. C
11. B	12. D	13. D	14. B	15. C	16. B	17. C	18. A	19. A	20. D
21. B	22. B	23. B	24. C	25. B	26. B	27. C	28. D	29. B	30. D
31. A									

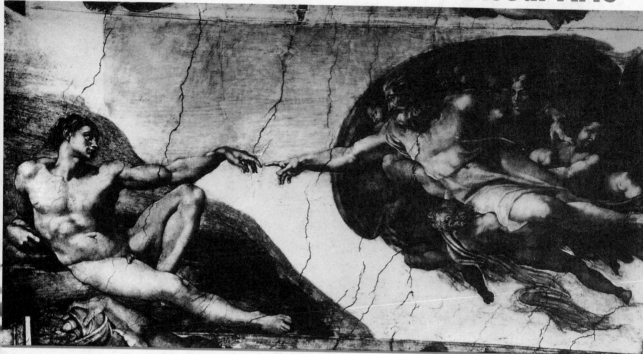

Though they may seem to capture pure and timeless beauty, the visual arts—painting and sculpture and their offshoots—always convey essential elements of the culture that produces them. Art also matters because it provokes conflicts. When it shows us beauty in an unexpected place, art makes us wonder what beauty is. When it makes things that are familiar to us seem suddenly strange, art makes us reconsider how we experience the world around us. When it presents us with the achievements of someone in a remote time period or culture, art makes us both reaffirm our common humanity and acknowledge the massive differences time and place produce.

1. A *kouros* is a statue of

   (A) a reclining woman
   (B) a slave
   (C) a standing boy
   (D) an animal

The **kouros,** of the Greek Archaic period, was a statue of a nude standing youth, its weight distributed symmetrically, one leg striding forward. The *kouros* often had a grinning facial expression (called by art historians the "Archaic smile"). The corresponding female figure was the **kore,** a clothed girl, also often smiling. In the fifth century B.C. the smile gradually vanished, while the rigid pose was replaced by the more natural **contrapposto,** in which weight is unevenly distributed, and the body is twisted along its central axis into an S-curve.

Ancient Greek representations of the human body are a benchmark for all Western art, and since nearly all Greek paintings (with the exception of vase paintings) have disappeared, the progress of the nude is usually traced back to Greek sculpture. The representation of the nude developed from the Egyptian rigidity of the *kouros* (nude standing boy) of the seventh century B.C., to relaxed, muscular, idealized figures of the **Classical period**, such as the *Poseidon* of the fifth century B.C. The **Hellenistic period**, the third century B.C., produced realistic, expressive forms that invite the viewer to look at them from several viewpoints. Paralleling the rise of Greek theatre (p. 542), art of the Hellenistic period was emotional and dramatic, often showing dynamic movement, as in the statue *Winged Victory of Samothrace*. The concern of the philosopher Aristotle (p. 386) for understanding the laws of the natural world was also reflected in the increasingly relaxed, naturalistic style of sculpture. Ancient Greek society valued and respected individual artists, but in ancient Rome artists became anonymous laborers, seemingly working in groups to produce unified projects. Roman sculptors mainly produced copies of Greek originals, many of which are the only record we have of missing Greek works. The famous *Laocoön Group*, however, depicting the powerful, writhing bodies of the Trojan priest Laocoön and his sons as they are strangled by serpents, is now thought to be a Roman work done in a Hellenistic style.

Laocoön Group

Winged Victory of Samothrace

2. **The early Renaissance painter known for breakthroughs in three-dimensional realism is**
   (A) Botticelli
   (B) Giotto
   (C) Titian
   (D) Tintoretto

Giotto di Bondone (1267-1337) is the artist held responsible for moving painting past the "Greek" or **Byzantine** style, ushering in the era of **three-dimensional realism**. Strictly speaking, Giotto painted during the **Gothic period**, which lasted from the twelfth to fourteenth centuries, but since artists of the **Renaissance** built on his foundation he can be considered an early Renaissance figure. Gothic art was produced mainly for religious purposes—to deliver biblical messages to a mostly illiterate public. Breaking free from the old decorative, stylized, flat-looking representation, Giotto created a new sense of the space of the picture. His scenes seem to get at the heart of a story through the gestures and expressions of his human figures, who all have a real physical presence. There is controversy about how many fresco cycles he painted, especially over whether he painted the *Life of St. Francis* series at the church of St. Francis in Assisi. But it's certain that he painted the Arena Chapel in Padua, considered his greatest work.

In Siena, **Duccio** and his student, **Simone Martini**, rivaled Giotto in developments like fluidity and the capacity to tell a story, but their work still had a flatness reminiscent of the Byzantine style. Yet Duccio, Simone, and others of the Sienese school took smallness and decorativeness to new places. Simone gives his figures opulent, beautifully colored, delicately folded clothing, enhancing the graceful yet passionate quality of paintings like *The Angel and the Annunciation*. Simone traveled to the papal court in Avignon, France, where he was influential in the development of an **International Gothic** style of courtly, decorative, lyrical painting. Fusing elements of Italian style with Northern European naturalism and concern for detail, International Gothic artists like **Gentile da Fabriano** and **Antonio Pisanello** painted large-scale pictures with big casts of characters and lots of action going on simultaneously. Gentile's *The Adoration of the Magi* is a good example of the style, depicting an animated group of travelers, replete with exotic animals and servants, waiting to see the Christ child.

International Gothic artists were also well-versed in sculpture, architecture, and jewelry design. In 1401, a competition was held to pick the artist to design the **relief** (sculpture that projects from a background surface rather than standing freely) for the gilded bronze doors of the

The term "Gothic" originated as a misnomer. It was coined as a derogatory term by Renaissance critics who wrongly labeled medieval architectural styles barbaric—the product of the Gothic tribes who had invaded Rome and destroyed most of its art.

Fresco is a method of painting used in antiquity that became popular during the Italian Renaissance. To paint a fresco, pure powdered pigments, mixed only in water, were applied onto a fresh, wet ground of lime-plaster. The colors soaked in and became part of the wall. The artist had to have a steady hand and work very quickly, before the plaster could dry—corrections are just about impossible. Colors were limited, also, and became lighter when they dried, making dark tones difficult to achieve. Frescoes can only be painted in a dry, warm climate like Italy's—Northern European Renaissance artists did not do frescoes. There are also examples of fresco painting in China and India.

Baptistery of Florence (the building in which the city's infants were baptized). The city's best talents submitted entries, and **Lorenzo Ghiberti** defeated a group that included the celebrated architect Filippo Brunelleschi (p. 40). Depicting twenty episodes from the life of Christ, the doors took several years to complete and required a large workshop of goldsmiths and artists, some of whom, like **Masolino** and **Paolo Uccello**, went on to become outstanding painters of the period. Another of Ghiberti's students, **Donatello** (1386-1466), became a revolutionary sculptor whose innovations influenced painters and led the way away from Gothic elegance to Renaissance monumentality in sculpture. Building on the technique of classical sculpture, Donatello's work was emotional and forceful, and the artist boldly broke new ground: his standing *David*, done in bronze, is thought to be the first nude statue since antiquity. Donatello's technical breakthroughs included a careful incorporation of the angle from which a statue would be seen, so that he adjusted proportions if a statue was to be seen from below, or used more forceful lines if a statue was to be positioned at a distance from viewers.

The sculptural realism Donatello achieved is at the heart of Renaissance painting, influencing especially pioneers of three-dimensional form and perspective like the Florentine painter known as **Masaccio** (1401-1428). Though he died at only twenty-seven years old, Masaccio (his nickname means "Sloppy Tom," supposedly because of his lack of attention to his appearance) is the first truly Renaissance Italian painter, building on Giotto's intuitive use of perspective to create a precise, scientific approach to it. His greatest work, the fresco cycle in the Brancacci Chapel in Florence, was studied closely by later Renaissance artists for its technique and powerful emotionalism. Masaccio's most immediate descendant was the Dominican friar known as **Fra Angelico** (1400-1455), who is regarded as saintly and inspired but was also a very professional, confident artist, able to achieve impressive effects of light and perspective.

3. *Birth of Venus* was painted by
   (A) Sandro Botticelli
   (B) Giovanni Bellini
   (C) Piero della Francesca
   (D) Jan van Eyck

One of the most famous images in Western art, *The Birth of Venus*, was painted by another Renaissance Florentine, **Sandro Botticelli** (1445-1510), who reacted against the scientific naturalism of Masaccio to develop a

Birth of Venus

lyrical, graceful, idealized style. In *The Birth of Venus* (sometimes referred to as Venus on the Half-Shell) we can see Botticelli's interest in secular, mythological subjects, which were fashionable among his patrons, who included members of the powerful **Medici** family. Botticelli later turned to religious subjects, though his figures still had an intense, moody sensuality. Botticelli was most likely a student of the wayward friar named Fra Filippo Lippi, whose adventurous life story includes a scandalous love affair with a nun who bore him two children (they were later released from their vows and married, though Lippi defiantly kept the "Fra" before his name). Lippi's work is characterized by graceful lines that he seems to have passed on to his son, who also became a painter, Filippino Lippi.

Piero della Francesca (1420-1492) is a Renaissance figure who was rediscovered in the twentieth century and is now acknowledged as one of the great painters of all time. Born in the quiet, hilly central Italian region of Umbria, Piero was able to impart a feeling of silence and stillness to his paintings. In works such as the fresco series *The Legend of the True Cross* and the fresco *Resurrection of Christ* (which has been called "the perfect painting"), colors are muted but clear and distinct, and the white light that

 In 1966, a flood in Florence damaged a number of frescoes, but the restoration ended up providing new insight into fresco-painting technique. The *sinopia* technique, in which red ochre was used to draw initial guides for the day's work, was exposed, revealing that artists often introduced changes between the initial plan and the final work.

evenly bathes the figures adds to the feeling of serene gravity. Patronized by the duke of the powerful Renaissance city of **Urbino, Federico da Montefeltro**, whose famous portrait he painted, Piero was also a devoted mathematician, reflected in the precision and scientific approach to perspective of his painting. The first great Northern Italian artist was the strong-willed **Andrea Mantegna** (1431-1506), whose grasp of perspective and foreshortening was also unsurpassed. As court artist for the **Gonzaga** family of Mantua, Mantegna painted the Ducal Palace with boldly done courtly scenes and portraits of the family, as well as stunning **illusionistic** painting—designed to trick the eye into taking the painting for something "real"—of architectural details, such as a ceiling painting of a skylight that opens up to the sky as angels peer over the edges.

Mantegna's brother-in-law **Giovanni Bellini** (1430-1516) went on to become a central figure of the Renaissance **Venetian School** of painting. Venetian painters were less preoccupied with problems of perspective and sculptural form than Florentine-influenced artists, focusing instead on color and light. Bellini was especially famous for his paintings of the Madonna and child, such as the *Madonna of the Meadow*, in which the Madonna's robe glows a beautiful blue and harmonizes with the earth tones of the landscape behind her.

4. **The painting of Jan van Eyck is notable for its**

    (A) employment of scientific perspective
    (B) use of the grotesque
    (C) minute, realistic detail and control of light
    (D) emotionalism and pathos

In Northern Europe, the fifteenth century saw a movement toward pictorial realism that reached its peak in the work of **Jan van Eyck** (1390-1441). Northern painters wanted to paint people just as they were, in everyday settings, with meticulous atttention to detail. Van Eyck, the court painter to the Duke of Burgundy, Philip the Good, brought the technique of **oil painting** to new levels of technical mastery. His control of light and flair for minute detail stand out in works such as the commissioned painting *The Arnolfini Wedding (plate 1)*. As the couple stands, exchanging wedding vows, every detail of the scene is scrupulously recorded and has symbolic value: the dog in the corner symbolizes fidelity; the single burning candle above the couple symbolizes God's all-seeing eye; the shoes by the groom's feet indicate that he is standing on holy ground, symbolizing the sanctity of marriage. Amazingly, the tiny convex mirror behind the couple contains their reflection as well as that of the man performing the ceremony and van Eyck himself painting it. Above the mirror, written in legal style, are the Latin words "Johannes de eyck fuit hic"—"Jan van Eyck was here"—which could be interpreted to mean that van Eyck served as witness to the marriage, or may just be a playful touch.

Among the most imaginative, fantastical artists who ever lived is the Dutch painter **Hieronymus Bosch** (1450-1516) who emerged from the meticulous Northern tradition to blaze a trail all his own. Bosch used unique, vivid, often bizarre symbolism to create crazy, nightmarish images that seem to come from deep within some collective unconscious. There's something strangely modern about his horrific vision of the state of humankind, and in fact twentieth-century **Surrealists** claimed Bosch as an inspiration. In *The Temptation of Saint Anthony*, for example, among the riotous detail we can see Saint Anthony tormented by demons with human bodies and strange animal heads, an animal with an urn for a body, and boats that are half fish, while *Hell* is crowded with bodies and random body parts in grotesque sexualized configurations. Much of Bosch's symbolism would have been recognizable to his contemporaries from Flemish proverbs and religious terminology, and in his day Bosch was a popular figure, reflecting the terrors and anxieties of an uncertain time.

In fifteenth-century Germany, where artists worked mainly in isolated cities and small courts, **Albrecht Dürer** (1471-1528) brought the Renaissance to Northern Europe. The son of a goldsmith, Dürer spent his early career practicing the art of **woodcut**, in which the artist draws a design on a smooth block of wood, then gouges away the parts that are to stay white, applies ink and creates an impression in reverse on a sheet of paper. An avid student of perspective and proportion, Dürer wanted to move past the medieval view of the artist as craftsman, still prevalent in Germany. His paintings have a psychological intensity that reveals the inward state of his subjects; his greatest painting, the *Four Apostles*, reflects his commitment to the Reformation (p. 494). Less religiously inclined than Dürer, the enterprising **Lucas Cranach the Elder** (1472-1553) painted both sexy nymphs that were all the rage with

WOODCUTS FOR EVERYONE

Woodcuts became a hot commodity in the sixteenth century among the bourgeoisie, who were newly able to become consumers of art in the style of aristocrats of old. The development of woodcut was also helped along through its increasing use in the illustration of books, which, due to the invention of the printing press, could now be owned by common people. The woodcut didn't see much action again until the late nineteenth century, when it was rediscovered by artists such as Gauguin and Munch. Twentieth century German Expressionists were also especially attracted to woodcut.

Albrecht Durer, *Adam and Eve* (engraving)

his aristocratic patrons and religious scenes that were quickly copied for sale to the public by members of his workshop in Wittenberg. **Hans Holbein** (1497-1543) left Germany for Switzerland, where he met Erasmus, who arranged patronage for him from King Henry VIII of England. As court painter, Holbein developed a dignified, realistic style that revealed little of the inner life of his sitters. An exception to Holbein's usually impassive figures is the sad, revealing, personal note struck in a portrait of his wife and children, in which they seem lonely and worn down. The Northern **landscape tradition** reached its height with the so-called "peasant painter," the Flemish **Pieter Brueghel** (1525-1569), who despite his nickname was a cultured and well-traveled man. Influenced by Bosch, Brueghel tended toward crowded panoramas, though his scenes of peasant life, like *The Wedding Feast*, with its fat, plain, complacent bride and undistinguished guests, reveal the humbling, pathetic state of humanity through a devastating realism rather than Bosch's symbolism. Bruegel's many landscapes of the Alps (p. 137) are his major triumph, conveying a complex, grand, and vast universe.

5. By the end of his career, Leonardo da Vinci saw painting as

   (A) a poor method of conveying his ideas about the world
   (B) the truest revelation of God's will
   (C) a lucrative profession
   (D) a good road to scientific discovery

The period known as the **High Renaissance** gave birth to the idea of the artist as genius, and no artist so fits the mold of genius as **Leonardo da Vinci** (1452-1519), the definitive "**Renaissance Man**." His talents were incredibly diverse—from mathematical and mechanical wizardry to a beautiful singing voice. The illegimate son of a Tuscan lawyer and a peasant girl, Leonardo had a restless, independent spirit, and art and the patient dedication it required never sat well with him. He left many paintings unfinished; he was more interested in conveying his ideas through the drawings he used to solve scientific problems and design contraptions such as his well-known flying machine. Leonardo actually painted very few pictures for a painter of his stature. What he did paint, however, has an amazing singularity. The *Mona Lisa* is so well known that it is hard to see it any more, but in Leonardo's other portraits of women, such as the portrait known as the *Lady with an Ermine*,

Da Vinci's *The Last Supper*

you can notice Leonardo's wistful, luminous perfection, achieved through his pioneering use of the technique of **sfumato**, the "smoke-like" blending of colors into each other so subtly that no transitions are perceptible. He also pioneered the technique of **chiaroscuro**, the bold contrasting of light and dark later perfected by **Rembrandt**. Leonardo's achievements in beautifully balanced composition also defined Renaissance style, most notably the *Last Supper* fresco (which has required endless restoration and is still in horrible shape because Leonardo used an experimental fresco technique that didn't hold up well).

Michelangelo Buonarotti (1475-1564), another High Renaissance master, was also something of a reluctant painter—it was sculpture that held his interest first and foremost, and he had to be coerced by Pope Julius II to undertake the

Michelangelo's *David*

Lives of the Most Eminent Painters, Sculptors, and Architects (last ed., 1959), by painter and architect Giorgio Vasari. It was first published in 1550; the revised and enlarged version, published in 1568, contains over two hundred biographies. It has affected how we view the Renaissance and how the Renaissance viewed itself, and despite its inaccuracies and apocryphal incidents, it remains a valuable source of information. Vasari believed that art was revived by Giotto and reached its zenith with "the divine Michelangelo."

painting of the **Sistine Chapel ceiling**. Michelangelo's early statues, including his famous *Pietà*, are powerfully expressive yet polished and refined, and his famous nude *David*, huge and self-assured, came to symbolize Florence at its most self-confident. Work on the Sistine Chapel ceiling took Michelangelo nearly four years, most of them spent lying on his back on a scaffold, and at its completion in 1512 he was again hailed as the greatest artist of his day. With an intense, complicated, yet calm energy, the ceiling depicts scenes from Genesis (p. 487), from the story of Creation to Noah. At each corner of the central scenes are beautiful nude youths (called the *ignudi*), and flanking the scenes are seated figures, Hebrew prophets and pagan sibyls, who predicted the coming of the Messiah. The recent cleaning has revealed another dimension to the ceiling—the vivid, bold colors that Michelangelo used that were obscured by centuries of grime. Twenty-nine years after finishishing the ceiling Michelangelo came back to paint *The Last Judgment* (plate 2) on the west wall of the chapel, and the later work reflects the pessimism and despair of his later years, times of political and spiritual unrest in Italy: the mood is troubled, the figures wrathful and threatening.

6. Raphael is famous for painting

    (A) madonnas
    (B) *The School of Athens*
    (C) portraits
    (D) All of the above

A LOVER

In contrast to the reclusive Leonardo and to the pious, conflicted Michelangelo, Raphael was courtly and gregarious; Vasari called him "gracious Raffaello." Unlike his two older contemporaries, Raphael was a lover of women. Vasari considered him amorous to a fault, and reported that, after an excess of lovemaking, Raphael went into a violent fever, and doctors bled him (a popular remedy at the time). His death, at age thirty-seven, soon followed.

Raphael (1483-1520) is the third great High Renaissance artist, most famous for his many madonnas, among them the *Sistine Madonna*, and insightful portraits. Raphael, who was also an architect, had the ability to incorporate and synthesize the many movements and developments in art into his own work, so much so that more than any other artist his style seems to define the High Renaissance style. His clearest influences were Leonardo and Michelangelo, yet rather than their intellectual turbulence Raphael conveys a sense of

Raphael imagines Aristotle.

well-being, sweetness, and balance. His monumental fresco in the Vatican, *The School of Athens*, depicting a lively scene of ancient Greek philosophers (many of them portraits of Raphael's contemporaries, including a self-portrait) is one of his greatest works, with its lively, balanced figures, sophisticated composition and masterful use of perspective. After Raphael's early death (on his thirty-seventh birthday) his reputation continued to soar, and through the nineteenth century he was considered the greatest painter who ever lived.

7. **The Renaissance painter of the Venetian school famous for his pioneering use of bold color was**

   (A) Caravaggio
   (B) Titian
   (C) Tintoretto
   (D) El Greco

The Venetian painter **Titian** (1490-1576) had a long career in which his style developed through several periods, moving from a vigorous earthiness to a sad yet profound sense of freedom. Titian revolutionized oil painting technique, using a free, bold brushwork and sweeping strokes, often discarding the brush altogether and using his fingers, and is revered most of all for his daring use of rich, shimmering color. He also has a claim as the first great Renaissance artist to focus all his energies on painting, unlike his predecessors who were accomplished in other crafts as well. Along with many portraits, such as *The Daughter of Roberto Strozzi* (plate 3) and religious scenes, Titian produced a celebrated series of seven erotic mythological subjects, including *Venus and Adonis* and *Rape of Europa* (plate 4). Titian's influence on later painters was great, and his most direct follower was **Tintoretto** (1518-1594), who declared that his aim was to combine Titian's color with Michelangelo's drawing. Tintoretto's paintings are explosive, especially his crowded, dramatic *Crucifixion*, and his compositions are strikingly original, full of strange poses and exaggerated touches.

Tintoretto's inheritor was the painter known as **El Greco** (1541-1614), actually a Cretan named Domenicos Theotikopoulos who settled in Spain in 1577. El Greco often abandoned the Renaissance ideal of three-dimensional realism, creating a style based on intentional distortion. His figures, and everything else in his paintings, are elongated, as if the whole painting is being pulled upward. In his famous *Burial of Count Orgaz* the scene of earthly mourners beneath a celestial crowd seems almost like a hallucination. El Greco's strange, moody, apocalyptic style has inspired several

 In the Renaissance, oil paint was made by grinding pigments into vegetable oils, usually derived from walnuts, sunflower or poppy seeds, or linseed, in contrast to tempera paint, in which the pigment is mixed with water-soluble stuff such as egg yolk. Titian's innovations brought out not only oil paint's richer color potential but also its potential to have a wide variety of surface textures, allowing the artist to develop more of a "signature."

theories—that he was insane, or that he had a problem with his eyesight, for example, but he's best understood as a visionary, ahead of his time, whose stormy spirituality shaped his art.

8. **Which of the following best characterizes art of the baroque period?**

(A) Restrained and pared down
(B) Delicate and detailed
(C) Abstract and other-worldly
(D) Ornamental and emotional

Baroque art, which developed in the seventeenth century, had its detractors right from the start—the term itself was derogatory, coming from a Portuguese word for a misshapen pearl. The baroque style developed as a reaction against mannerism, a sixteenth-century style of elegance, sophistication, and artificiality. Mannerism reflected the pessimism of Italy at the time of the counter-reformation, the zealous Catholic response to Protestantism, and was in marked contrast to the idealism of the High Renaissance. Tintoretto, El Greco, and Michelangelo in later years worked in the mannerist style, as did Parmagianino, whose *Madonna with the Long Neck* seems eerily distorted and asymmetrical beside one of Raphael's perfectly balanced Madonnas. The word "mannerist" or "mannered" now transcends its original historical period to mean anyone who eagerly adopts the "tricks" or outward signs of a particular style but lacks the real substance. For that matter, "baroque" has also come to be used as a term beyond its original time period, meaning anything overwrought, overly emotional, overly florid.

Going for Baroque: Bernini's *The Ecstasy of Saint Teresa*

The sculptor, architect, and painter **Gianlorenzo Bernini** (1598-1680) is a major figure of baroque art. Bernini sculptures such as *The Ecstasy of Saint Teresa*, with its depiction of Teresa in a spiritual trance resembling an orgasmic state, have been used as prime examples of baroque excess, but nonetheless they hold your attention. Bernini statues seem to bring sculpture together with painting and architecture into one decorative whole. His architecture and outdoor sculptural architecture, including many famous fountains, left an indelible mark on the face of Rome.

Michelangelo Merisi da **Caravaggio** (1573-1610) is the painter who best defines the naturalistic strain of the baroque style. His painting of a lush, rosy-cheeked *Bacchus* seductively and impertinently offering a glass of wine to the viewer stands in contrast to the solemn dignity of Raphael. The baroque period came during the counter-reformation, and Caravaggio's uncompromisingly realistic works got him in constant trouble with Catholic authorities. *The Death of the Virgin,* for example, shows a dead Mary looking, well, *dead,* with her feet stuck out unceremoniously and sallow, sagging skin. This kind of brutal realism is used to stunning effect by one of the most passionate and intense female artists before the twentieth century, **Artemisia Gentileschi** (1593-1652), daughter of Caravaggio's follower **Orazio Gentileschi**. In her *Judith Slaying Holofernes,* she takes a popular Old Testament subject—Judith's murder of the tyrant Holofernes, which saved the Jewish people—and makes you see the act in all its goriness. The head is severed directly in the foregound of the painting, and blood spurts upward out of the neck and drips down a white mattress in rivulets. At nineteen, Artemisia Gentileschi was raped by a friend of her father's, but while he was eventually acquitted she was tortured during the legal proceedings, and the powerful painting is said to be her symbolic revenge.

In Northern Europe the decorative, theatrical tendency of the baroque style was strongest in Flanders, the stronghold of Catholicism in a Protestant region. Influenced by the Italian Renaissance, the ambitious and prodigious **Peter Paul Rubens** (1577-1640) was an extremely popular figure in his native Antwerp. Rubens was appointed court painter to King Albert and Queen Isabella of the Netherlands, and ran a bustling, profitable workshop. He also designed tapestry, book illustrations, and festival decorations—in fact his artistic output is so huge that the catalogue currently being completed of his work is expected to reach thirty volumes. Rubens painted every subject conceivable, from huge religious works like *Descent from the Cross* that express his energetic Catholicism to the luminous portraits of nude, full-figured, white-skinned women for which he is most famous today. His almost-nude portrait of his charming, rounded second wife, *Helena Fourment,* captures perfectly what has come to be called **Rubenesque** beauty. Another Flemish Baroque painter, Anthony van Dyck, developed a less robust, more refined style, specializing in portraits that lent an air of dignified elegance to his sitters.

A Fighter

Caravaggio's life was as violent as his paintings. He was a brawler, constantly getting into skirmishes with the law, and counting on patrons in the church and the aristocracy to get him out of trouble. After killing a man, following a disputed tennis match, he fled Rome, and went on the run, to Naples and Malta, awaiting a papal pardon. He was returning to Rome when he was falsely arrested, in a case of mistaken identity. Several days later, he was released, but it was too late—he had contracted malaria. He died a few months short of his thirty-seventh birthday, without knowing that the pope had pardoned him.

9. **Who is the seventeenth-century painter famous for his paintings of the Spanish court that include dwarves and children?**

   (A) Diego Velázquez
   (B) El Greco
   (C) Francisco de Goya
   (D) Pablo Picasso

The greatest painter of the **Spanish school, Diego Velázquez** (1599-1660), painted with a commanding presence and complete technical mastery. Appointed Court Painter to King Philip IV at only twenty-four years old, Velázquez painted religious and mythological scenes for Philip as well as many court paintings, including portraits that conveyed the dignified humanity of the dwarves Philip kept around for amusement. Velázquez's contemporary history painting *The Surrender of Breda*, depicting reconciliation after battle, stands out, but it's another Velázquez that was recently voted "the world's greatest painting" in a poll of artists and critics—*Las Meninas*, "The Maids of Honor." This renowned painting cleverly depicts a scene from the Court: The Princess, Margarita Teresa, is at center, surrounded by her maids, her tutor, her dog, and a dwarf. To the left is Velázquez himself, painting the portrait of the King and Queen, whom we can just make out in a mirror on the distant wall. The King's eye-view of the moment is an ingenious tribute to Philip, as well as a portrait of his daughter and a statement of Velázquez's own claim to artistic importance and pride—on the far wall are two pictures by Rubens obscured in the distance. The picture seems like a game of illusions, with a sense of spontaneity, but everything is worked out with amazing precision. You can also see in *Las Meninas* Velázquez's characteristic brush strokes, which seem random and fuzzy up close but miraculously cohere into perfect realism when viewed from a distance.

A seventeenth-century painter with a deep and sensitive feeling for humanity that has made him one of the most beloved artists in history is **Rembrandt van Rijn** (1606-1669). His style is rooted in a very Dutch practicality. He was fascinated by the human face, and his many commissioned portraits all reveal a probing but compassionate psychological awareness. Rembrandt is never more honest than in his many self-portraits through which you can chart his emotional progress. He evolved from the brash, half-shadowed youth in *Self-Portrait at About Twenty-One Years Old*, to the beaten, sad, knowing face of his later years in *Self Portrait* (plate 5), done in 1660, after he had lost a fortune and buried several children

Rembrandt was one of the greatest practictioners of etching, a method of engraving in which an etching needle is used to scratch an image onto a wax-coated metal plate. The plate is then immersed in acid to eat away at the image where the scratches are. Etching is still popular today, often used for book illustrations.

Rembrandt was also a gifted storyteller, able to capture the essence of a story. *The Anatomy Lesson of Dr. Tulp* conveys the personalities of all eight sitters—though the corpse manages to steal the show—yet they are subordinated to the composition as a whole. In the mysterious painting called *The Jewish Bride* he conveys emotional depth and intensity alongside tenderness. Rembrandt used the brush boldly, especially as he got older, and on some paintings he's said to have used the butt-end of the brush to scrape through the paint. His subtle and precise use of light and dark is amazing. Another great seventeenth-century Dutch painter is the enigmatic **Jan Vermeer** (1632-1675). Only about forty of his paintings are known today. Vermeer's focus was on serene, harmonious interior images, done with delicate details and clear, vibrant light such as *The Artist in his Studio* (plate 6). His one landscape *View of Delft*, is a radiant view of the city.

10. The rococo style originated in

    (A) France
    (B) Holland
    (C) Italy
    (D) Prussia

The style known as **rococo** emerged in France in the eighteenth century and spread to the rest of Europe. Rococo is another artistic label that was coined as an insult, combining the words *rocaille* (ornamental design made of crushed shells) and barocco (baroque). The rococo style was accused of excessive, tasteless ornamentation. The style grew out of the baroque but rejected baroque heaviness in favor of an elegant, spirited playfulness, fragile beauty, and decoration. The somber baroque reds and greens were replaced by pastels and lots of white by rococo artists. **Antoine Watteau** (1684-1721), a central figure of rococo art, took on as his main theme a genre that came to be known as *fête galante* ("courtship party"), paintings of well-to-do young people in beautiful formal dress flirting and frolicking in idealized pastoral settings. The frivolity and elaborate artifice of French court life in the mid-eighteenth century was best captured by the painter, engraver, and opera and theatrical set designer **Francois Boucher** (1703-1770), who rejected nature as "too green and badly lit." Boucher's most famous pupil was **Jean-Honoré Fragonard** (1732-1806), whose delicate coloring and playful eroticism in paintings like the four canvases of *The Progress of Love* are truly characteristic of the rococo style. The coming of the French Revolution altered the

David's dramatic yet controlled *The Death of Socrates*

public's attitude toward art along with everything else, and Fragonard was among those artists ruined when tastes turned against rococo levity.

The late eighteenth century saw the rise of two movements, both rejections of the rococo, that were almost diametrically opposed to each other, yet often cross-pollinated in particular artists. **Romantic painting**, like romantic literature (p. 258), celebrated the imagination and freedom of the artist, emphasizing the influence of nature on both. **Neoclassicism** sought to convey serious, elevated ideas like Honor and Justice, and reached back toward the simplified styles of ancient Greece and Rome. In France especially, these ideals took hold against a backdrop of the **Enlightenment**, and the desire to restore ancient values of reason, order, and self-sacrifice into civic life that culminated in the Revolution. The heroic grandeur and clarity of form in the work of **Jacques-Louis David** (1748-1825) made him a central neoclassical painter. With his serious, often classical, subject matter and austere mood, David captured a spirit of moral revolt against rococo values in paintings like *The Death of Socrates*. David, who was involved in the Revolution, voting for the execution of Louis XIV, painted a portrait series of "martyrs of the Revolution," which included his famous *The Death of Marat*, a passionate work of political propaganda. David's student, **Jean-Auguste-Dominique Ingres** (1780-1867) eventually eclipsed him as the major figure of neoclassicism, with ideas about perfection and proportion so strong that he often disregarded reality altogether to achieve them. For example, the long, graceful backs of his female nudes, like *Odalisque with a Slave* (plate 7) and *The Bather*, were accused of having extra vertabrae.

In England, elements of neoclassicism and romanticism coexisted in the late eighteenth century. The unique work of **Thomas Gainsborough** (1727-1788), most famous for his elegant portraits, leans toward the romantic. In portraits such as *Mr. and Mrs. Andrews* the sitters are almost eclipsed by a lyrical landscape, while several portraits of his daughters convey an innocent freedom that is also quite emotional. **Sir Joshua Reynolds** (1723-1792), is responsible for the **Grand Manner** of English portraiture, which, he explained in several treatises, aimed for a balance and elevation above the vagaries of nature. Reynolds often copied his poses from classical sculpture, and his ability to capture tiny nuances of expression inspired Gainsborough's famous remark, "Damn him! How various he is!"

American artists of the late eighteenth century took on a neoclassic style in an attempt to lend stature and a feeling of historical importance to their fledgling nation. Yet the lingering American Puritanism could not fathom paintings of, say, George Washington in a toga, and combined with the dearth of established artists as teachers and a congenital Yankee mistrust of creative spirits, the results are peculiarly stiff. However, the greatest American painter of the colonial era, the self-taught **John Singleton Copley** (1738-1815), did rise above the ranks of American portraitists to produce naturalistic, lively portraits. Copley left America for England at the onset of the Revolution, where he had some short-lived success, especially for his action-filled history paintings. One of Copley's Boston students, **Charles Willson Peale** (1741-1827) went on to become the most successful portraitist in America after Copley's departure. Peale fought in the Revolution, and developed his wide-ranging talents as an inventor, naturalist, watchmaker, saddler, and silversmith. Peale had seventeen children whom he named for Renaissance artists, and several of them went on to become artists themselves, including Raphaelle Peale, who specialized in still lifes, Titian Ramsay Peale, a naturalist like his father, and Rembrandt Peale, whose huge painting *The Court of Death* became a national phenomenon, touring the states for over fifty years.

Life of Johnson (1791), by James Boswell. This is an immense biography of the witty, eccentric writer and personality Samuel Johnson, and it is one of the most celebrated literary works of the eighteenth century. It was dedicated to Sir Joshua Reynolds. Reynolds was friends with literary types more than with artists, and his artistic theories were comparable to Johnson's literary theories.

John Singleton Copley, *Paul Revere*

11. **Which Romantic poet was also an important artist?**
    - (A) Eugène Delacroix
    - (B) Joseph Turner
    - (C) John Constable
    - (D) William Blake

The work of **William Blake** (1757-1827), artist, philosopher, and poet, embodies the visionary strain of romanticism. After working as a commercial engraver, Blake developed a new method of printing the illustrations for his *Songs of Innocence and Experience* (p. 259) in color, so that the handwritten text of the poems and the illustration were engraved together, forming an inextricable whole. With their precise, linear, flowing lines, his engravings for *The Book of Job* and Dante's *Divine Comedy* (p. 249) express his conviction in the spiritual reality behind the ordinary world. The Romantic landscape genre was taken to new places by a proud cockney, **Joseph Mallord William Turner** (1775-1851). Turner began with watercolors and took the abstract, airy sense of movement into his later oil works, such as the powerful *Shipwreck*. In his free treatment of space and his objects almost completely dissolved into light, Turner anticipated the **impressionists**, but with a romantic sense of symbolism.

> **"** *The first virtue of a painting is to be a feast for the eyes.*
>
> —— *EUGÉNE DELACROIX* **"**

In France the romantic theme of man against nature was conveyed with vivid realism in the painting *The Raft of the Medusa* by **Théodore Géricault** (1791-1824). The painting depicts the survivors of a notorious shipwreck in 1816, who were left to drift for thirteen days on the Atlantic before they were rescued. All but fifteen of the 150 died, and rumors held that the survivors had resorted to cannibalism. In Géricault's rendition, the all-male surviviors writhe in agony but are still muscular, and a charged energy seems to bind them together on the raft. The painting's cool reception had as much to do with its implicit political criticism—the ship's incompetent captain, who absconded in the only life raft, was a government appointee—as its graphic treatment of gruesome subject matter. Géricault's successor as leader of the romantic movement, **Eugène Delacroix** (1798-1863), conveyed a vital, animated expressiveness even when death was his subject, as in *Death of Sardanapalus*, inspired by the poet Byron (p. 259). Sardanapalus, an ancient Assyrian king, learning that his enemies are about to overtake him, has his wives, slaves, and horses slain, as he watches impassively. After a visit to Morocco Delacroix seized on the exotic subject matter he'd gathered, and produced works such as *The Sultan of Morocco*. Late in life he took up mural painting, and received commissions for murals that still adorn several Parisian public buildings.

The Spanish painter and graphic artist **Francisco de Goya** (1746-1828), defies categorization into any school. Goya's psychological penetration is rivaled perhaps only by Rembrandt, whom he cited as his influence (along with Velázquez). Goya was fascinated by people in all their specificity; portraits such as *Doña Maria Soledad* (plate 8) and *Don Fray Miguel* (plate 9) show enormous attention to expression and posture. He adds a decorative touch to his portraits that is almost baroque and seems to offset a bit the potential cruelty of his penetration into character. This is especially evident in his portraits of the family of King Charles IV of Spain, for whom he was appointed Court Painter. Goya's *The Family of Charles IV* is an unsparing portrait of a haughty, dull-looking royal family, yet the delicate, shimmering intricacy of decoration on their clothing gives the painting the sparkle that their personalities cannot. Goya's political painting *The Third of May, 1808*, depicts a faceless line of French soldiers gunning down Spanish hostages, a dark view of human brutality that transcends the politics of the moment. Goya, who had been left totally deaf after an illness in 1792, had a fascination with the savage and macabre aspects of human existence. He had a fierce artistic freedom, and in his old age he produced fourteen large murals, called the *Black Paintings*, done almost all in browns, grays, and blacks, depicting nightmarish visions with a universality that is strangely modern.

The mid-nineteenth century saw the formation of the **pre-Raphaelite Brotherhood** in England, who traced the downfall of art back to the academic style of Raphael, a figure worshipped in art circles at the time. The pre-Raphaelites wanted to recapture the simple, sincere roots of Italian art. A poet as well as a painter, Dante Gabriel Rossetti, son of an Italian ex-revolutionary and brother of the even better poet Christina Rossetti, was a central figure of the group, along with John Everett Millais and William Holman Hunt. Pre-Raphaelite artists painted serious, often religious subjects, and favored intense, almost acidic colors and clear details.

GUILDING THE LILY

Sometime pre-Raphaelite William Morris (1834-1896) had an influence on design that continued in the twentieth century. Morris founded an English decorating and manufacturing firm in 1861 that harked back to the idea of the medieval guild, in which craftsmen both produced and designed the work. Morris's firm put out products including furniture tapestries, carpets, and wallpaper, and his wallpaper designs are still produced today. A socialist, Morris had a vision of art made available for everyday use, by ordinary people, but his carefully handmade products ended up being affordable only to the well-off.

12. Which of the following artists is considered the leader of the impressionist movement?

(A) Edgar Degas
(B) Auguste Renoir
(C) Claude Monet
(D) Henri Matisse

In the second half of the nineteenth century, France once again was the birthplace of an influential, controversial artistic movement, **impressionism**, which was less a unified school with a clear artistic agenda than a loose association of like-minded artists who showed their work together when they were rejected by the official salons. The style we identify as impressionist was not adopted by all the artists we think of as impressionist at all times in their careers. **Edouard Manet** (1832-1883), for example, began as a realist, and like the realist writers (p. 262) of the nineteenth century, sought to portray modern life in paintings such as *The Balcony* (plate 10) and *The Monet Family* (plate 11), not an idealized mythological world or the romantic's inner world of his own emotions. The elegant, well-to-do painter sought official recognition, and never exhibited with the impressionists. Yet his dark-toned paintings of the 1860s, with their flattened perspective and shocking subject matter, outraged the critics and the public as much as his impressionist colleagues would do a decade later. In Manet's famous *Déjeuner Sur L'Herbe,* he presents a scene of three contemporary people, two men and a woman, enjoying a lovely al fresco lunch. The woman, however, is stark naked, and not in the guise of a nymph or goddess but as a real, contemporary person. The traditional scene—it's even based on a work by Raphael—is startlingly modern and risqué. Two years later, Manet's *Olympia,* a scandalously and directly sexual reclining nude woman based on a Titian painting, was similarly attacked as offensive. **Edgar Degas** (1834-1917) also came from an upper-middle-class background and was also associated with the Impressionists. Influenced by Manet, Degas turned from his interest in classical themes to scenes of contemporary life, focusing especially on the worlds of the ballet, theatre, circus, and horse racing. His scenes of cafe life, like *L'Absinthe,* with its droopy, sad woman surrounded by stark table tops, had a biting realism. When women are his subject, especially his ballet pictures like *Dancers Practicing at the Bar* (plate 12), and his pictures of women at their toilette, Degas conveys a voyeuristic quality—he seems to like to capture his subjects engaged in some private gesture, unaware that they are being watched. Although he worked in many media, pastel was his favorite; he also experimented with modeling in wax, including the sculpture *Little Fourteen-Year-Old Dancer*, dressed in a real tutu.

The term "Impressionist" was first used in 1874 as a derogatory label for the work of **Claude Monet** (1840-1926), the unofficial leader of the movement. Monet sought not finish and polish but a real correspondence with nature, and he eschewed working in studios in favor of setting up his canvas outdoors so as to get the most direct experience of a subject, a "radical" practice soon adopted by others as well. Light is the key ingredient of impressionism as practiced by Monet, and it's in order, paradoxically, to render faithfully the play and movement of light on an object that the impressionist style seems fragmented and abstract. In his series paintings, such as those of *Rouen Cathedral*, Monet painted the same scene at different times of day and in different weather, capturing the changes of color and light in an object we assume is static. The *Water Lilies (plate 13)* series is his style at its peak: small, quick, fluid, choppy strokes that ignore incidental details to capture brilliant patterns of color and light. The impressionist **Berthe Morisot** (1841-1895), was a close associate of Monet who later married his brother. Morisot shared

Ukiyo-E

Many artists associated with impressionism, including Mary Cassatt, Van Gogh, Gauguin, and Lautrec, were influenced by the Japanese technique of ukiyo-e, which means "pictures of the floating world." The decorative flat blocks of color, expressive patterning, unusual perspective, and cropped composition of the prints, which typically took as their subject matter the theatrical world, prostitutes, and bathhouse girls, were a revelation to Europeans. Celebrated artists of ukiyo-e included Ando Hiroshige and Kitagaro Utomaro, who inspired many themes in Cassatt's art. European artists were also inspired by ukiyo-e to begin making color lithographs, a technique of printing that uses a design drawn onto a stone with a greasy crayon and chemically treated so that the drawing is fixed, then transfered (in reverse, like all prints) to paper. In America, lithography reached a mass public in the late nineteenth century by way of the decidedly unprovocative Currier and Ives prints. These were a series produced by the firm of Nathaniel Currier and James M. Ives, advertised as "colored engravings for the people," and sold cheaply. The prints depicted the wholesome range of American life, from railroads and steamboats to sporting events to patriotic subjects. Though they were common and not valuable in their day, many of them are now collectors items.

Monet's interest in delivering the nuances of light and movement, and used the impressionist feathery brushstrokes and light palette to great effect, especially in her domestic and seaside scenes. Monet's closest ally, **Auguste Renoir** (1841-1919) turned toward depicting people rather than focusing on nature. Renoir communicates a delight in the spectacle of humanity, especially the female half of it, in lively, upbeat works like *The Luncheon of the Boating Party*. The scene seems like a glancing impression, yet Renoir paints all the specificities—the remains of the lunch spread on the table, the flirtatious conversations, the woman nuzzling her dog. His flickering, light touches of paint make his technique seem close to

Monet's, but by the 1880s Renoir gravitated toward more classical, defined form in paintings like *Les Parapluies*.

Mary Cassatt's *The Boating Party*

Camille Pissarro (1830-1903), born in the West Indies of a Creole mother and a Jewish father, was the only artist who exhibited at all eight impressionist shows, and with his generous personality and gift for teaching became something of a father figure to the rest. He painted mostly landscapes, and devoted his life to studying the effects of light in nature. **Alfred Sisley** (1839-1899), born in Paris of English parents, was, with Monet, the most consistently impressionist of all the Impressionists. But more than Monet, he conveyed the underlying structure of landscape, not reducing it to vaporous effects. The American **Mary Cassatt**, who spent most of her life in Paris, painted scenes of refined society and of mothers and children. Her style, solid yet delicate, was much admired by her friend and mentor Degas. Paintings like *Girl Sewing* show Cassatt's light brushwork that nonetheless conveys a grounded sense of physicality and power. The wealthy Cassatt persuaded upper-class Americans to buy impressionist works, introducing European innovation into the usually moribund taste of the nineteenth-century American upper class.

Camille Claudel (1988), starring Isabelle Adjani and Gerard Depardieu. This is the story of the sculptor whose personal and professional relationship with Rodin led to her demise.

The French sculptor **Auguste Rodin** (1840-1917), considered the greatest sculptor since Bernini, was in some ways the sculptural equivalent of an Impressionist—like impressionist painting, his sculpture was dismissed as "unfinished." That unfinished quality was precisely Rodin's aim, because it called attention to his process of production. Commissioned to make a bronze door for a proposed museum, Rodin produced his greatest work but never finished the entire project, and instead many of the individual

Ponderous ponderer: Rodin's *The Thinker*

sculptures have gone on display independently. The most famous of this group is *The Thinker*, a massive seated man lost in serious thought, intended to be placed over the Gates of Hell. *The Thinker* conveys Rodin's characteristic intensity and power. Rodin considered his bulky, forceful *Monument to Balzac* (p. 262), which was rejected by the literary society that commissioned it, his greatest work. One of Rodin's assistants, Camille Claudel, went on to a daring but stormy career of her own, though she was wracked by personal and professional controversies with Rodin.

13. The prominent nineteenth-century American movement in landscape painting was called

   (A) The Mississippi school
   (B) The Frontier school
   (C) The Hudson River school
   (D) The New England school

American painters turned to their native land with a new vigor in the mid-nineteenth century, as American intellectual independence from Europe, and nationalist sentiment, were taking shape. **The Hudson River school** produced landscapes that captured the remote, wild, natural beauty of the New World. **Thomas Cole** (1801-1848) set the movement in motion with his passionate attitude toward the Catskill Mountains on New York's Hudson River. In his later paintings Cole increasingly turned away from natural depictions to allegorical historical themes expressing the ideology of the burgeoning nation. His four-panel series *The Course of Empire,* for example, presents a triumphant, devastating view of the "inevitable" progress of white civilization and demise of Native Americans. In the West, the **Rocky Mountain school**, led by **Albert Bierstadt** (1830-1902), brought the spirit of the Hudson River school to the awesome scenery of the Rocky Mountains.

Flamboyant American painter **James Abbott McNeil Whistler** (1834-1903) travelled widely, including four years in Paris, but eventually settled in London and only flirted with impressionist style. His paintings are more subdued and subjective than those of the

FROM *THE GENTLE ART OF MAKING ENEMIES*

Art should be independent of all claptrap—should stand alone, and appeal to the artistic sense of eye or ear, without confounding this with emotions entirely foreign to it, as devotion, pity, love, patriotism, and the like. All these have no kind of concern with it, and that is why I insist on calling my works "arrangements" and "harmonies."

——James Abbott McNeill Whistler

Impressionists, more concerned with capturing a mood than with capturing light. Whistler's most famous image, *Arrangement in Grey and Black: The Artist's Mother* (plate 14), conveys the mixture of strong balance and subtle expressiveness for which he was renowned. An American artist who contrasts strongly to Whistler is **Winslow Homer** (1836-1910), who aims for a more solid, realist style. Winslow was praised for his vivid, original pictures of the rugged Maine coast and other scenes such as *Boys in Pasture* (plate 15). Considered by many to be the greatest Ameican painter of the nineteenth century, **Thomas Eakins** (1844-1916) trained in Europe but spent most of his life in his native Philadelphia. Eakins' Realism got him into trouble with that tenacious strain of American priggishness when he insisted on scientifically studying the body, including working with nude models, and he was forced to resign from the Pennsylvania Academy for Fine Arts after he had his coed class draw from (gasp!) a nude male model. Later, his painting *The Gross Clinic* was attacked for its realistic depiction of surgery, and it was only near the end of his life that Eakins's unsparing depiction of American life was recognized for its brave ingenuity. Among the American upper class, a portrait of yourself or your loved one by the English-based American **John Singer Sargent** (1856-1925) was the thing to have. Sargent's commissioned portraits captured the opulence of the staid society immortalized in the fiction of Edith Wharton (p. 288), but his heart lay in landscape watercolors, and he also showed a surprising depth of passion in his late tragic painting *Gassed*, inspired by World War I.

14. **Which post-impressionist artist is famous for his South Seas paintings?**

    (A) Paul Gauguin
    (B) Paul Cézanne
    (C) Georges Seurat
    (D) Camille Pissarro

Impressionism was the starting point for a varied group of artists later known as post-impressionists, most of whom, such as **Paul Gauguin** (1848-1903), started out associated with impressionism. Gauguin soon moved toward the pure, flat, symbolic use of color and the primitive shapes that mark his greatest work. After fleeing France and his family in 1891 for the South Seas, Gauguin produced his most daring work, rendering the Polynesian women as goddesses and expressing the total freedom he felt there in paintings like the allegory of life *Where Do We Come From? What Are We? Where Are We Going?* Gauguin was a major figure of the **symbolist** movement, originally a movement in French poetry, which saw the imagination as primary, and saw symbolic images as inte-

FROM "NOTES SYNTHETIQUES"

Painting is the most beautiful of all arts. In it, all sensations are condensed; contemplating it, every-one can create a story at the will of his imagination and—with a single glance—have his soul invaded by the most profound recollections . . . everything is summed up in one instant.

——*Paul Gauguin*

grally connected to the material world. Gauguin's painting *Nevermore*, borrowing symbols and its title from the poem "The Raven" by Edgar Allan Poe (p. 264), is a characteristic symbolist work, with its sensuous but remote nude Polynesian woman reclining, lost in thought, while a raven, the "bird of death," perches on a windowsill. From a different culture but influenced by Gauguin's simplified forms and use of artifical-seeming colors, the Norwegian artist **Edvard Munch** (1863-1944) traveled throughout Europe. His sense of the disillusionment and alienation in modern life is captured best by *The Scream*, with its distorted, anguished, wailing figure set in a whirling, dizzying pattern. Himself suffering from mental instability, Munch turned artists' attention to the tortured psychology of the modern individual, and was quoted as saying that while da Vinci dissected corpses to study human anatomy, "I dissect souls." Another symbol-

Oh no! Did I leave the oven on?

ist-influenced artist who broke with the establishment of his country was the Austrian **Gustav Klimt** (1862-1918). In the 1890s, Klimt was a leader of the *sezession* (secession) movement in Germany and Austria, in which groups of artists broke away from the hidebound art academies to present their own avant-garde exhibitions. Klimt's style is elegant, highly decorated, and ornamental, and he often treats mythological or archetypal

The art nouveau style of decorative art, developed by poster artists along with architects, jewelers, and potters, rose to prominence in Europe and America from the 1890s to World War I. Art nouveau used naturalistic, organic forms and fluid, sinuous line.

Vincent and Theo (1990), directed by Robert Altman. This emotionally charged movie looks at the close relationship between Vincent and his brother Theo. Altman's direction takes the movie beyond the typical "tortured-artist" biography.

subjects. He was a great lover of women and womanhood in general, conveying his sense of feminine mystery, beauty, and power. Typically, Klimt paints faces realistically and then goes to town on the clothing and background, using intricate, ornate, sumptuous patterns influenced by **art nouveau**.

Georges Seurat (1859-1891), who believed art should be theoretical and scientific, was the central figure of the school of **neo-impressionism**. Seurat developed a technique called **pointillism**, which used small, evenly sized dots of color set next to each other so that they blend together in the viewer's eye, rather than on the canvas. Dutch-born **Vincent van Gogh** (1853-1890), he of the severed ear and stormy life, is also considered a post-impressionist. Van Gogh lived most of his life in isolated poverty, often undernourished and battling mental disturbances, selling only one painting in his lifetime. His artistic ideals were high, explained at great length in letters to his devoted brother Theo. He came to reject the Impressionists' fidelity to realistic appearances, like Gauguin using color for symbolic effects. Van Gogh experimented with the delicate brush strokes of Seurat's pointillist technique, but he gravitated to the broad, sweeping, rugged strokes that characterize paintings like *Starry Night*. This painting was done during the last years of his life when he lived in an asylum near Arles, painting at a ferocious rate. Other well-loved works come from this period as well, such as *Sunflowers* (plate 16) and *The Artist's Bedroom*, which poignantly depicts his spartan bedroom, with two chairs set out in anticipation of the visit from Gauguin that ended badly in a fierce argument and van Gogh's slicing of his own ear. Van Gogh was an admirer of the simplicity of Japanese art, as was **Henri de Toulouse-Lautrec** (1864-1901), who revolutionized the art of the **poster**. The scion of a wealthy family, Lautrec, who became deformed after two childhood accidents and stood less than five feet tall, escaped into the seedier side of Parisian nightlife, which became his main subject—especially the **Moulin-Rouge**.

Considered the source of much modern painting, the French post-impressionist **Paul Cézanne** (1839-1906) left a legacy for several twentieth-century movements. It was Cézanne's intention to make of impressionism "something solid and enduring, like the art of the museums." Breaking from the impressionist focus on fleeting light and movement, Cézanne became interested in the underlying structure of objects—you can rarely tell what season or time of day it is in a Cézanne. His *Still Life on a Bureau* (plate 17), for example, conveys a solidity and mass through gradations in color and precise angles. Cézanne liked to identify discrete shapes in a scene, urging artists to "See in nature the cylinder, the sphere, the cone." His landscapes, such as *Mount St-Victoire,* use intense colors and find an underlying geometric structure in the natural world. Cézanne's greatest breakthrough, which led to the development of **cubism**, was the idea that the artist's varying viewpoints on an object can be incorporated into the painting itself; in other words, Cézanne rejected the idea that the artist must have a fixed point of view, since in real life you can see an object from several different points of view by changing your position. In his later paintings he often breaks up the predictable line of an object.

15. **Early in his career, Matisse was associated with the style of painting called**
    (A) fauvism
    (B) realism
    (C) cubism
    (D) colorism

One of the first avant-garde movements of the turn of the century was known as **fauvism**, and the dominant figure was **Henri Matisse** (1869-1954), who is often said to be one of the two greatest twentieth-century artists (the other being Picasso). The fauves used intense, brash color and wild patterns and shapes. The name fauvism was coined as a witticism by an art critic, who declared upon walking into a gallery filled with new paintings and one classical-style sculpture, "Donatello au milieu des fauves!" ("Donatello among the wild beasts!"). Fauvism was actually a short-lived movement—its steam was generated mainly by Matisse, who soon moved through it to a more controlled, serene style that marked his long career.

After fauvism, Matisse continued to use strong color, and he was attracted

---

FRIENDS AND NEIGHBORS

Matisse and Picasso were friendly rivals, from their first meeting in 1906 until Matisse's death nearly fifty years later. As did many young artists, they met in Paris at the home of the American brother and sister, Leo and Gertrude Stein (p. 272), *collectors of modern art. Leo Stein described Picasso: "His short, solid but somehow graceful figure, his firm head with the hair falling forward, careless but not slovenly, emphasized his extraordinary seeing eyes." Stein described Matisse as "bearded, but with propriety; spectacled neatly; intelligent; freely spoken, but a little shy." He compared the two men: "Matisse was a social person rather than a convivial one. Picasso was more convivial than social. Matisse felt himself to be one of many, and Picasso stood apart, alone." Matisse was the king of the fauves; Picasso, eleven years his junior, would soon take the spotlight as a founder of cubism. Despite their rivalry, they respected each other as peers. Matisse brought African sculpture to Picasso's attention and introduced him to wealthy collectors. Years later, as old men, they were neighbors in the south of France.*

to calligraphic patterning and sensual, simplified forms. He spent many years in Nice, where his paintings developed a languid, luxurious style that reflects the warm clarity of light on the Riviera. Matisse's use of contrasting patterns stands out, as in the many **odalisques** (paintings of female slaves or concubines), such as *Odalisque With Raised Arms,* in which the contrasting, richly colored patterns of the chair, window, rug, a screen—even her sheer skirt is patterned at the bottom—play against the woman's creamy skin, dark hair, and rosy nipples. Matisse's interest in rhythm and color came through clearly in the famous *The Dance* (plate 18). Late in his life, Matisse was confined to bed and a wheelchair after two operations for duodenal cancer, and in this period he produced some of his most imaginative, striking work in the **cut-outs**, collages of brightly colored cut paper arranged into striking, vibrant, abstract creations. Matisse saw his art as separate from politics and history and once wrote that he wanted his art to be "like a good armchair in which one rests from physical fatigue." His art was meant to express *The Joy of Life,* as one of his early paintings is called. The always productive Matisse also sculpted, made prints, designed a church in Venice, and illustrated books.

16. **Which of the following statements best describes the aim of cubism?**

(A) To represent different points of view of a single object
(B) To represent the geometrical incorporation of several objects into one
(C) To represent the movement of an object in space
(D) To represent the movement of an object over time

I am only a public entertainer who has understood his time.

——*Pablo Picasso*

Cubism, one of the major turning points of Western art, was developed in the first decade of the twentieth century by the Spaniard **Pablo Picasso** (1881-1973) and the Frenchman **Georges Braque** (1882-1963), working closely together. The third great cubist was the Spaniard **Juan Gris** (1887-1927), who was perhaps the most absolute of the three in his dedication to the style. Building on Cézanne's experiments with breaking up the field of the picture and influenced also by African masks and sculpture, Picasso and Braque produced works that abandoned traditional perspective such as Braque's *Femme à la Mandoline* (plate 19). Their aim was to present an object not as it appears at a particular moment, but in a way that incorporates different points of view of the object simultaneously: an object was broken down into geometrical planes, then reconstructed, presenting the different points of view. This early phase of cubism is known as **analytical cubism**. In a way, analytical cubism was realistic rather than abstract, since it depicted real objects, but realistic in a conceptual way, interested in the *idea* of the thing more than the thing itself.

The painting that galvanized cubism was Picasso's controversial, rebellious *Les Demoiselles d'Avignon* (plate 20), a depiction of five prostitutes, two of them with faces derived from African masks. With its flattened, shattered forms, the discordant mix of angularity and curves in the bodies of the women, and the strange mix of flesh tones, pinks, and icy steel blues, the painting seemed ugly and brutal even to some of the artist's friends who saw it in his studio in 1907. As Braque did in *The Portuguese*, Picasso stenciled letters to his cubist arrangements, which gave the viewer a clue as to what was being represented and reinforced the flatness of the painting's surface, as in *Ma Jolie (Woman with Guitar)*, where the words "Ma Jolie" refer to the words of a popular song. Braque and Picasso's cubist style gradually became less fragmented and ambiguous. They reintroduced color into their compositions, sometimes mixed sand with their paint, and employed the technique of **collage**, in which scraps of material are glued to the canvas. These changes mark the beginning of the second phase of cubism, known as **synthetic cubism**.

 An often-repeated story, retold by Roland Penrose in his biography of Picasso: During the German Occupation of Paris, a Nazi officer paid a visit to Picasso's studio. Seeing a photograph of *Guernica* lying on the table, the German asked, "Did you do this?" Picasso replied, "No, you did."

Picasso's *Guernica*

Picasso was the most versatile and prolific figure in twentieth-century art. The melancholy Blue Period and the less somber Rose Period, his ventures in Symbolism, had preceded his cubist phase. In the 1920s he alternated between cubism and a classical style, the latter producing the harmonious *Mother and Child*. In the late 1920s, influenced by surrealism, he worked in a looser, more expressive style. In 1937, enraged by the terror-bombing of the town of Guernica during the Spanish Civil War, Picasso produced a mural-sized painting combining cubist and surrealist elements and using only shades of black, white, and gray. *Guernica* has become a symbol of the brutality of modern warfare. The many women in his life provided inspiration for Picasso's changing styles. The young, voluptuous, and passive Marie-Thérèse, for example, inspired some of his most beautiful, pacific work, such as *Nude Woman in a Red Armchair*, in the roundedness of her body conveying an innocent yet maternal quality, while the brilliant and neurotic Dora Maar inspired expressive, anguished pictures such as *Weeping Woman*. Picasso also produced significant work as a sculptor and graphic designer, conveying in these media as well the many sides of his powerful personality and his unbounded vitality.

17. Which of the following things would a futurist consider beautiful?
    (A) A Michelangelo sculpture
    (B) A speeding car
    (C) Rolling green hills
    (D) An ocean storm

 Two twentieth-century artists who never joined any movement were the friends **Amedeo Modigliani** (1884-1920) and **Marc Chagall** (1887-1985). Both Jewish emigrés to Paris in the 1900s (Chagall from Russia, Modigliani from Italy), they have easily identified styles. Modigliani painted voluptuous, elongated figures that have a languid sensuality, a combination of the classical and the primitive. Chagall, who went on to a long career after Modigliani's early death, painted images of buoyant fantasy, with cubist-influenced spatial dislocations and vivid, fauve color.

The **futurist** movement began in 1909, with the publication by the Italian poet **Filippo Marinetti** (1876-1944) of the first **Futurist Manifesto**, which declared a radical break with all the dusty, convential things of the past, and embraced the heady danger of the modern technological world. "We intend to sing the love of danger, the habit of energy and fearlessness," read the Manifesto. "We affirm that the world's magnificence has been enriched by a new beauty: the beauty of speed." A roaring racing car, it went on, is more beautiful than the *Winged Victory of Samothrace*. Marinetti's manifesto was soon followed by two Manifestoes of Futurist Painting, written by a group of artists including Umberto Boccioni and Gino Severini, which declared, "All subjects previously used must be swept aside in order to express our whirling life of steel, of pride, of fever, and of speed." Futurists eventually adopted cubist techniques in order to express movement in space. Boccioni's sculpture *Unique Forms of*

Continuity in Space, a futurist reinterpretation of the *Winged Victory of Samothrace*, conveys the dynamic motion of modern machinery.

18. **Expressionists saw art as expressing the artist's**

    (A) emotion and inner world
    (B) engagement with the outer world
    (C) intellect and reason
    (D) direct response to nature

The term "expressionism" is used broadly to refer to art that expresses the artist's emotion and inner life, rather than directly representing the natural world. However, **expressionism** also refers to a movement that began in Germany at the beginning of the twentieth century. Building on the intense emotional distortions of nature by van Gogh, Gauguin, and Munch, expressionists were preoccupied with the dark, sinister elements of human psychology. Like futurists, they revolted against established art and celebrated the idea of violence and rupture. From the first group of expressionists, called **Die Brücke** (The Bridge), who wanted to be a bridge to the future, **Ernst Ludwig Kirchner** painted images of the modern city done in harsh colors and tortured forms. **Max Beckmann** (1884-1950) fought in World War I and brought his horrendous war experiences to his art. His paintings, including many self-portraits, are full of disturbing, distorted images and acidic colors. Graphic artist and sculptor **Käthe Kollwitz** (1867-1945) brought strong moral convictions to her expressionist art, protesting the working conditions of peasants in her series of etchings *Peasants' War*; like Beckmann, she was expelled by the Nazis.

Austrian expressionists included **Oscar Kokoschka** (1886-1980) and the short-lived but fascinating **Egon Schiele** (1890-1918). Kokoschka rejected all harmony in his paintings, conveying instead a visionary intensity that he brought to landscapes as well as portraits. Schiele expresses his vision through nervous, distorted, but strangely beautiful portraits. His figures are twisted, wild, and intense, yet vulnerable, conveying a raw, innocent sexuality.

Expressionism moved emphatically toward the abstract with the group that called itself **Der Blaue Reiter** (the Blue Rider), after a painting by their leader, **Wassily Kandinsky** (1866-1944). The group wanted to bring spiritual values into their work, though their agenda was never dogmatic or precise. The Russian Kandinsky gave up a law professorship to move to Germany, where his painting became increasingly

DEGENERATE ART

The Nazis promoted government-controlled, traditionally styled art with a strong ideological message. They attacked modern art as subversive, ugly, and "degenerate," and in 1933 began to organize exhibitions ridiculing it. In Munich in 1937 they presented a "degenerate" exhibition that displayed works by prominent artists alongside works by the mentally ill. Among the artists shown were Picasso, Mondrian, Beckmann, Kirchner, Chagall, and Kandinsky.

non-representational. A pioneer of **abstract art**, Kandinsky broke new ground in his series of *Compositions and Improvisations*, painted between 1910 and 1913. In these works, Kandinsky conveys a rapturous wildness, using bright colors and free brush strokes. Later in his career Kandinsky moved toward restraint and geometricization, creating art that claimed no direct connection to the natural world but existed as pure abstraction, the reflection of the artist's "inner and essential" feelings. The mystical Kandinsky also wrote prodigiously about his artistic and philosophical theories, and has been a major influence on twentieth-century artists. Another member of the Blue Rider group, Swiss-born **Paul Klee** (1879-1940), was one of the most inventive and influential twentieth-century painters. He worked on a small scale, moving freely between abstraction and representation and conveying poetic beauty through symbolic arrangement and luminous color. *The Golden Fish* captures his early, light-hearted style. Late in his life, as he was wasting away from a rare disease, he created somber, bitter images like *Death and Fire*.

> 66
>
> *The joy of life is the irresistible constant victory of the new value.*
>
> ——WASSILLY KANDISKY
>
> 99

Another important abstractionist was the Dutch painter **Piet Mondrian** (1872-1944). Mondrian developed a style he called **neoplasticism** and teamed up with the architects to form the De Stijl movement (p. 56). He is most famous for geometric works such as *Composition with Red, Blue, and Yellow,* with its boxes of primary colors and white outlined with bands of black. The result is a look of a non-symmetrical balance that seems easy to produce, but it actually required painstaking effort.

A self portrait in woodcut by Paul Klee

19. The dada movement was named for

(A) a childish word for "father"
(B) its founder, Josef Dada
(C) the German word for "freedom"
(D) a childish term for "hobbyhorse"

The disillusionment of World War I made itself felt in art most strongly through the **dada** movement, which attacked reason and order, and aimed to jolt the complacent public. The movement's choice of name illustrates its anti-rational stance: according to one account, a pen-knife was inserted at random into a dictionary and landed on the French word "dada," which means "hobbyhorse." Dada didn't have a specific style or aesthetic principle, but rather was conceived as **anti-art**, emphasizing the randomness of artistic creation and mocking the traditions of Western art and society as a whole. **Marcel Duchamp** (1887-1968) introduced the concept of the **ready-made,** in which a manufactured object is chosen and displayed as art. This is not the same thing as a **found object**, an ordinary (usually discarded) object displayed for its inherently interesting or pleasing qualities. Duchamp claimed that any object was art if an artist selected it and declared it to be so; among his selections are a bottle rack and a urinal (entitled *Fountain*).

Surrealism combined dada irrationality with a Freudian (p. 230) influence—the sense of the richness of the unconscious, with its fantastic images and desires unrestrained by reason. Surrealists claimed influence from the purely creative, untutored art of children and the insane, and mined meanings from absurd images. In his long and varied career, the Spanish artist **Joan Miro** (1893-1983) integrated surrealist principles with his own personal mythology. His paintings tapped the unconscious in fluid, curvy, amoeba-like shapes and symbolic figures. The Belgian **René Magritte** (1898-1967) represents the more purposefully bizarre face of surrealism, juxtaposing strange images in startling ways, but often with a humorous touch, like the diginified men in bowler hats raining down from the sky in *The Fall*.

Man Ray (1890-1977), a painter, photographer, object-maker, and filmmaker, was central to dadaism; he later painted in a surrealist style, but gained his greatest fame as a photographer. Man Ray developed several innovative photographic techniques, such as **solarization**, the partial reversal of the tones of a photographic image.

Man Ray surrounded by his creations

CULTURESCOPE

 Un Chien Andalou (1928), by Dali and Luis Buñuel. As Buñuel said, "We relentlessly threw out everything that might have meaning." Yet the editing in this avant-garde and surreal film startles the viewer into making unexpected emotional and intellectual connections.

The Spanish painter, sculptor, and graphic artist **Salvador Dali** (1904-1989) is the most notorious surrealist, and his painting *The Persistence of Memory* (plate 21), with its stark landscape of melting watches, captures brilliantly the essential strangeness of the modern world. Dali called his method "critical paranoia," in which the artist cultivates a sort of paranoid delusion while keeping an awareness of reason and "reality" alive, though latent, in the back of his mind.

20. **The Mexican artist known for murals with Marxist revolutionary themes is**
    (A) Diego Rivera
    (B) Frida Kahlo
    (C) Fernando Botero
    (D) Rufino Tamayo

ART AND POLITICS

"One can analyze epoch after epoch—from the stone age to our present day—and see that there is no form of art which does not play an essential political role . . . What is it then that we really need? An art extremely pure, precise, profoundly human, and clarified as to its purpose."

——*Diego Rivera*

"

Art is Power.

——HENRY WADSWORTH LONGFELLOW

"

The Mexican artist **Diego Rivera** (1886-1957) spent time in Europe and was influenced by cubism and expressionism, and also by the severe, simplified style of native Indian art. Driven by the ideals of social and economic justice that inspired the Mexican Revolution, Rivera created huge didactic murals aimed to inspire a still mostly illiterate public. His themes were frankly Marxist, as in *The Struggle of the Classes* (plate 22), with its depiction of a fat, decadent bourgeois class and noble, rebelling peasants. His murals, often packed with people and with a sort of undulating motion, combine traditional and modern subjects in striking ways such as in *The Grand Tenochtitlan* (plate 23). **Rufino Tamayo** (1899-1991) painted many murals but eventually moved away from Rivera's direct didacticism toward a unique blend of European and indigenous folk-art influences in vigorous still-lifes, paintings of animals, and portraits. Rivera's second wife, **Frida Kahlo** (1907-1954) also a painter, has developed something of a cult following recently for her symbolic, searing self-portraits. Characteristically, Kahlo lays bare her most intimate emotions and desires, while looking out at the viewer with a controlled expression. She depicts herself as a man, with her severed hair strewn all over the canvas, in one self-portrait, *Self-Portrait with Cropped Hair*, while in another, *The Two Fridas* (plate 24), has two identical "Fridas" joined by a vein running between their visible hearts; one Frida is dressed in European style, the other in native Mexican dress, representing her dual Mexican and German heritage. Kahlo's compelling paintings lay bare the impulse of art as self-disclosure that underlies much twentieth-century art. Another Latin American painter of note is the Colombian **Fernando Botero** (1932-), whose sardonic parodies of the Old Masters and distinctive figures that look like blow-up dolls have earned him an international reputation.

21. **The ashcan school artists are known for**
    (A) abstract compositions of found objects
    (B) symbolic mythologies derived from ordinary objects
    (C) still lifes
    (D) scenes of everyday life

A group of artists later known as the **ashcan school** emerged in America in the first decade of the twentieth century under the guidance of **Robert Henri** (1865-1929). Rebelling against the staid National Academy of Design, these artists painted modern urban life, including the lives of the poor and outsiders. In the 1920s, the movement known as **American scene** painting also focused on the everyday reality of American life. The most significant artist to emerge from the movement was **Edward Hopper** (1882-1967), who denied any interest in social issues, saying "I don't think I ever tried to paint the American scene; I'm trying to paint myself." Yet Hopper's images of desolate streets, such as *Early Sunday Morning*, or the isolated woman in *Eleven A.M.* (plate 25) convey a sense of the lonely disconnectedness of modern American life.

Shaped by the social realist movements and the exhilarating communal intellectualism of the Harlem Renaissance (p. 276), the African American artist **Jacob Lawrence** (1917-) documented African American life in flat, colorful, stylized images. His works range from early scenes of social life like *Pool Parlor* to the *Migration of the Negro* series, sixty panels that tell the story of black migration to the North in the twentieth century, with Lawrence's characteristic sharp line and bold color. Another American painter who became central to the twentieth century was **Georgia O'Keeffe** (1887-1986). Her singular style begins with a realistic image and turns it highly abstract. O'Keeffe's intensely close-up paintings of flowers, such as *Black Iris III* (plate 26), which use rich, dense colors and sexual imagery, were followed by a focus on the desolate beauty of the New Mexico desert landscape.

Georgia O'Keeffe

22. The founder of *Camera Work* magazine was

(A) Alfred Stieglitz
(B) Robert Mapplethorpe
(C) Ansel Adams
(D) Henri Cartier-Bresson

In 1907, Alfred Stieglitz was sailing on an ocean liner to Europe when he wandered into the steerage section, where the poorest passengers were quartered. He was attracted to its natural atmosphere—so unlike his stuffy first-class section—and he photographed it. He was not making a political statement. Of *The Steerage* he later recalled: "I saw shapes related to each other. I saw a picture of shapes and underlying that the feeling I had about life."

The artist who did the most to establish photography as an independent art form was **Alfred Stieglitz** (1864-1946), who approached photographic art not as a method of documenting reality but as akin to painting in its expression of the artist's philosophy. Stieglitz was also a hugely influential art dealer who brought the European avant-garde to America and also championed American artists like Georgia O'Keeffe, whom he later married. From 1903 to 1917, Stieglitz edited *Camera Work* magazine, the major forum for photographic innovation, and experimented with various forms of photographic abstraction. **Margaret Bourke-White** (1904-1971) made an impact in this "straight photography" vein with pictures that suggested multiple levels of meaning, such as her famous Life magazine cover photograph of the Fort Peck Dam in Montana.

In France, however, **Henri Cartier-Bresson** (1908-) was perfectly happy with the label of photojournalist, though his pictures have seemed more

Margaret Bourke-White in 1931

Wall Street: Trinity Church Yard, by Margaret Bourke-White

aesthetic than journalistic. Cartier-Bresson emphasizes "the decisive moment," seeking to capture and organize an event at its peak moment of action and expression. During the 1930s, American photographers worked in the more photojournalistic mode yet produced deeply affecting, aesthetically solid pictures—many of them, for example Dorothea Lange, worked as Farm Security Administration photographers, responding daily to the terrible social problems of the Depression (p. 87) in their work. The continuum between photography as documentation and photography as pure "art"continues to enliven photography today in the daring, controversial work of Robert Mapplethorpe, Cindy Sherman, and others.

23. **A founder of the school of abstract expressionism is**

    (A) Jasper Johns
    (B) Jackson Pollock
    (C) Louise Nevelson
    (D) Frank Stella

With **abstract expressionism**, the American art movement that emerged after the Second World War, New York replaced Paris as the capital of the art world. **Jackson Pollock** (1912-1956), a leading figure in the movement, adopted the surrealist notion of **automatism**—art produced automatically, without conscious control of the hand. After working as a muralist for the Federal Arts Project during the Depression, Pollock moved to the completely abstract "drip-and-splash" style, known as **action painting**, in well-known works such as *One (#31)* (plate 27). Pollock laid his huge canvases out on the floor, moving above them in an almost trance-like state. "On the floor I am more at ease, " Pollock said. "I feel nearer, more a part of the painting." The works that emerge graphically record the process of their own creation. The second leading abstract expressionist painter is **Willem de Kooning** (1904-), who often uses figurative elements in his works. Even some supporters of abstract art were initially shocked by the impulsive freedom of de Kooning's furious, visceral brush strokes. **David Smith** (1906-1965) was the most prominent sculptor of the abstract expressionist generation. Smith used industrial materials and techniques to make sculpture that was constructed, rather than carved

Willem de Kooning

or modeled. In works such as Hudson River Landscape, Smith used welded steel with the freedom previously employed by painters, in a method he called "drawing in space."

Mark Rothko (1903-1970) represents another tendency within abstract expressionism. His **color field paintings** use big rectangular or square expanses of color stacked on top of each other to express aesthetic or emotional experiences. Rothko was sensitive to the charge that his seemingly simple works were just exercises in color relationships. The sense of doom, for example, conveyed by darker rectangles pressing down on lighter ones, or the serenity and ecstasy conveyed by hovering, nuanced shades of gray and white, are examples of the emotional weight his works have. The second-generation abstract expressionist **Helen Frankenthaler** (1928-) developed a less somber, less intellectualized style using a stain technique in which thin washes of color are worked into an untreated canvas, so that color doesn't "sit on" the canvas but actually becomes part of it.

The heyday of abstract expressionism was the 1950s, while the 1960s saw a reaction away from the emotionalism of abstract expressionism toward a pure, pared-down ideal that was, in the words of painter **Ad Reinhardt** (1913-1967), "Non-objective, non-representational, non-figurative, non-imagist, non-expressionist, non-subjective." **Frank Stella** (1936-) produced controversial works that included strips of unpainted canvas arranged in geometric patterns, and he used strangely shaped canvases. Stella sought to emphasize the painting as a real object, eliminating any attempt at illusion. In sculpture similar impulses led artists to the technique of **assemblage**, as in the work of **Louise Nevelson** (1899-1988), who assembled cut and scrap pieces of wood and other materials into abstract, mysterious forms, usually painted black all over at the end of the process.

Other painters reacted to abstract expressionism by returning to the representation of objects. In this vein **Jasper Johns** (1930-) produced his famous *Three Flags* (plate 28), one of several works that play on the American

Louise Nevelson, *Transparent Sculpture VI*

flag. **Robert Rauschenberg** (1925-) incorporated three-dimensional objects like tires or radios into paintings in what he called **combine paintings**. Both of these artists aim to force you to question the difference between art and reality, paving the way for the ascendence of **conceptual art** in the 1960s. In conceptual art the idea behind the work is what matters, and the work as a physical object comes after the fact. Often conceptual artists create works that are bland and neutral in appearance, to focus attention on the idea alone. An example is Joseph Kosuth's *One and Three Chairs,* in which a chair, a full-scale photograph of a chair, and a blown-up dictionary definition of "chair" are set side by side.

24. Andy Warhol's *Marilyn Diptych* is an example of
 (A) pop art
 (B) realist art
 (C) rolk art
 (D) linear art

Yet another reaction to abstract expressionism emerged in the 1960s: **pop art**, which celebrated rather than deplored the consumerism and materialism of post-war culture and sought to explode the difference between "high art" and the "low art" of comic books or magazines. **Andy Warhol** (1928-1987), about whom opinions range from "a genius" to "the perpetrator of the greatest scam in Western art," was interested in all that was not only familiar but banal, repetitive, and "machine-like" in modern life. He called his workshop **The Factory** and employed the **silk-screen** process, traditionally used for printing commercial images, in his painting. Warhol first came to public attention with paintings like *Campbells Soup* (plate 29) and others of objects like Coke bottles, monuments to a commercialized mass culture. His *Marilyn Diptych*—repeated, slightly varying images of Marilyn Monroe—exemplifies his fascination with the twentieth-century cult of celebrity. Pop artist **Roy Lichtenstein** (1923-) blew up comic-book images to enormous sizes, creating heavy blocks of color with the dot patterns used in the process. Lichtenstein expressed an archetypal force in works such as *Wham!,* with its pure, streamlined power. British artist **David Hockney** (1937-), now living in California, also began his career with whimsical pop art works. The movement known as op art, short for optical art, also emerged in the 1960s. Op artists like Bridget Riley aimed to create the illusion of movement by playing with the known responses of the eye, ultimately raising questions about how and what we see.

The Velvet Underground and Nico (1967) by the Velvet Underground, produced by Andy Warhol. The "house band" at Andy Warhol's Factory, the Velvet Underground, led by Lou Reed and John Cale, went on to become underground legends.

Representational art has continued to flourish despite the popularity of abstract art. The British painters **Francis Bacon** (1909-1992) and **Lucian Freud** (1922-), for example, are both strikingly modern, yet neither is abstract. Bacon produced violent, jarring images of human despair, often smudged and blurred on the canvas as if to record the act of painting itself as a struggle. Freud, a grandson of Sigmund Freud, paints frighteningly realistic nudes, almost grotesque, paradoxically, in their adherence to the physical reality of the human body. His typical subjects are lumpy, fleshy, blotchy, and caught in awkward, unflattering positions, yet his paintings seem luminous and soft.

FROM A *SUNDAY TIMES MAGAZINE* INTERVIEW

....

One thing which has never really been worked out is how photography has completely altered figurative painting. I think Velasquez believed that he was recording the court at that time and certain people at that time. But a really good artist today would be forced to make a game of the same situation. He knows that particular thing could be recorded on film; so this side of his activity has been taken over by something else.

——*Francis Bacon*

---

25. Richard Estes' *Nedick's* is an example of

  (A) ashcan painting
  (B) photo-realism
  (C) surrealism
  (D) environmental art

Painters have used photography since its invention in the mid-nineteenth century, but the **photo-realists**, taking from pop artists an appreciation of mass-media images, use photographs in a new way. **Richard Estes** (1936-) projects a photograph on the canvas, then paints over it, using the photograph as a guide. The result has the shimmering quality of a photograph, rather than the appearance of traditional painting. The giant portrait heads of **Chuck Close** (1940-), based on photographs, have been made into paintings in a painstaking manual method that recreates the photographic process. Close gives new meaning to Warhol's statement, "I want to be a machine." The sculptor **Duane Hanson** (1925-), casting from models, makes realistic figures out of painted polyester and fiberglass. His subjects are types we take for granted—tourists or a construction worker or a museum guard, for example. Like the images of Close and Estes, they seem unnervingly real.

In another offshoot of pop art, some artists incorporate urban graffiti into their work. Two such artists, **Keith Haring** (1958-1990) and **Jean-Michel Basquiat** (1960-1989), led tragically brief lives. Haring began his career in the New York subways—not on the trains, but in the stations, where he painted simplified figures on the black panels where ads had not yet been placed. Later he found that his graphic style could be applied almost anywhere, and achieved wide appeal in all manner of media, from murals and sculptures to posters and T-shirts. **Basquiat**, a sophisticated, formally trained artist, made paintings that seem deceptively primitive. His vibrant canvases incorporate, among other things, graffiti-like scribbling and spray-painting, cartoons, mass-media images, words, stick figures, and African masks.

Spoonbridge and Cherry, by Claes Oldenburg and Coosje van Bruggen

Many artists find traditional techniques of painting and sculpture too confining, and expand their work into the gallery space or the environment. Practitioners of **installation art**, such as **Richard Serra** (1939-), create site-specific works, limited in duration to the length of the exhibition. Serra confronts the viewer with massive metal plates, balanced against each other or the gallery wall, with no parts attached. **Christo** (1935-), a Bulgarian-born **environmental artist**, wraps natural sites and buildings with cloth, his most recent project being the German parliament building, the Reichstag. Other artists go beyond traditional visual-art media, incorporating such elements as video or performance into their work. One of the most successful **performance artists** today is **Laurie Anderson** (1947-), whose performances

BLOCKBUSTER BIENNIALS

The Whitney Museum of American Art has been holding survey exhibitions of contemporary art since 1932. The exhibition, now held biennially, is a way for the American art world to take measure of itself. It features works by both established artists and newcomers, often organized around a common theme. Though no prizes are awarded, inclusion is helpful to a young artist's career. Another important survey exhibition is the Venice Biennale, international in scope, which has been held on odd-numbered years since 1895. The Venice Biennale includes a pavilion from each participating country, with each pavilion featuring a leading artist from that country. Winning first prize at the Venice exhibition can cement an artist's reputation, as it did for Robert Rauschenberg in 1964.

combine wry humor, graphic art, music, and electronic effects. **Nam June Paik** (1932-), the Korean-born video artist, makes installation works with stacked television sets. Paik has stated, "As collage technique replaced oil paint, the cathode-ray tube will replace the canvas." Visual artists have always employed the most advanced technology at their disposal, and it's conceivable that Leonardo da Vinci, if alive today, would be working with video cameras and computers.

ANSWERS

1. C	2. B	3. A	4. C	5. A	6. D	7. B	8. D	9. A	10. A
11. D	12. C	13. C	14. A	15. A	16. A	17. B	18. A	19. D	20. A
21. D	22. A	23. B	24. A	25. B					

The chronicle of the wars the U.S. has fought in its short existence is a revealing, if unsettling, way to approach American history. As with any world power, rarely have more than a few years gone by during which the nation has not been involved in at least one bloody military conflict. Each generation of Americans has had a war through which to define itself, making the history of the nation's wars a window into the culture's psyche.

1. Which of the following correctly identifies the five members of the League of Iroquois?

   (A) Shoshone, Pomo, Shawnee, Miwok, and Paiute
   (B) Mohawks, Oneidas, Onondagas, Cayugas, and Senecas
   (C) Calusa, Seminole, Utina, Yamasee, and Biloxi
   (D) Crow, Arapaho, Cheyenne, Pawnee, and Omaha

The **calumet**, also called a **peace pipe**, was an elongated and decorated pipe used by Native American tribes of the Eastern woodlands and Great Plains to ratify treaties and settle conflicts. Agreements made with the calumet were considered sacred and inviolable.

The **League of the Iroquois** consisted of five tribes living in what is now the northeastern United States. Under the leadership of Hiawatha, a Mohawk chief, the Oneidas, Onondagas, Cayugas, Mohawks, and Senecas united as the **Hodinonhsioni**—"people of the longhouse." Each tribe sent representatives to the Council House, a longhouse (p. 42). The Council typically consisted of fifty **sachems**, or representatives, from villages and clans of the member tribes. The Council had the power to ratify treaties, receive embassies, arbitrate intertribal conflict, and decide upon peaceful settlements of disputes. They could not, however, intervene in the internal affairs of any member tribe. Military leadership of the League remained under the auspices of war chiefs.

Sorry bud, you've got the wrong continent.

In theory, no member of the Council could go to war without League approval. League members were widely feared for their military prowess.

Prior to the arrival of Europeans, League members used bows and arrows, clubs, and wooden shields in battle. They occasionally practiced cannibalism on their victims, in the belief that one could "eat" an enemy's valor, and also practiced scalping. The most common military tactic was to ambush the enemy in a surprise attack. To protect their villages, League tribes constructed long palisades surrounded by deep ditches and other earthworks. Women handled the adoption and assimilation of prisoners of war into the culture.

After the arrival of Europeans, League members employed iron tomahawks and guns in battle. They fought several wars with and against whites, and more frequently engaged in scalping since Europeans sometimes paid per scalp.

2. **What was King Philip's real name?**
   (A) Wamsutta
   (B) Metacom
   (C) Hiawatha
   (D) Albert

Battles between Native peoples and European settlers punctuated the colonial period. **King Philip's War** (1675-1676) was one of the bloodiest prerevolutionary conflicts. In the early 1600s, most settlers viewed neighboring tribes as a direct threat to their survival and ability to obtain land. In the northeast, the battling over land use led the English to nearly exterminate the Pequots. Afterward, a period of peace between colonists and other neighboring Native Americans followed due to an alliance forged among English settlers, the Narragansett, and Massasoit, chief of the Wampanoag. Massasoit even took his two sons before a Plymouth court to receive English names—hence, **Metacom** became Philip.

Upon the deaths of his father and older brother, Metacom became chief of the Wampanoag. Not sharing his father's trust for the English, Metacom believed his people would either be overwhelmed by colonists or should push the English back to the ocean. Vowing to destroy the English, Metacom spent thirteen years preparing for war, only to have his Native American confidant, John Sassamon, reveal his plans to an English governor who later tried and hanged three Native Americans for Sassamon's murder. The Native Americans retaliated, killing eleven colonists. War quickly followed.

Metacom promised to "burn every house, destroy every village and kill every white man." Equipped with guns and armor from trade, Metacom's warriors fiercely battled the colonists, attacking fifty-two and destroying twelve of ninety white settlements. But without a base of operations and ready access to food and supplies, Metacom's men began to desert, and in some cases, side with the enemy.

Colonists had superior numbers, employed wholesale massacre battle tactics, and enlisted the support of five hundred **Mohegans**, blood rivals of the Wampanoag. On July 20, 1676, in a bloody siege, colonists captured Metacom's wife and son and sold them into slavery in the West Indies. Less than a month later, after a concerted manhunt, colonists raided a village where Metacom hid. Alderman, an Native American traitor, shot and killed Metacom, whose head was then displayed on a pole. King Philip's War had reached an end.

The Invasion of America: Indians, Colonialism and the Cant of Conquest (1975), by Francis Jennings. This book treats European "discovery" as an invasion, and considers, from that viewpoint, Indian-colonist relations.

3. **Who was Nat Bacon?**

(A) A wealthy farmer from Virginia
(B) A freed slave who returned to Africa
(C) A rebellious merchant in Boston
(D) A radical student at Harvard

The pugnacious Nat Bacon

While King Philip's War raged in the northeast, an up-and-coming young farmer from Virginia named **Nathaniel Bacon** (1647-1676) grew increasingly frustrated with "timid" governmental Native American policies. After a Native American killed his plantation overseer, Bacon raised a militia of five hundred men and attacked the peaceful Occaneechee tribe, instantly becoming a local hero among whites. Bacon then composed his *Declaration of the People* (1676), a document that, among other things, criticized the government for not protecting frontiersmen against Native Americans by organizing armed detachments. **Governor Berkeley** (1606-1677), who was angered by the uproar, chastised Bacon, yet pledged changes, and Bacon subsequently apologized.

However, Bacon soon believed the Governor wasn't pursuing the Native Americans as promised. Gathering troops, including lower-class planters, servants, freed slaves, and slaves, Bacon headed for Jamestown and burned the city, causing Berkeley to flee. In turn, a naval squadron was dispatched by the Crown and pursued Bacon, who died of **dysentery** before capture. Upon arrival at Bacon's garrisons, English troops found nearly seven hundred armed Englishmen, alongside servants, slaves, and other poor. British rulers feared such united forces. The Virginia government responded by passing a law making it illegal for white servants to rebel, thus preempting white-black and rich-poor alliances. The first of more than eighteen such popular rebellions, primarily between landowners and impoverished farmers and slaves, Bacon's rebellion was simultaneously both anti-Native American and anti-aristocrat.

FROM WILLIAM BRADFORD'S *HISTORY OF THE PLYMOUTH PLANTATION*

"It was a fearful sight to see them thus frying in the fryer, and the streams of blood quenching the same, and horrible was the stincke and sente thereof, but the victory seemed a sweet sacrifice, and they gave the prayers thereof to God, who had wrought so wonderfully for them . . ."

Dysentery, an infection of the large intestine, occurs in two strains, amoebic and bacterial. Both cause severe diarrhea and dehydration; amoebic dysentery can cause permanent liver damage. The disease occurs most often in tropical climates. Although today we have anti-bacterials and other treatments, dysentery continues to kill many people, particularly children, in developing countries.

4. Which European power gained tremendous influence
   in the Americas after the French and Indian War?

   (A) Spain
   (B) England
   (C) France
   (D) Holland

The **French and Indian War** (1756-1763) was a direct extension of the **Seven Years' War** (also 1756-1763) taking place in Europe. The conflict arose among European countries vying for power in colonial territories that would bring them greater wealth, access to resources, and markets for exports. One-and-a-half million English colonists vastly outnumbered the sixty thousand French, but the French had superior organization, experienced fighters, and the support of Native Americans from the Iroquois League. In fact, the war's name reflects the strong alliance between the French and the various tribes who were eager to avenge English colonists' years of cruelty. (Few Native Americans fought on the English side.) Despite the alliances, the war concluded with England securing substantial power throughout the North American colonies.

A depiction of the French and Indian War

The French and Indian War is traced to a battle between British troops led by a young lieutenant named **George Washington** (1732-1799) and French troops at Duquesne, located in disputed territory in Ohio country. In retreat, Washington and his troops quickly assembled at Fort Necessity, where they were again routed and sent tramping back to Virginia on the Fourth of July, 1753. Two years later, once the war had officially commenced, English Major General Edward Braddock planned to assault four strategic French bases—Duquesne, Fort Niagara, Crown Point, and Acadia—simultaneously. His troops succeeded only at Acadia.

In fact, the English lost most of the war's early battles, both in America and worldwide. Things continued to go badly for the English until **William Pitt** (1759-1806) took command of English forces. Pitt's emphasis on naval warfare and his reliance upon new and aggressive generals turned the war around. Jeffrey Amherst, one of Pitt's generals, instituted an early form of **biological warfare**: while negotiating with Native Americans, he gave them blankets from a smallpox hospital.

Several important English victories from 1758 to 1760 finally secured British control over the American colonies. Montreal fell to the English in 1760, giving the British control over Canada as well. The **Treaty of Paris**, signed in 1763, secured official British dominion in North America, including land stretching from the Atlantic Ocean to the Mississippi Valley, from Florida to the North Pole, and several Caribbean islands. Another result of the war was that American colonists realized the importance of intercolonial cooperation, a lesson that would serve them well in their fight for independence.

5. Who coined the name "Sons of Liberty"?

(A) Paul Revere
(B) A British parliamentarian
(C) George Washington
(D) The French leftists

DO THE LAUNDRY ALREADY

Paine wrote, "Until an independence is declared, the continent will feel itself like a man who continues putting off some unpleasant business from day to day, yet knows it must be done, hates to set about it, wishes it over, and is continually haunted with the thoughts of its necessity."

 Numerous pamphlets circulated among the colonies, debating issues of independence and the war. *Common Sense* (1776), written by Thomas Paine (1737-1809), argued compellingly for secession from England. Widely read throughout the colonies, *Common Sense* convinced many colonists that America must become a separate nation.

In order to repay debts incurred by years of war as well as to finance the management of their vast empire, England's Parliament passed several tax acts (p. 78), including the **Stamp Act**, on goods such as sugar and tea. American colonists found themselves heavily burdened by what they called the **Intolerable Acts**. Numerous rebellions ignited, including the **Boston Tea Party** (1773), in which colonists, dressed as Native Americans, dumped tons of tea into Boston Harbor, and the **Boston Massacre** (1770), in which British soldiers fired upon colonialist demonstrators. One of the first persons to be killed at the massacre was a former slave named Crispus Attucks. Within Parliament (p. 397), a British dissenter of the tax acts called American colonists **"Sons of Liberty,"** a name quickly assumed by many colonists. In 1774, colonists formed the First Continental Congress in protest of British actions.

The death of Crispus Attucks

6. **What did one lantern in the belfry at Christ Church Boston signify?**

   (A) The start of Sunday Service
   (B) The British redcoats' arrival by land
   (C) The death of Paul Revere
   (D) The official beginning of the Revolutionary War

In Massachusetts, the British governor, attempting to avert armed rebellion, began seeking out hidden caches of arms. Meanwhile, colonists, under the guidance of patriot leaders, began drilling with muskets. Ready to pick up arms and fight at a minute's notice, the Sons of Liberty came to be known as **minutemen**. To signal the arrival of British **redcoats**, **Paul Revere** (1735-1818) devised a system of early warning. One lantern in the belfry at Christ Church Boston meant troops arrived by land, two lanterns signaled arrival by the Charles River. Late at night, on April 18, 1775, Revere received the signal: two lanterns. He rode off to alert the militia at Lexington, but unfortunately, he was arrested along the way and couldn't deliver his warning.

Fighting started in Lexington, where an unordered shot rang out as redcoats and minutemen faced off. A battle ensued, leaving eight minutemen dead. The first shot fired at Lexington became called **"the shot heard 'round the world."** Shortly afterward, in Concord, a better orches-

READY . . . FIRE!

British soldiers employed typical European battlefield strategy. Lines of infantry wielding muskets fought in the open against the opponent, who also lined up. Each side marched toward the other, loading, advancing, firing, and reloading. A musket's range was limited to a few hundred feet; its firing was inaccurate, leaving the final work to the bayonet. Thus, the British drill did not include the word "aim."

The Battle of Princeton

trated battle commenced. As the redcoats proceeded in line formation, minutemen spread out and fired from hidden positions, employing the guerrilla tactics they had learned from fighting with Native Americans. By day's end, seventy-three redcoats lay dead.

As a result, the Second Continental Congress met in Philadelphia on May 10, 1775, and produced the **Declaration of Independence** and the **Articles of Confederation**. On June 15, 1775, George Washington, the Virginia congressional delegate, took charge of the Continental army.

7. **What was the first battle of the Revolutionary War?**

(A) Battle of Bunker Hill
(B) Battle of Bennington
(C) First Battle of Saratoga
(D) Morristown Mutiny

The first significant battle of the Revolutionary War, the **Battle of Bunker Hill**, took place at Breed's Hill in Boston on June 17, 1775. This battle is called Bunker Hill because, in an offensive move, Colonel **William Prescott** (1726-1795) received orders to fortify Bunker's Hill (as it was then called). Without apparent reason, he fortified Breed's Hill instead. While the redcoats won, their victory was less than resounding, and the British replaced Colonel Thomas Gage with Sir William Howe.

In most of the early battles of the war, the British cleaned up. However, on Christmas Day, 1776, Washington led his troops in a surprise attack on Trenton, New Jersey. American morale lifted. The English miscalculated colonial commitment to freedom

The Battle at Breed's (not Bunker) Hill

rom the Crown, and fighting lasted longer than they anticipated. To maintain the war, the British had to ship most of their troops and supplies. Needing still more soldiers, they hired nine thousand mercenaries, known and feared for their brutality, from the Hesse-Kassel region of Germany.

In the winter of 1777, Washington's men took quarters at **Valley Forge**, Pennsylvania, arriving there exhausted and bedraggled. They passed a difficult winter with inadequate supplies. In the face of this adversity and with the help of Prussian Baron von Steuben, Washington drilled his army. When they emerged in the spring, Washington's forces were a well-trained, cohesive unit.

Radicalism and the American Revolution (1993), by Gordon S. Wood. Wood offers one of the more recent studies of conditions of the Revolution and its leaders.

8. **Who acted as American envoy to France during the revolution?**

   (A) Thomas Paine
   (B) Benjamin Franklin
   (C) Paul Revere
   (D) John Adams

Although the colonists largely won the Revolution because of their military tactics, assistance from European countries, notably France, greatly aided the American effort.

Benjamin Franklin (1706-1790) acted as American ambassador to France, where he was hailed as a great figure of the Enlightenment (p. 396). Franklin managed to convince the French to provide support for Americans even though France, like England, was heavily in debt from previous wars. Since May 1776, the French, in part to undermine their longtime rival England, had secretly supplied munitions and arms to the colonies. After a decisive American victory at Saratoga, New York, in October 1777, where British General John Burgoyne surrendered five thousand troops to American General Horatio Gates, the French openly supported America and formally recognized its sovereignty. By the end of

Nathan Hale, captured by the British, was hanged for spying without a trial. It was rumored, but never documented, that he said bravely, "I only regret that I have but one life to give for my country."

Ben wanted the national bird to be a wild turkey.

1779, France, along with Holland and Spain, declared war on England. The end of the Revolutionary War was in sight.

9. **What treaty brought an end to the Revolutionary War?**

   (A) The Treaty of Versailles
   (B) The Warsaw Pact
   (C) The Peace of Paris
   (D) The Declaration of Independence

Deborah Sampson, using the name Robert Shurtleff, enlisted in the Continental army in 1782. She is the only woman known to have served. The Fourth Massachusetts nicknamed her Molly because of her hairless face. Sampson's identity was revealed in 1783 when she contracted a fever. Upon discharge, she received a small pension, and later, her heirs received a full pension. In 1802, Sampson went on a lecture tour describing her experiences in the war. She was one of the first women in America to go on a lecture tour.

General Cornwallis in his finest topper

Throughout 1781, the British now fighting against the colonists, the French, the Spanish, and the Dutch, lost many decisive battles especially in the South. To make matters worse, French and American ships maintained a blockade of supplies coming from England. Finally, on October 19, 1781, **General Charles Cornwallis** (1738-1805) along with eight thousand troops surrendered at Yorktown. England signed preliminary peace treaties with all warring factions throughout late 1782 and early 1783. The United States and England signed the **Peace of Paris** on September 3, 1783, formally ending the war, and Congress ratified the treaty in January 1784.

10. **Against what country did the U.S. fight the Barbary Wars?**

    (A) Portugal
    (B) Cuba
    (C) Tripoli
    (D) Mexico

U.S. merchant ships conducted a swift business across the Atlantic and throughout the Mediterranean Sea. Without naval protection, American merchants fell prey to marauding pirates from the Barbary Coast stretching across northern Africa. Pirates raided ships, held sailors captive, and demanded high ransoms from the U.S. government. By 1801,

Stephen Decatur: the first Navy Seal

the U.S. had paid more than $2 million to the governments of Tunis, Morocco, Algiers, and Tripoli for the release of Americans and the assurance of safe passage. Demanding, but unable to obtain even more cash, the Pasha of Tripoli declared war on the U.S. in 1801.

In response, President Thomas Jefferson initiated a massive build-up of naval forces, and, in 1804, he dispatched Commodore **Edward Preble** (1761-1807) to assault Tripoli. A battle ensued during which Americans lost their key ship *Philadelphia*. Later that same night, a young navy officer named **Stephen Decatur** (1779-1820) slipped aboard the ship and set it ablaze to embarrass the Pasha. Decatur became an instant hero. Further land and sea assaults led to the fall of Derna, and soon the young American flag held sway over an old-world country for the first time. The Pasha requested peace. The war against the Barbary pirates, also known as the Tripolitan War, ended on June 10, 1805, yet the Barbary practice of extortion persisted until 1816.

 The U.S. Marine Corps, established in 1775, incorporated the military duties of both the navy and the army. These soldier-sailors frequently land on hostile territory in advance of the navy. Today, the marines number more than 170,000—the largest marine force in the world.

11. **What British practice contributed to the start of the War of 1812?**

(A) Four o'clock tea
(B) Impressment
(C) Taxation
(D) Fur trading

The **War of 1812** arose out of collisions between American expansionist zeal and British imperialist actions. The Napoleonic wars left England desperate for men. They boarded ships at sea and forced men, including many Americans, into military service. This practice was called **impressment**. Further antagonizing Americans, the British provoked Native American attacks on western settlers, who continued to forge westward and northward into English and Spanish territory. Some Americans, in fact, urged war with England in the hope of acquiring Canada.

Many Westerners supported a war with England, but the U.S. government faced dissension by Northeastern Federalists (p. 404), who opposed the war on grounds that it would adversely affect trade with England and other countries. In the end, American troops assaulted a force of British-Canadians who had the support of one thousand Native Americans. By December 1812, the British had instituted a naval blockade that eventually stretched along the entire Atlantic coastline. With only twelve thousand troops, the U.S. was poorly prepared for war and lost many early battles. But, surprisingly, America won a number of sea victories against Britain's strong navy. Commodore Isaac Chauncey and Captain Oliver Hazard Perry began building warships on Lake Erie, in preparation for controlling the Great Lakes.

The war of 1812 comes to an end—in 1814.

Peace negotiations commenced in August 1814, but fighting continued unabated. In fact, in late August, the British marched into Washington and burned the Capitol (p. 46) and other important civic buildings to the ground. Finally, on December 24, 1814, the U.S. and England signed the **Treaty of Ghent** to end the war. The settlement included the establishment of clear boundaries between Canada and the U.S. Having defeated British forces that had recently defeated **Napoleon**, Americans saw themselves as a people destined for greatness.

After the war, the U.S. implemented the Monroe Doctrine (p. 412), stipulating that America would not tolerate any European nation exerting power in the Americas, and, in turn, that the U.S. would not interfere with existing colonies or European governments. America at that point officially recognized many emerging South American countries. This doctrine, through varied interpretations, would provide a basis for later U.S. interventions in Central and South America.

Shortly after the Treaty of Ghent was signed, the British, unaware of the new peace, attacked the troops of **Andrew Jackson** (1767-1845), who had been fighting Native Americans in the South. **The Battle of New Orleans** proved devastating for the British, who lost more than two thousand men, and was a decisive victory for the Americans, who embraced Jackson as a hero. Jackson's fame later catapulted him into the office of the presidency.

Americans aimed to acquire much of Britain's northwest territories, extending to the latitude 54' 40". During the war of 1812, soldiers used the rally cry **"54-40 or fight!"**

Francis Scott Key (1779-1843), observing a battle in which Americans prevented the British from entering Baltimore, wrote the U.S. national anthem, **"The Star-Spangled Banner."**

12. **What happened to many Native Americans after the War of 1812?**

    (A) They were "given" a large spread of land west of the Mississippi.
    (B) They were granted citizenship.
    (C) They were recognized as independent and sovereign nations.
    (D) They became subjects of an accelerated genocidal policy of the U.S. government.

Prior to the War of 1812, a Shawnee chief named **Tecumseh** (c. 1768-1813) along with **Tenskwatawah** (c. 1773-1837), called "the Prophet," traveled throughout the Ohio region, organizing tribes into a union intended to preserve the Ohio River as a boundary between white settlers and Native Americans. Tecumseh's death during the War of 1812 was a heavy blow to Native Americans who, after the war, became subjects of continued assaults by settlers heading westward under the banner of Manifest Destiny (p. 176). By the end of the War of 1812, Andrew Jackson had initiated a "removal" policy. One product of this policy was the Cherokee movement westward to Oklahoma along what came to be called the Trail of Tears (p. 176)

13. **How many Texan settlers fought against more than 3,000 Mexicans at the Alamo?**

    (A) 24
    (B) 178
    (C) 1,000
    (D) 12,000

By 1830, more than twenty thousand white settlers and their slaves lived in Texas, a region belonging to Mexico, which had earned its independence from Spain in 1821. Upon learning of Texan plans to secede from Mexico and join the U.S., Mexican leader **Antonio Lopez de Santa Anna** (1794-1876) marched three thousand troops into Texas, where he won several skirmishes. He finally arrived at the **Alamo**, where 178 whites held off his troops for ten days. Santa Anna's forces eventually killed all of the whites. Invoking the courage of those settlers, many whites later used the phrase **"Remember the Alamo"** as a rallying cry. Texas claimed its independence, which lasted until the **War with Mexico** in 1846.

So far from God, so close to the U.S.

——*Mexican Proverb*

CULTURESCOPE

So Far From God: The U.S. War with Mexico 1846-48 (1989), by John Eisenhower. The book is chock full of graphic battle scenes and primary source material.

At the start of the war with Mexico, many Americans supported fighting. However, dissension arose, especially in the Northeast. Vehemently opposing the war, Henry David Thoreau (p. 264) refused to pay his taxes and went to jail, where Ralph Waldo Emerson (p. 263) visited him. Emerson asked, "What are you doing in there," to which Thoreau responded, "What are you doing out there?" Soon afterward, Thoreau wrote *Civil Disobedience* (p. 264)

James Polk (1795-1849), who became president in 1846, aimed unabashedly to expand the U.S. to the Pacific, engulfing California and other Mexican territory. Polk ordered General **Zachary Taylor** (1784-1850) to take troops to the Rio Grande, well inside Mexico. On April 25, 1846, in response to the American aggression, Mexicans fired the first shots, thus starting a war that quickly developed into a rout. U.S. forces, led by many members of **West Point's** class of 1846, including **Robert E. Lee** (1807-1870), **Jefferson Davis** (1808-1889), and **William Tecumseh Sherman** (1820-1891), swept victoriously through Mexican territory. Polk admonished Congress to quickly declare war.

The Alamo, remember?

Several bloody and vicious battles occurred throughout northern Mexico. U.S. troops took Monterrey and many other cities as they progressed toward Mexico City. In what is now the western U.S., American forces were consistently victorious. U.S. troops arrived at the Mexican capital and claimed victory in September 1847. (In fact, the first line of the Marine Corps anthem begins, "From the Halls of Montezuma," referring to their arrival at the Mexican capital.) In 1848, Mexico and the U.S. signed the **Treaty of Guadalupe Hidalgo**, which granted nearly half of Mexico's land to the U.S. and defined the border along the Rio Grande. In return, the U.S. paid Mexico $15 million. An American journalist announced, "We take nothing by conquest . . . Thank God."

14. **Which state was the first to secede from the Union?**

(A) South Carolina
(B) Virginia
(C) Georgia
(D) Maryland

Within days of the 1860 election, South Carolina's state legislature voted to secede from the Union. By Abraham Lincoln's (p. 409) inauguration in 1861, five more states had seceded. Together with South Carolina, they formed the **Confederate States of America** and drafted their own constitution that emphasized states' rights and the legality of slavery. In 1861, **Jefferson Davis** (1808-1889) was elected president of the Confederacy. The North seemed destined to win the war against the South with more than twenty-two million people, 70 percent of the railroad system, and three times the financial wealth of the South. However, the South had military advantages, including better trained leaders and militia, familiarity with the battle terrain (since much of the fighting was done in the South), and wider popular support. The North relied upon conscripts who were primarily poor urban immigrants or farmers' sons.

Battle Cry of Freedom: The Civil War Era (1989), by James McPherson. Events leading up to the Civil War are covered in this prize-winning, nonfiction piece.

The Gray and the Blue

Many spoke little English, had no familiarity with weaponry, and carried Bibles in their breast pockets for protection.

On April 12, 1861, the first official engagement of the war occurred at U.S. Fort Sumter in Charleston, South Carolina, where **General Pierre Beauregard** (1818-1893) faced off with the federal troops. The fort fell the next day, due largely to lack of supplies. The North was outraged, crying "The Union forever!" Lincoln had barely arrived in Washington. He immediately ordered a blockade to prevent the South from exporting cotton or receiving vital supplies and munitions from abroad.

15. **Who was appointed head of the Union Army after the First Battle of Bull Run?**

    (A) "Stonewall" Jackson
    (B) Pierre Manassas
    (C) George McClellan
    (D) Henry Halleck

The Civil War, a documentary series by Ken Burns. This award-winning documentary made Ken Burns a household name. Get it on video and plan to sit on your couch for a few days—it's worth it.

Who sits in Grant's chair?

On July 21, 1861, the first major battle of the war, called the First Battle of Bull Run by the North and First Manassas by the South, took place in Virginia. The Union troops were routed by **General Thomas J. Jackson** (1824-1863), whose brigade earned him his future sobriquet for standing "like a stone wall." The Union lost 2,900 men, the South lost 2,000. The loss was a wake-up call for the North, which lacked effective military leadership, and led to the appointment of **George B. McClellan** (1826-1885) as head of the Union Army in November. The battle also made clear to the North that the war would not be over soon. To raise money for further fighting, Congress instituted the first income-tax law and increased enlistment from ninety days to two years. Throughout the rest of 1861, the Union suffered one defeat after another.

At the start of 1862, Lincoln issued General War Order Number One, demanding a Union offensive, which McClellan ignored. In exasperation, Lincoln stated, "If General McClellan does not want to use the army, I would like to borrow it." In March 1862, Lincoln replaced McClellan with General Henry W. Halleck. Meanwhile, **General Ulysses S. Grant** (1822-1885) commenced a Union offensive with great success outside Nashville, Tennessee.

General Robert E. Lee

16. **How many people died at the Battle of Shiloh?**

    (A)   156
    (B)   2,000
    (C)   28,000
    (D)   50,000

Grant moved his victorious troops on to Pittsburg Landing, Tennessee, where General Albert S. Johnston's troops attacked. On April 6 and 7, 1862, the **Battle of Shiloh** raged. The Union nearly lost, but reinforcements arrived just in time to drive off the Confederates off. Each side suffered staggering losses; in total, 28,000 men died. More died at Shiloh than all the soldiers who died during the Revolution, the War of 1812, and the Mexican War collectively. Shortly after this devastating battle, Robert E. Lee took command of the Confederate Armies of Northern Virginia.

> "
>
> *Universal suffrage, furloughs and whiskey have ruined us.*
>
> ——GENERAL BRAXTON BRAGG
> OF THE UNION, AFTER SHILOH
>
> "

17. **After which battle did Lincoln issue the Emancipation Proclamation?**

    (A)   Second Bull Run
    (B)   Gettysburg
    (C)   Antietam
    (D)   Shiloh

Fighting throughout the summer months of 1862 did not go well for the Union, although McClellan almost captured Richmond, which would have ended the war in early July. Lee's forces drove the Union back from Richmond to Washington. Continually dissatisfied with his military leaders, Lincoln reinstated McClellan as general-in-chief.

Shortly thereafter, Lee's battle plans fell into McClellan's hands. Anticipating Lee's strategy, McClellan led his men to Sharpsburg, Maryland, where they were victorious in the **Battle of Antietam**. This

Southern loss increased European reluctance to recognize the South's independence. With the Union's success behind him, Lincoln issued his historic Emancipation Proclamation.

Published on September 23, 1862, in Northern newspapers, the proclamation didn't officially free the slaves. Legally, Lincoln could only free slaves in rebel territory; Congress reserved the power to address universal emancipation in the U.S. But the document, officially signed on January 1, 1863, clarified the political positions of France and England; both finally agreed not to recognize the South. In the North, people now perceived freeing the slaves as the war's pivotal issue. Whereas Northerners previously fought to "save the Union," many now refused to enlist, forcing the government to pass the **Conscription Act** in March 1863. Riots ensued, especially since mainly the poor were forced to serve while the act allowed wealthy men to pay for a substitute.

 African Americans had served in all the major previous conflicts until a 1792 law barred their participation. On January 26, 1863, the Secretary of War, desperate for men, authorized the Governor of Massachusetts to recruit black troops. The 54th Massachusetts Volunteers was the first black regiment. By the war's end, more than 185,000 black soldiers, many from Louisiana, Kentucky, and Tennessee, served in 166 all-black regiments. Black regiments were frequently assigned the least desirable tasks and were paid less than white soldiers.

18. Who led U.S. forces at Gettysburg?

(A) Grant
(B) Sherman
(C) Schwarzkopf
(D) Meade

The **Battle of Gettysburg**, by most accounts, was not a victory for either side—it was a bloodbath. More than 50,000 men died in three days of fighting that stretched across Cemetery Ridge from one hill to another. Both sides, suffering immense losses, received reinforcements throughout the engagement. The Confederates had arrived at the town shoeless; they retreated with no remaining hope for international recognition. This battle is perhaps best known for the **Gettysburg Address**, the memorable speech given by Lincoln at the dedication of the military cemetery, where mounds of bodies were separated by state origin and buried in mass graves.

A few of the 50,000 soldiers that died at Gettysburg

The Gettysburg Address

"Fourscore and seven years ago our fathers brought forth on this continent a new nation, conceived in Liberty, and dedicated to the proposition that all men are created equal. Now we are engaged in a great civil war, testing whether that nation or any nation so conceived and so dedicated can long endure. We are met on a great battlefield of that war. We have come to dedicate a portion of that field as a final resting-place for those who here gave their lives that that nation might live. It is altogether fitting and proper that we should do this. But in a larger sense, we cannot dedicate, we cannot consecrate, we cannot hallow this ground. The brave men, living and dead, who struggled here have consecrated it far above our poor power to add or detract. The world will little note nor long remember what we say here, but it can never forget what they did here. It is for us the living rather to be dedicated here to the unfinished work which they who fought here have thus far so nobly advanced. It is rather for us to be here dedicated to the great task remaining before us—that from these honored dead we take increased devotion to that cause for which they gave the last full measure of devotion—that we here highly resolve that these dead shall not have died in vain, that this nation under God shall have a new birth of freedom, and that government of the people, by the people, for the people shall not perish from the earth."

While Lee and General George Meade faced off at Gettysburg, Grant sustained a long siege at Vicksburg and was appointed head of the Union forces in the West, where unorganized fighting had erupted. In March 1864, Lincoln, in acknowledgement of Grant's victories, appointed him head of the Union armies. General Sherman also met with great successes throughout the South.

19. **Where did General Sherman conclude his devastating march from Atlanta?**
    (A) Little Rock
    (B) Washington, D.C.
    (C) Tallahassee
    (D) Savannah

Sherman devised a strategy to divide the South in half, and on January 14, 1864, headed for Atlanta from Mississippi. Along the way, he led his troops in a devastating march, during which they burned, pillaged, and destroyed anything that might contribute to the continuation of the South's war effort. When Sherman arrived at Atlanta on September 2, 1864, most of the city was already in flames. In the North, morale lifted.

> **"**
>
> *I have come to regard the death and mangling of a couple thousand men as a small affair, a kind of morning dash . . .*
>
> —General William Tecumseh Sherman
>
> **"**

Sherman then proceeded from Atlanta to the coastal town of Savannah, Georgia. This swath of carnage left by Sherman and his troops earned Sherman the nickname "Attila of the West." Just before Christmas, he arrived at Savannah, having successfully bisected the South.

The Red Badge of Courage (1960), by Stephen Crane. A great war novel and psychological portrayal of violent emotion.

20. What did Lincoln do when he toured Richmond, the capital of the Confederacy, on April 2, 1865?

(A) Attended a theater performance
(B) Sat in Jefferson Davis's chair
(C) Met with abolitionist leaders
(D) Declared peace

As Sherman and Grant swept across the South, Lincoln made his second inaugural address in 1865, in which he spoke of finishing the "work we are in." On April 4, 1865, he toured the Confederate capital of Richmond and sat assuredly in Jefferson Davis's chair. Four days later, April 8, 1865, surrounded and starving, Lee surrendered to Grant at the **Appomattox Courthouse** in Virginia. The South was left in ruins. In total, more than 600,000 men lost their lives. More than three million had fought in the war.

Gone With the Wind (1939), starring Clark Gable and Vivien Leigh. This is the classic story of a Southern belle and the fall of the South.

FROM LINCOLN'S SECOND INAUGURAL ADDRESS

"With malice toward none, with charity for all, with firmness in the right, as God gives us to see the right, let us strive on to finish the work we are in, to bind up the nation's wounds, to care for him who shall have borne the battle and for his widow, and his orphan—to do all which may achieve and cherish a just and lasting peace among ourselves and with all nations."

21. Why did Custer take his troops into battle against the Sioux and Northern Cheyenne?

(A) For buffalo hides
(B) For gold
(C) For guns
(D) For ghost shirts

Twelve years after the Civil War had ended, **President Rutherford B. Hayes** (1822-1893) shifted the last of the old Union troops still "occupying" the South to fight Native Americans throughout the West. From 1866-1891, the U.S. army, along with settlers, fought a sustained and brutal war against various tribes, eventually killing most of their leaders and bringing their population to less than 250,000. As settlers moved westward along wagon trails, they passed directly through land occupied by Great Plains tribes, including the Sioux, Arapaho, Apache, and

Little Big Man (1970), starring Dustin Hoffman. Hoffman plays a 121-year-old man reminiscing about his life. A couple of his more impressive feats are surviving the Little Big Horn and drinking with "Wild Bill" Hickok.

> *We had buffalo for food, and their hides for clothing and for our tepees. We preferred hunting to a life of idleness on the reservation, where we were driven against our will. . . We preferred our own way of living. We were no expense to the Government. All we wanted was peace and to be left alone. Soldiers were sent out in the winter, who destroyed our villages. Then 'Long Hair' [Custer] came in the same way. They say we massacred him, but he would have done the same thing to us had we not defended ourselves and fought to the last.*
>
> ——*Crazy Horse, 1877*

Comanche, and often settled, displacing Native Americans and forcing them to live on reservations (p. 177).

Protesting development of the Bozeman trail that took settlers to gold-rich California, the Sioux, led by **Red Cloud** (1822-1909), attacked the U.S. government forts along the trail in one of the last battles of the Native American Wars. Fighting concluded in 1867 with the signing of a flimsy treaty that allowed the U.S. to proceed with the trail.

A few years later, **Colonel George Custer** (1839-1876) and a host of white trespassers discovered gold on a Sioux reservation in Black Hills, South Dakota. Throughout 1875, a rush to the territory ensued. The U.S. government ordered the Sioux off the reservation land promised to them only a short time before. In response, the Sioux decided to fight. Led by **Sitting Bull** (c. 1834-1893) and **Crazy Horse** (1849-1877), and joined by the Northern Cheyenne, the Sioux concentrated their men at the **Little Big Horn River**. On June 25, 1876, ignoring specific orders against attack, Custer led 250 men directly into the assembled Native Americans, now a force of more than 3,000. The Native Americans destroyed Custer's troops, leaving only one man alive. On the east coast, journalists described the battle as the heroic "last stand" of Custer. An infuriated public demanded all-out war upon Native Americans. Thus, while the **Battle at Little Bighorn** was a rout for the Native Americans, it also led to their rapid demise.

> 66
>
> *I should welcome almost any war, for I think this country needs one.*
>
> ——TEDDY ROOSEVELT
>
> 99

In the face of these wars and such extensive losses, many Native Americans began following a religious movement led by a Paiute named **Wovoka** (c. 1856-1932), whose **Ghost Dance** conjured up the spirits of dead warriors and promised a return to Native American paradise. The Native Americans wore **ghost shirts**, thought to protect them from bullets. Alarmed at this religious zeal, the U.S. army continually engaged with Native Americans and arrested many of their leaders, including Sitting Bull and **Big Foot** (yes, Big Foot). Three days after Big Foot's arrest, his people were captured by the Army and encamped at **Wounded Knee** where they were forced to surrender their weapons. While the Native Americans were turning in their arms, a deaf Native American named Black Coyote apparently misfired his gun. The U.S. soldiers immediately opened fire on the disarmed Native Americans. As many as three hundred Native Americans died at Wounded Knee, which some call the Native Americans' "last stand."

"How could I have been so stupid?"

22. **What were Teddy Roosevelt's troops in the Spanish-American War called?**

(A) Big Sticks
(B) Rough Riders
(C) Teddy's boys
(D) American pawns

The **Spanish-American War**, fought under the pretense of assisting Cuba's struggle for freedom from imperialist Spain, provided America with an opportunity to resuscitate its flagging economy, flex military muscle, and gain territories abroad for trade and resources. Most business and military leaders clamored for this war; the newspapers especially wanted war because it would boost their circulation. In fact, **William Randolph Hearst** (1863-1951) dispatched a photographer on assignment in Cuba to get pictures, saying he would "furnish the war." In contrast, the Spanish and U.S. **President William McKinley** (1843-1901) didn't seem to want war. However, McKinley eventually gave in to the persistence of **Henry Cabot Lodge** (1850-1924) and **Theodore Roosevelt** (1858-1919), and sent the U.S. battleship *Maine* to Havana's harbor.

On February 15, 1898, the *Maine* mysteriously exploded, killing 260 Americans. The newspapers cried, "Remember the *Maine*! To hell with Spain." Congress responded by unanimously appropriating $50 million for national defense. In April, Spain requested peace negotiations but

 As the U.S. prepared for war in Cuba, it dispatched the *U.S. Oregon* from California. The vessel took nearly two months to arrive at Cuba. When Roosevelt assumed the presidency, he revived an old idea to build a canal through Panama, Colombia. The Colombians, however, asked "too much" for the land, so the U.S. sponsored a revolution in Panama in November 1903. The new Panamanian government then sold a strip of land to the U.S. for $10 million plus an annual rent of $250,000. That was nice of them.

McKinley had already given in to internal political machinations and delivered his "War Message" to the public on April 11. Spain declared war on April 24 and Congress formally adopted a war resolution on April 25.

Throughout April, responding to Congress's **Volunteer Army Act**, thousands enlisted. The papers christened these soldiers the **Rough Riders**. Teddy Roosevelt was commissioned to lead this brigade.

The war lasted only a few months, and was fought in Cuba, the Philippines, and Puerto Rico. In May, a fierce naval battle at Manila Bay ended after the U.S. sunk all of Spain's ships. 657 marines landed at Guantanamo Bay, Cuba in June, commencing the official U.S. invasion. On July 1, the battles of **El Caney** and **San Juan Hill** took place. Sustaining heavy casualties, including deaths from **yellow fever** and malaria, the U.S. eventually defeated a much smaller Spanish force. Roosevelt, having led his triumphant men, became an instant hero. Fame would later propel him to the White House. Spain finally requested peace, and on August 9, 1898 McKinley formally accepted.

WHERE THE BOYS ARE, 1850-1900

Date	Place	Action
1852-53	Argentina	Marines arrive in Buenos Aires to protect American interests during revolution
1853	Nicaragua	Marines sent to protect American interests duing political upheaval
1853-54	Japan	Perry expedition, U.S. uses warships to force Japan to open its ports to the U.S.
1853-54	Bonin Islands	Ryuku and Perry lands to access ports for trade
1854	Nicaragua	Battles at Greytown to avenge insults to American Minister
1855	Uruguay	Forces arrive to protect American interests during attempted revolution in Montevideo
1859	China	Forces arrive to protect interests in Shanghai
1860	Angola	Forces sent to protect interests during uprisings at Kissembo
1893	Hawaii	Forces deployed to protect U.S. interests and involvement in provisional government
1894	Nicaragua	Forces sent to protect interests after a revolution

In the course of the war, the U.S. lost more than 5,000 men and gained control of Puerto Rico, Guam, Wake Island, and occupation of the Philippines. Cuba won its independence. America, now an imperialist force in its own right, soon faced a bloody insurrection in the Philippines.

23. On what country did Austria declare war after the assassination of Archduke Ferdinand?

   (A) Russia
   (B) Serbia
   (C) Turkey
   (D) Germany

On June 28, 1914, Gavrilo Princip, a student radical, assassinated **Archduke Francis Ferdinand**, heir to the Austro-Hungarian throne. Princip acted on behalf of a group that wanted to separate from the Austrian empire to join independent Serbia. Immediately following the murder, Austria declared war on Serbia. In turn, Russia, Serbia's ally, mobilized troops. Germany then declared war on Russia and its ally, France. England, defending its alliances, declared war on Germany, whose troops were already pushing into France and Belgium. Eventually, Turkey, Japan, the United States, and Italy, among numerous other countries, would become involved in the **Great War**.

Trench warfare

The forces leading to the war varied from rising nationalism, complicated alliances (notably the **Triple Alliance** of Germany, Austria, and Italy and the **Triple Entente** of France, England, and Russia), stakes in colonial territories, and centuries-old antagonisms. Many of the countries stood to gain or lose significant, resource-rich colonies throughout Africa, Asia, and the Middle East.

This **"war to end all wars"** brought to the battlefield advanced weaponry, including mustard gas and flamethrowers; new military hardware, including U-boats and tanks; and introduced the devastating and prolonging tactic of **trench warfare**. World War I was a technological tragedy; new tools of destruction prolonged and exaggerated the devastation of war.

TRENCH WARFARE

The introduction of machine guns to the battlefield made massive and rapid artillery attacks possible. In turn, trenches made it possible to escape artillery fire and prevent rear strikes. Thus, each side sat in a defensive position, unable to assume an offensive, which would entail running straight on at the opponents' machine-gun fire.

The first major battle occurred in France at the **Marne River**, on September 5, 1914, where French and British forces fought for seven days and stunted an ambitious German assault intended to attack unprepared Allies. Troops from both sides retreated into trenches, establishing a four-hundred-mile line that stretched from the North Sea to the French-Swiss border. For the next four years, most of the major battles of World War I, including Ypres and Belleau Wood, occurred along this line—the **Hindenburg line**.

24. **Why did the Germans sink the Lusitania?**

(A) It carried top-level British spies.

(B) It carried ammunition and weapons.

(C) It passed into German territory.

(D) It was an act of brutal civilian warfare.

All Quiet on the Western Front (1930), directed by Lewis Milestone. An adaptation of Erich Maria Remarque's novel, this Oscar-winning film vividly captures the German soldiers' experience in World War I.

German **U-boats** (*unterseeboot*) competed with Britain's superior navy throughout the war. Retaliating against the English blockade and declaring the sea surrounding England a war zone, Germans published civilian warnings in foreign papers and proceeded to sink several ships, including many carrying non-military supplies and civilians. On May 7, 1915, Germans torpedoed the British liner *Lusitania* off the coast of Ireland, killing 128 Americans. They claimed, correctly, that the ship carried ammunition and weapons. Outraged Americans did not believe that weapons were on the ship and clamored for war. President **Woodrow Wilson** (1856-1924)

OCEAN STEAMSHIPS.

CUNARD

EUROPE VIA LIVERPOOL

LUSITANIA

Fastest and Largest Steamer now in Atlantic Service Sails
SATURDAY, MAY 1, 10 A. M.
Transylvania, Fri., May 7, 5 P.M.
Orduna, - - Tues., May 18, 10 A.M.
Tuscania, - - Fri., May 21, 5 P.M.
LUSITANIA, Sat., May 29, 10 A.M.
Transylvania, Fri., June 4, 5 P.M.

Gibraltar—Genoa—Naples—Piraeus
S.S. Carpathia, Thur., May 13, Noon

ROUND THE WORLD TOURS
Through bookings to all principal Ports
of the World.
Company's Office. 21-24 State St., N. Y.

NOTICE!

TRAVELLERS intending to embark on the Atlantic voyage are reminded that a state of war exists between Germany and her allies and Great Britain and her allies; that the zone of war includes the waters adjacent to the British Isles; that, in accordance with formal notice given by the Imperial German Government, vessels flying the flag of Great Britain, or of any of her allies, are liable to destruction in those waters and that travellers sailing in the war zone on ships of Great Britain or her allies do so at their own risk.

IMPERIAL GERMAN EMBASSY
WASHINGTON, D. C., APRIL 22, 1915.

American Line

AMERICAN STEAMERS

BIOCHEMICAL WEAPONS

In the spring of 1915, Germany began using chemical weapons, specifically mustard gas, on the battlefield. The human devastation led to the Geneva Protocol and other international agreements governing the usage of chemical weapons. Such weapons, including tear gas, create a cloud of fine particles which are inhaled or absorbed by the skin. These weapons kill people, but they don't destroy property, so the aggressor is able to capture usable facilities.

offered several diplomatic notes requesting reparations and a disavowal of further attacks on civilian ships. The sinking of the *Lusitania* has often been identified as the primary reason America entered the war; however, two years passed before the U.S. formally engaged in battle.

In July, 1915, a German professor exploded a bomb in the U.S. Senate and then shot J.P. Morgan, further aggravating anti-German sentiments. Furthermore, in July, Secret Service agents found papers revealing a German spy ring with plans to subsidize **American films**. By August, partly in response to growing anger toward Germany, several private military camps opened in the U.S. to begin training troops.

 The human slaughter of the war was largely kept a secret from British civilians. They received reports, instead, that stated "All quiet on the Western Front."

25. **What was Woodrow Wilson's 1916 campaign motto?**

(A) "He kept us out of war."
(B) "He fights for liberty and justice."
(C) "He defended freedom of the seas."
(D) "He speaks softly and carries a big stick."

Wilson won the election of 1916 with the slogan **"He kept us out of war"** on the "Peace and Preparedness" platform. Shortly after his inauguration, Wilson went before Congress and called for a "league of peace" to assist in the resolution of international conflicts. From the outset of the war, he had urged peaceful settlement, declared American neutrality, and volunteered diplomacy. But he also built up troops and fostered alliances. Many business leaders who considered war good for the economy placed pressure on Wilson to fight.

Advocates of entry into the war were galvanized by the interception of the **Zimmermann telegram** in February 1917: a telegram from the German Foreign Ministry to the German Ambassador in Mexico offering to help Mexico recover Texas, New Mexico, and Arizona from the U.S. in exchange for Mexico's entering the war on the German side. Finally, on April 2, 1917, Wilson asked Congress to declare war on Germany, citing continued German naval aggression as just cause. He was greeted with hearty applause. On December 7, 1917, claiming protection of free seas and democracy, Wilson declared war on Austro-Hungary, and the United States joined forces with **the Allies**—France, England, and Russia.

> " *My message [to Congress] today was a message of death for our young men. How strange it seems to applaud that.*
>
> ——PRESIDENT WOODROW WILSON
>
> "

26. What was one result of the 1917 Espionage Act?

(A) Spying in the U.S. ended.
(B) All Germans were put under house arrest.
(C) The act was used to silence dissenters of the war.
(D) The Rosenbergs were executed.

To divert British attention away from the war in Europe, Germans supported the Easter Uprising in Ireland by providing ammunition and other assistance to the Irish leadership.

In May 1917, Congress passed the **Selective Service Act**, authorizing a draft of men aged twenty-one to thirty to ensure a continuous supply of troops. In June, Congress acted again with the passage of the **Espionage Act**. The act was also used for silencing war critics, among them socialist Eugene Debs (p. 191), who was arrested and imprisoned for ten years for delivering a speech the government claimed "obstructed recruiting." The government also instituted a massive public information campaign, training 750,000 "four-minute men" who delivered thousands of propaganda speeches to arouse hatred toward Germany and sympathy for the Allies.

Where's the pipe, Mac?

With the U.S. officially at war, Wilson still actively pursued peace. He went before Congress in January 1918 to present his **Fourteen Points**, which called for an international association of nations (what would later become the **League of Nations**) to establish mutual guarantees of peace and freedom. His Fourteen Points received little support.

The Russian Revolution of 1917, meanwhile, was well under way. On March 15, 1917, the Tsar abdicated and the U.S. recognized Aleksandr Kerensky's government, which was then overthrown by the **Bolsheviks** in November. The new government allied itself with Germany. In August, 1918, American and Japanese forces invaded and occupied territory reaching into Siberia.

Senator George Norris, speaking against the war, argued that Wall Street wanted a war because it was good for profits. He said, "Their object in having war and in preparing for war is to make money. Human suffering and sacrifice of human life are necessary, but Wall Street considers only the dollars and cents . . ."

In Europe, the trench stalemate was coming to a close. Americans, led by **General John J. Pershing** (1860-1948) and **Colonel Douglas MacArthur** (1880-1964), arriving late to the war, were received as heroes in France. In September, 1918, the American **"Doughboys"** participated in the final Allied offensive, forcing Germany to retreat past the **Hindenburg Line**, a line of fortifications built in 1916-1917. Within a month of the offensive, Germans formed a parliamentary government and the Kaiser abdicated. By the end of October, Austria surrendered. In 1918, on the eleventh hour of the eleventh day of the eleventh month, fighting ended. Germany signed an armistice treaty.

27. **What did the Treaty of Versailles require of Germany?**

(A) Payment of $32 billion in reparations
(B) Admission of guilt
(C) Return the Alsace-Lorraine region to France
(D) All of the above

Wilson's Fourteen Points provided a template for the **Treaty of Versailles**, signed by all parties on June 28, 1919, exactly five years after the assassination of Archduke Ferdinand. The treaty stipulated many harsh conditions for Germany, which shouldered most of the blame for the war and its devastation. The Allies required that Germany pay reparations of more than $32 billion, surrender its overseas colonies, return Alsace-Lorraine to France, and severely restrict its rearmament. The Allies also redrew the global map. Austria became a sliver of its former self. Turkey, a small and impoverished state, was all that remained of the Ottoman empire. Yugoslavia, Czechoslovakia, Poland, the Baltic states, and other Eastern European countries became independent entities. The Allies divvied up territories in Africa, and Britain took control of much of the Middle East, including Palestine.

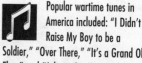

Popular wartime tunes in America included: "I Didn't Raise My Boy to be a Soldier," "Over There," "It's a Grand Old Flag," and "Johnny Get Your Gun."

In Our Time (1925), by Ernest Hemingway. This collection of short stories marks the debut of a fine writer and discusses the period of war in the United States. Difficult moral issues are conveyed in simple, straightforward prose.

Representatives of the Western powers at the Versailles Peace Conference, 1919

CULTURESCOPE

MAJOR PLAYERS IN WORLD WAR I

	Reason for Getting in War	Reaction to Treaty of Versailles	Total Combat Casualties
Central Powers			
Germany	Because Russia declared war on Austria	Pissed (lost 13 percent of its land)	1,800,000
Austria-Hungary	Invaded Serbia to get the ball rolling	No official reaction (ceased to be a nation)	1,200,000
Ottoman Empire	In cahoots with Germany	Ditto	325,000
Allied Powers			
France	Germans declared war against them first	Giddy (reacquired Alsace-Lorraine region)	1,357,000
England	Had a treaty with France	Pleased as punch (picked up most of the Middle East)	908,000
Russia	To defend Serbia from Austria-Hungary	Didn't care (quit war in 1917 after Bolshevik Revolution)	1,700,000
Italy	Had to pick a side	Displeased (left out of most of the spoils)	149,496
United States	Mad at Germany	Clammy (sick of bickering Europeans and glad to be done)	130,174

The treaty also established the League of Nations (p. 415). However, because Wilson left the Republican-dominated Senate out of treaty negotiations, they refused to ratify it, meaning the U.S. would not become an official member. Without American support, the League was ultimately doomed.

28. **What were Mussolini's paramilitary troops called?**
    - (A) The Mafia
    - (B) The Blackshirts
    - (C) Rain of Terror
    - (D) The Communards

A few years after World War I, **Benito Mussolini** (1883-1945), also called *Il Duce* (the leader), established a fascist (p. 415) regime in Italy, focused on military development, economic revival, and imposition of order. Mussolini blamed post-war ruin on foreigners and promised Italian revitalization. Under his leadership, the nationalistic **Blackshirts**, a paramilitary group, suppressed leftist movements considered a threat to the order of the state. Mussolini led his country into a series of military exploits in Africa and supported Spanish **General Francisco Franco's** (1892-1975) rebels.

In Germany, **Adolf Hitler** (1889-1945) rose to power on a platform of blame. He claimed that Jews, Marxists, and foreigners were collectively responsible for Germany's economic depression and the political embarrassment of World War I. His party, the **National Socialist (Nazi) party**, gained enough seats in the German parliament, the **Reichstag**, to appoint Hitler Chancellor in 1933. Soon afterward, Hitler seized total power and boldly announced the reunification of German-speaking people, previously separated by the revised map of 1918. Pledging to rebuild Germany, he commenced a massive military build-up. At this point, Hitler's racist rhetoric was put into action, as he began to formulate his so-called **"final solution"** to "the Jewish question." Germans began systematically murdering "enemies of the state," including Jews, homosexuals, and Gypsies. The Holocaust, resulted in the deaths of six million Jews, along with ten million others. Victims were starved, tortured, worked to death, shot, or herded into gas chambers for mass executions at euphemistically named **concentration camps** such as **Auschwitz**, **Dachau**, and **Treblinka**.

Claiming that Germans needed *Lebensraum* (living space), Germany annexed Austria in March 1938. Hitler then demanded the immediate return of the **Sudetenland** region of Czechoslovakia. Britain and France consented to his request at the **Munich Conference** in order to secure "peace in our time." By 1939, Hitler had consumed all of Czechoslovakia. With Poland as his next target, Hitler entered into the **German-Soviet non-aggression pact**, ensuring support from the eastern side of Poland. France and Britain could no longer look the other way. They declared war on Germany on September 3, 1939.

The German military successfully initiated a *blitzkrieg*, a lightning war, swiftly moving through Denmark, Belgium, Norway, the Netherlands, and France. With France defeated, the German **Luftwaffe** began bombing Britain. The charismatic new Prime Minister, **Winston Churchill** (1874-1965), rallied the British to stage a valiant resistance.

Japan also witnessed the rise of a fascist leader, **Emperor Hirohito** (1901-1989), who, like Mussolini and Hitler, intended to claim military and political power for his country. In 1931, Japan invaded China and, in July 1937, conquered Peking. Shortly

 Schindler's List (1993), directed by Steven Spielberg and starring Liam Neeson. This is a polished and haunting look at a Catholic Pole who saved the lives of a thousand Polish Jews by putting them to work in his factory. In the smooth hands of Spielberg, the film's black-and-white quasi-documentary look is surprisingly innovative and riveting.

 The Diary of Anne Frank (1945), by Anne Frank. The diary of this intelligent, fiercely honest, talented young writer facing adolescence in hiding from the Nazis during the Holocaust has just been reissued. Originally cut by her father before publication, several sections of the diary that deal with her awakening sexuality and family tensions have been restored.

Emperor Hirohito makes Eagle scout.

afterward, Japanese forces swept into Shanghai. The League of Nations condemned Japan, which promptly withdrew its membership.

29. **What was the Japanese code name for the attack on Pearl Harbor?**

    (A) D-Day
    (B) Tsunami
    (C) Zero Hour
    (D) Infamy

Until the end of 1940, Americans attempted to maintain an isolationist position. **Franklin D. Roosevelt** (1882-1945) enacted the **Lend-Lease Bill** and other initiatives intended to provide direct military support to the Allies, but America maintained a reluctance to enter a foreign war similar to its reticence in entering World War I. All of that changed, however, when the Japanese attacked Pearl Harbor.

Some argue that Roosevelt, preoccupied with the war in Europe, failed to pay adequate attention to Japanese intention or ability. If he anticipated a Japanese attack, he didn't expect it at Pearl Harbor, and he didn't find their threats sufficient to warrant additional protection in the Pacific. Others suggest that Roosevelt was seeking a way into the war and, anticipating a Japanese assault, viewed it as just the propellant needed. Some Americans did, in fact, know of the Japanese **"Zero Hour,"** the code name for the attack on Pearl Harbor on **December 7, 1941**. The Japanese sank eighteen ships, including eight

The destruction at Pearl Harbor

battleships, killing 2,400 people and destroying nearly 200 planes.

On December 8, Roosevelt went before Congress to deliver his war message: "Yesterday, December 7, 1941—a date which will live in infamy—the United States of America was suddenly and deliberately

Congress passed the declaration of war by a vote of 388-1. The lone dissenter, **Jeanette Rankin** (1880-1973) of Montana, was the first woman elected to the House of Representatives.

American racism distorted thinking about Japanese military intentions and abilities. Many American strategists dismissed Japanese air force capability, presuming Japanese pilots nearsighted.

With the Lend-Lease Bill, Roosevelt assumed unprecedented power to assist any country in its military defense, as deemed necessary to defend the U.S. America could now legally "lend" military equipment to the allies that would be returned "in kind" after the war. Critics compared this deal to lending chewing gum—you wouldn't want it back afterward.

attacked by naval and air forces of the Empire of Japan . . . . Yesterday, the Japanese Government also launched an attack against Malay. Last night, Japanese forces attacked Hong Kong. Last night, Japanese forces attacked Guam. Last night . . . ."

30. **Which act made it illegal to advocate the violent overthrow of the U.S. Government?**

   (A) The Neutrality Act
   (B) The Homestead Act
   (C) The Alien Registration Act
   (D) The Oppenheimer Act

While war raged in Europe, Americans shifted from a position of isolationism to one of preparation. In October 1939, Roosevelt approved a secret mission to develop an atomic bomb (p. 374). In November, he signed the **Neutrality Act**, which allowed America to send aid to Britain and France. By mid-1940, the **Smith Act**, also called the **Alien Registration Act**, required all non-American citizens to register with the government. This act also made it illegal to advocate the overthrow of the government.

In an ugly extension of fear of the enemy, the U.S. forced 120,000 Japanese-Americans into internment camps (p. 195) located along the West Coast. Many of those interned lost their homes and possessions.

Rosie the Riveter is an icon for women who took jobs during World War II.

"Rosie the Riveter" represented women who took labor-intensive jobs, such as truck driving and riveting, during the war. She contradicted notions that women, previously relegated to typing and light work, were weak. Gains made for gender equality during the war were short-lived; when men returned from combat duty, women relinquished their jobs.

In June 1942, the U.S. established two new agencies, the Office of War Information, a propaganda machine employing numerous writers and film makers, and the Office of Strategic Services, the precursor to the Central Intelligence Agency.

At the end of 1940, Roosevelt told the country it would become an "arsenal of democracy," converting factories to war production mode. When the U.S. formally entered the war, its production capabilities went into overdrive. Factories poured forth equipment. This mobilization produced more than $47 billion worth of war materials. America simply outproduced the enemy.

At home, the government imposed rationing, sold war bonds, and instituted a draft. Requiring "all hands on deck," Roosevelt issued an executive order declaring it illegal for government contractors to discriminate based on race.

31. Where did the Bataan death march take place?

(A) Iwo Jima
(B) The Philippines
(C) Thailand
(D) India

The Bridge On the River Kwai (1957), starring William Holden. British soldiers are held in a Japanese prison camp and forced to build a bridge. The film won seven Oscars.

Japanese **Kamikaze** ("divine wind") pilots flew suicide missions on which they would load their planes with ammunition and explosives, and fly directly into their targets.

In January 1942, holding more than 10 percent of the Earth's surface with territories extending throughout the Pacific region, the Japanese attacked the Philippines. General MacArthur led the American defense of the American colony. Intensive fighting, coupled with shortages of supplies and soldiers, crippled the American effort. Still, Americans and Filipinos held out for more than a year against the Japanese. When the Americans surrendered, Japanese leaders forced survivors to march more than 100 miles through the jungle in what came to be known as the **Bataan death march**. Nearly 10,000 soldiers died during the march due to harsh conditions and Japanese brutality. MacArthur, who had been removed from the islands by Roosevelt, returned on October 20, 1944, to lead a fierce and victorious retaliation.

Throughout the Pacific, the Allies, led by American troops, conducted a military strategy of "island hopping." They moved from one island to another, fighting the Japanese until they secured each island. Famous battles occurred at **Iwo Jima**, **Midway**, and **Okinawa**.

Bataan death march

32. What did Hitler do on June 22, 1941?

(A) He committed suicide.
(B) He invaded the Soviet Union.
(C) He made peace with England.
(D) He met with Churchill, Roosevelt, and de Gaulle.

Hitler made a grievous military error when he invaded the Soviet Union in June, 1941. He not only violated the non-aggression pact, making an enemy of the USSR, but he also involved his troops in an extended battle that lasted into a long and difficult winter. Germany was now fighting a **two-front war**.

33. Where did Germans think the Allies would land on D-Day?

(A) Paris
(B) Calais
(C) Normandy
(D) Dover

On June 6, 1944, Allied forces commenced the largest and most powerful invasion in history, landing on the shores of **Normandy** and aiming to recapture Europe from Germany. The invasion, a stroke of military genius called **Operation Overload**, duped the Germans, who thought the attack would take place at Calais. The night before the actual attack, paratroopers dropped into France to cut off German supply lines. An **amphibious** force followed to construct artificial pontoon harbors for the landing. The following day, Allied forces landed 15,000 troops; within a month, their numbers were more than one million.

During the war, Americans used the Navajo language as a military code.

For the next year, the Allies fought against the German and Italian armies, eventually sweeping upward from Sicily and eastward from

I want to ride my bicycle!

The Longest Day (1962), starring John Wayne. The Allied invasion of Normandy is the topic of this epic packed with international stars. The film won two Oscars (for cinematography and special effects).

Normandy. The Allies liberated Paris on August 25, 1944, and **Charles de Gaulle** (1890-1970), the leader of free France, returned to the city. By early 1945, Germans were retreating back into Germany, and the Allies began fierce firebombing campaigns, wiping out cities and civilian populations. Nearly 100,000 Germans died in Dresden alone. In April, when Berlin came under heavy assault, Hitler committed suicide. Germany formally surrendered on May 7. The war in Europe ended on **V-E Day**, May 8, 1945.

In the course of eight years of warfare, more than thirty-eight million people had been killed.

34. What was the name of the plane that dropped the atomic bomb on Hiroshima?

(A) The Lindy Hop
(B) The Enola Gay
(C) The Jefferson Airplane
(D) The American Spirit

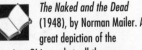

The Naked and the Dead (1948), by Norman Mailer. A great depiction of the American GI in combat, all-the-more-impressive because future Pulitzer-Prize winner Mailer was only twenty-five when he completed this book, his first published novel.

On August 6, 1945, the *Enola Gay*, a B-29 bomber, dropped the first atomic bomb on **Hiroshima**, Japan. Three days later, Americans dropped another atomic bomb, this one made from plutonium rather than uranium, on **Nagasaki**. Both cities were utterly devastated with over 150,000 casualties. Death rates continued to grow as people died from radiation poisoning. These assaults on Japan concluded the deadliest war on record.

Since those fateful attacks, many have argued about Truman's rationale for dropping the bombs. On the one hand, Truman, having recently

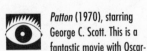

Patton (1970), starring George C. Scott. This is a fantastic movie with Oscar-winner Scott effectively portraying Patton's powderkeg temperment.

The Enola Gay lands after its fateful flight.

replaced Roosevelt, believed that the bombs would bring a rapid end to the war, thus saving thousands of American lives that would be lost in an invasion of Japan. On the other hand, it appears that the Japanese were ready to surrender because the Soviets would also soon be fighting against them. Some argue that the bombs were dropped as a show of force to the world, and particularly to **Joseph Stalin** (1879-1953). Truman suspected that Stalin planned to create a buffer of socialist states in Eastern Europe, and Truman may have wanted to flex military muscle.

 The atomic bombs dropped in Japan used **fission**; new bombs use **fusion (p. 381)**, which is much more powerful. The use of the bomb, or rather the horrific display of its capabilities, shifted the notion of a weapon from a tool for killing to a tool for deterring killing.

35. **Who coined the term "Iron Curtain"?**
    (A) Stalin
    (B) Eisenhower
    (C) Churchill
    (D) Schwarzenegger

At the end of the Second World War, Stalin, Churchill, and Truman agreed to divide Germany into eastern and western halves. While the U.S. implemented the **Marshall Plan** to help rebuild Western Europe, the USSR took Eastern European into its "sphere of influence." Stalin, believing in worldwide socialism, broke his earlier promise to allow Eastern European countries to determine their own governments and forcibly instituted communist regimes throughout the regions bordering the USSR In 1946, Winston Churchill delivered a speech, saying "From Stettin in the Baltic to Trieste in the Adriatic an **iron curtain** has descended across the Continent." In 1961, the Berlin Wall became the curtain's literal symbol.

 Julius and Ethel Rosenberg, tried for spying and executed on June 19, 1953, may well have been communists and spies, but their case was unfairly handled by a judge in league with the prosecution and a list of prosecution witnesses who were themselves confessed spies. Albert Einstein, Jean-Paul Sartre (p. 568), and Pablo Picasso (p. 604) appealed to Truman on behalf of the Rosenbergs.

Meanwhile, the U.S. busily exerted its influence in Western Europe by way of the Marshall Plan, airlifting thousands of tons of goods into Berlin. To counteract the communist **Warsaw Pact**, the U.S. spearheaded the organization of **NATO** (North Atlantic Treaty Organization). The Cold War between the U.S. and the U.S.S.R.—the world's remaining superpowers after World War II—was well under way.

In response to a leftist uprising in Greece, Truman delivered a speech to Congress, arguing that the U.S. must "support free peoples who are resisting attempted subjugation by armed minorities or by outside pressures." (He then sent military advisors and armaments to support a right-wing dictatorship in Greece.) This notion became the **Truman Doctrine**, which essentially allowed the U.S. to act as another kind of "outside pressure." The theoretical basis for this doctrine was derived from George Kennan's concept of **containment**, meaning the U.S. would act to contain the spread of communism.

 From 1948-1954, Hollywood produced more than forty anti-communist films.

THE YALTA CONFERENCE

In February 1945, knowing the end of the war was at hand, Churchill, Stalin, and Roosevelt met in the Soviet Union to arrange postwar settlements. Roosevelt insisted on the development of a United Nations and a Soviet commitment to declare war on Japan. Land divisions were agreed upon, and Stalin promised to ensure the freedom of Eastern European countries.

Lenin with his ruthless successor Stalin

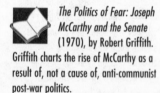

The Politics of Fear: Joseph McCarthy and the Senate (1970), by Robert Griffith. Griffith charts the rise of McCarthy as a result of, not a cause of, anti-communist post-war politics.

In the United States, the red scare (p. 194) quickly spread. The hysteria was based upon a fear that communists lurked everywhere and threatened American well-being. A pamphlet distributed by the U.S. government titled "One Hundred Things You Should Know About Communists" included this tidbit: "Where can Communists be found? Everywhere." Looming over this fear was a dark mushroom cloud. At any moment, communists might destroy Americans with the bomb. In a perverse extension of this fear, Senator Joseph McCarthy (p. 422) initiated a campaign in 1950 to identify and **blacklist** American communists. Many were called before the **House Un-American Activities Committee** to confront accusations and defend themselves.

The **Cold War** arose, in part, out of the economic boom that World War II brought to the U.S. Happy with the effects of war productivity, General Electric President Charles E. Wilson suggested the U.S. should have a "permanent war economy." **Dwight D. Eisenhower** (1890-1969) later called this relationship the **"military-industrial complex."** Without a war, how could the U.S. sustain economic growth and productivity? The Cold War provided just the situation.

36. **Which general was in charge of military operations in Korea?**

    (A) Dwight D. Eisenhower
    (B) Sun Myung Moon
    (C) Douglas MacArthur
    (D) Robert McNamara

During the **Potsdam Conference** at the end of World War II, the peninsula of **Korea**, then a Japanese possession, had been divided at the **38th parallel** into two separate nations. The North fell under the Soviet sphere of influence, the South under the American. On June 25, 1950, ninety thousand Soviet-trained North Korean troops invaded South Korea, intending to unite their divided country under a socialist government.

Within a week, Truman sent U.S. forces to fight alongside South Koreans. The U.S. never declared war; instead, this conflict was considered a **police action**.

The United Nations acted on a second resolution (the first being a cease-fire) to support South Korea, and they authorized the use of UN forces. Douglas MacArthur took control of the troops and Truman instituted a naval blockade. MacArthur led an amphibious assault far into North Korea at Inchon. Seoul was then quickly recaptured from the Northern forces. By September, the South, with the assistance of UN forces, pushed the North back to the 38th parallel, presumably completing their military task.

In a shift from containment to a complete overthrow of the communist government, UN forces invaded the North in October 1950. For several months, under the leadership of MacArthur, troops moved forcefully into North Korea and headed straight for China. They planned to return deposed Chinese Nationalist leader **Chiang Kai-shek** (1887-1975) to the mainland. The U.S. imposed an embargo on China and initiated an army build-up. Despite these moves, Truman attempted to negotiate peace and removed MacArthur for defying orders. The American public, viewing MacArthur as a hero, was outraged. However, Truman successfully shifted back to a containment policy in mid-1951. Throughout 1952, the battles of Heartbreak Ridge, Bloody Ridge, and Punchbowl reached bloody stalemates reminiscent of World War I. Truce talks continued.

An armistice was reached on July 27, 1953, and the line dividing North and South Korea remained at the **38th parallel**. More than fifty-four thousand Americans and nearly two million Koreans died during the war, but nothing effectively changed for Korea. Back home in America, however, the military-industrial complex continued to churn out armaments and other materials, and the economy kept thriving.

M.A.S.H. (1970), the movie and "M.A.S.H.," the TV series. The movie is a leaner and meaner look at the daily comings and goings of an American mobile hospital in Korea, but the TV show has Klinger in a dress. You decide.

Chiang Kai-Shek

37. Who assisted Fidel Castro in the Communist-backed takeover of Cuba in 1958?

(A) Fulgencio Batista
(B) Howard Hunt
(C) Che Guevara
(D) Sam Giancanna

Ernesto "Che" Guevara, an Argentine doctor turned revolutionary, fled Argentina in 1953 when the right-wing dictator Perón was in power. An orthodox Marxist, Che first went to Cuba to assist Castro, then went to the Congo to fight against white mercenaries. In 1965, he was assassinated in the Bolivian jungle while trying to raise a peasant resistance there.

Since the Spanish-American War, Cuba had been an economic territory of the U.S. American companies maintained almost total control of the island's cattle, sugar, mining, and oil wealth. Havana was a flashy American hot spot, filled with luxurious Mafia-controlled casinos and hotels. In 1958, **Fidel Castro** (1927-) and **Che Guevara** (1928-1967) swept down from the mountains and sent the American-backed dictator **Fulgencio Batista** (1901-1973) into exile. Castro established an iron-fisted socialist regime backed by the U.S.S.R., and Cuba suddenly became an archenemy of the U.S.

In 1962, **Allen Dulles** (1893-1961) and his colleagues at the **Central Intelligence Agency** devised a plot to assassinate Castro and reclaim the island in the name of democracy. Dulles concocted a plan to train and arm a troop of Cuban exiles that would be deployed at the Bay of Pigs to rendezvous with CIA-planted insurgents. The invasion was a disaster. The invaders and insurgents were captured, later to be ramsomed by the U.S. for $53 million in money and medicine. Attempting to hide its involvement, the U.S. never even formally acknowledged the deaths of four American fliers. Soviet leader **Nikita Khruschev** (1894-1971), having witnessed this debacle, began shipping weapons to Cuba and building offensive installations.

In October, 1962, after American spy planes photographed evidence of Soviet missiles in Cuba, President **John F. Kennedy** (1917-1963) demanded that the missiles be dismantled and returned to the U.S.S.R. He also instituted a naval blockade of Cuba and prepared for a full-scale invasion of the island. The ensuing stand-off brought the superpowers to

Cold warrior Nikita Kruschchev

the brink of all-out war. Finally, on October 28, **Radio Moscow** announced that the missiles would be sent back to the Soviet Union. Kennedy had recovered from the embarrassment of the Bay of Pigs and proved to the world he was willing to fight the spread of communism.

Dr. Strangelove (1964), directed by Stanley Kubrick. This is a funny and bizarre depiction of the sense of paranoia resulting from the Cold War.

38. **Which country was a colonialist power in Vietnam before U.S. military involvement?**

    (A) England
    (B) France
    (C) Spain
    (D) Japan

In the 1950s, after the French withdrew from **Indochina** (the collective name for **Cambodia**, **Laos**, and **Vietnam**), Vietnam split into two warring factions. Seeking both to stop the spread of communism and to gain access to Vietnamese resources, the U.S. sent arms, money, military advisors, and other support to the anti-communist South Vietnamese government in **Saigon**. In 1963, the CIA began sending trained guerrillas into North Vietnam on sabotage missions. To support these missions, the U.S. stationed American ships in the **Gulf of Tonkin**, located within Vietnamese waters. In August 1964, the U.S. *Maddox* and *Turner Joy*, fired upon Vietnamese patrol boats without being fired upon themselves. **President Lyndon Johnson** (1908-1973), setting aside his own doubts about the situation and wanting to appear hawkish during the 1964 campaign, ordered air raids over North Vietnam. He requested the passage of the **Gulf of Tonkin Resolution**, which granted him the ability to "take all necessary measures" to repel attacks against the U.S. With this resolution, Congress effectively turned its power to declare war over to the President. Near the war's end, in November 1973, Congress passed the **War Powers Act** that, in turn, restricted Presidential ability to use U.S. troops overseas without Congressional approval.

I believe that history will record that we have made a great mistake in subverting and circumventing the Constitution.

——SENATOR WAYNE MORSE, SPEAKING OF THE GULF OF TONKIN RESOLUTION

Platoon (1986), directed by Oliver Stone and *Full Metal Jacket* (1987), directed by Stanley Kubrick. *Platoon* won an Oscar, and is horrifying. *Full Metal Jacket* didn't win an Oscar, and is also horrifying.

39. What did President Johnson call U.S. troop involvement in Vietnam?

(A) A police action
(B) A secret war
(C) American intervention
(D) An anti-communist mission

President Johnson proceeded to involve the U.S. in a full-scale war, but referred to American involvement as a **police action**. In March 1965, the first two battalions of U.S. Marines arrived in Danang; by the year's end, more than 200,000 troops were in Vietnam. The total number of Americans who served in Vietnam reached one million by 1975.

While peace negotiations between North Vietnam and South Vietnam and its allies (Australia, New Zealand, Thailand, the Philippines, and the U.S.) commenced, fighting continued through 1966-1967. Americans found themselves at war against a guerrilla force willing to die in great numbers to preserve, even unify, their country. Like the British during the Revolutionary War, Americans had to ship troops and supplies over a great distance and fight on unfamiliar terrain.

In early 1968, **Lieutenant General William Westmoreland** (1914-), commander-in-charge of operations, decided to attack the **Ho Chi Minh Trail**, aiming to destroy the North's supply route. This massive four-month siege was televised nightly into thousands of American living rooms, greatly affecting public perception of the war: for the first time in history, the horrors of battle became a graphic reality to the average person back home.

"Fortunate Son," by Creedance Clearwater Revival, *"Volunteers,"* by Jefferson Airplane, and *"Fixin' to Die Rag,"* by Country Joe McDonald. Three great anti-war tunes by three great hippie bands.

40. Who resigned shortly after the Tet Offensive?

(A) Richard Nixon
(B) Lyndon Johnson
(C) Robert McNamara
(D) Le Duc Tho

In late January 1968, there was a brief respite from battle to celebrate the Vietnamese New Year, called Tet. In a surprise move, the North launched a massive offensive throughout the South. The **Tet Offensive** was a literal and symbolic defeat for the South and the United States. Unable to tolerate governmental policy and certain that the U.S. was fighting a losing battle, **Defense Secretary Robert McNamara** (1916-) resigned. Later that year, Johnson announced a halt to air bombing and renewed peace talks in Paris.

Television allowed Americans to witness the war nightly. Reporters regularly delivered up the "day's count," of how many Americans were wounded or killed in battle that day. These same-day accounts helped stir anti-war sentiment.

When **Richard Nixon** (1913-1994) became president in 1969, he ordered that secret bombings in Cambodia resume. Nixon simultaneously announced his "Vietnamization" plan, which entailed turning the war over to the South. Fighting abated throughout 1970-1971 and American casualty rates declined. Yet, in 1972, fighting erupted again when the North launched a major offensive in the demilitarized zone. Americans stepped up bombing until the North agreed to both a cease-fire and a commitment to peace negotiations.

In January, 1973, National Security Advisor **Henry Kissinger** (1923-) negotiated a cease-fire agreement with North leader **Le Duc Tho** (1911-1990). On March 29,1973, the last American troops evacuated Vietnam; prisoners of war—**POWs**—held in Hanoi were released on April 1. A Senate investigation disclosed the secret bombing campaign in Cambodia, which then ceased on August 14.

Although the war seemed to be over, in a furious six-month offensive at the beginning of 1975, North Vietnamese troops swept into the South and Cambodia. President **Gerald Ford** (1913-) called the war finished and arranged for the remaining Americans in Vietnam to be airlifted out of Saigon on April 29, 1975. The U.S. had lost the war. Vietnam united under a communist government. More than 55,000 American troops died in Vietnam. Between two and three million Vietnamese died in the war.

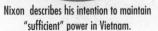

Nixon describes his intention to maintain "sufficient" power in Vietnam.

THE MY LAI MASSACRE

*In March, 1968, Charlie Company was sent into My Lai, a Vietnamese village suspected of being a **Vietcong** stronghold, to "clean the village out." Under the leadership of Lieutenant **William L. Calley**, they didn't find enemy personnel. Instead, . they massacred 560 Vietnamese, including women and children. This provided further proof that the war was unjust and that the U.S. presence in Vietnam was as destructive, if not more so, than a communist takeover.*

 To spot the enemy more easily, the U.S. began using chemical defoliants, particularly Agent Orange, to destroy plant cover. This chemical, while not considered a chemical weapon, inflicted severe damage to both Vietnamese and Americans soldiers.

41. In what city did massive demonstrations against the Vietnam War take place during the Democratic convention of 1968?

(A) San Francisco
(B) New York
(C) Washington, D.C.
(D) Chicago

 During the Vietnam war, America dropped seven million tons of bombs—more explosive power than was dropped on Europe and Asia during World War II—on a country the size of Massachusetts.

 The Deer Hunter (1978), starring Robert De Niro and Meryl Streep. This is an arresting film that looks at the lives of some steel workers and their families before, during, and after the Vietnam War.

 In 1995, after twenty-seven years of silence, former Defense Secretary Robert McNamara publicly admitted that the Vietnam War was morally unjust and a military disaster. He did not, however, apologize for his role.

Throughout the course of American involvement in Vietnam, anti-war demonstrations and draft protests occurred on college campuses and in major cities. The first march on Washington, organized by **Students for a Democratic Society** (SDS), took place on April 15, 1965. At the start of the **1968 Democratic Convention** in Chicago, thousands of demonstrators converged on the city in protest of President Johnson's policies (despite the fact that Johnson wasn't running for a second term). As a result of these protests, eight key leaders, including **Abbie Hoffman** (1936-1989), were arrested, and tried for conspiring to incite riots in a trial that turned into a courtroom circus. (Bobby Seale, a Black Panther, [p. 200] was tried separately.) In 1970, nervous National Guardsmen opened fire and killed four students during anti-war protests at **Kent State University** in Ohio. This riveting event catapulted anti-war sentiment to an all-time high. The anti-war movement was no longer limited to college campuses and localized groups.

Kent State

Raging against the injustices of the war (as well as to save their own skins—remember, the draft was still effective), protesters from all walks of life placed tremendous pressure upon the government to get out of Vietnam. Their actions led directly to changes in U.S. policy in Vietnam and helped to end this "police action" that looked, smelled, and killed like a war.

42. What United States governmental organization has conducted numerous covert wars against developing countries during the last forty years?

(A) The FBI
(B) The CIA
(C) The IRS
(D) The FDA

Reagan snaps one off.

Throughout the 1980s, the United States, frequently operating through the CIA, intervened in the internal affairs of several countries, especially in Central America and the Caribbean, claiming to be protecting American interests and guarding against the spread of communism. Many of these countries were undergoing civil wars, and, as a rule, the U.S. intervened on the anti-communist side. In El Salvador, the U.S. provided arms and other military support to the government that was combatting leftist guerrillas. Meanwhile, in Nicaragua, the U.S. supported **Contra rebels** who fought against the Marxist **Sandinista** government which took control of the country in 1979. Worried about the Cuban influence in the tiny nation of **Grenada**, where an extremist group had overthrown a moderate Marxist government, the U.S. invaded that marginal country in 1983. Operation Urgent Fury eliminated the Grenadian resistance within three days. Eighteen Americans died in the conflict. According to President **Ronald Reagan** (1911-), the zealous invasion was necessary to save the lives of several American medical students.

In the 1980s, in addition to these anti-communist actions, the U.S. also acted militarily to preserve its political and economic interests. In 1989, the U.S. invaded **Panama** to remove **Manuel Noriega** (1940-), the president of the country and a suspected drug dealer, from power. Commanded by

A Vote for Ollie North is a Vote for . . .

In the summer of 1985, the Reagan administration agreed to trade arms for hostages in a deal with an Iranian arms trader. This deal led to further arms sales to free other American hostages in the Middle East and improve relations with Iran. Meanwhile, the Reagan administration was also shipping arms and providing military support to the Nicaraguan Contras. When Congress passed an amendment making such support illegal, the administration looked overseas to find money for the rebels. **Oliver North** *(1943-), along with CIA and Pentagon officials, created a system by which they would sell arms to Iranians and funnel the money to the Contras. The whole deal circumvented Congressional oversight. Congress, discovering this covert operation, commenced the* **Tower Commission**. *In the end, Oliver North was the only conspirator tried. He was convicted on felony charges of obstructing Congress, mutilating documents, and taking an illegal gratuity. Since the hearings were so widely televised, however, Congress decided to drop the charges on appeal, citing that it would be impossible to give him a fair trial. North later lost a close race for the U.S. Senate in 1994.*

General Maxwell Thurman, **Operation Just Cause** landed 12,000 troops in Panama City. After a three-week siege, U.S. authorities secured Noriega and transported him to the U.S. where he stood trial on drug charges.

More recently, the U.S. invaded Haiti to reinstate **Jean-Bertrand Aristide** (1953-), Haiti's first democratically elected leader, who had been in exile in the U.S. since his overthrow by military dictator General Raoul Cedras. This invasion marks the latest episode in a tense military relationship between the U.S. and Haiti.

43. What kind of government does Kuwait have?
  (A) A monarchy
  (B) A communist regime
  (C) A democracy
  (D) A military dictatorship

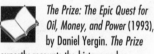

The Prize: The Epic Quest for Oil, Money, and Power (1993), by Daniel Yergin. *The Prize* expertly recounts the history and development of political and economic relations in the Middle East.

In 1990, **Saddam Hussein** (1937-) pushed his Iraqi troops into Kuwait in a land grab. By annexing Kuwait, Saddam controlled a substantial portion of the Middle East's oil supply. The international community, under the auspices of the UN, immediately deployed troops in Saudi Arabia. American General **Norman Schwarzkopf** (1934-) commanded the forces and initiated an unrelenting bombing raid. Saddam, however, did not back down. In February 1991, Americans implemented **Operation Desert Storm**, an all-out high-tech display of U.S. armaments. It was a rout. The U.S. claimed it got involved largely to preserve Kuwait's monarchy and national integrity, but it's more feasible that Americans actually intended to stop Saddam from controlling Kuwait's massive oil supply.

High-tech warfare or low-tech trash removal?

44. Which Soviet leader paved the way to the fall of the Berlin Wall and the Iron Curtain?

(A) Khrushchev
(B) Gorbachev
(C) Stalin
(D) Yeltsin

In the late 1980s, **Mikhail Gorbachev** (1931-) instituted a policy of *perestroika* (restructuring) in the Soviet Union. He implemented widespread economic reforms, moving the country from a communist to a capitalist system. In part, Gorbachev realized his country could no longer sustain the costly **arms race**. The United States had out-produced its enemy again. The Cold War was over, and relations between the U.S.S.R. and the U.S. quickly improved.

Perestroika resulted in the collapse of the Soviet Union, which dissolved into several smaller countries including **Russia, Belarus**, and Kazakhstan. In late 1989, East and West Germany reunited and pro-democracy demonstrators tore down the **Berlin Wall**, the icon of the Cold War. The **Eastern Bloc**, European coutries dominated and run by the Soviet Union, also began to dissolve. The domino-effect led to the dismantling of their communist regimes, which split along centuries-old tribal and communal lines in a process called **balkanization**, after the ethnic and political unrest that plagues the Balkan peninsula of Southeast Europe. Most of these countries experienced bloodless revolutions, with the major exception of Yugoslavia.

ANSWERS

1. B	2. B	3. A	4. B	5. B	6. B	7. A	8. B	9. C	10. C
11. B	12. D	13. B	14. A	15. C	16. C	17. C	18. D	19. D	20. B
21. B	22. B	23. B	24. B	25. A	26. C	27. D	28. B	29. C	30. C
31. B	32. B	33. B	34. B	35. C	36. C	37. C	38. B	39. A	40. C
41. D	42. B	43. A	44. B						

Index

Note: Italicized page numbers indicate main discussions.

Aaron, Hank, 444
Abdul-Jabbar, Kareem (Lewis Alcindor), *451*, 452
abnormal psychology, 244
abolition, 103, *181-182*, 409, 505
abortion rights, *201*, 428
Abraham, 486
absolute monarchs, 392
absolute sovereignty, 392
abstract art, 608
abstract expressionism, 613-615
Abu Bakr, 496-497
Academy Awards, 103
    "x"-rated films, *121-122*, 130
acceleration, 351
acid rain, *378-379*, 380
acids, in food, 369-370
Acropolis (Athens), 35
"action film" genre, 123
action painting, 613
activist government, 422
Actors' Studio (New York City), 557
actuarial tables, 344
ACT-UP, 203
AD (assistant director), 111
Adam, 493
Adams, Abigail, 187
Adams, John, 187, 405
Adams, John Quincy, 406
adaptive radiation, 150
Adderley, Cannonball, 313
Adler, Dankmar, 49
ADR (automatic dialogue replacement), 103
Adventists, 507
advertising
    radio, 516
    television, 531-532, 537
Aeschylus, 542
affective (mood) disorders, 244
Affirmative Action, 204
Africa
    colonialism in, 159
    slave trade and, 160, 178, 179
African Americans
    in baseball, 442, 444-445
    in basketball, 451-453
    "blacksploitation" films, 122-123
    in boxing, 461-462
    and civil rights movement, 196
    concentration of, 166-167
    education of, 186
    in feminist movement, 202
    films and, 103
    in football, 449

Jim Crow laws and, 102
literature of, 186, 254, 265-266, 271, 276-277, 282-283, 286-287
migration to cities, 316-317
minstrel shows, 564-565
music of, 307-317, 321-322, 324-325, 329-331, 504-505
race and, 210
religion of, 504-505
in the Senate, 183-185
See also slavery
African Methodist Episcopal Church, 505
Afro-Cuban jazz, 314
Age of Reason, 554-555
aging, 234-235
agon, 435
agoras, 36-37
agrarian societies, 70
Agricultural Adjustment Agency (AAA), 420
agriculture
    centers of, 163
    dependence on oil, 171
    origins of, 68-70
ahimsa (non-violence), 476
AIDS (acquired immune deficiency syndrome), 168, 203, *213*, 232
Alamo, 631
Alaska, 139
Alberti, Leon Batista, 41
alcohol, 241
    Prohibition and, 272, 309, *418*
Aldrin, Buzz, 338
Aleutians, 137
Alexander Nevsky (film), 104
Alexander the Great, 159
algebraic notation (chess), 464
Ali, Muhammad (Cassius Clay), 461
Alien Act, 405
Alien Registration Act (Smith Act), 651
Allah, 495
allegories, 249
allergies, 232
Allies
    World War I, *414-415*, 645-648
    World War II, 650-655, 652
Allison, Dorothy, 282
All That Jazz (film), 124
"Alphabet Soup," 420
alpha decay, 374
alpha particles, 374
Alps, 584
Alsace-Lorraine, 647
Altman, Robert, 121, 130
aluminum, 372
Alzheimer's disease, 234-235

Amazon forest, 146
amber, 207
American Anti-Slavery Society, 181-182
American Bowling Congress, 465
American Broadcasting Company (ABC), 519-521
American Federation of Labor, 190
American Football League, 447
American Indian Religious Freedom Act (1978), 500
American Renaissance, 263-265
American Revolution, 258, 401, 503, 593, *626-628*
    causes of, 78, 624
        Native Americans and, 175
American scene painting, 611
American Transcendentalism, 263-265
America Online, 349
"Amos 'n' Andy," 517
amphibious force, 653
Analects, 483
anal stage, 237
analytical cubism, 605
anarchism, 79, 193-194
anatta (soul) doctrine, 481
Andersen, Laurie, 575, *617-618*
Andes, 137
Andre the Giant, 390
anesthetics, 225, *227-229*
Anglo-Saxon (Old English), 249-250
animal rights activists, 67, 218-219
Animals, The, 326
animal testing, 218-219
animated musicals, 107
animism, 470
anorexia nervosa, 227
antacids, 370
Antarctica, 140-141
antennae, 514
Anthony, Susan B., 188
anthropic cosmological principle, 335
anti-art, 609
antibiotics, *212, 214, 215*
antibodies, 232
Antietam, Battle of, 636-637
Anti-Federalists (Democratic Republicans), 404-405
antigens, 232
antigravity, 338
antinovels, 279
antitrust laws
    film industry and, 107, *108-109*
    football and, 447
Antonioni, Michelangelo, 117
anxiety-based disorders (neuroses), 244
Apocalypse Now (film), *124-125*, 267
Apollo, 292
apostles, twelve, 488

Appalachia, *157-158*, 165, 318-319
Appomattox Courthouse, 639
aqueducts, 38
Aquinas, St. Thomas, 493-494
Arabian Peninsula, 137
Arahant, 498
Arawak Indians, 150, 173-174
Arbuckle, Fatty, 109
arcades, 36
archaeology, 373
arches, pointed, 39
Archimedes, 50
archipelago, 149
Arctic Ocean, 139
arete, 435-436
Ariosto, Ludovico, 251
Aristide, Jean-Bertrand, 664
aristocracy, 386
Aristophanes, 543
Aristotle, 141, 248, 364-365, *474*, 578
    on Atlantis, 156
    on politics, *386-387*, 395
Arjuna, 475-476
arms race, 665
Armstrong, Henry, 460
Armstrong, Louis "Satchmo," *309*
Armstrong, Neil, 338
Arnold, Matthew, 267
Arnolfini Wedding, The (painting; van Eyck), 582-583
Arrangement in Grey and Black: The Artist's Mother
    (painting; Whistler), 600
Artaud, Antonin, 574-575
art deco style, 59
arteries, 233
Arthur C. Nielsen, 526-227
Articles of Confederation, *401*, 402, 404, *626*
artificial insemination, 223
artillery warfare, 41, 643
Artist in his Studio, The (painting; Vermeer), 591
art nouveau movement, 53, 602
arts and crafts movement, 52-53
asceticism, 479
asexual reproduction, 223
ashcan school, 611
Asian Americans, literature of, 282
asides, 561
Asimov, Isaac, 283
aspirin, 215
assemblage, 614
assumptions, 345
Astaire, Fred, 107
asteroids, 206
AstroTurf, 443
Athena, 35

Beauregard, Pierre, 634
bebop, 280, *311-314*
Bechet, Sidney, 307
Beckett, Samuel, 569-570
Beckmann, Max, 607
Becquerel, Antoine Henri, 372
Beecher, Henry Ward, 508
Beethoven, Ludwig van, *301*
behaviorism (learning theory), 237-238
Behrens, Pieter, 56
Beijing, pollution in, 148
Belarus, 665
Belgium
    art of, 589
    colonies of, 158
Bell, Alexander Graham, 358
bell curve (normal distribution), 343
Bellini, Giovanni, 582
Bellow, Saul, 280
bends, 379
Bering Strait, 139-140
Berkeley, Governor, 622
Berle, Milton, 522
Berlin, Olympics (1936), 111, *437-438*, 440, 441
Berlin Wall, 60, 429, 655, *665*
Bernini, Gianlorenzo, 588
Bernstein, Carl, 426
Bernstein, Leonard, 305
Berry, Chuck, *323*, 325
best boy, 121
beta decay, 374
Betamax, 535
beta particles, 374
Bhagavad Gita (Song of the Blessed), 475-477
Bhakti Yoga, 477
Bible, 251
    creationism, *508-509*
    printing press and, *494*
Biblioteca Laurenziana (Laurentian Library, Florence), 41
bicycles, in Cuba, 150
biennials, art, 617
Bierstadt, Albert, 599
big bands, *309*, 331
Big Bang theory, *334-335*, 337
Big Foot, 641
Big Sleep, The (film), 125
big stick era, 412-413
Big Three (networks), 519-521
Bill Haley and the Comets, 323
billiards, 464
Bill Monroe and his Bluegrass Boys, 319
Bill of Rights, 402-403
Billy the Kid, 174-175
binary logic, 345

biological warfare, 624, 644
biomes, 146-147
bipeds, 208
Bird, Larry, 452
birth control, 189, 216
birth control movement, 189
Birthday Party, The (Pinter), 573
Birth of a Nation (film), 102-103
Birth of Venus (painting; Botticelli), 580-581
Bishop, Elizabeth, 274
bits, 354
Black, Clint, 321
Black American Christianity, 505
Black arts movement, 277
Blackbeard, 151
Black Codes, 184
black holes, 337
Black Iris (painting; O'Keeffe), 611
blackjack, 467
blacklists, 86-87, *114*, 656
Black Mountain Poets, 275
Black Muslims, 200
black nationalism, 200
Black Panthers, *200*, 330, 662
Black Power, *200*, 438
Blackshirts, 648
"blacksploitation" films, 122-123
Black Tuesday, 87-88
Blackwell, Elizabeth, 189
Blake, Eubie, 307
Blake, William, 259, 594
Der Blaue Reiter (The Blue Rider), 607
Bleeding Kansas, 409
blitzkrieg (lightning war), 649
blood donor programs, 196
blood types, 233
bluegrass music, 318-319
blues, 276, 307, 308, 311, 316
Blue Velvet (film), 125
Bogart, Humphrey, 125, 151
Bohr, Niels, 362
boiling, 366
Bolsheviks, 646
Bombay, 164
Bonds, Barry, 445
"Bone Key," 151
bones, connections to muscles, 224
Bonnie and Clyde (film), 125-126
Bonnin, Gertrude (Zitkala-Sa), 177
Bontemps, Arna, 276
boogie-woogie, 316
Book of Mormon, The, 506
Boone, Pat, 322
Bordeaux region, France, 166

Camera Work magazine, 612
Camp, Walter, 446
Campbells Soup (painting; Warhol), 615
Camp David accords, 153
Camus, Albert, 201
Canada
    largest province of, 162-163
    North American Free Trade Agreement (NAFTA), 95-96
    official game of, 432
cancer, 230-231
Cannes Film Festival, 117
cantilevered structures, 52
Cantonese, 154
capitalism, *79-82*, 397, 401
    assumptions of, 79-80
    laissez-faire, 81, 411
    markets in, 80-81
    Marx and, 84, 245
    movement toward, 81
    origins of, *79*
Capitals of columns, 35
Capitol, U.S., *46*, 630
Capone, Al, 107, *418*
Capra, Frank, 111
captivity narratives, 255-256
Caravaggio, Michelangelo Merisi da, 589
carbohydrates, 227
carbon cycle, 218
carbon dioxide, as "greenhouse" gas, 378
carbon-14 isotope, 364
carbonization, 207
card games, 467
Carlyle, Thomas, 78, 260
Carnegie, Andrew, 410
Carolingian Dynasty, 389
Carpetbaggers, 184
Carson, Pirie, Scott Building (Chicago), 50
Carter, Jimmy, 439, 509
Cartier-Bresson, Henri, 612-613
cartilage, 224
Cartwright, Alexander, 442
caryatids, 38
Casablanca (film), 126
Casa Milá (Barcelona), 53
Cash, Johnny, 320
Cash, June Carter, 320
casinos, 466-467
Cassatt, Mary, 598
castes, *477*, 479
Castiglione, Baldassare, 251
cast-iron architecture, 47-48
Castro, Fidel, *86-87*, 150, 424, *658*
catalysts, 372, 377

cathedrals, *39-40*, 53
Cather, Willa, 270
Catholic Legion of Decency, *108*, 110
Cat on a Hot Tin Roof (Williams), 571, 572
Cats, 306
CAT (computerized axial tomography) scan, 231
cattle, 164-165, 171, 378
CBGBs, 328
CBN (Christian Broadcasting Network), 509
CD-ROM, 284
cell membranes, 211
cells, 211
Cenozoic interval, 139, 206
censorship
    film industry, 109-110, 114-115
    film ratings in, 108, 121-122
    McCarthyism and, 114-115
Central Intelligence Agency (CIA), 658-659, 659, *663-664*
central nervous system, 229
central nervous systems, 224
Central Park (New York City), 54
Central Powers
    World War I, *414-415*
    World War I and, 643-648
ceramics, 368
Cervantes, Miguel de, 251
cestus, 434
Cézanne, Paul, 602-603
Chagall, Marc, 606
Chamberlain, Wilt, 451
chamber music, 297
Champagne region, France, 166
Chandler, Raymond, 113, 125, *278*
Chaplin, Charlie, *106*, 114, 116, 127, 130-131
chariot races, 436
charismatic theory of states, 384
Charlemagne (Charles the Great), 251, *389*
Charles, Ray, 317
Charles the Bald, 389
Charleston (dance), 417
Chartres Cathedral (France), 39-40
chaturanga, 463
Chaucer, Geoffrey, 250
Chavis, Boozoo, 331
Chechnya, 157
Checker, Chubby, 323
Cheever, John, 279
Chekhov, Anton, 556
chemical bonds, 365
Chernobyl nuclear disaster, 170
Cherokee Nation, 176-177
chess, 72, *463-464*
Chestnutt, Charles, 271
Chiang Kai-shek, 148, 657

Cochran, Eddie, 323
Code of Hammurabi, 228
cognition, 239
cognitive psychology, 239
"cold fusion," 381
Cold War, 422, 423, 429, 439, *656*
    Cuba and, 86-87, 150-151
    film industry and, 114-115
    McCarthyism, 114-115
Cole, Nat "King," 321
Cole, Thomas, 599
Coleman, Ornette, 313
Coleridge, Samuel Taylor, 259
collage technique, 605
collective bargaining, 192
Collins, Michael, 338
Colombia, 641
colonial America, 621-628
    American Revolution, *626-628*
    architecture of, 43-44
    nations involved in, 77
    Native Americans and, 621-624, 626
    religion in, *500-502*
    theater in, 552-553
colonialism
    in Africa, 158-159
    in America, 175
    of Spain, 77, 147, 175
colonnades, 36
color field paintings, 614
color television, 525
Colosseum (Rome), *37*, 38, *433-435*
Colossus (computer), 347
Coltrane, John, 313
Columbia Broadcasting System (CBS), 519-520
Columbus, 42
Columbus, Christopher, 77
    arrival in New World, 141, *173-174*
    circumference of Earth and, 141
    Cuba and, 150
columns, 35
combine paintings, 615
comedies, film, 107
comedy genre, 107
Committee to Re-elect the President (CREEP), 426
common, village, 44
communism, 79, *84, 401*
    containment policy, 422-423
    McCarthyism and, 114-115
    Red Scare, 656
compounds, 365
compression, 47-48
Compromise of 1850, *181*, 408

computers, *346-349*
    architecture and, 62-63
    chess and, 463, 464
    literature and, 284-285
    origins of, *347*, 374
Conan Doyle, Sir Arthur, 278
concave lenses and mirrors, 361
concentration camps, 649
concepts, 209
conceptual art, 615
concerto, 299
concrete, 38
concrete operational stage, 240
condensation, 366
conditioned response pairs, 237-238
conductors, *352*, 353
Confederate States of America, *409, 633*
Confucianism, *483-484*, 485
Confucius, 483-484
Congregationalists, 501
Congress, U.S., 154
    Emancipation Proclamation, 636-637
    gerrymandering and, 161
Congress of Industrial Organization (CIO), 190
Connolly, Maureen, 455-456
Conrad, Frank, 515-516
Conrad, Joseph, 267
Conscription Act (1863), 637
conservatism, 398-399
Conservative Judaism, 488
Constantinople, 546
Constitution, U.S., *402-404*
    Bill of Rights, 402-403
    Eighteenth Amendment, 418
    Equal Rights Amendment (ERA), 189, 201
    Fifteenth Amendment, 185
    Fourteenth Amendment, 185
    framers of, 401-402
    income taxes and, 92
    Nineteenth Amendment, 189
    separation of church and state, *501-502*, 503
    slavery and, 408-409
    Thirteenth Amendment, 182, 185
    Twenty-First amendment, 418
consuls, 387
consumers, 80
containment policy, *422-423*, 655
contemplation, 51, *482*
contemporaneous geological levels, 206
Continental Congress
    First, 624
    Second, 626
continental drift, 136-137

Davis, Miles, 300, *312-314*
Davis, Rebecca Harding, 268
Davis Cup, 455
Dawes Severalty Act (1887), 177-178
DDT, 216
Death in the Afternoon (Hemingway), 458-459
death of the author, 279
de Beauvoir, Simone, 201
Debs, Eugene V., 85, *191*, 646
decathlon, 440
Decatur, Stephen, 629
December 7, 1941 (Pearl Harbor), 650-651
Declaration of Independence, 394, *626*
    slavery and, 179, 182
    women's rights and, 188
"Declaration of Sentiments," 188
declarative knowledge, 239
deconstruction, 60, 61, 119, *279*
deficit spending, 91
Def Jam, 329-330
Defoe, Daniel, 256
de Forest, Lee, 515
deforestation, *143*, 147
Degas, Edgar, 596-597
de Gaulle, Charles, 654
de Kooning, Willem, 613
Delacroix, Eugène, 595
delta-blues, 315
deltas, river, 142
demand and supply, *66-68*, 518
demand curve, 67
dementia, 240
democracy, 386
Democratic National Committee, 426
Democratic Party, 427
Democratic party, *407*, 411, 662
Democratic Republicans (Anti-Federalists), *404-405*
Democritus, 364
Les Demoiselles d'Avignon (painting; Picasso), 605
Dempsey, Jack ("Manassa Mauler"), 460-461
Denishawn school, 566
density, 366
dentistry, 225
deoxyribonucleic acid (DNA), 220-222
Depo-Provera, 216
deposition, 366
depressions, worldwide, 415
Derrida, Jacques, 279
desertification, 142-143
designated hitters, 443
De Stijl movement (Holland), 56, *608*
detective fiction, 277-278
detective shows, 529
determination, cellular, 211

Deutscher Werkbund, 55-56
deviant behavior, 243-244
dharma (righteousness), 476
Diaghilev, Sergei, 558-559
dialectical concepts, 400-401
Diamond Way, the (*Vajrayana*), 481
diaspora, 487
Dickens, Charles, 260
Dickinson, Emily, *266*, *285-286*, 506, 567
Dickson, W. K. L., 98
Diddley, Bo, 323
Didriksen, Mildred "Babe," 440
diet
    acids and bases in, 369-370
    changes in, 171
    kosher, 486, *487*
    nutritional deficiencies in, *227*
digestive systems, 227
DiMaggio, Joe, 444
Dimucci, Dion, 323
dinosaurs
    extinction of, 206
    world geography in time of, 135-137
Dion DiMucci, 323
Dionysus, 542
dirges, 301
disco, 328
discrete variables, 343
diseases, 70, 169-170, *212-214*
dismal science, 78
Disney, Walt, 107
diverging lenses, 361
Divine Comedy (Dante), 594
divine right, *390*
divine theory of states, 384
division of labor, 52, *80*
DJ (disk jockey), 329
Doctorow, E. L., *279*, 419
Dr. Strangelove (film), 127
documentary fiction, 279
documentary films, 119-120
"domestic dependent nations," 176
domestic novels, 264
domestic violence, 201
Domino, Fats, 317, 321
Doña Maria Soledad (painting; Goya), 595
Donatello, 580
Don Fray Miguel (painting; Goya), 595
Donne, John, 252
Doors, The, 328
Doppler effect, 357
Doric order (Greek architecture), *35*, 37, 38
Dorsey Brothers, 310
Dostoyevsky, Fyodor, *262*, 490

emperor (Rome), 388
Empire State Building (New York City), 59
endothermic events, 370
energy
    conservation of, *351-352*
    nuclear, 170-171, 381, 655
    oil and gas reserves, 142, *144*, 207
    renewable resources and, 380-381
L'Enfant, Pierre Charles, 46-47
Engels, Friedrich, *84*, 398, 400-401
England
    American Revolution, *626-628*
    architecture of, 47, 48, 52-53, 58
    art of, 592-593
    in colonial America, 77
    literature of, 249-253, 256-258
    socialism in, 85
    theater in, 547-552
    War of 1812, 629-630
    World War I and, 643, 645
    World War II and, 651
English Park movement, 54
ENIAC (electronic numerical integrator and computer), *347*, 374
Enlightenment, 44, 258, *396-397*, 503, 592, 627
Enola Gay, 654
entablatures, 35
enthalpy, *370*
entropy, *335*, *352*, *370*
environmental art, 617
epic verse, 248
epistolary novels, 256
epithelial cells, 230
equality, *399-400*
Equal Rights Amendment (ERA), 189, 201
equations, 342
Erasmus, *251*, 584
Eratosthenes, 141
Erdrich, Louise, 282
Erving, Julius, "Dr. J," 452
Espionage Act (1917), 646
estates, feudal, *73*, 75
Estes, Richard, 616
ether, 228
Ethiopia, 137
    desertification, 143
ethos, 292
Etruscans, 36, *387*, 475
Eugenics, 194
euhemerism, 473
Euphrates River, 70
Euripides, *542-543*
European Union (European Economic Community), 95
Eurydice, 293

Evangelism, 509
Evans, Gil, 314
Eve, 493
evolution, *219-220*, 508
executive branch, *403*
exile, 501
existentialism, 201, *507-508*, 568-569
exothermic events, 370-371
expiration (breathing out), 225-226
exports, 623
expressionism, *607-608*
    in theater, 555-556
Eyck, Jan van, 582-583

Fabriano, Gentile da, 579
factories, American, first, 46
factors of production, *80*, 400
Factory, The (New York City), 615
Falling Water (Pennsylvania), 51, *52*
Falwell, Jerry, 510
family values, 542
fascism, *415-416*, *648-650*
fats, 227
Faubus, Orval E., 197
Faulkner, William, 125, 255, 272-273
faults, 138
fauvism, 603-604
Federal Bureau of Investigation (FBI), 198
Federal Communications Commission (FCC), 519, 525
Federal Deposit Insurance Corporation (FDIC), 420
Federal Emergency Relief Administration (FERA), 420
Federalist Papers, 404
Federalists, *404-407*, 630
Fellini, Federico, 117
Feminine Mystique, The (Friedan), 200-201
feminist movement, *200-202*, 271
Femme à la Mandoline (painting; Braque), 604
Ferlinghetti, Lawrence, 281
Fermat, Pierre de, 344, *345*
fêtes galantes (courtship parties), 591
fetishes, 471
fetus, 223
feudalism, *73-76*, 389-390
fiat, 71
FIDE, 463
fiefs, 73-74
field goals, 447
Fielding, Henry, 256
Fields, W. C., 107
"54-40 or fight!," 630
"Fight the Power," 330
Film Corporation, the, 103
film editing, 104
film noir, *113*, 133

Furness, Frank, 49
fusion, nuclear, 171, *381*, 655
fusion jazz, 313-314
Futurist Manifesto, 606
futurist movement, 55, *606-607*

GI Bill, 423
gabled roofs, 43
Gabriel's Rebellion, 182
gaffers, 115, *119*
Gagarin, Yuri, 338
Gainsborough, Thomas, 592-593
Galapagos islands, 149-150
Galileo, 336
Galvani, Luigi, 371
Galvanic coatings, 371
gambling, *465-468*
gambrel roofs, 51
game shows, 530
gamma rays, 364, 374
Gandhi, Mohandas Karamchand, 197, *476*
Gandil, Chick, 446
gangsta rap, 330
gangster films, 107
Garden of Eden, 395, *493*
Garland, Hamlin, 268
Garrison, William Lloyd, 181-182
Garvey, Marcus, 199
gases, 366
Gaskell, Elizabeth, 260-261
Gates of Heaven (film), 128
Gauguin, Paul, 600-601
Gautama, Siddartha (Buddha), 479-482
Gaye, Marvin, 324
Gay Men's Health Crisis, 203
gay rights movement, 203
Gehrig, Lou, 443-444
gems, 368
General, The (film), 128-129
General Agreement on Tariffs and Trade (GATT), 95
General Will (Rousseau), 395-396
genes, *220-221*
Genesis, Book of, *487*, 586
Genet, Jean, 569
genetic engineering, 222
genetics, *220-221*
Geneva, 153
genocide, *649*
    Holocaust, 487
genomes, 220-222, 346
Gentiles, 488-489
Gentileschi, Artemisia, 589
Gentileschi, Orazio, 589
geological intervals, 139, 206

geological record, 206
geometry, 340-342
George III, king of England, 179
Georgia, Cherokee Nation and, 176
geosynchronous orbit, 339
geothermal energy, 380
Géricault, Théodore, 594
Germanic tribes, 73, *389*
German-Soviet non-aggression pact, 649
Germany
    architecture of, 55-56
    art of, 583-584, 601-602, 607
    capitalism in, 81
    colonies of, 158
    films of, *110-111*, 441, 645, 646
    post-World War I, 88, 649
    theater in, 555, 567-568
    World War I and, 644-645, 647
    World War II and, 653-655
germ layers, 211
Gernsback, Hugo, 283
gerontology, 234-235
Gerry, Elbridge, 161
gerrymandering, 161
Gershwin, George, 305
Gettysburg, Battle of, 637
Gettysburg Address, 637-638
Getz, Stan, 313
geysers, 145
Ghent, Treaty of (1814), 630
Ghiberti, Lorenzo, 580
Ghost Dance, 499-500, 641
ghost shirts, 641
Gibson, Josh, 444
Gibson, William, 284
Gilberto, Joao, 331
Gillespie, John Birks "Dizzy," *311-312*, 313
Ginsberg, Allen, 281
Giotto di Bondone, 579
Giovanni, Nikki, 275
Gipp, George, 447
glaciers, 140-141
gladiatorial combat, 37, *433-435*, 543
glass, 366
Glass, Phillip, *304*
Glass Box aesthetic, 59
glass ceiling, 201-202
Glen Miller band, 310
global warming, 147, *377-378*
Glorious Revolution, *394*
Gnostic Gospels, 489
God, *395*
Godard, Jean-Luc, 116, *117*, 119
Godfather, The (film), *129*, 153

H. D. (Hilda Doolittle), 274
Hagen, Walter, 462-463
Haiti, *664*
    refugees from, 160
Hajj (pilgrimage to Mecca), 495
Halacha (rabbinic law), 488
Hale, Nathan, 627
Haley, Bill, 323
half-life, 364
hallucinogens, *241-242*
Hamilton, Alexander, 404
Hamlet (Shakespeare), 344
Hammerstein, Oscar, 305, 564-565
Hammett, Dashiell, 113, *278*
hammock hits, 521
handedness, 230
Handel, George Frederick, *298*
hand-held cameras, 117
Han Dynasty, 72-73
Hanson, Duane, 616
hard bop, 313
hard-core music, 329
Harding, Warren G., *416-417*, 516
hardware, computer, 346
Hardy, Thomas, 261
Haring, Keith, 616-617
Harlan, John Marshall, 185
Harlem Renaissance, *276-277*, 611
Harpers Ferry, Virginia, 183
harpsichords, 297
Harrison, William Henry, 407
Hasidism, 487
Haussman, Georges-Eugène, 47
Hawaii
    forests of, 147
    rain in, 142
Hawks, Howard, 107, 116, 125
Hawley-Smoot Tariff, *95*, 430
Hawthorne, Nathaniel, 263
Haydn, Franz Joseph, *300*
Hayes, Rutherford B., 639
Haymarket affair (1886), 193
Hays Office (Motion Picture Producers and Distributors of America), *109-110*, 113-115
HBO (Home Box Office), 535
Head Start program, *425*
Hearst, Patty, 255
Hearst, William Randolph, 641
heart, 233
    artificial, 235-236
    transplants, 236
heartburn, 369
heart-lung machines, 235
heat, *355-356*

heat capacity, 356
heaven, 34
Hebrew Bible, 477, *485-486*, 487
Hebrews, 384
Hecht, Anthony, 275
Hegel, G. W. F., *400-401*
Heisenberg uncertainty principle, *362*, 364
"He kept us out of war" (Wilson), 645
heliocentric (sun-centered) model, 336
Hellenistic period, 578
Hemingway, 458-459
Hemingway, Ernest, 151, 272, *286*
Hendrix, Jimi, 327, *328*
Henie, Sonja, 440-441
Henri, Robert, 611
hepatoscopy, 475
Herbert, Frank, 283
heresy, 220
heretics, *491*
Hesiod, 473
heterogeneous mixtures, 365
High Renaissance, 584-588
"highrise downtown," 54
Hillerman, Tony, 278
Himalayas, 137
Hinayana Buddhism, 479
Hindenburg Line, 644, 646
Hindu-Arabic number system, 72
Hinduism, 155, *476-478*
hip hop, 285, *329*
hipped roofs, 51
Hippodamos of Miletus, 36
Hirohito, Emperor of Japan, 649
Hiroshima, Japan, 654
Hitchcock, Alfred, 116, 131-132
Hitchcock, Henry-Russell, 57
Hitler, Adolf, 384, 416, *649*, 653
    film propaganda and, *110-111*, 441
HIV, *213*, 232
HMS Challenger, 379
Hobbes, Thomas, *393-394*
Ho Chi Minh Trail, 660
hockey, *453-454*
Hockney, David, 615
Hodinonhsioni ("people of the longhouse"), 620
Hoffa, Jimmy, 85
Hoffman, Abbie, 662
hogans, 43
hogs, 164-165
Holbein, Hans, 584
Hollander, John, 275
Holliday, Billy, 312
Holly, Buddy, 323, 324
Hollywood Ten, 114-115

Indus River, 375
industrial noise music, 329
Industrial Revolution, *81*, 87, 163, 398
    architecture and, 46, *47-48*
    coal in, 144
    second, 97
Indus Valley, 70
    as cultural hearth, 154-155
inertia, 350-351
infanticide, 167
inflation, causes of, 90-91
infomercials, 537
information-processing theory, 239
infrared (IR) radiation, 363
Ingres, Jean-Auguste-Dominique, 592
Inn-Danube River, 152
Inquisition, 336, *491*
insecticides, 216
inspiration (breathing in), 225-226
installation art, 617
insulators, *352*, 353
integrated circuits (ICs), 353
intelligence, 242-243
interaction, 239
interactive books, 284
International Gothic style, 579
International Ladies Garment Workers Union, 192
International Olympic Committee, *437*
International Style, *57*, 59, 60
Internet, *347-349*, 539
    architecture and, 62
"internment camps," 195
interstate commerce clause, 420
Intolerable Acts, 624
invisible hand, 80
in vitro fertilization, 223
involuntary process, 225
Ionesco, Eugène, *569*, 570
Ionic order (Greek architecture), *35*, 37, 38
IQ (intelligence quotient), 242-243, 342
Iran
    Cuba and, 151
    Islam in, 496-497
Iran-Contra affair, 526
Iran-contra affair, *663*
Ireland
    Great Britain and, 156
    potato famine, 214
Iron Age, *368-369*
Iron Bridge, The (England), 47
iron curtain, 655
iron lungs, 235
Iroquois Confederacy, 42, *619-620*
irrational numbers, 342

Irving, Washington, 263
Islam, 200, *495-497*
Islamic laws, 142
isotopes, 364
Israel, origins of, 71, *487*
Italy
    art of, 579-582, 585-587
    colonies of, 158
    film industry, 117
    post-World War I, 648
Iwo Jima, battle of, 652

Jackson, Andrew
    "Indian removal," *176*, 258, *631*
    as President, *406-407*
Jackson, Helen Hunt, 177
Jackson, Michael, 317
Jackson, "Shoeless" Joe, 446
Jackson, Thomas J., 635
Jacksonian Democracy, 406-407
Jacobi, Mary, 189
Jacobs, Harriet, 265-266
Jamaica, slavery and, 150
James, Etta, 317
James, Henry, 270-271
James, P. D., 278
Janácek, Leos, 304
Japan
    architecture of, 55
    continental drift and, 137
    economic position of, 429
    economy of, 82
    Hiroshima/Nagasaki, 654-655
    natural resources of, 143-144
    neomercantilist system of, 82
    post-World War I, 88, 649-650
    post-World War II, 82
    territorial expansion of, 159
    theater of, 545-546
    ukiyo-e art, 597
Japanese, "internment camps" of World War II, *195*, 651
Jarvik 7 heart, 235
Jay, John, 404
jazz, 276, *306-309*
    improvisation, 308, 311
Jazz Age, 87, 109, 272
Jefferson, Thomas, 266, 404
    in American Revolution, 629
    architecture and, 45-46
    as President, *405-406*
    slavery and, 179
Jefferson Airplane, *327*
Jeffersonian Democracy, 406
jen (essential goodness), 484

Krishna, 475-476
KRS One, 330
Krushchev, Nikita, 658
Kubrick, Stanley, 118, 133-134
Ku Klux Klan, 103, *184-185*, 417
Kundera, Milan, 279
Kurds, 156
Kuwait, 144, *664*
Kyogen, 545-546

L. L. Cool J, 330
labor, *80*
labor movement, 190-191
Labor party (Great Britain), 85
labor reform movement, 190-191
lacrosse, *432*, 466
laissez faire, 411
laissez-faire economics, *81*, 411
Lake Yellowstone, 145
La Mama Experimental Theater Club (New York City), 575
Lamarck, *219-220*
lambada, 331
LaMotta, Jake, 461
landed gentry, 83
landscape painting tradition, 54, 584
Lang, Fritz, 110, 116
languages
	in Canada, 162-163
	components of, *209*
	diversity of, 153-154
Laos, 148, *659*
Lao Tzu, 484, 485
lasers, 359
Last Judgment, The (painting; Michelangelo), 586
Last Supper, *492-493*
Las Vegas, gambling in, 467
Latifah, Queen, 330
latitude, 141
Laurasia, 136
law of conservation of energy, 351
Law of Demand, 66-67
law of diminishing marginal productivity, 78
Law of Supply, 66-67
law of universal gravitation (Newton), 336-337
Lawrence, D. H., 267
Lawrence, Florence, 106
Lawrence, Jacob, 611
League of Nations, *415*, 646, 648, 650
League of the Iroquois, 42, *619-620*
Leakey, Louis, 208
learning theory (behaviorism), 237-238
Leaves of Grass (Whitman), *266*, 289
Lebensraum (living space), 649
Lee, Robert E., 183, *632*

Lee, Spike, *123*, 184, 199
legislative branch, 403
Le Guin, Ursula K., 283
Lend-Lease Bill, 650
Lennon, John, *325*
Lenny (film), 129
lenses, *360-361*
Lescaze, William, 58
Letterman, David, 534-535
Lever House (New York City), 59
levers, 349
Levertov, Denise, 275
Levittowns, 55
Lewis, Carl, 224
Lewis, Jerry, 116
Lewis, Jerry Lee, *323*, 324
li (respect), 484
liberalism, *397-398*
Liberator, 181
Lichtenstein, Roy, 615
life, liberty, and property, rights to, 394-395
ligaments, 224
light, 359-362
limited sovereignty, 394
Lincoln, Abraham, *409*
	Civil War, 633-635, 637
	Gettysburg Address, 637-638
lines of scrimmage, 446-447
Linnaeus, Carolus, 216-217
lintels, 40
liquids, 366
Liston, Sonny, 461
literary criticism, 248
literary salons, 285
lithography, 597
Little Big Horn River, 640
Little Richard, *323*, 325
Little Rock Central High School, 197
Little Tramp, 127
Little Walter, *316*
livestock, 164-165, 171, 378
lobotomy, 240, 241
location settings, 117
Locke, John, *394-395*
Lodge, Henry Cabot, 641
logic, 345
Lombardi, Vince, 449
London, Jack, 269
longhouses, *42*, 620
longitude, 141
lords, feudal, 73-75
Los Angeles
	first permanent movie theater, 100
	Hollywood film industry
	San Andreas fault and, 138

mass (religious), 295, *492-493*
mass culture, 278
mass suicide, 510-511
Mather, Cotton, 254
Matisse, Henri, *603-604*
matter, 365
Matthew, gospel of, 490
Mayas, 34, 432
Mayflower, 501
Mays, Willie, 445
MC5, 328, 329
McCarthy, Joseph, 114-115, 203, *422-423*, 523, 656
McCarthy, Mary, 280
McCarthyism, 114-115, *422-423*, 656
McCartney, Paul, *325*
McClellan, George B.,, 635-636
McDaniel, Hattie, 103
McGovern, George, 426
MCI, 539
McKim, Charles Follen, *45, 47*
McKim, Mead, and White, *45, 47*
McKinley, William,, 641-642
McNamara, Robert, 660, 662
Mecca, 199, 494, 495
Medea, 542-543
Medicaid, 425
medical ethics, 219
medical shows, 529
Medicare, 425
Medici family, 581
meditation, 482-483, 498
Megalopolis, 168
meistersingers (minstrels), 296
Mèlies, Georges, 100
melting, 366
Melville, Herman, 264, *287*
Mendeleyev, Dmitri, 367
MENSA, 243
mercantilism, 75-77
merchant class, *70*, 74, 75
Mercury, 335
merengue, 331
Mesoamerica, 140
    architecture of, 34
    See also Native Americans; *specific tribes*
Mesopotamia, ancient, 340-341
    architecture of, 33-34
    as cultural hearth, 154-155
    demise of, 71
    first civilizations in, 70
Mesozoic interval, 139, 206
Messiah, 488-489
Metacom, 621
metals, 368

metaphysical poets, 252
method acting (the method), 556-557
Metropolis (film), 110
Mexican Revolution, 610
Mexico
    art of, 610-611
    illegal immigrants from, 196
    North American Free Trade Agreement (NAFTA), 95-96
    war with (1846-1848), 631-632
Mexico City
    Olympics of 1968, 438
    problems of, 168
Micheaux, Oscar, 103
Michelangelo Buonarotti, 40-41, *585-586*
microeconomics, 65
microscope, 211
microwaves, 363
Middle Ages, 390
    feudalism, 73-75
    literature of, 249-250
    music of, 294-296
    theater of, 544-545
middle class, origins of, 74
Middle English, 249
Middle Passage, 179
Middle Way principle, 479
Midnight Cowboy (film), 121-122, 130
Midway, battle of, 652
Midwest, U.S., 48
    architecture of, 49-52
    population of, *154*
migration, 159-160
Miletus (Greece), 36
"military-industrial complex," 656
Mill, John Stuart, *398*
Millennialists, 506-507
Miller, Arthur, 572
Miller, Henry, 280
Miller, William, 506-507
Milton, John, 253
mimetic art forms, 299
minerals, 227
Mingus, Charles, 197, *313*
minimum wage, 421
Ministry of International Trade and Industry (MITI; Japan), 82
Minoan civilization, 137, 156
minstrel shows, 564-565
minutemen ("Sons of Liberty"), 624-625
miracle plays, 544
Miro, Joan, 609
mirrors, 360-361
mise-en-scène, 115, 116

Nabokov, Vladimir, 279
Nagasaki, Japan, 654
Naismith, James, 450
Napoleon, 301, *413*, 630
Napoleon III, 47
narcotics, 241-242
"narrative" films, 100-101
"Nashville Sound," 319
National Association for the Advancement of Colored People (NAACP), 186
National Baptist Convention, 505
National Basketball Association (NBA), 451-452
National Broadcasting Company, The (NBC), 518-520
National Endowment for the Humanities (NEH), 425
National Football League, 447
National Hockey League (NHL), 453-454
National Industrial Recovery Act, 89
nationalism, 303, *393*, 437
National Labor Relations Act, 192
national media coverage, 453
National Negro League, *442*, 444
National Organization for Women (NOW), 201
national parks, U.S., 145-146
National Park Service, 145, 146
National Woman Suffrage Association (NWSA), 188
nations, *156*
nation-states, 75, 156
    origins of, *389*, *392-393*
Native American Church, 500
Native American Renaissance, 282
Native Americans
    after War of 1812, 631
    animism of, 470-471
    architecture of, 42-43
    arrival in North America, 139-140
    and captivity narratives, 255-256
    Christianity and, 499-500
    in civil rights movement, 204
    Columbus and, 174-175
    games of, *432-433*, 453, 466
    land ownership and, 175
    League of the Iroquois, 42, *619-620*
    mythology of, 282, 470
    oral literature of, 281-282
    pan-Indian movement, 177
    population decline among, 174-176
    "removal" of, *176-178*, 258, 425, *631*, 640
    war with, *639-641*
nativism, 194-195
NATO (North Atlantic Treaty Organization), 655
natural gas, 144
naturalism, 269-270
natural rights, 397-398
natural selection, 219

natural theory of states, 384-385
Navarre, Marguerite de, 251
naves, 38
navicular bone, 224
Nazis (National Socialists), 88, 416, *469*
    art and, 607
    eugenics and, 194
    film propaganda and, *110-111*, 441
    Olympics and, 437-438
NBC, 525
Neanderthals, 208-209
negative reinforcement, 238
Nelson, Willie, 321
neoclassicism, 555, *592-593*
    in architecture, 44-46, 54
    in music, 304
    in theater, 546-547
neoconservatism, 428
neo-impressionist movement, 602
neomercantilist economic systems, 82
neoplasticism, 56, *608*
neorealism, 117
Neotaoism, 485
Neptune, 335
Netherlands
    art of, 583, 584-585, 608
    colonies of, 158
"neti . . . neti" ("not this . . . not this"), 478
neuroses (anxiety-based disorders), 244
Neutrality Act (1939), 651
neutralization, 370
neutrons, 364
Nevelson, Louise, 614
Nevermore (painting; Gaugin), 601
"new architecture," 48
New Deal, *89*, 192, *419-422*
"New Democrats," 427-428
new music, 304
"New Negro," 276
new novels, 279
New Orleans, 170
    Battle of, 630
    music of, 308
newsgroups, 348
newsreels, 119
New Testament, 489-490
Newton, Huey, 200
Newton, Sir Isaac, *350-351*, 396
    first law (law of inertia), 350-351
    law of universal gravitation, 336-337
    second law of motion, 351
    third law of motion, 351
new wave movement (film), 104
new wave music, 329

One (#31) (painting; Pollock), 613
One Flew Over the Cuckoo's Nest, 131
O'Neill, Eugene, *563-564*
On the Origin of Species (Darwin), *219-220*, 508
On the Waterfront (film), *131*, 305
OPEC, 145
open-mike poetry readings, 285
opera, 297, 299, *302-303*
Operation Desert Storm, 144, *664*
Operation Just Cause, 664
Operation Overload, 653
operetta, 564
opiates, 215
opinion polls, 342-343
Oppenheimer, Robert, 476
opportunity costs, 68
optics, 360-361
oral stage, 237
oratorio, 297, *298*
orders (architecture), 35, 37-38
organic chemistry, 372-373
organisms, 217
organized crime, 418
organized labor, *85*, 411
    See also trade unions
original sin doctrine, 493
Orpheus, 292-293
Orr, Bobby, 454
Ortega y Gasset, Jose, 385
orthodontics, 225
Orthodox Judaism, 487-488
ostracize, 501
Oswald, Lee Harvey, 424
Otis, Elisha, 50
Otto, Frei, 60
Ottoman Empire, 496
    World War I and, 414, *415*, 647, 648
Ouimet, Francis, 462
Outerbridge, Mary Ewing, 455
l'Ouverture, Toussaint, 182
Ovid, 249
Ovitz, Michael, 123
ovum, 223
Owen, Robert, *83*, 399, 408
Owens, Jesse, 111, 440, *441*
oxidation, 371-372
ozone, *376-377*
ozone layer, *376-377*, 378, 380

PA (production assistant), 120
Pacific Ocean, 137, 139
Pacific Rim, 148
Page, Jimmy, 326
Paige, Leroy "Satchel," 445

Paik, Nam June, 618
Paine, Thomas, 624
paleontology, 136, *207*
Paleozoic interval, 139, 206
Palestinians, 156
Palestrina, Giovanni Pierluigi da, 296-297
Paley, Grace, 280
Palladio, Andrea, 45-46
Palmer, A. Mitchell, 85-86
Panama, 663-664
Panama Canal, *413*, 641
pancratium, 436
Pangaea, 136-137
pan-Indian movement, 177
Pantheon (Church of Ste-Geneviève, Paris), 44
Pantheon (Rome), *38*, 46, 475
pantheon of Greek deities, 472-473
Papua New Guinea, language in, 153
Paradise Lost (Milton), 253
Paramount Case, 108-109
paranoid schizophrenia, 241
Paris
    Treaty of (1763), 624
    urban plan for, 47
Paris Review, The, 276
Parker, Charlie "Bird," *311-312*, 313
Parker, Dorothy, 273
Parks, Rosa, 197
parliamentary systems, 392, *397*, 624
Parson Capen House (Massachusetts), 43-44
Parthenon (Athens), 35
partial lobotomy, 240
"party conventions," 414
party platforms, 414
Pascal, Blaise, 225, *344*
passion plays, *544*
pastoral poetry, 248
Paths of Glory (film), 131
Patriarch of Constantinople, 493
patricians, 387-388
Pavlov, Ivan, 238
Pax Romana ("Peace of Rome"), *388*, 475
Payton, Walter, 450
Peace Corps, 424
Peace of Paris (1783), 628
peace pipes, 620
Peale, Charles Willson, 593
Pearl Harbor, 128, *650-651*
Peckinpah, Sam, 120
"peculiar institution," 179-180
pedal steel guitar, 318
pediments, 40
Pele, 457
Peloponnesian War (431-404 B.C.), 436, *543*

women's rights convention, 188
Women's Tennis Association (WTA), 456
Wood, Ed, 116
woodcuts, 583
Woodstock, 245, *327*
Woodward, Bob, 426
Woolf, Virginia, 271-272
Wooster Group, 575
Wordsworth, William, 259
Works Progress Administration (WPA), *89*, 91, *420*
World Boxing Organization, 460, 461-462
world cop role, 413, 657, 660
World Cup, 457, 458
World of Forms (Plato), 473, *474*
World of Matter (Plato), 474
World Series, 109, 446
World War I (Great War), 87, *413-415*, 515, *643-648*
    Modernism and, 272
    music following, 308
World War II, 415, 422, *650-655*
    Japanese defeat in, 82
    Japanese "internment camps," *195*, 651
    Korea and, 148
    literature following, 278
    Manhattan Project, 374-375
    music during, 316
    post-World War II economy, 165
    radio in, 517-518, 523
    theater and, 572
World Wide Web (WWW), 349
Wounded Knee, Battle of, 177, 499, *641*
Wovoka, 499-500, *641*
Woyzeck (Buchner), 555-556
Wozniak, Steve, 347
wrestling, 436
Wright, Frank Lloyd, *50-52*, 56, 57
Wright, Richard, 276
wrought iron, 47

"x"-rated films, *121-122*, 130
X-rays, *231*, 355, 364

Yahweh, *485*
Yalta Conference (1945), 656
Yardbirds, The, 326
yeasts, 214
Yeats, William Butler, 267
yellow fever, 170, 642
"Yellow Peril," 195
Yellow River, 375
Yellowstone National Park, 145
Yezierska, Anzia, 272

Yin/Yang symbol, 485
yoga, 476-477
Young, Brigham, 506
Yugoslavia, collapse of, 161-162

Zakat (almsgiving), 495
Zappa, Frank, 328
Zazen (seated meditation), 482
Zen Buddhism, 482-483
zero, 496
"Zero Hour," 650
Zeus, 435, 472-473
ziggurats, 33-34
Zimmerman telegram, 645
Zitkala-Sa (Gertrude Bonnin), 177
Zohar, 498
Zola, Emile, 269
Zydeco, 331
zygotes (embryos), 211, 223

(by chapter, in order of appearance)

Architecture

UPI/Bettmann
The Bettmann Archive
UPI/Bettmann
The Bettmann Archive
Collection of The New-York Historical Society
UPI/Bettmann
The Bettmann Archive
The Bettmann Archive
The Bettmann Archive
The Bettmann Archive
The Bettmann Archive
The Bettmann Archive
The Bettmann Archive
The Bettmann Archive
The Bettmann Archive
The Bettmann Archive
UPI/Bettmann
The Bettmann Archive
The Bettmann Archive
The Bettmann Archive
UPI/Bettmann
The Bettmann Archive
The Bettmann Archive
UPI/Bettmann
Reuters/Bettmann

Economics

Amalie R. Rothschild/The Bettmann Archive
The Bettmann Archive
UPI/Bettmann
The Bettmann Archive
The Bettmann Archive
The Bettmann Archive
The Bettmann Archive
The Bettmann Archive
The Bettmann Archive
Reuters/Bettmann
The Bettmann Archive
UPI/Bettmann
UPI/Bettmann
UPI/Bettmann
UPI/Bettmann
Reuters/Bettmann
The Bettmann Archive
The Bettmann Archive

Film

The Bettmann Archive
The Bettmann Archive
The Bettmann Archive
UPI/Bettmann
The Bettmann Archive
The Bettmann Archive
The Bettmann Archive
The Bettmann Archive
The Bettmann Archive
The Bettmann Archive
UPI/Bettmann
Negative #67150
Collection of The New-York Historical Society
Springer/Bettmann Film Archive
Springer/Bettmann Film Archive
UPI/Bettmann
UPI/Bettmann
Springer/Bettmann Film Archive
Springer/Bettmann Film Archive
Springer/Bettmann Film Archive
Springer/Bettmann Film Archive
Springer/Bettmann Film Archive

Geography

The Bettmann Archive
The Bettmann Archive

Human Rights

AP/Wide World Photos
The Bettmann Archive
UPI/Bettmann
The Bettmann Archive
Collection of The New-York Historical Society
Collection of The New-York Historical Society
The Bettmann Archive
The Bettmann Archive
UPI/Bettmann
Collection of The New-York Historical Society
The Bettmann Archive
The Bettmann Archive
UPI/Bettmann
UPI/Bettmann Newsphotos
The Bettmann Archive
UPI/Bettmann
UPI/Bettmann
UPI/Bettmann
UPI/Bettmann
The Bettmann Archive

Life Sciences

The Bettmann Archive
Neg. No. 261417   Courtesy Department Library Services
   American Museum of Natural History
UPI/Bettmann Newsphotos
The Bettmann Archive
UPI/Bettmann
The Bettmann Archives
The Bettmann archive
The Bettmann Archive
The Bettmann Archive
UPI/Bettmann
The Bettmann Archive
Reuters/Bettmann
Reuters/Bettmann
UPI/Bettmann
The Bettmann Archive
The Bettmann Archive
The Bettmann Archive
Reuters/Bettmann
Reuters/Bettmann

Literature

The Bettmann Archive
The Bettmann Archive
The Bettmann Archive
The Bettmann Archive
The Bettmann Archive
The Bettmann Archive
The Bettmann Archive
The Bettmann Archive
The Bettmann Archive
UPI/Bettmann
The Bettmann Archive
The Bettmann Archive
The Bettmann Archive
UPI/Bettmann
The Bettmann Archive
The Bettmann Archive
The Bettmann Archive
Springer/Bettmann Film Archive
UPI/Bettmann
The Bettmann Archive
UPI/Bettmann
UPI/Bettmann
UPI/Bettmann Newsphotos
The Bettmann Archive
The Bettmann Archive
UPI/Bettmann
The Bettmann Archive
The Bettmann Archive
UPI/Bettmann
The Bettmann Archive

Music

UPI/Bettmann
The Bettmann Archive
The Bettmann Archive
The Bettmann Archive
The Bettmann Archive
The Bettmann Archive
The Bettmann Archive
The Battmann Archive
UPI/Bettmann Newsphotos
UPI/Bettmann
The Bettmann Archive
The Bettmnann Archive
UPI/Betmann
The Bettmann Archive
The Bettmann Archive
UPI/Bettmann Archive
The Bettmann Archive
UPI/Bettmann
The Bettmann Archive
The Bettmann Archive
UPI/Bettmann
Amalie R. Rothschild/The Bettmann Archive
UPI/Bettmann
UPI/Bettmann
UPI/Bettmann
The Bettmann Archive
UPI/Bettmann

Physical Sciences and Technology

The Bettmann Archive
UPI/Bettmann
UPI/Bettmann
The Bettmann Archive
UPI/Bettmann
The Bettmann Archive
UPI/Bettmann
The Bettmann Archive
The Bettmann Archive
UPI Bettmann Newsphotos
The Bettmann Archive
The Bettmann Archive
UPI/Bettmann Newsphotos
The Bettmann Archive
UPI/Bettmann

Politics

UPI/Bettmann
The Bettmann Archive
The Bettmann Archive
The Bettmann Archive
The Bettmann Archive
The Bettmann Archive
The Bettmann Arhcive

The Bettmann Archive
The Bettmann Archive
The Bettmann Archive
The Bettmann Archive
The Bettmann Archive
The Bettmann Archive
The Bettmann Archive
The Bettmann Archive
Collection of The New-York Historical Society
The Bettmann Archive
The Bettmann Archive
The Bettmann Archive
The Bettmann Archive
The Bettmann Archive
UPI/Bettmann Newsphotos
The Bettmann Archive
UPI/Bettmann Newsphotos

Recreation

UPI/Bettmann
The Bettmann Archive
The Bettmann Archive
The Bettmann Archive
The Bettmann Archive
The Bettmann Archive
The Bettmann Archive
UPI/Bettmann Newsphotos
The Bettmann Archive
UPI/Bettmann
The Bettmann Archive
UPI/Bettmann
UPI/Bettmann
UPI/Bettmann
UPI/Bettmann
UPI/Bettmann
UPI/Bettmann
UPI/Bettmann
UPI/ Betmann Newsphotos
UPI/Bettmann
Reuters/Bettmann
UPI/Bettmann
UPI/Bettmann
UPI/Bettmann
UPI/Bettmann
UPI/Bettmann
Reuters/Bettmann
UPI/Bettmann
UPI/Bettmann

Religion

UPI/Bettmann
The Bettmann Archive
The Bettmann Archive
The Bettmann Archive

UPI/Bettmann
UPI/Bettmann Newsphotos
The Bettmann Archive
Collection of The New-York Historical Society
The Bettmann Archive
Collection of The New-York Historical Society
The Bettmann Archive
The Bettmann Archive
Neg. No. 108781   Courtesy Department Library Services American Museum of Natural History
UPI/Bettmann Newsphotos
UPI/Bettmann

Television

All photos for this chapter provided courtesy of The Bettmann Archive

Theater

The Bettmann Archive
The Bettmann Archive
The Bettmann Archive
The Bettmann Archive
The Bettmann Archive
UPI/Bettmann
The Bettmann Archive
The Bettmann Archive
The Bettmann Archive
The Bettmann Archive
The Bettmann Archive
The Bettmann Archive
Springer/Bettmann Film Archive
UPI/Bettmann
The Bettmann Archive
Springer/Bettmann Film Archive
UPI/Bettmann

Visual Arts

Scala/Art Resource, NY
Scala/Art Resource, NY
Scala/Art Resource, NY
Scala/Art Resource, NY
The Bettmann Archive
Scala/Art Resource, NY
The Bettmann Archive
The Bettmann Archive
The Bettmann Archive
Cassatt, Mary (1844-1926) The Boating Party 1893/93 oil on canvas, .900 x 1.173National Gallery of Art, Washington, Chester Dale Collection
The Metropolitan Museum of Art, Gift of Thomas F. Ryan, 1910. [11.173.9]
Scala/Art Resource NY
Scala/Art Resource NY
The Bettmann Archive

The Bettmann Archive
The Bettmann Archive
UPI/Bettmann
UPI/Bettmann
UPI/Bettmann
Collection of Whitney Museum of American Art, New York
Collection Walker Art Center, Minneapolis Gift of Frederick
    R. Weisman in honor of his parents, William and Mary
    Weisman, 1988

War

Collection of the New-York Historical Society
The Bettmann Archive
The Bettmann Archive
The Bettmann Archive
The Bettmann Archive
The Bettmann Archive
The Bettmann Archive
UPI/Bettmann
The Bettmann Archive
The Bettmann Archive
The Bettmann Archive
The Bettmann Archive
The Bettmann Archive
The Bettmann Archive
The Bettmann Archive
The Bettmann Archive
The Bettmann Archive
The Bettmann Archive
The Bettmann Archive
The Bettmann Archive
Collection of the New-York Historical Society
UPI/Bettmann
The Bettmann Archive
The Bettmann Archive
UPI/Bettmann Newsphotos
UPI/Bettmann Newsphotos
The Bettmann Archive
UPI/Bettmann
UPI/Bettmann
The Bettmann Archive
The Bettmann Archive
UPI/Bettmann
UPI/Bettmann
UPI/Bettmann Newsphotos
UPI/Bettmann
Reuters/Bettmann

Color Insert

Plates 3, 4, 6, 7, 8, 9, 10, 11, 15, 17, 19, 22, 23, 24, 25
provided courtesy of The Bettmann Archive

Author Biographies and Acknowledgments

ARCHITECTURE

Gregg Pasquarelli is a graduate of Columbia University's Graduate School of Architecure and lives, writes, and practices architecture in New York City. Kimberly J. Holden is also a recent graduate of Columbia University's Graduate School of Architecture. She lives and works in New York City and Winter Harbor, Maine. They would like to thank John Dohlin for his expert editing and Eric Banks for fact-checking.

ECONOMICS AND POLITICS

Eric Owens graduated from Cornell College with a BA in Philosophy and Economics, and has worked for The Princeton Review since 1994. He would like to thank Lee Elliott, Chris Kensler, John Katzman, Maria Russo, Doug McMullen, the Felker family, Marsha Clark, his Mom and his Dad, his best friends, and everyone who ever believed in his abilities

FILM

Leland Elliott graduated from Dartmouth College where he majored in both English and Film. He has worked in the publishing department at The Princeton Review since 1992 and became the Managing Editor and served as the Director of the department. Leland suddenly decided to turn the tables on the department and become an author as well, because it was an opportunity for Leland to prove his long-standing thesis that degrees in both English and Film can afford you chances at gainful employment. The author plans to continue pursuing careers both in writing and in the grand illusion of film. The author would like to thank his department for not making too much fun of him when the boss missed his own deadline.

GEOGRAPHY

Susan Cohen graduated from Boston University with a BA in Anthropology. She has since worked as a writer for newspapers, magazines, books, radio, television, and interactive media on subjects ranging from painting to politics. She would like to thank PJ Waters for his expert editing and the design staff for their great maps and diagrams.

HUMAN RIGHTS

Miles Shapiro has a BA from Yale University and an MA from Temple University. He has published two biographies on Bill Russell and Maya Angelou in the Chelsea House Black Americans of Achievement series. He received the New York Public Library's Best Book for the Teen Age Award for Bill Russell. His short fiction, essays, reviews, and articles have appeared in various papers, magazines, and journals around the country. He would liketo thank Maria Russo for her expert editing. He would also like to thank Barbara Heffernan and Rachel Shapiro, his wife and daughter.

LIFE SCIENCES AND PHYSICAL SCIENCES AND TECHNOLOGY

Kyle Alexander holds numerous degrees from the University of Michigan and has completed either some or lots of post-graduate education in anthropology, business, chemistry, computer science, education, electrical engineering, materials science and engineering, mathematics, physics, and psychology. He is also the holder of several patents in chemistry, physics, and engineering. He has worked as an educator (elementary school through graduate school), bartender, bicycle mechanic, chemist, consultant, convenience store cashier, cook, delivery driver, dishwasher, engineer, flower arranger, husband, laboratory rat for psychological studies, medical experimentee, records clerk, salesman, slave (read "graduate student"), waiter, and writer. He would like to thank Debbie Guest for her expert editing and fact-checking.

LITERATURE AND VISUAL ARTS

Maria Russo, a graduate of Georgetown University, is completing her PhD in English at Columbia University. She would like to thank John Cauman for his expert editing and fact-checking, Pat Crain, Sarah Cusk, Janet Dean, Michael Elliott, Meredith Goldsmith, and Patrick Horrigan.

MUSIC

Peter Spagnuolo is a poet living on the Lower East Side in New York City. He plays banjo, guitar, and other fretted instruments. He would like to thank Ian Carleton for his expertise on ancient and classical music and Holly Williams for her input on rap and hip hop.

RELIGION

Lenora Todaro is a freelance writer completing work on a book entitled *Saints Through The Centuries*. She wishes to thank Professor James Carse, Director of Religous Studies at New York University, for looking over her initial outline and offering suggestions; Alys Cohen for reading and offering suggestions for the section on Judaism; and Donna Todaro, an infinite source of wisdom, who answered many questions and offered suggestions regarding the Eastern faiths. Thanks finally to Professor George Saint Laurent, Professor of Religious Studies at California State University-Fullerton, for his expert editing.

RECREATION

Bruno Blumenfeld attended SUNY-Binghamton and then the School of Visual Arts, from which he graduated with a Bachelor of Fine Arts degree. He has worked for The Princeton Review since 1993. Many thanks are due to Lee Elliott and Chris Kensler for their confidence and support. Thanks also to Eric Banks for his fact-checking, Tashi Ridley for her unparalleled hospitality, and to Stacey Matthias for her unparalleled computer.

TELEVISION

Woody Thompson graduated from Colgate University and is a television producer and writer living in New York City. He has written and produced segments for Linda Ellerbee's "Nick News," the Dupont Award winning kids news magazine show on Nickelodeon, and Brandon Tartikoff's "Last Call," a syndicated late night show. He would like to thank Les Brown, Louis Phillips, Burnham Holmes, Erik Barnouw, Anne, mom and dad, Linda Ellerbee, Tad Low, and the remote control.

THEATER

Cornelia Cocke has a BA in English from Dartmouth College and an MFA from Columbia University. She once met Arthur Miller at a cocktail party. Big thanks to Doug McMullen for his expert editing and fact checking, Thomas Wilson Glass for his *bon mots* on dance, and to Christopher Baumer, Mr. Theater.

WAR

Alexandria Giardino has a BA in Journalism from the University of Oregon and an MA in English literature from Mills College. She is currently editing a book about children of 1960s radicals. Living in New York City has provided her with plenty of experience to draw upon for the War chapter. Antonio Garza provided much wisdom and perspective on the United States, and for that she is grateful.